DATE DUE

MY 5'98			
1 8 98			

DEMCO 38-296

The World of Opals

The World of Opals

ALLAN W. ECKERT

John Wiley & Sons, Inc.

New York • Chichester • Weinheim • Brisbane • Singapore • Toronto

On the dust jacket are shown spectacular pieces of the magnificent 25,586-carat Bonanza Opal, which was accidentally unearthed by Keith Hodson while operating a bulldozer in 1976 at his Bonanza Mine in Virgin Valley, Nevada. The huge stone was solid precious opal, alive with play of color, without any dead spots or foreign inclusions of any kind. Pictured are some of the five principal chunks into which this massive gemstone broke: the largest piece weighed just over 2 pounds, and the next largest, just under 2 pounds. The full account of this remarkable discovery begins on page 123. (Photos by the author)

This text is printed on acid-free paper.

This publication is designed to provide accurate and authoritative information in regard to the subject matter covered. It is sold with the understanding that the publisher is not engaged in rendering legal, accounting, or other professional services. If legal advice or other expert assistance is required, the services of a competent professional person should be sought.

Library of Congress Cataloging in Publication Data:
Eckert, Allan. W.
   The World of Opals / Allan W. Eckert
      p.   cm.
   Includes bibliographical references and index.
   ISBN 0-471-13397-3 (cloth : alk. paper)
   1. Opals.   I. Title.
TS755.O73E25   1997
553.8'73—dc21   97-1825
0-471-13397-3

Printed in the United States of America

10 9 8 7 6 5 4 3 2 1

To the Hodsons—Agnes and Keith—who introduced me to the glorious and fascinating world of opals and who then gave me an even greater and more treasured gift—their friendship

and to Alan A. Vogel, who has so often shared with me the joys of the world of opals and, in the process, has become so dear a friend.

Contents

Foreword   The Queen of Gems   ix

ONE   What *Is* an Opal?   1

TWO   A New Look at Opal Formation   17

THREE   Opalized Fossils and Pseudomorphs   39

FOUR   A Chronological History and Mythology of Opals   53

FIVE   Famous and Otherwise Noteworthy Opals   119

SIX   Types of Opals   161

SEVEN   The World's Major Opal Fields   187

EIGHT   Opal Occurrence Worldwide   263

APPENDIX   A Glossary of Opal-Related Terms   373

NOTES   387

BIBLIOGRAPHY   Principal and Secondary Sources   397

Index   419

Foreword

THE QUEEN OF GEMS

Just as the iridescent blue morpho butterfly is the flying sapphire of the insect world, so the precious opal's beauty is singular among all the gorgeous gemstones of the earth, and it can justifiably be called the Queen of Gems. By far the most changing, the most remarkable, clearly the most breathtaking, the opal is undoubtedly the most inherently different of the five principal jewels considered "precious" gemstones—diamond, ruby, emerald, sapphire, and opal.[1] Those first four will initially quite often look much like rather misshapen, dull, generally ugly lumps of glass until their clear or colorful beauty is brought out by the lapidarist. But the opal has an incredible beauty that is often visible and fills one with awe from the moment it is first seen, even before it is removed from the ground. And however much a miner might thrill to that unforgettable instant when the tap of his pick uncovers the glint of gold or the unmistakable presence of a crystalline gemstone, it hardly compares with that stunning moment when, in a level of tan-colored sedimentary sandstone or gray volcanic clay, what stares back at him, winks back, gleams back, is an array of incredibly iridescent, constantly changing colors and patterns emanating from the precious opal he has just exposed (see figure on page x).

It was probably about A.D. 75, only a few years before his death in the eruption of Mount Vesuvius in A.D. 79, that the Roman scholar Gaius Plinius Secundus—more familiarly known as Pliny the Elder—wrote in his exalted encyclopedic work, *Historia Naturalis,* a comparison of opal with the other precious gemstones, saying: "It displays at once the piercing fire of carbunculas (ruby/sapphire), the purple brilliance of amethystos (amethyst), and the sea-green of smaragdus (emerald), and all these glittering colors mixed together in an incredible way. Some opali carry such a play within them that they equal the deepest and richest colors of painters. Others again simulate the flaming fire of burning sulphur, yet, and even the bright blaze of burning oil."[2]

That sense of wonder and captivation by the beauty of the colors displayed

ix

A sight to gladden the heart of any miner; a fine black opal, rich in play of color, protruding from the montmorillonite clay opal level at the Northern Lights Mine of the Royal Peacock Opal Mines, Virgin Valley, Nevada. The stone, an opalized limb section, when carefully excavated and cleaned off, measured 5″ [127 mm] in length and, across the face, 1.75″ × 1″ [44.5 mm × 24.5 mm]. June 1995. (Photo by the author)

by the opal was very apparent to Australian writer Frank Leechman, who wrote *The Opal Book,* the first relatively comprehensive book about opals, even though centered primarily upon the opals of Australia. In it he wrote of this gemstone: "Surely there can be few things in this world more strikingly beautiful; perhaps the most lovely flowers, the most delicate paintings, the most exquisite sunrises come near; but there is nothing that shows the sudden bright nuances of a really fine opal, the blazing crimson reds, the wonderful deep greens that only emerald can approach, the pulsating royal blues and purples; there is nothing else that can offer these in such a way as the opal flaunts them in our eyes."

The opal is by far the softest of the five precious gemstones, unequivocally the most fragile, particularly sensitive to heat, all too easily scratched or cracked, the only one of the five that does not have a characteristic crystalline structure, and definitely the riskiest as an investment. So, just what is it about the opal that, since the time of the ancient Romans and even earlier, has so caught the imagination and delight of humans? Unquestionably it is not only the incomparable brilliance of its colors, those indescribably dazzling pure hues so intense they seem to burst from the stone, but equally its infinite variety.

Where all the other precious gemstones look essentially alike within their own species—one diamond, apart from a few color variations, looks pretty much like another, one ruby looks like another, et cetera—no two opals are *ever* exactly the same. Not only do they differ from stone to stone, but also they have shifting colors and patterns within the individual stone that cause it to look dazzlingly different depending on the angle from which it is viewed and the type of light source illuminating the stone.

A fine-quality gem opal that exhibits brilliant broadflash red when perceived from one direction will change to scintillating green or blue or orange if tilted only a few degrees; and in that tilting its very pattern also becomes wholly different from what it was before. No other gemstone in the world can display all the colors of the spectrum with such infinite variety of tints and shades, brilliance, and patterns—all of which will change as well depending on whether the light source is a simple candle, a tungsten or halogen bulb, a fluorescent tube, ordinary daylight, or direct sunlight. Often several colors are visible at the same time in a particular pattern of placement and, when moved only a fraction, the patterns shift and overlap, appear and disappear, and those colors change to several entirely different colors in a remarkably lively display. It is this element, known as play of color, that makes the opal unique as a gemstone. There are, of course, numerous other stones that exhibit phenomena induced by light—stones such as cat's eyes, star stones, and chatoyant stones—but however beautiful they may be, they have a predictably constant similarity one to another. Only in the opal is the play of color consistently entirely different from stone to stone, as well as within the individual stone itself. Evidently this is what prompted John Ruskin to write of the opal: "It's beauty shows the most glorious colors seen in the world" (Color Plate 2).

Obviously, a stone that is so dramatically affected by outside influences of angle of light source, direction of light source, pattern, play of color, and other factors must, in the end, be unquestionably the most difficult stone in the world to properly evaluate for the market. While this is true, the opal simultaneously remains the most marvelously enigmatic and different gemstone occurring in nature.

The love of opal clearly affects all levels of those who become involved with the stone, often with an intensity remarkable to a point virtually beyond defining. As Frank Leechman put it, "Opal is like gold: once the fever gets into your blood, they say, you can never get away from it. When you expose and unearth an opal, what a feeling of success that is! How the heart lifts and the world seems good as you gaze into a really fine piece! How the colors flash and change, how brilliant, how far beyond those of any other stone!" There are some who use the American slang term, opalholic, to embrace those so thoroughly captivated and enchanted by the stone's unique beauty, irrespective of at what level of incidence they encounter them: those who prospect for and mine the opals, those who initially buy and sell the rough material, those who cut and polish them, those who fashion the polished opals into exquisitely designed jewelry, those who enjoy owning lovely gemstones in fine settings, and those who collect the most superb examples of this jewel of nature's bounty.

Dick Turley, sometime opal miner, after digging in an opal level in Virgin

Valley, Nevada, and uncovering a large and beautiful stone, wrote: "It is an indescribable feeling to at one moment be staring at the dull clay bank, and the next to have a fiery opal eye gleaming at you! . . . Your adrenalin level skyrockets, you can hardly believe what you see. Slowly, carefully, you extricate the gem from its home of 14-million years."

Years ago, when discussing opals with the man who introduced me to opal mining, Keith Hodson, I made a comment with which he emphatically agreed: "I think one of the more fascinating things about the opal is the fact that here you have a stone which may have the liability of being unpredictable, but it also has the *joy* of being unpredictable." And an American jewelry designer, Paula Crevoshay, once said, "Opal is so inspiring because each stone is like a painting. Quite often I find pieces that look like Monet created them; they look almost like an impressionist painting."

Arabian legend says the opal was imbued with its marvelous colors through falling to earth from heaven in lightning flashes. To the ancient Romans, the opal symbolized purity and hope, and ancient Greeks attributed to it powers of foresight, imbuing the owner with an ability to accurately predict future events. Belief was also widespread that the opal was beloved of the gods and a talisman that, when worn, could ward off disease to the owner, or in other ways protect him. It was—and in some cases still is—a stone that embraced the spirit of truth and, as such, was considered among many Orientals as sacred.

The two foremost popular periodicals on the American market today dealing with gemstones, minerals, and various lapidary pursuits are *Lapidary Journal* and *Rock & Gem*. In addition to having a continuing succession of pieces about opals in their pages throughout the year, each devotes an entire issue during the year solely to opals: the June issue of *Lapidary Journal* and the October issue of *Rock & Gem*.

Little wonder, then, that a stone of such incredible beauty and variability, with such a background of myth, adventure, and intrigue, and one that evokes such a continuing interest has attracted so broad and appreciative a following on a worldwide scale and has resulted in a great many lovers of fine gemstones now considering the finest black opals to be the most desirable, the most valuable, the most precious of *all* gemstones (see figure on page xiii). There can be no doubt that the precious opal deserves its title as the Queen of Gems.

ACKNOWLEDGMENTS

In preparing a work of this scope, with research extending well over a decade, scores of people assisted me in one way or another—some with very pertinent information, some with photography, some with companionship in the field, some with generous hospitality. The list would be far too long to name them all here, but there are a few whose help was constant and whose contributions were

A mixed bag of Lightning Ridge opal doublets cut by the author. (Photo by the author)

many and cheerfully given throughout the process of putting this work together. Therefore, very special thanks go to

Alan A. Vogel, of Mequon, Wisconsin, who journeyed with me many thousands of miles to the opal fields and elsewhere, who provided much information, many fine photographs, excellent jewelry work, and intelligent, delightful company in the field as well as in his home and mine.

The Hodsons—Agnes and Keith—proprietors of the Rainbow Ridge Opal Mine in Virgin Valley, Nevada, who introduced me to the joy and wonder of opals initially, provided bountiful information, and opened their home and hearts to me in innumerable ways.

Bill Harris, of Sarasota, Florida, for material, information, encouragement, companionship, and a willing helping hand, and for always just "being there."

The Carrolls—Lisa and Peter—of Lightning Ridge, New South Wales, who introduced me to Australian opal mining, provided extensive hospitality and information, and became good friends in the process.

Len Cram, also of Lightning Ridge, whose insight, intelligence, vision, and down-to-earth wisdom were invaluable, whose photography was stunning, and who opened many doors for me, especially in New South Wales and Queensland, and for his friendship as well.

Kevin Lane Smith, of Tucson, Arizona, who introduced me to Oregon opals, provided important information and fine photography over a period of years, and who, as a premiere opal cutter, stone carver, and fine jewelry designer, provided me with new insights into the world of opals.

George Munzing, paleobotanist of Brigham Young University, Provo, Utah, for valuable information about opals and fossilized, opalized wood and many other pertinent matters.

Mary Ann and Walter Wilson of Virgin Valley, Nevada, for their help in so many ways and at whose mines I dug some of the most gorgeous opals occurring anywhere in the world.

Michael C. Hansen, of the Ohio Geological Survey, for the abundant data and multitude of contacts with which he provided me.

And Tanya and Eddie Maguire of the Yowah Opal Field in Queensland, Gene Favell of Klamath Falls, Oregon, Gene Sharp of Denio, Nevada, Mario Antolovich of Surfers Paradise, Queensland, Herb West of Roswell, Georgia, Virgil Patterson of the New Coocoran Opal Field near Lightning Ridge, New South Wales, Serjean and Paul Vaillant of Reno, Nevada, George Hewitt of Virgin Valley, Nevada, and Paul Reeve of Cottage Grove, Oregon, all of whom were of considerable assistance, and to the host of others I met and who helped me along the way.

Allan W. Eckert

ONE

What Is an Opal?

Precious opal is, of course, a glorious gem, exhibiting a variety of colors, incredible patterns, and an inner fire that no other gemstone in the world can rival. But while that is what we see when we gaze at the beautiful stone, exactly what is it?

It is perhaps easiest to understand what an opal is by discovering what it is not. It is not, for example, a crystal; unlike the other four precious gemstones—diamond, ruby, sapphire, and emerald—opal does not have crystalline characteristics. Therefore, it is not a mineral, as those stones are, since the very definition of being a mineral means having a crystalline composition. Instead, opal has long been held by many scientists to be, crystallographically, an amorphous substance—the term amorphous meaning *without form,* in other words a solidified gel of silica. The atoms have not linked together in an organized pattern sufficient to give it a regularly recognizable crystal form, so it is classed as a mineraloid. In its basic structure, it most resembles such solidified gels as the glass produced by nature that we know as obsidian—volcanic glass—and man-made glass in its myriad forms.

In its chemical composition, opal is quite simple: It is a hydrated form of silica having the chemical formula $SiO_2 \bullet nH_2O$, which is silicon dioxide and a variable amount (indicated by the n) of loosely bound molecules of water. As silica, it belongs to a large family of stones that is broken into four major divisions: *coarsely crystalline silica,* containing the quartz varieties of clear quartz, smoky quartz, rose quartz, citrine, and amethyst; *microcrystalline silica,* better known as chalcedony and including agate, carnelian, chrysoprase, chert, flint, jasper, prase, and some varieties of petrified wood; *granular quartz silica,* which takes in primarily the grainy forms of quartz, such as quartzite; and *opaline silica,* containing some varieties of petrified wood, tiger's-eye opal, cat's-eye opal, and, most important to our purposes here, both common opal and precious opal.

Of those latter two basic forms of opaline silica, the former is exactly what its name indicates: a very common form of opal, commercially of little value, that is found widespread around the globe in a variety of types. Precious opal, on the other hand, is an extremely rare variety of the same stone. To be classed as the gemstone known as precious opal, the stone must exhibit what is termed play of color—an extraordinarily brilliant display of a pure spectral color, or combination of colors, in a variety of patterns. These colors and patterns change in hue, shape, and dispersion as the stone is rotated or looked at from different angles and under differing light sources.

As an example, a precious opal that may show an array of flashing red streaks from one angle, if moved only a fraction, may become a display of equally brilliant green lines or flashes or smudges that are entirely different in placement. Turned again just a bit, it may show incredibly bright orange or purple or blue in patterns that can vary from small dots of fire (called pinfire) to broad splashes (called flashfire or broadflash) to surprisingly well-organized, aligned, and defined blocks of color (called harlequin), and so forth, with all sorts of gradations in between. Such incredible variety of constantly shifting patterns and intensely colored hues constitutes, of course, the fundamental joy and beauty of the precious opal. There are a few other color-change stones whose basic body color will change from one hue to another as a light source is changed, such as kunzite, chrysoberyl, and especially alexandrite. But such stones are still limited to two colors and only show one of those colors at a time. Where diamonds, sapphires, emeralds, and rubies are, for the most part, predictably alike from one stone to the next within their species, precious opals can display many colors simultaneously and no two are ever exactly alike. And no other gemstone can even come close to displaying the degree of dazzling, scintillating, pure color that a fine opal exhibits.

Virtually all of the texts refer to this appearance of brilliant color in an opal as play of color, but that term is something of a misnomer, because by itself it does not take into consideration the equal importance of the opal's play of pattern. It is the wonderful combination of these two traits that gives precious opal its uniqueness among the gemstones of the world. To save time and space in these pages as well as to possibly coin a new word that could in the future be used with more accurate foundation than the usual play-of-color term embraces, the author is taking the liberty in this book of referring to the combined attributes of play of color and play of pattern by a new acronym: *POC*.

So what is this mysterious force or property that causes POC in an opal and makes it a precious variety? For hundreds, perhaps thousands of years, no one knew the answer to that, although there were many theories advanced, ranging from the utterly ridiculous to some that were surprisingly close to the truth—a truth that was not definitely revealed until the mid 1960s. Some, like the ancient Arabs, believed the stone to be endowed with the brilliance of lightning and the color of fire and then dropped from the heavens as a gift of the gods. Some believed the stone was simply imbued with magical powers that manifested themselves in these amazing arrays of shifting patterns and intense colors. Others, of more pragmatic inclination, believed oil to be trapped within the stone and emitting its interference colors and patterns, as occurs when a drop of oil is placed on the surface of water. Yet others, noting the prismatic effect caused by a crack in crystal or glass, were claiming that the remarkable POC attributes of precious opal were caused by a myriad of tiny internal cracks that were catching and refracting rays of light entering from an outer source. And, because opal holds varying amounts of water, there were many—scientists among them—who believed that it was this water content in opal that caused the play of color and play of pattern, a theory that could not stand because common opal also had similar water content.

Many respected texts have, in the past, attributed opal's POC to internal cavities or impurities, and others have stated with decided authority that the POC was derived from quasi-crystallization of quartz internally (with some "authorities" substituting for the quartz such high-temperature silica minerals as cristobalite and tridymite.) Probably the two attributed causes that came closest to the truth were those of Sir David Brewster of England and mineralogist H. Behrens of Germany. Brewster theorized that the colors came from a multitude of microscopic cavities in the stone which caught the white light, broke it up prismatically and reflected it in spectrographically pure colors. Behrens, in his 1871 paper entitled *Structure of Opals*, stated in his own way that POC was caused by a series of extremely small, thin curved plates—referred to as lamellae—acting as internal diffraction gratings.

One could describe play of color (POC) as merely being a variegated pattern of patches or lines or sprinkles of bright spectral colors that change or disappear as the stone is rotated, but that would be little more than a description of the visual aspects, the effects rather than the causes, and would hardly do justice to the complex structure that induces the POC phenomenon. It was in the mid 1960s that the true cause of POC in precious opals was discovered. The discovery was made by a pair of scientists at the Commonwealth Scientific Industrial Research Organization (CSIRO) in Australia, John V. Sanders and Peter J. Darragh. Through the use of electron microscopy at 30,000 × magnification and greater, which ordinary microscopes could not accomplish, they found opal to be constructed of tiny spheres as large as four ten-thousandths of a millimeter (0.0004 mm) to as small as five one-hundred-thousandths of a millimeter (0.00005 mm), less than a millionth of an inch (Figure 1).

The spheres in both common opal and precious opal are generally similar, but with some significant differences. Those of the common opal are of varying sizes, sometimes not perfectly spherical and always rather haphazardly tumbled together with no sense of alignment, like a scoopful of marbles tossed into a jar. The base color in common opal, which covers a wide range, is normally caused by impurities, rather than by the stone's molecular construction, as is the case in precious opal. The spheres in precious opal, by comparison, are perfectly aligned in neat rows and identical in size within their rows. They are always

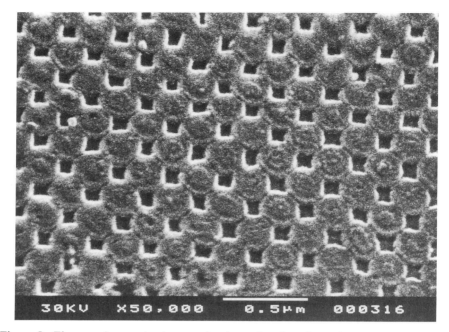

Figure 1. Electronmicroscopic photography shows that the spheres that make up the basic structure of the opal have particles consisting of a nucleus ranging in size from 30 to 40 nanometers in diameter that are surrounded by one or more concentric shells. The number of these shells determines the final size of the spheres, and that final size is ultimately the determining factor in the color of the spectrum to be emitted. In the specimen pictured here, originating from Bulla Creek, Queensland, Australia, the spheres consist of three concentric shells of primary particles and the voids between the spheres appear as dark, squarish shapes. (Photo courtesy of Dr. J. Van Landuyt, University of Antwerp (RUCA); Photo by RUCA Center for High Tension Electronmicroscopy)

within a range of 200–300 nm (nanometers)[1] and they are stacked in a three-dimensional gridwork of lattices, one atop another (Figure 2). The voids—that is, the spaces between the neatly gridded spheres—form a series of similarly hexagonal shapes. These spheres and voids together create a sort of latticework that is a three-dimensional diffraction grating.

One Australian source contends that each silica sphere is made up of a central nucleus with one or more concentric shells of primary silica particles, the number of shells determining the color of the gem. This is really a somewhat misleading simplification. Actually, the different colors result from variations in the size of both the spheres and the gaps—a condition that causes a very delicate balance of light diffraction and interference. No POC will be apparent if the spheres are imperfectly stacked, or if the spheres are not perfectly spherical, or if they are not stacked together in rows and layers of precisely the same size. If

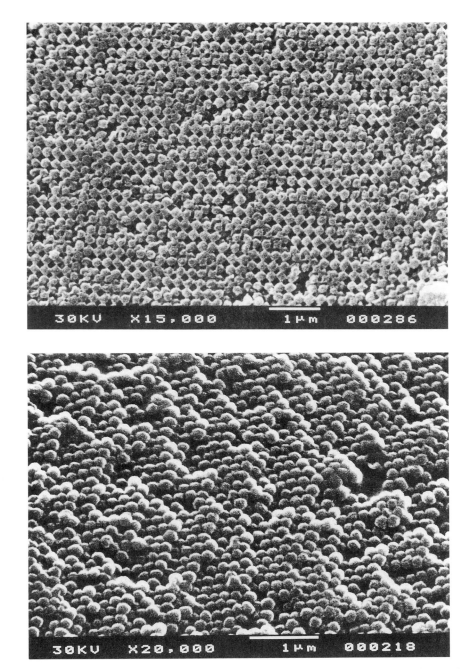

Figure 2. In the formation of the opal, as in this precious opal from Coober Pedy, South Australia, not only are the spheres neatly aligned side by side and in precise adjoining rows, but also they are stacked atop one another in a three-dimensional gridwork, sometimes (*top,* 15,000 ×) in square patterns of stacking and sometime (*bottom,* 20,000 ×) stacked in hexagonal patterns. (Photos courtesy of Dr. J. Van Landuyt, University of Antwerp (RUCA); Photo by RUCA Center for High Tension Electronmicroscopy)

the spheres are unequal in size, the light that enters the stone becomes overly scattered as well as diffracted, resulting in what is termed opalescence or, more commonly, a pronounced milkiness of the opal. Should the difference in size become more pronounced, it results in more of the incoming light being scattered and reflected rather than diffracted and the end result is no POC. Only a perfect stacking of perfect spheres that are identical in size—whereby the voids between the spheres are not silica-filled—allows any play of color. It becomes obvious, then, that the voids between the spheres are as crucial as the spheres themselves to the occurrence of POC in precious opal. In this forming of a uniform honeycomb type of pattern between the silica spheres, a distinctly three-dimensional diffraction grating is also created. It is the variation in the size of the spheres and the gaps throughout the stone, sometimes adjacent to one another, and the angle of incident light that results in the different colors and patterns that become visible.

To get a better grasp on what transpires to create the POC of the precious opal, consider the spheres to be an array of a number of transparent Ping-Pong balls neatly laid out side by side and layered one atop another. The surfaces of these transparent spheres scatter the light waves passing through and emerging from them, so that the lattice becomes an optical diffraction grating. So long as there is a difference in the refractive index of the voids and the spheres, some form of color will be produced. The closer together the refraction index of the two are, the more glasslike the opal itself becomes. This is why one can see into most volcanic types of opal, leaving the impression of the color coming from deep within, whereas most—*but not all*—sedimentary-type opal gives the appearance of the color floating across the top surface.

Diffraction occurs when the light waves entering the opal pass the edge of the sphere and become slightly bent in such passage—the same phenomenon of light-bending so commonly witnessed in the water of a swimming pool. When two close-together edges of the spheres create a narrowed gap, the light waves, after bending slightly around both as they pass, spread out again in a fanlike manner and begin overlapping. It is the overlapping that creates interference. Now, with diffraction and interference occurring together in passing through a multitude of narrow gaps and voids, the light separates into its prismatic components and the pure, scintillating colors of the spectrum appear in a sort of fan, with the lower speeds of vibration, the reds, at one end and the fastest, violet, at the other. These separated colored wavelengths of light leave the internal lattice in different directions and then are further separated at the surface of the opal by angles of refraction.

It is at this prismatic separation of the spectrum colors that the size of the aligned spheres becomes very important. Using the Ping-Pong ball allusion, add to it other arrangements of spheres occurring in levels all the way up to the size of beachballs. No matter how tightly and neatly the spheres are packed, they cannot fill all the spaces, and those spaces—or voids—between the spheres form a honeycomb lattice that varies in size according to the size of the spheres themselves. There are sharp limitations as to size and this is where the rarity of precious opal becomes understandable: When the transparent silica spheres exceed 350 nm, the incoming light rays pass through them with virtually no diffraction and, thus, no resultant POC; when the silica spheres are less than 200 nm, the waves of light strike the spheres and are reflected and scattered by them and so, again, no POC results.[2] Only when the sphere size falls within the 200- to 300-nm range will the light waves passing through the spheres and those traversing the voids bend with diffraction and intersect each other. It is as the light rays pass the spheres that, in the voids, they subsequently merge and interfere with each other, an overlapping that results in the release of the purest prismatic colors of the spectrum.

The smallest of the neatly stacked, uniformly sized spheres—those with a diameter down to 1500 angstroms—and their similarly small hexagonal voids allow passage and diffraction of only the shorter wavelengths of light, producing colors from indigo blues to the deepest violet end of the spectrum; medium-sized spheres and voids create the purest royal blues and emerald greens, ranging gradually into the yellow and orange range; and finally the largest of the spheres—with a diameter up to 3500 angstroms (350 nm)—and their respective voids, allow all the color wavelength diffractions to occur, up to the most intense red, for which the spheres must be relatively large—one millionth of an inch in diameter (Figure 3). Since most precious opal consists of spheres measuring less than 0.00025 mm (0.0000097 inch) in diameter, red is not a common color. If red does appear, then the other shorter wavelength colors will appear at other angles of the viewing. While such diffracted beams of light can show a variety of colors of the spectrum, more often one or two colors will predominate, depending on the size and placement of those spheres in the latticed gridwork formation. The colors emitted are also dependent on the angle of the incoming incident light and the viewing angle, since only slight movement to a different angle can cause the POC to change drastically or even disappear. Certain varieties of common opal consist of silica spheres having diameters as small as 0.0001 mm (0.0000039 inch), which, even if the spheres were regularly arranged, is too small to initiate diffraction effects in visible light.

Some scientists are convinced that if the precious opal dehydrates to the point where the water content is no longer sufficient to fill the voids, the light waves will no longer be diffracted and the rays that are refracted will be white light without POC. In the case of common opal, because of the haphazard size of the spheres, their lack of gridlike stacking, and their differently sized and shaped voids, the incoming light deflects at angles inconsistent with exhibiting visible color and so no POC is apparent[3] (Figure 4).

While the combination of diffraction and interference is necessary in the

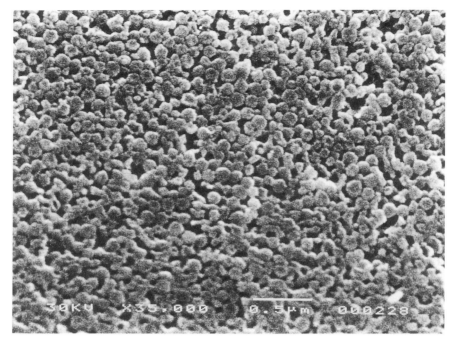

Figure 3. Haphazard stacking of the spheres in common opal—potch, as in this pictured material (35,000 ×) from the Andamooka opal field in South Australia, results in neither equal-sized nor equidistant voids between the spheres. The conclusion is, of course, that only a perfect alignment and stacking of the spheres provide the conditions that cause play of color to occur. (Photo courtesy of Dr. J. Van Landuyt, University of Antwerp (RUCA); Photo by RUCA Center for High Tension Electronmicroscopy)

opal to separate the prismatic colors, interference colors alone are something quite apart. These colors are induced by double reflection, like the colors seen swirling in soap bubbles or oil slicks on water. Part of the incident light is reflected from the upper surface of a thin film and part from the lower. Prismatic colors, as already noted, are caused by the fanning out of the components of light, with separation of the colors into their purest wavelengths, running from the slowest vibrations—infrared—on one end of the spectrum to the fastest wavelength vibrations—ultraviolet—on the other.

While some common opal varieties will fluoresce under longwave or shortwave ultraviolet light, most—including precious opal—usually do not fluoresce to any appreciable degree.[4] Some fire opals fluoresce from an olive-greenish color to brown and certain deposits of milk opal will fluoresce from very pale blue-white to pale green-white. As a matter of fact, the series of very rich opal mines grouped under the name Royal Peacock Opal Mines in Virgin Valley, Nevada, were actually "throw-ins" so to speak when the properties were initially purchased by the Wilson family in 1937 (Figure 5). As Walt Wilson related to

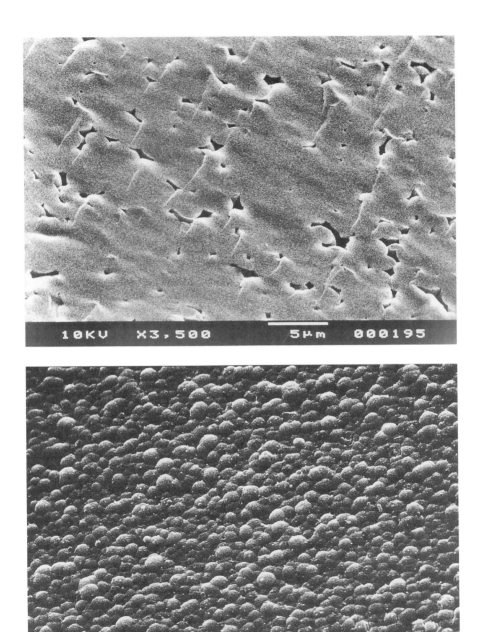

Figure 4. The deformity of the spheres in common opal, such as (*top*, 3,500 ×) in this potch from Coober Pedy, results in a severely disorganized plane that prevents the diffraction of light rays and therefore prohibits play of color. The same is true when (*bottom*, 750 ×) the spheres are not the same size and tiny spheres can pack themselves into the voids between larger spheres, as in this common opal from White Cliffs in New South Wales, thus preventing diffraction and its resultant play of color. (Photos courtesy of Dr. J. Van Landuyt, University of Antwerp (RUCA); Photo by RUCA Center for High Tension Electronmicroscopy)

Figure 5. The fluorescent opal level at the Royal Peacock Opal Mines. While the level is 4 feet thick and very extensive, best quality material occurs in a band a foot thick in the center. This opal, which fluoresces brilliant green, was initially the only opal being commercially mined in Virgin Valley, as it was once very popular in the European market. Even today a substantial amount of rough is mined and shipped overseas periodically by the mine's proprietors, Mary Ann and Walter Wilson. (Photo by the author)

the author, the money-maker at that time was the individual mine that was producing a translucent, faintly greenish-beige common opal that fluoresced to brilliant pastel green and was much in demand in the eastern United States and in Europe. The Virgin Valley black opal does not fluoresce and the other mines, with their marvelous deposits of incredibly beautiful precious black opal, were simply included as part of the purchase deal, since there was no market for the Virgin Valley precious opal at that time.

The refraction index of opal is generally listed as being between 1.435 and 1.455, but, again, this is variable depending on water content and the size of the spheres that comprise the stone. When pinned down to a definite figure for a refractive index for opal, most texts make it 1.44–1.46, although some will show Australian stones at a solid 1.47 and Mexican stones at a definite 1.37.

Opal is known to frequently carry a variety of impurities or inclusions—bits of clay, pieces of petrified wood, minute red spots, tiny bubbles, patches of hyalite, and sometimes even silver. But these occurrences have nothing to do with the visible color emitted from a precious opal.

Considerable confusion exists in differentiating some species of common opal with precious opal. Common opal almost always shows the same color when viewed from any angle, and some of the transparent common opals reflect white light. The Mexican fire opal, as opposed to the Mexican *precious* fire opal is a case in point. While the latter has a distinct and very beautiful POC in a base color of transparent red-orange to yellow-orange, the common fire opal variety has a similarly beautiful base color, resulting from the presence of iron oxides, but with a total absence of POC. The fact is, the base color of precious opal varies from transparent to white, as well as various hues: yellow to yellow-ish-brown, beige, orange, red, green, blue to violet, light gray to medium gray to black. Its POC can also vary widely, as can its clarity, which may range from absolute transparency through translucency to being entirely opaque.

Generally speaking, common opal is considerably hardier than precious opal in practically all respects. Common opal can more easily withstand the vagaries of atmospheric conditions in natural settings or changes of environment, temperature, and the like under artificial conditions, such as those to which the stone is subjected by the lapidarist. Precious opal tends to be considerably more fragile than the other precious and semiprecious stones in a variety of ways. While it does not have a cleavage plane as seen in many gemstones, such as topaz, it is a decidedly brittle stone that can easily crack or break or chip when subjected to sharp knocks or vibration.[5] When it chips, the break occurs in what is usually described as a conchoidal fracture, as seen in glass and obsidian, although certain authorities have classified opal fracturing as subconchoidal and undulating. A good example of a conchoidal fracture is the cone-shaped piece of glass that is knocked out of a window pane that has been struck by a BB from an air rifle. The opal conchoidal fracture has one aspect peculiar to opal only: The fracture surface itself under slight magnification, frequently shows a series of radiating lines that are tipped, on one side only, with tiny triangles, making them appear to be a number of harpoons. Also, when found in the mine, the precious opal is often discovered because of the brilliant colors it shows where it has been fractured in the mining process, having broken with a smooth and shiny surface that scintillates with an incomparable brilliance no less beautiful than the final cut opal will exhibit in a piece of jewelry.

The luster exhibited by opal varies from this vitreous (glassy) aspect to subvitreous to vitreous waxy to pearly to greasy to resinous to dull, depending on the individual opal's porosity, which in turn is dependent on the size of its molecular makeup. In precious opal, the luster tends more to the vitreous (glassy) than to the duller aspects, which are more often applied to common opal. Actually, many of the forms of common opal take their names from the type of luster they exhibit, as in wax opal, resin opal, pitch opal, and so on.

In habit, opal—which is most often opaque to translucent—occurs as massive material, often reniform (kidney-shaped), frequently as seam material, in certain areas as nodules, sometimes botryoidal (formed like solid bubbles or partial bubbles), often as filling in gas pockets or other cavities in volcanic rocks, sometimes pseudomorphic (as a replacement of other minerals or fossil remains), and, in some types of opal—such as geyserite, also known as siliceous sinter—as thin coatings over other rock material.[6] The specific gravity (relative density) of common opal normally runs from a low of 1.98 g/cm^3 to a high of 2.25 g/cm^3, but precious opal falls within these bounds at 2.1 to 2.2. Because of the porosity of some stones, there are those that will exhibit a density that is considerably lower, and others will register a higher density due to the amount of water contained within the individual stone.

The basic hardness of the stone can vary somewhat, with an opal that has larger internal spaces being softer. However, on the Mohs scale of hardness for minerals, opal, is usually listed as a hard stone, with a rating of 6, though it generally ranges between 5.5 and 6.5 (approximately the same as turquoise) and, in some cases, can be as soft as 4.5. To compare, quartz is listed at 7 on the Mohs scale and calcite is listed at 3. Hardness may also vary among types of opals. Volcanic opals and sedimentary opals are of the same family, but should not be considered identical in the matter of hardness or other elemental factors.

Certain types of precious opal—particularly opal that occurs as vug or gas bubble fillings in hard volcanic rock such as rhyolite or basalt—is extremely difficult to extract without severe damage to the stone. This is true as well with the most prevalent opal of Queensland, Australia—the boulder opal—which occurs in such thin veins and coatings in the matrix of ironstone that normally it cannot successfully be removed and is therefore polished with matrix adhering to it.

Precious opal is also notoriously heat sensitive, which often causes it to crack—sometimes even disintegrate—during the cutting process. Occasionally, even a sudden change in ordinary temperature can instigate cracking. Heat sensitivity during cutting is particularly common during the dopping process as well as during all phases of grinding, sanding, and polishing and is partly due to opal's high levels of water content, recorded as high as 21% but normally averaging between 6% and 10%. These negatives concerning working with opal frighten many amateur cutters into not even *attempting* to cut opal, but the stone's problems are not insurmountable. Kevin Lane Smith, a friend and easily the most skilled gem cutter the author has encountered, says in regard to cutting opal: "It can be as forgiving as harder materials when treated properly." The big problem, of course, is that a would-be opal cutter really views with trepidation the prospect of overcoming the pitfalls of opal cutting by practicing on rough gemstone material that may cost hundreds of dollars per carat or more.

Water content in opal tends to be the basis for most of the problems in opal cutting. The rule of thumb seems to be, the higher the water content in the stone, the greater its instability. The opals with the greatest stability today seem to be the sedimentary opals that are mined in Australia at Coober Pedy, Mintabie, and Lightning Ridge. The water content in this opal averages about 6% to 9% and in some areas is as low as 5%. The water content in volcanic opal, such as that from Mexico and Virgin Valley, Nevada, averages close to 10% and not infrequently is as high as 13% and the incident of opal fracture during cutting runs very high. For that reason the majority of the opals from Nevada—which are among the most beautiful opals in the world—are usually not cut but are, instead, kept as specimen pieces in liquid-filled containers.

Normally the liquid used for such storage of specimen opals is ordinary tap water, but some collectors swear by distilled water. Others store their opals in pure glycerin, transparent mineral oil, or liquid silicone. Since silicone is quite a viscous solution and is closest to the refraction index of opal, it not only can protect the stone, it can also cause any cracks visible in it to seemingly disappear. They do not actually disappear, of course, but are only masked by the liquid. The big drawback with silicone is that it is very expensive to use for such a purpose. Glycerin, too, has a pronounced ability to hide cracks, but despite being relatively inexpensive, it is not held in high favor because it has been shown actually to increase what cracking is already occurring in the stone and also to induce new cracking. Mineral oil is favored by some collectors, who claim its viscosity helps to protect the opal, which is true, but it has the disadvantage of being gradually absorbed into the opal—at least into its surface. Eventually the oil and the stone turn yellowish, which diminishes the opal's POC.[7] Because of this propensity of some (not all!) opals to absorb fluids, even though it may be but surface absorption, it is wisest not to bring them into contact with any types of oils or detergents. In the final appraisal, water—either distilled or ordinary tap water—seems to be cheapest, safest, and best fluid in which to store and display specimen opals that are not to be cut. It is a good idea, however, to add two or three drops of ordinary bleach to the container of water to prevent the formation of algae.

While a great many of the Nevada opals are stored and displayed in water, this is not to say that Virgin Valley opals cannot be cut and polished into fine gemstones, since a good many of them have been. Nevertheless, Virgin Valley stones have gained a reputation—often much worse than deserved—for producing opals more than ordinarily subject to cracking and crazing (Figure 6). So pronounced is this bad reputation that many opal cutters are afraid to work with them. The author has cut scores of these stones, most of which he mined himself in Virgin Valley, and would estimate that, with care, perhaps one-half of the stones can be successfully cut and, of the cut stones, the majority have not subsequently developed any cracks. Mexican precious fire opals, too, have a reputation for instability that easily rivals the reputation of the stones from Virgin Valley, yet by far the greater percentage of Mexican precious fire opal is sold

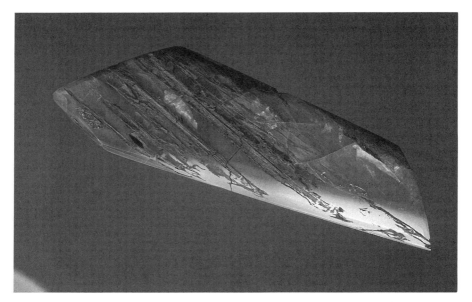

Figure 6. This Virgin Valley wood opal cut in 1993 by the author cracked a few days later, but the cracking stopped and never resumed. (Photo by the author)

for cutting in the Orient and, so far as can be determined, stands up reasonably well in the cutting process and afterward.

Opal, being somewhat more brittle and softer than other precious gemstones and more often translucent or opaque than transparent, is rarely faceted. Rather, it is cut and polished into cabochon mountings that emphasize the flashing, flowing, shifting nature of the POC much better than faceting permits. That having been said, the author must add that he has seen some superb faceted opals cut from transparent (and even translucent) material showing good POC. If faceting is contemplated, the critical angle for opal in that circumstance is 43°.

Quite often the cracking and crazing phenomenon to which opals are subject—a phenomenon, as noted, to which volcanic opal is more vulnerable than the so-called sedimentary opal—may occur spontaneously and so devastatingly that the opal will actually self-destruct. The prevailing belief is that the retention of substantial percentages of water in the opal's basic structure can often mean that application of heat or even just exposure to excessively dry conditions—or sometimes even ordinary atmospheric conditions—can cause fractures to develop in the stone, often within a short time of its being removed from the ground, if the opal is not quickly placed in a water-filled container.

It is unfortunately true that a fair amount of mined opal crazes, cracks, and even self-destructs within hours—sometimes within minutes!—of being dug out. This, as noted, is most often blamed on moisture loss, but that, according to opal expert Len Cram of Lightning Ridge, is incorrect. Cram contends, "While moisture can be lost from an opal exposed to the atmosphere, the process is very slow, even in arid conditions, and cracking or crazing so induced is not apt to show up for weeks, months, perhaps even years. Actually," Cram adds, "the greater majority of such rapid cracking and crazing in opal is more directly due to abrupt exposure of the newly unearthed stone to direct sunlight or excessively bright artificial light, since this will excite its ions into such increased acceleration that the vibrations generated can become intense enough to cause the opal to crack or even disintegrate. This often occurs—as many can attest, to their regret—even if the opal is stored in water, thus obviating the contention that the self-destruction is exclusively the result of drying out."

The author has developed a process that, while not guaranteed to entirely stabilize opals prone to crack or craze, such as those from Mexico and Virgin Valley, nevertheless goes a long way toward doing so; certainly it makes a great many stones safely cuttable that heretofore would most likely only have been consigned to water containers as specimen opals. That process is as follows.

Immediately upon unearthing what appears to be a good opal, keep it out of bright daylight or artificial light. Place it temporarily in water in a container that light cannot penetrate, but leave it there only long enough to get it back to the camp or shop or home that is its destination. There, working in dim light and with the stone immersed as much as possible or being held under running water, carefully remove all extraneous material—mud, clay, opal dirt, debris, etc. Dental tools are especially handy for such a job.

When the stone is as clean as it can be made under the circumstances, place it in a zip-type poly bag that can be resealed. Fold an ordinary paper towel, into as small a square as possible and saturate it in fresh water. Place this inside the plastic bag with the opal and then zip the bag closed. On the outside, in waterproof marking pen, write the date. Then put the bag and its contents, along with others similarly prepared, into a closeable cardboard box or other lidded container that will keep out most (but not necessarily all) of the light. Actually, a bit of rather dim ambient light is recommended.

Do not open the container for at least 6 months. At the end of that time, take the plastic bag out and look at the contents without opening it. It should be wholly dry by then, including the paper towel. However, to be certain, without opening the plastic bag, place it for a minute or so in lightly shaded sunlight. If moisture condenses on the inside of the plastic bag, put the unopened bag back into the storage box for another 3 months. If no moisture appears, unzip the plastic bag and inspect the stone for cracks of any kind. If no cracks are evident, the opal can be considered stabilized and stored dry thereafter, to be carefully cut at your convenience. If some cracking has become evident, make a note of where the cracks are situated on the stone and repeat the saturated paper towel treatment in the zipper poly bag for another 6 months.

Normally, one 6-month treatment will suffice. Occasionally a stone will show new cracks on the first inspection and require yet another 6-month treatment. Rarely, a third treatment may be necessary. And even more rarely, you will occasionally have a stone that simply will not stabilize and should then be permanently stored in water as a specimen stone. In the author's experience, about half of the stones stabilized in such manner can be successfully cut into excellent gemstones, not only of fine, lasting quality, but also of high value.

In discussing what comprises an opal, it would be remiss to fail to point out that opal is the only gemstone in the world that, in addition to being formed geologically, is also known to be formed both as an animal-produced product and as a vegetable-produced product (as opposed to pseudomorphic opal, which is another thing entirely). Animal opal is found in the stingers of female mosquitos (where it keeps the tip sharp.) Vegetable opal is found in microscopic diatoms, from which is formed such opal material as Fuller's earth and tripoli, and in stinging nettles, again where nature uses it to keep the points sharp. There is also another form of vegetable opal known by the name of tabasheer— a product that forms as small nodules (sometimes called pearls) in the joints of bamboo while it is still growing. It is most apparent in bamboo species that grow in China, South America, India, and Myanmar (formerly Burma). If the bamboo plant is injured, a form of liquid silica is produced and settles as a small nodule in the joint. When dried out these little nodules are opaque or translucent white, sometimes with a faint hint of blue, and bear a resemblance to seed pearls. They are often used in the Orient as jewelry. Like hydrophane opal, or cachalong, these little stones are extremely porous; so much so that they will adhere if touched with the tip of one's tongue. Because of such moisture-seeking properties, this type of opal was used in the Middle Ages to suck venom out of snake bites and was known there as snake stone. In South America, some of the tribes similarly use it to suck out poison from dart or arrow wounds.

A New Look at Opal Formation

It is not common for the long-held theories of how an elemental substance forms in nature to be proven to be so incorrect that all subsequent textbooks and scientific descriptions must be changed, but that is precisely the case in regard to the formation of opals. And it all happened because of a man named Len Cram of New South Wales, Australia. That name will be familiar to many who are interested in opals, since Cram is not only renowned as an opal expert, he is author of eight volumes concerning the beautiful opals of Australia and is currently writing what must become the definitive history of Australian opal.

Throughout the study of opals, the scientific papers and textbooks have told that the process of opal formation requires tens of thousands of years, perhaps hundreds of thousands . . . and some have even suggested millions. Not true. They have told us that a substance called silica gel percolates through the soil and when it finds a cavity left by a gas pocket in volcanic rock, it seeps into that cavity and fills it and then starts an eons-long process of drying and hardening into opal. Not true. They have told us that a similar process occurs in sedimentary areas where buried branches or logs or even animals decay away and leave behind a cavity mimicking the form of the original object. The silica gel seeps into such cavities, fills them, carefully reproducing the shape of the wood or even animal matter that was there before, and then begins the long hardening process to create opalized wood or opalized fossils. Not true. In fact, almost all that we have been taught about the basic formation of opals is based on theories that are now proven to be incorrect, at least in part if not in full.

The refutation has come about because of the experiments carried out by the self-taught individual named above, Len Cram, (Figure 7). Before getting into exactly what those experiments were, it would be fitting to take a brief look at the kind of person Cram is. Although I had been familiar with his writing and excellent photography for years, it was not until October of 1995 that I finally met Cram in Lightning Ridge and found him to be a friendly, gregarious chap who is uncommonly generous with both his time and his knowledge, a character trait that, unfortunately, has often been taken advantage of by others and that at times has brought him to the brink of disaster. Born in Newcastle,

Figure 7. Len Cram of Lightning Ridge, New South Wales—a remarkable man in many respects and a truly lateral thinker. (Photo courtesy of Len Cram)

New South Wales, and raised there on the shores of Macquarie Lake, he left home for Queensland in 1952 when he was 18 and went to work at the Hayricks Opal Mine, 1500 miles distant and one of the foremost producers of boulder opal in the world. There he gained a decade's worth of experience about opals that would stand him in good stead for the rest of his life.

Cram subsequently returned to Newcastle, married, and then settled in Lightning Ridge where he initially took out claims and mined for black opal, but eventually became a buyer. He, along with another chap named Les Taylor, opened the Japanese market for Lightning Ridge black opal, generally selling it in Japan for a 50% profit over what he had paid the Lightning Ridge miners for it. Cram steadily built up the Japanese market he'd created and eventually went into partnership with an overseas dealer, as well as making arrangements with two Lightning Ridge miners, which he admits was a serious mistake. It not only cost him a small fortune but he lost his business, his airplane, and almost everything else as well. Since that time he has worked alone, not only in mining and opal buying but in a relatively new adjunct to the field, photographing opals, at which he has become quite expert.

Cram describes himself, quite justifiably, as "a lateral thinker." He has a penchant for questioning things that others of us accept as fact, simply because we have encountered them proclaimed as such. His mind seems to reach out and not only enfold the elements of a subject, but automatically question their validity and assess how it might possibly be improved. A case in point was an auto Cram had at a time when every penny was dear. The car was a 253-V8 Holden, which gave him 19 miles to the gallon at 70 mph and a lot less with in-town driving. He thought it should do better and that two things were needed: better engine performance and better fuel economy.

"I've tinkered with many things, while laterally thinking," Cram told me, "and some of 'em I've researched—such as hydrocarbons, like petrol, and if you understand the way carburation works in a carburetor, you can start to do a few modifications. I decided that with a couple of little inventions, I might be able to accomplish both. Now, then, the fuel goes through a carburetor, and it's in gobbets. They say it's atomized, but it's not—it's only sort of vaporized and if you were to get it under an electronic microscope, you'd see it's like sausages and odd-shaped-balls and spheres. I thought of these vaporized gobs of fuel in the carburetor as being the size of basketballs and said to myself, 'If I can break that fuel up, say into eight balls the size of baseballs instead of one the size of a basketball, the surface area of the fuel that's going to burn will be increased by nearly 200 percent for the same volume of fuel!' And I figured if I could spin the air that was going into the manifold, without having any revolving parts and without putting any resistance into it, maybe I could improve the fuel economy.

"I drew a number of rough sketches and sat down with some thin copper pieces, which I rolled and soldered into tubes the correct size to fit into the intake manifold beneath the carburetor. With fine tin snips I cut out little vanes around one end of the tube. The angles in it looked a bit like the vanes of a jet engine, and the only resistance they gave was the thickness of the copper I used, which was about fifteen thou. They fit neatly under the carburetor and it took a few prototypes before I got what I was looking for. But eventually, when I had the angle and size of the vanes correct, the auto took off like a rocket. It accelerated to 120 miles per hour with great facility and everything—*everything!*—functioned better at all speeds; the vehicle's whole performance was greatly improved. I used the system for a number of years, besides putting it into the autos of a few selected friends."

That was the first invention, but there was another. Cram said he drew some rough sketches and then went down to the trash heap where some carpenters had thrown away pieces of flat galvanized iron off the new buildings. "I sat down on the floor with that stuff," Cram went on, "and I marked it all out with a pencil. I think I worked on it a couple of days. Obviously I needed the use of certain carburetor parts that I couldn't manufacture—the idle-inject, the accelerator pump to help start the motor, and the butterfly—but I didn't want the metering jet and the main jet, so I closed them off. And I built a float chamber on the bottom of the device."

Cram grinned as he continued. "The principal was this: I had a sponge that the petrol hydrocarbons wouldn't dissolve, right? It was a piece of that black spongy stuff that they put under the old typewriters to help muffle the noise, and it didn't dissolve in petrol. The float chamber that I built held 1.2 liters and I measured out that much fuel in a beaker and put it in there and then I just set the sponge in it. Of course, it sucked up quite a bit of the petrol into it. A tube went up through the center and there were two holes on either side of the bottom just above the float chamber—that's where the air went in—and there was just a little space for the air to run fast over the face of that spongy matting so that, while it was passing, it could drag away fine particles of fuel. Then the air carrying the fuel came up around and out of the hole in the top and went straight through the carburetor into the intake manifold. So there it was, and you couldn't get it any simpler than that.

"The whole thing, housing and all, was about that round and about that high," Cram continued, using his hands to indicate a size that was about one foot by eight inches, "and because I figured I should give it some kind of a name, I called it a compillary fuel converter. I had designed it to fit between the fender and the engine and the radiator—there's a place where it could sit. So I attached it and got everything in place. At this point there was no connection between the gas tank and the carburetor, because I had closed off the main jet and metering jet. The only fuel was the 1.2 liters that I had poured in by hand."

Cram chuckled, remembering. "Now, I didn't know if the thing would even start," he told me, "and I have to admit I didn't have the foggiest notion that it would ever run—it just seemed to me that it ought to, you know? It was just a dream. But I put it on the car and started the car up and the motor roared like an airplane taking off and I couldn't believe it!"

Cram said he took the car out on a test run and was amazed that it even ran. Because of the limited fuel, he drove only eight miles before turning around and coming back home and, as he put it to me, "I drove back in there and I switched that motor off as quickly as I could. Then I grabbed that converter out and took it into the shed and I poured what was left of the fuel back into the beaker. And . . . I was amazed! I had driven sixteen miles without stopping, and I calculated it out to 69 miles to the gallon, but I was so excited, I forgot about the fuel that was still soaked up in the sponge! It must have had a quarter of a liter of fuel in it, and that means the mileage could've been anywhere up around 80 or 90 miles to the gallon."

Cram said he cleaned the compillary fuel converter and put it into a box in his shed, intending to do some modification work on it later on, but somehow other things intervened and he never got back to it. That was nearly twenty years ago and, having only been used that one time, this amazing little device still sits gathering dust in Cram's little storage shed, which is where I saw it, held it in my hands and marveled at its simplicity.

The point in telling this has been simply to exemplify the type of mind Cram has and how he tends to analyze and question the things that people normally take for granted. It was in this same respect that he began to question what everyone else was accepting as fact—the long established theory as to how opal forms in nature. First, let's take a quick look at the theory that has been held in such esteem for so long.

Putting it in rather simple form, the old theory states that beginning in the late Cretaceous Period, some 70 million years ago and extending about 35 million years into the middle Tertiary Period, vast beds of sedimentary and volcanic ash material were subjected to extensive acid or alkaline rains. These caustic rains were alleged to seep into the compressed volcanic ash deposits or muds or country rock, turning them into kaolinite—clay.

As the solution percolated deeper into the ground material, it became, through chemical action, very heavy with soluble silica dissolved in water at 120 parts per million. It continued the downward percolation, sometimes following and filling pathways made by cracks or faults, at other times slowly steeping itself through the ground material and eventually filling all the cavities encountered. Then, over an extensive period of time covering eons, the silica gel filling the cracks and cavities finally hardened. And if, in this process of settling and hardening, the opal molecules managed to align themselves in very orderly, overlapping fashion, the resultant opal, instead of being merely common opal, became today's very precious variety.

Sounds like a reasonable theory? Sure it does, at least superficially. But to accept that theory, one really does have to overlook some very perplexing anomalies, which is invariably something Cram refuses to do. A variety of questions plagued him. For example, if the silica solution percolated through the soil until it reached a cavity and then filled it, why, as so frequently occurs, would one cavity be filled and others around it and closely adjacent to it have no trace of opal in them? If the silica gel merely filled a cavity, how then could it reproduce perfectly the internal cellular structure of the object that had been there in the first place?

How could the soluble silica possibly have percolated through such extremely hard materials as igneous rocks—the basalts and rhyolites, for example—and snugly fill the vugs and gas pockets with amygdaloidal nodules called amygdules, especially in beds of such dense material that had no cracks or fissures for the silica gel to follow? How could the silica gel fill a cavity and remain a gel—a state in which it is occasionally found—through hundreds, thousands, or millions of years, as frequently occurs? How could the gaps or cracks or cavities in soft sediments possibly remain open for ages, simply waiting for the happenstance of a silica gel percolating through the soil to fill them? How could the silica solution lay itself down in one part of the cavity as common opal, then on top of that form a layer of precious opal and, on top of that, another layer of common opal? Why would the percolating silica gel form a whole deposit of fine precious opals in one small area, but not in an area adjacent to it that was identical in every respect, so far as could be determined? If it took eons for the silica gel to harden, why was that gel not squeezed out of the cavities through normal earth pressures? Why did the opal form so differently in different places—pipe opal here, boulder opal there, nobbies or blobs or seams in other places?

Filled with all these unanswered or poorly answered questions about opal, Len Cram began looking at opal and its formation—and the *speed* of its formation—in an entirely new light. He had always been fascinated by the way opal had replaced not only fossil woods, but also, in some cases, fossil animals. Miners at White Cliffs and Lightning Ridge in New South Wales and others at Coober Pedy and Andamooka in South Australia were finding fossils of prehistoric creatures that had been replaced by opal, such as the several completely opalized skeletons of the marine reptile called plesiosaurus. It was unfortunate that most of these, instead of being preserved for their scientific value, had been broken up and sold for their opal content, but such was the case.

What really had a greater impact upon Cram, however, were the cases where far more modern remains were being found, also opalized. One such case involved the skeleton of a cat. This animal, the pet of a miner, had died in 1896. The miner had placed the dead animal in his own hat, sorrowfully buried it in the floor of his mine and soon afterward abandoned the dig. The mine remained unworked for 50 years, when a new miner came in and reclaimed it. Soon after beginning his own digging, he uncovered the hat and it's contents. Only skeletal residue of the cat remained, but that entire skeleton had been transformed into a pale pink precious opal.

As if that were not enough, Cram learned that fenceposts erected in volcanic opal country some 80 years ago were being discovered, when the fence needed replacing, to have their buried portions turned into opal. It also happened in Victoria, thousands of miles away. To others, these discoveries were simply unusual and interesting; to Cram they further underlined the anomalies involved in the prevailing theories of the genesis of opal. How could a cat, buried only five decades earlier, be discovered again and its entire skeleton found to have been turned into precious opal? How could fenceposts sunk in opal dirt have their subsurface portions transformed into opal, some of it precious?[1] How . . . well, the list goes on and on and only if one is willing to overlook these prevailing inconsistencies can the percolation-and-cavity-filling theory hold up. These anomalies triggered a definite response in Cram, encouraging him to toss those existing theories aside, put his lateral thinking in gear, and start looking for new answers.

By this time Cram was convinced that not only did opal form with infinitely greater swiftness than previously believed, it had little or nothing to do with cavities being filled by a percolating liquid—a silica gel—that, over eons, hardened into opal. To the contrary, he believed the formation of opal had to be accomplished through the process termed ion exchange or, more properly, perhaps, atom migration; a process in which, when a proper chemical mix has occurred involving feldspar, alumina, and all the other minerals found in the opal clay, besides water and an electrolyte, a transference of ions occurs spontaneously, in which electricity passes through virtually any kind of matter from one place to another. It is, therefore, the electrolyte itself—a liquid bearing a particular acid or alkali—that not only *permits* the migration of ions from one place to another, but actually *encourages* such a migration to take place, generating an electrical field in which opal spontaneously *replaces* the original matter, i.e., the transformation of opal dirt to precious opal, or the alteration of fossil material, animal and vegetable, into precious opal.

As Len Cram himself put it to me: "In all the equations, atom migration is involved. During my geological studies, traveling around the world and Australia, up to this point, I have discovered four separate ways in which the formation of opal occurs, and they are all interrelated through ionization. In all, the nucleus is the attraction or starting point. The electrolyte is the conductor which operates in the groundwater in which the movement of positive and negative ions becomes the conduction. In chemistry, a group of atoms that have either lost or gained electrons and have thereby acquired a positive or negative charge are properly termed ions. Such ions are capable of chemical recombinations, known as ion exchange or atom migration, allowing them to form new compounds. Hence, opal dirt, when subjected to an electrolyte—that is, a liquid carrying a chemical that generates an electrical pathway through anything—spontaneously changes to opal, beginning at the nucleus and expanding outward, with the process continuing unabated until all of the electrolyte present has been used up. This satisfactorily answers the question that has perplexed so many, about how opal could occur, for example, as amygdules in gas bubbles or pockets within dense deposits of rhyolite, basalt or other volcanic rock, in which there are no cracks to permit access by a percolating liquid. There doesn't have to be: As long as the chemical conditions are correct and an electrolyte is present, the opal grows spontaneously from the inside out, through the process of atom migration.

"Now then," Cram went on, "what initially made me think laterally, away from the tunnel vision that we've been taught, is that the models we've been taught with have got gaping holes in them. These holes are not written up in the models, and being an experienced opal miner and with maybe an analytical mind in everything I do, I recognized these omissions and simply said to myself, 'Why haven't we been told about these things? Why aren't they there? Why are they simply left out of the equation, as if they don't even exist, when it is perfectly obvious that they *do* exist?' The answer is a blot on scientific research: There were no known answers for these anomalies; and, since they just wouldn't work in the existing equation, they were simply ignored. Instead of being acknowledged and investigated, it was more convenient to merely leave them out. So that made me question the accepted theories and prompted my research into 'em: you give me the challenge and I think I can go on and grab it."

"So what it all boils down to," I commented to Cram, "is that the most accepted existing theory—that acid or alkaline rains chemically reacted with volcanic ash to form a silica gel, which, in turn, percolated down through the ash and into cavities or pockets in sedimentary soils or volcanic rocks or in deteriorated or fossil wood or other plant or animal matter—that this is not really true?"

Cram shrugged. "Ninety-eight percent," he replied, "or ninety-five percent, is not true. Okay, look at it this way: For an electrolyte to work, you've got to have water for it to travel through, right? Then you've got to have a nucleus—any one of a number of things, depending on what it's going to attract that ion to, right? Now, in the opal dirt, as any opal miner knows, you are going to have holes occurring that are empty, while right alongside them, sometimes even surrounded by them, are similar cavities wholly or partially filled with opal. Or vice versa. Or there may be a bit of wood that is opalized, with a similar one right alongside it—or maybe even part of it—that is not. Now, the logic of it . . . just the simple logic of it disputes this contention: If, as the existing theories state it, the silica was dissolved by the alkalies or acids and precipitated downward through the soil as a silica gel, and you have two pieces there within inches of each other, and one has a big tube of wood in it, partly opal and partly potch, and the other's so dry and empty that a rabbit can crawl up it, what would be your conclusion?"

"That the empty hole would also have been filled?"

"Right. You don't even have to go to school to answer that one. And if it had wood in it, it would slowly rot away and leave a hollow. Now, if that wood had been dissolved with salts and water and seeped out and left a hollow and then that hollow had later filled up with silica gel as the theory contends, can you explain to me why all the configurations of the bark, the design and the shape of it, is all preserved in solid opal? Can you explain why the basic cellular structure of the wood has been reproduced in the opal?"

"No. That's what I don't understand at all and what I'd like you to explain to me."

"Okay," Cram replied, nodding. "What has happened is a process has taken place that is commonly known in physics as atom migration. We don't know for certain what the natural electrolyte was that occurred there, but it becomes clear that the wood didn't simply dissolve away and leave a cavity to be filled with percolating silica gel that could eventually harden into opal. Actually, there's a neutral ion electrolyte at point A and there's an attraction in the wood at point B, and so what happens is a flow of ions from point A to point B that results in the atoms of the wood becoming rearranged in molecule structure without actually being disintegrated—an atom migration and then a re-arrangement of these atoms.

"So it's a form of metamorphosis?"

"Yes! It's absolutely perfect metamorphism. Now think: Most opal is composed of at least two point five percent aluminum oxide, so let's ask ourselves a very basic question. What is aluminum oxide? Well, it's the second hardest thing in nature—sapphire. So how does it get into the opal? You can't transform an oxide into a plain water solution, not even in a lab. That means it certainly can't be flowing along in solution with a silica gel and get trapped in the opal. And that was one of the things that got me thinking. That was what made me get onto the ionization process as the possible answer for how the aluminum oxide gets into the opal. And it turns out that is the only answer: It can *only* get into opal as ions in an ionic migration. And, if aluminum oxide can be formed from alumina and oxygen during the ion exchange process, also know as atom migration, then everything else can exchange as well, providing conditions are exactly right for such an exchange to occur.

"In the case of opals," Cram went on, "the altered volcanic ash has become a clay, a kaolinite or montmorillonite that we call opal dirt, and in that clay is found naturally the alumina atom: Al. Now, all that is necessary for ionic migration to take place within the subject material—whether it be a bone or wood or shell or anything else, including even the ordinary opal dirt itself—all you need to do is have those atoms available and be able to pick up, for every two of those Al atoms, three oxygen atoms, which are hardly traveling at all, and lock into it. When you do that, you've got aluminum oxide—Al_2O_3. And the same elemental process occurs with all the other materials that are in that wood and in the traveling ions that are involved."

"So doesn't that mean," I pointed out, "that for the formation of opal, there is still a necessary process of percolation of water through the soil or ash or clay?"

"Absolutely," Cram agreed. "There has to be water present for any electrolytic action to take place—for ion exchange to occur. Now, you say, well it doesn't occur everywhere, and that's perfectly true; it doesn't. Which only goes to show that there are still a number of factors involved in opal formation that no one yet understands. If it formed in one place but not in another, was this because where it didn't form there was a lack of an electrolyte? Was it because of the lack of a nuclearite in a target subject or area? Obviously, if you haven't got somewhere for the ions to be attracted to, you are not going to have the atom migration—which is closely related to ion exchange—so you need both of them, and then you need the water to act as the conductor for the electrolytic process."

Having given careful consideration to all these factors, Cram, in 1987, ambled down a few hundred yards to the west end of Pandora Street—the street on which he lives in Lightning Ridge—to the place where a still partially worked opal field exists. It was a field that years earlier had been a good producer of precious opal. There, from the old mullock heaps, he collected some of the opal dirt and brought it home. In his little makeshift lab in a shed behind his house, he mixed up a solution he thought might emulate the type of natural electrolyte he believed caused the generation of opals. Putting some of the opal dirt and some water into a jar, he mixed it thoroughly and then he poured in a portion of the liquid electrolyte he'd concocted. Cram then shook it up well so that the electrolyte was evenly dispersed all through it and put the jar on a shelf and forgot about it for a few months. When next he checked, he was overjoyed to find that a certain limited amount of ionization had definitely occurred and that a small layer of opal had formed within the opal dirt in the jar (Figure 8). It was not much, but it proved him correct in his belief that the existing theories about the formation of opal were incorrect and his own postulations seemed to be the answer. Still, he determined to carry his experiments even further to be certain.[2]

It was at about this time that an old friend of Cram's, a scientist named John V. Sanders, visited him. The scientist didn't want anyone to know that he had terminal cancer and was paying a last visit to many of his friends, including Len Cram. He had planned to spend only a few hours but wound up remaining for three days. Some time before, Sanders and his colleague, Peter Darragh, renowned scientists of the Commonwealth Scientific Industrial Research Organization (CSIRO), had collaborated on a scientific paper entitled "The Genesis of Natural Opal."[3] In that paper, which Cram states "is the bible on the genesis of opals all over the world," the two scientists reiterated a new slant on the old silica gel percolation theories to explain how opal formed. In a good-natured way, Cram and Sanders had debated that very issue over the years, with Cram pointing out the inconsistencies in their theory. Cram said, "As I've mentioned, it was the holes in this model that had got me thinking laterally about opal formation to begin with. It was not only that there simply could not be the kind of hollowed-out sedimentation they propounded, a sedimentation that was just sitting there waiting over X-amount of millions of years for an opal gel to come percolating down and fill those hollows, it also had to do with the faulty physics involved in the whole thing; there were a number of aspects of physics that were just absolutely incredible, that just couldn't happen under any circumstances."

Figure 8. One of the earliest of Len Cram's experimental opals, grown in a glass jar in his little backshed laboratory in Lightning Ridge, New South Wales. (Photo by Len Cram)

It was at that juncture, chuckling to himself, that Cram had led Sanders out to his shed and showed him that first trace of opal he had grown in the jar. Sanders was absolutely stunned and, as Cram laughingly put it, "I think he got a terrible shock. His eyes practically popped out and he dug out that 10-power glass of his and studied the opal through the glass of the jar. I think he forgot I was even there because he was whispering under his breath, 'Amazing! Amazing! Amazing!' and I don't think he even knew he was saying it. Finally, he seemed to catch himself up and he turned and looked at me and asked if I had written down the experiment. When I told him I hadn't, he reached out and grabbed my arm and said, 'Len, you've got to get it written down! Puh-lease! If you don't want to show anyone, at least write it down so it won't be lost!' "

As it turned out, Cram said, he and Sanders sat up talking most of that night and all the next two days and Cram explained how the holes in the existing theories regarding opal formation had really bothered him and he had begun searching around for answers on his own. "I told him," Cram recalled, "that since it just wasn't possible for opal to have been deposited the way they had written in their paper, there had to be another way. I told him what happened then: that I had thought it over and thought it over—lain in bed and thought about it, played around with it in my mind and eventually I came up with this theory. I didn't tell John just then what the theory was, but I knew that somehow it must have something to do with ion exchange, and that I then decided to experiment. Now it's the only scientific experiment I think I've ever put together and the way I went at it probably wasn't according to regular scientific protocols—I didn't have to do hundreds of experiments and throw them away when they didn't work. But I had a lot of experience from the work I was doing and I had a lot of theories, based on my mining experience over so many years, and from my research with opals out in my shed. So I was able to put all these together and come up with that theory that it had to be ion exchange. The long and the short of it was that I came up with this particular electrolyte and mixed it up, put it in a bottle, and it worked . . . to a degree. Finally, I said to him, 'Johnny, if I tell you what's going on, do you promise you will never tell Peter or anybody else down there? Not a living soul?' He said, 'I promise you, Len, I promise you!' I said, 'Okay, I will, John.' I said, "It's ionic exchange. Now this is what I'm doing. . . ." and I told him the kind of electrolyte I was using and how I was doing it and all. And then he shook his head and said to me—and I don't disbelieve the man—he said, 'Len, I have to tell you that when we put that paper together, *The Genesis of Natural Opal,* we considered ionic exchange but we . . . uh . . . discarded it.'[4]

"That's what he said, and what I deduced from that was that if they'd've followed that line of thought it would've upset a lot of geologists around the world. Now, coming back to my own work, after Sanders left I decided that since only a *little* bit of the dirt had changed into opal, I would make the next one a rather bigger experiment. I had a 1 ¼-liter bottle which I'd cut the top off of and made a considerable amount of dirt and electrolyte and I mixed it all up and threw it in it. And I did expect *something* to happen, because of the first experiment, but I never expected to get what I got.

After a little while, color started to show . . . and . . . and I forgot all about it, because I'd put the experiment on a shelf above me head and I used to walk past it and forget it and not even look up there. And after a number of months I looked up, and there was what looked like a huge amount of opal in it. I suppose 40% of what was showing in the bottle appeared to be opal, and the rest was opal dirt with water on top. Day after day I looked at it but it was staying constant, without further change and so, I thought, I will siphon the water off the top and let it slowly dry out, just see what I have. I put a little hole in the plastic cover and siphoned the water off and *again* I forgot all about it . . . for some months—probably three or four. One day I looked up there and got the shock of my life—it was *all* opal . . . just a few little spots of dirt around the sides, just an odd spot, y'know? I suppose it was three-quarters of an inch thick and, in diameter, the same as the jar—I suppose about 3 inches. And probably weighed about 6 ounces."

"Oh, my word! Len, what an accomplishment!"

Cram nodded. "Anyway, I looked at it and I was in shock. Absolute shock.

I got it down very quickly, but I couldn't get it out of the bottle, so I smashed the glass. It still had quite a bit of moisture in it, but it hadn't blown up or anything like that. My eyes were seeing it, but my mind wouldn't accept it. Absolutely shocked. What I had believed in theory I wasn't prepared to accept in reality."

"I shouldn't wonder! My gosh, Len, it had to be one of the most exciting moments of your entire life!"

He nodded and continued, "So, after a few minutes I walked over into the house just to get a drink of water. My wife was working in the kitchen and she said to me—I didn't even look at her, I don't think—so she said to me, 'Are you sick?' And I said, 'No, but I've just turned opal dirt into opal and I find . . . , I can see it but my brain won't accept it.' Now she takes absolutely no interest in that shed, but she said 'What?What?What?What!' and went hurrying out and went into the shed. She said, "Where is it?" and I pointed and said, "There it is." She picked it up, put it in her hand like that. 'Oh,' she said, 'it's much heavier than all your other opal, isn't it?' And she put it down and walked out and she never came back."

"And that was it?" I asked. "An incredible accomplishment like that, one of the greatest discoveries *ever* in mineralogy, and that was the only reaction you got?"

"That was all she ever said," Cram murmured, shaking his head. He then went on to tell me that he had been, at that time, making some "floating opal" jewelry pieces and, "I thought to myself, 'This will make fantastic stuff,' and, like an idiot, I broke that piece up."

"Oh, Len, you didn't! What a shame!"

"Yes," he agreed ruefully, "but the basic thing was this—and I think this is the crucial thing in the whole experiment—there was a period of time from when I siphoned all the water off it to when I took it out. And it was then all opal dirt on the top half. But then there came a period of time when the viscosity of that opal dirt got within given parameters. And when this happened, that ion exchange just took off like lightning. See? So, it had been up there a long, long time with all the water sitting on top of it and the process had gone as far as it was going to go. Until I siphoned the water off of it and the dirt started to dry out, and away it went, and all the remaining opal dirt turned into opal."

It's true. With opal dirt from different opal fields around Australia and even different locations around the world, Len Cram can grow opals in an amazingly short period of time. He has grown boulder opal potch in varying designs and colors like the specimens found in boulder opal locations in Queensland, black opal identical to that of Lightning Ridge, light opal and crystal opal indistinguishable from that which occurs at Coober Pedy, and beautiful green-blue opal that cannot be differentiated from Andamooka opal. He has even been successful in growing specimens from opal dirt gathered from the mines in Virgin

Valley. The opals grow with the same kinds of patterns, veinings, color bars and other attributes found in natural opals mined in the fields.

Among the many long-held beliefs involving opal formation is the one that asserts the black opal nobbies of Lightning Ridge are actually fossils. Due to their odd, often conical shape, the nobbies have been likened to seed pods of a type of water lily. Cram's experiments have proven this—and many other similar suppositions—to be incorrect. Using opal dirt from areas of Lightning Ridge where fine black opal nobbies have previously been mined, Cram introduces the electrolyte and at once a compact little core of opal begins forming. It quickly grows outward from this center point and forms itself into a concretionary shape that soon takes on the typical nobby configuration, complete with the so-called "cap of white porcelain" and interior of brilliantly beautiful black opal. So it is clear, now, that the black opal in no way a fossil. Why it takes that distinctive shape, however, remains a mystery and, as Cram puts it, while ionization answers the fundamental question of *how* opal forms, it opens up a whole new field of inquiry into *why* it forms into the specific shape of nobbies here, boulder opals there, pipe opals elsewhere, and the many other particular shapes it assumes in different places and under certain circumstances.

"We have only barely opened the door to understanding the true nature of the opal," Cram says.

One of the most strongly established theories in regard to opal formation is seemingly proven incorrect by Cram's experiments—the theory of how seam opal forms in sedimentary deposits. Prevailing belief has it that the sedimentary beds of clay were interlaced with a variety of cracks, most less than an inch in height but often as much as 30 feet wide and frequently overlying one another. These cavities, so the theory goes, lay waiting for hundreds of thousands—perhaps millions—of years until at last conditions became right for the percolation of silica gel through the soil. When the gel reached the cavities, it spread out, filling them and subsequently, over more thousands of years, hardening into broad flat seams of precious opal. So the theory went.

Even before his experiments, Cram thought that theory was ridiculous, maintaining that it would have been impossible for the unstable clay to remain suspended this way for even a short period, much less eons. Further, most of the seam opal from these deposits is permeated with bits of the clay, which the miners usually refer to as sand. The clay bits, Cram contends, being much lighter than the opal gel, would soon float to the top of the gel rather than be held in suspension all through it while the hardening process took place over greatly extended periods. The fact that they didn't, he says, indicates not only a much swifter hardening than previously believed but also that, just as the opal grows into seams when forming in Cram's jars, so in the sedimentary beds, when the opal formed through ion exchange, it actually created its own seams in the process, usually following a horizontal plan of the silicon atoms' preferred force to build molecules in this way. The same seems to hold true for the long strands of rootlike pipe opal, though why one opal form spreads out in a broad, flat seam and the other in a tubelike shape remains another of the many unanswered questions.

Another set of theories about opal that are obviated through the proofs inherent in Cram's work are those involving color in opals—more specifically, the base color of the opal as opposed to the POC. In 1965 it was shown through electron microscopy by Drs. Sanders and Darragh of CSIRO that it was the neat alignment of the spheres and voids in precious opal causing diffraction of light rays that resulted in POC, but what about the base color? Most scientists involved theorized that the base color of any given opal was the result of microscopic impurities, an explanation that sounded quite reasonable and that was generally accepted. Cram's work, however, has proved that supposition incorrect.

Early on he experimented with adding dyes to the liquid involved in growing the opals. All this resulted in was that the opal, selecting its own color or transparency, grew in layers apart from the color that had been added. If, for example, the opal dirt was from an area that produced light opal stones and Cram added a black dye to the initial mix in order to try to grow a black opal, the opal would form as a transparent or white layer *beneath* the dye-bearing liquid. What this points out, in essence, Cram contends, is that light and black opal appear to start out the same. As Cram told me, "Dyes were only used in my very early work and never in any work with opal dirt. Also, opal dirt from black opal areas does *not* necessarily produce black opal [in the lab]; this has happened on only one occasion. We must always remember that light and black opal are always mined together; rarely do you find black totally by itself (Figure 9). Some of the greatest crystal opals the world has ever seen have been found alongside black opals. Also, it is not uncommon to find an outstanding black gem attached to a piece of poor-quality light opal. All this has a reason and I personally believe from my research in growing opals that all Lightning Ridge black opal was once light. Certain molecule changes took place before the opal had reached a given hardness which allows a certain amount of white light to be absorbed. Hence, I was able to develop all the different types and colors of opal without adding any dye. It is true that I originally used dyes in my work in trying to grow opal, but without success. I first realized that black opal had no natural dye in it many years ago when I started crushing samples of pure black potch. They always changed to a light dirty gray. It is a very simple test for any base color of opal, no matter where it comes from. If it contains a mineral dye, it should not change color when crushed."

Len Cram has since, of course, discovered that opal dirt from black opal-producing areas results in true black opals being formed; opal dirt from Andamooka produces the lovely blue-green opals for which that field is famous, and

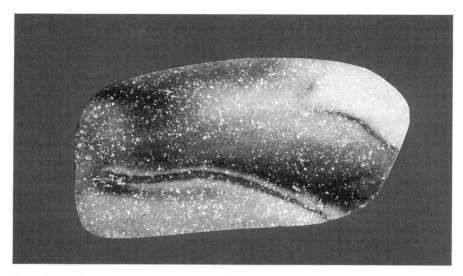

Figure 9. A piece of opal recently grown by Len Cram combines black opal and light opal in one piece, as so often occurs in nature, and glitters with multicolor pinfire POC. (Photo by Len Cram)

so on. Cram's conclusion is that the chemical composition of all opal—black, white, transparent, crystal, green, whatever—is identical. It is likely that the combination of the electrolyte, the molecular structure of the opal dirt, and perhaps even the speed of generation and rate of opal growth determines what the ultimate base color will be, but that's not a definite finding and an indisputable answer remains yet to be found.

Undoubtedly one of the most important elements of Cram's work is the fact that through his questioning of the inconsistencies in the widely accepted theories regarding opal formation—and in the face of opposition from very influential people and organizations behind them—he has single-handedly enlightened the mineralogical world and scientifically proven every step of the way the correctness of his own conclusions. Though in his own words he thinks of himself as "just a backyard scientist," to further encourage acceptance of his work, Cram, now possessor of an honorary doctorate in recognition of his outstanding work with opals, is preparing to present papers to the scientific community outlining the proofs that substantiate his efforts.

Cram's little outer shed workshop laboratory is rustic to say the least—a long, narrow walk-in closet of a room, probably no more than 6 feet wide and perhaps 15 feet long. Several shelves hold dozens, even scores, of containers in which opal is being grown: jelly jars, soft drink bottles, mason jars, baby food jars, condiment bottles, peanut butter jars, etc. (Figure 10). As noted, much of

Figure 10. A wide variety of bottles and jars are used by Len Cram in his opal-growing experiments, each carefully marked in his own cryptic system of identification. Opals of different types and in various stages of growth can be seen here. (Photo by Len Cram)

the opal, as it grows, spreads itself out in seams of its own creation through the electrolyte-impregnated opal dirt, just as occurs naturally in the opal dirt levels in the opal fields. Eventually, assuming enough electrolyte has been mixed with the dirt, nothing but solid precious opal will remain. Attached to each container is a piece of paper on which is cryptically logged the salient details of that particular experiment. Numerous other jars are filled with lumps and chunks of brilliant, beautiful precious opal in all colors and sizes—the impressive results of past experiments.

While Cram still engages in some variant experiments in regard to opal growing, much of what he does these days is pretty well proscribed. Once he has put together the opal dirt, water, and electrolyte and mixed them well, as the mixtures settles and begins to clear, the first play of color becomes visible within as short a time as three days, although he has been able to produce color in as little as 15 minutes in his lab. Before very long the dirt all settles on the bottom and the solution clears. Hairlike seams of opal become apparent threading through the opal dirt, and these seams, virtually identical to the seams opal has formed naturally underground, widen and spread during the weeks that follow. (Figure 11). By the end of 3 three months, a half-inch of pure, beautifully patterned and colored precious opal has grown in the dirt itself rather than, as one might suspect, in the bottom of the container. "In many cases," Cram added, "it forms a crockery potch on top of the color, as is the case with many nobbies."

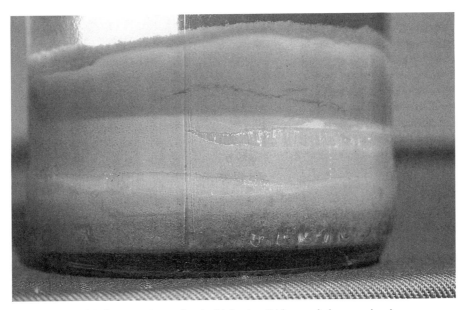

Figure 11. 1996, Seam opal growing in Lightning Ridge opal clay, creating its own seams as it grows, as it undoubtedly does in nature. These specimens are only two of the large number of opal-growing experiments being carried out by Len Cram in his backshed laboratory at his home in Lightning Ridge. (Photo by Len Cram)

Eventually, usually by the end of 5 or 6 months, the growing process slows drastically, sometimes stopping altogether. The opal in the container is, at this point, an inch or more thick, abnormally heavy because it is super-saturated, and so soft that it is wholly unusable for jewelry of any kind. The remaining liquid is thereupon carefully siphoned off through a small hole in the container's cover, allowing direct air contact in order to dry the stone—a process that takes about 6 months. It is during this drying process that the viscosity of the mixture again reaches a critical point and the remaining dirt in the container very quickly begins its restructuring, altering to precious opal, the process continuing in some cases until no dirt remains and the opal has markedly intensified in color and pattern and hardened substantially. The degree of hardness is predicated upon the amount of aluminum oxide formed during the process and the majority of the water content in stone being squeezed out. While Cram's opal is, at this stage, still not quite as hard and stable as the majority of the naturally formed opal at Lightning Ridge or Coober Pedy, it is now marginally cuttable as a gemstone. But it is also through this process of accelerated drying that the newly formed stone sometimes exhibits a proclivity toward cracking, a problem Cram is currently striving to solve.

Cram is convinced that while the opal formation process in nature takes a considerable while, the span of time involved is nowhere near so long as most experts have for many years contended. Conditions must, of course, be exactly right for the process of ionization to begin naturally—the correct amount of silica, moisture, subsidiary chemicals, and the all important electrolyte. But Cram believes—and his experiments bear testimony to the validity of his belief—that once begun, the ion exchange occurs rapidly and continues in the wood or fossil or opal dirt for as long as the supply of electrolyte lasts and while the critical chemical balance is maintained.

In 1994 Cram went on a world tour, visiting some of the best known and most productive precious opal-producing areas. Among those he visited were the Mohave Valley volcanic opal mines in California, the black opal mines of Virgin Valley in Nevada, the rhyolitic Spencer opal mining area in Idaho, and the first known opal mines in the world, those in the Carpathian Mountains of southeastern Europe, where for centuries the so-called Hungarian opals were mined and supplied to the world.

It was while he was on this tour that Cram spent a day in Lucerne, Switzerland, with one of the foremost gemmologists in the world, Edward J. Gübelin, discussing opal generally and its formation in particular. Upon his return home, Cram found a letter awaiting him from Dr. Gübelin, who wrote, in part:

> Let me tell you that I have the feeling that I should not let another day pass by without cordially thanking you for the honour you bestowed upon me by your interesting visit on Monday afternoon, as well as for your kindness of presenting me with two indescribably beautiful and informative publications on beautiful Australian opals composed by your good self.
>
> It was with keen interest that I followed your highly interesting and instructive elaboration about opal in general and your own experiments and scientific projects in particular. I have never experienced such a very informative talk about opal and after you had left I felt I had learnt so much more about opal within the short period of your visit than ever before during my entire career as a gemmologist. I agree with you that opal is the most beautiful and most exquisite gemstone, because it encompasses all the finest colours of the other most precious gemstones in one individual specimen, yet exchanging these colours in a highly vivid play, which no other gemstone is able to do. I could, of course, never specialise myself in opal because I was obliged to let each important gemstone share my interest, although I prefer a few to many others.
>
> Your tale about your adventurous journey to all of the most important and even some less important and exhausted opal deposits impressed me highly, and therefore I bid you much success in, as well as the necessary health for, the continuation of your field research, so that you may gain ever more valuable knowledge from your visits; and I also bid you continued success in your scientific experiments through which you will fill so many gaps in our knowledge about this mysterious petrified rainbow.

The ramifications of what he has accomplished and the responsibility he now carries is not lost on Len Cram. His process for growing opal remains a closely held secret to this very day. He realizes only too well that his knowledge, if it ever became public, could be devastating to the opal industry on a world-wide scale, but most particularly in his own native Australia.

Unlike the zirconium oxide-based, unnaturally bright synthetic Gilson opals or the imitation Slocum opals and others of that ilk, that are created through the use of pressure and heat and are easily detectable, what Len Cram appears to have accomplished has nothing to do with substitute opals; he contends that they are neither clever fakes nor well made synthetics but, instead, are opals as truly as any opal occurring naturally anywhere in the world. What, if anything, will this very enterprising, self-taught individual do with the knowledge he harbors? No one can answer that yet, not even Len Cram himself, at least not fully.

Because of the rather momentous significance of Cram's experiments and his accomplishments that have become so important in the field of gemology, the author posed to him a rather tough multiple question about his home-grown opals and if, in fact, they are truly identical to natural opals, as some sources have stated. The question was this: "Len, has your opal, grown at home, ever been submitted for analysis to Australia's Commonwealth Scientific Industrial Research Organization (CSIRO) or, even more importantly, to the Gemological Institute of America (GIA)? If not, why not? If so, what was the result? Were they able to determine under close analytical examination a difference in your opals from opals that occur naturally in the earth?"

Cram considered this for a long moment and then answered in a careful and deliberate manner as follows:

"The plain answer to the question is no, there has been no scientific analysis conducted yet on my opals, for reasons I will come to in a moment. First, I should say that a problem has arisen from the fact that many of the people who have seen my work have made the statement—some in writing—that the Cram opals are indistinguishable from natural opal, *meaning by sight only.* It has been the general comment of many eminent people, but has left the impression on some occasions that the material has been analytically compared, which is not the case.

"Dr. John Sanders of CSIRO," he continued, "did all my analytical work on my early research up until his death. Unfortunately, he lived just long enough to see my first experiments with electrolytes and was the only person I ever confided in. Now, there are a number of reasons why an analysis has not yet been done. First, the work is far from completed and is still in its infancy. Since Dr. Sanders' death I have yet to find someone I can fully trust for this work—someone who won't publish or pass on information. The trouble in the academic world is everyone wants to have the honor of testing and being the first to write a paper on the subject. I have had many offers for my work to be analyzed, even from as far away as France. Second, there needs to be a lot more work done with the electrolytes before I hand over work to someone reputable enough not to publish the results. The driving force behind all this is, of course,

I want to publish them myself! And why shouldn't I? I have made all the break-throughs. I have often wished I had kept it to myself until it was totally completed, then hit the world with one great bombshell instead of in this fragmented manner.

"As you also know," he continued, "I am putting together a large book on the history of opal in the world. Surely I should have the privilege of publishing the results in a special chapter on the geology and chemistry of opal. My research is a lot deeper than anything we, you and I, have ever talked about during our discussions. I have on-going experiments which probe deeply into pseudo-morphism, using animal bones and wood in opal dirt. I expect them to be extremely exciting and to put to bed a lot of myths with regard to opal when completed. I have even started a series of experiments on healing crazed opal, and I don't mean by filling the cracks with some foreign material: the principal is to create atom migration within the stone to heal itself, remembering that it is atom migration in the first place which causes opal to crack, with light being one of the more common things to start them on their way. Atom migration is common in all types of opal, the most commonly seen being webs and scums which grow sometimes very fast, especially in the volcanic varieties. My experiments in this line are currently in the dawning stage and one of them is already showing promise."

Evidently feeling he had already said more than he should, Cram fell silent and did not comment beyond that. Whatever lies ahead in the world of opals, there will undoubtedly be exciting developments soon to come and it would seem that surely Len Cram will play a major role in whatever is in store.

THREE

Opalized Fossils
and Pseudomorphs

While many people consider a pseudomorph to be a mineral of one species that takes the form of another, pseudomorphism is not limited strictly to minerals. Very often various types of flora and fauna are involved, and in all of nature, few formations are quite so remarkable—and stunning!—as opalized fossils of plants and animals, or parts of them. This does not mean fossils that have merely been coated with a sort of "skin" of opal of varying thickness, which happens in some cases, but solid animal or plant matter that has been partially or wholly *replaced* by solid precious opal through a cell-by-cell pseudomorphism.

Among the many fossils known to fall into this category are examples of the following: ammonites, bivalves such as fossil brachiopods and pelecypods (clams), gastropods (snails) (Color Plate 4), bones of various types, brachiosaurs, cephalopods (such as belemnites), corals, crinoids, crocodiles, dinosaurs, dogfish (sharks) and fish of other kinds, foraminifera (minute protozoic creatures whose name derives from foramina, or perforations, as are seen in corals), mammals and mammal parts (including human), marine creatures or their parts, plants of various kinds, plesiosaurs or other marine reptiles, protozoa, shells of a wide variety of species (including trigonias, a form of cockleshell), snakes, teeth and tusks of many kinds, tortoises or turtles, wood of a wide variety of species, and even wood borers, found at the ends of their tunnels bored through wood, the borers themselves just as opalized as the wood.

So how do such opalized fossils form? The answers are not yet all known, but far more is clear in this respect now than was true as short a time as a few decades ago. It used to be the prevailing belief—and one still held by many, because this is what they were taught—that the fossil of a plant, or a piece of wood, a small animal, or an animal part, occurred in one way only. It was believed that the plant or animal that was eventually opalized was in some way buried naturally shortly after death occurred. This burial might have been by volcanic ash or by muds of various kinds, but burial was one of the prerequisites. Then, as the material around the object hardened, it formed a sort of mold that retained the impression of the plant or animal within. At some later time—the time element always of a very nebulous nature—the actual remains of the object disintegrated; some say by ordinary decay but more commonly the belief has been that the object matter was attacked by strong acids or alkalis that permeated the deposit and simply ate the object away, dissolving out whatever was dissolvable, and leaving a cavity that faithfully became an exact mold of the object plant or animal.

Sometimes, in the case of wood, only a portion of the woody material decayed away and left a cavity. Then, so the explanation goes, the opal-formation process occurred as earlier described, with a silica gel slowly percolating downward through the ground material and filling every such cavity with a sort of viscous silica gel, which, we're told, took the exact shape of the cavity it filled. In other words, as it filled in the cavity where the plant or animal had once been, it became an exact duplicate of the original organism, but now in a gelatinous opal form that, in turn, over a period of time often calculated in the tens of thousands to hundreds of thousands or even millions of years, hardened and became solid opal. Actually, it all sounds fairly reasonable and that's why the theory was accepted for so long and why so many people, scientists included, *still* believe that this is exactly how opalized fossils form.

But the cat in the hat opalized skeleton mentioned earlier certainly was an anomaly to such a theory, since both cat and hat were only buried for five decades. It was, in fact this recognition of the anomaly involved in acceptance of the prevailing theories of the genesis of opal that made Len Cram, as earlier shown, toss the theories aside and start looking for new answers, and why he was eventually able to reproduce conditions in a given amount of opal dirt that would result in the spontaneous growth of precious opal by ion exchange; showing indisputably that it is through this natural electrolytic process that is called ion exchange that all opal is formed. And it is equally the reason why fossil materials in their entirety can transmogrify into precious opal without loss of original cellular identity. Finally, it proves that a great deal of the opal being mined today was deposited rather quickly in geological terms and did not require millions of years of slow formation.

Taking a little closer look at some of the fossils that have become pseudomorphs in opal, the greater majority by far come from those opal fields—particularly Australian—where the opal is sedimentary rather than volcanic. This does not preclude opal pseudomorphs from occurring in the volcanic opal fields, only limits them.

First we define what a pseudomorph actually is. The pseudomorph is simply the crystals of one mineral replacing the crystals of another mineral that may be totally different, yet retaining the shape of the mineral that is replaced. Such natural impostors have always led to a great deal of puzzlement in the study of mineralogy, for here suddenly is a crystal whose shape tells us it is one thing, but whose composition is something entirely different. A pseudomorph, then is a false form of a mineral, deriving from the Greek *pseudo* meaning false and the

Greek *morph* meaning form. Joining the two into the single word pseudomorph, in 1801, was the coinage of the Abbé René Just Häuy (1743–1822), who has justifiably been recognized as the father of crystallography. Studying petrified wood and petrified shells, he called them pseudomorphs, which, he said, are "bodies that have a false and deceitful shape." It is not known whether he ever saw fossils that were reproduced exactly in precious opal, but had he witnessed such phenomena, he would undoubtedly have classified them, along with petrified shells and wood, as pseudomorphs. In modern times, this has evolved and refined to be usually more exclusively crystal-to-crystal evolution, which tends to exclude opal, since opal is amorphous, without true crystal structure. Nevertheless, for our purposes here and for the better understanding of how fossils become opalized, the term pseudomorphism is quite satisfactory and appropriate in the original sense of the word as coined by the Abbé René Just Häuy.

Perhaps the most outstanding field in the world for the production of opalized fossils has been White Cliffs in New South Wales, where the very first were discovered in 1892. These were shells of a variety of species that had been filled with—or replaced by—a beautiful light precious opal, plus the flowerlike animals called crinoids, whose stems became opalized and whose individual stem sections were found as beautiful little disks of solid opal, which, even though too small and thin to be regarded as much more than curios, were so lovely that they were easily sold. A number of these early opal fossils, including a spectacularly beautiful opalized ammonite six inches across, became part of the collection of the Sydney Botanical Gardens but were destroyed soon after their acquisition by a severe fire that burned down the building in which they were housed.

One of the more frequently found opalized fossils at White Cliffs, and also at Coober Pedy, is the belemnite, an ancient squidlike creature, a cephalopod, that had a long, gradually tapering and horny body covering, which, in some instances, after the soft body parts were gone, filled with material that ultimately pseudomorphosed into opal. At first when this rather cigar-shaped precious opal was discovered, the miners erroneously thought it was a form of pipe opal.

Among the many types of opalized and ossified bones of various types that have been found at Lightning Ridge are a large number of vertebrae and some rather remarkable dinosaur bones, including the massive thighbone of a brachiosaur that was found 70 feet below ground level in 1989 and that measured 11.5 feet in length (3.5 m) and weighed several tons. It included no precious opal, but a fair portion of the bone had been transformed into common opal.

Some of the most spectacular of the precious opal bone finds have been the entire skeletons or isolated bones of a surprising number of the marine dinosaur called plesiosaurus—a fiercely toothed, long-necked, bulbous bodied creature that sometimes reached a length of 40 feet (over 12 m) and weighed upward of 30 tons. Plesiosaurs lived about 120 million years ago and probably the finest example of the opalized remains of this huge sea reptile is the complete skeleton of a small one, just short of 10 feet in length (3 m), its bones turned into solid reddish precious opal. The specimen, properly mounted, is displayed prominently at the showroom of Andrew Cody, Pty., Ltd., in Melbourne. One quite similar, also with the bones having turned to pure gem red crystal opal, is on display in Adelaide, while another, less complete and with some common opal but little precious opal, is displayed in an opal shop in Sydney. And an almost complete opalized backbone and several other bones from such a creature are presently in the Australian Museum in Sydney. Occasionally, a plesiosaur (or parts thereof) has been found at Lightning Ridge. One of these, fossilized but with little of the body structure pseudomorphosed into opal, is owned by Gieny Biesiada and is on display in her shop, Opal Flash, across from the post office on Morilla Street in Lightning Ridge.

The famous opal buyer at White Cliffs, Ted Murphy, told of a "most beautiful and perfect" plesiosaur specimen found just after World War I that had "gem quality opal bones and was complete except for the head." The opalized skeleton was quite small for a plesiosaur—only five feet long (1.5 m). When one of the world's great opal collectors, famed harp manufacturer Prosper Ralston of Canada, learned of it, he was on the verge of departure to Australia anyway to buy a spectacular gem called the *Pandora Opal,* that had been found by miner Jock McNichol at Lightning Ridge 7 years earlier and which had been cut from the opalized shoulder blade of a plesiosaur.[1] So he detoured to White Cliffs, certain the skull would also have been discovered by the time he arrived, and he was determined to buy that skull as well. To his chagrin, Ralston found that even though the miners had searched diligently for it, the skull was never found and was eventually assumed to have been bitten off, in life, by an even larger predator. As it was, Murphy said, the headless skeleton, was not worthwhile to keep whole and try to sell as a museum piece, and, as good opal was selling for £12 an ounce and since this particular skeleton, as a curio, "would fetch no more than £60, it was broken up and sold as opal, the first sale being £150 and several others at £50 each"—a total of about $1500.

That was far from the first time spectacular opalized fossil finds met such a fate. Some time after that, another plesiosaur skeleton was sold to a Hong Kong cutter and made into jewelry. Individual bones—some turned to pure precious opal, some to common opal and some merely petrified—are not uncommon in opal fields throughout the world and these bones, if of solid precious opal are almost always sold strictly for their gemstone content, to be cut up for jewelry.

When a once-in-a-lifetime fossil specimen is sold to be cut up for its gemstone value, one cannot help feel a pang that such a specimen should be forever lost. The miner, who is trying to make a living, cannot be blamed for selling it for the best price he can get and, unfortunately, probably no museum can compete with the price any buyer of opal in the rough will pay for a solidly opalized fossil specimen. Consider, for example, the wholly opalized tortoise (some say a turtle) that was found by a miner at the turn of the century at White Cliffs. It was some 4 or 5 inches across the widest part of its upper carapace. To his credit, the miner tried in vain to sell it whole to a museum, but when none could come anywhere near offering what he would get from gemstone buyers, he eventually cut up the magnificent specimen into fine precious opal cabochons, which he had no difficulty selling for the price he wanted.

Among the most remarkable accounts in regard to opalized fossils is one told to me by Len Cram—the account of a find in 1929 at Lightning Ridge of an opalized human skull. "I happened to be working with the chap that told me about it," Cram related, "and it was his mother and father who actually saw it. His name was Bobby Hands. He worked here for a long time and he's extremely reliable—he doesn't drink or swear, y'know; in fact, he's a very religious man and takes life very serious. And he told me, when he knew that I was searching these things out, that he thought his father and mother had dug up this human skull from the deep Three Mile (Figure 12), out of new ground in 1929. So, to find out, he wrote a letter to his mother, who was still alive, and he passed the letter on to me and I still have it. What *she* said is very interesting. It wasn't she and her husband who found it, although they did see it. The skull had been found by friends of theirs who, at that time, owned the claim alongside theirs. She verified that it was indeed an opalized human skull she and her husband

Figure 12. A directional sign at the Three Mile opal field of Lightning Ridge. (Photo by the author)

had seen, but they weren't the only ones. She said that just about everyone who was in the small community of Lightning Ridge at the time saw it. And she said it was the talk of the town! Such a talking point! It was completely opalized—apparently high quality opal. Unfortunately, it had far more value for the couple who found it to break it up and sell the black opal as gem material, and so that's what they did with it. They broke it up and cut it up and sold it."

"Now, was this a prehistoric skull?" I asked.

Cram shrugged. "It was found in the opal level, so you place the age of the opals or the strata here and that's where it come."

"This was not the skull of a miner, though?" I persisted.

"Oh, no, no, no! It came out of brand new ground. It was dug out like they dig out dinosaur bones and fossils here at Lightning Ridge."

"Okay. But what date do *you* put on it? What date would you *estimate* that it would be? Fifteen thousand years? Fifty thousand?"

Cram obviously didn't want to be pinned down. "I'm not even going to speculate at this stage," he said, shaking his head, "because there's so much of the geology of the opal strata of Lightning Ridge to be rewritten and a lot of studying to be compiled and completed before one could actually set a date, right? But it certainly doesn't fall into the category of millions and millions of years. That much, in my heart, I'm categorically sold on."

Cram was not finished. "Anyway," he added, "I heard of another man who might have seen the skull, a very elderly man, and I looked him up and asked him about it. He said he hadn't been here at the time, so he hadn't seen it, but he did see another kind of opalized human remains that were dug up seven years later, in 1936, at Angledool, a mining field of northernmost Lightning Ridge. He said it was a human hand, a small one, that had been opalized by potch, not by precious opal. He said they took it to the policeman—there was only one policeman here. And the old gentleman said that when the policeman saw it, he just shook his head and said, 'Go bury it again. You'll cause me all the work in the world, what with inquiries and all the rest. It came out of the level, so it's nothing recent, so just get rid of it. Break it up and get rid of it!' And so the old man said, since it was potch and not worth anything, they did what the policeman advised."

"Any other significant opalized fossil finds that you've been associated with or heard about, Len?" I asked.

"Well," he replied, "there's one more I can tell you about that you might find very interesting. And the man involved with this one, he's still alive here, in town. He told me that in 1956, at the Grawin—this was eight years before I came to live at Lightning Ridge on a permanent basis. He said what was found was in the level, between two billie boulders—a billie boulder is a sort of a level boulder, found now and again; we don't get many of 'em here—they're a very hard, very smooth, round siliceous rock. They get a lot of 'em at White Cliffs and they call 'em silcrete. But anyway, between these two level boulders they got—it was his mate, I think, who found it; they were friends—his mate dug out a perfect bat, of the type we know of today as flying fox bats—fruit-eating bats. And it was absolutely in perfect condition; it was opalized. Precious opal. And they broke the darned thing up and sold it."

Cram also remarked about the several opalized fossils that the famed buyer Ted Murphy was involved with, among which was an occasion when a miner sold him a complete opalized slender-bodied dog shark just over 3 feet in length. The miner had carefully dug it out of his mine at the 30-foot level and was jubilant at having been able to bring it to the surface without breaking it. The whole fish was pseudomorphic in good gemstone opal. "This," Cram said, "was when White Cliffs was still going in a big way. Actually, Ted Murphy fully documented this and you wouldn't get a more accurate man to document it than he. He said that since they couldn't get any museum or private collector interested in taking it, they finally broke it up for the gem content. Chopped it all up and sold it."

What it all comes down to in the end, Cram remarks, is that "No two ways about it, metamorphism—the development of an opal pseudomorph—is ionic exchange and nothing else. And so, all those old Granny stories that we're being fed in this book and that book, telling us that the formation of opal, and opalized fossils, is a process of silica gel percolating through the ground and filling cavities is just not so. Not so to the thinking man."

One of the more interesting fossil finds made at Lightning Ridge was that of a segment of crocodile jawbone in which were six very impressive teeth, the entire specimen changed into good-quality blue-black opal. Though of a species heretofore unknown, the crocodile's jawbone resembled that of the present-day saltwater crocodile of Northern Australia and it was subsequently named *Crocodilus selas-lopheosis,* Lightning Ridge crocodile.

The Australian opal fields do not have a monopoly on opalized fossils, however. Agnes Hodson, of the Rainbow Ridge Opal Mine in Virgin Valley, showed me the jawbone she dug out in their mine—a section of camel jawbone as long as her hand, with several teeth still in it, the bony portion of the specimen transformed into precious opal, but the teeth merely fossilized. Walt Wilson, on the other hand, has in his possession four fossil molar teeth—evidently from a carnivore and possibly from a prehistoric canine—that were found at one of the mines in his Royal Peacock Opal Mines group some ten crow-flight miles distant from Rainbow Ridge (Figure 13). Those teeth, found in conjunction with one another, still fit perfectly one against another but without any jawbone material, and every vestige of those teeth, including enamel and pulp, has been turned into precious jelly black opal, two very black and two lighter, but all of them filled with fire. I couldn't help feeling a sense of awe as I held these teeth, studied them and photographed them. And there have been many other teeth,

Figure 13. The completely opalized molar teeth of a carnivore found by Walt Wilson in Virgin Valley and still in his collection. (Photo by the author)

including tusks, partially or fully opalized, that have been found on the opal fields throughout the world.

Among other bones that have been found that were in whole or in part pseudomorphosed into opal have been reptilian bones—significantly those of snakes, including one three-foot specimen found at the Butterfly Diggings at Lightning Ridge—a snake skeleton, actually, that was entirely changed into quality gem opal. And fully opalized fossil fish are not at all uncommon there and at White Cliffs.

Ted Murphy and Tullie Wollaston, both early Australian opal experts, thought that the famed black opal *nobbies* of Lightning Ridge were actually opalized sponges or corals. In the years that followed, certain evidence surfaced that seemed to suggest the nobbies were more likely pseudomorphs of some sort of vegetative air bladder, such as those some seaweeds develop to raise their strands of vegetation to the surface. Some also suggested a podlike growth of the nature formed by certain water lilies. Now, however, comes Len Cram, who states that there is no way whatsoever that the nobby is a fossil. He claims that the nobbies actually often begin as small round lumps of hardened white opal dirt that the Lightning Ridge miners are familiar with as dog stones or angel stones, which are quite the same shape and size as the nobbies and which occur regularly throughout the opal levels there. When conditions become exactly right and electrolytic action can occur, the resultant ion exchange transforms these stones into the nobbies. When he duplicated in his own little lab, as closely as he could, the natural conditions, Len Cram actually grew a black opal nobby. Pretty difficult to come up with a stronger proof than this, that nobbies are not fossils of any type.

White Cliffs, as early as 1892, was noted for the beautiful opalized shells it produced, but it was overshadowed by those that subsequently were found at Coober Pedy, where individuals have been known to find bucketsful in a single day, all pseudomorphs in the most glorious precious opal. In one unusual piece, a whole cluster of opalized mussel shells were attached to an opalized piece of wood.

Where opalized plants are concerned—as opposed to opalized wood—there are many species that have been reported from the opal fields everywhere in the world. One form of opal, called bog opal, which was discovered in Virgin Valley by miner/scientist George Hewitt, was so named because it is a black base stone with a wide variety of identifiable bits of vegetation locked in the stone, the whole enhanced by a beautiful pinfire and broadflash play of color (Figure 14).

Figure 14. A 32-carat cabochon of bog opal mined by George Hewitt at his Cecilie Ann Opal Mine in Virgin Valley and cut and polished by his partner, Paul Reeves. The bog opal very often shows a wide variety of nonwoody plant matter—tiny blossoms, stems, leaves, seeds, bits of grass, and the like—all suspended in a dark brown jelly opal. (Photo by Paul Reeves)

Wood opal of various species, including hardwoods, palms, and pines, have been found fully or partially opalized in opal fields throughout the world, but especially impressive are those from Virgin Valley, where the entire structure of the wood has been preserved in magnificent precious opal.

The author was fortunate enough to have been on hand at the Northern Lights Mine (of the Royal Peacock Opal Mines) of Virgin Valley in June 1992, when an amateur collector who stopped by for a day of fee digging encountered one of the largest opalized logs ever found—a superb piece that was 35 inches long, 16 inches in diameter, weighed 130 pounds, and was estimated to contain no less than 30% precious opal. The species was identified by paleobotanist George Munzing as a ginkgo tree, hitherto unknown in the valley.

Most of the opalized fossil flora species found in Virgin Valley have been identified or at least classified within probable genera. Some, however, are new to science and one such was collected by the author on the tailings of the Rainbow Ridge Opal Mine in Virgin Valley in 1994. The author found an unusual five-chambered seed pod that had become a pseudomorph in hyalite opal, as if frozen in the clearest glass. The species was evidently previously unknown to paleobotanists, including Dr. Munzing, whose work with Virgin Valley species has been extensive. Other opalized wood species he's identified there are oak, hickory, pine, birch, sequoia, cedar, larch, spruce, elm, hemlock, and chestnut (Color Plate 5). Greater details of this find are discussed in Chapter 7 under the section devoted to Virgin Valley.

THE REMARKABLE WHITE CLIFFS PINEAPPLES

Probably no specific opal formation elicited as much interest and comment in the past as the so-called pineapple opal pseudomorphs that were found at White Cliffs in New South Wales . . . and nowhere else in the world (Figure 15). When first discovered, these amazing formations, which looked like clusters of crystals, astounded all who saw them. Buyer Ted Murphy wrote that they were "extraordinary formations, spiked all over and looking like opal or potch crystals—an impossibility, as opal will not crystalize. One beautifully colored specimen was valued at £100." Whether deemed impossible or not, nevertheless, there they were: opal pseudomorphs after radial crystal clusters of some sort that terminated in spiky crystal shapes. Such a specimen—generally oval, from 2 to 7 inches in diameter, and standing 4 to 10 inches high—actually averaging about 3.5″ × 4.5″ [89 mm × 114 mm] and weighing 3500 carats, and having the spiky crystal-shaped terminations on the exterior—superficially was reminiscent of a small pineapple and, at first, many miners actually believed them to be an opalized fruit that most resembled a pineapple, and so that is what they called them. The opal itself was sometimes entirely potch, sometimes potch-and-color and, on rare occasions, almost entirely solid precious opal that was rich with

Figure 15. One of the so-called opal pineapples mined at White Cliffs over the years, this fine specimen is in the collection of the Museum of Victoria at Melbourne. The specimen, a pseudomorph of ikaite, measures. 4.1″ × 3.55″ [105 mm × 90 mm]. (Photo courtesy of Dr. William D. Birch, Museum of Victoria, Melbourne)

POC over a light base coloration that generally shaded from pale greenish white to lavender or pale blue, the fire normally in patches throughout the nodule.

Such "pineapples" were never common and they quickly became highly sought-after by collectors, but not before a large number of them had been broken up for their opal content, precious opal as always being more valuable than scientific curiosities. It is estimated that probably not more than 200 of these unusual formations have been found, of which only a very small number remain whole in collections today. One Australian collector, Grant Pearson, became convinced in 1987 that he could find one of these pineapples himself if he really worked at it. Even though fewer than 10 specimens had been found over the previous 18 years, Pearson and two of his friends spent their vacation studying the played-out opal field at White Cliffs and making sample diggings. It paid off when they struck what Pearson terms a "nest" of about a dozen of these pineapples.

Murphy started on the right track when he became convinced that these pineapples were pseudomorphs of crystals that had become opalized, even though pseudomorphism was technically a crystal-to-crystal replacement. He was correct in that assessment, but he erred when he reckoned that the original crystals had been gypsum. Under closer study, it was decided that the original crystal material was actually glauberite—a calcium sodium sulfate mineral. This, then, was the explanation that was accepted for many decades. But it, too, was incorrect, since the replaced mineral was not glauberite after all. Nor was it, as others had been suggesting, aragonite, apophyllite, or apatite.

The correct identification was finally made in 1963 when a Danish geologist named Hans Pauly discovered a new mineral he called *ikaite*. This mineral is so fragile in its composition that it can retain its crystalline structure only when submerged in frigid waters. Pauly discovered it while working on a scientific ship mapping Greenland's southwestern coast in the Ika Fjord sea bottom, just under 5 miles south of Ivigtut, which had gained renown as a cryolite mineral locality. Members of the expedition noticed some strange looking crystalline reefs extending upward from the bottom some 66 feet and terminating only 3 feet below the surface. They brought some of the crystals up and those samples, as soon as they warmed up a bit, decomposed at once into a muddy substance that was porous, granular, and white. A quick check determined that the water temperature was only 37°F (3°C) at the bottom and 45°F (7°C) at the top of the reefs. Thermos bottles were then filled with the frigid water and specimens from the reef were kept in them at 39°F (4°C) for later study of a more detailed nature.

The results of that study were most interesting. The crystals, chemically analyzed, turned out to be a nearly pure transparent calcium carbonate that had crystallized with 6 molecules of water into a heretofore unknown form, immediately named *ikaite,* but physically identical to the spiky surface structure of the pseudormorphic opal pineapples of White Cliffs. At room temperature, of course, the crystals soon became opaque and within hours disintegrated into a muddy trigonal calcium carbonate—granular calcite and water. Since the pineapples have been found associated with glacial debris as well as marine fossils of many kinds, it seems likely that as glaciation occurred (or was disappearing) from the area that eventually came to be known as White Cliffs, conditions became right for electrolytic action to occur and in this process of ion exchange, the fragile *ikaite* was altered into far more stable opal—some precious, some common. Later, when the continental upheaval occurred that raised Australia from the sea bottom, the pseudomorphic opal after ikaite survived in the form of the so-called pineapples.

As if to validate the findings initiated in the waters of Greenland, 19 years later, in 1982, scientists aboard the German research vessel named *Meteor,* were taking core samples from the floor of the sea off the Bransfield Strait of Antarctica when they brought up glassy ikaite crystals 2.5″ long. These were very similar to the German pseudomorphs in opal called "barleycorns" or, more properly, *pseudogaylussite,* specimens of which had perplexed the experts for a century and a half. Quickly photographed, the clear crystals exhibited long monoclinic shapes with prominently stepped faces, indicating oscillatory growth, which is a characteristic that has been noted both in the German "barleycorn" opals and the opal "pineapples" of White Cliffs.

Only 2 years after that—in 1984—the scientific ship *Glomer Challenger* was working off the east coast of Japan in the Nankai Trough when it brought up specimens of transparent amber-colored ikaite, which, in the warm air, broke down within mere minutes into tiny mushy particles of calcite and water.

What it all amounts to is this: It is now fairly clear that the majority, if not all, of the opal pseudomorphs of this type found throughout the world, including

- The "barleycorns" of Germany, discovered at Obersdorf, Thuringia, in 1827
- The "jarrowite" found near Jarrow during construction of dockworks on the Tyne River in Newcastle County, England, in 1847
- The "glendonite" found by James Dwight Dana in 1849 at Glendon, New South Wales
- The "glendonite" also found by Dana at Astoria, Oregon, in 1868
- The "thinolite" discovered by his son, Edward S. Dana, in both Nevada and California in 1884
- The world famous "pineapples" of White Cliffs, first found in 1892
- The "White Sea hornlets" found by superstitious fishermen dredging near Archangel off Russia's Karelian Coast in 1930 and believed to have magical healing powers;

and perhaps more yet to be discovered, are merely different physical manifestations of opal pseudomorphs after ikaite.

FOUR

A Chronological History and Mythology of Opals

There would be little point here in spending much time discussing the history of opal beginning during the late Cretaceous Period to the Middle Tertiary Period when, evidently, most of the opal mined today was formed. It is enough to point out, for example, that the opals of Lightning Ridge, New South Wales, Australia, were formed about one hundred million years ago—**100 mya.** The opals of Opal Butte, Oregon, in the United States, were formed about **65 mya** and, in Australia, both the Canaway opal deposits in Queensland and those at White Cliffs in New South Wales were formed about **30 mya.** Volcanic activity leading to subsequent opal formation in Virgin Valley, Nevada, USA, occurred about **25 mya,** but the actual opal formation there did not begin until approximately **16 mya.**

What is more important here is the history of mankind's involvement with opal. The very first known evidence in that respect came as a result of a discovery made in 1939 in East Africa by the distinguished anthropologist and archaeologist, Louis S. B. Leakey. It was at that time, in a cave near Nakuru, Kenya, that Dr. Leakey found precious opal artifacts along with other materials and, with modern dating tests, established the fact that those artifacts dated from about **4000 B.C.** While Dr. Leakey said he thought there had to have been important opal mines in the vicinity, few precious opal mines have ever been discovered in the entire African continent. The nearest known natural occurrence to that discovery is a deposit of green precious opal discovered in Tanzania in 1962, but that material bears no resemblance to the opal in the Nakuru cave artifacts. The next closest reported site is nearly a thousand miles south on the border of South Africa and Zimbabwe at Beit Bridge, but, again, the Nakuru cave opal is an entirely different type than this. A third site for natural precious opal on the continent is much farther away, in Morocco, where there is an occurrence of a precious fire opal similar to the Mexican variety. Again, this bears no resemblance to the precious opal found in the cave in Kenya. Closer to Kenya, South Africa does have deposits of common opal and hyalite, but no precious opal. Finally, a relatively new and important precious opal source has been discovered and is now being developed in Ethiopia, details of which may be found in Chapter Eight under the heading "ETHIOPIA."

There is no known evidence to indicate human use of opal over the next 3500 years—until 593 B.C.—but there is a curious and rather fascinating reference to the black opal of what is now Virgin Valley, Nevada, in the United States, in one of the oldest Chinese literary works, a book written in **2250** B.C., called *Shan Hai King, The Classic of Mountains and Seas*. This work, consisting of over a dozen volumes, is a very detailed geographic treatise and was allegedly written by the great Yu, who subsequently became emperor of China in 2208 B.C. His *Shan Hai King* had been published 42 years earlier, about a century after the death of Almodad, the seventh-generation descendant of Noah, who "measured the earth to its extremities."

For about 1800 years after its publication, the *Shan Hai King* was regarded as a strictly scholarly scientific work, but around 420 B.C., when many Chinese records were being reevaluated and condensed, it was discovered that its geographical data did not correspond to any known lands. As a result, the *Shan Hai King* was reclassified as myth and relegated to an unimportant position in Chinese literature. In modern times, however, portions of the *Shan Hai King* have been reexamined and the data contained finally recognized once again as not only factual but amazingly accurate in respect to today's geographical knowledge. In the Fourth Book, entitled *The Classic of Eastern Mountains,* are four sections describing mountains located "beyond the Eastern Sea"—that is, east of the Pacific Ocean. Each section begins with a detailed description of the geographical features of a certain noteworthy mountain—its height, shape, mineral deposits, surrounding rivers, and types of plants and woody vegetation— then gives the direction and distance to the next mountain, and so on, until the narrative ends. By following the clues, directions, and distances provided, much as one would a road map, investigators have now ascertained beyond any doubt that these sections describe in detail the topography of western and central North America.

The first section begins in Wyoming on the Sweetwater River and proceeds southeast to Medicine Bow Peak; then in succession to Longs Peak, Grays Peak, Mount Princeton, and Bianca Peak in Colorado; to North Truchas Peak, Manzano Peak, and Sierra Blanca in New Mexico; then to Guadalupe Peak, Baldy Peak, and finally Chinati Peak, near the Rio Grande in Texas. The second section describes an expedition over an even more expansive area. It begins in Manitoba, Canada, at Hart Mountain near Lake Winnipeg, and proceeds to Moose Mountain in Saskatchewan; it goes from there to Sioux Pass (between Andes and Fairview) in Montana; to Wolf Mountain and Medicine Bow Peak in Wyoming; to Longs Peak, Mount Harvard, and Summit Peak in Colorado; then to Chicoma Peak, Baldy Peak, Cooks Peak, and Animas Peak in New Mexico; then on into Mexico, describing the Madero, Pamachic, Cukliacan, and Triangulo heights, and ultimately reaching the Pacific Coast near Mazatlan.

The third section is a tour of the mountains along the Pacific Coast: Mount Fairweather and Mount Burkett in Alaska; Prince Rupert and Mount Waddington in British Columbia; Mount Olympus in Washington; Mount Hood in Oregon; and Mount Shasta, Los Gatos, and Santa Barbara in California. The fourth and last section covers several peaks in a smaller area: Mount Rainier in Washington; Mount Hood, Bachelor Mountain, Gearhart Mountain, Mahogany Peak, and Crane Mountain in Oregon; and Trident Peak and Capitol Peak in Nevada.

Not only is *The Classic of Eastern Mountains* an explicit geographical survey, but the accounts in each section give the observations and experiences of the surveyors, from picking up shiny gold nuggets and beautiful black opals in what was undoubtedly Virgin Valley, Nevada, to watching the seals sporting on the rocks in San Francisco Bay. The exploring Oriental geographers were even amused by a strange animal who avoided its enemies by pretending to be dead: the native American opossum. There is a notable and accurate description of the Grand Canyon in the Fourteenth Book of the *Shan Hai King* and other parts of the work that are still being investigated and are said to be accounts of explorations farther to the east, in the Great Lakes and the Mississippi Valley areas.

The remarkable accuracy of the geographical details and personal observations in the *Shan Hai King* prove that not only did the Chinese make an extremely extensive scientific survey of North America almost 4500 years ago, they found beautiful black opals in Nevada in the process.

For roughly the next 1700 years, no more records of human involvement with opal are known to exist, but precious opal was evidently on the scene. Plato wrote in 393 B.C. that some 200 years earlier, in about **593 B.C.,** a shepherd in the employ of Gyges, king of Lydia, obtained a powerful magic ring under extraordinary circumstances and by twisting its bezel the wearer rendered himself invisible. Using this ring's magical power, Plato wrote, the shepherd soon found means to seduce the queen and then, aided by her, slew King Gyges and took possession of the kingdom. Although the legend does not *expressly* state that the ring was set with an opal, the use of the term bezel *(spheudoun)* suggests that some precious stone was the seat of the magical power the ring possessed. That the stone was most likely opal derives from the story that it was able to render its possessor invisible—a myth that has involved opal, and no other stone, throughout all of recorded history.

Almost a century later in Greece, in about **495 B.C.,** Onomacritus, poet and oracle of Athens, wrote a long poem about precious stones, including one he referred to as *paederos,* which means "Cupid's gem" and probably refers to the rose opal of France, a pink common opal usually but, on rare occasion, exhibiting POC; a stone that brings to mind the creamy, rose-suffused coloration in the complexion of a little child. Some scholars, however, contend that Onomacritus could also have been referring to rose quartz or pink chalcedony.

Although the precise date is open to question, it is about **400 B.C.** when the first verifiable mining of Hungarian opal (actually Slovakian) is initiated in open pit mines in the area of Opalbanya (present Dubnik) in the Carpathian Mountains. Seven years later, in **393 B.C.**, Plato penned his account of King Gyges of Lydia, as earlier mentioned. However, the name opal has not yet come into use. In fact, just over a century later, in **290 B.C.**, the Romans are calling opal *ceraunium,* meaning "thunderstone," the word apparently originating from the Bedouins of the Sahara, who believe opals, with lightning trapped within them, fall from the sky during thunderstorms and acquire their marvelous colors in the process. The Arabs, also well aware of these thunderstones, are convinced that anyone who has such good fortune as to find one of these heavenly jewels can, so long as the gemstone is in his possession, consider himself to be protected from all bodily harm. Present use of the word *ceraunium,* sometimes spelled *keraunios,* refers to meteorites.

Around this same time—perhaps in **287 B.C.**—small finds of precious fire opal, similar to the Mexican variety, are possibly being found in Arabia and rose opal is found in southern Egypt, yet these stones remain unknown to the pharaohs. It is at about this same time, however, that the Sanskrit word *úpala* is first historically noted—a word that was originally a rarely used generic term meaning "precious stone." According to some scholars, the Romans half a century later, greatly admiring the stone we know as opal, allegedly used that root word *úpala* to name the stone *opalus;* yet other scholars contend that the Roman *opalus* derived from the Greek *opallios,* which itself evolved from two roots: the first related to "seeing," as in our words opaque and optical; the second meaning "other," and has given us such words as alias and alter. Thus, the meaning becomes "to see an alteration or change in color," but such theorizing creates a substantial credibility gap, especially when one discovers there are scholars who contend that the Greeks didn't even coin their own word *opallios* until they derived it from the word *opalus* that was used by the Roman invaders in 180 A.D., and that the Greeks, until then, had called the stone *paederos.*

A credibility gap also exists in the theory that suggests Pliny's use of the word *opalus* could have derived from Ops, the Roman goddess of fertility and the wife of Saturn. The Roman celebration to honor Saturn was, of course, called Saturnalia and that portion of the celebration devoted to Ops was called Opalìa. From that, it is further alleged, the word *opal* subsequently derived. This Roman mythological version was long generally accepted as the true derivation. Yet, all these suggested sources seem to lose their validity in view of what occurred nearly a half-century later.

With the passage of another 37 years the Romans, by **250 B.C.,** value opal above all other gems, believing it combines within itself the beauty of all other precious stones. They also very frequently carry opal as a good luck charm or talisman, since they believe that the gem, like the rainbow, brings its owner good fortune. And it is in this year that they finally begin referring to it by the name of *opalus*—a name they get from the traders who are their suppliers of the stone. These traders, dealing with Roman merchantmen in the area of the Bosporus, where Constantinople will eventually be situated, convince the Roman merchants that the opals they are buying come from India and arrived at the Bosporus marketplace via the great eastern trade route.

Actually, it is now believed that the opal traders took those stones they purchased at the Carpathian Mountains mines to the Bosporus via Byzantium, down the Danube River and across the Black Sea to the great international marketplace, and then sold them from there as "Oriental" opals, specifically from India, because "Oriental" had an especially good significance in the European gem market even in these ancient Roman times. This is due to the prevailing Roman belief that gemstones ripened or cured better in hotter climates than those mined in temperate zones; thus the conclusion among the Romans is that Oriental gemstones are harder and purer than others and that those from India are among the very finest.

Actually, native opals are entirely unknown to India at this early time—and nearly so even now—and those early trade opals, eventually to be called Hungarian opals, originating from the Hungarian (what was to become eastern Czechoslovakian) open-cut mines in the Carpathian Mountains. Although these are most often referred to as Hungarian opal, that too is a misnomer, since while the Carpathians do extend into Hungary, the location of the mining—all open-pit mining at this time—is north of Hungary, west of Ukraine, south of Poland and northeast of Kosice (Kaschan). Even though highly prized, the opals of this time are, for the most part, a far cry from the beautiful opals of the twentieth century. While there are a few quite notable exceptions, by and large the Hungarian opals are small stones with a light base color—usually milk white to pale lavender—and exhibit relatively weak red multicolor POC in small flashfire patterns. Some of these Hungarian opals are stones that originate as thin seams of opal in andesite lavas near what is now Czernowitz, Slovakia.[1] Others are being mined from similar seams a small distance from there in a mountainous region southeast of Presov (Preschau). However, the greater majority of trade stones are opals that are being purchased by traders from miners near present Dubnik, Slovakia, which, in those early times, is known by the name of Opalbanya. All these sites are in the Slánsky highland, at the foot of the Simonka massif, in an area along the southern slopes of the Carpathian Range and these are the only known precious opal deposits of commercial significance in Europe, Africa, or Asia. It is the name of the actual gemstone source, Opalbanya, that becomes important in establishing where the modern name opal derives. In the Magyar language, which was the ancient Hungarian tongue, Opalbanya itself meant "opal mine" and S. B. J. Skertchly, former president of the Queensland Branch of the Royal Society, who was also an authority on ancient names, agreed that the original name for opal was probably Hungarian/Magyar in origin, rather than Sanskrit.

In final analysis, the great deception of the Romans by the traders is one practiced out of simple economics; the tentacles of what is soon to be called the Roman Empire are extending ever farther and though they are not yet in the region of the Carpathian Mountains where these Hungarian opals originate, it is known that if the Romans discover the true source of the opals, it will not take the Roman legions long to get there and confiscate the mines for Rome, thereby ending the independent opal trade and its wonderful profits for the traders.

It is in **41 B.C.** that one of the more famous stories involving opal unravels. In Rome, during the temporary reign of Mark Antony (Marcus Antonius), a wealthy senator named Nonius is in possession of a particularly fine opal—one of the finest ever reported. The stone, said to be as large as a hazelnut and mounted in a ring, is valued at 2,000,000 sesterces, which in 1997 values would have been just a bit less than a quarter-million dollars. The magnificent opal catches the attention of Antony, who thinks such a piece would make a wonderful and unique gift for him to give to Cleopatra, Queen of Egypt. He approaches Senator Nonius and offers to buy it, but Nonius, who likes neither the offer nor Antony himself, says the stone is not for sale. Furious, the emperor retaliates by ordering the death of Nonius and confiscation of all his property. Nonius, however, aware of what is occurring, takes his precious opal with him and secretly flees Rome into a self-imposed exile and out of the pages of history.

By **1 B.C.**, the Romans have elevated *opalus,* the precious opal, to the highest status among precious gemstones, and in **1 A.D.** the opal mines of the Czechs, Slovaks, Turks, Rumanians, and, some contend, Russians continue to supply Rome via the Byzantium route as they already had for at least two and a half centuries. But by this year a whole new mythology is springing up around the stone. In **3 A.D.** the belief is already prevalent throughout the Roman Empire that all gemstones—precious and semiprecious alike—possess medicinal attributes, most of which are based on the color of the particular stone. Such stones are ground to fine powder and mixed with liquid for consumption and prescribed by physicians as curatives for various maladies. The red stones, such as ruby, garnet, and carnelian, allegedly have healing properties associated with blood. Amethyst, because its purple color is similar to the color of grapes crushed for merlot or burgundy wines, is being used to lessen the effects of drunkenness or to ease the pain of a hangover. The green stones, emerald in particular, are allegedly a cure for a malfunctioning bile and various stomach ailments, while the blue stones, including sapphire, can reduce swelling associated with bruises. Opal, because it exhibits many colors, is the most highly valued medicinal stone and reputed to achieve great success in the treatment of a broad spectrum of maladies.

By **5 A.D.** opal has been nicknamed *ophthalmis lapis*—literally, the "eye-stone"—the stone that sees all, knows all, and imparts to its owner the power of generally foretelling the immediate future. Some decades later this belief in opal-induced prognostication has expanded to endow the opal's owner with the specific ability to warn of impending disaster, natural or man-made, and opal has become so highly esteemed in the Roman Empire that it is virtually all but priceless. Only the wealthiest of the Roman elite, by paying many times the stone's weight in gold, are able to obtain fine specimens of cut opal. It is at about this time, **75 A.D.**, that the famed scholar Gaius Plinius Secundus, commonly called Pliny the Elder, writes that

> The gem called opalus differs but little, or not at all, from beryllus. Lovers of precious stones and writers of books on precious stones have called opalus the most valuable of all precious stones, largely because of the difficulty of determining and knowing how to describe it. . . .

At this point he goes into the description of opal previously cited in the foreword. Pliny also, in this work, describes a sugar–acid method for dyeing agate black and, presumably, opal as well—a method still used by some today to make light opal appear to be the more desirable and much higher-priced black opal.

In recent years a point of contention has arisen about whether Pliny, in referring to *opalus* in 75 A.D., as quoted in the foreword, was actually referring to the stone we know today as opal, or was he referring to iris quartz? Some aspects of the argument in favor of iris quartz seem plausible, yet to anyone who has seen stones of both varieties there is no real comparison and it is highly implausible that Pliny could have been referring to iris quartz when he wrote his stirring description of *opalus*. Even less does it seem he could have been referring to iris agate, as some have contended.

Passage of the next three-quarters of a century result in very little being recorded about opal. In about **150 A.D.**, however, a saying becomes prevalent to the effect that "Fortunate is the person who finds the pot of gold at the end of the rainbow, but even more fortunate is he who finds the place where the beams of sunlight and moonlight join, for there he will find a chest filled with glowing opals." And in the **200 A.D.**, the Lithika of Orpheus states that opal "fills the hearts of the gods with delight."

Even after the fall of the Roman Empire in **284 A.D.**, the Byzantine opal traders continue to be successful in convincing European trading agents who come to Constantinople that the opal they are buying originated in the Orient, specifically India. So successful is this deception begun about 250 B.C., that it continues well beyond eight centuries. As late as the Seventh century, in **612 A.D.** Isidorus Hispalensis, Spanish prelate, scholar, and archbishop of Seville, who at the time is generally considered to be the world's most learned man, in his encyclopedia, *Originum seu Etymologiarum, Libri XX,* remains under the widespread illusion of Oriental opal and declares unequivocally that the gemstone opal occurs naturally only in India.

It is around **850 A.D.,** possibly even earlier, when the Aztecs, in what will eventually become Mexico, begin revering the opal. They give it the name of *quetza-litzle-pyollitli,* meaning "a stone appearing to have many colors which change with the direction of the light." They also dub it with the nickname *vitzitziltecpatl,* which means "hummingbird stone," after the flashing colors of that bird's plumage. It is the Spanish writer Sahagun who first tells of this in his 1380 book, *Historia General de las Cosas de Neuve España.* The Aztecs have extended their Empire some 200 miles [322 km] northward of the Valley of Mexico, where they conquer the Otomi and the Huasteca Indians in the region of Querétaro. It is apparently during this occupation that they first encounter opals, since in modern times this area has long been the largest and most productive of all Mexican opal areas.

Enamored of the stone, these Aztecs often bury their dead with funeral offerings that include opal and many of the opal specimens found in the ancient Aztec tombs are now housed in the collection of the National Museum of Mexico. One of these artifacts, its head carved of precious matrix opal, is the *Aztec Sun God,* which is presently in the collection of the Field Museum of Natural History in Chicago. Another fine stone found in the tombs is called the *Aquila Azteca*—Aztec Eagle—which is a magnificent 32-carat carving of the head of that bird and which, once owned by Emperor Maxmiliano, is now in a private collection.

The Arabs continue to highly treasure precious opal and in **984 A.D.** Arabian scholars write of the marvel of the so-called thunderstones, within which can be found the rare precious rose opal, which, they claim, endows its owner with good fortune and good health.

By the year **1020,** stipulations are being attached to the mythology of the opal. Instead of it simply being a stone that brings good luck to its owner, this is deemed true only if the owner is possessed of high ideals and purity of soul. To such a person, the opal is believed to induce visions that are valuable guides in decision making when faced with a dilemma. If, however, the owner of the opal is a person whose character is low and whose intentions are evil, then such visions will be deliberately misleading. It is about this same time that a new belief about opals has its genesis: that the owner of an opal receives effects from the stone that are distinctly beneficial to his vision. This is the beginning of a flurry of superstitions that are to rise about the opal in this respect.

Such superstitions reach a notable plateau when, about **1060,** an epic poem about gemstones is written by Marbodus, the Bishop of Rennes, northwest of Paris.[2] His poem is constructed of 743 hexameter lines in which he comments about the medicinal and magical attributes of some 60 gemstones. The work becomes very popular and, over the years, goes through 14 editions. Section 49, devoted to opal, states:

> *Though from the eyes each ail th'Opthalmius chase*
> *Yet 'tis the guardian of the thievish race;*
> *It gifts the bearer with acutest sight*
> *But clouds all other eyes with thickest night;*
> *So that the plunderers bold in open day*
> *Secure from harm can bear their spoil away.*

By Marbodus thus establishing the opal as the patron stone of thieves, it is quite possible that this point in history marks the beginning of the belief that springs up to the effect that possession of opals causes the owners to experience bad luck. Obviously, the gentry, being robbed by thieves who can escape detection through protection by opals, soon gives the opal an unsavory reputation.

Some 15 years later, in **1075,** continuing to write about opal, this time in his *Lapidarium,* Marbodus actually calls opal *patronus furum*—protector of thieves (referring in particular to purse thieves, today known as pickpockets)— since the Bishop of Rennes is himself convinced this stone is customarily carried as a talisman by thieves who firmly believe that having it not only sharpens the vision of the one carrying it, but simultaneously clouds the vision of others. To work, however, the opal must be wrapped in a fresh bay leaf and carried by the thief in his pocket. Allegedly, with such protection, a pickpocket can, with ease, become all but invisible in a crowd and thus, even in full daylight, be able to steal the purses and escape with his booty. These statements by Marbodus reach a wide audience and influence the public considerably. There are some who extrapolate the statements so far as to proclaim that the opal, properly wrapped and carried on one's person, imparts the mantle of total invisibility.

A century and a quarter later, in **1200,** there comes the first mention of a somewhat uncommon form of precious opal, the hydrophane—that word deriving from the Greek words for "apparent in water." Hydrophanes are precious opals that are opaque but, when placed in water, rather quickly absorb the moisture and become transparent, though with their POC still readily apparent (Color Plate 6). Taken from the water, the stone slowly dries and resumes its previous opacity. Stones such as these seem to have a mystical quality and soon a whole body of superstitions cloaks them. They are ascribed with magical powers and the belief sprouts and grows that within such an unusual opal resides a hidden eye that can see everything. The Romans dub it *oculus mundi*—eye of the world—and the Germans, with a word meaning the same, called it *weltauge* (Figure 16).

It is about this time, too, for no known reason, that the unusual beliefs

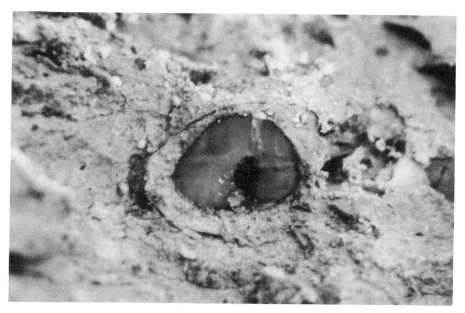

Figure 16. While not a hydrophane, this precious opal peering out of the bank at the Northern Lights Mine could well have been the inspiration for the stone the Romans called *occulus mundi*—eye-of-the-world. (Photo by Alan A. Vogel)

involving opal, which for centuries have been largely of a very positive nature, start becoming negative and the stone is gradually shrouded in various strange and decidedly bad superstitions. These only increase over the next two centuries and it is almost as if the whole European populace has discovered a ,convenient scapegoat to blame for all its ailments.

Even though such superstitions in regard to opal continue strongly, in **1280** they do not seem to be greatly affecting the production of Hungarian opals. In the area of Dubnik alone, some **300** individuals are actively employed in the mining of opals. In this same year, however, Alfonso X, Spanish king of Castile and Leòn, publishes his book entitled *Lapidario del rey,* in which, referring to opal as *optallius,* he reiterates the now ancient belief of criminal protection, saying that it

> keepeth and saveth his eyen that beareth it, cleere and sharp and without griefe, and dimmeth other men's eyen that be about, with a manner clowde, and smiteth them with a maner blindnesse, that is called Amentia, so that they may not see neither take heede what is done before their eyen. Therefore it is said that it is the most sure patron of theeves.

The reinforced nervousness this generates among the general populace, that opal is a bad luck gem, only increases with an outbreak of bubonic plague. As the Black Death spreads across the whole of Europe in **1348–1349**, there are a substantial number who blame the opal and, under such prevailing circumstances, the notion is not so outlandish as one might believe today: those experiencing this harrowing time soon notice that an opal worn by a victim is quite brilliant up to the point of death, but then it quickly loses much of its brilliance. They deem this to be evidence of the opal having malignant influence on the victim's fate and do not understand that it is the demise of the victim that alters the stone, due to a relatively rapid change from the warmth of the fever the victim was experiencing to the chill of death. Within a few short months the dire malady kills fully two-fifths of the population of a number of major European cities. Though to this time opal has always been a highly favored gemstone with European jewelers, following the plague they regard it as a badge of dread.[3]

The first truly remarkable individual opal to appear on the world scene after the Senator Nonius opal of 45 B.C. is a stone that is observed and held by Peter of Arles in about **1350**. So moved is he by its incredible glory that he later sits down and writes his feelings as follows:

> The various colors in the opal tend greatly to the delectation of the sight; nay, more, they have the greatest efficacy in cheering the heart and the inward parts and especially rejoice the eyes of the beholders. One in particular came into my hands in which such beauty, loveliness and grace shone forth that it could truly boast that it forcibly drew all other gems into itself, while it surprised, astonished and held captive without escape or intermission the hearts of all who beheld it. It was of the size of a filbert and clasped in the claws of a golden eagle wrought with wonderful art; and had such vivid and various colors that all the beauties of the heavens might be viewed within it. Grace went out from it, majesty shot forth from its almost divine splendor. It sent forth such bright and piercing rays that it struck terror into all beholders. In a word, it bestowed upon the wearer the qualities granted by Nature to itself, for by an invisible dart it penetrated the souls and dazzled the eyes of all who saw it; appalled all hearts, however bold and courageous; in fine, it filled with trembling the bodies of the bystanders and forced them by a fatal impulse to love. honor and worship it. I have seen, I have felt, I call God to Witness! of a truth, such a stone is to be valued at an inestimable amount.

In **1400**, for the first time after centuries of mining has occurred there, written mining records are inaugurated for the Hungarian opal mines still in operation in the Carpathian Mountains. And exactly a century later, in **1500**, relatively modern commercial Slovakian opal mining begins.

Another book about gemstones, written in **1502** by the physician Camillus Leonardus, in the service of Cesare Borgia, is entitled *Speculum Lapidium Clarissima Artium*. It furthers the vision superstitions regarding opal, a stone he refers to as

> Obtalus or Obtalmius, whose color is not assigned by the Learned, altho some say it is of many Colours. Wonderful is its Virtue in preserving the Eyes from various

Distempers. It sharpens the Sight of him that carries it, but darkens those of the bystanders, so that they are not able to see. If it be wrapped in a leaf of Laurel, and a Charm said over it, and carried cautiously, it has a wonderful effect.

The Mexican precious fire opal, noted for its base color raging from transparent yellow through orange to cherry red, makes its European debut sometime during the first quarter of the sixteenth century—perhaps as early as **1505,** following the fourth voyage of Christopher Columbus to the New World, when he first sights Mexico in 1503. However, it is more likely that such opals are not seen in Europe until about 1520 or 1521. While it is remotely possible that Columbus may have obtained opals from tribesmen of the jungles farther south as early as 1495, this is pure speculation and no concrete records to that end have been discovered. It is far more likely that it was a year or two before—and in the years after—the **1521** conquest of Mexico and destruction of the Aztecs by the Spaniards under Hernando Cortes that the Mexican opals begin appearing on the European market. As Cortes expands his control for Spain, it is equally likely that opals from Nicaragua and Honduras also reach Europe for the first time. By **1525,** Spaniards are regularly returning to Spain with superb lots of the fine rhyolitic opal from both Mexico and Central America.

The belief that opal improves eyesight remains widespread in **1554,** with a few interesting nuances added to the lore: Opal not only is now purported to possess *all* the virtues attributed to *all* the other precious and semiprecious stones, it also, beyond enhancing the owner's vision, is claimed to make the person who wears it a general favorite among those with whom he associates and it also shields him from committing suicide by alleviating whatever depression might envelop him. To these claims is added, in **1561** by Giovanni Porta, a list of attributes that includes the opal's alleged ability to prevent conception, stimulate the heart, protect the owner from "contagious and infected airs," provide a cure for despondency, and equally prevent fainting, malignant affections and heart disease.

Such claims apparently do much to remove the stain on opal's reputation that have been lingering since about 1060. But far beyond any expectations, and for no apparent specific reason, the popularity of the stone as personal jewelry soars in **1573** all over continental Europe. In England, too, in **1579,** opals again come into vogue well beyond anything previously experienced, but this time there is a good reason. This is when Queen Elizabeth I gives her favorite buccaneer and explorer, Sir Francis Drake, a remarkable and very expensive gift. It is a brooch for his cap that is stunningly beautiful—a ruby carved with the orb and cross, surrounded by eight fine opals and the whole enclosed in a rim festooned with alternating diamonds and opals. The gift becomes the talk of Europe and suddenly everyone, it seems, wants opals.

The popularity of the stone wanes slightly after this to a moderately high plateau that it seems inclined to maintain. Twenty-two years later, in **1601**, the stone once again surges to the forefront of public consciousness as a result of Shakespeare's reference to opal in his play, *Twelfth Night*. In it the Duke is constantly falling in and out of love and this causes the clown to say,

> *Now, the melancholy god protect thee;*
> *and the tailor make thy doublet of changeable taffeta,*
> *for thy mind is a very opal!*

There are a surprising number who take this comment about opal's changeability to be pejorative of the stone, depicting its inconstancy as undesirable. But, for the most part, opal remains in high esteem. This is clearly reflected by Anselm de Boot, Dutch court physician, who writes in his **1609** book, *De Gemmis et Lapidus,* that "Opal is the fairest and most pleasing of all jewels."

While in most of Europe opal enjoys its steady popularity, in Italy, where its prominence had been fostered even prior to the Roman Empire, it has slipped from favor somewhat over the past century or so. But in **1620** it regains considerable favor there because it has suddenly become very popular for use in rosaries and other jewelry for religious purposes and so becomes eagerly sought by the monastery workshops where religious jewelry is created.

After so many years of having enjoyed the good graces of the public, a bit of a black mark is lodged against opal in the fickle public mind in **1645** due to a story that originates in the court of Louis XIV. The emperor has five royal coaches that he has named after the five precious gemstones. On an evening when all five coaches are expected for a royal function in Paris, only those named Diamond, Emerald, Sapphire and Ruby reached their destination. The driver of the coach named Opal had become drunk before starting out and was involved in a collision en route. The coachman is fired and the royal vehicle repaired, but the coach named Opal coincidentally becomes involved in a series of minor accidents. Thereafter, when a guest is to be picked up by a royal coach, it is not uncommon for the prospective passenger to remark, "Thank you, but please don't send Opal. You see, it's so unfortunate." Oddly enough, this tongue-in-cheek story catches the public fancy and spreads widely across the continent and, in one way or another, the catch phrase of the period becomes "Opal is so unfortunate."

It is in **1666** when Anselm de Boot, the Dutch court physician who had written over a half-century earlier that opal is the fairest and most pleasing of all jewels, finally becomes the one to let the cat out of the bag concerning one of the best kept secrets of all time. In his book published this year, entitled *Gemmarium et Lapidarium Historia,* he becomes first to tell the European public that precious opals are found not only in the Orient, but that most of the stones seen by Europeans over a recent period are actually Hungarian opals that were mined in the Slovakian region. The term Hungarian opal at once becomes synonymous with the finest opals in the world.

The little besmirchment of the opal reputation inspired by the French royal coach story has gradually worn off and is all but a dim memory by **1748** when Sir John Hill writes in regard to opal that it

> has been esteemed by many in all ages of very great value, though at present it is of less price in proportion to its size than any of the finer gems. However, opal is softer than any other of the fine gems and is difficultly polished to any degree of nicety.

In **1788** the Slovakian government steps in and takes complete control of all the opal mines in the Carpathians. It inaugurates a program of systematic mining that is so restrictive and is combined with such penurious controls that the workers cannot tolerate it. Within a year the mines are abandoned. For the next two decades, what little mining is done here is carried out only by government workers.

Bad times of a sort return for opal popularity around the start of the nineteenth century. For reasons not clearly understood, the gemstone simply falls out of favor throughout Europe about the year **1800.** Through widely spread stories, mainly untrue, opal becomes associated with—and even blamed for— the fall of monarchs, the devastation caused by famine, and the horror of pestilence. It becomes, in fact, once again a very unlucky stone to have in one's possession. The problem is not eased by what is happening at the principal European source of opals. The open pit mines in the Carpathian Mountains that had been producing Hungarian opals for centuries were suddenly all but depleted and the Slovakian government, in an effort to preserve its monopoly, commences underground mining for the first time. Deep shafts are sunk to new opal levels and there is initially great excitement and joy when substantial new opal deposits are discovered. However, the opal being mined from far below ground level is found to be considerably less stable than that from the open pit mines and the large quantities of opal reaching the surface prove to be very prone to crazing—sometimes while being cut and, more to its detriment, often after it has been purchased by the consumer. There are soon a great many very unhappy opal owners and the demand for the stone diminishes so swiftly that before long even the government-controlled mines are nearly all closed. The opal that continues to be mined is brought to the surface in level by level stages over long periods of time, in an effort to give the stones a chance to stabilize. It is not a rousing success.

Whether done as a deliberate effort to restore precious opal to public favor in Europe is not certainly known, but only a few years later another of the world's most beautiful and famous opals appeared, in no less a place than the French court. Napoleon Bonaparte presents to his first wife, the Empress Josephine, who is one of the world's all-time great jewel collectors, what is undoubtedly the finest opal existing at the time. So captivated is the public with the romantic event and the stories circulating about this beautiful gemstone that the popularity of opal once again soars. The stone, a superb, 700-carat black opal with brilliant broadflash red fire across its entire face, is very aptly named the *Burning of Troy* opal—the first opal known to have been given a name. Reputed to have measurements of 4.5″ × 2.5″ × 0.5″ [114.3 mm × 63.5 mm × 12.7 mm], it is claimed to be a Hungarian opal mined at Czernowitz. Since this opal, both in color and size, is so out of character for the Hungarian opal mines, it has caused recent speculation that the stone actually originated from Honduras, where black opals are not uncommon. Whatever the case, Napoleon and Josephine are divorced in **1809** and she leaves the palace, taking the *Burning of Troy* with her.

This same year, after over two decades of absolute minimal activity in opal mining, the Slovakian government acknowledges its errors and resumes private leasing of the Slovakian/Hungarian opal mines. It is too little, too late. Even though many of the original workers return, the mines will never again reach their former productivity and prominence. But now a new source is breaking into the world market. In **1810,** after low-scale mining has been occurring in Mexico for centuries, modern mining techniques are introduced to the few precious fire opal mines still operating here and production rates climb dramatically.

Back in France, having been divorced from Napoleon for 5 years, the Empress Josephine in **1814** falls ill and dies. The extremely beautiful *Burning of Troy* opal disappears and is not heard of again . . . for 91 years.

The first lengthy scientific tract written specifically about opals is published in **1821,** an impressive work by a renowned French mineralogist named C. P. Brard. Among other things, he discusses the great value of precious opal in its various forms and lists as the most valuable types the harlequin (*arlequinines*) opal and the *opal à flammes* or fire opal. It is perhaps significant that he makes no mention of past superstitions concerning the opal's reputed magical and curative powers or that it was allegedly the patron stone of thieves, that it was an aid to prognostication, or that it was the harbinger of bad luck.

Six years later, in **1827,** an unusual opal discovery is made near Sangerhausen in Thuringia, Germany. Odd little precious opal pseudomorphs are discovered that are called *Gerstenkörner*—barleycorns. They are described in the scientific literature by mineralogist Johan Katrk Freiesleben, as "single rounded or acutely pyramidal crystals or groups of crystal that interpenetrate."

It is difficult to imagine in modern times that the publication of a novel in which an opal is cast in a suspect light could influence the popularity of the gemstone for nearly the next quarter-century and wreak havoc with its economic importance throughout all of Europe and much of the rest of the world. That, however, is precisely what happens in **1828** with publication of the novel by

Sir Walter Scott entitled *Anne of Geierstein,* the final volume of a very popular series called *The Waverly Novels.* In that story, it seems that a young woman named Hermione, the grandmother of Anne, habitually wears an exquisite opal on a ribbon in her hair—a stone bound to her by inexplicable physical and psychical ties. The opal clearly reflects her moods, flashing deep red when she grows angry, scintillating and brilliant when she is happy. When it happens, however, that, during the christening of her infant daughter, Anne's eventual mother, some holy water is inadvertently sprinkled on the stone, the opal shoots out a great spark and then instantly loses its color and Hermione falls unconscious. Carried to her room, she is placed on her bed to recover, but when someone checks on her later, nothing is found of her or the opal except a small mound of ashes on the bed.

Though it is just a fanciful tale, it is amazing how the reading public takes the story to heart. They blame the opal for Hermione's death and condemn the stone as being the incarnation of evil or it would not have been so affected by holy water, a condemnation that swiftly spreads to include all opals. Incredibly, despite the fact that the crown jewels of France contain many fine opals and the crown of the Holy Roman Emperor also includes a beautiful large opal, within a year the sales of opal fall by nearly 50% throughout all of Europe—a slump that lasts for 22 years! And even today, almost a century and three-quarters later, the reputation of opal as an evil, bad luck stone lingers in the minds of many and opal dealers today are still frequently asked by potential customers, "But doesn't owning an opal bring bad luck?"

As if a prelude of things to come, in **1841** a German geologist named Johannes Menge, discovers opal while prospecting some 50 miles northeast of Adelaide, South Australia. His find is made on the station (ranch) named Tarrawilla, near Angaston in the Flinders Range, close to where the great Murray River abruptly changes course from a western flow to run directly south. The opal he found is of little value, so almost no attention is paid to the discovery.

It is at a dock facility construction on the Tyne River in County Durham, England, during **1847,** close to the town of Jarrow near Newcastle, County Durham, that a find of small opal pseudomorphs is made. These are very much like the "barleycorns of opal" *(Gerstenkörner)* that were found near Sangerhausen, Thuringia, Germany, 20 years earlier. The new pseudomorphs are named jarrowite. And two years later, in **1849,** another find of little opal pseudomorphs quite similar to the barleycorns and jarrowite is made at Glendon, New South Wales, Australia, by the esteemed mineralogist, James Dwight Dana. This new variety is later (1905) named glendonite.

The continuing great slump in opal popularity finally comes to an end in **1850** when Queen Victoria, who adores opals herself and frequently wears them, not only presents beautiful opal rings to many of her friends, but gives exquisite opal jewelry to each of her five daughters—Victoria, Alice, Helen, Louise, and Beatrice—as wedding gifts.

Since the British monarch is indisputably the fashion setter for much of the world, opals abruptly become very popular once again and almost overnight the prices rise close to their former levels and the superstitions greatly abate. Numerous writers have stated that Queen Victoria deliberately flaunted her love of opals for the express purpose of promoting the new Australian opals into a world market item in order to, in this way, aid the Australian economy and the Australian opal miners in the newly discovered opal fields there. It's a nice, altruistic thought, of course, but patently untrue, since the Menge find of virtually worthless opals in South Australia and the little glendonites of New South Wales were the only Australian opal finds made to this point and the major discoveries Down Under still lay almost a quarter of a century in the future.

A bit of the old "bad luck" superstition comes back to haunt the opal for a few years, beginning in **1853** and extending into 1856. It stems from British soldiers, during the Crimean War, traveling through southeast Europe and pausing to buy the misnamed Hungarian opal mined in Slovakia. Because they have these stones in their possession when they are killed on the battlefield or when they fall victim to war-related disease, many resurrect the old "bad luck" label for the opal, holding the stone responsible. On the positive side of the ledger, however, during this same year, Australia comes up with another intriguing but short-lived precursor of things to come: A small but very rich deposit of precious opal is discovered in Western Australia near the shores of the Indian Ocean, some 20 miles east of the Dampier Archipelago—named after the infamous pirate/explorer. The deposit is found close to Roeburn, in an area today called Cossack. Unfortunately, it is a deposit that rather quickly plays out.

In **1855** the Querétaro opal deposit, destined to become the most important precious opal-producing district in Mexico and the foremost precious fire opal producing area in the world, is discovered in a rhyolitic volcanic flow by a field-working peon on the plantation of the Hacienda Esperanza, 150 miles northwest of Mexico City. The source also produces some very fine black opal, some with a true black base color, some a dark chocolate brown. Despite the excitement the find generates, no substantial mining is done for the next 15 years. Actually, the discovery of this volcanic opal in rhyolite is a rediscovery of the ancient Aztec mines, whose location had always been a carefully guarded secret. These mines had not been worked for over 300 years. At about the same time, a very similar discovery is made 32 miles to the east of the Hacienda Esperanza find and slightly to the south, at San Juan del Rio, also in the state of Querétaro.

In **1860** a deposit of lapidary grade precious opal, volcanic opal in rhyolite matrix, is discovered near Karamandjik (present Karaman) in southcentral Turkey, and the material mined there—which is still being mined to a moderate degree—is taken to the great world marketplace at Constantinople.

A decade after the discovery of rhyolitic precious opal in the state of Querétaro, Mexico, the Ontiveros Mine, first commercial precious opal mine known in the western hemisphere, opens in **1865** near San Juan del Rio. The mine is 32 miles east and slightly south of the town of Querétaro.

Following in the footsteps of his illustrious father, James Dwight Dana, mineralogist Edwards S. Dana, in **1868**, finds opal pseudomorphs at Astoria, Oregon, that are similar to those found by his father almost 20 years earlier at Glendon, New South Wales.

In **1870**, because of the success of the Ontiveros Mine, there is a flurry of opal prospecting activity in Mexico, resulting this year in the discovery of several more important precious opal occurrences and the establishment of new mines. One of these is the Santa Maria Iris Mine established by Don Jose Maria Siurob on the Hacienda Esmeralda near Querétaro early this year. La Carbonera Mine is another. Later this year, important opal workings are begun at Vila Seca, near Zimapan, north of Mexico City, in state of Hidalgo, and in the hills of Caja and Peineto, as well as a very little deposit at Tequesquipan and more at San Juan del Rio. One of the very largest of these newly established Mexican opal mines is the Jurado Mine—still in operation and producing gem grade opal today, a century and a quarter later.

The first truly significant and relatively permanent precious opal discovery in Australia occurs in **1872**. It is often touted in the literature as the very first discovery of opal in Australia but, as has been noted, this is not true. Nevertheless, it marks the beginning of a new era for Australia. This new discovery is high-quality boulder opal found in Queensland at Listowel Downs (Color Plate 7). The material occurs in sedimentary deposits along Blackwater Creek in the comparatively flat country 60 miles north of Adavale, where the hills and ridges, seldom exceeding 100 feet in height, are of sandstone, although just below the surface the rock is basalt. Fully 150 miles east of this site, another discovery of precious opal—this time volcanic opal in basalt—is found in a deposit of the Great Dividing Ridge at Springsure by a miner named Paddy O'Brien. In effect, these finds represent the vanguard of a multitude of discoveries that are to be made in the remote, harsh environment of the Queensland outback, where the opal fields cover an expanse greater in area than the American state of Texas. The following year, **1873**, even more finds of high-quality boulder opal are made in Queensland—a relatively important deposit on the Bulloo River near Thargomindah, and a few in the Kyabra Hills, where Joe Brindle establishes his mine on Breakfast Creek.

In **1874** the first Australian opal appears in the London market. It is not, as so many books suggest, the solid light opal from White Cliffs in New South Wales, but, rather, the boulder opal being actively mined by this time in

Queensland. The following year, **1875,** the very first Australian opal mining leases are taken out by Herbert Bond of Toowoomba, Queensland. He subsequently floats a company in London with offices at Pall Mall, a locality noted for security and wealth, basing his venture on the production of several Queensland mines, including two of the more famous, which are still in operation a century and a quarter later—the Aladdin Mine and the Little Wonder Mine.

This same year witnesses what is often described as the first discovery of opal in New South Wales, but such claims overlook Dana's discovery of opal pseudomorphs at Glendon in 1849. This new find occurs when miners, following up a thin gold seam in volcanic rock, discover a deposit of precious opal in the Blue Mountains just under 18 miles [30 km] south of Bathurst on the west side of Rocky Bridge Creek, just above its junction with the Abercrombie River.

At almost the same time, a similar find of precious volcanic opal is made some 1200 miles [1930 km] due north, in the far northeastern part of Queensland, in the mountains between Cairns and the Palmer River. In this area a new gold field has just been opened up and a wave of hopeful humanity has poured into the district—prospectors and miners, shopkeepers, tramps or hobos (called sundowners), Italians, Chinese, and many others. So rich are the deposits of both gold and opal that reliable reports have it that during the peak mining period some 55,000 men are on hand, 25,000 of whom are Chinese. And it is in respect to these Palmer River diggings that one of the more colorful Australian opal stories occurs.

Food—especially fresh meat—is in very short supply there and to ease the situation, a cattle herd is formed about a thousand miles distant at Wyndomen, the Delpard Station (or ranch) in southeastern Queensland, to be driven northward to the mines. The herd is placed under the supervision of a young Englishman, Clement Tyrell, who is assisting Mr. and Mrs Delpard and their two daughters, Laura and Lucy, to run the big ranch, which at the time is one of the more renowned stations in Queensland. Tyrell is very much in love with Lucy.

The cattle drive is a difficult one, following the coastal range northward via such towns and settlements as Gympie, Port Curtis, Mackay, Bullarenda, and Glenburndale Creek. They are still three days distant from the latter place when a young bull splits from the herd and races off, Tyrell in hot pursuit. As he overtakes the animal some distance from the herd, the young bull thuds to a halt, spins around in a spray of dirt, plants his hooves, lowered his head and tenses for a charge. As he stops, however, one of his hard hooves strikes a volcanic rock projecting from the ground and snaps off its top. Tyrell approaches cautiously and, with a few judicious sharp cracks of his whip in the air close to the young bull, convinces the animal to forget about charging and begin a run back to rejoin the herd. Tyrell is just starting to follow when he detects a fiery flash on the ground and investigates. It is the broken rock, which, inside the rough brown exterior, is solid, brilliant, breathtaking precious opal—a chunk that measures $2'' \times 1.5'' \times 1.5''$ [50.8 mm $\times$ 38.1 mm $\times$ 38.1 mm]. It is staggering in its beauty and a quick inspection shows a number of other rocks of the same type similarly projecting from the soil.

Realizing that just the stone in his hand is alone worth a small fortune, Tyrell passes the order to his men that the young bull is not to be sold as a meat animal as the others are soon to be, but be kept as a pet—and he names the animal Opal. When he finally completes his mission and returns to Wyndomen, he gives the stone to his love, Lucy Delpard. It is taken to a skilled lapidarist in Brisbane and there cut and set as a pendant the size of a small walnut and virtually a ball of fire. It astounds all who see it and becomes the talk of Brisbane, Sydney, Melbourne, and even London.

This same year sees Paddy O'Brien, the miner who discovered the opals at Springsure three years earlier, lease an area of his claims to a Mr. F. Batho who, in turn, is quite successful in mining his own stones, taking them to London on two different occasions (1879 and 1886) and selling them there. For one piece alone he receives £150 [over $750], which is quite a substantial sum and would today be the equivalent of about $7500.

The influx of opals into the world market from Australia, Mexico, and Central America very quickly has the Slovakian miners of Hungarian opal seeing the writing on the wall. Their monopoly in world trade opals is being invaded and there is really nothing they can do to thwart it except initiate a malicious whispering campaign, which is what they did in **1876,** stating that only the Hungarian opals were genuine and all those showing up from other localities around the world are absolute fakes. It doesn't work and the suffering economic situation among the Carpathian miners takes an even deeper plunge and more mines shut down. The mine at Dubnik is one of the small handful to remain alive, although by the following year, **1877,** there are only about 150 miners left actually working the mine, along with six men employed as polishers. It is quite a regression for the whole Carpathian opal mining industry, which at one time employed thousands. The end of Slovakian mining, after perhaps well over 2000 years, is suddenly a very distinct possibility, and everyone knows it.

In **1880** the popularity of opal in Europe takes another beating, from two unrelated causes. The first of these involves Francisco de Asís Fernando Pío Juan María Gregorio Pelayo, better known as King Alfonso XII of Spain. He had become king in 1874, but, prior to that time, had met and took as his lover the Comtesse de Castiglione, a renowned beauty, who was deeply in love with him. When later her lover becomes King, the Comtesse came to him, fully expecting to be made his Queen, only to discover him preparing to wed the Princess Mercedes. It is alleged that her great fury was well contained but it leads her to seek vengeance for what she considers a betrayal of her affections. As a supposed memento of their former closeness, she sends Alfonso a wedding present—a finger ring fashioned of fine gold, in the center of which is set a truly outstanding opal.

Overwhelmed by the beauty of the stone, Queen Mercedes asks Alfonso if she can wear the ring and he gives it to her. Only a few short months later she dies of a mysterious illness. The grieving Alfonso then gives the ring to his grandmother, Queen Christina, who dies soon afterward. Then Alfonso gives the ring to his sister, the Infanta Maria del Pila, who also soon dies, evidently a victim of the same mysterious affliction. The King's sister-in-law, youngest daughter of the Duc and Duchesse de Monpensier, asks for the ring, which he gives to her, and then she, too, dies. Finally, King Alfonso puts the ring on his own finger and very quickly is struck by the same illness and soon dies. The ring is then placed on a golden chain and hung about the neck of the statue of the Virgin of Alumdena, patron saint of Madrid, where it is reputed to hang to this day.

The second cause of the opal losing some popularity this year comes as a result of an outbreak of cholera that sweeps Spain, killing over 100,000 people and causing an upsurge in the belief that opal is at least partially the cause, in view of the tragedies so recently visited upon the family of King Alfonso XII.

Another discovery of precious opal is made in New South Wales in **1881,** this time at remote Milparinka in the northwestern corner of the state, but it is a small and relatively insignificant deposit and so is not commercially developed.

There is a significant upsurge in the amount of opal mining occurring in Honduras beginning in **1882** that allows the country to favorably compete on the international opal market, still centered in Europe. These Honduras opals include both white opal (light opal) and "flaming fiery opal" (precious fire opal) and, of particular significance some years later, a fair amount of top gem quality black opal. In his 1890 book, *Gems and Precious Stones of North America,* George Frederick Kunz, for whom kunzite is named, writes in regard to the Honduras opal: "The noble opal of Honduras are often exceedingly beautiful . . . A remarkable specimen of these weighed over a pound and, when cut, furnished a quantity of fine stones, some of the finest of which are in the collection of Dr. A. C. Hamlin (now at the Mineralogical Museum, Harvard University.)"

Some sources have stated that precious opal was discovered at White Cliffs in New South Wales in **1884,** but that the deposits were not mined for another five years after that. In view of the richness of the White Cliffs opal field and the quality of the opals initially found there, this really does not seem to be very likely and it is far more plausible that the field is not found until 1889, as most of the more authoritative sources contend. However, it *is* in 1884 when mineralogist Edward Dana finds and describes opal pseudomorphs he calls thinolite in Nevada and California. These specimens are similar to those he found at Astoria, Oregon, 16 years earlier.

One of the great figures in the history of Australian opals makes his appearance in 1888. This is Tullie Cornthwaite Wollaston, who is soon to introduce into the London gemstone market not only additional supplies of quality boulder opal but a new sedimentary seam opal—a light opal comparable to or even exceeding in beauty the Hungarian opals. He tells how all this came about in his 1924 book entitled *Opal: The Gem of the Never Never*, so only a very encapsulated version will appear here. Having heard highly encouraging stories of Joe Brindle's Opal Mine on Breakfast Creek in the Kyabra Hills of Queensland, Wollaston sets off for there from Adelaide, New South Wales, with a miner friend and a young black helper on 21 November of this year. It is a grueling journey of incredible difficulty in the face of terrible hazards. Traveling largely on camels through unmapped desert in the midst of summer's excruciating heat, it takes them 47 days to reach their destination on 9 January 1889. They peg some claims for themselves and Wollaston buys his first parcel of opals—61 pieces for £27 10s—and is thereby well launched on a great career as an opal buyer. Leaving his friend behind, Wollaston immediately returns to Adelaide and then is off to London with his gem opals. Unbeknownst to Wollaston, a prospector far to the north, George Cragg, discovers, this very same year, a precious boulder opal deposit in the Winton District of Queensland, that will become one of the greatest producers of boulder opal of all time—the site of the present Cragg Mine near where Opalton will soon be. Cragg determines to keep his find secret as long as possible.

The year **1889** becomes a signal year in the history of opals, as this is the year when a party of kangaroo hunters accidentally discovers one of Australia's first truly outstanding opal fields. The hunters—Alf Richardson, Charlie Turner, Wil Clouston, and George Hooley—are 60 miles [96.5 km] northwest of Wilcannia on Momba Station (Momba Pastoral Co.) in west central New South Wales when one of their horses kicks up an opal, a floater that has eroded out of the side of a hill. They look around and quickly find an abundance of them—fine solid opals that are of a color and quality similar to the Hungarian opals but generally much larger. Instead of in little pieces with matrix attached as the Hungarian opal normally occur, this is seam opal occurring in flat cakes free of matrix. Few people have ever heard of this location prior to 1889, but ever after its name is famous in the annals of opal. It is called White Cliffs.

This was not the end of the wonderful things that were occurring in regard to opal during this fateful year. More than 200 miles north of the Breakfast Creek claims, a deposit of magnificent black opal with amazing density of color and pattern, formed as pipe opal in round tubes, is discovered in what is to become the Jundah opal field in Queensland and the Black Mine is quickly established.

Meanwhile Wollaston, having successfully established a market for Australian opals in London, returns later in the year and is soon again buying opal in the Queensland fields. A single parcel that he buys from the Little Wonder Mine costs him £1000, which is quite a fortune in these days when the average wage is less than £10 a month. He is also soon contacted by Charlie Turner, one of the discoverers of the White Cliffs deposit, who offers him the first parcel of White Cliffs opal. Rather hesitantly, Wollaston buys it for £140 . . . and never regrets it. In fact, a short time after he turns it over to his London contact, whose six cutters quickly shape and polish the stones, Wollaston writes that "the cut product was selling as fast as they could turn it out."

One final event of considerable importance is yet played out in this eventful year. Late in 1889, on the other side of the world, a sheepherder in the western United States, on a hill known as Peters Butte in Morrow County, Oregon, finds some stones so different in appearance from any others he has previously seen that he smacks a couple of them together to see what is inside. The stones are what is now commonly known as thundereggs and inside he finds a core of high-grade, gem-quality opal (Figure 17). The secret is soon out and miners flock to the site. Very soon the name Peter's Butte is supplanted by a new name, which the hill still bears today—Opal Butte—and it promises great things to come.

It is on 21 March of **1890** that the first official claims at White Cliffs are registered and this, in actuality, marks the real beginning of extensive commercial opal production in Australia. Edward F. "Ted" Murphy, another of the men who will become famous on the Australian opal fields, arrives at White Cliffs as a 20-year-old prospective miner, but soon becomes an opal buyer in the employ

Figure 17. Freshly broken Opal Butte thundereggs with promising interior opal. (Photo by Kevin Lane Smith)

of Tullie Wollaston and excels in the job. And, not surprisingly, a sense of competition develops between the miners at White Cliffs and those in Queensland. It is the latter that makes a significant mark very quickly by turning out the first named opal from Australia—a superb 650-carat stone called *Gay Paree*. The value of Queensland opal produced this year is reported by the Department of Mines as being £3000. However, despite the promising beginning, by the end of the year Queensland's fortunes begin to decline, while those of White Cliffs are definitely in the ascendancy.

And this year, once again things of importance are occurring in the United States, this time in the state of Idaho on the Washington border. Here, near Whelan in Latah County, and very close to the town of Moscow, precious opal that is said to compare favorably with the best Hungarian opal is accidentally discovered in decomposed basalt during the digging of a water well. Very quickly an opal rush develops and almost overnight a whole new town springs up, called Gem City. During the following summer and fall of **1891,** more than $5000 worth of high-grade, gem-quality material is mined at Gem City. A little 3.5-carat gem sells for $500 and a chunk of rough weighing two ounces sells for $1200. While the principal deposit is in Idaho, most of the mining is being done on the Washington side of the border.

And Down Under, the fortunes of White Cliffs continue to rise, while those of Queensland falter badly. There is a trio of reasons for this: First, the White Cliffs opal is considerably easier to cut than the Queensland boulder opal and thus less risky; second, the White Cliffs supply of opal is much more reliable; and finally, while the White Cliffs opal can be relied upon to maintain its character, color, and brilliance from one mine to another, Queensland opal fields are not only widespread, each of the localities seems to produce a different type of boulder opal—even neighboring mines often produce different types—so there is less general acceptance of it by the buying public. Thus, White Cliffs is doing just fine. It starts this year with only 18 permanent miners, but in the months following, over 4000 others are attracted and by year's end more than 800 of these have also established claims. The town of White Cliffs has boomed to a population of some 2500 and it now has four hotels.

In the following year, **1892,** fossil shells and the oddly flowerlike animals called crinoids, all fully opalized, are found at White Cliffs and create quite a sensation. Some of the world's most beautiful and perfect opalized fossils are found here this year, including opalized tusks, vertebrae, and many other kinds of bones. Ted Murphy, now the most experienced and trusted buyer on the field, sees many of these opalized fossils and wishes they could have been sold whole as museum specimens, but they were far more valuable for their gemstone content than for scientific interest and no museum could match what the miner gets by breaking the fossil up and selling it piecemeal for cutting. Murphy buys many of these broken-up opalized fossils, as well as a few that are still whole, including at one time a perfect, fully opalized dog shark three (some sources say four) feet in length, which, unfortunately, is also subsequently broken up.

As if to outdo itself, White Cliffs in the next year, **1893,** becomes the source of the first so-called opal pineapple ever found—a strange formation that seems to be a fossil of some sort that has been transformed into pure precious opal, sort of spiky on the outside and roughly in the shape of a pineapple. Close examination by experts ascertain that it is an opal pseudomorph after some kind of a crystal cluster, but no one at first can say for certain what the original mineral was. They finally conclude that the opal pineapple it is a pseudomorph of glauberite and that is the way it is accepted for the next 69 years, until 1963, when it is proven that the pseudomorphed crystals had been ikaite—although even today many still call it a pseudomorph of glauberite. White Cliffs is not only the first source of these pineapple-like opal pseudomorphs, it is the only place in the world that they are known to occur.

Matters continue to improve this year for Australian opal. At White Cliffs, precious opal is being mined in such abundance, by over 1000 miners, that buyers are purchasing £10,000 worth monthly. And in Queensland, opal mining peaks at both Listowel Downs and Springsure. Overseas, the London firm of Treibs, Ltd. becomes the first established firm to invest in Australian rough opal. The first of that Australian opal rough soon reaches the professional gem-cutting shops of Idar-Oberstein in western Germany.

Also during 1893, an estimated $20,000 worth of opal is mined and sold from Opal Butte, Oregon—material that has intrigued buyers throughout the world. However, the opal endeavors at Gem City, Idaho, do not fare so well. The miners strike a solid layer of basalt so thick that it quickly discourages further mining and by the end of the year Gem City is a ghost town and the location is no longer even visited. There are other areas in the state where prospects are much better. Precious opal has just been discovered in basalt in Owyhee County in the area of Squaw Creek Canyon, just below where Little Squaw Creek empties into Squaw Creek, three miles above the Snake River and some eight miles southwest of Nampa. The initial mining consists of an open-cut and a 40-foot shaft. Another site is found at this time, fairly close by; two miles south-southeast of a place formerly known as Sommer Camp, and about 4 miles west of Enterprise. Initially about six pits are sunk within 200 yards of each other into decomposed whitish rhyolite interbedded with brownish glassy rhyolite. Much chalcedony and common milk opal are found here along with the precious opal. Finally, also in Owyhee County about 25 miles west of Mountain Home along Castle Creek, opal claims are filed at a point about six miles east of Oreana and, although some good opal is found, the difficulty of removing it from the rock without shattering it into useless fragments prevents profitable mining. A similar situation occurs about this same time in the extreme southwest of Owyhee County, where precious opal is found occurring as seams and cavity fillings in basalt on the Brace Brothers Ranch near Cliffs, about 40 miles from Boise. Unfortunately, the rock is so hard and dense that removing the opals without shattering them is almost impossible and mining endeavors are abandoned.

During **1894,** stockmen on Warrnambool Downs discover George Cragg's boulder opal find. After six years his secret is out and the opal rush he so wanted to avert begins. In a short time the town of Opalton has sprung up at the site.

While a brief resurgence of mining takes place this year in the opal digs at Gem City, Idaho, it quickly dies away and there has been no further mining of a serious nature there since then.

During **1895** it is discovered that the supply of precious opal at Opal Butte, Oregon, has diminished to such extent that most of the claims are abandoned before year's end. But this does not terminate production of opal from Opal Butte, for it will again make its mark in the gem world before the end of the twentieth century.

With precious opal now having been established as the October birthstone, immensely popular entertainer Sarah Bernhardt, born in October, prizes opal above all other stones and always wears them, influencing many other people, especially in the United States.

White Cliffs is, by this year, in the midst of its heyday, with some 2000 miners and a total resident population just topping 5000, while hundreds of transients come and go at the five hotels currently in operation, The Queensland opal fields, too, are still holding their own and boulder opal production reaches an early peak this year, resulting in the further development of such opal fields as Kynuna, Opalton, Kyabra, Yowah, Koroit, and Hungerford. Total Queensland opal production is recorded this year at £32,750.

And in South Australia, as a sort of footnote for the year but with considerable ramifications for the future, J. R. Hutchison, while trying to get to Coolgardie from Anna Creek, which is Hogarth and Warren's Station a dozen miles west of William Creek on the Oodnadatta line, encounters several good looking quartz reefs of which he makes mental note as being potential gold areas.

The year **1896** is not a good one on the world opal market due to the occurrence of a worldwide recession. Nevertheless, full-scale commercial production of precious opal begins at Opalton in Queensland, with the George Cragg Mine setting the pace. And, well to the south of here, in New South Wales, a new opal deposit is discovered in the Purnanga area, 31 miles [50 km] northeast of White Cliffs.

The discovery of new opal deposits continues in Australia in **1897** with the find of another volcanic precious opal deposit—this one in New South Wales in the Tooraweenah area, 5 miles [8 km] north of the main road from Gilgandra to Coonabarabran.

Opal mining continues its boom at White Cliffs unabated. The number of miners, including transient miners and prospectors, totals 3500 individuals, and scores of mines have been dug in a stretch a half-mile wide by nine miles long. A good number of very substantial finds of gem-quality opal are being made and everything—or nearly so—seems to be going wonderfully. The only fly in the ointment, actually, is that a major mining combine, composed mainly of men working with English capital and calling itself the White Cliffs Opal Mining Company, has formed and quickly buys or claims over 300 acres in the very midst of the most productive area of the opal field.[4] From this they will, for a certain fee, lease out tiny plots of ground to miners who can then dig on a tribute system and who are soon known as tributors. Each tributor is required to surrender half of the opals he finds to the company. It is the young buyer Ted Murphy who becomes the tribute collector at White Cliffs for what was nicknamed the English Company. At intervals, each tributor brings him his accumulated opal. Murphy weighs and values it and the company sells it. Troubles soon develop, however, as the miners want their own claims and resent having to share half the proceeds of all their hard work with an absentee company that is doing nothing but sitting there reaping profits. Murphy himself recognizes the unfairness of the situation and advocates termination of the tribute system. A Royal Commission investigates and the tribute system is abolished about three years after its commencement and is replaced by the Miner's Right, which permits miners to have individual claims.

Len Cram, the renowned miner, cutter, buyer, and writer of Lightning Ridge, related to me when I was there in 1995, the story of the richest pocket of opals ever found at White Cliffs. It occurs in this year of 1897 while the tribute system is still in effect. An old man named Saul arrives in a covered wagon with his wife and son and makes temporary camp behind Ted Murphy's hut. Saul approaches Murphy to acquire a tribute lease and Murphy, who thinks the man is a little too old for the usual hard work, takes him over to a flat depression on Block No. 7, marks out a claim and tells him he shouldn't have to sink a shaft any deeper than 6 feet to hit opal. When the other miners see Saul working out on the flat, they chuckle a bit among themselves, believing that Murphy has only put him there in order to get him off his hands, which is not an unusual occurrence with a newcomer at any opal field. At 6 feet, however, Saul strikes a patch of beautiful opal extending some 8′ × 10′. It takes him and his son 3 months to clear out the pocket and when he sells the opals he has accumulated, he clears a quite substantial £3290—equivalent in today's values to roughly $165,000. Ready to take his profits and leave, Saul puts his little claim up for sale and competition is keen among many potential buyers before it is finally purchased by Emil Treibs and Sam Levy. How well they did with it is not recorded.

The mining at the various fields in Queensland suffers a setback in **1898** when a severe and widespread drought occurs throughout this already arid outback country. Lack of water becomes a major problem and mining is sharply curtailed, especially in such areas as the Jundah field, and remains at a low ebb throughout the duration of the drought, which extends into the early twentieth century.

A setback of an entirely different and decidedly more deadly outcome begins occurring at White Cliffs this year, a situation that is eventually to sound the death knell for this first truly great opal field in Australia. It occurs with the introduction of what is called the candle-box trade. It is introduced by a man named Rosenove. Ever since the discovery of the White Cliffs opal field, the miners, by unwritten agreement, have kept the lower-grade opal off the market so as to enhance the value of better qualities. This low-grade opal is stored in the wooden shipping boxes in which candles had been shipped to White Cliffs. Early on, Rosenove started buying up those accumulations of less than top-quality opal for the usual field price of only 10 shillings (£0.5 per box) and several others had followed his lead. Now, in 1898, Rosenove readies his candle boxes of low-grade opal for shipment and again others follow suit. Literally *tons* of these opals tightly packed in the candle boxes are shipped to Germany, where they sell for an enormous profit of £3 per box. This, along with steadily diminishing opal production, heralds the forthcoming end for the White Cliffs market. Still, at the close of this year White Cliffs is flourishing and miners and merchants alike begin living underground to escape the searing heat of the outback. Even an underground pub has been established and the town's permanent population hovers at around 4000.

Early in **1899** a new opal field is discovered in New South Wales that is initially called the Bunker Field, but that later became just as well known by the name of Gemville, after the town that quickly develops here. At nearly the same time, in Western Australia, a small deposit of gem-quality opaline silica, dubbed byro opal, is discovered on Byro Station, one kilometer northwest of Iniagi Well and north of Meegea Hill, in jasperoidal silica cappings of the ultramafic rocks.

Finally, by the end of this year, the intensive mining that has been occurring in Queensland for boulder opal comes practically to a standstill. This hiatus in Queensland mining lasts for three-quarters of a century.

As **1900** begins, despite the slump that not only continues but worsens in Queensland opal mining, a significant amount of boulder opal mining is still being done at the Hayricks Mine northwest of Quilpie, one of the finest and most productive of all the Queensland mines. Yet, White Cliffs opal easily surpasses Queensland opal in production and prominence. Apart from being easier to cut, steadier in supply and less variable than the Queensland opal, the White Cliffs area is not undergoing the recent severe drought conditions that have all but curtailed Queensland mining operations. Thus, beginning this year Queensland opal mining becomes almost dormant until 1957.

On the other hand, the mining and opal production at White Cliffs continues at a strong pace, aided by outstanding finds that make big news. The so-called "pineapple" found this year by a former sheep shearer, Theodore Matthey, is touted as the finest, most perfectly formed opal pseudomorph ever discovered, alive with more play of color than ever seen in any other specimen. On 25 March, the White Cliffs post office opens (which is still in operation) and even more of the miners begin living underground, with subterranean attractions for their convenience, including the very popular pub, which is now in its second year, a large restaurant, and an excellent bakery. A newspaper is founded, called the *White Cliffs Opal Miner*. Yet, despite these improvements, all is not sanguinary at White Cliffs; various illnesses are taking a severe toll among miners and their families.

Across the Pacific in America a deposit of precious opal is discovered in Lemhi County, Idaho, nearly 30 miles north of Challis. Found in veins in both quartzite alluvium and Challis volcanics, it is called the Panther Creek Opal Occurrence and is located at an elevation of 6700 feet [2043.5 m] in the Gravel Range District along Panther Creek near mouth of Opal Creek, a tributary of the Salmon River.

But by far the most important event of 1900 in regard to opal occurred in New South Wales and goes unheralded at this time—the discovery of black opals at Lightning Ridge. Most of the accounts of how this discovery came about have been based on erroneous hearsay or the copying of earlier accounts that were initially in error. The fact of the matter is that a man named Jack Murray, employed as a boundary rider and ranch hand at Wallangulla Station, lives with his wife in a semipermanent camp at a slight rise called Lightning Ridge. This year, while setting a rabbit trap in the area he discovers some small oddly shaped stones on the surface, each about half the diameter of a walnut.[5] He breaks one open and finds startlingly beautiful precious black opal inside that is very different from the usual precious light opal that he's heard about; most of the stones have incredibly brilliant play of color in a dark gray to black base color on black potch, (Color Plate 8). It is perhaps the finest black opal that has ever been discovered, but at this time its value is a question mark. Murray has no idea whether the black opals will have value similar to the white opals but, on the off chance that they might, he begins a sort of desultory collecting of the stones on the surface during his days off from his job. He calls the stones nobbies and names the site where he is finding them Nobby Hill.

The year **1901** sees yet another discovery of opals in New South Wales, this one occurring close to the coast in the far northeastern corner of the state. The discovery of this volcanic opal is made by D. Munro hardly a mile south of the little community of Tintinbar. Unfortunately, most of the opals are soon found to be unstable and a disturbing percentage of them craze or disintegrate when cut, so early mining operations are suspended and not resumed until 1919.[6]

A few good stones are still showing up on occasion at White Cliffs, one of which is a superb 1100-carat beauty named *Mackenzie's Opal* after its discoverer. Nevertheless, finds such as this are rare indeed and there is very good reason why so many of the White Cliffs miners decide to abandon their claims and drift away. White Cliffs is now in the midst of very bad times. Not only have the opal resources diminished to almost nothing, but, from the onset of mining here to the end of this year, various water-related diseases have killed over 1100 people, including 500 children, most of whom have fallen victim to heat exhaustion, diphtheria, dysentery, and typhoid fever.

Meanwhile, at Lightning Ridge, Jack Murray continues searching throughout 1901 during his offdays—Sundays—for opals on the ground at Nobby Hill. By late in the year he has depleted the supply of stones on the surface and realizes if he is to find any more, he will undoubtedly have to sink a shaft. As the year comes to an end, he is spending his Sundays digging such a shaft at what he deems a likely spot near the eastern base of Nobby Hill.

The year **1902** is not very old when Jack Murray's employers discover that he is spending his off-days digging a shaft at Lightning Ridge. They immediately tell him he should find something better to do on Sundays and order him to cease. When he does not, they fire him, but he stays in the area, abruptly with considerably more time to spend in his digs. Still, it is hard work for a man alone and he soon realizes that he really needs some help and also some funds to keep him going. He reveals details of his find to three of his friends—Walter Hennissey, Peter Ferguson, and Bob Buckley—who become intrigued when they see the new kind of opals he is digging. The three buy into a partnership with him and work then progresses much more efficaciously with the shaft at Nobby Hill.[7] Before long they hit the opal level and begin finding nobbies of the same sort Murray had initially found on the surface. Three other men show up—the Canfell brothers, Jim, Tom, and Mick—and they peg their own Nobby Hill claims adjacent to Murray's.

Meanwhile, another individual arrives who is destined to become one of the greatest promoters of Australian opal. His name is Charlie Nettleton. When he sees what the miners at Nobby Hill are finding, he is very impressed. He visits an inn owner nearby named Joe Beckett and then sets about prospecting on his own. On 15 October of this year he pegs a claim and starts digging his own shaft near a place called Beckett's Tank (later called McDonald's Six Mile).

In **1903,** the several managers of the large stations (ranches) surrounding the Lightning Ridge area, adjuncts of powerful Sydney-based grazing companies, take closer notice of the mining that is going on there. They, along with Joe Beckett and other businessmen ultimately realize there might be big profits to be made here and so they form a mining syndicate, giving Murray and his mates—and other miners—the right to dig there in exchange for a share of the profits, which they anticipate will come both quickly and very substantially.

Early this same year, his laboriously dug shaft having proven to be a duffer (barren of opals), Charlie Nettleton gives up on it and, having joined the mining syndicate, goes back to Nobby Hill to see how Murray and his partners are doing. Murray, aware of Nettleton's extensive mining experience, which he feels can benefit them, confers with his partners and, with their agreement, invites Nettleton to join them as the fifth partner. He does so and the partners quickly put together a 5-pound [2.27-kg] parcel of beautiful rough-cut stones that Nettleton passes along to Mr. Ferris, leader of the syndicate, who forwards the parcel to a well-known Sydney dealer who is anything but impressed. All his remarks are not recorded, but he returns the opal parcel with an offer of a mere 10 shillings, saying it is far too young a form of opal and nothing more than a valueless form of black matrix.

Undaunted, Nettleton declares that the Sydney buyer does not know what he is talking about and that he himself is convinced Lightning Ridge black opal has a great future. He continues to work, accumulating a larger parcel of the black opal—a total of 8 pounds [3.6 kg]—which he persuades the syndicate to allow him to take to White Cliffs, where a number of buyers are operating, believing he can open up a new market for the black opal among them, most particularly with Ted Murphy, whom he trusts, and who is the field agent there for the most noted Australian opal merchant, Tullie Wollaston. The syndicate gives Nettleton permission to give it a try but tells him he is on his own, that they are not going to pay for his transportation there and back. The 41-year-old Nettleton agrees.

Together, Charlie Nettleton and Jack Murray make the arduous journey, arriving at the 435-mile [700-km] distant White Cliffs in early November. After greeting many of the miners he knows and boasting about the opal mining at Lightning Ridge—and also learning that the opal reserves of White Cliffs are declining with alarming rapidity—the pair meet with Murphy who, never before having seen black opals, gazes with wonder and appreciation at the parcel of stones, but who later admits "I had no idea of its value, if any." [8] Deciding to take a risk, he offers them a £15 downpayment, with additional payment to be made if Wollaston, in Adelaide, accepts them. It is much less than Nettleton and Murray have hoped for, but much more than the Sydney dealer offered, so they accept and the deal is consummated on 11 November. [9]

Nettleton and Murray then head back to Lightning Ridge, being followed by some of the White Cliffs miners, who reckon that the opal resources at White Cliffs will soon be entirely exhausted. But when they reach the Ridge and Nettleton reports to the syndicate what they have received for all the miners' great effort, the syndicate members are greatly angered, dissolve the syndicate and order the miners off the grazing lands. By this time Lightning Ridge is peppered with claims and the miners refuse to go, so the station managers begin doing everything they can to force them out, thus beginning a very bitter fight that will last for some three years.

Back at White Cliffs, however, immediately after buying the black opals, Murphy sends the parcel on to Wollaston in Adelaide, who becomes greatly enthusiastic over their exquisite beauty. He, in turn, instantly sends an order back to Murphy to buy all he can of the same material. In the end, as the fortunes of White Cliffs begin eclipsing, he eventually sends Murphy to be the resident buyer at Lightning Ridge. By the end of the year, black opals are selling for £1–2 per ounce in the rough, according to Wollaston.[10]

And in America this year, in the same general area where opal was discovered in Lemhi County, Idaho, 3 years earlier, very beautiful precious opal, along with much common opal, is discovered on the west side of Panther Creek Valley in a large porphyry dike that runs parallel to the creek some 6 miles below its head at an altitude of 7000 feet above sea level.

Not fully up to date with what is occurring at Lightning Ridge, the New South Wales Annual Report of 1903 declares that "In the parish of Wallangulla, prospecting has been carried on with apparently indifferent results."

Although the year **1904** sees a brief resurgence of mining efforts at the Gem City opal mines near Moscow, Idaho, in the United States, the effort is soon abandoned.

The end seems to be in sight this year for Hungarian opal as well. Australian opals so completely dominate the world opal market that all but a few of the Slovakian opal mines in the Carpathian Mountains have closed. The sole exceptions are those a half-mile west of Dubnik on the slope of Libanka Mountain.

In New South Wales, official statements have not yet caught up to reality and the Annual Report of New South Wales Department of Mines lists opal production at Lightning Ridge as £1000 for the year. It is the last time the area will be mentioned in so offhand a way. With the very sharp decline occurring in opal production at White Cliffs, a great many of the miners there have been leaving. Most, having heard about what has been occurring at Lightning Ridge, go there and peg their own claims and the rush is on, attracting other hopefuls from elsewhere in Australia as well. Some, having heard of a new deposit of precious volcanic opal recently found in New South Wales at Hyandra Creek, 13 miles [21 km] south of Dubbo, go there to mine but soon discover that, like so much of the volcanic opal, it is very unstable material. A limited number of the White Cliffs miners travel all the way to Western Australia where unofficial reports claim that a fine quality black opal deposit has been discovered some 3 miles [5 km] northeast of Coolgardie. It is a long journey made in vain, since the report is essentially groundless.

The year **1905** brings another significant discovery in the world of opals, this time in the United States. In northwestern Nevada a mining engineer named Marsden Nanson, while merely passing through Virgin Valley in Humboldt County, discovers precious opal that is clear black with a glorious array of the whole spectrum of color scintillating in its depths.[11] Within mere weeks of his filing his report, the first opal mine claim is filed in Virgin Valley and the Opal Queen Mine is established.

In Europe this same year, the *Burning of Troy* opal, once owned by the Empress Josephine and missing since her death nearly a century ago, is acquired from an unidentified source by the city of Vienna, Austria. Several hundred miles to the west, in southwestern Germany, the opal-cutting monopoly enjoyed for so many years by the firms of Idar-Oberstein comes to an end, although fully 90% of Australian opal is still being cut here.

In Australia, the opal pseudomorphs found at Glendon, New South Wales, in 1849 are finally officially named glendonite by T. W. E. David. And the more famous pseudomorphs of this state, the so-called "pineapples" of White Cliffs, are this year the subject of the first scientific description written of them, a paper by C. Anderson and H. Stanley Jevons, who believe them to be pseudomorphs after glauberite.[12] But, despite this interest in a by-product of White Cliffs, that area is in deep trouble; the field is all but defunct and most of the miners have left, many of them going to Lightning Ridge.[13] The renown opal buyer, Ted Murphy, is among those who have put White Cliffs behind them for good. Under instructions from Wollaston, Murphy reestablishes his opal-buying activities this year at Lightning Ridge. Despite the continuing fight there between the miners and the powerful station managers, the whole Lightning Ridge area is at this time experiencing a real boom in mining, with full-scale mining in effect, no less than 200 full-time miners already resident here and the year's production noted at £4000. Among the multitude of beautiful stones found here this year is the lovely *Dark Jubilee* opal, which has been cut into a stunning gemstone weighing 318 carats.

The three long years of bitter strife between miners and the station managers, who formerly made up the Lightning Ridge Mining Syndicate, finally ends in **1906** when at last the New South Wales Minister of Mines intervenes on behalf of the miners, giving them the right to claim land and mine for opals on it.[14] The on-going boom in opal mining here is so pronounced that by the end of the year there are 1500 resident miners, most of them living at the foot of Sim's Hill in humpies—crude shacks and shelters—in what is known today as the Old Town area, just over a mile [2 km] north of Nobby Hill (by this time generally called Old Nobby or Shallow Nobby). Ensuring the area's future even more, Charlie Nettleton arrives in London and will remain here for the better part of two years, convincing the gem merchants of the value of black opal and establishing that stone as the most desirable of all opals.

In the United States it has taken a while for news of last year's opal discovery in Nevada to spread. The Virgin Mine claim becomes the second opal mining claim filed in Virgin Valley—an important mine that will later be renamed the Bonanza Mine—and, following that, hundreds of claims are made. By the end of this year, a veritable patchwork of claims cover much of the ten-mile long valley in Humboldt County.

Early in **1907,** a New York jewelry merchant from Tiffany's, visiting in London, becomes intrigued by the beautiful black opals from Australia that Charlie Nettleton is promoting. He spends a considerable amount of time with Nettleton, purchases many excellent stones from him and, on returning to his Fifth Avenue shop in New York, devotes a full window and a whole interior showcase to displaying these most outstanding black opals in the loveliest imaginable settings with diamonds and the best enamels. For weeks crowds gather just to see the displays and there are major write-ups about it in newspapers and magazines. The American taste for opals, previously limited to light opals from either Europe or, more recently, White Cliffs, Australia, is tremendously stimulated and in a very short time the black opal has become the American public's favorite.

Nettleton returns to Lightning Ridge in late May of **1908** and finds the population has risen to about 3000, of which two-thirds are miners. All available spaces in the immediate Nobby Hill area are already claimed. Sim's Hill, adjacent to Old Town, is already pretty much abandoned and, in scouting around for a likely spot to peg a claim for himself, he discovers a pinhead-sized trace of precious opal on the ground surface three miles south of the Lightning Ridge community. He sinks a shaft and encounters a new opal deposit. Instantly there is a mad rush of miners to peg claims adjacent to his, or at least as near as possible. Others quickly start finding good opals and the rich new field, while still part of Lightning Ridge, is named the Three Mile Opal Field, more often merely called the Three Mile.[15] Inspired to do further exploration, the miners who have not yet pegged producing claims begin spreading out, prospecting new areas. They find them in a crescentic stretch extending some 10 miles [16 km] and soon Lightning Ridge has a whole new series of producing opal fields with such names as Angledool, Butterfly, Chum, Four Mile, Hawk's Nest, Iron Bark, Mehi, New Chum, New Nobby, Pony Fence, Pott's Point, Telephone Line, and others.

By the middle of **1909,** the Three Mile is generally deemed to be all but played out and practically all of the miners go elsewhere, most of them to the rush at the new Hawk's Nest opal field, 2 km southwest of the Three Mile. Three miners, however, continued digging at the Three Mile—Son Bruce, Jack Maine, and George Bailey. When their shaft reaches the opal level, 30 feet deep, they work the level for a week and find it barren. They then agree to dig down to the next opal level, at a depth of 54 feet, which takes them a week to do. Almost immediately Maine, to his great delight, finds one of the finest slabs of black opal ever seen—4″ × 2″ × 1″ [101.6 mm × 50.8 mm × 25.4 mm]. Further digging shows that the wall of their dig is actually peppered with opals, as thickly as currants in a fruitcake. It was that lucky occurrence that every miner dreams of and what they reverentially call "a jewelry shop" in Australia or a "glory hole" in the United States. For over two hours the three mates do nothing but carefully extract opals within arm's reach of the bottom of the shaft—320 of them and each a grand gemstone, including that first big black slab. When a buyer called Pappa Francis shows up and offers them £320 for the lot, they haggle back and forth over the price. The miners are hungry and really need the money so they soon give in and accept the offer. It was an incredible deal for Pappa Francis—paying £1 each for 320 top gem-quality opals.[16]

This same year another fine opal is found at the Three Mile—this one dubbed the *Eighty-Quid Opal* after the price the miner receives for it from a buyer in the field. It is not the only named stone found at Lightning Ridge this year. Another was discovered only a bit over a mile north of Nobby Hill, at an elevation called Bald Hill. A miner named Dunstan is invited by one of his miner friends, whose partner is hospitalized, to work with him on equal shares in the mine until the ailing partner returns.[17] This is in an area where several tentative shafts were sunk but soon abandoned when opal was not immediately discovered. Dunstan agrees and works there, without any significant finds being made, until the recuperated miner returns. They ask him to stay on but Dunstan refuses and elects to start a shaft of his own some 50 yards away. In mid-August, when his shaft is only 18 feet deep, which is only halfway to the opal level in this area, he uncovers a stone that, when first viewed, seems to be a piece of opalized wood with some play of color showing, but not really very promising. After being cleaned off a bit, it weighs 6.35 ounces—900.11 carats—and one of his miner friends suggests he try selling it as a specimen stone and, if lucky, he might get £20 for it. But Dunstan thinks there's a core of good opal inside that will be found if the stone is cut and he soon finds a buyer who agrees with him and pays him £100 for the stone in the field—a value equivalent in today's currency to about $2500. The stone is indeed cut and, as both Dunstan and the buyer suspected, there is a core of beautiful black opal on natural black potch. The final result is a smashing 27-carat rectangular black crystal opal cabochon presently valued at $250,000. Originally called just *Dunstan's Stone,* the opal, after being cut, is renamed the *Aurora Australis,* but because two stones (one found in 1938 and another in 1989) have also been given the same name, most people have resumed calling this one *Dunstan's Stone.*[18]

In **1910,** what is claimed to be some of the finest opalized wood in the world is discovered in America, originating in a unique deposit along Clover Creek east of Bliss in Gooding County, Idaho; logs of an extinct species of oak are found encased in hardened volcanic ash that must be blasted in order to free the wood. Specimens reach as much as a foot [304.8 mm] in diameter but the average is closer to 4″ to 6″ [101.6 mm to 152.4 mm]. Ranging from buff to brown and with black markings, the Clover Creek wood is notable for the beautifully preserved structure of the original wood; each pore and annular ring so characteristic of present-day oak wood is faithfully preserved in opal.[19]

It is believed by many that this year of 1910 is also the year when one of the largest solid opals ever found is discovered. Very little information is available about it beyond the fact that it is found at White Cliffs and is presently designated as the *White Cliffs Number Two Opal*. Hodge Smythe, former curator of minerals at the Australian Museum in Sydney, stated that the stone was discovered a dozen feet below ground level, was "a light opal of good color" and weighed 90.64 ounces—that's a shade over 5.5 pounds and fully 12,474 carats!

It is in April of **1911** when, in northwestern Nevada, a second major precious opal occurrence is discovered in the Virgin Valley area of Humboldt County by a rancher named Ed McGee. He makes his claims nearly 10 miles eastward from where the Opal Queen Mine and Virgin Mine (Bonanza Mine) are already located. The new area is on a slight elevation already rather prophetically known as Rainbow Ridge and the McGee Claim will subsequently become the world's first patented precious opal prospect, the Rainbow Ridge Opal Mine (Figure 18).

Figure 18. The entrance to the extensive tunnels of the underground portion of the Rainbow Ridge Opal Mine. (Photo by the author)

In the upper end of Virgin Valley, numerous claims are registered in **1912,** later to become known generically as the Royal Peacock Opal Mines, which will comprise not only scores of claims and prospects but also 14 working mines. Those mines include the Little Pebble, Northern Lights, Orion, Peacock One, Peacock Two, Peacock Three, Peacock Four, Pebble, Phantom, Royal Peacock One, Royal Peacock Two, Sand Pebbles One, Sand Pebbles Two, and Sand Pebbles Three.

Also this year, far across the ocean in New South Wales, Australia, the first of the rare, fully opalized fish skeletons is found at White Cliffs and, unable to be sold profitably as a museum or collector's specimen, is broken into bits and sold as gem-grade opal rough.

In **1913** there are no recorded momentous events concerning precious opal but a steady strengthening of opal interests and production in Australia, the United States, and Mexico. Where White Cliffs is concerned, however, both this year and throughout 1914, almost no mining is occurring. In fact, the White Cliffs opal field, for all intents and purposes, is abandoned and the town has become a ghost town; only 20 people remain and from this time forward, little work is done here.

In America, since no timber is available for supports in the entire region surrounding Virgin Valley, the miners who hope to strike rich deposits of precious opal have begun to dig their drives without benefit of properly supporting the tunnel roofs. As a result, already a number of miners have been badly injured in various cave-ins.

It is very close to the close of this year of 1914 when James R. Hutchison, of Adelaide, South Australia, working for the New Colorado Prospecting Syndicate, is sent out to try to relocate the quartz reefs he had noted during his outback travels 19 years earlier, in the hope they will be a source of gold. He sets out from Anna Creek with his 14-year-old son, Bill, called Willie, and two of his employees, P. J. Winch of Melbourne and Mel McKenzie of Port Augustus. They travel on camelback, but the desert conditions are very hard on them and the end of the year finds them at North Creek near the Stuart Range in the vacant, hostile outback, sorely in need of water. Conditions grow steadily worse for them and, as the year **1915** begins, they are spending more time looking for water than for gold. The situation becomes so crucial that on 6 February, when they are camped in the Stuart Range, the three men head out in different directions looking for water, leaving Willie at the camp. To say they were in the middle of nowhere is quite accurate. Their camp in the Stuart Range was some **470** miles northwest of Adelaide and **360** miles south of Alice Springs. When the three men return after dark that night, unsuccessful in their quest, they find Willie gone and are initially very fearful. However, a short time later the youth shows up, having found not only a good supply of water, but a very rich deposit of opals all over the surface.[20]

Within a month Hutchison's two helpers are back in Adelaide reporting his find and Jim Hutchison and his son show up on 28 March with his official report about the discovery. It does not take long before the first miners arrive on the field and set to work—in this case the O'Neil brothers, Dick and Jim, who are actually out gold prospecting when they learn of the Stuart Range opal discover. They go there and, by late in the year, are mining at a site they name Big Flat. They are first to sell stones from that field to Tullie Wollaston, who assumes these brothers are the discoverers of the Stuart Range Opal Mines.[21]

Across the ocean in the summer of this year 1915, an important figure comes on the scene in Virgin Valley. Learning of the discovery and mining of precious opals in Virgin Valley, some 400 miles distant to the northeast, the San Francisco *Chronicle* assigns a 59-year-old veteran reporter named Flora Haines Loughead Gutierrez—best known as Flora Loughead (pronounced Lockheed)—to go there and research information for a feature story.[22] She does so and, in the process, becomes so enamored of opals that she buys a dozen or more claims from Ed McGee, including the Virgin Mine (Bonanza Mine), Royal Peacock, Northern Lights, Pebbles, Rainbow Ridge claims, and others and spends the remainder of her life involved with the opals of Virgin Valley.

The following year, **1916,** Flora Loughead meets the very wealthy Mrs. Gardiner Hammond, of Hammond Organ fame, in Santa Barbara, California, at a social function and talks begin that will, within two years, result in a partnership in which Mrs. Hammond will finance an extensive Virgin Valley opal mining venture for Mrs. Loughead, whose contribution will be her Rainbow Ridge claims, acquired from Ed McGee, and her opal mining experience.

By this time, word of the discovery of the opal field in the Stuart Range of South Australia, has spread and numerous miners flock to the area. Although occasional black opals are being found—more in the earlier days than at present—by far the greater majority of opals mined here are a white base seam opal, much of it in large chunky pieces. Once again it is Tullie Wollaston who, this year, sells in the United States the first mined stones from what will become Coober Pedy, and the beautiful light opals find ready acceptance. It is lack of water at the Stuart Range Opal Mines that is the first concern, since there is almost none, and so the many miners already attracted to the field, even if not yet mining, band together and, aided by government funds, dig a great circular hole, 300 feet in diameter and 12 feet deep and line it with concrete—a water reservoir capable of holding half a million gallons. By the end of this year, Big Flat, just north of present Hutchison Street, has been well established by the O'Neil brothers as the principal mining area at the new field, but some of the other, smaller fields are the Four Mile, the Eight Mile, the Twelve Mile, Crowder's Gully, Post Office Hill, and the Jungle.

Meanwhile, at Lightning Ridge four truly outstanding precious opals are found at virtually the same time in the Telephone Line Diggings: the 800-carat *Flamingo*, the *Empress*, 504 carats; the *Pride of Australia*, 226 carats, and the *Black Prince*, 219 carats.[23]

In the spring of **1917**, a German mineral dealer named Schwalm claims that some small pieces of layered milk opal with attractive play of color at one end originated in the Kaiserstuhl in Germany, one of Europe's better mineral localities, but no more of this opal has ever shown up and it is believed Schwalm falsified the origin to protect the actual site, wherever it was.

And it is this year as well that the first two truly noteworthy black opals are discovered at Rainbow Ridge in Virgin Valley. The first, which later comes to be known as the *Grubstake Opal*—a 10,376-carat stone found early in the summer—ultimately becomes part of the collection of the American Museum of Natural History in New York. The second, discovered in November by a miner named Lew Thompson, who has been hired by Flora Loughead's mining supervisor in Virgin Valley, J. B. Oliver, is an incredibly beautiful red-in-black solidly opalized fossil limb section weighing 2665 carats, subsequently named the *Roebling Opal*, which is presently in the collection of the Smithsonian Institution in Washington, DC.

With entry of the United States into the Great War in **1918**, opal mining in Virgin Valley goes into a virtual hiatus, which lasts until the early 1940s. Nevertheless, the partnership in Virgin Valley opal mining between Flora Loughead and Mrs. Gardiner Hammond becomes actuality in April, resulting in the formation of the Rainbow Ridge Mining Company, and Flora Loughead and her brother, Allan Ledford, continue trying to hire men to do the actual mining.

The war has also been affecting the amount of mining being done at the Stuart Range Opal Mines, but something occurs in later April that stirs great interest—some aboriginals show up with a quantity of high-quality black opal to sell to buyers in the field. Initial attempts by miners to follow these aboriginals back to the source of their supply remain unsuccessful for five years. Because of that and the end of the war later in the year, a surge in opal mining interest occurs and some 300 applications to prospect in the area are received by the South Australian Department of Mines.

This year, too, in the Bald Hill diggings at Lightning Ridge, another gorgeous opal is found and named—the lovely 253-carat *Flame Queen*. Nevertheless, as miners return from the war in **1919** to resume digging and the lull in mining ends, it is the Stuart Range Opal Mines field in South Australia that this year takes over prominence from Lightning Ridge. A certain amount of mining of volcanic opal is occurring too, in new opal discoveries at Tintinbar and two other nearby localities along the northeastern coast of New South Wales, but the opal is very hard to extract undamaged from the volcanic rock (Figure 19). This same year, the city of Vienna, Austria—despite the fact that it is undergoing a period of pronounced financial difficulty following the Great War—refuses

Figure 19. The present opal diggings at Tintinbar in the northeastern corner of New South Wales. (Photo by the author)

to accept an offer of £25,000 for the *Burning of Troy* opal, which is still in its treasury.

In Nevada it was expected that there would be an upsurge of mining activity now that the war is over, but many of the miners did not even return and, with most of the surface opal deposits picked clean, Virgin Valley experiences a near total cessation of opal mining activity that prevails until 1942.

In Australia things are different. Here, ever more of the veterans of the Great War, returning home, have decided to try their hand at mining and a fair number of these have come, in **1920,** to the Stuart Range Opal Field. They bring along the idea of defeating the elements by living underground—an idea that has already long been quite successful at White Cliffs. They also form a Progress Committee, which agrees that since no one likes the name Stuart Range Opal Mines, they will rename the field something more appropriate and individualistic for their area. On 26 June of this year, they select the term that the Arabana aboriginals have been using for it since the white men arrived— *kupa piti*. In the aboriginal dialect being used here, *kupa piti* means "boy's waterhole," referring to the discovery made by Willie Hutchison here at the same time he discovered the opals in 1915—the discovery of the water being of far more importance to the aboriginals than the discovery of the opals. Very quickly that aboriginal terminology evolved—distorted among the white miners—to

Coober Pedy, which is the name that is now officially adopted and that is still used. Over the years, however, due to some early misinformation appearing in print, people got the idea—now the most prevailing belief—that Coober Pedy was the aboriginal term for "white man's burrow" or "white man in a hole," neither of which are correct. Desultory attempts are still being made at Coober Pedy to follow the aboriginals to their continuing source of black opal in the north, but the mining at Coober Pedy is consuming all the energy and man-power—with production of over £20,000 worth of precious opal reported this year. Many of the Lightning Ridge miners, believing the fields there are just about played out, abandon them this year and go to Coober Pedy.

It is during the following year, **1921,** that the *Burning of Troy* opal disappears from the treasury of the city of Vienna, Austria. Three-quarters of a century later—as of 1996—the fabulous stone has not reappeared, but since the first disappearance lasted for nearly a century, perhaps there is still hope.

At Coober Pedy this year the population fluctuates as miners come and go, but it averages around 200 miners, plus their families. A fair number of these miners are branching out, prospecting for new finds in the general area and it is because of this that one of the truly significant finds is made—the Twenty Mile opal field. By the end of this year the full extent of Coober Pedy covers some 40 miles [64 km] and production for the year surpasses £24,000.

The vagaries of opal mining continue in **1922.** In Queensland where mining has been practically dormant since 1900, the incredibly beautiful 432-carat *Living Fire* opal, also known as the *Red Show* opal, is found at the Old German Diggings near Quilpie in the southwestern quadrant of the state. In Slovakia, commercial mining for Hungarian opals finally ends entirely except for the mines at Dubnik, where only a few skeleton crews are kept on the site to continue mining and protect the mines from vandals. And in Australia, the story spreads that the opal deposits at Lightning Ridge are depleted and many of the miners leave and do not return until after World War II.

After five years of attempting to follow the aboriginals to their source of black opal somewhere to the north of Coober Pedy, several white opal miners are successful in **1923.** A party of the aboriginals, having sold a quantity of high-quality black opal to buyers at Coober Pedy, now unwittingly lead the trailing whites some 217 miles [350 km] northwestward to a site just west of Marla Station, which they call Mintabie. Claims blanketing the area are immediately pegged but not exploited, since no really productive mining for the black opal is carried out here for almost a decade.

The following year, **1924,** two occurrences cause a temporary influx of miners and others at Lightning Ridge; the first is the discovery of the lovely 2126-carat black opal called *Otto's Stone,* after the miner who found it; the second is publication of Tullie Wollaston's book entitled *Opal: Gem of the Never Never*. Despite these little bursts of interest, opal mining at Lightning Ridge continues in its quarter-century slump while production at Coober Pedy increases.

It is in **1926** that a form of opal pseudomorphs called pseudogaylussite are discovered at both Groningen, Holland, and Paris, France. These are pseudomorphs similar to the so-called jarrowite discovered in County Durham, England, in 1847, and directly related to the pseudomorphs called pineapples that are found at White Cliffs in New South Wales.

In September **1927,** the *Grubstake Opal,* originally mined at Rainbow Ridge in Virgin Valley, Nevada, is acquired by the American Museum of Natural History in New York, where it remains today as part of their gem collection.

One of the more significant finds of **1928** occurs at the Mehi opal field close to Angledool, some 25 miles [40 km] north of the town of Lightning Ridge, but still considered to be the far northern part of the main Lightning Ridge opal field. This was the discovery of the outstanding 709-carat *Pandora* opal, and the interest it evoked was augmented by a find much closer to the town of Lightning Ridge—the *Leonard Opal,* 138 carats of black beauty named after the miner who found it. And once again, this year, opal pseudomorphs similar in composition to the White Cliffs pineapples are found in the preserved frontal lobe of the skull of a fossil cave bear in the Tufra Mountains at Hermanecz near Neusohl in Hungary.

Coober Pedy has not only held its own, but actually increased opal production through these years while other opal fields in Australia were suffering severe doldrums. Now, in **1929,** as a direct result of the Great Depression, even this field goes into a steady decline until the outbreak of World War II.

The next big chapter in Australian opal history occurs in **1930** when precious opal floaters are discovered by a pair of young men, Sam Brooks and Roy Shepherd, on One Tree Hill in what is now the center of the town of Andamooka, South Australia, in the Flinders Range a few miles west of Lake Torrens, 186 miles [300 km] southeast of Coober Pedy. The name Andamooka derives from the aboriginal *Jantamuka* or *Jandarimoko.* The two men discover the field quite by accident. While they are working in low ground, a torrential storm begins flooding the gullies. They rush to nearest high ground, which is up a creek gully now called Opal Creek. The high ground where they take refuge has a solitary tree growing upon it and, hence, was called One Tree Hill.[24] Here, as they wait for the waters to abate, Sam Brooks picks up the first opal on the surface. Neither boy knows what they have, but they think they might be onto a good thing and start looking for more that might be worthwhile picking up. At the first opportunity, they take their find to their boss, Mr. Foulis, at "the big house" (homestead) and asked him about them. He knows what opal is and, ordering them to keep the place secret so there will not be a rush, he is soon planning systematic mining. He sends out two employees—Alan Treloar and Paddy Evans—to investigate and do some further prospecting. Even Foulis himself, whenever he goes out to see how they are faring, takes a different route each time so there will be no definite track that can be followed by others. The first actual work is done on One Tree Hill, with the three employees, including Sam Brooks, pegging out the spots they fancy best. They finally strike opal 18 inches down on what is now Treloar Hill.

Over the next few months they improve the diggings and the field is producing, but prices are down and initially they get very little for the opal. The opal here is mostly crystal but, unlike Coober Pedy, not in seams. It is found in odd lumps that the miners are soon calling blobs. There is also a matrix opal, as well as a form of opal called painted ladies, which occurs as large rounded pebbles of hardened purple sandstone, in which the opal is carried in a network of cracks or sometimes partly covering the stones like a coat of whitish opal. As this early mining effort occurs, Andamooka is considered to be an interesting, valuable field, but from the beginning it is obvious it will never become as large or as productive as Coober Pedy.

In this same year of 1930 White Cliffs is deemed by most miners to be entirely played out, but a little handful of miners remain and occasionally they get lucky. A beautiful 808-carat opal is found this year that is named the *Double G* Opal.

And before this year of 1930 is ended, another discovery of unusual opal pseudomorphs is made, similar in composition to the "pineapples" of White Cliffs and in appearance to the "barleycorns" of Thuringia. The new find is made by fishermen who are dredging the sea bottom near Archangel, off the Karelian Coast. These new finds are superstitiously attributed with healing powers and called "White Sea hornlets," a name by which they are still known today.

By the midpoint of the following year, **1931,** the Andamooka secret is out and a certain number of miners come to the area to give it a try—at first surreptitiously, then openly. With prices down as a result of the depression, however, there is not much of a living to be made in a new, essentially unproven opal field, so no one here is making much headway.

At the same time a certain amount of small scale mining is inaugurated at Mintable, eight years after the miners have finally ascertained the location of the South Australian field. Even here, however, mining was not very productive until open cut mining was initiated with heavy equipment in 1976.

It is not until September of this year that the first motor car, hailing from William Creek, arrives in Coober Pedy. Prior to this year all who came traveled on horseback, by camel, or on foot.

Finally, in **1932,** unable to keep up even a pretense of competing with Australian opal, all remaining Slovakian opal mining, including the Dubnik mines which have been in partial production for the last decade, ceases and all mines are closed permanently except for a minimal maintenance staff, although occasional rockhounds continue to prowl the old mine dumps. In the meanwhile, also this year, a breathtaking 150-carat opal named the *Green Goddess* is found at Lightning Ridge in New South Wales.

By the year **1933** mining operations are becoming pretty well established at Andamooka. Although the continuing worldwide depression is causing a general decline in all phases of the opal industry, Alan Treloar and Paddy Brooks bring out Andamooka's first mine-produced opal, a 1933 production figure that is recorded at £1000, which means it has very nearly overtaken Coober Pedy.

Elsewhere in the world, a precious opal deposit is found in Ankartra, Malagasy Republic, and there is the report of precious opals appearing at the Nairobi market that supposedly have been mined in Ethiopia, a report that was long thought to be spurious, since no other such claims were made until recently, when an important deposit was found. In the United States, a geologist named H. C. Dake publishes a scientific paper describing the Virgin Valley opal beds, and mine owner and former Basque shepherd Dan Archevaleta uncovers a beautiful black opal that is named the *Archevaleta Opal*.

By **1935** the precious opal production at Andamooka has risen to £2000; a number of different fields have been discovered in the general area and their opal resources are being exploited. Some of these include digs named Blackboy, Boundary Riders, Brooks (or Treloar's), Coster's Hill, German Gully, Gunn's Gully, Horse Paddock, Jubilee, Koska's, Lunatic Hill (or Grosser's), One Tree Hill, The Saddle, Stevens Creek, Triangle, Willis' Ridge, and Yahloo.

Because of the general disinterest in the opal mining at Virgin Valley, by **1936** many of the initial claim owners have defaulted in performing their annually required improvements and so have lost their claims, some of which are picked up by a newcomer to the valley, Mark Foster. It is in **1937** that the Harry W. Wilson family comes to Virgin Valley and buys numerous claims and mines from Foster, including the Royal Peacock Opal Mines (Figure 20).

Bad times have descended upon Flora Loughead, due to an erroneous magazine article that has caused a wave of trespassers to descend on Virgin Valley to pillage and vandalize the opal mines, particularly those belonging to the Rainbow Ridge Opal Company. It is also during this year that the first and only mining fatality occurs in Virgin Valley. A miner named Miller is killed in the cave-in of his drive, and his mine is ever after called the Dead Man's Claim.

The second beautiful New South Wales black opal to be named the *Aurora Australis* is found in August of **1938** at the Shallow Nobby (Old Nobby) opal field at the northeastern edge of the town of Lightning Ridge, practically on the same spot where black opals were first discovered at Lightning Ridge by Jack Murray in 1900.[25] An unidentified miner discovers the stone and sells it as a rub in the field for an undisclosed sum to an agent of the Melbourne firm of Altmann & Cherny, Ltd.[26] Cut into a magnificent red-on-black oval cabochon measuring 3″ × 1.8″ [76.2 mm × 45.72 mm], the stone weighs 180 carats. It has the distinct impression of a fossil starfish on its back.[27]

Figure 20. A view to the southeast across Virgin Valley from near the summit of Gooch Table. The workings of the Royal Peacock Opal Mines are visible on the opposite slopes. (Photo by Alan A. Vogel)

It is **1939** when the distinguished archaeologist and anthropologist, Dr. Louis S. B. Leakey finds, in a cave near Nakuru, Kenya, the oldest opal artifacts known to man—dating from about the year 4000 B.C. No source for these opals has ever been definitely ascertained, though it is now believed they may have originated in the recently discovered—or rediscovered—Ethiopian opal field.

Mexico's La Carbonera opal mine becomes involved in a major lawsuit over ownership, which, beginning in **1940** and lasting for six years, leaves the mine deserted and badly neglected for six years. Other Mexican deposits, however, are presently producing good precious fire opal. They include some brilliant orange material being mined 150 miles southeast of Mexico City, near Tlaxiaco in the State of Oaxaca; a good supply of topaz yellow to pale reddish opal, very clear and alive with strong yellow-red-green POC, from a feldspar porphyry near San Nichola del Oro in the State of Guerrero; some unusual salmon pink precious opal being mined north of Querétaro near Sisoquichic in the Sierra de Tarahaumare; a good red precious opal occurring even farther away, about 150 miles northwest of Querétaro in the Barranca de Tepezala, Cerro de las Fejas, Aquascaliente; and, finally, a quality milk opal with excellent play of color near Coacoyula. All these deposits are being regularly worked, with most of the recovered opal being purchased by Oriental buyers for shipment to the Far East.

Meanwhile, at this same time in South Australia, the 11-year decline in mining at Coober Pedy has leveled off with only 34 full-time miners left working the great field. And, at Lightning Ridge, another noteworthy stone has been found this year. It is called the *Big Ben* opal and weighs 4099 carats.

It is on 29 January of **1943** that Flora Loughead, never having fully realized her dream for the Virgin Valley opal fields of Nevada, dies at the age of 87 at the home of her daughter, Hope Loughead Ledford, in Berkeley, California. Now Harry Foulks of Stockton, California, primarily considering it an investment, acquires the six patented claims comprising the Rainbow Ridge Mining Company. Nevertheless, opal mining remains at a virtual standstill in Virgin Valley until late in **1945,** several months after the end of World War II. And in that same year, at Andamooka, a matrix opal is found that ranks as one of the 15 largest opals ever discovered—the 10,036-carat *Noolinga Nera.*

The end of World War II stimulates a spectacular increase in production at opal fields all over the world in 1946, but perhaps nowhere so much as in South Australia, and particularly at Coober Pedy. It is estimated that by the end of this year no less than 80% of the world's precious opal production is originating from the South Australian fields. One of that state's great discoveries this year is the beautiful *Andamooka Opal,* a lovely light opal of blue-green body color discovered at Andamooka's Stevens Creek diggings. Eventually cut to a beautiful finished cabochon weighing 205 carats, it is the first of three large stones so named. The other two are found in 1948 and 1970, but included a certain amount of matrix material along with the precious opal. This first stone is beautiful solid opal.

The year 1946 also saw a greater development of the Red Rock Opal Mine at Red Rock Canyon, California, which has just been acquired by the Janet Cowden family. The claim, now being worked with new machinery and better methods, is producing some very good gem-quality volcanic opal.

It is in **1947** when one of the better opal deposits is discovered at Coober Pedy. The find is made by an aboriginal woman who, with her white husband named Charlie, is looking for a place to take out a claim well apart from other diggers some eight miles from town. They are at Geraghty Hill when she sees a white stone protruding from the ground and digs it up with her spear. Underneath its thin, gritty clay coating, it is solid black opal. The pair file their claim and then take the stone to buyer Ernest G. Sherman, who gives them £2000 for it. A great rush of some 200 new miners results and there are those who still contend that the Eight Mile produced the best opal ever discovered at Coober Pedy, although others would give the adjacent Olympic opal field that honor. The only other major field to come close to emulating Coober Pedy's record is Lightning Ridge, in New South Wales, especially with such new areas being found there at intervals as the Mehi, Grawin, Glengarry, Coocoran, and New Coocoran. It is, in fact, at Lightning Ridge this year that another named stone is found—the beautiful *Duke of Devonshire* opal, which was still 100 carats after being cut.

Queensland, too, has a fine boulder opal found this year, an exceptional 2126-carat stone discovered near Quilpie and named, after the miner who got it, the *Schwencke Opal*.

It is this year, too, when a so-called "smoked opal process" is developed in the state of Jalisco in Mexico. When applied to the very porous hydrophane opals, it causes them to turn black, the resultant material bearing a resemblance to the black opal of Lightning Ridge, but easily detectable under close examination.[28]

The Spencer Opal Mine is accidentally discovered in **1948** by two deer hunters lost in fog on the side of a mountain in Clark County, Idaho, 15 miles south of the Montana border and 60 miles directly west of Yellowstone National Park as the crow flies. They know they are only a few miles east of the tiny sheeptown of Spencer, founded by Spencer Harwood in 1891, and so they simply settle down to wait for the fog to lift. While doing so, they begin looking at the multitude of pieces of thin-layered, milky-white porcelain-like rock that has weathered out of a rhyolite ledge and is littering the ground surface around them, and find that some of them have thin bands of brilliantly iridescent blue, green, red, and yellow. When the fog dissipates and the sun comes out, they take particular note of the spot and fill their pockets with samples, which they take to a competent lapidarist, who identifies the thin bands of colorful material as precious opal.

And late this year in Australia, renowned opal buyer Ted Murphy has his book published, entitled *They Struck Opal!*

The long dormancy in opal mining in Virgin Valley, Nevada, comes to an end in **1949** when members of the Hodson family—Glenn and Bea, along with their son, Keith, and his wife, Agnes—buy the Rainbow Ridge Mining Company claims from Harry Foulks and name the principal mine of those claims the Rainbow Ridge Opal Mine. This seems to initiate a distinct mining boom in Virgin Valley. And, as if this becomes an international signal, the following year, **1950,** in New South Wales, the quarter-century slump in opal production that has been plaguing Lightning Ridge abruptly ends and a whole new era of vigorous opal activity begins.

In **1952,** four years after the discovery of opal on the mountainside just east of Spencer, Idaho, the first opal mining claim occupies 10 acres of Forest Service land and is filed as the Lost Deer Hunters' Mine by Franklin W. Argenbright and Jesse Ray Bohney. At once they begin their initial dig, a hole that is 10″ × 20″ [3 × 6 m] and they quickly begin removing opal. Numerous other claims are soon made in the vicinity of theirs. The precious opal is primarily very bright, very colorful layers of precious opal in milky white common opal.

The layers are so thin, with much of it the thickness of a sheet of paper, that the majority of material brought out is suitable only for the making of opal triplets or, occasionally, doublets. The opal is quite stable and uncommonly beautiful, but little of it is thick enough to permit the cutting of solid stones.

Well to the southwest of there, in Virgin Valley, Nevada, Keith Hodson, working in the main drive of his Rainbow Ridge Opal Mine, discovers the magnificent opal that is first called the *Father's Day Opal,* but that is later officially named the *Hodson Opal,* which, at 14,288 carats, is (in 1997) the seventh largest solid opal ever discovered in the world. At about the same time, Hodson discovers a smaller black opal which he cuts into a rectangular cabochon and mounts as a bola slide, around which is fashioned a framework of beaten gold nuggets.

In **1954** the lovely *Andamooka Opal,* discovered at Andamooka's Stevens Creek dig eight years previously and still uncut, is now deemed a perfect gift to present to Queen Elizabeth II for her state visit to Adelaide. It is forthwith cut into a fine 205-carat pendant and, with matching earrings, presented to Her Majesty in Adelaide with much pomp and ceremony.

The Hart Mountain opal field of volcanic precious opal is discovered in south central Oregon, almost on the Nevada line, and not terribly far to the southeast of there, in Virgin Valley, the Hodson family buys the Bonanza Mine (formerly the Virgin Mine) from Mark Foster.

This year as well, the Australian Mining Act is passed, in which Miner's Right makes it legal for any person, on payment of a small yearly fee, to peg out a mining claim and to keep as his own any precious gemstones found therein. The Act abolishes the large holdings of the White Cliffs Mining Company and opens that ground to any miner who wishes to peg and claim it.

In 1955 the old Lost Deer Hunters Mine, which will one day become the Spencer Opal Mine, is now relocated by Jesse Ray Bohney and George D. Wright as a quartz claim, without any mention of opal. About the same time the Firestone Opal Mine (No. B) is established in the Santa Rosa Range some 20 miles north of Paradise Valley, Humboldt County, Nevada. The deposit is volcanic opal in basalt and very difficult to remove from the matrix without damage to the gemstone.

A gigantic solid opal with light base color and considerable beautiful pinfire is found in **1956** in a new, unnamed opal field adjacent to the Eight Mile opal field at Coober Pedy. The stone is, when found, the largest solid opal ever discovered anywhere in the world, weighing 17,707.41 carats (10.41 pounds). The new field, quickly object of a rush of miners, is immediately named the Olympic opal field in honor of the Olympic games being held this year in Melbourne. The remarkable stone, found by miner Frank Titheradge, is named the *Olympic Australis* opal, and is listed for 33 years by the *Guinness Book of World Records* as the largest solid precious opal ever found, until supplanted at last by the 11.61-pound (19,748 carat!) *Jupiter-Five* opal in July 1989. The *Olympic Australis* was bought in the field by an agent of Altmann & Cherney, Ltd. Opals in Melbourne, where the stone is still on exhibit today.

Lightning Ridge also has a superb stone found this year, a 1475-carat exquisite black opal discovered in the New Nobby opal field. Named after the miner who found it, the opal is called *Pat's Stone.*

Within mere feet of where the giant *Olympic Australis* was found last year, this year—**1957**—another large stone is found in the Olympic opal field of Coober Pedy. It is called the *Americus Australis Opal* and weighs 12,196 carats. As with its sister stone, this one is purchased by Altmann & Cherney, Ltd., but is brought to America by Mr. Altmann within a couple of years and sold to Fred Von Brandt of Napa, California.

In California, this year Leo Nowak, a reasonably well-known Los Angeles artist, becomes manager of the Red Rock Opal Mine for owner Janet Cowden, whose advanced age precludes any further active participation in its operation.

It is in **1959** at Spencer, Idaho, that Charles W. Casper buys out the interest of George D. Wright in the Lost Deer Hunters' Mine, becoming co-owner with Jesse Ray Bohney. Still another change takes place when Mark Stetler comes onto the scene and buys the interest of Bohney, making Stetler and Casper now the co-owners.

And, this same year, in Virgin Valley, Nevada, Glenn Hodson dies and his ashes are interred beneath a monument just above the entrance to the underground diggings of the Rainbow Ridge Opal Mine, now owned by his son and daughter-in-law, Keith and Agnes Hodson.

Some of the so-called painted lady boulder opals of Andamooka are bringing high prices and one alone, in **1960,** yields fully £1600 worth of precious opal. A renewal of interest in opals and rapid expansion in opal mining occurs throughout Australia, but particularly in New South Wales and South Australia, largely due to new heavy equipment being used and the availability of generous financing for large-scale operations; some small opal companies are actively prospecting new areas for opal. At both Andamooka and Coober Pedy, production figures are up as the demand for good-quality opals increases in the United States. A new sifting device called a puddler has helped increase production at Lightning Ridge and at the Grawin opal field, an exquisite stone is found that weighs 2268 carats and is named *Light of the World* (Figure 21).

The market for Mexican and Central American opal becomes much stronger in **1961** than it has been in previous years. The Santa Maria Iris Mine in the State of Guerrero, 150 miles northwest of Mexico City this year, after almost a century of operation, becomes a noted center and the reputation of the opal produced there rises considerably. These opals are noted for their dark bluishgray to almost black body color and exhibit an intense, brilliant red and green play of color. Also in Guerrero, a fine precious fire opal with topaz yellow to

Figure 21. Opal mines and mullock heaps amid the eucalyptus trees at the Grawin opal field. In one of the mines in this immediate area is where the famed Light of the World opal was discovered. (Photo by the author)

pale reddish play of color is being mined near San Nichola del Oro. Pure white base opal with good play of color is being produced near Coacoyula as well as at the Barranca de Tepezala, Cerro de las Fejas, Aquascaliente, some 150 miles northwest of Querétaro. La Carbonera remains the most productive mine, with the Santa Maria Iris Mine second in production and quality. Other operations, generally much smaller and producing equivalently smaller amounts of precious opal include Cerro Viejo, El Conejo, El Muerto, El Toro, Fuentezuelas, La Cuadrillera, La Jurado, La Peineta, and San Augustin. Among the newer locations this year are the mines in an opal-bearing area occupying a zone of low rhyolitic hills extending from the vicinity of San Juan del Rio to Colon, all in a narrow belt of country on the green slopes of the rugged mountains from the southern end of the Rocky Mountains to Panama.

Most of the Mexican opal cutting is still being done at Querétaro where a decade or so ago upward of 50,000 stones were turned out annually by some 20 native lapidaries in 3 opal cutting shops. As evidence of the increase in production, this year, 1961, the cutting shops have increased to 50. All the Mexican and Central American opals are volcanic in origin, with different varieties often found in the very same rhyolitic matrix. Milk opal, fire opal, precious fire opal, brilliant harlequin patterned stones, and common opal all frequently occur within an arm's length of each other.

In **1962** a significant deposit of green precious opal is discovered in Tanzania, one of the very few African deposits ever discovered, but it does not become commercially available for over two decades. At the same time a greater awareness and understanding of opals is developing in the United States, but also a wariness of the nation's volcanic opals, which are, by and large, more prone to cracking and crazing than opals found in sedimentary beds. In an effort to combat this, it is during this year that a sometimes miner at Virgin Valley named William Kelley develops his so-called Kelley Process for opal stabilization. Most of the old timers in the valley, however, are unconvinced of its value and by far the greater majority of the beautiful stones they mine are kept in liquid-filled containers as specimen opal rather than being cut as gemstones.

The same is not true, however, of the volcanic opal being mined in Mexico, most of which is being sold to agents for cutting shops in the Orient. So profitable is this enterprise, in fact, that a new series of volcanic opal mines have just been opened in the Magdalena District in the northwestern part of the State of Jalisco, including the Magdalena Mine, Tequila Mine, Hostotipaquillo Mine, San Marcos Mine, and Etzatlan Mine.

It is during this year of **1963** that the mystery is solved concerning the correct structural identification of various opal pseudomorphic oddities found in widely disparate places around the world, including the so-called opal pineapples of White Cliffs, the barleycorns of Germany, the jarrowite of England, the White Sea hornlets of Russia, the glendonite of New South Wales and Oregon, and the thinolite of California and Nevada. This long-standing mystery and its accompanying misinformation—in which these strange opal forms have usually been described as pseudomorphs after glauberite or gypsum—are resolved this year with the discovery of ikaite in Greenland by Hans Pauly, about which more details are given in the chapter entitled Opalized Fossils and Pseudomorphs.

One of the most significant developments in the study of opals occurs during **1964–19654** when modern electron microscopy studies in Australia reveal, for the first time, exactly what causes the play of color in precious opal. Through use of magnifications of from $30,000\times$ to $50,000\times$, it is shown that the structure of opal comprises a multitude of tiny spheres. In opals that exhibit play of color, these spheres are arranged in a very orderly gridwork of rows and layers, with equal-sized openings between them, through which colors of the spectrum are cleanly diffracted in their purest hues. Thus, the colors and size of the POC patterns and hues seen in precious opal are wholly dependent on the size of the spheres, their arrangement, the distance and uniformity between the rows and layers of spheres, and the angle of the light entering and being reflected. In common opal, where no play of color is evident, electron microscopy shows the spheres to be placed in a haphazard way, so randomly scattered that there is no orderly reflection, diffraction, or refraction of light.

It is during this same year that some renewed mining is undertaken at White Cliffs using a bulldozer and excavator, but this operation is abandoned in less than a year when results turn out to be minimal. Meanwhile, in the Winton

Formation area of Queensland, a new system of geophysical aerial prospecting for opals is inaugurated with encouraging early results.

And in Andamooka, an opal christened the *Painted Lady* is found that weighs 5103 carats. At almost the same time, across the world at Opaline, Idaho, a fine precious opal weighing 325 carats and named the *Idaho Shirley* is found at the Shirley Mine.

It is during this rather eventful year as well that an American, John Slocum of Rochester, Michigan, creates a synthetic opal that looks very good but that turns out to be highly unstable. Therefore, he ceases trying to create a synthetic and turns his efforts instead toward creation of an imitation opal.

In **1965,** Janet Cowden, whose family has owned the Red Rock Opal Mine for the past two decades, sells the operation to Leo Nowak, the former Los Angeles artist, who has been her mine manager for the past eight years. He now renames it the Last Chance Opal Mine and plans to open it for collecting by private individuals on a fee basis. It will later become better known as the Leo Nowak Fire Opal Mine.

An important innovation occurs at Lightning Ridge this year that is so good it quickly spreads to other mining areas throughout Australia and even to foreign countries. This is the invention by a miner named Eric Cattrell of the automatic self-tip bucket hoist for removing mined material from underground and dumping it on the surface—an operation heretofore laboriously carried out by hand with a windlass (Figure 22). The device is invented as a matter of necessity by Cattrell, who has become crippled to the extent that he can no longer remove the material from his mine in the conventional manner.

In **1966** a new opal field is discovered and opal mining begins and booms in Mexico's State of Jalisco, at the town of El Salvador, which is just north of Tequila.

After eight years of contention and the final settlement of several land cases in court, Mark Stetler, in **1967,** becomes sole owner of the Lost Deer Hunters' Mine near Spencer, Idaho, and the name is officially changed to the Spencer Opal Mine, with Jim Kontis acting as geologist. The Spencer Mine is one of 11 opal mining claims in the area, but the only one where the gemstones are dug commercially.

The following year, **1968,** Mark Stetler opens the Spencer Opal Mine to

Figure 22. The automatic bucket hoist or tipper was one of the great opal mining inventions, and there are two basic models: the type that brings up the opal dirt and debris in a large bucket from the mine, perhaps a hundred feet below, and dumps it *(top)* in a pile on the ground, called a mullock heap, as is occurring here at the Allah's Rush diggings of the New Coocoran opal field of Lightning Ridge, and which may later be taken to the agitators and tumbled in water for recovery of the opals; and the type that brings up the opal dirt and *(bottom)* dumps it directly into a truck to be taken immediately to the agitator, as is occurring here at Molyneux's, also at the New Coocoran opal field. (Photos by the author)

the general public on a fee-digging basis and opens a rock shop there, which becomes the mining company's headquarters (Figure 23, Color Plate 9). The operation is such a success that by the end of this year the mine has been visited by rockhounds from all but one of the United States—Mississippi being the only exception.

About 100 miles south of Virgin Valley, at the southern extremity of the Black Rock Desert, Ray Duffield, owner of the Little Jo Mine near Gerlach, finds a large and very beautiful precious opal—the 1744-carat *Duffield Opal*. And in Africa, this same year, a small but good deposit of precious opal is discovered on the border of Rhodesia (soon to be Zimbabwe) and South Africa, only a short distance from the border crossing at Beitbridge.

In **1969** five new small precious fire opal mines are established west of Penjamo in the southwestern part of the state of Guanajuato, Mexico.

Close on the heels of that, early in **1970,** the opal mining boom that has prevailed in Australia throughout the 1960s finally levels off and, in some area even shows a slight decline. Overall, however, the Australian opal industry continues its remarkable growth well into the 1970s. In Queensland, George Cragg's son, Fred, combines two 100-meter square claims to form the present Cragg Mine at Opalton. And southwest of Lightning Ridge, before the year is out, a fabulously rich deposit of opals is discovered at a dig immediately named Millionaire's Gulch, located four miles south of the Grawin opal field, at the Glengarry opal field.

On the other side of the world in Virgin Valley, Nevada, about the same

Figure 23. First called the Lost Deer Hunter's Mine, the Spencer Mine was the first opal mine at Spencer, Idaho. This is how it looks today. (Photo by Len Cram)

time, at Wilson's Royal Peacock Opal Mines—now a fee-digging area—a superb black opal, immediately dubbed the *Royal Peacock Opal,* is dug out of the montmorillonite clay and, before being cut, weighs 3.25-pounds—5528 carats. It is soon cut into several impressive stones, including a flawless 166-carat red-on-black cabochon that is called the *Black Peacock,* and a smaller but no less lovely 20-carat cabochon named the *Little Black Peacock.*

It is during the following year, **1971,** after very nearly three-quarters of a century of essential inactivity in Queensland boulder opal production, extensive mining is resumed. New mining methods combined with greatly improved and highly effective machinery makes mining the boulder opals profitable and a considerable swell of interest surges about these unusual, highly colorful stones that are suddenly selling well on a worldwide scale. And at the Millionaire's Gulch area, discovered last year as part of the Glengarry opal field, production is very high and new sites are constantly being prospected. Among the notable finds are two gorgeousnamed stones—the remarkable 222-carat *Orient Queen* and the truly spectacular *Calabah Flame* opal, which weighs 850 carats.

And this year, seven years after failing to produce a stable synthetic opal, John Slocum now announces to the gem world his creation of an imitation opal that some are calling "credible" and that is supposed to soon be marketed under the name Opal Essence. Slocum, however, not fully satisfied with his creation, continues working at improving it.

Lightning Ridge, in **1972,** is experiencing another boom in its mining, population, and town development. The town itself is bulging at the seams with newcomers, not only miners and opal business-related people, who are showing up in greater numbers, but service people as well who can cater to the needs of residents and tourists alike. Even a good many pensioners are coming to settle here to take advantage of lower living expenses and taxes. As an added impetus to this growth, many are attracted by the resultant publicity each time a new, beautiful opal is discovered that merits a name—such as this year's beautiful and unique 600-carat opal found here that is called the *Blue Web Opal,* in which the play of color is limited to one hue: a brilliant, scintillating blue in a fine spider-web pattern that is most attractive. This unusual opal is cut into two identical gemstones, one of which is presented to Princess Diana and the other is acquired by the Smithsonian Institution.

Blue seems to be the opal color of this year because it becomes prominent in America as well, when a deposit of high-quality blue-based precious opal is discovered near Marsing, Idaho. An operation at the site involving a dozen open-pit works and a few exploratory shafts is registered as the Tepe Mine and the opal recovered begins appearing at gem shows throughout the country.

On the heels of John Slocum having announced his creation of the Opal Essence imitation opal two years ago, now, in **1973,** another opal simulant—

this one made of plastic—is developed by others and called Opalite. However, it takes nine years for the new imitation to appear in significant quantities in the market.[29]

Slocum's perfected imitation opal, after three additional years of work, is introduced to the world market in **1974** under the name Slocum Stone. And at practically the same time, the first true synthetic opal appears as well—a stone developed and introduced by Pierre Gilson, who calls his creation Gilson Opal. Reaction varies throughout the world, with many liking the stone, but the greatest criticism seems to be that the colors in his opal are *too* bright and the demarcation of patterning too sharply and boldly delineated.

At Mintabie this year, the introduction of heavy mining equipment initiates a whole new era of much increased exploitation of the remarkable and quite extensive precious black opal resources here.

And in Queensland this year, boulder opal mining remains at a high peak as new areas are being discovered and developed regularly. One of these is a mine located 8 miles [13 km] east of Cowarna Station Homestead. Here, in a very short time indeed, 9.5 pounds [4.32 kg] of precious opal is recovered that is valued at $16,994. Involved in the finding of such new areas are new skills developing in the application of geophysical prospecting in order to locate zones that are decidedly favorable to the formation of opal, including such indicators as concentrations of ironstone concretions or bedding plane irregularities. Additionally, a certain amount of success is being achieved in locating new fields with instruments that generate more accurate magnetic and resistivity measurements.

Of course, any flagging interest in the Queensland opal mining is quickly rejuvenated when spectacular finds are made, and few are better in the boulder opal fields than the finding of the stone called the *Moyd Opal* this year. This awe-inspiring stone, alive with incredible colors in pinfire to broadflash POC and the third largest nonsolid opal ever found, was discovered 6 feet below the surface just outside Quilpie and tipped the scales at a whopping 39 pounds![30]

Also in 1974, halfway around the world, in the Bay of Fundy region of Canada, near Brunswick, Nova Scotia, a new find is made of opal pseudomorphs after ikaite, similar to the glendonites found a century and a quarter ago in New South Wales. These present specimens are called fundyite.

And at the Spencer Opal Mine in Idaho this year, Mark Stetler's daughter, Claudia, marries 24-year-old Doyle Haight, who was raised at Dubois, 13 miles south of Spencer. Haight runs the opal shop and takes over much of the day-to-day management chores at the fee-digging opal mine. Stetler begins to consider giving Haight a full partnership in the Spencer Opal Mine.

A very significant, though unheralded, event occurs at Lightning Ridge during **1975,** when Len Cram, the already introduced opal miner, buyer, and cutter, as well as renowned opal-book author, succeeds in growing opals under controlled conditions, but the resultant stones at first lack necessary stability. These stones are neither simulated opals nor synthetics, but actual opals that have been encouraged to form and grow under the same conditions required in nature—details of which are found in Chapter 1 of this book.

Despite the amazing growth Lightning Ridge has enjoyed over the past decade, the town is still, in 1975, bisected by a single dirt street on which there is a petrol station and a pub. Hand-dug mine shafts are all over the area. To the north of there, just north of Angledool and the Mehi opal field, the Billygoat opal field is discovered this year, almost on the Queensland border.

In the four years since the rejuvenation of interest in Queensland boulder opal was initiated, this year is the first where a slight downturn of opal mining activity is experienced. However, it rebounds very quickly.

And in Humboldt County, Nevada, late this year, the Firestone Opal Mine north of Paradise Valley, which was begun in 1955, is now abandoned due to the great difficulty constantly plaguing the owners in extracting the opal from its tough volcanic rock matrix.

In **1976** the Mintabie opal field, so long worked on only a very small scale (since 1931), or ignored, or simply held in abeyance for over half a century since its discovery in 1923, now becomes the site of a flurry of activity as heavy equipment is moved in and full-scale opal open-cut mining operations begin in earnest. The amount of quality gem material immediately discovered amazes many and there are those who are convinced that Mintabie will soon rival Coober Pedy as the largest and most dependable opal field in all of Australia. The only drawback seems to be that some—not all—of the Mintabie precious opal seems inclined to be, as the miners call it, "cracky"—that is, some of it is inclined to crack or craze upon being removed from the ground.

Andamooka, on the other hand, is not faring so well. By this year that field is all but deserted, the majority of the miners having gone elsewhere due to a variety of reasons, including bad weather conditions, frequent road closings, and a persistent lack of food supplies. While a few active miners remain at the site, overall opal production has fallen to a very low ebb.

Unquestionably the most outstanding opal event of the year 1976 is the discovery, in Virgin Valley, of the *Bonanza Opal,* one of the largest and very definitely one of the most absolutely gorgeous solid opals that has ever been found anywhere in the world. At the time it is discovered, only two solid opals are known to exceed it in size—the *Olympic Australis,* found in August of 1956, and the so-designated *White Cliffs Number Two Opal,* believed to have been found in 1910. Two other larger stones were added to the list between this present year of 1976 and 1996—the *Jupiter-Five* found in July 1989, and the *Irene Lovell Opal,* also from the Bonanza Mine, found in 1990. The story of how the *Bonanza Opal* was found by accident at the Bonanza Mine is told in this book's chapter on Famous Opals. This glorious stone—illustrated on the dust jacket of this book—weighed, in toto, 10.4 pounds, which is a whopping 23,587.2 carats.

By the midpoint of **1978,** the open-pit mining occurring at Mintabie has revealed a whole new series of important opal deposits—some of which is seam light opal very similar in deposit and appearance to the Coober Pedy opal, and some of which is a form of black opal that is very beautiful and fully rivals that from Lightning Ridge. Some, though not all, of this Mintabie black opal, however, is very susceptible to cracking and crazing. Such opals the miners sell at a low price, but that is a big mistake because it doesn't take long for *all* Mintabie black opal to get a bad reputation as being unstable. To get around this, some Mintabie miners are careful to put aside those black opals mined from areas where the "cracky" opals occur and take the others, which they know to be stable, by the sacksful to Lightning Ridge, where they surreptitiously sell them at a relatively low price to certain miners who, in turn sell them to regular buyers there as local material. While the price the Mintabie miners get for the black opals from the Lightning Ridge miners is low, it is much better than the price they can get for the same material from the buyers at Coober Pedy.

Quality black opals continue to be found in America's Virgin Valley as well. At the Royal Peacock Mine Number Two in June of this year a fee-digging woman customer finds a wonderful red-on-black stone that weighs 205 carats. And another good find of black volcanic opal is now being mined at the new Royal Rainbow Mine in the Black Rock Desert near Gerlach, Nevada.

In **1980** the Inamori Division of the Kyocera Corporation begins producing synthetic opals in Japan. These stones are said to be very similar to the Gilson synthetic opals.

At the end of this year, world production of precious opal is led by South Australia, New South Wales, and Queensland. White Cliffs, which has hung on for decades with a population of usually less than 50 and more often around 20, sees a sudden influx of prospectors, most of them from the Coober Pedy area, who hope that with modern equipment they can make finds that can be profitably exploited.

In Virgin Valley the Harry W. Wilson family receives its patent for the Royal Peacock Opal Mines and the Hodson family receives theirs for the Bonanza Mine. At the same time, black opals from the Birdlebough Mines, also in Virgin Valley, are appraised by the House of Opal in Hawaii, which rates their value as from $500 to $2500 per carat and states there is a strong demand in Hawaii and the Orient for opals of that type.[31]

While he still remains in titular charge of the Spencer Opal Mine, Mark Stetler more or less phases himself out of the operational work and puts it in the hands of his daughter, Claudia, and son-in-law, Doyle Haight. The latter, who estimates he has by this time cut at least 90,000 pieces of opal, is vociferous in favorably comparing the quality of Spencer opals with the quality of opals found anywhere else in the worlds[32] (Figure 24).

More opal pseudomorphs, found during **1981** in Canada, are similar in certain respects to the "pineapples" of White Cliffs and the fundyite of Nova Scotia. These, too, are opal pseudomorphs after ikaite. And only a few months later, in **1982,** scientists aboard the German research vessel *Meteor,* taking core samples from the Bransfield Strait in Antarctica, bring up additional opal pseudomorphs after ikaite, and similar specimens are discovered in the bed of the Nankai Trough off Japan by scientists aboard the *Gomer Challenger.*

During this year of 1982 as well, Agnes Hodson of Virgin Valley, Nevada, digging at the Bonanza Mine, finds a fine solid opal fossil limb section that weighs 2695 carats. As she is digging it out, one of their friends stops by, stunned by what she is unearthing, and gasps, "Agnes, that opal is your crowning glory!" When the opal is freed, cleaned off, and consigned to a large water-filled specimen opal dome, it is officially named the *Crowning Glory* opal.

In **1983** Mintabie continues to develop, its opal production continues to increase and a number of million-dollar opal finds have been made, with the promise of more to come. And this year the first book exclusively about Lightning Ridge and its miners is published under the title *Lightning Ridge, Home of the Black Opal,* by Gan Bruce.

At least two or three important new finds of blue, green, and green-and-blue precious opal are made this year at Piaùi, Brazil, but export is so tightly controlled that only a small percentage of the material finds its way to the world market.

A similar situation had existed in regard to the beautiful green precious opals discovered in Tanzania on the African continent in 1962, but in **1984,** those stones at last become available commercially worldwide.

It is during this same year that Queen Margrethe of Denmark, to her de-

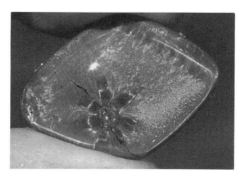

Figure 24. The beautiful Spencer Orchid Opal, mined at the Spencer Mine near Spencer, Idaho, is presently in the private collection of Cal and Leona Lichtenwalter. (Photo by Len Cram)

light, is presented with a fine opal brooch as a gift from the Danish community of Australia. She wears it often and is quite vocal in her advocacy of Australian opals.

The following year, **1985,** mining activity becomes even greater than what has previously been seen at Mintabie and more than 400 miners and their families now reside here. Mintabie and Coober Pedy together are this year proclaimed to rank first in the world's production of precious opal. Then, in **1986,** Mintabie alone produces more precious opal than Coober Pedy—the first time in the past 65 years that Coober Pedy has not ranked first in the world in opal production.

A flurry of excitement occurs when some of the miners who have returned to White Cliffs from Coober Pedy encounter a rather rich little pocket of quality gemstones. Unfortunately it turns out to be just that, a small, isolated pocket that is quickly depleted, and the excitement dies away.

Across the Pacific in America, Doyle Haight this year becomes a full partner with Mark Stetler in the ownership of the Spencer Opal Mine, with Stetler assuming more of an advisory status than anything else and the full operation of the fee-digging mine being handled by Claudia and Doyle Haight. Spencer opal, which lends itself to the making of doublets and triplets more than anything else, has been a favorite haunt of American rockhounds for many years.

And this year at Opal Butte in Morrow County, Oregon, where opal mining has been dormant since 1895, a flicker of interest returns as the opal mining rights are leased by West Coast Gemstones, Inc., from the Kinzua Corporation, a lumbering firm. During the following year, **1987,** a two-man mechanized open-pit opal mining operation is inaugurated and the precious opal recovered in this first year of mining here in the past 92 years is impressive—over 220 pounds of precious opal that is sold commercially.

At White Cliffs a miner named G. Pearson, convinced that there must be more of the pseudomorphic opal pineapples than the approximately 2000 that have been found over the years, searches diligently and turns up what he terms a whole "nest" of them—over a dozen of the unusual formations that are opal pseudomorphs after ikaite.

The open pit mining operation at Opal Butte in **1988** is producing a large number of precious opals in a wide variety, including rainbow opal, hyalite, contra luz, hydrophane, and crystal opal. Fire opal, blue opal, and dendritic opal are also found. The opals occur within rhyolitic geodes—thundereggs—embedded in a level of decomposed perlite. The recovered opal varies widely in stability, but the most stable precious opal makes excellent carvings cabochons and even faceted stones (Figure 25).

Also in 1988, the *Other Half* opal, weighing 851 carats, is found by Agnes Hodson at the Rainbow Ridge Opal Mine in Virgin Valley and fits exactly the broken edge of another large opal found by a fee digger at the mine 11 days

Figure 25. An opal cut by Kevin Lane Smith from opal material he found within rhyolitic geodes (thundereggs) that he mined in Opal Butte in Oregon. The elegant precious opal pendant is enhanced by the inclusion of botryoidal agate between the opal and matrix, and, without the gold finding, weighs 77 carats. (Photo by Kevin Lane Smith)

previously. And Keith Hodson, after 34 years of owning the Bonanza Mine, sells it. The new owners, in turn, sell shares and open the mine for share-owner digging only.

Meanwhile, across the Pacific in Australia, the Haan's Peak opal field is discovered at Coober Pedy, but the first opal finds are a lower-grade orange-green on white. And the New Field opal field, also at Coober Pedy, goes out of favor because it has been producing "cracky" orange-based stones that are generally unstable. At the same time precious opal mining of boulder opal in Queensland is once again on the rise and, by the end of this year, Queensland accounts for six percent of the value of all the gem-quality opal produced in Australia—over $6.6 million. Over the past 18 years, since 1970, it is conservatively estimated that Australia has produced several scores of millions of dollars worth of opal of all types.

The year **1989** turns out to be a banner year in the opal industry throughout the world, but particularly in Australia. It is at Coober Pedy, at the Haan's Peak opal field, that a new type of pneumatic tunneling machine is introduced this year that saves a phenomenal amount of hand digging—a machine that will soon be widely in use throughout Australia. Also at Coober Pedy, a massive dinosaur bone, partially opalized, is discovered. When wholly excavated, it turns out to be the 11'6″ thigh bone of a brachiosaur and weighs several tons. But most importantly, in the Jupiter opal field at Coober Pedy, during July two phenomenal opals are found in the same dig, within feet of each other; the stunning *Persephone* opal, weighing 765 carats, and, according to the *Guiness Book of World Records* (1991 edition), the new world record solid opal, the *Jupiter-Five,* which weighs 11.61 pounds—a whopping 26,331.48 carats! Greater details of these finds will be found in the Famous Opals chapter of this book.

Both Coober Pedy and Mintabie this year experience extensive heavy rains, receiving 3½ years' worth of rain in less than 3 weeks. In both fields, a large number of mines are so badly flooded that full-scale mining cannot be resumed for as much as 6 months. Yet, all is not gloom—at Mintabie, as soon as the temporarily suspended production ends, a major new find is made of beautiful red crystal precious opal that is valued in excess of $1 million.

Lightning Ridge, in this remarkable year of 1989, experiences a small increase in precious opal production, largely due to improvements in mining techniques. And, while its full significance is not yet realized, a major new Lightning Ridge opal field is discovered about a dozen miles west of town, just west of the vast, often dry Coocoran Lake, and is named the New Coocoran opal field. A full-scale rush occurs and hundreds of claims are pegged. Almost immediately some spectacular discoveries are made, including a number of incredibly beautiful stones valued as high as $9000 per *carat* or more. One stone—a glorious harlequin black opal—is reported to have brought $12,000 per carat! Another nobby is alone cut into three fine stones that sell for $6800 per carat! When the author visited here in late 1995, he found no sign of flagging of interest or production in this remarkable field.

Meanwhile, at the northern limits of Lightning Ridge, 28 miles [45 km] north of town, at the Mehi opal field close to New Angledool, the third opal to be named *Aurora Australis* (see also 1909 and 1938) is discovered in July. It weighs 900.11 carats 6.35 ounces and, never cut, is in the collection of the Smithsonian Institution in Washington, DC, valued at upward of $300,000.

At White Cliffs, even though only six mines remain active, an underground hostelry called the Dug-Out Motel, owned by Leon Hornby, goes into operation.

In Queensland, the remarkable boulder opal called the *Galaxy* is discovered in the Opalville Mine near Jundah. In its rough form it weighs over 700 grams—more than 3500 carats—but this is cut down to the final polished stone, which weighs 2615 carats. See Chapter 5 for greater details of this exceptional stone. Nevertheless, despite the discovery and cutting of the *Galaxy Opal,* the over-all Queensland boulder opal production declines this year, although this probably has nothing to do with the death of Des Burton, who is widely recognized as the father of modern-day boulder opal popularity.

Far away in the United States, this same year of 1989, a precious opal with Wedgewood blue base color has been discovered and this blue opal is being mined at the Gloria Dia Mine in the San Simon District of southern Arizona, close to the Mexican border, with over 30 pounds of precious opal removed from the ground in a short time. Coincidentally, a fine blue-based precious opal almost identical to the blue opal of southern Arizona is discovered in rhyolite matrix in Idaho. And in Louisiana, serious commercial mining activities begin with a type of attractive precious opal matrix known as Louisiana opal.

The year **1990** is only slightly less eventful in regard to opals than 1989 had been. Lightning Ridge's New Coocoran opal field remains the big newsmaker, with rather remarkable finds being rather consistently made. One Calweld drill sinking a 36″ shaft brings up half a million dollars worth of fine germquality opal, and a lone miner working his claim brings out $40,000 worth of precious black opal in a single day! Some of the opal being found remains at such high quality that it is selling for $9500 a carat. The result of such stirring finds is an even greater rush to the New Coocoran area, with over 200 mine leases registered in a single 5-day period and a total in the opal field now of over 5500 claims. As icing to this cake, black opal prices are up a full 20% this year and it is only late in the year that mining at the New Coocoran comes temporarily to a standstill as the result of 14″ of rain that causes Coocoran Lake to fill and overflow and bring about some severe flooding in the mines, as well as cutting off access to town. Farther to the north, the whole southern portion of Queensland is similarly deluged and flooded.

At Coober Pedy, too, particularly at the Olympic opal field, gem-quality opal production remains at a high level, producing beautiful, stable, red-fire-on-black precious opal. Even the Haan's Peak opal field, which had initially given up only a low-grade yellow-and-green precious opal, has abruptly been producing an excellent gem-quality orange-green precious opal. The nearby East Pacific opal field is also showing good results, particularly along the small fault lines called slips.

In Queensland, where the best boulder opal is claimed to rival the beauty of the best Lightning Ridge black opal, a setback is suffered with heavy, unseasonable rains that cause some serious flooding and suspension of the mining for several weeks, especially in the Winton area.

The White Cliffs area, to no one's surprise, remains essentially unproductive and the only real news concerning the area is that the uncommonly beautiful Theodore Matthey opal pseudomorph "pineapple" found in 1900 is finally sold.

Only Andamooka, of all the major opal fields in Australia, showed a very sharp decline in precious opal production this year.

And before the close of 1990, far away in Virgin Valley, one of the shareholders of the Bonanza Mine, Irene Lovell, finds a magnificent solid opal that weighs eight pounds—18,143.36 carats!—not much more than a stone's throw away from where Keith Hodson accidentally found the Bonanza opal at the same mine 13 years earlier. The stone is named the *Irene Lovell Opal,* and is still in possession of the Bonanza Opal Mine Corporation.

The year **1991** witnesses what at first appears to be a major opal discovery in Western Australia. A miner named Peter Milnic, mining at an undisclosed location not far from Coolgardie, is extolled for having found a precious opal weighing 36.4 pounds—82,552.29 carats! Closer examination, however, indicates that the piece is most definitely not solid opal but that by far the greater majority of its weight comes from the matrix material in which precious opal is lodged, but in quantity probably totaling less than 10% of the specimen's full weight.

Production of quality gem-grade opals continues apace at most other Australian opal fields and Queensland this year claims to have 69 active boulder opal mines, most of which are open-pit operations.

The biggest opal news of 1991, however, comes from the other side of the world as, for the first time, what appears to be a major deposit of precious opal is discovered in Canada. The discovery—subsequently named the Okanagan Opal Mine—is made by prospector Tony Grywacheski in British Columbia, where three different open-pit mining operations, called the Discovery Pit, the Bluebird Pit and the Caramel Pit, have each yielded precious opals peculiar to its own site. Bearing a resemblance to Mexican precious fire opals, all are volcanic opals in basalt and many appear much like the boulder opals of Queensland, but with the matrix material softer than the ironstone of the Queensland specimens. One of these three operations—the Bluebird Pit—has been opened to fee digging from mid-May to mid-October.

In **1992** a fee digger at the Royal Peacock Opal Mines, now being operated by Mary Ann and Walter Wilson, is working in the Northern Lights Mine when he uncovers an opalized log weighing 130 pounds, of which it is estimated that about 30%, roughly 39 pounds, is high-quality precious opal—primarily black opal, green opal, and the rather rare pink opal. This is the largest authenticated specimen of nonsolid opal ever recorded (although many tales exist of much larger specimens of both solid and non-solid precious opal). See the section dealing with Virgin Valley in Chapter 7 for greater details and illustrations of this incident.[33]

About a hundred miles to the south, the fee-digging Royal Rainbow Mine in the Black Rock Desert near Gerlach is sold to a miner named Berchtold.

Mining has increased this year by about 80% over last year at the Queensland boulder opal mines in Australia. A total of 123 full-time miners are now working the Queensland fields. But the greatest excitement in Australia this year is inspired by the discovery of a new opal field 56 miles [90 km] north of Mintabie and 224 miles [360 km] south of Alice Springs. The new location, called the Lambina opal field, consists of two separate digs just over a mile [2 km] apart, both of which are producing good gem-quality light and black opal. This new Lambina opal field is administered from Mintabie.

By **1993,** the town of Lightning Ridge now has a paved (sealed, the Aussies call it) main street—Morilla Street—lined with businesses and a few residences, as well as several side streets, some paved, some dirt, facing which are a variety of businesses, some well-built homes, plus a large number of "humpies"—shacks, shanties, and huts.

This year, too, the excellent Theodore Matthey "pineapple" opal pseudo-

Figure 26. A so-called Yowah nut in the rough—the nodule split in half but not otherwise cut or polished. Found at the Yowah opal field in southwestern Queensland, this one will make an exceptionally nice finished stone. (Photo by Len Cram)

morph after ikaite, found at White Cliffs in 1900, but not sold until 1990, is brought to the United States and displayed at Bill Vance's San Diego gem firm called the Rough Times Company.

Finally, this year ends with an unofficial report of gem-quality precious opal having been discovered in Ethiopia.

The world gemstone industry designates **1994** as the Year of the Opal, but they could hardly have selected a less propitious year, since no opal events of any great significance occur. In fact, the only opal-related events worth even passing notice this year include (1) the fact that the White Cliffs opal field is deemed to be no longer of commercial importance and is designated as strictly an opal "hobby" field, and (2) the Japanese imitation opal called Opalite is now being marketed in quantity.

In **1995,** the lovely *Coocoran Flame* opal is discovered at Lightning Ridge's New Coocoran opal field (see illustrations in the Foreword). It is cut and polished to a 30-carat cabochon. The author was fortunate enough to be on hand in Lightning Ridge when this stone was discovered, cut, and polished . . . and then photographed by Len Cram. Publication late this year of Cram's new book, *Beautiful Yowah, Black Gate & Koroit,* meets with such an enthusiastic response that the issue is sold out practically before the ink is dry and the Yowah opal field in southwestern Queensland and the beautiful Yowah nuts it yields gains in popularity far beyond anything previously known (Figure 26).

Also in 1995 the population of White Cliffs holds steady at 150 residents (as opposed to 4000 in 1900). There are about 130 dugouts and the government has curtailed allocating any land for more; thus, anyone wanting to try underground living there now must buy his dugout from an existing owner, and many of the old dugouts are now selling for $60,000–$70,000 each. White Cliffs has now, more than anything else, become a retirement community. There are even dugout galleries where resident artists display their endeavors. A small amount of mining is still pursued, usually between April and November, and in recent years small prospectors have had some success at White Cliffs, and some fine little parcels of crystal opal have been recovered. But, with last year's ruling making this an opal "hobby" field, a claim does not have to be worked on a regular basis. All a prospective claim owner must do is peg his claim so the points can be plotted from a survey peg, map it out roughly on paper, and send this to the mining office at Broken Hill with a check for $50 to cover registration fees. After that, all he has to do to retain the claim is pay an annual fee of $75. But there are still occasional old timers who look at the opal field with wistful eyes and remember the glory that was White Cliffs.

Famous and Otherwise Noteworthy Opals

There are a fair number of opals that are so large or so spectacular in their play of color or other attributes that they are given a name, by which they are ever afterward known. There are just as many, if not more, that have *not* been named, even though they may be of similarly significant size and beauty— many of which that have managed to remain whole in private collections or museums throughout the world. This section is an effort to list the relevant and sometimes quite fascinating details about the discovery, cutting, whereabouts, and value of a select number of these very significant stones.

Unfortunately, in many instances, details are sorely lacking, sometimes because they were not recorded in the first place and, in perhaps just as many cases, because the details are purposely withheld. Whatever the case, as much as can be determined about the stone will be included here.

The following stones are, obviously, opals of outstanding character, but they by no means represent all of the great finds ever made. One of the most unfortunate facts about opals is that more often than not, the very best, especially if they are particularly large, are deliberately cut up to make a number of smaller gemstones, This is true with opals far beyond that which occurs where other precious gemstones are concerned. The reason why most large, fine opals are cut down is one based on simple economics: a large single stone, while extravagantly beautiful, is also extremely difficult to sell—there may not be more than a handful of collectors in the world who could afford it—and the amount of its real value would almost certainly have to be reduced to make a sale economically feasible. If, however, that same stone were cut into smaller stones, not only could the full value of all the gem material can be realized, in some cases the ultimate profit would be considerably more than the whole original cut would be worth. One can hardly blame those involved for cutting the stones down, since the opal business is, in fact, a business, and all who are involved in the selling—first the miners, then the buyers, then the jewelers—quite naturally wish to get the greatest profits possible.

Sadly, this same situation exists in regard to by far the greater majority of the exquisite, opalized fossils that have been discovered—clams, belemnites, and ammonoids as well as plesiosaurs, land dinosaurs, and other reptiles. Museums, however much they would like to have them, are simply not in a financial position to buy such specimens at top gemstone prices.

The following, therefore, are those stones—named or not—that have managed to survive long enough to be noted as something very special . . . and even some of those, as will be seen, that did not survive whole for long, despite such early recognition.[1]

AMERICUS AUSTRALIS

One of the largest solid precious opals ever discovered, this stone, weighing 16,261.56 carats, was found in August 1957, 30 feet below ground level in the Olympic opal field of Coober Pedy within mere feet of where its sister stone, the giant *Olympic Australis,* weighing 23,609.88 carats, was found the previous year. The *Americus Australis,* as with its sister stone, was purchased by Altmann and Cherney, Ltd., of Melbourne, but was subsequently taken to America by Mr. Altmann and sold to Fred Von Brandt of Napa, California. Since its purchase, the *Americus Australis* has been displayed at more than 400 gem and mineral shows in the United States, mostly on the West Coast.

ANDAMOOKA OPAL

This exceptionally beautiful opal was named after the South Australian opal field in which it was discovered in 1946. The stone was found by a miner named R. Goldsworthy as he was working at a depth of about 30 feet in the Stevens Creek Diggings at Andamooka. In the rough, the stone weighed 6.25 ounces (885.94 carats) and its measurements were 4" × 2" × $5/16$" [101.6mm × 50.8 mm × 7.94 mm].

It was soon sold to a prominent Sydney opal dealer, who kept it uncut for over seven years. When it was announced in 1953 that Queen Elizabeth II was planning a trip to Australia and intended visiting Adelaide, the South Australian Government decided to have a fine opal prepared to present to Her Majesty. Tullie Wollaston's son was, as his father had been, an expert in opals and was asked to search for a fine specimen that had been mined in South Australia. He contacted the firm of Altmann and Cherney in Melbourne who, in turn, suggested the still uncut *Andamooka* as being the most suitable candidate. Wollaston agreed and, on his recommendation, so did the Government. The stone was purchased and then cut at Altmann and Cherney, with John Altmann himself doing the cutting and polishing, which was no easy task because it was desired to have a large but quite thin stone, so its weight would not be too much around the neck of the Queen. He turned the stone into an oval cabochon of 205.54 carats [1.45 oz], measuring $3^{1}/8$" × $1^{3}/4$" × 0.2" [81mm × 45 mm × 5 mm], plus matching 8-carat stones for earrings.[2] The magnificent stone was then incorporated into a beautiful necklace (with matching Andamooka opal eardrops) by Wendt's Jewelers of Adelaide. The colors are brilliant and the necklet is of 18-karat palladium in the most delicate design, with light graceful filigree work containing 150 matched diamonds. This was the set that was presented by the Government of South Australia to the Queen of England at a State banquet in Adelaide on 24 March 1954.

AURORA AUSTRALIS

Three different Lightning Ridge opals have been given this name over the years. The first, found in 1909, was originally called *Dunstan's Stone* after the miner who found it, and so, to avoid confusion, that name will still be used in this section. The second, an almost unbelievably beautiful black opal was found in 1938 by an unidentified miner working in the area of the Shallow Nobby (also called the Old Nobby.) It was purchased as a rub in the field for an undisclosed sum by an agent for the Melbourne firm of Altmann & Cherney and subsequently cut and polished by John Altmann into a magnificent red-on-black oval cabochon measuring 3″ × 1.8″ and weighing 180 carats [1.27 oz]. Still owned by the company, the stone, valued in 1995 at $1,000,000 U.S., is on permanent display at Altmann & Cherney in Melbourne (Color Plate 10).

The third *Aurora Australis* is also a black opal, this one found in 1989 at the Mehi opal field near New Angledool and weighing 900.11 carats [6.35 oz] in the rough. The stone is alleged to have been bought on the field for $200,000 and now, owned by the Smithsonian Institution, is valued at $300,000.[3]

BACKUS OPAL

This lovely, unusual Nevada opal from Virgin Valley was found in the mine tailings of the Rainbow Ridge Opal Mine—a fee-digging area—by Mrs. Standish Backus about 1970. A large piece of specimen rough with one end polished, the stone's base color is a light transparent brown, while the POC is a lively deep blue, green, and yellow-green. The stone, which measures 5″ × 4.75″ × 2″ [127 mm × 120.65 mm × 50.8 mm], weighs 3870 carats [1.71 pounds]. It is presently part of the collection of the Cranbrook Institute of Science in Bloomfield Hills, Michigan, to whom it was donated by an individual who did not wish to be identified. Valuation of the stone, past or present, is undisclosed.

BIG BEN

In its original uncut state, when found about 1975, this was a magnificent black opal—very likely one of the largest and most perfect ever to come out of the ground at Lightning Ridge in New South Wales. Sadly, this incredible stone was cut down to a number of smaller exceptionally beautiful gemstones with an aggregate weight of 5465.69 carats—2.41 pounds! Details of who found the original stone and when, and what the miner received were not kept. The finished gemstone pieces are now scattered in jewelry and collections throughout the world.

BLACK PRINCE

First named the *Harlequin Prince,* this beauty is a polished, freeform cabochon displaying POC of intense broadflash blue, with accompanying brilliant green, red, and yellow fire. The cut and polished stone measures 2.375" × 2.1875" × 0.25" [60.33 mm × 55.56 mm × 6.35 mm] and weighs 218.85 carats [1.54 oz]. This stone was bought by Sydney opal buyer Ernest G. Sherman, along with the *Flamingo,* the *Pride of Australia,* and the *Empress,* all in a single Parcel, in 1915. All four of the stones, which were found in the Phone Line Diggings of Lightning Ridge, were named by Mr. Sherman's sister. The *Black Prince* was then purchased by an American serviceman stationed in Australia, who brought it home and subsequently offered it for sale, through the Gem Starstone Company of New York, to The American Museum of Natural History at a very reasonable price. The museum's then Curator of Minerals, Frederick Pough, could not let such an opportunity pass and purchased the stone in January 1943, so it is now a valued specimen in that institution's collection (AMNH # G42855). Details as to purchase price or present valuation "are not for publication."

BLUE WEB OPAL

A precious opal originally found about 1972 at an unspecified dig at Lightning Ridge, New South Wales, this unusual stone is estimated to have been, in the rough, about 6" × 3.5" × 0.75" [152.4 mm × 88.9 mm × 10.1 mm] and weighed about 600 carats. It has a transparent bluish-gray base color and shows a quite attractive POC in a spiderweb pattern, with waves of brilliant blue and no other color. The *Blue Web Opal* is the only stone ever found known to have this unusual POC patterning. It was cut into two stones, one of which is now part of the precious gemstone collection of the Smithsonian Institution in Washington, DC. That cut half of the stone measures 2" × 1.1" × 0.44" [50.8 mm × 27.9 mm × 11.2 mm] and weighs 92.09 carats [18.42 g]. The cut stone was acquired in 1981 as a donation from Joff and Jonathan S. Pollon. According to Russell C. Feather II, in the Smithsonian's Department of Mineral Sciences, the original stone was well over double the dimensions of this particular cut, the other piece, approximately 100 carats [20 g], reportedly having been similarly cut and presented to Princess Diana.

BONANZA OPAL

The *Bonanza Opal,* three pieces of which are pictured on the dust jacket of this book, must be ranked as one of the largest and most spectacularly beautiful opals ever found anywhere in the world. The story of its accidental discovery in Virgin Valley, Nevada, in 1976, as told to the author by Keith Hodson, is fascinating.

Owner at that time of the Bonanza Mine, Hodson says that on the day he made his most spectacular opal find, he was in his D-7 bulldozer, a cable-rigged outfit, at that mine and was working all by himself in a high area where the ground was very hard—an area he did not at all consider to be one that would be productive of opal. The only reason he was leveling it was to gain access to another area he thought might be worthwhile to develop into an open pit excavation. The hard area he was trying to level was very tough and had resisted his efforts the preceding day. It was on a sort of high ledge and it was while he was pushing the debris over the side and down the steep slope that the unexpected occurred.

As Hodson himself put it: "It's an open ledge, and I got my Cat up on a high place and got the blade down first thing in the morning. I gave 'er the gun and, by golly, I *got* that hard spot. Got it. Usually the cable would ride it right up and I couldn't get it. But then I got it and poured the diesel to it and shoved it about twenty-five, thirty feet and over the edge—boom! And I backed 'er up and I looked, and I saw what I thought was a beer bottle, sitting right on the edge. And, I mean, it looked just like that kind of greenish glass, with the morning sun shining through this thing."

Had not that one piece managed to come to rest virtually teetering on the rim of that ledge, Hodson would never have seen it and he would have covered everything with his 'dozer's next shove of debris. But he did see it perched there precariously and he stopped. "Well," he continued, "I got off the Cat and I thought, 'That *can't* be a beer bottle up here, this is virgin ground,' you know, and I never threw stuff like that around. And I walked over there and stood facing the west with all this ground down below me and here, right on the very edge, here's this . . . this *opal* . . . and I looked at it and then I looked down and saw the rest of it. I'll tell you what—it took my breath away! I didn't even touch it. I went back to my Cat and had a drink of water and I looked back . . . and, yep! It's still there! I shut off the diesel and I said, "This is it!" I don't know why that one stayed on top. I guess maybe the good Lord just wanted me to have it, 'cause there was *nothing* between my push and the edge where that one was hanging up, and all the rest was scattered down below. I got the one on the edge—I have to tell you, it made me breathless!" Hodson said that he picked up the piece that was on the edge and, with it still in his hand, he looked over the edge and could see no less than three other pieces equally large or larger on the debris he'd pushed down the slope, including one that would be over two pounds by itself. "I then went down very carefully," he said, "and began picking up the others."

Hodson picked up the really big chunks first—five of them altogether, as it turned out, including the one that had balanced on the edge—and his first concern was to keep them from drying too rapidly and possibly cracking or crazing, and here he faced a dilemma. He did not have any kind of container to put them into, and so he used his hard hat and poured water over them.

"I used all my drinking water," he recalled. "Pretty near died of thirst before I got done that day. I poured it into the hat and, while I was doing this, the hat tipped over a little and I lost some of the water, and I thought, ' "Oh boy, what am I gonna do?' But even without being fully submerged, the stones held up okay and I worked quite a few hours recovering all I could. The five main pieces of the *Bonanza Opal* were easy enough to find, but then I spent a long time poking around looking for the medium and small chunks and chips, which I put into the empty wide-mouth quart-sized water bottle. And I just about filled that jar, which had just over a pound and three quarters of smaller pieces by the time I was finally finished."

All the pieces Hodson found had come from a single piece that had broken when struck by the bulldozer's blade. Hodson believes it had been a massive chunk of wood opal, even though it doesn't really look like typical wood opal and there is not the slightest residue of wood in the specimen—every piece was all solid, exceptional, gem-quality opal. The base coloration in the jelly opal was an uncommonly vivid bright blue to blue-green, with the POC composed of long flames or streaks of red and green (and shorter streaks of orange and blue) when viewed from the side and distinctly harlequin when viewed from the end—all of it some of the most dazzling solid opal he had ever encountered in many years of opal mining.

The largest of these five major pieces weighed 2.5 pounds; another weighed just a hair over two pounds, a third weighed a hair under two pounds, the fourth weighed a pound and a quarter and the fifth was just under a pound. These five main pieces together, then, weighed an aggregate of about 8.65 pounds—19,618.2 carats. The largest piece was sold to mineralogist Dr. Peter Bancroft. The next-to-smallest was eventually cut into smaller stones. The remaining three pieces—the smallest about 1.5 pounds, the other two, a hair over 2 pounds each—have never been cut and are still in the Hodson collection.

There was also at least a pound and three-quarters of chips, including 7 or 8 big ones and all these chips and bits totaling some 3969 carats. The largest of these so-called "chips" was a fine stone of itself, measuring 6½″ × 5″ × 4½″ [165.1 mm × 127 mm × 114.3 mm] and weighing 13 ounces. This piece was kept as a specimen piece in a water-filled dome and is valued at $75,000. The rest of the larger chips ranged from golfball size down to lima bean size, plus the residue of smaller chips. Thus, the full stone, before being broken, had to have weighed in excess of 10.4 pounds—an amazing 23,586.37 carats!

In all the pieces and chips, the opal is clear and without residue of any kind. In 1975, a 38-carat triangular cabochon, measuring 1.97″ [50.0 mm] to the side and 0.315″ [8 mm] thick, was cut and polished from one of the chips and set into a ring by Hodson for his wife, Agnes, who still wears it frequently and it is still as bright, unblemished, and uncrazed as when first cut over two decades ago.

"Of all the things that happened that day," Hodson told me, concluding his account, "there were two things that I've always sort of regretted. And one of 'em was that there was nobody there to share the experience with. You know, beauty can really be enjoyed . . . oh, at it's very best! . . . when you can *share* it! And the other thing—this is even worse—was, when I finally got all the pieces, I looked around and said aloud, 'Is that all there is?' I really did say that! 'Boy,' I thought, 'good Lord . . . don't . . . don't strike me down after all of this!' I mean, He left it hanging there for me and I get this biggest and best opal I will ever have found in my entire life, and I wind up saying, 'Is that all there is?' I thought about that afterwards," Hodson concluded, shaking his head ruefully, "and I thought, 'Boy! Greed is a vicious thing!' "

Keith Hodson took all the recovered opal home and came back later and looked around more for anything else he might have missed, but found nothing further. Even when he dug some more in that hard ground and checked it over very carefully, he only found one more piece of opal—a little, relatively nondescript piece.

Of the second smallest of the larger pieces—the one that was cut up for gemstones—and the bits and pieces (excluding the one still in the water-filled dome), some of the cut stones have held up very well and are still in great shape; but a few wound up cracking or crazing. "Why some of the stones cut from this opal have been perfect examples of stability," Hodson comments, "while others, cut from the same stone, have just gone to hell with cracking and crazing, is a mystery I still haven't figured out." Such mysteries are, of course, part of the fascination this remarkable stone called opal embodies.

Keith Hodson has no plans to either cut or sell the remaining pieces of the *Bonanza Opal* that he still owns. He says he likes the *Bonanza Opal* far better than the *Roebling Opal* and that if he were offered the quarter-million-dollar *Roebling Opal* in trade for it, he would not accept. No actual dollar value has been set on the *Bonanza Opal,* but while Hodson initially valued his three remaining large pieces of the stone at $100,000 for the three, in today's market the valuation would realistically be much closer to $200,000 each!

BRIAN HODSON OPAL

This large opal fashioned into a pendant was mined at the Rainbow Ridge Opal Mine in Virgin Valley, Nevada, then cut and polished by Brian Hodson, son of mine owner Keith Hodson. It is a polished freeform, essentially triangular in shape. The base color is orange-brown and the POC is broadflash red and blue predominantly, along with some green and yellow pinfire.

The polished stone is 1.25″ × 1″ × 0.1875″ [31.75 mm × 25.4 mm × 4.76 mm] and weighs 12.3 carats [2.46 g] It is presently valued at approximately $10,000, and was purchased from Hodson by Gene Favell of Klamath Falls, Oregon.

BURNING OF TROY

Undoubtedly one of the most famous black opals in history, the *Burning of Troy* gained its name because of the many red flames blazing brightly in its black depths. This stone once stirred great interest in the French court, since Napoleon Bonaparte, at the height of his power, bought it as a gift for the Empress Josephine and she wore it with great frequency.[4] At that time it was unquestionably the largest, most beautiful and most valuable opal in the world, weighing in its cut form about 700 carats [4.94 oz] and measuring 4″ × 2½″ × 1″ [101.6 mm × 63.5 mm × 25.4 mm]. Although most accounts allege this stone was mined in Slovakia, some experts have questioned that, saying it appears to be more typical of the Honduras opals because of its great size and the fact that it was a naturally black-backed black opal. In 1814, five years after her divorce from Napoleon, Josephine died and the *Burning of Troy* opal, if she still had it at that time, disappeared. It seemed then to be lost forever and yet, a hundred years later, this same stone abruptly appeared in Austria, having been acquired by the city of Vienna, though by what means remains secret. Officials of the city government valued it so highly that even when the Austrian capital city was experiencing severe financial distress immediately following World War I, they refused an offer of £25,000 for it. The *Burning of Troy* disappeared again at the outbreak of World War II and has not since resurfaced.

BURROUGHS OPALIZED LIMB

This specimen is an early Nevada piece from Virgin Valley and is precious opal with a transparent gray base color. It is presently in the collection of the Wilbur Greely Burroughs Geologic Museum at Berea University in Berea, Kentucky. Cataloged as a natural limb cast, it appears to be part of a branch replaced by opal, cracked open at the thin edge. Part of the thinner portion is common opal overlain with precious opal. Its POC is largely reds, greens, and the more unusual pinks in both pinfire and moderate broadflashes. The stone is 5.25″ × 1.63″ × 1.375″ [133.35 mm × 41.4 mm × 41.28 mm] and it weighs 810 carats [5.71 oz] Purchased from Ward's Natural History Establishment many years ago, the specimen is presently valued at $50,000.

BUTTERFLY

Also known as the *Red Admiral* (a distinct species of butterfly), this is not a huge opal; yet, even though it weighs only 46 carats [9.20 g] in its cut and polished state, it is truly a glorious stone. One of best opal appraisers and buyers ever in the field, Ted Murphy, unreservedly called it "the daddy of them all" in terms of form and beauty. Both the shape of the stone and its fine harlequin pattern rather remarkably resembles the upper surface of the spread wings of a Red Admiral butterfly—a vivid mixture of all colors with red predominating. It is a black opal having true POC, meaning that when it is tilted or turned, or when viewed from any angle or direction, it shows brilliantly vivid colors—there are no "dead" spots.

Where this incredible opal is claimed to have been discovered and where it was actually found seem to be two different matters. Here's the story as it seems to have occurred at Lightning Ridge in 1920: Jack Murray, as elsewhere noted, was the first to find opals at Lightning Ridge and sink a shaft there, that first shaft at the area now called the Shallow Nobby or Old Nobby. His son, Jimmy, took over where he left off and in 1920 Jimmy had four partners. One of the mates was Bill Ethridge, a World War I veteran; another was simply called Canada Bill. The final mate was not identified. They were busily at work not very far from the Shallow Nobby at a new spot called the Phone Line Diggings and, as they dug, they apparently discovered the opal that ultimately became the *Butterfly.* They realized instantly what a fantastic find they had made and were aware, as well, that as soon as word leaked out about the find, there would be a grand rush to the scene as other miners converged to peg claims on every inch of the ground adjacent to their mine.

To forestall and divert this, they evidently kept the stone hidden for a while and, as Bill Ethridge and the other miner were still working in the Phone Line Diggings, Jimmy Murray and Canada Bill moved off and started sinking a new shaft where no one had dug before, some 200 yards northeast. Other miners noticed and thought it curious, since such a splitting of partners normally only occurred when a serious rift developed among them, and none apparently had. Before long the new shaft had been sunk deeply enough to punch through the "steel band" and reach the opal level. Almost immediately the pair emerged, dancing about and chortling over their great find. Other miners came running to crowd around and gaze at probably the most magnificent opal they had ever seen. Word spread with astounding swiftness and before long, as they knew would happen, all adjacent space around them was pegged.

The area was quickly dubbed the New Rush Diggings, but kept that name only until the stone was cut and named the *Butterfly* (or *Red Admiral,* as many chose to call it), upon which the diggings where it was supposedly found immediately became known as the Butterfly Diggings, a name by which it is still known today. The likelihood is far greater (and many of the more experienced miners remain wholly convinced) that the astounding opal was actually found in the Phone Line Diggings, 200 yards to the southwest and close to where the *Empress* and *Pride of Australia* were found.

BUTTERFLY NO. 2

Found about 1923 at the Three Mile Diggings, this stone was said to resemble the original *Butterfly*, which had been found a few years earlier, except that this second *Butterfly* exhibited brilliant POC that was predominantly blue and green, with some orange and purple, on black. Details are lacking in respect to who found it or its size, apart from the fact that it was said to be quite large. It is rumored that this stone was ultimately cut into several smaller but still very beautiful gemstones.

CALABAH FLAME

A superb, huge Australian black opal weighing about six ounces—850.47 carats—the *Calabah Flame* was found in 1971 by Keith Hobden in the area called Millionaire's Gulch at Glengarry in the Lightning Ridge Opal Field. While no estimate is known of its value, it was the largest stone of a pocket of black opals, which also included the $150,000 *Orient Queen*. During handling, the *Calabah Flame* lost a 150-carat chip from one end. It is not known what ultimately happened to this stone but, since it was seen no more, it is believed to have been cut into smaller stones and sold.

CHRISTMAS BEETLE

This beautiful black opal gemstone was found by miner Colin O'Neil on Christmas Day 1974, in an old abandoned mine of the Three Mile Flat of Lightning Ridge. It was so named because in shape, pattern, and color, the finished elongated oval cab bears a striking resemblance to an Australian Christmas beetle. The value of the stone, now in a private collection, is undisclosed.

CORNUCOPIA

Quite appropriately named *Cornucopia,* this gorgeous black opal was dug from the Bonanza Mine in Virgin Valley, Nevada, in June 1992. It has a bicolored base coloration of blue and black and the POC pattern is an unusual triangular harlequin variety. The opal, beautifully carved by Kevin Lane Smith of Tucson, Arizona, weighs 59 carats [11.8 g] and measures 1¾″ long, 1½″ high and 1¼″ across [44.45 mm × 38.1 mm × 30.48 mm]. It was recently purchased for an undisclosed sum by a private collector in Germany.

CRANE OPAL

The *Crane Opal* is part of the colletion of the Field Museum of Natural History in Chicago and has for many years been on display there in the Grainger Hall of Gems. This stone is a slab of Australian black opal with one face polished. Believed to have originated from the Mintabie opal field in South Australia, the stone has outer dimensions of 2.145″ × 1.443″ × 0.312″ [54.48 mm × 36.65 mm × 7.93 mm] and a weight of 29.59 carats [5.92 g] The base color is black and the POC is broadflash blue and orange. This stone was donated to the museum by R. T. Crane, Jr. and, currently listed as Opal No. H-456, its photograph appeared in the booklet entitled *Gems, a Companion to the Grainger Hall of Gems,* written by Edward Olson and published by the museum.

CROWNING GLORY

This lovely stone was found in 1982 at the Bonanza Mine in Virgin Valley, Nevada, by mine co-owner Agnes Hodson. Working at her dig, she started exposing the stone and, after she had worked on it for a while and had it nearly free, another miner passed, gasped when he saw it and said, "Agnes, that's your crowning glory!" And that's how the stone was named. Its dimensions were 4″ × 3¾″ × 2¾ [101.6 mm × 95.25 mm × 69.85 mm] and it weighed 1.58 pounds—3583.31 carats! Still a part of the Hodson collection today, it is valued at $50,000.

CUAUHTEMOC OPAL

A huge piece of black basaltic opal had been carved into the bust of the Aztec god Cuauhtemoc (qwa-WHO-teh-mock), last of the Aztec kings, wearing a full ornate headdress of plumes wrought in silver, the silver alone weighing over 7 pounds. The carving weighs 16,875 carats. The silver, which includes the base, is not polished but, rather, burnished, so as not to detract from the subject, and the silverwork was done over a period of 4 months in 1930, according to one report, by the noted artist Alejandro Gomez. In the plumes of the headdress are inlaid 21 opal cabochons and there are also four opal cabs in each of the large silver earrings. The entire bust stands 19 inches high, including the silver headdress and the total weight of the whole piece is 18 pounds, 11 of which is the black basaltic opal. The original piece of matrix opal from which this bust is carved weighed 30,000 carats. At first the bust appears to be carved out of jade or black rock. Then the light hits it and millions of points of brilliant green, red, blue, and yellow in various shades and tints of precious opal sparkle throughout it. This piece may have come from the Sierra Madre Occidental Mountains where there is a rare deposit of basalt infused in this way with precious opal. It was found reported by—around 1920—in a vein nine feet wide, extending more than 160 feet up an exposed cliff face. The vein extended back into the cliff another 150 feet. It has now been totally mined out. The mine name was Luz Nueva—"New Light." Most of the material mined was relatively small, but the largest piece obtained became the carved bust of Cuauhtemoc, a carving executed in 7 months of work by the noted Taxco artist Rafael Tapia. The bust is now in the possession of the Kansas Newman College in Wichita, Kansas.

DARK JUBILEE

Apparently originating from Lightning Ridge, this Australian black opal has been cut into a freeform cabochon that was donated to the Smithsonian Institution by the Zale Corporation in 1981. Its base color is gray and the POC includes irregularly shaped broadflash green and yellow, with less dominant flashes of blues and reds. The stone weighs 318.94 carats [2.25 oz] and measures 3.29″ × 2.46″ × 0.49″ [83.57 mm × 62.48 mm × 12.45 mm]. Its value is undisclosed, but purported to be quite high.

DESERT BEAUTY

This piece of white translucent opal with brilliant pinfire POC was found in an undisclosed mine at Coober Pedy, South Australia, and cut into a long oval cabochon measuring 3.39″ × 1.51″ × 0.62″ [87 mm × 38.6 mm × 16 mm] and weighing 290.59 carats [2.05 oz] The *Desert Beauty* is presently in the collection of the Australian Museum, Sydney, New South Wales, and valued at $10,000. Details of the donation remain undisclosed.

DOUBLE G

This stone, found during the 1930s by a pair of miners named Gladstone and Gonevy at White Cliffs, weighed 808 carats [5.7 oz]. It was a squarish stone almost an inch thick and of exceptionally good color. It was sold in the field for £100, though had it been found a few years earlier, before the Great Depression, the White Cliffs *Opal Miner* reports it would have brought in a great deal more—probably five or six times as much.

DOWN UNDER

The *Down Under* opal is a relatively small gemstone—cut and polished to only 0.5″ [12.7 mm] square, 0.25″ [6.35 mm] thick, and weighing but 7 carats [1.7 g]. It wins its place among the "special" stones by being what is generally referred to as a "picture" opal—having a mainly brilliant yellow and green pattern depicting a remarkably accurate map of Australia, which includes Tasmania, the

Great Barrier Reef, and New Guinea. The present whereabouts and value of the stone have not been discovered.

DREAM CLOUD

This piece is a Queensland, Australia, boulder opal carving of "a winged female bust as personification of the dream," with the face turned well right, eyes closed. Face and neck are matte finished, wings and hair highly polished, with excellent use of the dark brown ironstone matrix to help define the subject. The base color of the opal ranges from creamy blue-gray through blue-green to blue. Its POC is predominantly blue and green, with some yellow and a little red. The entire carving weighs 1167 carats—a shade over half a pound—and its measurements are 3.35″ × 2.93″ × 1.37″ [85.09 mm × 74.42 mm × 34.8 mm]. This piece, presently in the collection of the Royal Ontario Museum in Toronto, was purchased in 1915 by John Junius Morgan (nephew of J. P. Morgan) from a Russian emigre, who evidently carved it. The stone was donated to the museum in 1987 by Mrs. J. B. MacNeill, of Weymouth, Nova Scotia, who was the niece of the lady who was a companion of J. P. Morgan's sister.

DUKE OF DEVONSHIRE OPAL

An Australian deep black opal from Lightning Ridge, this splendid stone with brightly spangled colors was cut into a low oval cabochon that weighs 100 carats [20 g] and measures 2″ × 1″ [50.8 mm × 25.4 mm]. The stone, mounted in a pendant, is owned by the estate of the Duke of Devonshire.

DUNSTAN'S STONE

Originally named Dunstan's Stone after the Australian miner who discovered it at Bald Hill in August 1909, this was the first opal of world significance to be found at Lightning Ridge. It subsequently also came to be known as the *Aurora Australis,* but that name has since been used for two other stones, so the original name remains more suitable. Details of this find are recounted in the History/Mythology chapter of this book, under year 1909.

EMPRESS

First named *Kaleidoscope Queen,* then renamed *Tartan Queen* and, finally, the *Empress,* this opal was the most strikingly colored of four major stones found in the same pocket in 1915 in the Phone Line Diggings at Lightning Ridge and it is generally considered to have been one of the most spectacular opals ever discovered in that opal field. Tom Irwin and his mate, George Brown, were the miners who were working the dig when the stone was first gouged out at a depth of near 30 feet. The weight and dimensions of the piece in its rough state were not recorded, but as a fairly well-shaped rubbing, its weight was about 504 carats [3.56 oz], making it too large to properly be termed a nobby. A rounded triangular in shape, after being rubbed at the site (probably by Walter Bradley), the three sides of the stone measured 3″ × 2.75″ × 2.25″ [76.2 mm × 69.85 mm × 57.15 mm] and it was no less than half an inch [12.7 mm] thick. The POC was positively stunning—a deep, rich black background all over, upon which played blazing broadflash patches of incredibly fiery red.

The stone was taken to the Lightning Ridge Hotel where miners from all directions quickly congregated to see such a beauty. As it was being passed from one miner to another to be admired, one of them, a former sheep-shearer-turned-miner, got fumble-fingered and dropped it. As ill fortune would have it, the opal struck a nail head in the flooring and split in two. A universal groan of utter dismay erupted from the men, but all was not lost. With some careful and truly exemplary cutting, one of the two pieces was worked into a pair of nearly matching pendants and the other large piece was cut into a third pendant both broader and larger than the other two. The two smaller, matching pendants were each nearly 2″ [50.8 mm] long and about 20 carats [4 g] apiece, while the larger pendant, which became the present *Empress,* weighs 55 carats [11 g] and is 1.75″ × 1.5″ × .6 [44.45 mm × 38.1 mm × 15.25 mm]. The aggregate value for the three pendants was close to what was estimated for the whole stone in the first place. The *Empress* (along with its companion stones, the *Flamingo, Black Prince,* and *Pride of Australia,* were all purchased in a single parcel by the well-known buyer, Ernest G. Sherman, and all four stones were named by his sister.

FAVELL ARROWHEAD OPAL

This precious opal had been knapped into a small but very nicely executed and deeply barbed arrowhead that, according to owner Gene Favell, was found in 1912 by a Basque shepherd in the Black Rock Desert of Humboldt County, Nevada (Figure 27). The base color is blue and the POC is blue, orange, pink, and red. The arrowhead is 1.25″ [31.75 mm] from point to base and 0.75″ [19.05 mm] across barbs. The weight is exactly one ounce—141.75 carats. The Basque shepherd who found it, kept the piece for four years until he sold it, in 1916, to H. H. Stuart, then living in Alturas, California. Half a century later it was purchased from Dr. Stuart by Favell, who still owns it and has it on display at the Favell Museum of Western Art and Indian Artifacts, Klamath Falls, Oregon.

This is the only native arrow point the writer has seen fashioned from precious opal and there have been few opal artifacts of any kind associated with most Native American societies. It is not clear whether this lack stemmed from

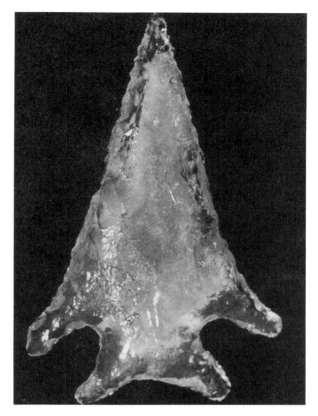

Figure 27. The Favell Arrowhead opal. (Photo courtesy of Gene Favell)

the difficulty of working the precious opal or because there was some sort of superstition that instilled a taboo on the stone. Because of its composition and rarity, the *Favell Arrowhead Opal* is considered by its owner to be "priceless."

FLAME QUEEN

This magnificent stone is surely one of the most renowned of all the great opals. The events leading up to its discovery in the Lightning Ridge opal field began with an unidentified miner who, sometime prior to 1914, dug a shaft in Bald Hill, some distance north of the town of Lightning Ridge and close to the Mehi dig where Dunstan had found his beautiful namesake stone a few years earlier, in 1909. The unidentified miner had no luck to speak of and in 1914, shortly after the outbreak of World War I, he abandoned the hole and went off to fight in Europe. When he did not come back after the Armistice, Walter Bradley, Jack Phillips, and Irish Haggarty claimed the hole as partners.

That was in 1918. The three mates started a drive along the level and when their tunnel reached the normal distance of about 25 feet away from the main shaft without their having encountered anything, they figured the hole was probably a "duffer" (devoid of precious opal) and were contemplating giving up on it when suddenly they began encountering some decent potch-and-color, so they pushed on considerably farther than usual. To aid in ventilating the over-long drive, they rigged a wind-chute to funnel downward any vagrant breezes that came along. At last, when they were close to 35 feet away from the shaft, Bradley's pick sang out with that unforgettable glassy-gritty sound caused when metal strikes opal and, sure enough, there it was—an enormous nobby. With contained excitement they carefully gouged it out of the surrounding opal dirt and squatted with it close to the candle. Using steel snips, they nibbled a small bite off one side and then carried it to the base of the shaft where, being midday as it was, the light was streaming down well. They were overjoyed at the brilliant flash of colors emanating from the little "bite" and for the first time realized they had made a spectacular find.

Bradley was given the job of doing the field cutting and polishing, since he had the best outfit for doing so and was acknowledged the best cutter of the trio. He worked it very carefully on the wheels and it more than met their expectations—a truly magnificent stone, the cut opal weighed 253 carats [1.78 oz] and was a flattened oblate in shape. Across the stone's face it measured 2.8″ × 2.4″ [71.12 mm × 60.96 mm] and at its thickest, on the well-rounded dome, was 0.5″ [12.7 mm]. Encircling the dome was a 0.375″ [9.53-mm] wide band of brilliant black and green, while the dome itself showed a large broadflash red-bronze POC, which gave rise to its immediately being dubbed the *Poached Egg Opal,* a sobriquet which, fortunately, did not last. *The Flame Queen* turned out to be a much more decorous and suitable name.

The three mates sold the stone to a buyer in the field for £93—£31 apiece, which was roughly $155 then or equivalent to perhaps $1500 today. At present, the *Flame Queen* is worth considerably more than a million dollars. Perhaps Frank Leechman rated it best in *The Opal Book,* where he said "It is, in fact, a priceless gem."

FLAMINGO

Part of the parcel of precious opals that included the *Empress,* the *Black Prince,* and the *Pride of Australia,* purchased by Sydney opal buyer Ernest G. Sherman, the *Flamingo,* after being cut and polished (and named by his sister) tipped the scale at 800 carats [5.64 oz] but further details are sketchy and it is rumored that the stone, after being sold by Sherman, was cut into smaller gemstones for jewelry.

FRENCH ROSE

A very rare rose precious opal from Quincy, France, this fine stone is in the collection housed in the Green Vaults at Dresden, Germany. There are almost no details available in respect to its size or value, but is said to have a highly transparent rose-pink base color that is shot through with a POC of broad, slightly misty flashes of deeper pink.

GALAXY

Because of the nature of boulder opal—usually a relatively thin layer of precious opal upon and through a dark brown matrix—not very many are given names or afforded a place in the annuals of "very special" stones. This is one of the exceptions and very justifiably so. It is a superb boulder opal that was found by a miner named Josip Grguranic in October 1989, in Queensland at the Opalville Mine, Lease No. 135, near Jundah, 621 miles [1000 km] northwest of Brisbane (Color Plate 11). In the rough it weighed 1.54 pounds [3500 carats] but was cut down by Michael Walsh to its present weight of 2615 carats, of which 550 carats is spectacular precious opal with incredible POC. It was named the *Galaxy* because "looking into it is like looking into a soaring heaven of glittering stars." Melbourne photographer Robert Campbell took hundreds of photos of this stone and finally admitted that "none comes close to doing justice to the Galaxy's real-life brilliance and vibrancy. It has to be seen to be believed!" Valuation undisclosed.

GALLOPING SIXTY

This was evidently a very good-looking Lightning Ridge black opal. Little has been recorded concerning its dimensions, weight, or anything else except an anecdote that a fair number of miners claim is the absolute truth. According to the story, it was named the *Galloping Sixty* because the roughly cut and polished nobby, "alive with color" was originally sold by the miner to a buyer in 55-mile distant Walgett for £60 . . . and the full amount went for whiskey that the miner bought for "the house," all of which was said to have been gulped down in a riotously galloping 60 minutes!

GAY PAREE

Queensland boulder opal rarely shows up in cuttable pieces of precious opal large enough for gemstones without including ironstone matrix. This one, however, found relatively early in Queensland's boulder opal history, was indeed an exception. With no matrix whatever, either attached to it or as inclusions any-where in the stone, this was a solid opal and, as reported in *Precious Stones and Gems* by E. W. Streeter, "was as large as a hen's egg and of excellent color, that sold in Paris in 1891 for £1000."

GEM OF THE WEST

Apart from glowing praise by editor R. Gray of the Walgett *Spectator* for its "extraordinary colors and brilliant fire" and the fact that it had been found at Lightning Ridge in the late 1920s and was "so outstanding that it has been given a name," almost nothing else is recorded about the black opal that was dubbed *Gem of the West*.

GOLDEN JUBILEE

This appropriate name was bestowed on the fine Lightning Ridge black opal found at the Deep Four Mine by the Galman brothers during the midst of a great rush that occurred at that site. The opal, field cut and polished, was a lovely, scintillating, 72-carat [14.4-g] triangular-shaped gemstone with a rare and beautiful moving pattern of broadflash POC in golden yellow over black, along with pinfire of red, orange, blue, and green.

GREEN GODDESS

Said at one time (with what may have been some of Hollywood's usual extrava-gance) to be "the world's largest and rarest opal," this opal's claim to fame, apart from its size and brilliant green POC, is that it was worn by actress Myrna Loy in the 1937 movie, *The Double Wedding,* co-starring William Powell. The gem, said to have been mined at Coober Pedy in South Australia, was then valued at £20,000.

GRUBSTAKE OPAL

The *Grubstake Opal* was obtained by the American Museum of Natural History on 19 September 1927 from the Lovelock, Nevada Mercantile Co. That com-pany, about 10 years earlier, was visited by a miner who had come in from Virgin Valley where he had found the excellent, very large opal, apparently in the Rainbow Ridge diggings. Down on his luck, he offered it as security if the company would grubstake him so he could return and mine for more, after which he would come back within three years and redeem the big stone with the proceeds of whatever else he found there during that interval. The Lovelock, Nevada Mercantile Company did, in fact, outfit the miner with all he needed and he quickly headed back to Virgin Valley . . . but he never returned and was never again seen. After waiting a full decade for the miner to show up, the mercantile firm allowed the stone, which it was now calling the *Grubstake Opal,* to be cut and polished so they could offer it for sale. The finished stone, alive with an extremely fine POC in brilliant green, blue, rare purple, indigo, and red, is a polished rectangular slab measuring 4″ × 2″ × 0.75″ [101.6 mm × 50.8 mm × 19.1 mm] and weighs 13,812.12 carats—just over 6 pounds. Amazingly, it was sold as part of a parcel of 15 opals to the American Museum of Natural History in New York for the incredibly low sum of $165.00. Its estimated value in 1927 remains a mystery, as does the identity of its discoverer. Its present value undisclosed, the *Grubstake Opal* is featured in the opal exhibit in the museum's J. P. Morgan Hall of Gems.

HARLEQUIN PRINCE

Another name for the *Black Prince*.

HEAD OF QUEEN VICTORIA

This carved precious opal is quite a lifelike representation of Queen Victoria in her younger days. It is said that the carving was presented to the Royal Family just prior to the death of the queen in 1901. Yet, oddly enough, a carved opal that was either the same stone or one extremely similar came up for sale in Hatton Garden, London, in 1959, and included with it was a newspaper clipping dated 1901 about the initial presentation of the stone years ago. If this truly was the same stone, the question becomes implicit: How did it come to be moved from the possession of the Royal Family to the auction block in Hatton Garden?

HELENA RUBENSTEIN NECKLACE

This necklace incorporates three cut and polished solid tear-shaped pendant opals, one large and two smaller, set in a necklace of platinum with eight large diamonds and each opal surrounded by numerous small diamonds (Figure 28). Base color of the opals is pale blue on the large opal and one of the smaller teardrop opals and darker blue-green on the other smaller teardrop opal. All three have POC of broadflash to smallflash blue, red, and green. Dimensions and weight of the set opals are not available. Valuation of the entire necklace was originally set at $12,000, but it is probably much more now. The piece was purchased by Gene Favell from an antique store in Atlantic City, New Jersey, and is presently on exhibit at the Favell Museum of Western Art and Indian Artifacts in Klamath Falls, Oregon.

Figure 28. The *Helena Rubenstein Opal* pendant necklace. (Photo courtesy of Gene Favell)

HODSON OPAL

Originally, this stone was named the *Father's Day Opal* when first discovered in 1952, but later renamed the *Hodson Opal*. Keith Hodson eyes twinkled as he related to me the story of its discovery in his Rainbow Ridge Opal Mine.

"I had been digging in the farthest reaches of the drive," he began, "when a jeweler named Dan Ronasco came to visit. He was interested in how the digging in the mine was done and how it looked in there, so I took him into the mine. In those days there weren't too many people around, so I was kinda' happy to see somebody, so I took him into it. I didn't let him dig, because I never let anybody dig in there, but I did take him in and I was showing him where I'd been digging there. As I pointed out a spot on the wall to him, I saw the glint of a little opal in the clay of the wall. Well, I showed this jeweler how an opal is removed when encountered in the digging; the pick is put away and, in those days, we used an ordinary screwdriver, sharpened to a point, to poke around, dislodge the clay and free the opal. Well, it was about the size of your little finger and I got it out okay, but just as I did, I ran into another that was bigger. I showed the jeweler the first opal—gave it to him, in fact. Later, after he left, I came back out and fooled around some more with that opal in the wall, being very careful as I dug the clay away."

He chuckled. "Well, let me tell you, it kept getting bigger and bigger and, of course, very colorful. I kept working on it for maybe a half an hour or so and I saw this was . . . well, you know, . . . not just any ordinary opal. Pretty soon it was sticking out quite a way. It was in the side of the drift there that I always kinda' called my Dad's spot.[5] It was a good spot and he only had a few weeks when he came visiting out here, and so I always liked to put him in a good spot to dig. So, anyway, I quit digging it and I just left it alone there, 'cause I knew he was coming out on Father's Day. For a while we called it the *Father's Day Opal*. Well, he came out and I never told him about the opal at all, but as soon as he got here, why, even though it was dark, I had to take him back in the mine. I could hardly wait!

"In those days we had a light plant—an old Army surplus light plant, gasoline—that we would use. Not all the time, but some of the time, and I turned it on and we went back. And a funny thing happened. A flycatcher bird was roosting right at the entrance and since it was a dark out, it flew toward where it was lighted, farther into the mine. The drive goes back quite a long way—three hundred feet—and then makes a turn to the left, and then still again to the left, where this *Father's Day Opal* was sticking out of the wall." Hodson laughed and slapped his knee. "And darned if this bird didn't fly all the way in and landed right on that opal! We were talking as we approached and I could see it perched on the stone and so, though I'm still not saying anything about the stone, I pointed and said, 'Oh, look at that bird!' Well, my dad looked and looked before he finally saw it . . . but what he *finally* saw was the bird, not the stone. Even when we got closer. I couldn't believe he couldn't see it. At last I just had to tell him to look at what the darned bird was sitting on. Oh, man! He saw it then and we walked closer. The bird flew off and then he could *really* see it and he was flabbergasted, y'know? Well, we dug for a little while that night, but it got pretty late and we finally left it. And, by golly, the very next day we spent almost a half a day taking it out.

"Now, when we first got it out, I guess it must have weighed about 12 pounds, but half of it, because it was on a little tilt, the upper half just wasn't as good as the bottom half, and it broke in half—a nice flat break—right where the two areas met, which was very lucky. Although I still have the bottom half, I don't ever feature it. The cleaned-up top half of the stone weighed over six and a half pounds. The gem-quality bottom half was six pounds three ounces."

"Okay," I said, "now, tell me how you'd describe the color of the *Hodson Opal*. It *is* a jelly opal, isn't it?"

Hodson shook his head. "No. Well, on one end, yes, I would say it's a jelly, but it's sort of white on the outside edge and then goes more to a clear opal in the center part. The upper piece, the not so good one, went into white opal and contra luz opal and it's just amazing, because if you looked at the two opals together, you wouldn't really think they were part of the same stone. Now, on the gem-quality piece, the one now called the *Hodson Opal,* the smaller end where it broke, which is the jelly-type of end, I would say is predominantly green, but it's all the colors. It's basically a tricolor opal—blue, green, and red and shaped about like a football except for being flat on that one end where it was broken, and on the other smaller end, there's been a chunk about three or four ounces broken out of it which I have, and which, if I ever sell the opal, will go along with it.

"For a long while I called the *Hodson Opal* the world's largest gem-quality opal and there was a good reason. When we went back to Washington, DC for a gem show in 1955, we took that opal along to display it as 'one of the largest' in the world, and it was seen by Dr. [W. F.] Folshag, who was the director of the Mineralogical Department of the Smithsonian Institute. He came to the show with Dr. [Frederick] Pough and they asked me, 'Why do you call it *one* of the largest?' And I said, 'Well, because I don't know what you guys have got down in the basement of the Smithsonian.' They laughed at that and then Dr. Folshag said, 'Well, we haven't got anything like that and if I were you,'—and, honestly, he said this—'I'd call it the largest opal in the world.' So that's why we started doing so and it kept that title for four years until the *Olympic Australis* was found. Now, of course, there are several others that have been found that are larger."

Still ranked as one of the largest, most colorful and most valuable solid opals ever found anywhere in the world, it weighs 6.3 pounds (14,288.4 carats!), and measures 9½" × 5½" × 4½" [241.3 mm × 139.7 mm × 114.3 mm]. Originally valued at about $250,000 when first discovered, its value today is estimated as being in excess of $1 million. It remains uncut in the Hodson Collection in Scottsdale, Arizona.

IDAHO SHIRLEY OPAL

It was reported in the *Australian Mining Journal* that about 1964 a fine *"flawless"* precious opal, described, much too extravagantly, as *"probably the largest first-class opal ever found in the World"* had recently been found and that it was *"about the size of a hen's egg and nearly the same shape."* The stone was found in the

Shirley Mine near Opaline in Owyhee County. After being cut and polished into a handsome freeform cabochon, it weighed 325 carats [2.29 oz] While it is a fine stone, there have been, of course, many other first-class opals in the world—in fact many others in the United States—that clearly outweighed and outclassed this Idaho find.

JUPITER-FIVE AND PERSEPHONE

An Australian opal miner named Steven Zager was working 56 feet underground in his mine at Coober Pedy on 4 July 1989, when he encountered a rough, hand-sized piece of sandstone, on one corner of which was a faint trace of opal play of color. He almost tapped it with his pick to break it, but then decided not to and dropped it into his specimen bag. Zager continued to work and a little while later he found a main column of opal. As he worked on it, a sizeable sand-encrusted rock dislodged from the wall above his head, struck his shoulder and nearly forced his head into his powerful tunneling machine. Irked, he almost kicked it into the blower, an enormous vacuum system used to clear away dust and rubble and circulate fresh air, which would have disintegrated it immediately into powder and blown it out of the mine. But, because it somewhat resembled the smaller, hand-sized piece found earlier, he tossed it into his bag with that first piece and later put those two chunks into a bucket in the back of his truck. There, next to some bags of Nitropil (a high explosive), they rolled about for a week, covered over only with a tarp.

They were turned over by Zagar some time later for cutting and polishing to a close friend called Ziggy, who was a sapphire cutter and noted as an honest jeweler. Ziggy started cleaning off the sandstone from the smaller of the two with his drills and diamond tip burrs, expecting the precious stone to quickly end and the remainder be sandstone. It wasn't. Actually it was all solid opal, lightly coated with a covering of sand adhering to the whole surface of the stone. After many laborious hours of cleaning away all the sandstone, the result was a superb, brilliantly colored and patterned stone, temporarily dubbed *Unnamed Lady*, which, when fully cut and polished, weighed 765 carats.

Before starting to clean the second stone, which was so much larger, they took the first one to an opal expert named Stuart Jackson, who was a senior lecturer in Lapidary and Opal Cutting at TAFE (Technical & Further Education College) to ask what should be done with it, since Ziggy was considering cutting it into smaller stones. Jackson confirmed to them (and also confirmed in letters to the Smithsonian Institution and the Guinness Book of World Records, UK) that the stone exhibited a brilliance and clarity of color unsurpassed by anything he'd seen in his 27 years in the opal industry, stating that "Considering its quantities and magnitude, I consider it to be an important, rare and most valuable discovery." News flashed around the world of it and the *Adelaide Adver-*

tiser newspaper did a story on it and held a statewide contest to name it appropriately and officially, with a 7-carat solid opal cab (found also by Zagar in the Jupiter opal field) as the prize. The winning entry, out of 2600, was *Persephone,* one of the daughters of Jupiter.

In the meanwhile, Ziggy set to work on the much larger stone, which he found to his astonishment was also solid opal under a thin sandstone crust. He finally got it all cleaned off and it turned out to be an exceptionally beautiful and incredibly large gem-quality opal weighing 11.5 pounds—a phenomenal 26,331 carats! Since it had been discovered in the Jupiter opal field of Coober Pedy, it was subsequently named the *Jupiter-Five* and appeared in the 1991 edition of the Guinness Book of World Records as the largest precious opal ever found, surpassing the previous record-holder, the 10.41-pound *Olympic Australis,* which had been found in 1956, and which itself had supplanted the *Hodson Opal,* found in 1952, as the record holder. Both *Persephone* and *Jupiter-Five* made their 1990 international debut 10–15 November at Christie's Ltd. in Geneva, after which they were in New York, London, and the Far East. A silent auction was eventually held in Switzerland and the stones were purchased by an anonymous collector for an undisclosed sum.

KALEIDOSCOPE QUEEN

Another name for the *Empress.*

LEECHMAN'S LOSS

Dubbed with this name by the writer after the Australian author, miner, lapidarist, and opal fancier, Frank Leechman, the stone might just as easily have been called the *Near Miss.* Many years ago Leechman put an open cut a few feet into Nobby Hill at Lightning Ridge, but after a week or two gave it up when he encountered nothing. A year or so later a newcomer named Paddy arrived on the scene and after looking around, decided to open up Leechman's old abandoned cut. He worked for a while and found traces of opal with a little color, but nothing very encouraging. The cut was near a path some schoolchildren used to take every day going to school. On their way home they would stop at the diggings for a while to have a word with Paddy. One fine evening one of the youngsters, sitting on the edge of the trench and swinging her legs, hit something extra hard with the back of her heel. Poking at it, she dislodged a stone from the wall. It turned out to be a precious opal as large and as square as the palm of your hand, It was not broken or chipped at all but had a lovely rounded surface all over, just like a big squarish bone. The color was fairly good in parts, with some reds, but mostly greens and dark inky blue, so far as could be seen without opening it, and should have cut into ten or a dozen 20-carat stones at least. Uncut, it weighed ten ounces on the village scale—about 1417 carats, nearly twice the weight of the *Flamingo*—and measured approximately 3.5″ × 3″ × 0.25″ [88.9 mm × 76.2 mm × 6.35 mm]. It was one of the largest precious opals ever recorded from Lightning Ridge.

LEONARD OPAL

This light opal, weighing 138.19 carats [0.97 oz] and 2.3″ × 1.5″ × 0.41″ [58.42 mm × 38.1 mm × 10.42 mm], is freeform polished stone from Lightning Ridge, New South Wales. The base coloration is a bright translucent white, with POC predominantly orange and gold, but having some green and purple. It is part of the collection of the Royal Ontario Museum at Toronto, and was acquired in 1933 through the bequest of R. W. Leonard. Valuation undisclosed.

LIGHT OF THE WORLD

Kurt Stevens and William Klein were partners in October 1928, working the Grawin opal field some 24 crow-flight miles southwest of the town of Lightning Ridge. They were working only 14 feet below ground in a false level when they found an opal that staggered their senses. In the rough it weighed a full pound—2268 carats—and measured 6″ × 3″ × 1″ [152.5 mm × 76.2 mm × 25.4 mm], which they described as being "as big as the flat of your hand." The POC was dazzling: broadflash green, red, and gold that blazed and flowed across the face of the stone as it was angled and tilted, as if it were trying to light the world with its fire, and that's what they named it—*Light of the World*. There was one major flaw—a deep slug of sand embedded in the center of the stone's face. There was only one way to attempt to satisfactorily remove the imperfection with minimal loss of precious opal. Slowly and carefully, a hollow was ground away in the center of the stone in a gentle curve until the sand was all cleared away and the stone had a concavity on the face that was fully a quarter-inch deep. They were delighted that the POC seemed unaffected by the treatment and followed up by sawing off a slice of the face to level the indentation, in the process of which they cut away an estimated £250 worth of the stone's value. However, even here they were lucky, because a section of the slice was cut and polished into a fine ring-sized stone in which the rolling POC was just as glorious as it had been on the original stone. The final cut on the big chunk of opal left them with a superb stone that weighed 252 carats and measured 2.5″ × 1.5″ × 0.875″ [63.5 mm × 38.1 mm × 22.2 mm] and was even more deserving than initially of the name *Light of the World*. Unfortunately, the stone of that name no longer exists. In 1960 it was sold and cut into three smaller stones that sold for more in aggregate than the value that had been set on the single larger stone.

LIVING FIRE

Discovered about 1912, this opal, found near Quilpie in Queensland at an abandoned German dig by Joe Knehr, was only one of a large number of fine opals from the same tight little spot—an incredible find of the kind all opal miners dream about encountering and which they admiringly call "a jewelry shop." Knehr, working in the abandoned dig, encountered a horizontal layer of so-called "concrete," which is a layer of silicified sandstone; this particular concrete exhibiting tiny sparkles of what is termed blue-bottle opal. He punched through the hard layer and almost immediately encountered an equally horizontal layer of precious opal that was approximately four feet long and "thick as a man's thigh," from which he was able to extract 75 *pounds* of very fine opal. One of the finer pieces was a stone that was amazingly brilliant broadflash blood-red fire on black—an opal that was subsequently named the *Living Fire*. Knehr sold the entire parcel of 75 pounds for £150—approximately $750. In today's market, the value of the *Living Fire* alone would probably have been somewhere around $750,000, and such a parcel would be worth at least $2.5 million. Whether this stone still exists is not known, but it was more than likely cut up into smaller stones.

LIZARD

This is the remarkably lifelike carving of a small lizard in Queensland boulder opal, believed to have originated in the Jundah area. The lizard, exquisitely carved in unusually thick precious opal, clings eternally to a brown log, which itself is the boulder opal matrix. Value and present whereabouts of this piece is unknown.

LOUIS XIII

More than likely, this was a Hungarian opal that has been reasonably well authenticated to have appeared at least as early as 1711 and probably somewhat earlier. It is a large precious opal cameo executed with great skill, depicting a fine likeness of King Louis XIII. The cameo is set in a gold filigree mounting and surrounded by small matched diamonds. This piece of jewelry is said to be presently in the Royal Collection at the Palace of Versailles.

MACKENZIE'S OPAL

Apart from the small account of this stone that appeared shortly after the turn of the century in the White Cliffs *Opal Miner* newspaper, little is known about it. The stone was found by two brothers named MacKenzie, who were working as tributors at a claim in Block Two belonging to the White Cliffs Syndicate. Had it been undamaged, it would have weighed about 1100 carats [7.76 oz] but, unluckily, it was found by being struck by a pick one of the brothers was wielding and was split in half. Even in this condition, the two pieces were still worth £700, which was no small amount at the turn of the century.

MEXICAN DRAGON

The *Mexican Dragon* is a magnificent 54-carat [10.8-g] Mexican contra luz opal, which stands 4″ high on a base of Arizona ironwood (Color Plate 12). By ordinary reflected light its POC is absent, but in transmitted light—with the opal between the light source and the viewer's eye—the POC comes vibrantly alive. This piece of opal, found in 1992 at the Magdalena Opal Mine in Mexico, was carved by Kevin Lane Smith of Tucson, Arizona.

MEXICAN SUNRISE

This is an exceptionally fine Mexican fire opal of vivid transparent orange that was originally mined in Jalisco. It was faceted into a standard brilliant cut by author and gemologist John Sinkankas that is 0.41″ [11.18 mm] across the crown and 0.66″ [16.77 mm] in depth. Purchased by the Smithsonian Institution, the beautiful stone is now part of that institution's gem collection.

MOONBEAM

This superb Lightning Ridge crystal opal with remarkable POC in broadflash red, blue, and green, and secondary yellow, is only about 18 carats [3.6 g] but, set beautifully in a platinum ring and surrounded by 16 small diamonds, it is a spectacular piece of jewelry. Its valuation has not been disclosed and its present whereabouts are undetermined.

MOYD OPAL

This piece is a fine specimen of boulder opal that was found at a depth of six feet just outside Quilpie in southcentral Queensland, Australia. The opal seam is uncommonly thick, 3.2″ [81.28 mm], with sandstone/ironstone matrix at top and bottom. It has a base color of translucent white with the POC predominantly orange to green, but with the full spectrum of red to violet visible, and with the POC pattern varying from pinfire to large broadflash, the seam itself banded with light brown common opal. The piece is 13″ long by 7.5″ wide and 8.7 thick [330.2 mm × 190.5 mm × 215.9 mm] and weighs 39 pounds [17.71 kg]—which is 88,452 carats—but that, of course, includes the ironstone. This remarkable piece is presently in the collection of the Canadian Museum of Nature in Ottawa, which acquired it as a donation from the former museum curator, Louis Moyd, who originally purchased it in 1976 from E. Gregory Sherman, Pty., Ltd., Sydney, New South Wales.

NAPOLEON

Almost nothing can definitely be determined about this named stone apart from the fact that it is a very lovely black opal from Lightning Ridge with broadflash scarlet fire on a solid black background, the POC forming a silhouette remarkably similar in configuration to a profile of Napoleon Bonaparte.

NONIUS OPAL

For a more detailed account of the superior opal owned by Senator Nonius of Rome, who chose exile over giving up the stone, see the History/Mythology chapter of this book under the year 41 B.C.

NOOLINGA NERA

This is a black opal whose name, in an aboriginal dialect, means "Dark Sun." Oddly, as its source, two locations are given that are on two different continents: One source says it is a stone from Andamooka, South Australia, while the other says that it originated in Virgin Valley, Nevada, and had been found at the Rainbow Ridge Opal Mine. The reason for the anomaly is that the stone is part of the collection of the Cranbrook Institute of Science in Bloomfield Hills, Michigan, where two different entries on the catalog cards conflict and no one seems to know which is correct. The card that identifies it as a South Australian stone states that it was found at a depth of 12 feet below ground level by some Australian aborigines who were camping near the Andamooka Opal Field—and the fact that it has an aboriginal name lends credence to this account. The entry identifying it as a Nevada stone has no other details about its origin apart from the fact that it was allegedly purchased sometime before 1946 by the former museum director, Dr. Goddard, at the Rainbow Ridge Opal Mine. Although the museum catalog card lists this as "the largest black opal in existence," the stone is actually not solid opal at all but rather a fractured skin on a quartzite matrix, which is a common base formation for Andamooka opal and not for Virgin Valley opal, which is normally wood opal and occasional rhyolitic vug opal. The base color of the opal itself is black and the POC is brilliant orange, red, blue, and green. The specimen, unpolished, is 20.5″ long, 5″ wide and 4.5″ thick [520.7 mm × 127 mm × 114.3 mm] and weighs 5.9 pounds—a staggering 13,381.2 carats. Although the stone was purchased by Dr. Goddard, no valuation is given. Cranbrook Institute authorities say that owing to the stone's tendency to craze, each year Dr. Goddard used to remove a layer of the outer skin, in which cracks were developing.

OLYMPIC AUSTRALIS

The *Olympic Australis* was found by miner Frank Titheradge in the Eight Mile Opal Field at Coober Pedy. The actual weight of this gigantic opal was 10.41 pounds, which is 23,609.88 carats. It was purchased in the field by Greg Sherman, agent for Altmann & Cherny, Pty., Ltd., of Melbourne. For the next 33 years, until 1989 when the *Jupiter-Five* opal was found, the *Olympic Australis* was listed by the *Guinness Book of World Records* as the largest gem-quality opal ever discovered anywhere in the world, and when first found with estimated worth of $1.8 million. The magnificent stone remains uncut today and, presently valued at $2.5 million, it is on permanent display in a security vault of the Altmann & Cherney main showroom at 120 Exhibition Street, Melbourne. For greater details about the discovery of this stone, see the section in this book dealing with Coober Pedy.

ORIENT QUEEN

Found in the same pocket that included the beautiful *Calabah Queen* in Millionaire's Gulch at the Glengarry Opal Field, Lightning Ridge, this excellent black opal was discovered in 1971 by miner Keith Hobden. It was cut and polished to a finished cabochon weighing 222.55 carats [1.57 oz] and measuring 2.5″ × 1.5″ [63.5 mm × 38.1 mm] and was sold for $150,000.

OTHER HALF OPAL

This opal was found by Agnes Hodson, co-owner of the Rainbow Ridge Opal Mine, Virgin Valley, Nevada, at the mine in 1982—11 days after a rockhound who had been fee digging at the mine found the first half. The two pieces, sections of the same wood opal limb replacement, were very similar in appearance. They were brought together for comparison weeks later and fit against each other perfectly, although the piece Agnes Hodson found was slightly better in respect to POC and lack of inclusions. The POC is broadflash orange and green. The greatest dimensions of the *Other Half* Agnes Hodson found are 4″ long by 3½″ wide [101.6 mm × 88.9 mm] and it weighs 6 oz—850.47 carats (Figure 29). Today it is kept as a specimen in a water-filled glass dome as part of the Hodson Collection and is valued at $10,000.

Figure 29. *The Other Half* opal. (Photo by the Author)

OTTO'S STONE

Beyond the fact of its weight and value—plus that it was honored with a name—little is recorded about the stone (presumably a black opal from Lightning Ridge) that is called *Otto's Stone* after the miner who found it. The opal was reported to have weighed a pound and a quarter—2834.9 carats—and was sold to a buyer in the field for £15,000.

PAINTED LADY

Presently housed in the collection of the Australian Museum in Sydney, New South Wales, this uncut specimen is a large seam black opal in sandstone matrix that was unearthed in a mine at Andamooka, South Australia. Its base color is black and gray and, because of the uncommon length of the stone, there is a considerable mixture of POC color and pattern, although the majority is broad-flash and pinfire in blue and green, with some reds, yellows, and oranges. The specimen is 14″ long and 4″ wide [355.6 mm × 101.6 mm]. Its thickness and weight are not recorded, but the museum has set a $20,000 value on it. Details of acquisition remain undisclosed.

PANDORA

There is an interesting story involved with the finding of the *Pandora* opal in 1928. It began on the north side of the Bald Hill Diggings at Lightning Ridge at noon on a hot, cloudless Thursday in November. The diggers were taking a lunch break and resting under the sparse shade provided by a few mulga and leopard trees. Jock McNichol, who had been working for weeks in his present drive without having found a smidgen of color, and feeling strongly that he never would get anything worthwhile out of it, announced he was "tired of working that hole" and decided he was going to sink a new shaft. Everyone started chipping in with suggestions as to where he should start the new en-deavor, most suggesting some spot very close by, and there was some validity to what they said; after all, only 50 yards away at the Mehi dig was where Dunstan had found the *Aurora Australis*—also known as *Dunstan's Stone*—a couple of decades ago, and even closer, on this very Bald Hill, was where Walt Bradley uncovered the magnificent *Flame Queen* 14 years earlier. Still, as the miners all knew only too well, those areas had been worked hard in the intervening years without much to show for all the effort.

Fred Bodell was one of the resting miners and he settled the matter. He dug in his pocket and extracted a ha'penny coin. "Here you go, Jock," he said, flipping the coin as high and as far as he could, and adding while it was still in the air, "just dig where it falls." Jock watched it twirl away and, when it hit, having no better idea of where to try, shrugged and said "Why not?" He went to the spot and marked a circle around the coin with his pick. Then he picked up the ha'penny and pocketed it with the remark, "At least I've already made a profit here." The miners roared with laughter and Jock started to work, clearing away brush and grasses within the circle and the surrounding area. By the time he finished it was midafternoon and he contemplated waiting until the morrow to actually start digging, but then shook his head. No, he reasoned, everyone knew that no good ship ever left port for a voyage on a Friday—that was defi-nitely bad luck—so he attacked the spot with pick and shovel and by quitting time had gone down to the hard sandstone. For several days thereafter he con-tinued sinking the shaft until he reached the opal level, but much sooner than expected. Instead of at 17 feet, where he had hit it in the hole he had abandoned, here he struck it at 14 feet—but only in half the diameter of the hole. In the other half he had to continue downward in a sort of step for another three feet, to that 17-foot level before striking the opal dirt.

Obviously, this was a major fault line and, not only that, right at his feet was a brilliant flash of color; in fact, several of them. One, however, was larger than the others—an elongated piece measuring 4″ × 2″ × 1″ [101.6 mm × 50.8 mm × 25.4 mm]. It was largely black opal and breathtakingly alive with POC. It weighed exactly 5 ounces—708.75 carats. He picked up all the pieces, of course, and immediately realized they were opalized pieces of a skeleton, which later was identified as plesiosaur. The large piece, which he had picked up first, was almost completely black on the back, light opal on the front and with a startling crimson-red POC line undulating across the entire lengthwise face of the fossil bone. He turned the specimen over to Harold Frazer, without doubt the best opal cutter on the field at this time. But it was Frazer's wife, Polly, under her husband's watchful eye, who cut the stone perfectly with a bare minimum of waste. The final weight of the cut and polished *Pandora* turned out to be 590 carats [4.16 oz] of top-quality gemstone, the entire light face ablaze with wonderful POC dominated by the longstreak red.

So phenomenal was the find that Frazer set up a special tent and charged admission for other miners—and buyers—to view the treasure. It is said, without verification, that McNichol sold it to a buyer on the field for £800. Shipped to England for sale, the price set on the stone was £2000 and lower offers were turned away, including one of £1750. The grand stone was finally sold (at slightly less than the asking price) to one of the world's great opal collectors, harp-maker and musician John Prosper Ralston of Canada, but only with the stipulation that the stone was never to be cut down to make smaller stones. And in that collection the *Pandora* remains to this day, still whole, still beautiful, and still one of the world's outstanding opals.

PAT'S STONE

It seems more than likely that the miner who found this excellent opal in 1956 was named Pat, but his surname was not recorded, nor were many details of the find, which was made at the New Nobby Diggings of Lightning Ridge. Fortunately, the uncut stone was weighed and measured—3.5″ × 3″ × 1″ [88.9 mm × 76.2 mm × 25.4 mm] and 1475.57 carats [10.41 oz]—because it was quickly purchased on the field by a buyer for an undisclosed amount and then was never again heard of, probably having been cut up for smaller stones.

PERSEPHONE

See details about this lovely opal and its companion stone, the *Jupiter-Five,* under the heading *Jupiter-Five* in this chapter.

PHOEBUS

Not too many Mexican precious opals make it into the annals of fame, but the *Phoebus* is certainly one of those wonderful rarities. This is one of the largest of the Mexican precious opals in private collections—in this case, the Hope Collection. The opal has been carved in high relief to represent the head of the sun-god, Phoebus, with sun rays emanating outward from the subject. Highly transparent and very rich in a vibrant topaz yellow body color, the stone's POC incorporates bold rays of red, blue, green, and yellow that are transected in different directions by bright flashes of brilliant blue and blood red. The carved piece weighs about 35 carats [7 g] and measures 1.75″ × 1″ [44.45 mm × 25.4 mm]. No date of discovery is recorded, nor is the site where the stone was found, but most likely it was at Querétaro within a few years after the turn of the century. (A second school of admirers suggests that the stone may have had its origin in Asia Minor or perhaps Arabia, since its mounting of black enamel and gold suggests the work of a Persian artisan.)

PRIDE OF AUSTRALIA

This stone was found at Lightning Ridge in 1915. Snowy Brown and Tom Irwin had a claim on the Phone Line Diggings near the crest of the main road from Walgett where it comes into Lightning Ridge. It was one of four large stones found in the same patch, including the *Empress,* the *Black Prince* and the *Flamingo.*[6] Of the four stones, the *Pride of Australia,* though largest, was probably the least worthy, since its color was not then considered to be of the best quality—mostly a brilliant green shot with orange. Cut and polished, it weighed 225.75 carats. Rumor says those four fine stones were sold together for about £2000. Today the *Pride of Australia* alone is valued at about $20,000. The parcel of four stones was bought by Ernest G. Sherman, whose sister named them.

RED ADMIRAL

See *Butterfly.*

ROEBLING OPAL

Unquestionably one of the finest true black crystal opals ever discovered, the *Roebling Opal*—a wood opal—was found in Virgin Valley, Nevada, in the United States in November 1917. The base coloration of the stone is deep transparent black (not brownish) and the POC shows dominant broadflash red, with green, yellow, and blue in irregular patterns. This is a large limb segment of solid crystal opal, 4.1″ [104.14 mm] long and tapering from 3″ [76.2 mm] in its greatest diameter to 2.2″ [55.9mm]. It weighs 3560 carats—1.57 pounds. The discovery was made in one of Flora Loughead's mines at Rainbow Ridge by one of her employees, a miner named Lew Thompson.[7] The stone was still in Flora Loughead's possession when the partnership between herself and Mrs. Gardiner Hammond became reality in April of 1918 and was subsequently sold by the partnership to Ward's Natural History Establishment in Rochester, New York. It was from Ward's that the stone was ultimately purchased, about 1922, by Washington A. Roebling, architect of New York's Brooklyn Bridge, for his collection. After his death, it was donated in 1927 to the Smithsonian Institution in Washington, DC by his son, John A. Roebling, as part of the Washington A. Roebling Gem Collection.

About 1968, after the stone had been out of the ground for over half a century and after having been in the Smithsonian's collection for over four decades with no cracking or crazing having occurred, it was decided by museum authorities to exhibit this exquisite opal, in such a manner that its magnificent internal POC of brilliant broadflash red in deep black could better be appreciated. A special display case was rigged with a high-intensity light aimed at the face of the opal so that the stone was not lighted at all times but could be lighted by museum visitors by pressing a button. It did indeed show the glory of the stone most satisfactorily and the brilliant light was switched on scores of times every day. Then it was noticed by concerned museum officials that the high-intensity lamp had caused some rather significant crazing to begin, whereupon the stone was removed from its new exhibit. Two queries sent by the writer to Smithsonian authorities, inquiring about the present condition of the stone—whether the crazing was successfully halted or if it has continued—have gone unanswered.

ROMAN LOVERS

This is an impressive carving of gem-quality precious opal depicting two nude figures in embrace. There is no matrix involved in the piece and the POC is primarily red, blue, yellow, and green. The opal carving weighs 50 carats and has been set in 18-karat gold with diamonds as a brooch/pendant and was last known to be in the possession of Andrew Cody, Pty., Ltd. of Melbourne.

SCHWENCKE BOULDER OPAL

This piece of boulder opal is in the collection of the Colburn Gem and Mineral Museum in Asheville, North Carolina, in the United States. It is shown as having been found in the Quilpie Artesian Basin of Queensland, Australia, and is quite impressive. It is cut flat on one side; polished somewhat but still largely in a natural state. The base color is blue, and POC is not mentioned. The stone is 3.75″ × 3.25 × 1.5″ [95.25 mm × 82.55 mm × 38.1 mm].

SPANISH GALLEON

A lovely 48.20-carat [9.64-g] cut black opal, this stone has a dark gray base color and POC in brilliant green, gold, and blue. It was discovered in the Canfell's Hill Diggings at Lightning Ridge by Garry Stone and Oxford Terry in May 1990. They named it *Spanish Galleon* because of its shape and the fact that when held at a certain angle, the POC exhibits what appears to be a remarkably good abstract picture of an ancient Spanish galleon with billowing sails. Without losing this picture, the stone was cut into a high cabochon. Valuation undisclosed.

STAR OF BETHLEHEM

This small but very choice stone was worn as a tie pin by the most famous of the early buyers in the Australian opal fields, Tullie Wollaston. It was a piece of jewelry of which he was especially fond because of its unrivaled brilliance. Ted Murphy, in his excellent book, *They Struck Opal!*, tells of the time Wollaston was in a darkened bank vault and the red glow of the stone reflecting the minimal light was so pronounced that he could see it quite well, even though he could not discern the features of the person holding it. So wonderful was the stone and so attached to it was Wollaston that, at a time when the best black opals were selling for £15 per carat, he several times refused offers of £100 per carat for it. The present disposition of this stone is unknown.

SUN GOD OPAL

Now displayed in Chicago's Field Museum of Natural History as part of the Grainger Hall of Gems Collection, this opal cabochon has been fashioned into a brooch, gold mounted, face curved on opal. Unfortunately, no record exists of the origin of this stone, which measures is 1.4″ × 1.33″ × 0.585″ [35.56 mm × 33.78 mm × 14.86 mm]. The stone was donated to the museum by H. N. Higginbotham (Opal No. H-447) and is so outstanding that its photograph was used on the cover page of the booklet, *Gems, a Companion to the Grainger Hall of Gems,* written by Edward Olson, published by the Field Museum of Natural History.

TARTAN QUEEN

See the *Empress*.

TRIPP OPAL

Presently in the collection of the Field Museum of Natural History in Chicago, this is a Lightning Ridge, South Australia, black opal polished slab set in a gold-rimmed mount that can be worn as a necklace or brooch. The base color of the stone is black and it has vivid red and green POC in broadflash. It is 1.99″ × 1.09″ × 0.156″ [50.55 mm × 27.69 mm × 3.96 mm]. The weight of the entire brooch is 109.16 carats. This piece (Catalog No. H-1633) was donated to the Field Museum by Chester D. Tripp and is on exhibit in the Grainger Hall of Gems. A photograph of it was used in the Field Museum's 1985 calendar entitled *The Year of the Gemstone*.

UNNAMED ANDAMOOKA OPAL

Similar to the *Noolinga Nera,* this opal was found in a dig on Lunatic Hill. It is approximately the same size as the *Noolinga Nera* but is said to have more matrix material involved. The full weight of the uncut piece is 13,608 carats—roughly 6 pounds.

UNNAMED HUNGARIAN OPAL

This noteworthy opal with magnificent colors and as large as a man's fist is in the collection of the Imperial Treasury in Vienna. One of the largest Hungarian opals ever reported, it is purported to weigh 3197.77 carats [1.41 pounds], but no valuation is listed.

UNNAMED OPALIZED CLAMSHELL

No special name has been given to this opalized clamshell, which was found in the Coober Pedy Opal Field of South Australia. Now part of the collection of the American Museum of Natural History in New York City (AMNH No. G96230), the stone is cut and polished and exhibits fine POC in green, yellow, red, and blue flashes. Measuring 1.63″ × 1.44″ [41.4 mm × 36.57 mm], it weighs 69 carats [13.8 g] It was donated to the museum by mineral collector Mabel Lamb of New Canaan, Connecticut. Its valuation is not for publication.

UNNAMED OPALIZED DINOSAUR JAWBONE

In the collection of the Australian Museum in Sydney, New South Wales, this is the jawbone of the dinosaur *Steropodon galmani,* wholly replaced by precious opal. Where the specimen was found is not disclosed, but is believed to have been at White Cliffs, New South Wales. Base coloration of the opal is white and the POC predominates in a lovely violet broadflash that is frequently seen in White Cliffs specimens. Height of the piece is 1.02″ [25.91 mm], but other dimensions and weight are undisclosed. No valuation has been set on this intriguing specimen, since it is unique. It was originally purchased, but details of the transaction remain undisclosed.

UNNAMED PINEAPPLE OPAL PSEUDOMORPH

Presently in the collection of the Australian Museum at Sydney, New South Wales, this beautiful piece is one of only a limited number of these so-called "pineapples" remaining in the world. Such specimens are actually opal pseudomorphs of ikaite, which, in this "pineapple" form, are known only from the White Cliffs Opal Field in northwestern New South Wales. The base coloration is opaque to translucent white with a very vivid POC that is high in lavender tones. This particular specimen, which varies from precious opal through common opal to hyalite, is about 5″ [127 mm] high and 4″ [101.6 mm] at its greatest thickness. Its weight is undisclosed. Acquired through purchase, the details of which are undisclosed, the specimen is valued today in excess of $5000.

UNNAMED VIRGIN VALLEY OPAL

This lovely black opal, originating from Virgin Valley, Nevada, is a cut and polished oval cabochon. Base color is transparent black and the outstanding POC predominates in red, green, yellow, and blue, but with other colors also evident—gold, orange, purple, lavender, etc. Patterns in the POC occur as harlequin, broadflash, and pinfire. Truly an outstanding opal, the cabochon measures 2.29″ × 1.73″ [58.17 mm × 43.94 mm] and is 1.14″ [28.96 mm] thick. The stone weighs 355 carats [2.5 oz] and is part of the Washington A. Roebling Collection, which was donated, along with the famed *Roebling Opal,* to the Smithsonian Institution in Washington, DC, in 1927 by his son, John A. Roebling. Of this black opal cabochon, writes Russell C. Feather II of that institution's Department of Mineral Sciences, *"the outer one-fourth of this stone is crazed around the girdle,"* but, nevertheless, he adds, *"This is the prettiest opal I have ever seen."*

UNNAMED WHITE CLIFFS OPAL NO. 1

Hodge Smythe, former curator of minerals in the Australian Museum at Sydney, New South Wales, reported that this exceptional light opal, which was collected in the White Cliffs Opal Field not long after the turn of the century, had breathtaking multicolored POC and weighed a remarkable 9344.16 carats [4.12 pounds].

UNNAMED WHITE CLIFFS OPAL NO. 2

Another of the remarkably large and spectacularly beautiful light opal specimens found at the White Cliffs Opal Field prior to 1913 was, according to former Australian Museum curator of minerals, Hodge Smythe, one of the largest solid opals ever recorded in Australia. Uncovered about a dozen feet below ground level, it weighed 17,122.80 carats—that's a hair over seven and a half pounds!

Some of the largest or best-known opals (wholly or partially of precious opal)

Name	Weight (ct.)	(lb.)	Date
Virgin Valley Log*	294,840.00 ct	130.00 lb	06/1992
Archevaleta Opal*	90,720.00 ct	40.00 lb	/1933?
Moyd Opal*	88,452.00 ct	39.00 lb	/1974?
Milnic Opal*	82,555.20 ct	36.40 lb	04/1991?
Unnamed Andamooka #1*	41,572.44 ct	18.33 lb	01/1970?
Jupiter-Five	26,331.48 ct	11.61 lb	07/1989
Olympic Australis	23,609.88 ct	10.41 lb	08/1956
Bonanza Opal	23,587.20 ct	10.40 lb	/1976
Lovell Opal	18,143.36 ct	7.99 lb	/1990
Unnamed White Cliffs #2	17,122.80 ct	7.55 lb	/1912?
Americus Australis	16,261.56 ct	7.17 lb	06/1957
Hodson Opal	14,288.40 ct	6.30 lb	06/1952
Grubstake Opal	13,812.12 ct	6.09 lb	/1917
Unnamed Andamooka #2*	13,608.00 ct	6.00 lb	/1948
Noolinga Nera*	13,381.20 ct	5.90 lb	/1945?
Unnamed White Cliffs #1	9,344.16 ct	4.12 lb	/1904?
Royal Peacock	7,370.74 ct	3.25 lb	07/1970
Painted Lady Opal*	6,803.76 ct	3.00 lb	/1964?
Big Ben Opal	5,465.69 ct	2.41 lb	/1975?
Vienna Imperial	3,991.54 ct	1.76 lb	?
Backus Opal	3,870.00 ct	1.71 lb	/1970
Crowning Glory	3,583.31 ct	1.58 lb	/1982
Roebling Opal	3,560.00 ct	1.57 lb	11/1917
Galaxy*	3,500.00 ct	1.54 lb	10/1989
Eighty-Quid Opal	3,401.88 ct	1.50 lb	07/1909
Unnamed Hungarian	3,197.77 ct	1.41 lb	/1775
Light of the World	3,016.33 ct	1.33 lb	/1960
Otto's Stone	2,834.90 ct	1.25 lb	/1924
Schwencke Opal*	2,834.90 ct	1.25 lb	/1947
Duffield Opal	2,335.96 ct	1.03 lb	07/1968
Light of the World	2,268.00 ct	1.00 lb	10/1928
Pat's Stone	1,475.57 ct	10.41 oz	/1956
Leechman's Loss	1,417.45 ct	10.00 oz	/1952?
Dream Cloud*	1,167.00 ct	8.23 oz	/1915?
Mackenzie's Opal	1,100.00 ct	7.76 oz	/1901
Aurora Australis #3	900.11 ct	6.35 oz	07/1989
Other Half, The	851.00 ct	6.00 oz	/1988
Calabah Flame	850.47 ct	6.00 oz	/1971
Tyrell Opal	850.47 ct	6.00 oz	/1875
Burroughs Opalized Limb	810.00 ct	5.71 oz	?
Double G	808.00 ct	5.70 oz	/1930
Flamingo	800.00 ct	5.64 oz	/1915
Waite Opal	776.00 ct	5.47 oz	/1981?
Persephone	765.45 ct	5.40 oz	07/1989
Pandora	708.75 ct	5.00 oz	/1928
Burning of Troy	700.00 ct	4.94 oz	/1795?
Gay Paree	650.63 ct	4.59 oz	/1890?
Empress	504.00 ct	3.56 oz	/1915

(continued)

Field	State	Country
Virgin Valley	Nevada	United States
Virgin Valley	Nevada	United States
Quilpie	Queensland	Australia
Coolgardie	Western Australia	Australia
Andamooka	South Australia	Australia
Coober Pedy	South Australia	Australia
Coober Pedy	South Australia	Australia
Virgin Valley	Nevada	United States
Virgin Valley	Nevada	United States
White Cliffs	New South Wales	Australia
Coober Pedy	South Australia	Australia
Virgin Valley	Nevada	United States
Virgin Valley	Nevada	United States
Andamooka	South Australia	Australia
Andamooka	South Australia	Australia
White Cliffs	New South Wales	Australia
Virgin Valley	Nevada	United States
Andamooka	South Australia	Australia
Lightning Ridge	New South Wales	Australia
?	?	Slovakia
Virgin Valley	Nevada	United States
Virgin Valley	Nevada	United States
Virgin Valley	Nevada	Australia
Jundah	Queensland	Australia
Lightning Ridge	New South Wales	Australia
?	?	Hungary
Lightning Ridge	New South Wales	Australia
Lightning Ridge	New South Wales	Australia
Quilpie	Queensland	Australia
Gerlach	Nevada	United States
Grawin	New South Wales	Australia
Lightning Ridge	New South Wales	Australia
Lightning Ridge	New South Wales	Australia
?	Queensland	Australia
White Cliffs	New South Wales	Australia
New Angledool	New South Wales	Australia
Virgin Valley	Nevada	United States
Glengarry	New South Wales	Australia
Glenburndale	Queensland	Australia
Virgin Valley	Nevada	United States
White Cliffs	New South Wales	Australia
Lightning Ridge	New South Wales	Australia
Mintabie	South Australia	Australia
Coober Pedy	South Australia	Australia
Lightning Ridge	South Australia	Australia
?	?	Honduras
?	Queensland	Australia
Lightning Ridge	New South Wales	Australia

(continued)

Some of the largest or best-known opals (wholly or partially of precious opal) *(Continued)*

Name	Weight (ct.)	(lb.)	Date
Living Fire	432.34 ct	3.05 oz	/1922
John Roebling Cabochon	355.00 ct	2.50 oz	/1920
Idaho Shirley	325.00 ct	2.29 oz	/1964
*Dark Jubilee**	318.94 ct	2.25 oz	/1898?
Desert Beauty	290.59 ct	2.05 oz	/1962?
Flame Queen	253.00 ct	1.78 oz	/1918
Pride of Australia	225.75 ct	1.59 oz	/1915
Orient Queen	222.55 ct	1.57 oz	/1971
Black Prince	218.85 ct	1.54 oz	/1915
Andamooka Opal	205.54 ct	1.45 oz	/1946
Black Princess	205.54 ct	1.45 oz	06/1978
Aztec Sun God	199.52 ct	1.41 oz	/1500?
Aurora Australis #2	180.00 ct	1.27 oz	08/1938
Black Peacock	165.85 ct	1.17 oz	07/1970
Green Goddess	150.26 ct	1.06 oz	/1932?
Leonard Opal	138.19 ct	0.97 oz	/1928?
Blue Web #1	100.00 ct	20.00 g	/1927?
Duke of Devonshire	100.00 ct	20.00 g	/1947?
Blue Web #2	92.09 ct	18.42 g	/1972?
Peon Black	90.00 ct	18.00 g	/1958?
Nonius Opal	80.00 ct	16.00 g	45BC?
Queen of the Earth	75.00 ct	15.00 g	/1921?
Golden Jubilee	72.00 ct	14.40 g	/1949
Unnamed Clamshell	69.00 ct	13.80 g	/1935?
Cornucopia	59.00 ct	11.80 g	06/1992
Mexican Dragon	54.00 ct	10.80 g	/1992
Roman Lovers	50.00 ct	10.00 g	?
Spanish Galleon	48.20 ct	9.64 g	05/1990
Butterfly (Red Admiral)	46.00 ct	9.20 g	/1920
Phoebus	35.00 ct	7.00 g	/1903?
Aztec Eagle	32.00 ct	6.40 g	/1500?
Dunstan's Stone	32.00 ct	6.40 g	08/1909
Christmas Beetle	30.00 ct	6.00 g	12/1974
Tripp Opal	30.00 ct	6.00 g	?
Crane Opal	29.59 ct	5.92 g	/1922?
Fire Bird	25.00 ct	5.00 g	/1973
Magpie	23.00 ct	4.60 g	02/1993
Little Black Peacock	20.00 ct	4.00 g	07/1970
Moonbeam	18.00 ct	3.60 g	?
Black Rock Arrow	13.00 ct	2.60 g	/1912
Brian Hodson Opal	12.30 ct	2.46 g	?
Mexican Sunrise	10.00 ct	2.00 g	/1977?
Down Under	7.00 ct	1.40 g	/1988?
Southern Princess	5.00 ct	1.00 g	09/1992?
Lapkalle	5.00 ct	1.00 g	07/1991

Note. Measurements are in avoirdupois weight.
* Not solid precious opal.

Field	State	Country
Quilpie	Queensland	Australia
Virgin Valley	Nevada	United States
Owyhee Co.	Idaho	United States
Lightning Ridge	New South Wales	Australia
Coober Pedy	South Australia	Australia
Lightning Ridge	New South Wales	Australia
Lightning Ridge	New South Wales	Australia
Glengarry	New South Wales	Australia
Lightning Ridge	New South Wales	Australia
Andamooka	South Australia	Australia
Virgin Valley	Nevada	United States
?	?	Mexico
Lightning Ridge	New South Wales	Australia
Virgin Valley	Nevada	United States
Lightning Ridge	New South Wales	Australia
Lightning Ridge	New South Wales	Australia
Lightning Ridge	New South Wales	Australia
Lightning Ridge	New South Wales	Australia
Lightning Ridge	New South Wales	Australia
?	?	Mexico
?	Opalbanya?	Slovakia
Lightning Ridge	New South Wales	Australia
Lightning Ridge	New South Wales	Australia
Coober Pedy	South Australia	Australia
Virgin Valley	Nevada	United States
Magdalena	Jalisco	Mexico
?	?	Australia
Lightning Ridge	New South Wales	Australia
Lightning Ridge	New South Wales	Australia
?	Querétaro?	Mexico
?	?	Mexico
Lightning Ridge	New South Wales	Australia
Lightning Ridge	New South Wales	Australia
Lightning Ridge	New South Wales	Australia
Lightning Ridge	New South Wales	Australia
Lightning Ridge	New South Wales	Australia
Lightning Ridge	New South Wales	Australia
Virgin Valley	Nevada	United States
Lightning Ridge	New South Wales	Australia
Gerlach	Nevada	United States
Virgin Valley	Nevada	United States
?	Jalisco	Mexico
Lightning Ridge	New South Wales	Australia
Lightning Ridge	New South Wales	Australia
Lightning Ridge	New South Wales	Australia

VIENNA IMPERIAL OPAL

A magnificent uncut Hungarian opal found in 1775, this stone is presently part of the collection of the Hof (Natural History Museum) in Vienna. It exhibits superb POC and, shaped like a thick wedge, measures 4.75″ × 2.5″ [120.65 mm × 63.5 mm] across the face surface and, in thickness, tapers from 0.5″ to 3″ [12.7 mm to 7.6 mm]. There is no matrix involved with the piece, which weighs 1.76 pounds—3991.54 carats. Published values vary from £50,000 to £70,000.

WAITE OPAL

A large freeform polished slab similar to a knife blade in shape. Originally mined at Mintabie, South Australia, the opal's base color is a transparent gray and its POC is a remarkable combination of broadflash red, green, blue, and purple. When viewed In transmitted light, the whole stone becomes a pale transparent orange. The stone measures 6.4″ × 2.5″ × 0.5″ [162.56 mm × 63.5 mm × 12.7 mm] and weighs 776 carats [5.47 oz]. Presently part of the collection of the Royal Ontario Museum at Toronto, this excellent stone was purchased at a Sotheby's Auction in 1984, in part with funds provided by friends of the late G. Grant Waite, who was a well-known lapidary in Toronto, specializing in opals, and who was also a research associate at the Royal Ontario Museum for many years. Valuation undisclosed.

Types of Opals

There is some easily understandable confusion in nomenclature on the part of the public in respect to what constitutes a "type" of opal. The reason for such confusion is that there are a number of adjuncts to the meaning of "type." There are, for example, types involving color (black opal, light opal, gray opal, etc.), types involving pattern (harlequin opal, broadflash opal, pinfire opal, etc.), types involving value (black opal, light opal, harlequin opal, etc.), types involving location (Lightning Ridge opal, Virgin Valley opal, Mexican opal, Hungarian opal), types involving formation (boulder opal, nobby opal, nut opal, sandstone opal, seam opal, pipe opal, matrix opal, etc.), types involving clarity (transparent opal, translucent opal, opaque opal, etc.), types involving genesis (volcanic opal, sedimentary opal, vegetable opal), types involving cuts (baroque, calibrated, freeform, etc.), and the list goes on and on with more categories and subcategories.

Indicative of the whole problem of what it is we're really talking about in regard to types of opal is the fact that even while basically, there are only two real types of opal—precious opal and common opal—precious opal itself (the opal that is so valuable as a gemstone) is very often erroneously referred to by people as fire opal. Yet true fire opal does not even have play of color (POC), or, if it does, then it must properly be called *precious* fire opal. Then there are many types of precious opal and, equally, many types of common opal. But there are two *fundamental* types of precious opal, which deal with its genesis— volcanic opal and sedimentary opal—and those headings are themselves further broken down into different types, as are other categories of opals.

Because of these ambiguities, the considerable overlapping of terms, and the confusion that occurs as a result, it is important to know what the various types of opals are and the accurate meanings of the terms insofar as it is possible to establish them. With that in mind, and in the full knowledge that there will be some overlapping, following are different types of opals.[1]

abanderos opal Also called *abanderado*. From the Spanish word *bandera*, meaning flag or banner and referring to the Mexican flag opal, which exhibits its POC of red, blue, and yellow in bands, streaks, or stripes, like a flag.

agate opal (1) A form of common opal that is banded like agate; (2) a form of agate that has bands of opal.

agaty potch A blue-gray variety of potch (common opal) that is colored in parallel bands similar to a particular species of blue-gray banded agate.

alluvial opal Also called floaters or *wasch* opal, these are pieces of relatively fair-quality precious opal that are found lying loose on the ground surface on slopes and in dry water courses where they have weathered down from the outcropping stratum in which they originally occurred and have frequently led to the discovery of hitherto undiscovered precious opal deposits.

amatite opal A variety of siliceous sinter or perlite.

amber opal A transparent to translucent common opal in which the body color of the stone is generally amber, ranging from brownish to golden.

amber potch Australian designation for a yellow to yellowish-brown variety of potch (common opal) more properly designated as Mexican fire opal.

amygdaloidal opal Alternative name for volcanic opal.

angel stone An Australian designation having two different meanings: (1) a form of hard, white, baked clay in which expansion lines have manifested themselves in a haphazard network of cracks that have become filled with precious opal that can be polished as solids or formed into doublets or triplets; (2) synonymous with the so-called steel band that overlies the opal level, which may reach a foot in thickness but is commonly thinner; the name angel stone was first used at White Cliffs, where miners felt the layer of very hard, usually pure white stone overlying the opal level was protecting it, as might a guardian angel garbed in white (although the steel band at Lightning Ridge is normally a dark gray); in some cases precious opal forms in angel stone, in cracks of the coarse, gritty sandstone that comprises the steel band, or even suffuses itself within that sandstone layer, imparting a vague blush of opal POC.

arananjado opal Spanish for orange, this is Mexican opal with base coloration of orange and ranging from transparent to slightly translucent and, unlike the amber opal variety of Mexican fire opal, exhibits POC in bright displays of red and blue and, to a lesser degree, green and yellow; it is properly called precious Mexican fire opal.

assembled opal Precious opal that has been glued together, either with common opal or another material. [See also doublet and triplet.]

azule opal or azules A Spanish term meaning "blue stones" and used to describe the transparent blue phase of the precious Mexican fire opals that exhibit an azure blue opalescent base coloration and show remarkably vivid flashes of bright hot red and intense cool green; the manner in which the POC moves through the transparent body is not seen in any other type of opal; some refer to azules as girasol opals, although girasol is more frequently used in association with the yellowish-orange to red variety of precious Mexican fire opal.

banded opal (1) a form of common opal ranging from white to gray in its base coloration, which is banded (or sometimes mottled) in black, gray, cream, pink, or peach; this material is apparently found only in an area running adjacent to the east shore of the Imperial Reservoir of the Colorado River in Yuma County, Arizona; (2) a brownish to red-orangish banded common opal, sometimes referred to as onyx opal, that is usually found in seams (although sometimes in ill-defined masses) in deposits of hard, dense porphyry indigenous to Latah, Lemhi, and Owyhee counties in Idaho.

bandfire opal A precious opal named after its POC pattern of colors, which appear in wavering, parallel bands, the colors changing from one to another swiftly as the stone is turned; similar to banner opal or flag opal, but not as predictably patterned.

bar opal A precious opal in which the POC consists of a thin bar of color running through common opal (potch).

baroque opal An opal cut to follow the natural contours of the stone to minimize loss of precious opal; also called a freeform or freeshape opal.

black crystal opal In general terms, a transparent to semitransparent black opal that exhibits exceptionally good POC; under the Lightning Ridge Miners Association Tone Scale, it is defined as a solid opal that is translucent to transparent with POC when viewed from the top and is graded as at least a Number 3 Black.

black jelly opal A transparent black opal that exhibits a reasonably good POC; the term often applied to some forms of Virgin Valley black opal.

black opal Also called dark opal; generally defined, the black opal is any transparent, translucent (Color Plate 13), or opaque precious opal whose base color ranges anywhere from jet black through dark blue, dark brown, and dark green to medium dark gray, with the POC occurring against or within the dark base color; in the black opal type occurring at Lightning Ridge the precious opal often occurs in a light crystal opal color band or bar upon a dark gray or (ideally) black potch background, which imparts a dark appearance to the light opal, and even high-quality black opals may have only a very thin color bar occurring naturally on black potch; under the guidelines of the Lightning Ridge Miners Association Tone Scale, a black opal is defined as one that is opaque, with an appropriately dark gray to blue-black to black general background coloration, and that, when viewed from the top has a POC graded at least as Number 3 Black; in the case of Virgin Valley black opals, however, the black coloration is an integral part of the transparent or translucent body of the opal; Lightning Ridge black opal most often forms in a nodule called a nobby, in which the POC can manifest itself in a wide variety of patterns and scintillating colors that are greatly enhanced by the dark or black background; the black jelly opal and the crystal black opals are considered by many to be the most beautiful, since the transparency allows the subsurface colors to become visible; where the jelly black opals are concerned, many are called sunflash opals because of their ability, under strong light, to intensify color emanating from deep within the stone; black opal is also sometimes called night stone, because high-quality black opal does not require direct sunlight or strong artificial light to show good POC, since a truly good black opal should literally sparkle with POC even in the light of only a single candle in a darkened room; lower-quality black opals generally have electric blue POC, while finer grades may be green or orange, and the best are the intense reds on black.

black potch A common black opal, which, when it forms a natural background for a precious opal color bar or band, is ideal, the potch itself having a certain value as a backing material for mounting thin slices of fragile precious opal into doublets or triplets; the black potch is believed to be stained by ferrous sulfides in the muds that originally formed the opal dirt; often found in the form of nobbies at Lightning Ridge.

blackmorite A name once seriously considered for a variety of orange translucent common opal that occurs near the summit of Mount Blackmore in Gallatin County, Montana; a name never officially adopted.

block opal A variety of precious opal named after its pattern of POC that is exhibited in large, blocky, usually irregular sections of color.

blue opal In precious opal it has a sky-blue to powder-blue base coloration, with POC normally of multicolored scattered pinfire; in common opal it is generally opaque to vaguely translucent and is usually of a medium blue hue, although one quite attractive darker blue variety has been described.

boulder black opal A natural Queensland boulder opal that, when cut, faces as a black opal as defined by the Lightning Ridge Miners Association Tone Scale (Color Plate 14).

boulder brown opal A natural Queensland boulder opal with crystal or semicrystal opal on brown ironstone background.

boulder matrix opal Another name for Queensland boulder opal, but also technically considered to be a combination of opal and ironstone, where the opal is mixed through the ironstone rather than merely appearing in seams or as coatings.

boulder opal (1) A nodule or concretion of ironstone or sandstone matrix shot through with thin veins of common or precious opal, which itself is often colorless; the concretions vary from horizontally occurring bands to boulders ranging from round to elongated ellipsoids and, with few exceptions, are found in well-defined levels within sandstone strata and have a matrix color that can range from a deep dark chocolate brown, when heavy with iron oxide, to relatively free from the iron oxide staining and, in such case, merely sandy colored and called boulder white opal; the matrix may sometimes have pockets that are filled with opal, either precious or common; the opal veining, which can be black or light, is often very thin but often with uncommonly beautiful POC and quite valuable; in those specimens referred to as solid boulder opals, the top surface is almost entirely covered with precious opal; the most valuable boulder opals are those with a dark body color and broadly exposed precious opal with a regular surface, its brilliance being the most important factor, with lower qualities mainly blue, higher qualities having green, orange, or red hues; true boulder opal occurs only in Queensland, Australia; (2) a cut opal that incorporates both ironstone matrix and precious opal. [See also boulder matrix opal, fun stone opal, and Yowah nut.]

boulder white opal A natural Queensland boulder opal with its precious opal occurring as veining or coating in a light-colored ironstone (or sometimes sandstone) background.

Brazilian opal A precious opal, usually having a pure white to cream body color but sometimes jelly or crystal opal, and normally having a pinfire pattern of POC; and a stone that, of course, originates in Brazil (Figure 30).

broadflash opal An opal named after its pattern of broadly flashing POC, which, in some cases, may even cover the entire surface of the stone, in which case it is sometimes referred to as sheen; a pattern of opal in which red is always highly desired and even more rare and valuable are purple or violet, colors that may flash across the surface of the stone in broad, parallel bands or streaks, almost as if they are flames; sometimes a stone showing bright red is referred to as a fire opal, but this is erroneous and confusing, as the true fire opal is Mexican and does not show fire in its orange transparency unless termed precious Mexican fire opal; broadflash opal is sometimes called broad flashfire opal.

brown-and-gray opal another designation for the common opal usually referred to as liver opal [q.v.]

brown crystal opal A precious opal that has a transparent brown base color.

cachalong opal Sometimes spelled cacholong; a variety of very porous common opal, which, when dry, has an opaque base color ranging from dull, pure milk white (usually) to faintly discolored and opaque blue-white, sometimes even creamy, yellowish, or reddish, and the outer texture of which may be distinctly chalky, but which becomes translucent to transparent when immersed in water, because the water quickly fills the pores of the stone, making it possible for light to pass through with less interference; cachalong is often confused with hydrophane, but there is a very important difference: as with hydrophane it is a thirsty opal— a water-hungry stone so absorbent of water that it will adhere to the tip of one's tongue; however—and this is the big difference—where hydrophane clearly exhibits POC when wet,

Figure 30. A 168-carat Brazilian jelly opal with columnar fire and broadflash red POC, cut by the author. (Photo by the author)

cachalong does not (some authorities have suggested that cachalong does, on occasion, exhibit color when immersed, but that is not true, for, if such were the case, it would then actually be hydrophane opal); because of this remarkable ability to change, cachalong and hydrophane alike were once believed to have magical powers, so it was commonly called the Magic Stone; cachalong was so named because it was found among the pebbles along the Cach River in Bucharia on the Caspian Sea—the name cachalong meaning "beautiful stone" and possibly derived, as well, from the Tartar *kaschts-chilon;* these stones were sometimes banded in agatelike layers and so have also been called kalmuk-agate or kalmuk-opal; when they have a gray, mother-of-pearl luster, they are termed by the Germans as being perlmutter opal, which is held in value as a material that lends itself well to the carving of cameos.

calibrated opal An opal that has been cut to a standard dimension so as to be set in standardized mountings, for example a 10 × 14-mm oval; compare with freesize or freeform opal.

candlebox opal A pejorative term for precious opal of a quality so low that in the early days of Australian opal mining it was initially stored in old wooden candleboxes and in that manner kept out of the marketplace, so it would not have a deleterious effect on the world opal market values; later, however, as the supply of quality opal diminished, this material was sold to western Germany's mass-production cutters at Idar-Oberstein, where it brought a decent price and was soon appearing in jewelry stores around the world.

celestial opal Oriental name for moonstone; see also Ceylonese opal.

ceraunium opal An ancient Latin designation meaning "thunderstone," which was applied to opal that was believed by some to fall from the sky during thunderstorms, with the lightning preserved within in the stone, a belief shared by the Bedouins of the Sahara; present use of the word refers to meteorites.

Ceylonese opal Not an opal at all, but an Oriental name for moonstone; also called celestial opal.

chaff opal An opal named after its pattern of POC, in which small blocks of color—most commonly yellow—give an appearance of scattered straw chaff.

chamälconstein opal See hydrophane opal.

cherry opal One form of the Mexican fire opal—a transparent red-orange to bright red opal, that lacks POC; most often found in Mexico but also occasionally found in Honduras and in certain southwestern United States locations; named after the body color of the stone; if POC occurs, the stone should be called precious cherry opal.

Chinese opal A name that has been used indiscriminately in the past to mean tabasheer (vegetable opal), white chalcedony, and moonstone.

Chinese writing opal An opal named after its pattern of POC, which is often green against black and in which the green POC appears to take on the distinctive configuration of Chinese characters.

chloropal A common opal similar to prase opal but with a body color that is lighter green than that of prase opal.

chrysopal A common opal basically similar to prase opal and chloropal, but with a golden-green body color.

claro opal A shortening of the Spanish *claro-o-translucente* as a designation for the Mexican opal that is exceptionally clear to slightly translucent, sometimes with pale body color (though most often colorless or vaguely misty white) and that exhibits its POC in an array of fiery red, sparkling green, intense blue, and vibrant yellow.

claro-o-translucente See claro opal.

cloudy opal A type of opal seemingly unique to the Spencer Opal Mine in Idaho, in which the transparent water-clear faintly bluish opal base color shows varying amounts of a white mistiness, giving a remarkable effect of clouds.

columnar fire opal An opal named after its patter of POC, which appears as needles of fire when the normal pinfire pattern of POC is viewed from the side rather than straight on; some stones are cut to specifically show this pattern rather than the pinfire.

common opal Also known as potch; any of a variety of opal types, forms, patterns, and colors that do not exhibit any POC, even though some may show a general or partial opalescence; included among common opals are cachalong, hyalite (Müllers glass), resin opal, wax opal and numerous others.

confetti opal An opal named after its POC pattern, which appears as colorful bits of confetti afloat in a transparent sea; this exciting, breathtaking pattern is quite rare and usually occurs in only a small portion of the gem-quality seam opal mined in Honduras.

conk opal A very stable type of wood opal sometimes found at Virgin Valley, Nevada, in which the interior of the wood cells were originally eaten away by disease and eventually refilled with opal that may or may not be precious; it is also called white speck opal because it tends sometimes to show small white specks on the surface of the rough material (Color Plate 15).

contra luz opal A type of precious opal that differs from the usual precious opal in that the POC is not visible in reflected light (usually), but becomes visible when viewed in transmitted light; i.e., the light source behind the opal instead of behind the viewer; there are exceptions, however, where some opal will show both normal POC and contra luz; *contra luz* is Spanish for "against the light" and, while the base color may be almost anything, it appears most often to occur in translucent white, transparent clear, transparent orange, or a transparent deep root beer brown; contra luz is also known in some quarters as iris opal, although this is usually confused with iris quartz or iris agate; the POC exhibited is usually of pinfire pattern, although in some cases harlequin, broadflash, and other patterns are noted (Color Plate 16).

Coober Pedy opal A characteristically light opal with excellent POC and usually splendid stability, which originates from the various opal fields in the area of Coober Pedy, South Australia.

corencite opal A type of gold-green common opal similar to chloropal.

crystal opal Term used when an opal is transparent or very translucent and the clarity of color is sharp; actual hue has little to do with the terminology, since crystal opal can be clear, red, orange, black, etc.; the term crystal opal applies when the diffracted colors are visible both on the surface of the stone and from within the stone (Figure 31); a crystal opal can be a transpar-

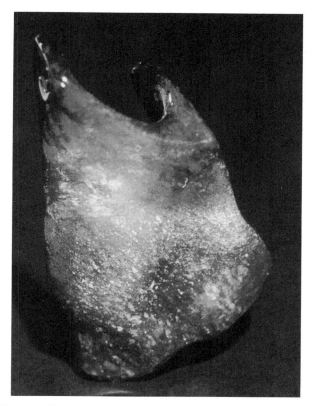

Figure 31. This magnificent 52-carat freeform black opal—the *Desert Hope Flame*—was cut by Kevin Lane Smith of Tucson, Arizona. It is 1.83″ [47 mm] high and 1.09″ [28mm] wide. The stone was dug in 1992 from the opal level at the famed Bonanza Mine in Virgin Valley, Nevada, and is still in Smith's private collection. (Photo by Kevin Lane Smith)

ent to semitransparent stone, sometimes even grading into translucent, whereas a jelly opal is always transparent, although some people use the terms crystal opal and jelly opal virtually synonymously; some sources claim that crystal opal has a stronger POC than jelly opal; much confusion results from the fact that the opal that is normally termed crystal opal in Australia is normally termed jelly opal in the United States.

dark opal   The terms light opal or dark opal signify, very broadly, the opal's body tonality; a dark opal is an opal that, when viewed from above, has a tonal quality (irrespective of color) that ranges from medium gray to the densest black; opals are classified into three major body-color tone types: transparent, light, and dark, and these categories, in this sense, have nothing to do with the opal's diffracted colors or its pattern; lightness or darkness in opal is caused by the degree and type of base color present in the stone, with base tones ranging from colorless and white, through the shades of gray, to black; light opal includes all those, of any color, to as dark as a medium gray tone; black opal incorporates those tones, in any color, from medium dark gray to black; dark opal can be transparent, translucent, or opaque; some opal properly termed dark actually has a light crystal color bar on dark opal potch, giving the otherwise light opal a dark appearance.

dendritic opal   An opal, usually common opal and most often translucent or opaque, that can be either clear or variously colored, that displays one or more dense black spots or delicately branching stemlike inclusions (dendrites) of manganese oxide or other impurities; some dendritic opal may properly be termed moss opal, but not all; some of the dendrites may create rather spectacular scenic effects.

diatomaceous opal   Also called fuller's earth, diatomaceous earth, diatom opal, diatomite, keiselguhr, tripoli, or infusorial earth; this is a mineralized white to tan to sometimes reddish siliceous powder formed of skeletal remains of minute marine plants (actually algae) called diatoms; it is very useful, in a particularly pure nature called tripoli, as an abrasive powder for metal and gemstone polishing (including opal); often mined and used in less refined form for its value as a filtration agent, as insulation, and as fertilizer.

dyed opal   Opal that has been treated with chemicals (sometimes in combination with heat and/or acid) to render its body color black in order to give it an appearance similar to true black opal.

eisen opal   A type of ferruginous jasp-opal.

enhydro potch   A small nodule of common opal (found on rare occasions in Australian opal fields) in the center of which is a little hollow core containing a small quantity of what appears to be water but which some people claim to be silica gel not yet hardened into opal.

eye-of-the-world opal   one of several superstitious designations for hydrophane opal, which is also called *oculus mundi* in Latin and *weltaug* in German. [See also cachalong opal.]

exploding flash opal   An opal with a pattern of POC in which the colors appear as a broad-flash pattern in a sudden burst, as if out of nowhere, and then disappear quite as suddenly when the stone is turned.

fan harlequin opal   An opal with a pattern of POC that forms in tiny adjacent colored squares that spray out across the face of the stone in a general fan shape.

fancy pattern opal   Precious opal in which the POC forms patterns that are not among those most commonly seen; includes such unusual configurations in pattern as blockfire, straw, ribbon, and mackerel sky.

fanfire opal   An opal pattern that sprays out from a central point in a fanlike manner. (Also called fan opal.)

fiorite opal A variety of siliceous sinter, also called geyser opal, which forms around the rims of thermal springs.

fire opal The term all too often incorrectly applied to any opal that exhibits POC, when the correct term for that is precious opal; actually, fire opal—closely associated with Mexican opal, but not exclusively such—is a type of transparent to semitransparent opal having a strong predominant base color ranging from water-clear transparency through distinct transparent bluish to transparent pale yellow through yellow-orange, light orange through yellow-orange, bright orange through red-orange to cherry-red, and from brownish-red to reddish-brown; that base color, while bright, is devoid of play of color; where POC *does* occur in such opal, however, the stone is then referred to as precious fire opal; ordinary fire opal is common to the Mexican opal mines and is also found in lesser abundance in other opal sources throughout the world, such as Australia, Nevada, California, British Columbia, Oregon, Honduras, and Guatemala; American buyers most often trade in the deeply orange or cherry red stone—the latter usually called cherry opal [q.v.]—of transparent to translucent body color and from no POC to abundant green and red fire; oddly, much of the pure orange fire opal is notably unstable and crazes within minutes of exposure to air and light; but the dark red material seems to exhibit greater stability.

flag opal see abanderos opal.

flagstone opal An opal having a pattern of POC exhibiting very distinctively defined patches of color with the appearance of flagstone paving; similar to the harlequin opal, but with the pattern not so regularly laid out.

flame opal A precious opal whose pattern of POC shows in red bands or streaks like flickering flames, especially notable when the opal is turned in the hands and much like flash opal except for the patches of fire being generally smaller.

flash opal Also called flashfire opal, this type has a POC pattern closely akin to (and sometimes synonymous with) broadflash or rolling flash, in which a large area of the opal is arranged in a brilliantly iridescent pattern that changes or "flashes" across the stone, or even abruptly disappears and reappears, as the piece is turned or moved; the flash pattern shows POC in spots of color that are larger than those appearing in pinfire and flame opal but smaller than broadflash; these colors range through the entire spectrum, from blue, which is the least valued in flash opal, through green, yellow (which is rare), and gold to red and, occasionally, to violet or purple; the flash pattern in red is considered by many to be the very finest and most attractive, and the best and most abundant stones of this type are found in Australia and Nevada.

flashfire opal See flash opal.

fossil opal This type of opal includes opalized shells, bones, and wood (or other plant matter) as well as belemnites and vertebrate animals such as tortoises and the more rare but very spectacular finds of marine dinosaur remains such as plesiosaurs.

freeform opal Also called baroque opal and freeshape opal, this is a precious opal that (usually to preserve as much value as possible) has been cut and polished in an irregular shape instead of into a calibrated opal, which may mean a cut following natural contours of the stone.

freeshape opal Another designation for freeform opal.

freesize opal Any opal that has been cut into a regular geometric shape—square, rectangle, round, triangular, and, especially, oval—but that is of a nonstandard, noncalibrated size. [Compare with calibrated opal.]

fun-stone opals This is an Australian colloquial term used to designate certain small boulder opals with abundant ironstone on the outer surface and only a small amount of precious opal visible; dubbed fun-stone opals as a result of their being used by early miners as payment to prostitutes.

gelite opal Any kind of opal (or sometimes chalcedony) that has been deposited as an accessory mineral and appears, usually, as a bonding agent in sandstone or similar material.

gem opal A term synonymous with gem-quality opal and which is most frequently applied to opal rough that can be cut into stones of gem quality.

gem-quality opal Synonymous with gem opal and signifying a precious opal that is of the highest quality—one having brilliant POC, fine body color, and an absence of imperfections.

geyser opal Also called geyserite; synonymous with siliceous sinter [q.v.].

geyserite Also called geyser opal. Synonymous with siliceous sinter [q.v].

Gilson opal A synthetic opal originally synthesized by Pierre Gilson of Paris, France, first produced in Switzerland and now produced in Japan.

girasol opal Also known as rainbow opal and hyacinth opal, this is the orangy-reddish to yellow precious fire opal, which shows its dormant colors when turned in the sunlight, or whose color appears to follow the sun as the stone is turned around; in Mexico they are called *Iluviznados;* the precious fire opal is an opal that is usually transparent to semitransparent opal and has a strong predominant base color ranging from water-clear transparency through distinct transparent bluish to bluish-white, transparent pale yellow through yellow-orange, light orange through yellow-orange, bright orange through red-orange to cherry-red, and from brownish-red to reddish-brown; the colors change as the angle of illumination changes, with red light being bent more than blue light; the base color is always bright and the stone in all cases exhibits a distinct POC, which is usually characterized by especially vivid red and green flashes; although yellow and orange flashes occur as well, they are less common; girasol means, literally, "turn-to-sun" and is used to describe a precious fire opal that shows its dormant colors when turned in the sunlight or whose color appears to follow the sun as the stone is turned around; such opals also lend themselves to being cut as faceted gemstones; almost certainly the poor reputation of girasol—the precious Mexican fire opal—results from the widespread distribution of inferior stones with little POC, or ordinary fire opal without POC, leading to an impression that precious Mexican fire opal is dull and lifeless, but that is not so; fine stones are rare and no great number are available, even on the Mexican market, but those who are familiar with the finest examples will attest they are unsurpassed in beauty and unique character. [See *azules* for the blue phase of the precious Mexican fire opal.]

glass opal See hyalite.

gold opal A decidedly gold-colored form of common opal and named after the body mass color of the stone; some gold opal will blend into an amber color.

gray opal Australian term for any opal with a base coloration varying in tonal density from light gray to medium gray, although technically it can be any precious opal with a background color varying in density from light gray to near black; the true gray opal, almost always opaque to translucent, is found on virtually all Australian opal fields, and has a grayish, sometimes smoky appearance that is easy to distinguish from all other types, as it appears to have a sort of liquid gray floating through the POC, no matter how bright; it is sometimes called semiblack opal, although the term is not all inclusive, since some semiblack opals show no trace of gray.

green opal A bright green common opal, ranging from opaque to translucent, that is said to have been colored by chromite or nickel to the point where it may well rival the superb color of top grade chrysoprase.

green-and-yellow opal　A nicely colored common opal that occurs in the vicinity of Oamaru, New Zealand.

gummisteen opal　See hyalite.

half-opal　Alternative name, seldom used, for semi-opal.

harlequin opal　An opal named after the pattern of POC that was itself named from the traditional harlequin patchwork bodysuit costume of the medieval clown or jester; it is one of the rarest and most valuable patterns of POC occurring in precious opal; a reasonably regular pattern in which clear, intense, and different individual colors are arranged in small, equally sized checkerboard squares, rectangles, diamond shapes, pentagons, or similar geometric patterns; most often the individual pieces average about a tenth of an inch square and fit together like multicolored tesserae of a mosaic and, in this respect, an opal so patterned is sometimes called mosaic opal; always a collector's piece whenever encountered. [See also fan harlequin pattern.]

heliotrope opal　Another name for pyrophane; heliotrope is applied both because of its reddish-lavender to purplish color and because the word also means "turn to the sun," and when the opal is turned to the sun, the colors become most vivid; heliotrope, however, is also the name of another stone unrelated to opal—a dark green chalcedony with red spots, which is also known as bloodstone.

Honduras opal　A type of volcanic precious opal that is said to have exceptional character, yet is only sporadically mined in the San Antonio Mountains of Honduras near Erandique; many of the very early Honduras opals—some of them apparently very high quality black opals—were sold on the European market but listed as Hungarian opals.

honey opal　A transparent to translucent opal with a base color about the hue of honey and which may or may not exhibit POC; the opal is usually found as vein or vug material in hard, compact porphyry.

huevos opal　Spanish for "egg opal" and used to designate an unusual nodule of rough opal (or a faceted or otherwise polished opal) in which the center is cloudy or hollow, an aspect taken advantage of in the cutting to create interesting or striking effects.

hummingbird stone　Aztec term for opal, which appeared as *vitzitziltecpatl* in the Aztec tongue, the stone named by them after the similarly brilliant iridescence of the hummingbird's plumage.

Hungarian opal　Any precious opal having been mined in the area of the present Czech Republic, Slovakia, Hungary, or adjacent areas; the name is usually applied to opals mined prior to the twentieth century and perhaps as far back in antiquity as prior to the Roman Empire (Figure 32).

hyacinth opal　Another name for girasol, the orangey reddish-to-yellow precious Mexican fire opal; however, the name hyacinth is used in connection with other gemstones as well, such as a variety of zircon.

hyalite opal　One of the most common nonprecious opals in the world, it is also known as Müller's Glass, glass opal, or gummisteen; formerly (and normally) considered to be a transparent, water-clear opal having no POC, which usually occurs in botryoidal incrustations on older rocks or minerals and looks like drops of molten glass; now, however, also including a form of smoky opal occurring in the vicinity of Zacatecas, Mexico, which forms in the same manner as hyalite; the smokiness, however, is in clearly transparent form, since no opal with any suggestion of milkiness or translucency can properly be considered hyalite; all hyalite fluoresces a brilliant yellow-green; the best is considered to be the pale ethereal blue transparent stone that is surprisingly stable and very well suited for faceting and carving; when faceted,

Figure 32. A piece of Hungarian opal rough from the Dubnik mines in Slovakia. The matrix material is andescite. (Photo courtesy of Dr. Petr Korbel, Prague)

it reflects yellow light off the pavilion faces, even though the stone is blue; much hyalite contains zones or layers of bright orange.

hydrophane opal A type of opal that, when dry (regardless of whether polished or rough), is opaque and usually cloudy milk-white or dull-colored but that, when immersed in water, quickly lets the water soak in and fill the pores of the stone, allowing light to pass through with less interference and causing the opal to then become translucent or even as transparent as hyalite, but displaying quite brilliant POC; when dried, it returns to its dull, opaque appearance; hydrophane opal is quite similar to cachalong opal, except that cachalong, when soaked, while it becomes translucent and sometimes even transparent, does not exhibit POC; the name hydrophane derives from the Greek words for "apparent in water," and this ability to become transparent and exhibit POC gave rise to the superstition that such a stone contained a magic "hidden eye" capable of seeing everything; for this reason, it was also called *oculus mundi*, from the Latin for "eye of the world"; German lapidaries, who finished especially fine examples of the stone, called it *weltaug*, meaning "world's eye", and sold it as a potent charm to buyers in the East Indies; it has also been referred to in past times as *lapis mutabilis* and *chamälconstein* and in some superstitious circles it is still referred to in English as Magic Stone and worn as a special magical charm; the incipient transparency can be induced for more extended periods through immersion in thin oil, but there is a risk that the oil will accumulate in the pores after a time and darken or yellow it, diminishing or even ruining its POC; another method of inducing the transparency is to soak the stone in hot clear wax; when cooled and dried in the air, a stone so treated will be opaque, but will begin to show some degree of transparency when warmed up; hydrophane has also erroneously been called pyrophane; some of the clear hydrophane is unstable when wet, but becomes stable when it dries out; conversely, some dry, usually white, hydrophane may crack if suddenly immersed in water.

Icelandic opal A nonprecious porous opal that is a form of siliceous sinter (geyser opal) that is deposited in layers around hot springs; it is also incorrectly called Icelandic agate or layered obsidian.

imitation opal A manufactured imitation of opal, usually of plastic, glass, or resin; not the same as synthetic opal; synonymous with simulated opal.

indivisible quartz A former terminology for opal, not quartz; the "indivisible" refers to the opal being amorphous rather than crystalline and having no cleavage planes.

infusorial opal See diatomaceous opal.

iridot A name first applied about 1880 as a euphemism to precious opal, when the name opal bore connotations about bad luck; the term iridot lasted for only a little over a decade, by which time opal had regained acceptance and respectability.

iris opal see contra luz.

isopyre Some of the older mineral books refer to a mineral called isopyre, first described from a quarry near Dover in Morris County, New Jersey; a dense dark material, sometimes red-spotted, so dark green as to almost be mistaken for black; it was occasionally cut into cabochons, but after many years of designation as a mineral in its own right, closer studies finally showed it to be nothing more than a very impure form of common opal.

jasp-opal A jaspery chalcedony in which the cementing material or veining is opal, not quartz; the material has also been called jasper opal and opal jasper.

jasper opal See jasp-opal.

jelly opal Precious opal that is ordinarily quite transparent, imparting a gelatinous appearance, generally water clear but often with blue iridescence throughout, or sometimes exhibiting faint base color traces and with POC ranging from light to dark green and blue and sometimes, depending on the stone's quality, exhibiting bright red; often called water opal because of its great clarity; when colored instead of water clear, the POC it exhibits almost always evinces a vague general haziness and, as such, that POC is not so concentrated or pronounced as the POC in crystal opal; to accurately be termed jelly opal, it must be either iridescent transparent blue or exhibit POC to some degree, or both; the term jelly opal is often incorrectly applied to any transparent stone, water-clear or colored, without POC.

kalmuk agate See kalmuk opal.

kalmuk opal Also called kalmuk agate, the material is a type of banded opal that occurs at Kalmuk near Astrakhan and the Caspian Sea; both terms refer to a form of cachalong opal exhibiting layering, as in banded agate.

kaschts-chilon opal Derived from the Tartar term for cachalong opal.

keraunios See ceraunium opal.

kieselguhr opal See diatomaceous opal.

lapis mutabilis See hydrophane opal.

layered opal See Icelandic opal.

lechosos opal The Spanish term for milk (or milky) opal, the word itself from the Spanish word *leche,* meaning "milk," and used to describe a type of opal with a milky white decidedly opaque base color and relatively strong POC. [See also milk opal.]

lemon opal Named for its brilliant, transparent lemon-yellow coloration, this type of volcanic opal originally came from Kootenai County, Idaho, and ranged in size up to 100 carats or more, but more typically in the sizes between 20 and 50 carats; the stones, recovered from vugs and pockets in rhyolite, were particularly suitable for faceting and some were said to show some degree of POC, usually in faintly discernable broadflash; mining for these stones ceased about 1955 when it was deemed marginally unprofitable.

levin opal A light opal variety characterized by a POC pattern of long, thin lightning-like flashes, which caused ancient superstitious beliefs that opal was not an earthbound mineral, but one that fell from the heavens.

light crystal opal Opals in this subcategory of light opal are those that are either wholly transparent or extremely translucent, allowing diffracted colors to be detected from within the interior of the stone.

light opal One of the major types of opals where tonality is concerned, where all opals are classed as either light opals or dark opals; light opal includes any precious opal having a base coloration (body color) from clear or white or a very pale grayish tone through a medium grayish tone; actual diffracted color comprising the tonality of the stone is inconsequential, as is pattern or degree of transparency; light opal simply includes all those to medium gray, and dark opal includes all those from dark gray to black; light opal is not the same as white opal, the latter term being properly used only when the base coloration of the stone is actually white, as in milk opal.

Lightning Ridge opal Basically, it is the extremely valuable black opal that is most closely associated with Lightning Ridge, although considerable light opal comes from this field as well.

lithoxyl opal Wood opal in which the woody structure remains clearly evident.

liver opal Known also as menilite opal, liver opal is so-called due to the deep, gray-brown, liver color it exhibits; it was named menilite because it first became recognized from deposits at Menil-Montant, near Paris, France; it normally occurs in rounded lumps somewhat similar to the Yowah Nuts of Queensland, Australia, and not unlike another variety called neslite opal.

Iluviznados opal Pronounced u-vees-nah-doze, this Spanish term literally means "sun on raindrops" or, more liberally, "fire-rain"; it refers to the prized high plateau precious Mexican fire opals, also called girasol, which have a transparent body ranging in color from water clear, faintly bluish, or very pale yellow, and decidedly enlivened by narrow bands of POC in scintillating shafts that may be yellow-orange, orange, red-orange, red, red-brown and brown-red; this fire often appears boldly, but sometimes simply as tiny scattered pinfire specks glittering like stars in the bluish or topaz opalescence.

mackerel sky opal Named after the pattern of POC it exhibits that shows a repeated, wavering, ribbonlike quality, usually in vibrant electric blue against a black body color or, occasionally, some other color against a blue base coloration; similar to ribbon opal.

magic stone A superstitious name sometimes applied to cachalong opal, but more properly applied to hydrophane opal.

magpie potch A common opal exhibiting black-on-white or black-on-gray patches and which occurs with some abundance in the Sheepyard Opal Field near Lightning Ridge.

man-made opal Synonymous with synthetic opal.

matrix of opal Not the same as matrix opal, this is not a type of opal but, rather, the mother rock in which opal is found and which encloses the opal forming in it; in volcanic deposits, this matrix of opal is usually rhyolite or basalt; in sedimentary opal it is usually montmorillonite clays or sandstones.

matrix opal Matrix opal is a type of opal-bearing rock with many subvarieties, all with their own peculiarities and embracing the following: (1) a brown to brownish-gray ironstone riddled with opal-filled cracks, known as Queensland boulder opal (which includes Yowah nuts) and in which the opal-filled cracks or veins are too thin and fragile to separate from the dark brown mother stone, so matrix and opal are polished together; the precious opal in such specimens found mainly between concentric layers on the underside of the nuts, or as a network of thin veins through the ironstone concretion; more correctly, however, the opal and matrix material are mixed together like a pudding, as in (2) a very hard siliceously cemented sandstone, basalt, or rhyolite that is speckled throughout with brilliant points of precious opal, or, more simply, precious opal bits mixed throughout a parent rock, in which the silica gel has spread throughout the porous iron sandstone, basalt or rhyolite of Queensland, Andamooka, Virgin Valley, Louisiana, and other sources, hardening into myriad iridescent specks of color radiating from a darker colored background, with such material, early on, being called mother-of-opal or *prime d'opal,* terms that are no longer in vogue; (3) a very dark gray basalt from Honduras which is liberally peppered with bits of brilliant green POC; matrix opal is also (4) a term used occasionally, but inaccurately, by Lightning Ridge miners in referring to a porous white impurity in black opal.

menilite opal See liver opal.

Mexican fire opal A nonprecious but highly attractive form of opal that is usually very transparent and that occurs in a wide range of colors, some of it bluish-white but far more commonly in the range of warm colors, from pale yellow through deep yellow, yellow-orange, orange, red orange, bright cherry red, and deeper red; lends itself equally well in jewelry work to cabochons or faceted stones; not the same as precious Mexican fire opal, which is also called girasol.

milk opal Also called milky opal and *lechosos,* this type of opal is milk white in base coloration and probably owes its color to the opal having formed in a pure white clay; some references claim that POC does not occur in milk opal since, if POC is present, it is no longer properly called milk opal but, instead, referred to as white opal; that, however, flies in the face of the many authorities that state that some milk opal does have very strong POC; in this respect, the Spanish word for milk opal, *lechosos,* derives from the word *leche,* meaning milk, and *lechosus,* as already noted is a type of opal with an opaque milky white base color and relatively strong POC; milk opal, even with POC, is normally the least desirable of all forms of precious opal and typically has only scattered specks of color throughout the pure white stone; with or without POC, milk opal is one of the more common types of opal world wide.

Mintabie opal Opal from the important Mintabie opal field in South Australia, which is characterized by its light base coloration of pale green to pale blue or blue-green.

mosaic opal A name sometimes erroneously applied to precious opal that exhibits the harlequin pattern but that is actually small pieces of carefully selected precious opal fitted together to form a design or picture.

moss opal (1) A nonprecious opal that has a generally clear base color in which dendrites and/or mossy or fernlike patterns are formed from inclusions of oxides of manganese; also known as dendritic opal; (2) a specific form of common opal that resembles mocha stone or black moss agate and that occurs in Trego County, Kansas, and is sometimes referred to as Trego opal.

mother-of-opal Alternative name for *prime d'opal,* a material consisting of bright specks of opal in porous matrix.

mother-of-pearl opal Layered Kalmuk opal (or agate) much used for the carving of cameos.

mountain opal Alternative name for volcanic opal, a precious opal that is found in pockets, vugs, or cracks in rhyolite or other igneous rocks and usually very difficult to remove without damage to the opal.

Müller's Glass opal See hyalite.

multicolor opal A precious opal that exhibits no less than three distinct colors in its POC but usually with one color dominating, in which case it might be referred to as a red multicolor, a green multi-color, etc. [See also multifire opal.]

multifire opal Since most people speak about opals more often by their predominant color, it is convenient to group them accordingly; the terms red, orange, and green fire refer to the dominant color in the stone, and multifire is a precious opal that exhibits three or more colors in its POC (and usually most colors of the spectrum) without any particular color predominating in the POC display; as intensity and brilliance increase, so does quality and value.

myrickite opal See opalite.

neslite opal A type of opal quite similar to menilite but with a grayer color and which, because of its weight and peculiar grip, was once very popular as a material used for the carving of fine sword handles.

night stone opal A precious opal whose POC shows up better in conditions of low light than under the full light of bright direct sunlight or artificial light—which occurs only with truly superior stones; a phenomenon that occurs when, in full light, so much light is diffracted from the stone that one's eye cannot sort it all out and so perceives it as white light; but under low light conditions, one's eye is not overloaded and the true magnificence of the opal is perceived.

noble opal An early designation for precious opal that is still used on rare occasions today.

oculus mundi Latin name for hydrophane opal, the Latin term meaning "eye of the world."

onyx opal A common opal that is banded and somewhat resembles onyx.

opal By itself, this to the miner generally signifies common opal, as opposed to precious opal, which is referred to by that name or as "noble opal"; common opal is found in relative abundance throughout the world; it is, with but few exceptions, valueless, uninteresting, and, in Australia, referred to disparagingly as potch.

opal jasper Synonymous with jasp-opal.

opal matrix Alternative term for matrix opal.

opaline (1) A term sometimes used for matrix opal; (2) any material that is at least in part opalized; (3) an old term for Australian opal.

opalite Not a recognized variety of opal and, in fact, the very word opalite is a considerably abused term used in the United States to rather indiscriminately describe various forms of chert (chalcedony) and/or, incorrectly, common opal; (1) opalite may also be called myrickite when it shows red streaks or red areas caused by cinnabar (ore of mercury) and many other colors of opalite are found in the California deserts; (2) in Australia, opalite denotes a manufactured black glass (as opposed to obsidian) that is used for doublet backing material; (3) an Australian yellow-green potch with black dendritic inclusions is referred to by some as opalite; (4) an imitation opal created from resin and produced in Hong Kong under the trade name Opalite first became available in 1976 but was not marketed in quantity until the early 1990s—it is a well-constructed imitation, which has much the same appearance of a Mintabie opal (its POC emanating from minute styrene plastic spheres embedded in the resinous material) but an imitation that can be detected easily enough because of its feathery lightness and its inherent softness of only 2.5 on the Mohs scale.

opalized wood Alternative term for wood opal (Figure 33).

opallion (or opallios) A Greek name for opal adapted from the Roman *opalus*.

opalo The Spanish name for opal.

opalus The oldest known name for opal, which was used by the Romans in the first century B.C. There are those who believe it has its origin from the Sanskrit word, *upala,* which means a special or valuable stone of any kind and has been said to be the oldest name known to civilization for the gemstone we call opal. However, evidence now points more conclusively to the name opal being derived from Opalbanya, the Magyar Hungarian (Slovakian) name for opal mine. [See the chapter on opal History/Mythology for greater detail.]

ophthalmus lapis A term used in the Middle Ages for opal and eyed agate; the literal translation being "eye" and "stone," as opal was known then as the "eye-stone."

orange opal A nonprecious solid opal, which may be transparent but which is more often translucent to opaque and has an orange to orange-red base color; synonymous with certain Mexican fire opals, although also found in other locations, such as at Opal Mountain near Mojave, California, in Virgin Valley, Nevada, and at the Okanagan Mine in British Columbia, Canada.

Oriental opal A term used in Sri Lanka, like celestial opal, for moonstone.

orphanus opal A name meaning "the orphan" and used to denote pyrophane opal; the term refers to the stone's POC, which wanders about loose and at random; the name is sometimes improperly applied to girasol opal.

Figure 33. This excellent wood opal alive with POC is what was inside a limb removed from the montmorillonite clay opal level at the Northern Lights Mine. (Photo by Alan A. Vogel)

paederos A name given to a precious stone—almost surely opal—by the ancient poet Onomacritus, writing about 675 B.C., in his long poem concerning precious stones; paederos means "Cupid's gem," and probably referred to the rose opal (quinzite) of France, a common opal (usually) whose coloration was reminiscent of the rosy complexion of a little child; Oonomacritus could also, however, have been referring to rose quartz or pink chalcedony.

painted boulders See painted lady opal.

painted lady opal (1) A type of boulder opal exclusive to Andamooka that is composed of a thin layer of opal that occurs associated with hard sandstone, sometimes on the surface and sometimes coating a fracture line that may split readily; usually sold as specimens rather than jewelry opal; (2) tan-colored sandstone-quartzite boulders containing veins of precious opal and often painted with scenes that either utilize or attempt to enhance the opal.

palette opal An opal named after the pattern of POC it exhibits, in which the colors are so blotchy and so intense that they tend to resemble an artist's colors on his palette.

patronus furum A Middle Ages term for opal, meaning "protector of thieves," since it was carried as a talisman by pickpockets who believed that possessing it not only sharpened the owner's vision, but dulled that of others; thus, the thief could become all but invisible in a crowd and easily escape with whatever he stole; some have interpreted this to mean that opal could make its owner invisible if the stone was wrapped in a fresh bay leaf and carried in a pocket.

peacock's tail opal An opal that exhibits a POC pattern in which the colors spread across the stone in a relatively regular arrangement of scintillating greens and blues in "eyes" much like those that occur at the end of peacock's tail feathers.

pearl opal Alternative name for the vegetable opal called tabasheer.

perlite opal A variety of siliceous sinter [geyser opal] that is also called amatite or fiorite.

pebble opal A variety of rounded, pebbly-appearing nodules that occur in at least two locations in Virgin Valley, Nevada; though more uniformly round, these little nodules are similar in size to the nobbies of Lightning Ridge of New South Wales. As described by George Munzing, paleobotanist, who has studied Virgin Valley opalized wood for years, the so-called pebbles are actually "pseudomorphic opal replacements after wood—the cores of rounded pieces of wood opal that originally formed with an outer layer of white material which is nothing more nor less than oxidation"; that layer or shell was, he said, fairly thick in some, "but so fragile that, in digging them out of the bank, the rockhounds invariably lost the outer covering and all they recovered was the nicely rounded inside core, and these they called pebbles."

perlmutter opal The German term for a type of cachalong or hydrophane opal that, because its luster is similar to that of mother of pearl, is particularly desirable for the carving of cameos.

picture opal A precious opal whose POC creates a picture, sometimes in conjunction with inclusions, remindful of a particular object, as in the Chinese writing opal, or which suggests a familiar subject; those that suggest landscapes are usually termed scenic opal [q.v.].

pineapple opal Exclusive to the White Cliffs opal field in New South Wales, Australia, and always a very rare collector's item, the so-called "pineapple" is a cluster of opalized crystals that are pseudomorphic of the mineral ikaite; they are transparent to translucent opal, often with a pronounced lavender color, generally in the form of a small pineapple. [For greater details, see the section devoted to these formations in the chapter dealing with fossils and pseudomorphs.]

pinfire opal An opal named after the small pattern of POC it exhibits, which resembles intensely colored pinpoints of fire that are sparsely to densely scattered across the opal, some-

Color Plate 1.

The hallmark of precious opal lies in its amazing variability in play of color and shifting patterns, not only between stones from widely separated major opal fields of the world, but also among stones that may have been mined in the same opal field, sometimes even from the same mine. These 16 opals, all cut, polished, and photographed by the author, originated from four different locations. They are not meant to represent the highest quality opals available from these sites, but merely a small representation of the variance that occurs among opals everywhere in the world. All of these stones are in the author's collection unless otherwise noted.

These stones originated in Virgin Valley, Nevada. *Clockwise from top left*: A 16-mm × 11-mm free-form opal solid with translucent tan base color and red-green pinfire, this stone weighs 5.68 ct.; a 1.51-ct. black opal solid, cut in a 13-mm × 10-mm half-round free-form, exhibits red multicolor shortflash and pinfire play of color; a light opal with green base color, this 1.94-ct., 18-mm × 7-mm oval opal solid has a play of color that is brilliant red multicolor broadflash and pinfire; this nice black opal free-form doublet, 10 mm × 7 mm, with multicolor fire in a straw pattern, weighs 4.47 ct. (*continued on overleaf*).

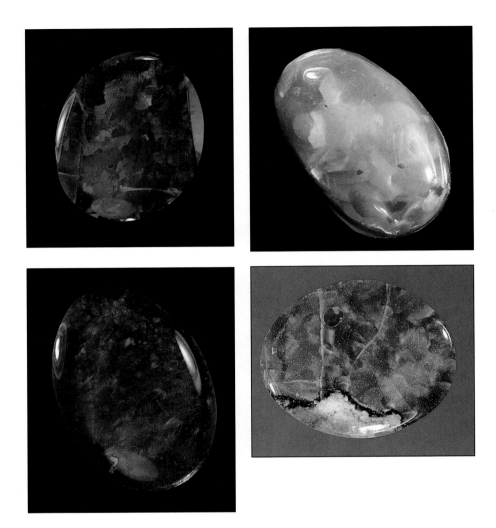

All four of these opal triplets were cut from opals originating at the Spencer Opal Mine, Spencer, Idaho. They are, *clockwise from upper left*: A 5.05-ct., 12-mm × 10-mm oval exhibiting red-orange-blue-green ripple and pinfire play of color on a gray base coloration; brilliant red-green-blue-orange shortflash play of color on a gray base highlights this 9-mm × 6-mm oval now owned by Sue Ann and Harold Early of Bellefontaine, Ohio; with green base color and combined red-green broadflash and pinfire, this 17-mm × 12-mm oval weighs 7.45 ct.; a scenic opal such as this one, which the author calls "Arctic Peak" and which is not uncommon at Spencer, is a 17-mm × 12-mm oval, with gray base color and red-green ribbon and pinfire pattern, and weighs 4.59 ct.

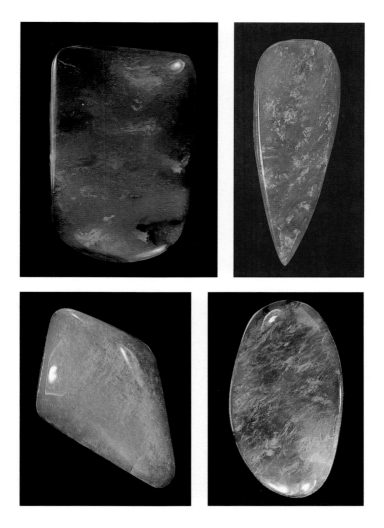

Opals mined at Coober Pedy, South Australia, range through a wide spectrum of color and pattern, as can be seen in these four specimens mined there, which are, *clockwise from upper left*: A 21-mm × 14-mm rectangular free-form opal solid with one end rounded, having a gray base color and red-green pinfire, weighs 6.5 ct. and is presently owned by Harold and Sue Ann Early of Bellefontaine, Ohio; this teardrop light opal solid weighing 3.24 ct. measures 25 mm × 10 mm and shows good multicolor pinfire play of color; with a pale blue-green base color, this diamond-shaped free-form opal doublet, measuring 18 mm × 11 mm and weighing 7.44 ct., exhibits a sparkling green pinfire play of color; a 15-mm × 8-mm oval jelly opal solid exhibiting blue-green pinfire, this stone weighs 1.83 ct.

Four opals from Lightning Ridge, New South Wales, Australia, these stones are, *clockwise from upper left*: a 9.92-ct. rounded triangular opal solid with base color of transparent gray, measures 18 mm × 12 mm and exhibits a strong rolling orange broadflash and green-blue pinfire; a 16-mm × 14-mm oval light opal solid weighing 6.23 ct. displays vivid multicolor pinfire play of color; a black opal doublet with attractive blue-green smudge and pinfire is a 12-mm × 8-mm oval weighing 5.22 ct. and presently owned by Virginia G. Lebo of Hamburg, New York; intense blue-green broadflash play of color highlights this black opal solid cut as a 24-mm × 12-mm oval, weighing 10.05 ct. and presently owned by Kelly Tanner of Hollywood, Florida.

Color Plate 2.

Part of the mystique of precious opal lies in the fact that the color and pattern change dramatically with the angle of the light striking the stone. As it is tilted or turned, these changes are breathtakingly apparent, as in these five different views of the same beautiful *Coocoran Flame* opal, mined in the autumn of 1995 at the New Coocoran opal field of Lightning Ridge, New South Wales. (Photos by Len Cram)

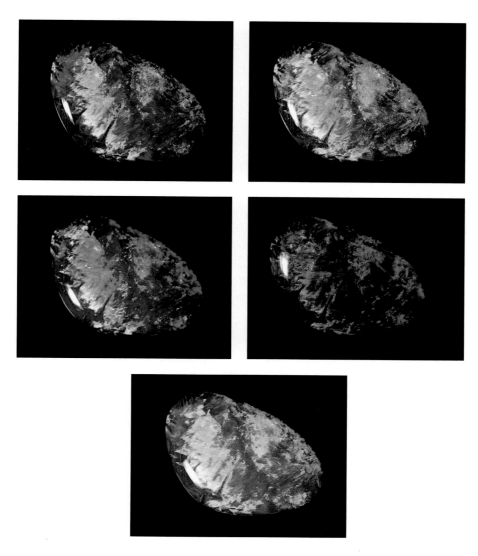

Color Plate 3.

This fine blue-black opal found by Kevin Lane Smith in 1992 at the Northern Lights Mine in Virgin Valley, Nevada, was cut by him into this 6-carat pendant. (Photo by Kevin Lane Smith)

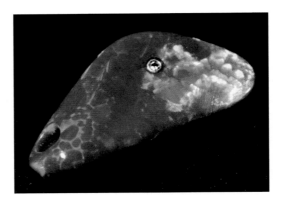

Color Plate 4.

An opalized fossil snail (gastropod) with all original parts of the shell replaced through pseudomorphism with precious opal. This specimen, in the Brian Shelton Collection in the Museum of Victoria's Department of Mineralogy and Petrology, measures 0.6" × 0.6" [15 mm × 15 mm]. It was discovered at Coober Pedy in South Australia. (Photo by F. Coffa, courtesy of Dr. William D. Birch, Museum of Victoria, Melbourne)

Color Plate 5.

Opalized Virgin Valley wood from the tailings of the Rainbow Ridge Opal mine. These specimens were collected, prepared, and identified, and some were polished by paleobotanist George Munzing of Brigham Young University, Provo, Utah. *Shown here from left to right and top to bottom*: (1) *Abies* at 250 ×; (2) *Abies* at 120 ×; (3) *Pinaceae* at 500 ×; (4) *Abies* at 120 ×; (5) *Sequoiadendron* brown wood at 250 ×. (Photos by George E. Munzing, Ph.D.)

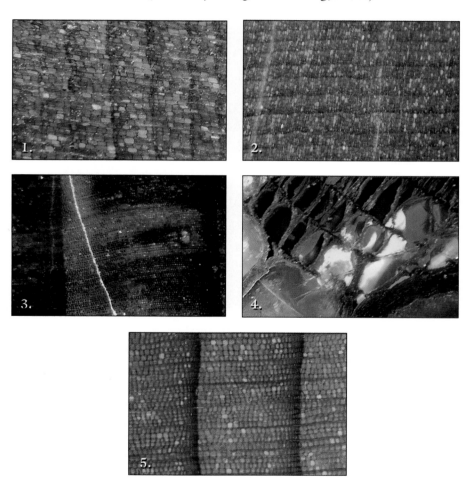

Color Plate 6.

Rainbow Ridge hydrophane opal, 0.47" × 0.35" [12 mm × 9 mm], and 2.74 carats, found, cut, and polished by the author: (a) translucent, with POC, when dry; (b) half-transparent, with POC, after soaking 15 minutes; (c) fully transparent, with POC, after soaking 30 minutes. (Photos by the author)

 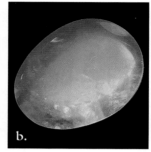 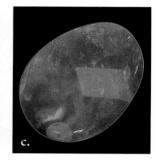

Color Plate 7.

The *Mariora Star* is the name of this outstanding 60-carat Queensland boulder opal cabochon, presently in the Mariora collection. (Photo courtesy of Mariora, Surfers Paradise, Queensland)

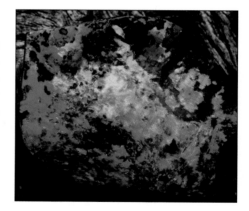

Color Plate 8.

Lightning Ridge solid black opal cabochon. This fine unnamed 11-carat stone with natural color separation line is owned by Peter Carroll Opal & Gems of Lightning Ridge and is valued at $10,000. (Photo by Len Cram)

Color Plate 9.

A trio of Spencer opal triplets cut by the author. (Photos by the author)

Color Plate 10.

The *Aurora Australis* opal. (Photo courtesy of Altmann & Cherny, Melbourne)

Color Plate 11.

The remarkable *Galaxy Opal* is considered by many to be one of the most spectacular boulder opals ever found. Melbourne photographer Robert Campbell took hundreds of photos of this stone and finally admitted that "none comes close to doing justice to the *Galaxy's* real life brilliance and vibrancy. It has to be seen to be believed!" (Photo courtesy of Dr. William D. Birch, Museum of Victoria, Melbourne)

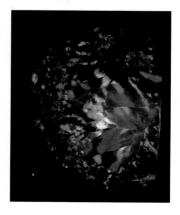

Color Plate 12.

The carved *Mexican Dragon Opal.*
(Photo by Kevin Lane Smith)

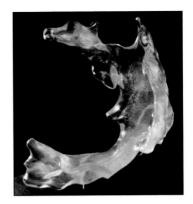

Color Plate 13.

This excellent black opal with green
line-fire POC is called *Green Rain*
and was found in 1990 at the
Rainbow Ridge Opal Mine, Virgin
Valley, Nevada. Carved into this
handsome pendant by Kevin Lane
Smith of Tucson, Arizona, it is $1\frac{1}{4}$"
[31.8 mm] long, $\frac{5}{8}$" [15.9 mm]
wide, and weighs 10.5 carats. (Photo
by Kevin Lane Smith)

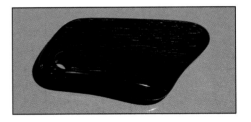

Color Plate 14.

A beautiful example of Queensland
boulder opal is this 42-carat polished
piece that is alive with a brilliant display of green and blue play of color.
(Photo courtesy of Mariora, Surfers
Paradise, Queensland)

Color Plate 15.

Conk opal from a limb section found
by Keith Hodson at his Rainbow
Ridge Opal Mine in Virgin Valley,
Nevada, and cut by him into this
polished free-form that is $\frac{5}{16}$" [2.5
mm] thick and $2\frac{7}{8}$" × 2" [73 mm ×
50.8 mm] across the face. It is valued at $2,180. (Photo by the
author)

Color Plate 16.

This lovely 92-carat contra luz pendant was cut from Opal Butte opal by Kevin Lane Smith in his Tucson, Arizona, workshop. Smith says that he finds contra luz opal is always a "very challenging" material with which to work. (Photo by Kevin Lane Smith)

Color Plate 17.

This exceptionally beautiful Opal Butte scenic opal carved by Kevin Lane Smith is called *Aquarium*. It utilizes matrix for both scenic inclusions and a natural well-polished pedestal. (Photo by Kevin Lane Smith)

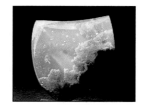

Color Plate 18.

A pair of interesting "scenic" Spencer opal triplets cut by the author: (1) 25.44-carat *Oriental Ocean*; (2) 10.38-carat unnamed stone. (Photos by the author)

Color Plate 19.

Queensland boulder opal is every bit as brilliant with POC as any other type of opal known, and it continues to grow in popularity worldwide. (Photo by Len Cram)

Color Plate 20.

Mixed triplets—from Spencer, Coober Pedy, and Lightning Ridge—cut by the author. (Photo by the author)

Color Plate 21.

Opals are used in fine jewelry in a variety of ways, sometimes to advantage with other precious stones. (a) A superb necklace fashioned with a beautiful black opal as a centerpiece, complemented by rubies and diamonds. (Courtesy of Gemological Institute of America); (b) This excellent pendant, designed and executed by Laurie M. Donovan, shows how the matrix material of Queensland boulder opal from Australia can be utilized to enhance the beauty of the stone. (Courtesy of Gemological Institute of America); (c) Fine craftsmanship is evident in this 14k yellow gold ring by Kabana, in which a trio of diamonds is enhanced by striking opal inlays. (Courtesy of Crescent Jewelers)

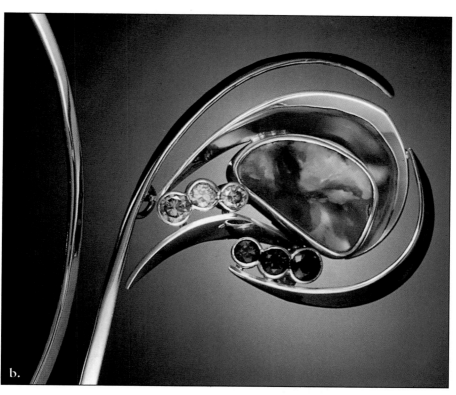

b.

c.

(d) In this Carolyn Typer Designs necklace, rendered by a Balinese craftsman, the beauty of this blue opal is nicely emphasized by the increasingly popular granulated gold from Bali. (Courtesy of Gemological Institute of America); (e) An exquisite butterfly brooch by Bulgari expertly ulilizes the intense colors provided by precious opal, ruby, diamond, and demantoid garnet set with 18k gold. (Courtesy of Gemological Institute of America) (All photos have been provided by the Gemological Institute of America.)

d.

e.

Color Plate 22.

This selection of opals exemplifies in a very small way, the tremendous variety of type, color, and pattern that appears in this remarkable gemstone, not only from different locations globally, but also among stones from the very same mine. (a) A magnificent example of black opal, this cabochon weighs 25 carats. (Photo by Robert Weldon); (b) A 0.76-carat chatoyant opal, also called cat's-eye opal, shows, as the stone is tilted or turned, a moving line of brilliant white against light brown, known as the milk-and-honey effect. (Photo by Robert Weldon); (c) The play of color in this contra luz opal cabochon is visible only in transmitted light (light from behind the stone) rather than with reflected light in front of the stone, as in the case of other opals. (Photo by Robert Weldon, courtesy of Richard Lua); (d) Some experts contend that the presence of copper may be the cause of the turquoise blue base color in these opal cabochons cut from material reportedly from Peru. (Courtesy of Gemological Institute of America)

(e) This bullet-shaped pink opal cabochon weighing 15.54 carats was cut from opal rough obtained in the Acari copper mining area near Arequipa, Peru. (Courtesy of Gemological Institute of America); (f) Some opals will even exhibit distinct chatoyancy, as in these Brazilian cat's-eye opal cabochons weighing 6.62 carats and 1.47 carats; (g) This high-domed, 16-mm-long, 4.87-carat cabochon displays the distinctive rosette-like markings that resemble a leopard's color, which is why it is called leopard opal. This specimen was mined in the state of Hidalgo, Mexico. (Photo by Maha DeMaggio); (h) A dozen cabochons from the GIA stone collection, cut from Mexican opals, gives an idea of color variances from just one location. (Courtesy of Gemological Institute of America) (All photos have been provided by the Gemological Institute of America.)

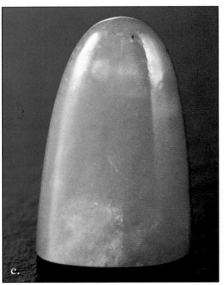

times fairly equally arranged and often differently colored, and that, as the stone is tilted or rotated, appear or disappear, glittering like tiny stars; generally the least valuable of the various patterns in precious opal, unless the points of the POC are all very small and close together and are mostly red, when, as such, it can be very valuable.

pink opal This is a lovely pink common opal that occurs in Tairua, New Zealand. [See also rose opal.]

pinpoint pattern Alternative name, used mainly in Australia, for the precious opal pattern exhibiting pinfire POC.

pipe opal Opal—much of it precious—that has formed into long (and, in cross section, slightly oval-shaped) cylinders in sandstone or volcanic clays, those holes, contrary to widespread belief, much more often horizontal than vertical; while large examples might be 6 feet long and as thick as a man's arm, the greater majority are less than half that length and usually little more than the thickness of a man's thumb; at the extremes, some of the so-called pipe opals will be as small as a sixteenth of an inch in diameter and no longer than a pencil, while the largest on record, according to Len Cram, was one that supposedly was 11 feet in length and as thick as a man's thigh. The origin of these pipes has been the subject of various theories that include steam vents through the soil, roots of trees that decayed away and left hollows that became opal-filled, prehistoric borings of snails, seaworms, or other sea creatures, and water drainage holes, but there is no evidence to support any of these claims. A certain cylindrically shaped fossil found occasionally at Lightning Ridge and White Cliffs is sometimes incorrectly termed pipe opal, when it is actually the opalized remains of the squidlike creature called a belemnite. Even though pipe opal is not noted for tapering as roots are inclined to do, some of them have been known to swell and thin or coalesce with others to form knotted masses.

pitch opal A variety of common opal that is similar to wax opal, but with somewhat more of a resemblance to pitch.

potch An Australian term, largely, signifying common opal, which may be almost any color, from black to pure white—but never, of course, with diffracted color, whichis play of color; when of a colored variety—usually a pastel color—potch is sometimes cut into cabochons or otherwise used in jewelry; the greens often are tinted from iron silicates, the blues from ferrous bisulfides, and the reds fromhematite; the pure white may be just as brittle and hard as fine china, and thedarker gray or black varieties, also quite hard, are often used as a backing for doublets or triplets; a clear amber form of potch has been found at Lightning Ridge; some potch may be entirely free from mud discolorations and almost transparentOcasionally the potch will be softer and so porous that it will, as cachalong does, adhere to the tip of the tongue; potch is sometimes called "snide" in Queensland.

potch-and-color Australian term for pieces of opal that are mostly potch, but have some areas exhibiting POC.

prase opal A dark green variety of common opal, usually translucent but sometimes opaque, which bears a resemblance to the prase variety of cryptocrystalline quartz; a particularly lovely green prase opal that has been colored by nickel is still mined at Silesia, Poland.

precious fire opal See girasol.

precious opal The highest quality gem-grade opal; in essence, opal in which the minute silica spheres of which it is formed are arranged and stacked in a precise latticelike formation, the placement and size of which, as well as the manner in which they and the voids associated with the spheres diffract the light, causing the stone to exhibit a scintillating, intensely colorful play-of-color in a wide variety of patterns and sizes; as the stone is turned or tilted, those colors and patterns appear and disappear or change dramatically from one pure color of the spectrum to another.

prime d'opal   Also called mother-of-opal; a precious opal filling the spaces in porous sandstone or ironstone grit, and showing bright specks of color. [See matrix opal.]

pyrophane   A type of precious opal in which the POC appears to wander about haphazardly and appear at random; also variously called heliotrope opal, waise opal, orphanus opal, and zeazite opal; the name pyrophane is also at times incorrectly applied to both girasol opal and hydrophane opal.

quartzite opal   An attractive looking quartzite stone that, with opal infused throughout, is closely akin to matrix opal and, while it can be cut, it normally does not take on a high polish, though it lends itself to carving and also for the cutting of spheres; value is determined by the amount of POC visible.

Queensland opal   An alternative terminology for boulder.

quetza-litzle-pyollili   A term used by the Aztecs to designate precious opal and meaning, literally, "stone that changes color with light."

quinzite opal   A very fine rose-colored opal peculiar to Quincy, France, and also known as rose opal, it is usually common opal, but on rare occasions precious opal specimens have been found.

radio opal   See radiolite opal.

radiolite opal   Smoky-colored opal in which the smokiness has been caused by organic inclusions and impurities, particularly radiolaria, which apparently suffused the opal gel before it hardened; also called radio opal.

rainbow opal   An opal named after the pattern of POC it exhibits, in which the colors align in curved bands alongside one another, much in the manner of a rainbow. [See also girasol opal.]

randannite   A diatomaceous opal similar to tripoli.

red flash opal   A type of precious opal exhibiting a POC pattern of sudden brilliant red flashes that just as swiftly disappear.

red-on-black opal   A type of densely black opal that exhibits a POC of nothing but brilliant red, making it extremely valuable.

red opal   A form of common opal, named after its color and useful in cabochon making due to its attractive translucency; indigenous to Arizona where it is found in weathered concretions in Santa Cruz County.

resin opal   A form of common opal that, because of its yellowish-brown to brownish-black resinous luster, looks very much like resin from pine trees and bears a slight resemblance to both wax opal and pitch opal (Figure 34).

ribbon opal   An opal named after its pattern of POC, which appears as a repeated, sometimes wavering, ribbonlike series of scintillations that move across the surface of the stone in parallel bands, those patterns manifesting themselves in almost any color; if associated with blue, however, the POC may be termed mackerel sky opal.

rolling blue dot opal   An opal named from its POC pattern in which highly iridescent blue spots seem to move across the face of the stone as the opal is tilted or rolled.

rolling flash opal   Also called rolling flashfire opal, this opal exhibits a relatively unusual POC pattern consisting of large flashing areas of color that appear to roll along with the movement of the stone as it is rotated.

rolling flashfire opal   See rolling flash opal.

rose opal   A type of opal also known as quinzite and named rose opal after the color of the body mass of the stone; it is known from Egypt, Idaho, and Quincy, France, where it occurs in a freshwater limestone matrix; a precious variety of rose opal is discovered on rare occasions,

Figure 34. Resin opal in matrix. (Photo by the author)

a magnificent specimen of which was in the famous Green Vaults in Dresden prior to World War II.

rough opal Uncut opal in the state in which it was originally found or mined; in the case of precious opal, it is opal of gem quality that shows play of color on surfaces or in fractures but that has not been cut, carved, worked, or polished in any way.

rubbed opals Also called rubs, these are rough opals, particularly nobbies, that have had all or a portion of the rough surface rubbed—i.e., ground down on a grinding wheel—to form a "window" of sorts into the stone's interior, to expose enough of the opal hidden beneath the rough exterior to give the prospective cutter an idea of the opal's extent and quality and how best to proceed with the cutting; virtually all Lightning Ridge nobbies that are not cut into gemstones in the field are sold as rubs.

rubs See rubbed opal.

rumanite A name once in vogue for opal mined in Rumania.

sandstone opal A partially opalized montmorillonite clay called sandstone, closely related to—and normally found only in the vicinity of—such sedimentary varieties as seam opal, nodular opal, and pipe opal; it is formed by replacement of the clay "sandstone" matrix, through impregnation of that ferruginous material, usually less than a foot above the opal seam; it is extremely hard and known by most of the miners as the "band" or the "steel band."

santillite opal A silicious sinter [geyser opal] that is similar to fiorite opal.

scenic opal Opal, usually with a water-clear base color transparency, in which certain inclusions from rhyolitic matrix or other material depict forms, landscapes, seascapes, and other scenes that are often very attractive; some scenic opal may also derive from an especially attractive network of crazing or cracking and, while these tend to create a pronounced instability in the stone insofar as cutting is concerned, if the cut can successfully be made, the result can be quite spectacular (Color Plate 17); certain opals from Opal Butte, Oregon, are especially noted for their remarkable scenic attributes; scenic opals may or may not display POC [see also picture opal]; Spencer opal from Idaho also frequently has a tendency toward scenics or pictures (Color Plate 18).

scintillation opal Opal named after its pattern of POC, which is an irregular but extremely brilliant display that tends toward very hot, shimmery patterns in reds and oranges.

sea opal A misleading term used to designate the brilliantly iridescent paua shell of New Zealand, which is frequently used in jewelry; paua (pronounced "power") is not, of course, opal in any form but rather an iridescent seashell.

seam opal (1) The most common type of opal formation in Australia, which is found at virtually all sedimentary opal fields throughout Australia; essentially, it is opal that occurs underground in a seam of varying thickness and length, that seam a thin (usually one inch or less), wide-spreading deposit running horizontally through another material, usually sandstone, clay, or altered volcanic ash; not all the opal that forms in seams becomes precious opal, and common opal frequently makes up a portion of the deposit; the extent of the precious opal may vary from a small placement to a rather extensive length; while the seam is usually horizontal or parallel to the surface, it may abruptly change direction and move straight up or straight down toward another level, in which case the opal is sometimes termed vertical opal; seam opal is the most common type of precious opal and its brightest POC occurs in planes vertical to the plane of the seam itself; thus the pieces of rough that are mined most often are flat segments of varying thickness; (2) a form of opal in Queensland that is found in thin ironstone seams or bands called casings, which are up to 5 cm (1.97") thick; these casings are found at the contact between sandstone and underlying fine-grained sediment, and in some places the upper surface of the seam has rounded, botryoidal protrusions up to about an inch across; both the seam and these protrusions commonly contain thin, horizontal veins and random flecks of brilliantly colored precious opal; opal dirt is commonly found immediately above the seam.

semi black opal A precious opal that has a base coloration lighter than a black opal but darker than a light opal; in some instances it is referred to as gray opal.

semicrystal opal An opal that exhibits enough translucency so as not to be as transparent as crystal opal, but that shows more transparency than a wholly translucent opal.

semi-opal Also called half-opal; these designations have been carelessly applied not only to common opal as a whole but to various types of common opal such as wax opal, resin opal, and other nonprecious types of opal, in most cases where the opal in question is found in matrix in conjunction with some other mineral.

siliceous sinter A form of opal without POC that manifests itself as encrustations and fibrous growths of a porous white to gray amorphous silica deposited in the throats and around the mouths of deep-seated hot springs and geysers, as well as on the basins and terraces created by those springs and geysers; synonymous with geyserite and geyser opal.

simulated opal Also called a simulant; synonymous with imitation opal; it has no connection with true opal whatsoever, common or precious, except that it may bear a certain visual similarity.

Slocum opal More commonly referred to as Slocum Stone, this is an imitation opal created by John Slocum of Rochester, Michigan.

snakeskin opal An opal, precious or common, that, due to its pattern or to a gridwork of crazings, takes on the scaly appearance of a snake's skin.

snakestone Alternative name for tabasheer [q.v.].

solid opal (1) A pure natural opal in one piece and without the presence of any other type of stone; (2) precious opal that has been formed into a cut piece that is solid opal; a piece of gem-quality opal that, apart from being cut and polished, has in no way been backed, capped, or otherwise treated.

speck opal Shortened form for white speck opal, meaning conk opal.

straw opal An opal that exhibits the relatively rare POC pattern in which the colors in the opal resemble straws that often overlap or overlie one another.

sun opal A flexible term that can signify honey opal, Mexican fire opal, or a type of amber common opal that occasionally shows flashing color.

sun stone A precious opal that exhibits its POC only in bright sunlight.

sunflash opal (1) An opal named after its POC pattern in which the colors flash with especial brilliance when the stone is rotated in direct sunlight; (2) a term used at Lightning Ridge to refer to a dark jelly opal, which, under strong light, seems to have its internal POC considerably intensified; (3) a term sometimes incorrectly used to refer to black opal.

synthetic opal An opal synthesized under controlled conditions, usually in a laboratory; not the same as imitation or simulated opal.

tabasheer opal This is the only known vegetable opal, sometimes called pearl opal, which forms only in the injured joints of a certain bamboo species occurring in Burma, South America, and India; the injury to the bamboo joint causes the plant to secrete a clear liquid containing silica, which, upon drying in small nodules, becomes translucent to opaque bluish, imparting a somewhat nacreous appearance, hence the alternative name of pearl; because of its high degree of porosity (so pronounced that it will stick firmly to the tongue until saturated), it has also become known as snakestone as a result of its use during the Middle Ages when applied to a snake bite to pull out the venom; it had a similar curative use in South America when applied to a wound to suck out arrow poison.

thunderegg opal Opal, both precious and common, that is found in the interior of the nodules commonly called thundereggs, prevalent in Oregon and other western locations.

thunderstone opal See ceraunium.

translucent opal Opal of any body color that allows light to pass through it, but is not transparent; in precious opal, translucency allows diffracted colors to be visible both on the surface of the stone and from within the stone.

transparent opal Opal of any body color that can be seen through clearly and, if precious opal, whose diffracted colors are visible through the stone from all sides.

treated opal Any opal whose appearance or structure has been altered or in any manner artificially enhanced by the introduction of chemicals, dyes, acids, or heat.

Trego opal A dendritic form of common opal that occurs in Trego County, Kansas. [See also moss opal.]

tripoli A fine powder manufactured from tripolite [q.v.], which is a diatomaceous earth and which, in refined state, is used in the polishing of metals and gemstones. see diatomaceous opal.

turtle opal See turtleflash opal.

turtleflash opal Also referred to as turtle opal; an opal whose pattern of POC seems unique to the Spencer Opal Mine in Idaho, one in which the POC is irregularly shaped in small pentagonal flakes that align themselves much like the scale pattern on a turtle's shell and impart a distinct domelike appearance.

twinkle opal an opal exhibiting a POC pattern that is similar to pinfire, but with the points of light somewhat larger and relatively evenly scattered throughout the stone.

vein opal Opal, precious or common, that occurs in veinings of any matrix material, but especially in thin veins in the sandstone above the seam or in the mudstone below.

vermilite opal A type of common opal characterized by a vermilion body color.

vertical opal A form of seam opal rather than pipe opal, since this is opal that originally filled seam fissures running horizontally but in which the lead changed direction to run vertically for a time, occasionally moving upward many feet from one opal level to another; this form of opal is often banded due to layering that occurred during deposition of the silica gel; also called vertical seam opal.

vertical seam opal See vertical opal.

Virgin Valley fire opal A misnomer for Virgin Valley precious opal, which should never be referred to as fire opal, since the term "fire" refers only to the POC locked within it; the true fire opal is a reddish, translucent opal that most often does not have the opalescent play of color and that is most commonly seen in the Mexican fire opal.

Virgin Valley opal Usually referring to the precious opal that is, in most cases, wood opal of volcanic origin that has formed in the layers of montmorillonite clay indigenous to the region.

vitzitziltecpatl Aztec name for opal, the word meaning hummingbird stone and so named after the iridescent brilliance of the hummingbird's plumage.

volcanic opal Opal that has formed in and lies embedded in rock of volcanic origin—igneous rocks—or in a matrix material, such as montmorillonite, that is of volcanic origin, such as pseudomorphs of wood in the clay; when the matrix material is basalt or rhyolite or other similar hard rock materials in which opal has formed as nodules in vugs or gas pockets, those opal nodules are then referred to as mountain opal or amygdaloidal opal; such opal ranging from water-clear to translucent, rarely opaque, and exhibiting a high degree of POC, but also notoriously unstable when exposed to light and when incipient pressure is released and moisture allowed to escape, any one of which (or all three in combination) engenders a particular vulnerability to cracking and crazing that is sometimes so pronounced that the stone will actually self-destruct.

waise opal A German name, meaning "waif" or "stray" that is applied to the opal called pyrophane [q.v.], because its POC seems to wander about loose and at random.

wasch opal Synonymous with floaters or alluvial opal.

water opal An alternative term for jelly opal.

wax opal A form of common opal referred to as semi-opal, which has a distinctively waxlike surface.

weltaug opal A German designation for hydrophane opal, the term meaning "eye of the world" or, more literally, "world's eye."

White Cliffs opal A generally light opal of high quality that was among the first deposits of precious opal mined in Australia, the quality and abundance of which was so superior to Hungarian opal that the European opal sources could not compete and ultimately failed.

white opal The lightest base color of a precious opal; in most cases synonymous with milk opal [q.v.], with a background (or base) coloration that is usually pure white but which can also be an off-white; this opal has a translucent to semitranslucent white body color, which differs from milk opal in that milk opal exhibits no POC, while white opal always exhibits some degree of POC, most often a display in strong light of deep green points of color scattered throughout the stone; such POC may become diminished with prolonged soaking but will return when the specimen is dried; white opal is the least valuable of all the precious grades of light opal. [See also milk opal.]

white speck opal Alternate name for conk.

wood opal Opal in which the structure and appearance of wood has been replaced with opal or in which the opal is closely aligned with, surrounded by or intermingled in fossil wood of varying degrees of hardness; such opal forms in the ash-origin clays, in the so-called opal dirt or in the mudstone underlying a seam; the opal may or may not exhibit POC, but if it does, it is correctly referred to as precious wood opal; commonly called opalized wood, wood opal is petrified wood with the structure of opal and easily identified by its vitreous luster on a fracture surface, as opposed to the more dull, waxy luster that occurs on ordinary petrified wood (cryptocrystalline quartz); when it clearly shows the woody structure, this opal is also called lithoxyl.

yellow opal An opal, precious or common, which may be transparent, translucent, or opaque, whose base color ranges anywhere from the faintest yellowish tint to the darkest yellow shade; most yellow opal is common opal, but that which occurs in transparent aspect is especially favored for faceting.

Yowah nuts Technically termed to be ironstone concretions that are small (usually walnut-sized), round to egg-shaped boulder opals, rarely as large as a lemon and bearing a superficial resemblance to nuts, these Yowah nut concretions are found massed in foot-thick clay seams only at Yowah, northwest of Eulo, Queensland, Australia; these deposits of concretions form what are termed nut bands, which are commonly associated with layers of mudstone (clay) clasts occurring in a ferruginous sandstone matrix called opal dirt; the mudstone clasts, which are actually clay pellets, have in some areas been replaced by iron oxides to some degree and this iron nut band usually is found in the lowest portion of the opal dirt level, which is itself likely to be located immediately above a contact between sandstone and underlying mudstone, or sometimes within that sandstone, and may have been deposited in what geologists term an intraformational breccia or conglomerate; some 7–10% of these little dark brown boulder opals, when opened, are found to contain kernels or swirls or lines of mainly transparent precious opal, some with amazingly beautiful POC, often between concentric layers on the underside of the nuts, or as a network of thin veins throughout the concretion; the ironstone matrix, which is not normally removed from the opal, is itself an attractive chestnut red to red-brown color, very hard, and polishes to a high gloss, providing a pleasing setting for the precious opal contained within it; Yowah nut opal has become more favored in recent years and its popularity is greatly on the upswing.

zeazite opal Another name for pyrophane, but also a term that has sometimes been mistakenly ascribed to girasol.

SEVEN

The World's Major Opal Fields

T he major opal producing areas in the world today are located in Australia (including New South Wales, Queensland, and South Australia), United States (including California, Idaho, Nevada, and Oregon), and Mexico (including Guerrero, Jalisco, and Querétaro.) This chapter provides a look at some of the more important specific areas, presenting them here alphabetically by name.

ANDAMOOKA, SOUTH AUSTRALIA

Andamooka, one of South Australia's major opal fields, is in located in the low mountains known as the Flinders Range some 155 miles [250 km] almost due north of Port Augustus, 373 miles [600 km] north and slightly west of Adelaide and 186 miles [300 km] southeast of Coober Pedy.

This unusual opal field remained unknown until a heavy rainstorm struck the area one day in mid-1930. A pair of young men who were on hand—Roy Shepherd and Sam Brooks—were employed to look after the sheep belonging to the nearby Andamooka Station homestead.[1] Seeing the waters rising in gullies nearby, they decided to head for the nearest high ground, which happened to be a short distance up the unnamed stream they were presently following—a stream that in the near future would be given the name Opal Creek.

Except for one feature, the hill they were ascending was little different from other low hills in the area. The single difference was that this one had, close to its summit, a tree growing all by itself. It was because of that tree that the knoll had long been known as One Tree Hill and the two young men decided they would camp beneath it until the waters receded.[2] They did so and it was as they rested that they picked up some of the smoothly rounded, purplish-colored sandstones common here—they called them gibbers—and made a game of rolling them at a larger rock they selected as a target. It was Sam Brooks' turn and he was just ready to bowl the gibber when he noticed the one he was holding had a vein running through it in which extremely brilliant colors of the spectrum glittered. They looked at it closely and, though neither had any idea what it might be, they figured it was worth more than mere passing interest and began looking for more. They found several others, including some that instead of the colorful veining, had a thin coating of whitish glassy material on the surface in which the same kind of colorful highlights twinkled.

When the waters finally receded and they finished their work, the young men headed back to the homestead, taking a number of the stones with them to show to their employer, the Andamooka Station manager, a Mr. Foulis. He studied the rocks closely and nodded, knowing what opal was and recognizing it in these rocks, which were obviously float from a source in that area. He also realized what a rush of miners would transpire once the word got out about the discovery and he was determined to prevent that from happening for as long as possible. After questioning Brooks and Shepherd closely about the exact location where they found the stones, he cautioned them to keep quiet it about it and set them off on another task elsewhere.

As soon as the pair were gone, Foulis got together with two more of the employees. Again, these were young men, but a pair he had known longer and whom he may have considered more reliable—his bookkeeper, Alan Treloar, and Treloar's good friend Paddy Evans—both of whom had previously had some experience in prospecting. He showed them the rocks, explained where they came from, outfitted them and sent them out to try to find the source, warning them to maintain secrecy. Foulis was careful himself about secrecy and each time he checked on the pair to see how things were going, he went by a different route so as not to establish a path that could be followed by others.

Treloar and Evans went directly to One Tree Hill and each pegged his claim. It was Paddy who first encountered opal, a piece of matrix speckled with opal bits, but he was unable to find a lead to the source. Soon, however, he found more small pieces of float and immediately sank a 6-foot shaft right there but found nothing further. It was left to Treloar, some days later, to hit the jackpot. Finding a piece of float he started to dig and had gone down only 18 inches when he ran into a good seam of opal. The hill was subsequently renamed Treloar's Hill and the site was named the Andamooka opal field.

Mr. Foulis was delighted and very soon had inaugurated some systematic mining, but mainly as spare-time work, since Andamooka Station had some 3000 sheep to tend as its primary business. Within a few months they had amassed a significant amount of opal with the promise of lots more to come. As Treloar put it, they "uncovered quite a lot of opal, but at that time the price was very poor and we practically gave it away for nothing!" In a few months the field was improved and producing. By the end of a year, however, the secret slipped out and a few miners began showing up before 1931 was ended, including at least one party who dug surreptitiously and, for the most part, unsuccessfully.

Over the next year Andamooka became established as a bona fide new opal field and other miners came until some 250 were on hand and digging. But

Andamooka did have its ups and downs. Production for 1933 was recorded at £1000, and by the end of 1935 it was £2000. Then, in the middle 1930s, the harshness of the worldwide depression hit here, the opal industry declined, and few people could afford the necessities, to say nothing of luxuries. After a decade of minimal production and another great World War in that period, a very strong increase in opal mining and sales began in 1946 and fed off itself, as major new finds stimulated even more mining. Since that time Andamooka has done quite well for itself as one of Australia's principal opal fields and one of the four most important in South Australia, along with Coober Pedy, Mintabie, and Lambina.

From the very beginning it was obvious that the primary opal found at Andamooka differed from that found at Coober Pedy. Though both were crystal opal, the Andamooka variety did not normally occur in seams as the Coober Pedy opal did. While some seams were encountered, far more often the opal was being found in rather misshapen flat lumps that the miners had quickly dubbed "blobs." These were not at all like the nobbies from Lightning Ridge, which were generally smaller and more definitively formed. The blobs, being larger, produced more opal per specimen than the Lightning Ridge nobbies, though not of such consistent high quality as the latter. But the Andamooka opals, reputedly because of the way they were formed, won an especially grand accolade—a well deserved reputation for never cracking after having been cut.

These formations so casually referred to as blobs are actually, geologically speaking, lenses—pancake-sized formations relatively thin near the edges, thickened and raised in the center on both sides—that consist of solid opal inside. The opals derived from them quickly became renowned for their beauty. The stones were similar to Coober Pedy's, in that they were light opal, but there was a significant difference. The Coober Pedy precious opals were characterized by an over-all whitish-with-red base coloration, whereas the Andamooka stones were whitish-with-green in base color and with beautiful crisp POC in blue, blue-green, orange, and red. More than any other combination in POC, the Andamooka stones are renown for their scintillating blue-green in a jelly base. Many of these are still found, as beautiful as ever, in some of the older pieces of opal jewelry. That some of these are truly fine gemstones was evidenced by the magnificent Andamooka Opal obtained by the South Australian government from the Australian Gem Trading Company as a gift for Queen Elizabeth II. The stone was cut into a superb 205.54-carat [1.45 oz] oval cabochon by John D. Altmann and, complemented by matching 8-carat earrings from the same piece of Andamooka opal rough, was presented to the Queen during her 1954 visit to Adelaide.

In addition to the blobs, there were more stones of the type that had first been found by Brooks and Shepherd—the smooth streambed type of quartzite boulders generally called river rocks. Such rocks, usually about the size of a man's fist, often had cracks in them. If the rocks were close enough to the opal level, the cracks would more often than not be filled with precious opal, exactly like those found by Shepherd and Brooks. Mixed in this area are boulders of quartzite the miners call river rock, because they are rounded and polished as if they had been smoothed in a streambed. Occasionally when these quartzite boulders are near the opal level they will have lines of opal filling their cracks or thinly coating the surface. Because there was no good way to extract the opal from these unusual boulders, some of the people drawn to Andamooka began collecting them and painting scenic pictures or portraits on them that incorporated the visible opal into the art, supposedly as a means of enhancing the stone's natural beauty. Though done initially as a hobby, the stones were, to the surprise of most, an item that sold well as souvenirs. They were soon being called "Painted Ladies" and the raw stones were eagerly sought. These painted ladies became an Andamooka tradition that spread, in time, to Coober Pedy.

That is not to say that all these unusual boulder opals were worthless for any other purpose. To the contrary, some were very valuable stones with veins or surface coatings large enough to fashion good solid opals from them. One of these, found at Andamooka in 1960, was carefully cut apart and the precious opal removed in pieces that ultimately sold for £1600. In recent years such boulders suitable for making painted ladies, with opal in the cracks, have become very scarce and the artisans now glue bits of opal onto the boulders before painting them, creating imitation painted ladies that are common at both Coober Pedy and Andamooka.

Finally, there was plenty of the opal mixed with matrix material that was soon being called opal matrix—an opaque material with scattered POC. Its base color was usually white or honey-beige, only rarely a natural grayish-black. Though hard enough to take a polish of sorts, it was also soft enough, because of its porosity, that the polish took on a sort of silky sheen. It was not extremely attractive material until someone thought of dying it black. A number of different processes were invented to create the black-dyed opal, but the most popular was, and remains today, a variation of the sugar-acid process that was first described by Pliny the Elder almost 2000 years ago. In that process, the stone was thoroughly dried, then soaked in a sugar solution. This is followed by boiling it in sulfuric acid, which blackened the sugar that has absorbed into the pores of the stone. The result was an enhanced material that, to the uninitiated, appeared to be similar to black opal. In fact, some was so convincing it was actually sold on occasion as black opal by the unscrupulous. Most often, though, it sold simply as what it was—black-dyed opal matrix. It, too, sold very well, perhaps because of the low prices set on it.

In addition to these various forms of opal found on a regular basis, a number of rather fine opalized fossil remains have been found on occasion at Andamooka, including an entire plesiosaur skeleton in pure red pseudomorphic opal of gem quality; a magnificent specimen that is still displayed in Adelaide. An almost identical intact specimen of plesiosaur, again a gem-quality opal pseudomorph, was sold to a Hong Kong buyer and eventually cut into cabochons for jewelry.

In most instances the material the miners were digging into at Andamooka was different from that of any other Australian opal field; a matrix of decidedly weathered Cretaceous Period sandy claystone that the miners call kopi. There is, at the base line at of the kopi, a distinct band containing pebbles, fist-sized smooth-surfaced rocks, and some boulders. The actual opal level is between this band and an underlying layer the miners call mud, but which is a grayish-brown claystone. It is in this level where most of the opal occurs as in-fillings in cavities and cracks, although there is no known means of detecting its presence before actually encountering it.

Also, in most cases the area immediately above the opal level is a peculiar little stratum of sand and sandy crystal that has been glued together by opal. The miners call it concrete and, though it is quite porous and decidedly light, it can be cut. It can also be dyed with a sugar-acid treatment that turns it black, from which bits of precious opal exhibit POC as if from black opal.

Among the many digs that were developed at Andamooka in those earlier years were the Blackboy, Boundary Riders, Brooks's (also called Treloar's), Buza, Christmas, Coster's Hill, Four Nations, German Gully, Gunn's Gully, Halfway, Hallion, Hard Hill, the Horse Paddock, Koska's, the Jubilee, Lunatic Hill (also called Grosser's), One Tree Hill (Treloar's Hill), Saddle, Stan's Hill, Stevens' Creek, Teatree Flat, Triangle, Warden Hill, White Dam, Willis's Ridge, Yahloo Extension, Yahloo South, and Yahloo West.[3] While Andamooka grew over the years and production increased, the town never became as large nor the diggings so extensive as at Coober Pedy. Yet, Andamooka had one asset that was lacking at Coober Pedy and other opal fields—it had an ample supply of water, as Opal Creek was a year around running stream, which, while not of great size, was of great dependability.

Andamooka vied with Coober Pedy for many years in opal production, but in 1976 hard times came. The Andamooka deposits seemed to be playing out, roads were closed because of bad weather, and food was not received in the quantity needed. One by one the miners and their families began drifting away. There was not much incentive for them to remain when they could make just as much money or more by working on the big sheep farms, by prospecting for and mining gold or wolfram or uranium, or by getting big-paying jobs, in far more comfortable and attractive conditions, at the 68-mile [110 km] distant government-operated Woomera Rocket Base.[4]

Nevertheless, a resurgence of interest in Andamooka was sparked by some rather spectacular new opal finds in the late 1980s and a respectable amount of mining has been going on there ever since. On several occasions open-cut mining has been tried, despite the fact that at $100 per hour when moving dirt, it can become a very expensive operation. Among the first of these were two bulldozer cuts begun in May 1992, by Willis Murray, better known locally as Murray the Miner, and his son, at the location called Stevens' Field, which is noted for top gem-quality red-and-green opals in blobs, as well as good matrix material, and where the opal level is located at a depth of only 18 feet [5.5 m]. The Murrays were among the few who made their operation pay.

In such open-cut mining, the object is for spotters to follow on foot in the cut the bulldozer is making, watching for the glint of opal, but it's a dangerous job. It is up to the spotter to watch out for the bulldozer to avoid being run over as it backs up or makes other maneuvers, since the driver is busy and cannot keep track of people on the ground around him. Some on-foot workers have been killed because they became too absorbed in watching for the opal and did not realize the heavy equipment had reversed direction and was bearing down on them.

Many of the open-cut mining projects have quickly run into difficulties, because one of the greater dangers of bulldozing at or near an established opal field lies in encountering a shaft or drive as overburden is removed. Doing so can mean considerable damage to the heavy equipment and possible injury to the operator. As a result, such open cuts have rarely proven to be very worthwhile and most have quickly been abandoned. However, if they are lucky and the 'dozer does uncover opal, then the machinery is stopped and every clump of mud and every bit of the so-called concrete must be checked for opal, since it is all too easy to miss valuable pieces if great care is not taken.

Far more commonly, the Andamooka precious opal is mined underground, as at Coober Pedy and Lightning Ridge, in drives tunneled off main shafts at depths of usually 70 to 100 feet. Because the ground at Andamooka is not so firm and strong as at Coober Pedy and other places, the tunnels are kept very narrow to help prevent collapse. For that reason and because of frequent encounters with large hard boulders, tunneling machines cannot be used effectively. In the underground mining, as soon as the smallest trace of opal is discovered, the immediate area is enlarged in search of a pocket of opals, ordinarily with some success. The areas that are so broadly opened are referred to as ballrooms, and it is not uncommon for such a ballroom to become a hub for drives that move out spokelike into adjoining areas.

Andamooka, with a fluctuating population of miners and their families that is rarely less than 600 and seldom exceeds 1000, has grown to be a town that can supply its miners and visitors with almost anything they require, but it is still a rough and raw mining community in many respects.[5] The town itself is little more than a collection of scattered houses and humpies that have been erected without plan or order along unnamed streets that are little more than paths and a main street that is the bed of Opal Creek. Yet, despite this primitive type of development, Andamooka Township at present boasts four motels, two hotels, a guest house, a trailer (caravan) area with camping facilities, a post office, a pharmacy (chemist), a restaurant, a few tiny opal shops and souvenir shops, a general store, and adequate medical services for common ailments and small injuries. In addition to various attractions and available field trips, there are areas open to visitors both for mining and fossicking and the finding of good specimens by novices is not at all uncommon. The mining laws in effect are the same as those presently observed at Coober Pedy and Mintabie. Bus service to the area is available on a regularly schedule basis from Adelaide via Port Augustus, Roxby Downs, and Woomera, and tourism has increased significantly since by far the greater portion of the dirt road leading there from Roxby Downs has now been paved.

BRAZIL

Surprisingly little seems to be known about Brazilian opal, considering its excellent stability, unusual hardness, generally large size, and interesting POC. What is known about it seems to derive largely from hearsay, so the data related here should not be accepted as incontrovertible. The opal appeared abundantly for a time in the early and mid-1970s and met with considerable favor worldwide, as it was said to rival in many respects the very best of Australian opal, not only in color but in the variety of patterning, some of which is quite distinctive. A few sources claim the color to be slightly more pastel than that in Australian opal and attribute the Brazilian stone with a Mohs scale hardness of 7, which is the same as quartz.

A beautifully translucent white-base opal, it has POC that is usually of the pinfire variety, but can vary to shortflash, longflash, and broadflash. While blue and lavender tend to predominate in the POC, there are also orange and green flashes and occasionally deep purple. Even in the base color there always seems to be a tinge of very palest lavender. The material has definite color bars separated by wider bands of the base color and so requires a judicious eye in cutting to take best advantage of those color bars. While much of the material is relatively large chunky pieces broken from more massive material, occasionally one encounters a solid nodule of the opal upward of 6–7″ in diameter, without trace of matrix or foreign matter. Such pieces lend themselves well to carving and the author has one such nodule that weighs over 4.5 pounds and will ultimately be used for that purpose.

In addition to this white-base opal, Brazil also produces a virtually optically transparent variety of so-called crystal opal rich with POC that seems to hang and twinkle starlike in the clarity of the material. It is sometimes compared to the crystal opal that occurs in Australia and in Oregon, though said to be more stable than either of those. This opal has an uncommonly low water content—

some contend about 3–4%—and is thus rather amazingly stable and can, as a rule, withstand abrupt changes in temperature, light, and humidity without showing any deleterious effects. Pieces of the material have been thrust directly into flame without turning milky or cracking; similarly it has been abruptly doused from room temperature into icewater without apparent damage.

It was in 1983 that again some excellent precious opal appeared on the world market that was touted as having originated in mines in the rather remote state of Piauí. The base coloration ranged from green to blue and the POC was quite rich and varied. One of the more important of these opal mines is the Pedro II Mine. Over 120 opals from this mine were studied and closely analyzed as to chemical content, thermal analysis, infrared spectroscopy, and X-ray diffraction analysis and how these related to the matrix material, which in some cases was sandstone, in others claystone, and, in still others, dolerites. Close attention was also paid to aluminum content, since aluminum appears to influence the order and packing structure of the silica spheres. Those opals from a sandstone matrix ranged in base color from a pale yellow to a dark yellow, had poor aluminum content and a reasonably well-ordered structure of silica spheres. Those occurring in claystone deposits were aluminum rich, their silica spheres more loosely packed, and the white base coloration had a decided blue iridescence. The doleritic opal, which was aluminum poor, was bright blue to dark blue in base coloration and exhibited violet and blue POC. All these varieties are said to be harder, tougher, and more stable than even Australian opal, but more difficult to orient for the most advantageous cutting.

Under tight governmental controls, little of the Piauí opal—also called *ceara*—has come onto the market in recent years, but why such stringent export restrictions were established seems to be anyone's guess. Other types of Brazilian opal seem to be suffering from the same rather incomprehensible governmental regulations that have all but stymied opal production and exportation efforts. In fact, it is rumored that most Brazilian opal still being mined today is surreptitiously sent to Australia, where it is allegedly cut and sold as Australian opal, but all that seems rather farfetched.

Officially, production of Brazilian opal is now down to almost nothing. There are many rumors about why this is the case—none of which even suggest that the opal resources have been exhausted. Perhaps one day we shall see more of this very interesting and beautiful material.

BRITISH COLUMBIA, CANADA

The first precious opal occurrence of any real significance in Canada was discovered as float on 14 October 1991, in a deposit just north of Vernon, British Columbia, overlooking the Okanagan Valley. That initial piece—a chunk of basalt bisected by a seam of scintillating green precious opal—was found by Carolyn Grywacheski, daughter of Tony Grywacheski, who had himself originally discovered common opal in the area some weeks earlier and, with his friend, Bob Yorke–Hardy, had explored the area, marked the corners, and registered claims.

The material found on the surface, considerably fractured from repeated freezings and thawings, was volcanic yellow-orange crystal opal exhibiting excellent red and green POC in a matrix of relatively soft, deteriorated, medium-gray basalt. Careful test diggings were made and two more deposits of gem-quality opal were found nearby. All three sites are now being actively mined under the name of Okanagan Opal, Inc., Bob Yorke–Hardy, president. The greater portion of the opal-bearing area in the near vicinity of Okanagan Opal is now well staked with claims.

The original site has been named the Discovery Pit. The first cut here removed a foot of overburden and, in a basalt stratum 3 feet thick, exposed several small precious opal seams and two relatively parallel, 30-foot-long seams of common opal in which precious opal was visible every few feet. These seams are much like those that appear in the boulder opal from Queensland, Australia, but the basalt here is considerably softer than the ironstone of the boulder opal. There were, as well, some small basaltic nodules containing precious opal and baseball-sized pieces of a dark brown common opal. Finally, there was also some mixed opal and matrix much like the opal matrix mined at Andamooka, South Australia, but the matrix here a bit softer than Andamooka's.

A high percentage of the opal near the surface is hydrophane—transparent and full of POC when damp and first removed from the ground, but gradually losing water content when exposed to air and turning opaque white, but with bright POC still evident. The opal encountered at greater depths is found to be mainly solid precious opal but not hydrophane.

While the greater portion of this Canadian precious opal exhibits brilliant red and green POC, there are also numerous occurrences of transparent nodules of yellow and orange faceting grade opal comparable to Mexican fire opal. Much of the opaque common opal—base colors, ranging from clear and blue-green to yellow, yellow-orange and deeper orange—has been found suitable for cutting into pleasing solid-color cabochons. Gem-grade precious opal is reported to comprise about 5% of the total opal mined in the three deposits and it is stated to be quite stable, with no reports of any significant cracking or crazing occurring in the years following cutting. Much of the frost-fractured material found on the surface is said to be excellent for the production of precious opal doublets and triplets.

The second deposit was named the Bluebird Pit, after a bluebird nest adjacent to it in a dead aspen tree, and the third site is called the Caramel Pit after the first opal found there, which was a richly caramel-colored common opal laced with black dendrites and rimmed with precious opal. The Caramel Pit at

Okanagan produces some clear transparent orange opal ideal for faceting and much like the fire opal from Mexico. Also, that pit is now producing clear blue and clear green faceting opal and crystal opal, with the same green and red POC as material found in the Bluebird Pit.

The Bluebird Pit area of the Okanagan Mines has been turned into a fee digging operation at $30 per day (Canadian) and is open to the public for 5 months each year, beginning in the middle of May. This is a generally rewarding location for those willing to subject themselves to the difficult work of hard-rock mining. Inquiries can be made to Okanagan Opal, Inc., in Vernon, British Columbia, at 604-542-5173.

COOBER PEDY, SOUTH AUSTRALIA

On Monday, 1 February 1915, a 14-year-old boy named Willie Hutchison discovered precious opals at a place in South Australia that was first called Stuart Range Opal Field, but which, just over 5 years later, was renamed and became what it is today—Coober Pedy, 466 miles [750 km] north by northwest of Adelaide.[6] Details of events leading up to the discovery and certain things that followed are found in Chapter 4.

Coober Pedy very quickly became one of the premiere opal sources in all of Australia and certainly the most productive, with the opal occurring in seams in the light mauve-colored, quite porous so-called sandstone—actually Cretaceous Period clay—which constitutes the horizontal opal level, a level often known to suddenly become vertical and plunge to some 80 feet below ground level. Not infrequently, a number of opal levels occur, one below another, but none of the levels are truly consistent throughout the field or even from one claim to the next.

Over the ensuing years following its discovery, Coober Pedy has become the foremost source in the world for the production of precious opal. The opals that come out of the ground here are generally of a light base color—often called white or milk opals—similar to the old Hungarian opals, but individually larger and with far more spectacular POC (Figure 35). As more than one visitor has exclaimed upon seeing what kind of opals are mined here, "They are *gorgeous!*"

Actually, not all Coober Pedy opal can be so categorized, since the opals found here include specimens in all grades, from very poor stones with almost no precious opal to very valuable stones with bright colors, but still usually retaining a generally white—or at least light—base coloration.

An opal also occurs here that has a light gray base color, which on occasion shades into a much darker gray and occasionally even into black, but this is quite rare. The area also produces a transparent opal, which, in lower-quality stones is referred to as jelly opal and in higher-quality stones is known as crystal opal.

Figure 35. A beautiful, colorful Coober Pedy triplet about 2.5″ long and shown to advantage with simple gold wire wrapping. Notice the color separation lines, which are sometimes mistaken for cracks by the uninitiated. This stone is presently in the collection of American miner Stan Bryn. (Photo by Alan A. Vogel)

Most of the Coober Pedy opal sold in the United States is light base material. And, as with other opal fields around the world, Coober Pedy produces its share of colorful transparent contra luz opal, which only shows that beautiful color when viewed with the stone held between the viewer and the source of light.

As soon as it became known that quality opals similar to but better than Hungarian opals were being found at the Stuart Range Opal Field, miners came flocking in from all over Australia. As had been done earlier at White Cliffs, many of these men and their families began living underground to escape the fierce 130°F summer heat of the area (which may cool down to only 100°F at night)—a style of living continued to this day, where the temperature remains constant at a pleasant 72°F all year around. At present quite a few of the old abandoned mines have been converted into comfortable, modern homes with virtually all the conveniences for good living (Figure 36).

Figure 36. Large, individually owned water cisterns are common place in Coober Pedy, serving both those who live above ground and those who live below. (Photo by Alan A. Vogel)

The opal level at Coober Pedy is not terribly deep—averaging about 15–20′ below the surface. Vertical shafts are sunk to the opal level and then areas cleared into spacious rooms where disassembled mining machinery can be brought down and assembled for underground use. This same process is followed in other opal fields throughout Australia—particularly at Andamooka, Mintabie, Lambina, and Lightning Ridge. Tunneling machines became especially useful, because they are able to bore at a wonderful pace horizontally while the operator watches and listens closely for the telltale gritty clink that signifies opals have been encountered (Figure 37). When that occurs, the machine is immediately shut off to avoid damaging the opals and the stones are carefully dug out by hand.

No other opal field anywhere developed so rapidly or resulted in the establishment of so many subsidiary opal fields and mines as Coober Pedy. Within two years the amazing Big Flat opal field had been discovered and was being exploited. Within five years the Coober Pedy field extended 25 miles—19 miles north and 6 miles south of the original opal discovery point found by Willie Hutchison. The Twenty Mile Field, discovered in 1921, was unbelievably rich and so was Geraghty Hill—also called the Eight Mile—which was discovered a quarter-century later and produced what many claimed to be the finest opal ever discovered at Coober Pedy. Such praise was justified, because even better things

Figure 37. One of the greatest labor-saving devices in Australian opal mining in recent years has been the hydraulic digging machine, which can dig out drives in opal levels with great facility and speed, as illustrated by the machine-gouged material falling here. But as soon as precious opal is encountered, the machine is stopped and the digging proceeds carefully by hand. The activity here, being observed by the author *(left)*, is occurring in the drive along the opal level in Mike's Mine at the Allah's Rush opal field on New Coocoran. (Photo by Len Cram)

were poised to come, on that portion of the Eight Mile field that would soon be renamed and forever after be called the Olympic field, famed for opals with excellent stability and beautiful red POC.

Among the multitude of subsidiary opal fields within the Coober Pedy field are those with such colorful names as Benito's Folly, Big Flat, Black Flag, Black Point, Crater, Crowder's Gully, Dead Man's Gully, Deadman's Dugout, Digger's Gully, Dingo, Dora Gully, East Pacific, Eight Mile, Emu, Flats, Four Mile, Fourteen Mile, Geraghty Hill, German Gully, Greek Gully, Haans Peak, Hopeful Hills, Jewelry Box, John Deere, Jungle, Larkin's Folly, Lennon, Old Four Mile, Olympic, Perfecto, Piping Lane, Pluto, Post Office Hill, Prospect, Russo's Folly, Saddle, Seventeen Mile, Shell Patch, South Pacific, Thirty-two Mile, Twelve Mile, Turkey Ridge, Two Mile, Twelve Mile, Twenty Mile, Venus, Vino, and Zorba.

Many unusual stories float about on these opal fields and among them is the one that says the Australian aboriginals, since as far back as the Dreamtime, have always been fearful of opals, assiduously avoiding them if they happened to see them glinting on the ground in the sunlight. Tradition says they considered opal to be a manifestation of the devil, who, in an alter form, was half human, half serpent, lived in a hole in the ground, and lured men in with flashing colored lights that were evil magic personified. That such stories have little or no basis in fact, seems to be borne out by the fact that the aboriginals were mining black opal at Mintabie and selling it at Lightning Ridge just after World War I, years before the whites even suspected Mintabie's existence; by the fact that the aboriginals are themselves miners at Andamooka; by the fact that one of Coober Pedy's greatest opal fields, the Eight Mile, was discovered in 1947 by an aboriginal woman who saw a white stone protruding from the ground there and pried it out with her spear, found it to be a spectacular opal, and wound up selling it to the renown buyer Ernest G. Sherman for £2000. Hardly evidence of the aboriginals fearing and avoiding opals.

Often "traditions" or "stories" involving the aboriginals and opal tend to surface *after* the fact. Coober Pedy is a case in point. There is nothing to suggest that the aboriginals had any knowledge of Coober Pedy or its opals prior to the field's discovery in 1915 by Willie Hutchison. Yet, about 1930 a supposed "ancient" story surfaced that was allegedly handed down by the aboriginals for many generations. It is the story of what happened during the "Dreamtime" in Australia when, supposedly, the goddess Kingfisher, who had a rainbow-colored body, traveled a great distance searching for a place to lay her eggs. Here and there she stopped and created a waterhole or a hill or a stream, but she always moved on until at last she found the ideal spot to lay her multicolored eggs. You guessed it: Kupa Piti—Coober Pedy—even though the field was not given that name until more than five years after the opal deposit was found.

The discovery of the Eight Mile field was to have far-reaching ramifications. It was just 6 years after that, in 1953, when a 27-year-old Adelaide man named Frank Titheradge arrived at Coober Pedy, little realizing that he would soon discover a solid opal that would be, for many years to come, the largest gem-quality opal in the world—the *Olympic Australis*. The odd thing was that he came here not as a miner but as a photographer assigned to shoot a 16-mm documentary film on unusual occupations—in this case about the men and women who lived and worked underground. When he finished, he sent the film in for processing but, since he now had to wait a couple of months for it to come back, he decided to try his hand at opal mining.

When I interviewed Titheradge 42 years later on 12 May 1995, he remembered the details as if it had all happened only yesterday. "I made out so well with the mining," he told me, "that I thought this was the thing to do and I never went back to filming after that and have been mining ever since. I'd been mining for about 3 years when I found the *Olympic Australis*. Nevertheless, I was still a fairly new chum to the fields. It was in 1956—on August 9, in fact, at 8:30 p.m. I had Bert Wilson as a partner. He was an oldtimer and I was the young buck who did all the hard work. I was about 30 then. We were working the far edge of the Eight Mile field and he pointed out the place to dig and so I dug. Actually, it was an old hole, about 4 feet deep, that someone had started and then abandoned a long time ago. I cleaned out the bush and bush snakes and began to dig and kept loading a four-gallon bucket, which Bert winched to the top and went through for traces. As luck would have it, we sank the shaft right on top of it. It took one week to reach the opal level at 28 feet deep and there it was. It was rather exciting, you know? And it did create quite a stir, but there were only a few other miners around in those days—probably only 10 to or 12 other digs being worked at the time, as compared to about 3000 now."

Titheradge shook his head and chuckled, remembering. "There were," he went on, "a number of opals that we hit all at once there, big ones: two 80-ounce stones, four 60-ounce stones, and four 40-ounce stones, plus a number of others. Altmann [the buyer, John Altmann] still has two of the stones from that lot—an 11-ounce stone and a 13-ounce stone. The big thing, though, was the *Olympic Australis*. When I gouged it out, it was about the size of a loaf of bread and covered with a crust of sandstone. I just couldn't believe it was all solid opal, so I broke off a few pieces of the crust to see if there was any good color underneath. Every place I broke it off showed this wonderful depth of color, but I still couldn't believe the whole thing could be entirely of such fine quality, so I used my pick and split the stone and there it was, free of potch or any imperfections and all perfect gem-quality solid opal clear through—a sort of milky rose color and just flashing brilliant pinfire with every color possible. Took it up top then and we measured it: 10½ inches long by 5½ inches wide and 5 inches thick. It weighed almost 10½ pounds! But there weren't any buyers on hand right then and I guess we just couldn't really comprehend the value of the piece. We actually used it as a doorstop for two weeks before Greg Sherman, Altmann's field agent, showed up on a buying trip. I won't say what he gave us for it, but we considered it a very fair price at the time. And it was Greg Sherman who named it the *Olympic Australis,* the first name in honor of the Olympic Games which were being held in Melbourne that year, and the second for the Aurora Australis—the southern polar lights—which is what the brilliant pinfire that occurs throughout the stone looks like."

The leading opal firm of Altmann & Cherney Pty. Ltd, of Melbourne is still the owner of that incredible stone. The actual carat weight of the *Olympic Australis* totaled out at 10.41 pounds—23,610 carats—and it was listed by the *Guinness Book of World Records* as the largest solid gem-quality opal ever discovered anywhere in the world and they estimated its value as $1.8 million. Its present value is $2.5 million. As for the hole at Eight Mile that produced this opal, Titheradge and Wilson continued digging there for a while. They got a few more stones in the months that followed, but nothing of any real consequence and the mine finally played out completely and they abandoned it before the close of 1956.

After holding the record for 33 years as the number one gem-quality precious opal in the world, the *Olympic Australis* was finally supplanted by another—this one also a Coober Pedy stone, found in that subfield of the Eight Mile that was being called the Jupiter opal field. Details of this stone's discovery may be found in the chapter dealing with famous and noteworthy opals.

The Coober Pedy opal field continues to be one of the great phenomena of the opal world. The records it continues to set place it in a special niche all its own, not only for the size and the abundance of the opals it produces but for the quality of them (Color Plate 1). Not very long ago at the Two Mile field, one miner was regularly bringing opal to the surface that was valued at $4000 per day. At the Seven Mile, a parcel valued at $100,000 was put together from two digs in just 3 weeks. Several of the mines have been producing superior stones that have been sold to buyers on the field for between $2500 and $5000 per *carat*. The Eight Mile field, in its prime, had shafts that went down 85 feet and a series of 20′-wide drives on three different levels—drives that produced over £1,000,000 worth of opal at a time when just £1 was equivalent to $5 in American money, which at that time was itself worth 10 times more than it is today; ergo, that £1,000,000 worth of opal then would be equivalent to about $50 million in today's market!

There have been a variety of disasters, financial and otherwise, on this great opal field over the years, but Coober Pedy has managed to overcome them. When the New Field area was discovered, a rush of miners converged there and many started finding the light orange-based stones with good fire, but the field quickly went out of favor when it was discovered that these new opals were very unstable, especially during and after cutting, and were suddenly giving Coober Pedy opals a bad reputation. By the end of 1988 the New Field was all but abandoned, and no opal miner of integrity cared to dig there. About a year later, in 1989, one of the worst disasters to strike Coober Pedy occurred when the normally arid area was struck with extremely heavy rains over a 3-week period—during which more than 3½ *years* worth of rain fell and caused numerous mines to be flooded and the collapse of quite a few. Practically all opal mining was brought to a standstill for many weeks and some of the mines did not get back into operation for half a year or more. Yet, when full-scale mining resumed, production was even better than it had been before. Therefore, it came as a deep shock to the Coober Pedy miners when the Mintabie opal field, 168 miles [270 km] to the northwest, surpassed theirs in opal production beginning in 1986.

Coober Pedy, it seems, has always been beset by problems, small and large. Some of the small problems include annoyances that may range from a lack of water or severe dust conditions whenever the wind blows to infestations of flies that virtually coat a miner as they search for moisture on his skin.

Along with the distressing occurrences, major or minor, some good things were happening, too. The Haans Peak opal field was discovered in 1988 and created quite a rush, until it was found that the thousands of ounces of opal being brought out were primarily middle- to low-grade material with orange-green POC on a white base. Most of the newcomers here left but a few persisted with the digging and were rewarded 2 years later when the orange-green material abruptly turned into excellent gem-quality crystal opal better than any other seen at Coober Pedy in a number of years.

Today Coober Pedy remains a very lively community of more than 6000 people who originate from all over the globe—the United States, Greece, Korea, Germany, France, Hungary Sweden, Japan, Russia, China, Italy, Turkey, Canada. . . . Many consider it to be the ultimate: an opal field larger than any other in the world, with mines as far away as 25 miles [40 km] from the center of town; an opal field that supplies the world with 80% of the light precious opal it desires; the most consistent opal-producing field in South Australia, or perhaps the world; an opal field supporting a flexible number of miners—depending on what kind of discoveries have been made lately—from as few as 200 to as many as 3000. The town itself caters to tourists and provides good services: cafes, restaurants, supermarket, general stores, opal shops, motels, backpacker hostels, resident doctors and nurses, ambulance services, rescue operations, and the like. For uncommonly serious illness or injury, the Flying Doctor from Ceduna, 400 miles distant, will fly in as soon as notified by radio-telephone.

Visitors wishing to prospect for opals can do so by obtaining a Precious Stone Prospecting Permit from the mine office on the field, which allows the permit holder to prospect and peg claims anywhere within the boundaries of the mineral field where the ground is not already claimed. However, neither machinery nor explosives may be used until the claim is officially registered. If, on the other hand, the visitor only wants to poke around recreationally among the mullock heaps (Figure 38), looking for opals that may have been overlooked, the South Australia mining laws do not apply to that pursuit, which is called fossicking, so long as the stones collected are for personal use only. The visitor should, of course, get permission from miners of the area before engaging in fossicking on their mullock heaps.[7]

HONDURAS

There is quite possibly no greater untapped source of precious opal in western hemisphere—perhaps even the world—than the deposits that lie in the moun-

Figure 38. Thousands of mullock heaps dotting the ground surface at Coober Pedy at the Olympic opal field give mute testimony to the incredible network of tunneling existing far below and the countless superb gemstones that have been found in them. (Photo by Alan A. Vogel)

tainous regions of Central America and the core of all this seems to be in western Honduras. Although numerous opal mines exist in the Honduran highlands, even though opal-bearing outcrops occur in considerable numbers, very few are seen in the entire stretch of largely geologically unexplored mountainous territory that forms a rugged rocky spine running from the Mexican border south to Colombia and connecting the Rocky Mountains to the Andes, its only break occuring in the Canal Zone of Panama. Even in Honduras, despite the fact that producing opal mines have existed here for probably no less than 500 years, mining occurs in a very haphazard manner, largerly with hand tools rather than modern mining equipment and considerable quantities of excellent material are ruined through simple ignorance and carelessness.

There are opal resources of considerable variety and value in Honduras and other Central American countries but the great problem with tapping them is, of course, the general inaccessibility of the areas where the deposits occur. There are few, if any, roads in most areas and the mountainous terrain, cloaked with rainforest jungle, makes passage very difficult, even on foot, much less on horseback or in vehicles. Obviously, lines of communication are limited in the extreme. Therefore, a minimum of prospecting, location work, and mine development has been done. As a result, the mining that is being accomplished today differs very little in scope, methods, and productivity from that which existed a century or more ago.

The opal of Honduras is volcanic in origin, a good portion of it found in the two ranges called Sierra Opalaca and Sierra de Celaque and occurring in vugs, fissures, and cavities of igneous rocks, in the alternating strata of andesite tuff, red vitreous trachyte, and occasional altered porphyry, as well as lava flows of both basalt and rhyolite—all these outcropping from elevations as low as 3000 feet to as high as 6000. Precious opal has been found to the north as far as a few miles south of the Guatemalan border, just north of Santa Rosa in the sate of Copán, to the slopes overlooking that arm of the Pacific Ocean called the Gulf of Fonseca.[8] While precious opals are mined in the vicinity of the towns of Gracios à Dios, Las Piedras, Goascoranand, Le Pasale, Yukasapa, La Esperanza, and Intibucat, the finest opals and richest deposits are in the center of that stretch, in the appropriately named Cordillera Opala—the Chain of Opal Mountains—that runs through the state of Intibucá, and most specifically in the area of the village of Erandique.[9]

The mines that occur in this region have been producing for a very long time and it has now been proven that for at least two or three centuries prior to the discovery of opals in Australia, the Honduran opals were the only opals actively competing with the so-called Hungarian opals on the world market.[10] In fact, they had been a part of the competition in that market—if not in numbers, certainly in quality—since the conquest of Mexico by Cortes, and with good reason: There was much similarity between the stones except in the matter of value, since Hungarian opals were always automatically priced much higher than those from Honduras. Little wonder, then, that many Honduran opals were sold in Europe as Hungarian opals.[11] Oddly enough, although there has been ample opal jewelry found in Aztec burial sites, the colorful gemstone is absent from the burial deposits of the Mayas, which are often rich with jewelry and carved ornaments of obsidian, turquoise, and jade.

The opals of Honduras are often extremely beautiful, ranking with some of the finest in the world, and some are of impressive size. One grand specimen weighing over a pound was cut into a large number of very fine smaller gemstones, some of which may still be viewed in the A. C. Hamlin Collection in the Harvard University Mineralogical Museum.

The precious opal that occurs in Honduras comes in a variety of forms: thick seams in one area, thin veins in another, fist-sized nodules here to huge lumps there to amygdules elsewhere. There are even exceptionally good occurrences of matrix opal, with the bits of opal peppered through black basalt as if they are colored stars in a dark galaxy, its greatest problem being the softness of the basalt, making it difficult to get a high polish on a specimen. The best of this black matrix material occurs just beyond the town limits of Erandique, at the Tablon Mine. In the same formation that produces the black matrix, occasionally will be found a delicate, fragile, easily cracked, but especially beautiful wandering vein opal. Usually it is too thin to use as anything more than triplets or, occasionally, doublets. Once in a great while the veins become thick enough that individual opals can be cut as solids, in which the POC is as vividly beautiful as any opals anywhere, and it was in describing these that mineralogist Henry E. Lindhe once wrote: "If ever a rainbow was captured by a gem, that gem would be the Honduras precious opal."

Each of the many Honduran forms of gem opal takes on its own particular character. There is, in some of the basalt, an unusual vein opal with a base color best described as milky-black and another vein opal occurring in red trachyte that is pearly gray-white with red POC. And in some areas, well scattered over the ground surface, there is an abundance of wood opal of a character similar to some of the material from Virgin Valley.

In the San Antonio Mountain area near Erandique, there is an occurrence of beautiful colorless transparent opals that are alive with flashes and ribbons and dots of POC. Sadly, it is material almost impossible to cut as a solid stone; less than 1% will survive such cutting without crazing. Even when used for doublets or triplets, crazing will still occur. They are, however, said to last "for a long while" when stored in water as specimen opal.

Near Las Colinas the precious opal occurs in seams varying in thickness and occasionally expanding in large masses that can yield several pounds of very colorful gem quality material that is surprisingly stable.

While much of the Honduran opal occurs in vugs within volcanic rocks, some very lovely water-clear vein opal rich in POC occurs threading through the basalt or rhyolite. This material, especially in the dark brown to dark gray to black basalt, cuts into beautiful gemstones much in character like the Australian boulder opals of Queensland and, in vividness of color, quite similar to the black opals of Lightning Ridge. Technically, it must be classed as a boulder opal, not a black opal.

There is black opal, however, in two varieties, each of which can compare with the best black opal found anywhere in the world. One is the solid black, brilliantly fire-filled opal that occurs in seams and large amygdules of the volcanic rock; the other, similarly brilliant, occurs in cavities in the andescite and it is said when a number of these filled cavities are close together, the piece becomes a decided collector's item.

Another opal, called black opal by the residents, but not truly so, is an uncommonly lovely stone that occurs as a small vein—usually only an eighth of an inch thick at maximum—that has a base color of transparent to milk white translucent. It is found in blocks of weathered-out basalt at the base of cliffs and it is very tough material. The POC in the opal is multicolored broadflash and shortflash, and very brilliant, the color appearing in quarter-inch-wide bands in some areas, but spread out fairly evenly in others. It is very desirable material and, because of the difficulty of freeing it from the matrix, priced very high.

The milky-black opal mentioned earlier is found in an adjacent cliff to the one above, also in blocks of weathered-out basalt. But unlike the clear or white opal of the above material, it is black with a slightly grayish cast and the POC occurs in very broad, amazingly brilliant bands. It is a breathtaking type of opal.

The white opal occurring in the Erandique area is found in the cliffs in veins that vary rather widely in thickness. Much of this material, which has excellent multicolor POC and bears a resemblance to Brazilian opal, can be picked up as float at the base of the occurrence cliffs and in creek beds. Normally such pieces will have matrix on one side.

San Antonio area mines are most productive of a very light-colored precious fire opal that most resembles the Mexican variety. It has a transparent to translucent pale yellow base color and exhibits very fine POC in pinfire, shortflash, broadflash, or combinations of these. Other opals of this type occur at a number of locations throughout the country, with one of the most important sites close to the capital city of Tegucigalpa. The stones here, mainly found loose on the ground surface, have a colorless transparent center which turns to transparent citrine yellow and, finally, near the outside edges to a transparent light brownish-orange. The majority is used for faceting purposes.

In his book, *Gems and Precious Stones of North America,* George Frederick Kunz mentioned another type of Honduras opal.[12] He wrote:

Another remarkable deposit of opal was found by Mr. Wright about five miles east of Villa San Antonio in the plains of Comayagua, which though not of high value, may be used for ornamental purposes, being of fine red color with transparent amethystine bands. It occurs in veins of gray porphyry, sometimes several inches in thickness, and may be procured in large quantities.

Contra luz opals, generally in large pieces and showing color by transmitted light rather than reflected light, are also found in substantial numbers in the various Honduras digs, where they are referred to as Iris opal. These stones are always in demand for faceting.

The amygdaloidal gem-quality opal occurs primarily in a pinkish rhyolite matrix, solidly filling vugs that may be as small as a pinhead to as large as a golf ball, but most often about 20 mm—roughly 3/4-inch—in diameter. They are very beautiful stones that may be water-clear jelly opal in one vug and milk-white in the vug beside it and crystal blue-green in another vug an inch or so away—all of it next to impossible to remove from the rhyolite matrix without rather severe damage to the opal.

There is also a very white to nearly transparent seam opal, uncommonly rich in a sort of confetti POC, that normally occurs in brown rhyolitic matrix.

While in most cases it is too thin to cut into solid stones, it does make exceptionally beautiful and very flashy doublets and triplets.

Even more importantly, much of the Honduran opal occurs in nodules, which, even to inclusions and matrix intrusions, are uncommonly similar to the so-called thunderegg opal nodules that originate in the perlite opal beds of Opal Butte in Morrow County, Oregon. Interestingly enough, the Oregon nodules also occur in perlite beds. The principal difference seems to be one of size, since the Oregon thundereggs seem to run a little larger on the average than the Honduras nodules, which, at the Azacualpa diggings, well above the Rio San Jose Lepasite, average about 1½ to 2 inches in diameter. While these are not the most valuable opals in Honduras, they are the most frequently mined because of the ease of doing so with rudimentary tools. Inside the rough dark skin of the Honduras nodules, especially those recovered at Las Colinas Mine, the transparent precious opal ranges from water-clear to a bright sky blue and may or may not exhibit POC. Occasionally this POC will show the very valuable harlequin pattern. The Indian worker normally digs with his machette and when he encounters a nodule, he lops off a piece with the same blade and if no POC is seen inside, the nodule is thrown away. Much beautiful opal still remains in many of the discarded pieces. Also, even if there is quality opal inside, it is often fractured by the machette blow. Gemstones cut from the nodules are said to be rather strongly prone to crazing within days or weeks of the cutting.

There are also many different varieties of common opal all throughout mountainous Honduras.

LIGHTNING RIDGE, NEW SOUTH WALES

Lightning Ridge has become synonymous not only with the extraordinarily beautiful black opals, but equally with some of the most valuable gemstones being produced in the world today and, reasonably enough, some of the most famous opals ever found throughout recorded history. The town itself, named after the extensive low ridge on which it is situated, has become virtually a focal point for the world opal industry. Other opal fields, such as Coober Pedy and Mintabie may produce more opal, and others may also produce *some* black opal—Mintabie, Lambina, Virgin Valley, Erandique—but none produce black opal so consistently, of such overall fine quality, of such reliable stability, and of such remarkable value as Lightning Ridge. Lightning Ridge black opals have become virtually synonymous with high-quality jewelry. Some of the finer of such black opals are officially recorded as having been sold for over $10,000 per carat—which approached the per-carat value of a top-grade diamond at that time.[13]

The name Lightning Ridge stems from a tragic incident that occurred about 1870, some 5 miles due south of where the town of Lightning Ridge would one day be situated in northcentral New South Wales 30 miles south of the Queensland border (Figure 39). In that early year, when the area was called Wallangulla, a shepherd herding a flock of over 600 sheep paused for the night on a high point of ground of the ridge he was following.[14] During the night a severe storm came up and at its onset a great bolt of lightning struck, killing the shepherd, his dogs and, because they were so tightly massed together as they slept, the entire flock of sheep.

From that time forward the ridge has been known as Lightning Ridge—a name officially adopted both for the ridge and the town on 5 September 1963. The Ridge, as most of the residents now refer to it, may be low, but it is very extensive. Most of it was initially owned in a few vast parcels by absentee owners or companies in Sydney or Brisbane or other more civilized places, who hired managers to run these huge cattle stations as they were called—comparable to the great western ranches in the United States. Lightning Ridge itself rises in a gradual slope to some 50 feet or more above the surrounding broad plains and, formed in a somewhat vaguely crescentic shape, runs from—using today's landmarks—just above the area of Billygoat Hill and Mehi and Angledool in the north, southward through the town of Lightning Ridge and the New Coocoran field to the Grawin, Glengarry and Sheepyard fields in the south; roughly 70 miles north to south and to as much as 20 miles east to west.[15]

Since much of the history of the discovery of opals and subsequent events

Figure 39. The spot that gave Lightning Ridge its name. Here in the late 1870s, a shepherd, his sheepdogs, and 600 sheep were killed by a tremendous bolt of lightning during a severe storm. This site is on the east side of Route 55 exactly 2 km south of the intersection with the road to the present town of Lightning Ridge. (Photo by the author)

at Lightning Ridge has already been covered in Chapter 4, that event will only be touched on briefly here. Suffice to say that the majority of the numerous stories of how black opal was first found here are incorrect. That includes the two most prevalent tales: (1) that the children of boundary rider Jack Murray initially found the stones and played with them as if they were marbles, and (2) that it was Charlie Nettleton who discovered the Lightning Ridge black opals. Jack Murray himself, as indicated in Chapter 4, discovered the opals as float on the ground surface while setting a rabbit trap. Familiar only with the light opals of White Cliffs, he was intrigued by the beauty of these black opals, which exhibited such brilliant POC in a dark gray base color on top of black potch. Sensing that something so beautiful had to have great value, he spent his off-time from work during the first year or even longer simply searching the ground for all the little opal nodules, which he called nobbies. He found the majority of these in the area where he finally dug his first shaft for the mine he named the Nobby, after the shape of the opal (Figure 40).

After having refused to sell the first parcel of black opals to the Sydney dealer who made such an insultingly low offer and then finally selling them for a better price, though still rather low, to Ted Murphy at White Cliffs, Nettleton

Figure 40. Warning sign such as the one on the left, alerting people to the presence of both active and inactive opal mines, and the one on the right, warning motorists about kangaroos crossing the road, are abundant in the Lightning Ridge opal fields. The rusting hulk of a truck cab straddles an inactive shaft to prevent anyone from accidentally falling into it. (Photo by the author)

reported to the Lightning Ridge syndicate of station managers, who were very upset at not reaping huge profits immediately. They immediately ordered all the miners off the land. The miners refused to go and a war of sorts broke out that lasted for years. The managers did everything they could, short of murder, to drive the miners out. Included among their various "inducements" was shooting horses and mules belonging to the miners, fencing some of the waterholes desperately needed by the miners and their animals, and, at the waterholes that were unfenced, posting signs of warning that the waterholes had been poisoned in an effort to eliminate rabbits. The long, intensely bitter struggle was finally decided in favor of the miners in 1906 by the New South Wales Minister of Mines.

While Charlie Nettleton did not discover black opals at Lightning Ridge, as some stories have it, he *did*, a few years later discover another opal deposit, quite rich, about 3 miles south. A mad rush of miners to the vicinity followed and the entire area surrounding his claim was quickly pegged. The field was named the Three Mile and it produced many excellent stones. Soon the miners were spreading out even more and establishing new, quite productive mines with a variety of colorful names, including, eventually, such major diggings as Airport Rush, Angledool, Bald Hill, Beckett's, Berlin Rush, Bill the Boer, Billy-goat, Black Knobby, Bullockies, Bullock's Head, Butterfly, Canada's, Canfell's Hill, Carter's Rush, Chum, Con's Rush, Coocoran, Darby's, Deep Belars, Deep Four Mile, Foley's Six Mile, Four Mile, Four Mile Flat, Frog Hollow, Frying Pan, Glengarry, Grawin, Gully, Hawk's Nest, Hearts and Spices, Holden's, Hornet's Rush, Indian's Lookout, Iron Bark, Kingfisher, McDonald's Six Mile, McNamara's, Millionaire's Gully, Nebea Hill, New Chum, New Coocoran, (Figure 41), New Nobby, New Year's Rush, Nine Mile, Old Chum, Old Nobby, Old Town, Palestine, Phil Herbert's Rush, Phone Line, Pony Fence, Potch Point, Pott's Point, Poverty Point, Pumpkin Flat, Rosso's, Seven Mile, Shallow Belars, Shearer's Rush, Sheepyard, Sim's Hill, Snowy Brown's, Ten Mile, Thorley's Six Mile, Three Mile Flat, Walsh's, and numerous others.

Despite occasional periods of stasis occurring over the years, Lightning Ridge continued a steady growth that went into a great upsurge beginning in the early 1970s and even increased beyond that as newer and better mining techniques and equipment were introduced in the late 1970s and early 1980s. Quite dramatic changes have occurred since then, with most of the town's streets becoming paved, better services of all kinds made available, soaring opal prices, and greatly increased mining and production that has risen to an annual figure in the many millions of dollars.

That such powerful events should all have been occasioned by the discovery of a black stone with bright colors predicates a closer look at such a stone. As noted, when first attempts were made to sell black opals, they were so foreign to the buyers that most wanted nothing to do with them and many even

Figure 41. Even with a guidepost like this, the author found it difficult to locate particular opal fields at the Coocoran—and almost impossible, without a guide, to locate specific mines. (Photo by Len Cram)

thought they were regular opals that had been dyed to look different. That first prospective buyer in Sydney thought they were young opals that hadn't ripened. Through the efforts of men such as Nettleton, Murphy, Wollaston, Sherman, Cram, and others, the glory of the black opal became generally known and this stone now easily occupies the highest pedestal in opaldom on a worldwide scale.[16]

The standards established by the Lightning Ridge Miners' Association (LRMA) require that in order to be a true black opal, the stone must have a base color that is no lighter than slate gray and that may be any tone darker, ranging down through dark gray and dark charcoal to jet black. It *must* show a dense black background when viewed from the top of the stone. Thus, even though it might look white, or beige or differently colored from the back side, so long as it looks densely black from the top, it meets the criterion for a black opal. The stone absolutely may not have an artificial dark or black backing of any kind, as in a doublet or triplet, nor can it be a dyed stone or a stone made to look dark by any other artificial means.[17] The very best black opal is one that gives a hint of deep navy to midnight blue on the dense black and with the pattern(s) and color(s) forming above this. Technically speaking, black opal is an opal in which the POC shows in brilliant pure spectral colors against a body color that can be dark blue, dark gray, or dark brown, but which is ideally black.

According to the LRMA standards, which are a bit more stringently specific, there are only three classes of black opal: the deepest, darkest pure black is rated as a Black #1; the dark gray base color black is rated as a Black #2; if the base color is slate gray, the stone is rated as a Black #3. Apart from that, a medium-gray base-colored stone is called a Gray. A translucent white stone is called a White. Finally, a water-clear stone is called a Crystal Opal in Australia and a Jelly Opal in America.

Certain Lightning Ridge black opals are designated *sunflash* opal because they have the ability, under strong artificial light or direct sunlight, to intensify the visible colors. But then, most opals will show up best in that type of light. What sets a top-quality black opal apart is its ability to exhibit its colors in twinkling beauty under very poor light conditions, as in a dark room where the only light source is a single candle.

As for what causes an opal to be a black opal, there have been many theories, foremost among which is that carbon material from decomposed or burned organic matter stained the silica gel at the time the stone was forming. The fallacy of such a theory becomes apparent in view of the experiments conducted by Len Cram, mentioned earlier, where he tried to grow black opal through the use of dyes and failed; but that black opal nobbies had then formed by themselves in untreated opal dirt from a specific black opal level when correct conditions were established, through the addition of water and an electrolyte, to promote ion exchange.

Just as it is important to know what visually constitutes a black opal in Lightning Ridge, it is important to know where and how such an opal is normally encountered and what shape it takes. First, it should be understood that while Lightning Ridge is the world's foremost producer of gem-quality black opal, it is not the only type of opal that occurs here. Light opal occurs in seams with considerable frequency and is of a character not differing greatly from that of the light opal from White Cliffs or Coober Pedy. A fair amount of opalized fossils also occur at Lightning Ridge, both animal and vegetable material, including a variety of opalized woods and infrequent opalized skeletal remains of both prehistoric and more modern creatures.

The black opal, however, reigns supreme and is usually found in opal levels occurring between 6 and 18 meters (roughly 19 to 60 feet) beneath the surface. Such levels, however, are not necessarily continuous or always horizontal. In most areas there are usually only two or three opal levels, but in some areas as many as a dozen levels have been encountered by shafts sunk as deeply as 33 m—100 feet. These shafts, formerly dug by hand, are now mainly dug by a powerful truck-mounted Calweld drill, which can do in 2 or 3 hours what it would take a man many days or even weeks to accomplish. Usually before such a 30″- or 36″-diameter shaft is sunk, a 9-inch bore is put down and the debris brought up is closely checked for bits of opal that may indicate the presence of a good pocket.

Once the shaft has been dug and goes through the hard level called the steel band, which often lies just above the opal level, a horizontal drive is excavated that follows the opal level, digging away the soft and sometimes slightly damp clay. Sometimes this is done by hand, sometimes with tunnel digging machinery. The excavated debris, which may have opals in it, is lifted to the surface by one of three methods: (1) a windlass arrangement operated by hand; (2) an automatic self-dumping bucket hoist that drops the debris into a truck or a mullock heap; or (3) a powerful blower which sucks it up from the mine floor in vacuum cleaner fashion and blows it out at the surface into a truck, to be taken to the agitators, much like cement mixers, which will wash away the dirt debris and leave only hard material, hopefully including opals (Figure 42).

What is most often being searched for is the peculiar little formation commonly called a nobby. This is a nodular formation ranging in size from as small as an olive to as large as a walnut. It is often topped with a peculiar little conical cap of white porcelainlike material. If the digging is being done by a tunneling machine, the device is turned off as soon that telltale clinking sound indicates an opal has been encountered. At that point the digging continues carefully by hand.

Whatever nobbies are collected are brought to the surface but, unlike most of the opal mined in Queensland or South Australia they are not sold and shipped away in their rough form.[18] The Lighting Ridge black opal nobbies are always cut and polished—or at least rubbed—in the field before ever being offered for sale anywhere. As soon as they are brought to the surface, they are carefully snipped along the edge with a pair of strong nippers to see if the opal material inside shows any trace of POC. If so, the stone is then carefully put to a grinding wheel and the sandy clay-encrusted coating rubbed away to some

---

Figure 42. Trucks loaded with opal dirt come to the agitators (1), which line a high bank over a waste area and draw their water (2) from a pond behind them. The dirt from the trucks (3) is loaded into a hopper, which, in turn (4) sends it up a conveyor belt and into the big agitator, where it will be washed and tumbled for several days. At the end of that time, the stones remaining after the dirt has been washed away are (5) released down a ramp onto the sorting table, and (6) each stone is checked carefully for opal content and those showing indication are (7) put into a bucket. Later, the best in the bucket (8) will be rubbed for closer inspection. Several stones in this load (9, 10, 11) show good promise, and one (12) is an excellent stone with a good color line sandwiched in black common opal. The best stones will be further cut or sold as is to a buyer. (Photos by the author)

Figure 42 *(Continued)*

Figure 42 *(Continued)*

Figure 42   *(Continued)*

Figure 42 *(Continued)*

Figure 42 *(Continued)*

extent. This results in what is called a rub. If, at this point, there is some color showing, that rub, along with others of similar quality, may be taken to a professional cutter on the field or in town. Anywhere from a small handful to 100 or more rubs may be turned over to the cutter at one time. For his services, the cutter is usually paid a flat sum on a per-stone basis, that flat rate dependent on the size of the stone and the established rate the cutter has set up, which may be as low as $5 per stone or as much as $25. If the stone shows good black or deep gray potch inside with a color bar atop that, it could turn out to be a very valuable stone. If such early promise becomes evident, then the cutter may announce that he will cut it only for a percentage of the value—usually no more than 2%, and often only 1%. The cutter then estimates the stone's minimum value and the miner must agree with that estimate before any further cutting resumes. If the stone proves to be worth more than the initial estimate, the cutter still gets his percentage of the total amount of final set value. If it turns out to be worth less, the cutter get's his percentage of the minimum value estimate originally made.

With these details seen to, the cutter then rough grinds the entire surface of the stone to determine as best he can which side will be the top. The entire interior of the nobby may be potch, which means it is worthless. Hopefully, it will show some color if it has not already done so. When the stone does have color, it is most often a bar of color going through the nobby and surrounded by potch. He then grinds down that top side enough to dome the stone and expose the fire, but not too deeply, since more will have to be taken off. The shape of the stone is then decided upon—most often an oval or, secondarily, a round—and the stone is cut to that shape. It is then dopped and the final shaping and smoothing is accomplished. The least valuable black opals will be those that finish out with predominantly blue POC. If the miner is lucky, the seam is clear crystal with rich POC of green and orange and the potch is a deep black with a somewhat bluish iridescence. That's the kind of nobby that will result in a top-of-the-line finished stone. And if the miner is *extremely* lucky, the POC will be a very hot, brilliantly rolling and broadflashing red-on-black with limitless depth from whatever direction viewed—the type of stone that can net him a small fortune.

In some cases, the color bar will be thick enough, that the cutter may be able to carefully saw the stone in half horizontally through the color bar and wind up with two very good stones instead of one. At any rate, when the stones are finished and have been turned into gem cabochons by the cutter, the miner pays him his fee and then takes the cut stones to a buyer he trusts. That buyer then studies them carefully, stone by stone and makes an offer. Usually, if indeed the buyer is one with whom the miner has dealt with previously and trusts, there is little haggling over what is a fair price. The buyer, of course, must be very skilled in estimating what he can afford to pay the miner for such stones as compared to what he can expect to sell those same stones for to jewelers, collectors, stone setters, or whomever.

The caliber of the exceptional stones that originate at Lightning Ridge can be seen in the large number that have earned that rare honor of becoming a named stone—stones such as the *Aurora Australis,* the *Black Prince, Queen of the Earth, Empress, Light of the World, Butterfly, Flame Queen, Flamingo, Dunstan's, Pride of Australia, Pandora, Duke of Devonshire,* and many others, details of which are found in Chapter 5.

Each time there is a bit of a lull in production at Lightning Ridge and a little sense of nervousness rises in the miners accompanied by a feeling that the fields are playing out, something seems to happen that restores their confidence. One of the most remarkable and stirring of such incidents occurred in early 1989 with the discovery of the New Coocoran field (Figure 43). Very quickly some of the most outstanding finds ever made in Australia were being made here—black opal of such high quality that it became the talk of the entire gem world and made New Coocoran black opals the most sought after stones ever to be found Down Under. Many of the parcels and individual stones began selling for previously unheard of prices. Each new story outdid the one before it and all were true; there was no need to exaggerate in light of the amazing things that were occurring. By late April, cut nobbies were selling for close to $7000 per carat. By June many hundreds of claims had been pegged in the area; 200 new mine leases in a single five-day period and, by late August, over 5000 fresh claims being worked. Everyone, it seemed, was finding opal that was not just good, it was outstanding—gorgeous red-on-black material as fine as anything ever found in Lightning Ridge to that point. Some miners reported bringing up to the surface between $30,000 and $50,000 worth of black opal daily for weeks. A Calweld drill, boring a new 36-inch shaft, brought a half million dollars worth of opal to the surface before the digging of the shaft was completed, and a mine about a half mile distant yielded a solid $8 million worth of black opals in one day (Figure 44).

Black opal values continued to increase and by the time 1990 rolled around, the top-quality material had increased upward of 20% over what it had been just a year previously. In February 1990, several of the individual New Coocoran miners each were selling Lightning Ridge buyers upward of three dozen stones apiece per week, with each cut stone valued in the neighborhood of $100,000. The New Coocoran field, now seven years old at this writing, still consistently produces black opal of the highest quality as a result of the steady development of new claims, new shafts, new drives, and great new opal discoveries.

The town of Lightning Ridge makes no population claim. Because many miners are very reticent about announcing their presence in the area due to wariness over possible taxes being levied, census reports are rare and unreliable. However, it is clear that the town itself has a floating population of around

Figure 43. Looking west over the great expanse of Coocoran Lake, with the Coocoran opal field on the other side and the New Coocoran field to the left (south) of that. This great expanse of lake bed is more often than not a vast field of wheat rather than a body of water. Only in especially wet springs does the lake reappear and then usually not for very long. (Photo by the author)

6000 and perhaps half that many more miners and their families living in camps among the mines throughout the length and breadth of Lightning Ridge. Many will neither allow their picture to be taken nor divulge their true name, and are known, even to their own neighbors, only by such sobriquets as Kangaroo Bob, Dirty Tommy, Fat John, Brisbane George, Benthose, and other colorful but unrevealing terms.

Tourism has become quite a substantial secondary business and visitors are catered to in a variety of ways. Certain sites have been set aside as fossicking areas where visitors can look through the mullock piles for opals that have previously missed detection—a surprising number of which are found—and tours among, and even into, the mines are available. There is an excellent health center, an ambulance service, and two resident doctors. In addition there are now good motels and hotels, over half a hundred shops of all kinds, including a number selling a variety of opal jewelry or finished stones, hot artesian bore baths, camp grounds and caravan (trailer) parks, bowling club, airport, racecourse, parks, a drive-in theater, olympic-size swimming pool, and many other attractions. The numerous wild kangaroos are interesting for visitors to see, but they can be distinct hazards to motorists, especially at night. Lightning Ridge, soon to celebrate its 100th year, is clearly a most remarkable opal field that is poised to step into the twenty first century with confidence and anticipation for what the second hundred years will bring.

Figure 44. When a 9″ exploratory drill rig is moved into position and prepared to drill, heavy-duty hydraulic jacks stabilize the rig and actually lift the wheels of the truck well off the ground, as has occurred here at the Dead Bird opal field of the New Coocoran near Lightning Ridge. When the drill has bored down to the opal level and opal dirt becomes visible with the excavated material, samples of this dirt are shoveled into the rig's built-in agitator, where it is thoroughly washed and any hard material in it is carefully washed free of dirt. After the washing, the operator of the rig inspects the pebbles remaining in the agitator to see if there are any traces of opal. If precious opal is found, a 36″ diameter shaft will be sunk to the opal level and a new mining operation will begin. (Photo by the author)

LAMBINA, SOUTH AUSTRALIA

At this writing, not a great deal has yet been divulged about Lambina, South Australia's newest opal field—one of the most remote in all of Australia. The new field was discovered in 1992 some 56 miles [90 km] northeast of Mintabie on the expansive grounds of Lambina Station. The nearest town is Marla, which lies 64 straight-line miles southwest of Lambina, but by road it is almost exactly twice as far.[19]

There are presently two separate-diggings at the site and they are yielding some very good gem-quality opal that is reputed to be quite stable. Rich in

POC, the opal—both black and light varieties—is favorably comparable to that which occurs at Mintabie. The opal level—a Cretaceous Period claystone called Bulldog Shale—is normally encountered some 36 feet (10 m) below the surface, and the precious opal itself occurs in joints and seams in that level as well as sometimes as smaller veinlets in the overlying stratum of Tertiary Period jasper breccia.

The opal mining at Lambina is administered out of Mintabie and originally six well-established companies from Mintabie set up operations at Lambina, of which four soon left, though the reason for their departure is unclear. The field is said to hold such great promise that it may, at some future time, be as productive as Mintabie itself.

MEXICO

There are many occurrences of opals in Mexico, ranging from just south of the United States border—where it occurs as a translucent sky blue variety in the state of Sonora and a nonprecious cherry opal in Chihuahua—to just north of the Guatemalan border where crystal and black volcanic varieties occur in the states of Oaxaca and Chiapas. In between those four states are a dozen others that have significant opal deposits and where mining of some degree occurs, of which two are principal sources that are the most commercially important on a worldwide scale. Located in central Mexico, they include the extensive, centuries-old diggings of the famed Mexican precious fire opal and black opal some 160 miles north-northwest of Mexico City in the state of Querétaro and well westward from there in the more recently discovered similar deposits closer to Guadalajara in the state of Jalisco.

The most productive Mexican mines at present are the older operations in the area of San Juan del Rio in the eastern part of the state of Querétaro—such as the Santa Maria Iris Mine and others, some of which have been worked steadily since 1865, five years after their rediscovery by one of the peons working on the Hacienda Esperanza—and the newer mines, those in the vicinity of Magdalena in the northwestern part of the state of Jalisco, such as the Magdalena Opal Mine, which have been in operation since about 1962. All are open-pit mining operations in jungle mountain areas at elevations over a mile and where the mineral is freed by blasting, much as in the manner of stone quarries. The problem with this, of course, is that a great deal of good opal is shattered in this process and also in the process of using sledgehammers to break up the blocks of rhyolite freed in the principal blasting. Almost all the mining is done by hand—a very slow and difficult process.

The gem quality of the Mexican opal is approximately alike in both areas and is actually much better than those in the trade normally give it credit for being. The general low esteem in which the Mexican opals have been held is due to three principal reasons. First, through the years there has been rather widespread selling of inferior Mexican stones exhibiting weak or nearly absent POC, resulting in the conclusion that Mexican opals are essentially lifeless. That, of course, is not true, as the fine Mexican precious fire opals will compare with fine-quality opals from anywhere else in the world. Second, even if they're high-quality gemstones, the majority of the Mexican opal production stones are of a generally yellow-to-orange-to-red base color, which appears to be something of a turnoff to opal collectors and fanciers in western cultures, who are much more inclined to the black and light opal types. The third, and by far the most deleterious, reason for low esteem derives largely from the reputation Mexican opals have garnered for instability. While it is true that certain opals from specific areas are known to have a definite propensity for cracking and crazing, it is patently unfair to paint all Mexican opals with the same brush. A good percentage of them are as stable as opals from anywhere else in the world and the market for them is very pronounced, most particularly in the Orient and especially in Japan, which imports by far most of the $4 million worth of Mexican opals exported every year.[20]

Although a small amount of Mexican opal is found in sedimentary deposits of both inorganic and organic material, most of what is being mined today, as in the past, is of volcanic origin and is almost always found in vugs, pockets, cracks, and cavities of igneous rocks, most particularly rhyolite and basalt. Most commonly it is recovered from a rhyolitic matrix—ranging in its own coloration from pink to a deeper reddish brown—in which, as nodular masses, it usually fills gas pockets so completely that the only way it can be removed is to break the rock itself, which all too often breaks the opal as well. By far the most beautiful and desirable of the opals recovered are those that are found either only lightly attached or even actually loose within the pocket. Such stones, which have an appearance of being lightly tumbled, are generally very stable and rich with POC and, as a result, make top-quality cutting material. The opals, whether or not attached to the matrix material, rarely exceed 50 carats in weight.[21] Of the opal occurring in sediments, much is pseudomorphic after various fossils and, frequently, crystallized minerals such as calcite, apophyllite, gypsum, apatite, aragonite, ikaite, and others. There is also quite a bit of opalized wood throughout Mexico, but its colors are subdued and it is rarely used for anything.

Precious fire opal, with its base color ranging from pale sherry and deep honey through brilliant transparent yellow to equally brilliant transparent cardinal red—hot red-orange undoubtedly being the favorite—has a richness made even more breathtaking by its POC, which seldom occurs in the familiar pinfire or broadflash seen in opal from other parts of the world, but most often as small, scintillating flakes of color that often seem to be arranged in rather vertical configuration that gives the unusual impression of a rainfall of colors. It is this type that modern Mexican miners call *Iluviznados*—literally, "sun on raindrops" or, in a more liberal sense, "fire rain." John Sinkankas, renowned gem cutter and author, very aptly described it as "intense color descending like a shower of raindrops through the rays of the setting sun." The ancient Aztecs, seeing it more as the colors seen in the tropical hummingbird, called it *vitzitziltecpatl*—which means just that.

Not uncommonly, the base color of the opal may grade into a deeper orange-brown. Sometimes the transparent opals will have a faint bluish cast—a touch of cool to complement the warmth of fire. Such stones, which may tend toward a translucent misty sky blue, are particular favorites of the Japanese buyers and are rapidly overtaking the reddish precious fire opal as the most desired variety. To many, these latter are simply superb stones that easily rival the fine translucent white opals of Coober Pedy in Australia. Even when they tend toward greater transparency and still retain the bluish cast, they are very popular and are referred to by the locals as *azules*—blue stones.

As noted, it is the red-orange variation with red, green, and yellow POC that is the type most accurately labeled precious fire opal. If it has only the bright transparent base color but no POC, then it is properly termed fire opal without the word precious. The deeper, pure red variety is often called cherry opal, while those with the base color tending more toward the tan or yellowish brown hues are termed honey opal. Some of this nonprecious fire opal is very porous, exhibiting a propensity toward being hydrophane—losing its transparency as it dries and becoming quite translucent, a transparency that can be regained time after time by merely immersing the stone in water for a short time, although the translucency will return as it dries.

Mexico also produces an exceptional water-clear opal in rather large chunks. This opal, properly called hyalite, closely resembles chunks of glass. In recent years this same type of material has been found that exhibits POC and it has become extremely popular, especially for faceting. A related type that is very common in the Mexican opal mining is the often—but not always—water-clear variety that shows no POC in reflected light, but when viewed in transmitted light, with the stone held between the light source and the viewer's eye, becomes alive with the colors of the spectrum. It is, of course, the variety called *contra luz*, meaning "against the light."

An opal closely resembling, in its base color of dark gray to black, the black opal of Lightning Ridge in Australia, occurs near Huitzuco in the state of Guerrero, but little organized mining has been done for this stone that harbors such truly remarkable red and green POC, an opal that may turn out to be a significant hidden asset for Mexico.[22]

Mexican opal's reputation for instability has, as already mentioned, been blown considerably out of proportion to actuality. Admittedly, in some mines the opals are notoriously susceptible to cracking, crazing, even self-destruction, but those mines are few and far between, and by far the greater amount of opal mined is reasonably stable. A bit more care might be required in the cutting of Mexican stones as compared to Coober Pedy stones, perhaps, but it is not an insurmountable problem. The very fact that millions of dollars worth of Mexican opal is purchased each year by Japanese buyers and sent to the Orient for cutting indicates that they are not intimidated by the reputation; they wouldn't be buying the stones if the opals couldn't be successfully cut. Equally, a great many opals, mined and cut by the Aztecs centuries ago and found in their tombs, remain uncrazed to this day. Many other antique opals also continue to hold up very well. Of the different varieties of Mexican opal, it is the precious fire opal that appears to be most stable and the white and jelly opals that are most prone to fracturing. Some buyers will not even consider buying either white or jelly opal varieties in Mexico.

The highest-quality Mexican opal is often referred to as "Japanese grade" because it is bought almost exclusively by Japanese buyers and very little of the top gem-quality material ever makes its way to the United States. Cutters in the United States are reluctant to pay the relatively high per-carat prices that the Japanese pay without quibble for top of the line material. Little wonder that so few opal fanciers in the United States have any real conception of what truly good Mexican opals look like.[23] The limited amount of Mexican opals that are seen for sale at the gem and mineral shows in the United States are often low-grade rough that has been bought from dealers, street vendors, and so-called "bottle merchants" in the Plaza Obregon of the city of Querétaro, where very little high-quality opal ever shows up. In these days, many of the opal mines in Jalisco and some in Querétaro are Japanese owned and operated.

The majority of Mexican opal not sold to the Japanese, which means only about 10–15% of the total opal mined, is sold by the miners to opal cutters in the opal-cutting capital of Mexico, the city of Querétaro. These individuals normally cut and polish the stones in their homes or work in tiny cutting shops that employ only a few people and are frequently family operations. More often than not, the grinding, sanding, and polishing machines are foot-treadle driven. The stones are normally cut into high-domed cabochons, sometimes with matrix attached if circumstance calls for it. The finished stones are then sold to buyers or dealers who visit by appointment. Despite the rather primitive cutting methods, the more than 100 cutters produce between 100,000 and 250,000 cuts stones each year.

The principal difference at Magdalena is that the opal-bearing rhyolite, after being blasted free, is sold to buyers without being further broken up. Those buyers then study the material they have bought and hire men to further break down the rhyolite for the best opal pieces visible. What remains is sold to Magdalena opal cutters, who break the rough down even further and cut what opal they can retrieve into high-domed cabochons.

Details on more specific Mexican opal deposits and mining operations may be found in the segment dealing with the occurrence of opal worldwide.

MINTABIE, SOUTH AUSTRALIA

It was in 1919 that aboriginals began showing up at Coober Pedy with parcels of black opal to sell to the buyers at that field. It was quality material—as good as the best black opal being found at Coober Pedy—but the aboriginals refused to say where they were getting it. Attempt after attempt was made by Coober Pedy miners to follow them during the ensuing years, but all were initially unsuccessful. The aboriginals traveled northwestward from Coober Pedy on the Stuart Trail leading toward Alice Springs in the Northern Territory, but they always disappeared from sight some 148 miles [238 km] after leaving Coober Pedy.[24] Finally, in 1928, the effort succeeded. Just north of a little camp called Marla, the aboriginals turned sharply west through some hills and traveled 22 miles [36 km] more before reaching a ridge where others of their people were searching the ground surface and finding black opals. The Aboriginals referred to the site as Mintabie.[25]

The miners returned to Coober Pedy and reported their finds. It was the most remote opal field yet discovered—168 miles [270 km] northwest of Coober Pedy and clearly land owned by the aboriginals. Negotiations were opened up with the Aboriginal Council at Alice Springs and a lease was finally granted by them to the white miners under what is now called the Pitjantjatjara Land Rights Act. Actual mining by whites began in 1931 on a small scale and it soon became clear that this was a very major opal field. The remoteness of the location, however, made mining very difficult and, despite the abundance of opal there, production remained low for many years.

The opal being found was very beautiful—both light opal and black. The seams of light opal were more extensive even than those at Coober Pedy and the quality of that light opal equally good. Black opal was less abundant, but it was beautiful material. There was also crystal, semiblack, and white pinfire opal, most of which compared quite favorably with the best of those types of opal from other Australian opal fields.

There was one major drawback with the Mintabie opal. Some of it was, as the miners termed it, "cracky," meaning it was susceptible to crazing after being removed from the ground and, while the affected opal was only from one small area, all the opal of Mintabie suffered from the bad reputation, which considerably lowered the value of Mintabie opal with the buyers at Coober Pedy. Production remained at a low level while mining was done in the usual method, in hand-dug shafts and drives. These mines were dug through coarse-grained kaolinitic sandstone to the opal level of montmorillonite, following the seams as they ran shallowly—from the surface down to 30 feet below ground level and sometimes plunging steeply downward in verticals to level off again as deeply as 82 feet below the surface. Mechanized drilling is done now to sink the vertical shafts and bulldozers are still used for what open-cut mining is done. In both types, however, all the work is done with hand tools as soon as precious opal is encountered.

A great lull in production—almost a total cessation, in fact—began in the late 1930s and lasted through World War II and the years that followed until 1976, when heavy earth-moving equipment was inaugurated there and open-cut mining began. Immediately production zoomed to great heights. Nevertheless, prices paid for the Mintabie opal at Coober Pedy were still very low, so some of the Mintabie miners began taking sacksful of their better black opal all the way to Lightning Ridge and selling it to miners there, who in turn sold it to buyers in their field as Lightning Ridge black opal. The Lightning Ridge miners didn't pay the Mintabie miners a great deal for it, but they did pay them much more than they could get from the buyers at Coober Pedy. This process continued for a number of years and the bad reputation cloaking Mintabie opal only gradually wore away. It has never completely disappeared.

New finds of exceptionally good black opal were discovered at Mintabie in the late 1970s and early 1980s and many so-called "million-dollar finds" were made. Much of it was said to rival the best from Lightning Ridge. With the discovery of better water resources in the field in 1978, more miners flocked to the Mintabie area and the little settlement there continued to grow, with production increasing dramatically.

It came as a great delight to the Mintabie miners and a great shock to those at Coober Pedy when, in 1986, the 400 miners living and working in the Mintabie opal field produced more opal than Coober Pedy, the first time since assuming world opal dominance many years ago that Coober Pedy did not lead the world in opal production. Today, Mintabie, boasting a population of over 1500, still justifiably proclaims itself as being the largest opal field in the world, though no longer the most productive, since Coober Pedy has once again become number one in that respect.

Heavy rains caused extensive flooding at the Mintabie opal field in 1989, halting some of the work, but when the waters receded and things dried out, a new open cut was made that produced actual hundreds of pounds of top gem-quality crystal opal with brilliant red POC—a find that ultimately became worth more than a million dollars. New diggings were discovered and given names like Crystal Valley and Grasshopper. They produced well for a while, but then they, too, played out as the original ridge before them had. By 1990 many miners were predicting that Mintabie's opal resources would be entirely depleted within the next 3 to 5 years. That didn't happen and Mintabie continues to produce abundant opal of high quality. In fact, recent new finds of large quantities of gray base opal and black opal have occurred—similar in quality to the opal produced at the Grawin opal field of Lightning Ridge—from which top-quality black opal gemstones are cut. after originally selling at very low prices, these are now valued at prices equaling or surpassing those for the same type of material at Coober Pedy.

The time is drawing near now when the lease on the Mintabie land, obtained from the aboriginals, is due to expire and all efforts to this point to get the council to grant an extension to the existing lease or inaugurate a new one on previously unleased portions of the Mintabie field have failed. What the outcome will be remains yet to be seen.

Tourism has become a substantial business in recent years at Mintabie and, though the town is not so well attuned to the tourist trade as Coober Pedy, it does have a post office and hotel, a number of stores, a decent restaurant, and an adequate medical center. Those who might wish to visit must first obtain a tourist permit from The Administrator, Anangu Pitjantjatjara, 37 Bath Street, P.O. Box 2584, Alice Springs, 5750, Northern Territory.

OPAL BUTTE, OREGON

While a number of deposits of opal—both precious and common—have been discovered in Oregon, the only one of significance in a worldwide commercial sense is the Morrow County occurrence at Opal Butte in the north-central portion of the state. Here, and extending eastward through the whole of northeastern Oregon in the Columbia River basin, there are extensive Tertiary Period volcanic flows of basalt and rhyolite. It is within these 60- to 65-million-year-old rhyolitic flows that 8-foot thick zones of perlite occur—perlite in this area being the clay resulting from the alteration of a dark green, silica-rich porphyry rock into a decomposed glassy material known to geologists as vitrophyre, but more commonly referred to as perlite.

In considerable abundance within these layers of clayey perlite—and nowhere else—occur rhyolitic geodes that are often roughly egg-shaped and range in size from only an inch or so through the thickest portion to as much as over a foot in thickness and much too heavy to pick up. These formations are called thundereggs. One such giant measured 4 feet in length, 3 feet in width, 1½ feet thick, and weighed over a ton, though not much of value was inside. Generally speaking, the smaller geodes do not have empty space in the interior and therefore are actually nodules; larger geodes, however, will be almost wholly hollow inside the initial outer layer of rock, the cavities not infrequently comprising up to 75% of the geode's total volume. There seems to be no real correlation between the size of the geode and the amount of opal it may contain, except that it has been noted that the smaller geodes may contain solid precious opal of decided gem-quality opal, while the largest of the geodes contain primarily common opal. The best seem to be those that range in size between the diameter of

a football and that of a beachball; these geodes often containing interior formations of a variety of different types of opal, both common and precious.[26]

It is in one such location, south of the town of Heppner, which itself is 60
miles southwest of the city of Pendleton, that there is a low mountain, well
rounded and only 5000 feet high, that was initially called Peters Butte. In
November 1889, a shepherd was tending his flock on the western slope of
that butte some 300 feet below the summit, at an elevation of about 4700 feet
[1400 m], when he saw a couple of the egg-shaped stones he was familiar with
as thundereggs. Knowing that they sometimes had within them some clear
quartz crystals or stalactites of agate—although more commonly just some colorful chalcedony patterns or banded agate—he decided he'd check their insides,
picked them up and smacked them together, breaking them. His eyes widened
as a burst of iridescent color such as he had never before encountered leaped
from the broken pieces. He had no idea what they were but, thinking it was
possible they might have some value, he shoved the pieces into his pack to take
back down the mountain with him and show to a friend of his named Levi
Shaner, whom he knew to be a rockhound.

Shaner's eyes widened, too, when he saw the broken, glassy pieces in which
spectacular pure colors of the spectrum—reds, yellows, blues, greens, oranges,
and purples—appeared and shifted and disappeared in glittering array. Never
having encountered such stones before, he learned the particulars of where the
shepherd had found them—an area with which he was vaguely familiar—and
then he took them to a lapidary he knew who was much more experienced
than he. The lapidary had no difficulty identifying the pieces immediately as an
especially beautiful precious opal.

Even though the land was largely privately owned, Shaner quickly began
staking claims at the site, but the word was out and others followed in a rush
and also made claims until most of the hill—which everyone was now referring
to as Opal Butte—was peppered with them.[27] Little actual digging was done at
first, since most of the material initially found was on the surface, exposed
through erosion and in some areas, where the thundereggs were sent rolling
down the slopes by the rain, there were actual piles of these ovate rhyolitic
rocks. The 1893 edition of the U.S. Geological Survey Report showed that
some $20,000 worth—equivalent to well over $100,000 worth in today's market—was sold from Opal Butte, with a fair portion of what was bought being
sent to cutters overseas.

Not surprisingly, the surface material was very quickly depleted and so, too,
were those geodes only inches below the surface. Ever more digging was being
done, often creating dangerous overhangs. Some of the miners began tunneling,
following the perlite zones so doggedly and so extensively that sometimes they
actually tunneled entirely through the butte and emerged on the opposite side.
Now the amount of opal being recovered was greatly diminished and many of

the miners began leaving, until before long only a dogged core of them remained. Their surface diggings, with the resultant overhangs and the tunnels themselves, were very unsafe and a number of accidents occurred, ranging from mild to serious. To the landowners it was clear that it was only a matter of time until someone got killed in a cave-in. They systematically dynamited all the digs and mine entrances, successfully terminating the opal mining operations. Now even the rockhounds stopped coming and opal hunting on Opal Butte had ended . . . at least for a long time.

Opal Butte lay dormant for decades. Then, in the early 1930s the heavily forested hill was leased from its owners by a logging operation called Kinzua Pine Mills. Oddly enough, it was this firm's work that caused a renewal of interest in the opals. As the huge logs were dragged to loading areas, they left behind significant gouges, exposing a number of perlite deposits—and their rhyolitic thundereggs. As this news spread, rockhounds once again converged at Opal Butte and numerous new digs began appearing. Kinzua did not seem to care, so long as the digging did not interfere with the logging activities. For two decades more this kind of prospecting and digging continued, with a fair amount of opal being found, but with the hill once again gradually becoming so unsafe that even many of the rockhounds themselves, early in the 1950s, began going to less hazardous places. Those who remained, however, continued prospecting and digging. Kinzua, acquiring full ownership of Opal Butte in 1953, began to fear lawsuits if any of the rockhounds they were allowing onto the land were hurt or killed, so they ordered all the diggers away, enforcing their ruling with regular patrols.

This was the situation that existed for the next third of a century. It was in 1986, however, that two young men, having studied the old records, reckoned that with a more systematic approach and modern mechanized equipment, they might be able to make opal mining at Opal Butte a profitable enterprise once again. The two were Kevin Lane Smith, a graduate geologist and skilled lapidary, and Dale Huett, who owned a John Deere 550 bulldozer equipped with a backhoe. Establishing themselves as West Coast Gemstones, they approached officials of the Kinzua Corporation with a request to lease part of the hill and initiate opal mining with the heavy equipment, a method not previously attempted. Late in that same year, Kinzua agreed that once the pair determined where they wanted to start such an operation, provided it did not interfere with the logging in any way, they could have permission to engage in an exploratory dig for a 2-week period.

For a year Smith and Huett studied Opal Butte in an effort to determine where best to establish their dig. They finally decided on a spot where there was a good deposit of perlite and began their mechanized exploratory open-cut digging in November 1987. The results were immediate and good, the exploratory work quickly showing that commercial opal mining was indeed feasible.

So impressed were the officials at Kinzua that the lease for West Coast Gemstones was extended for a year.[28]

During that first full year, ending in November 1988, Smith and Huett recovered 220 pounds [100 kg] of top-quality precious opal. Today, although Smith is no longer closely associated with the operation and retains only some slight side benefits, Huett, as West Coast Gemstones, is continuing with the operation and, during the summer of 1996, plans to open the operation to the public on a fee-digging basis. Certainly it is the most important opal mining operation in all of Oregon.[29]

Among the many varieties of opal occurring in the Opal Butte thundereggs are translucent light opal (crystal opal), transparent water-clear, or transparent colored opal (jelly opal), girasol (referred to as rainbow opal here), hyalite, blue opal, contra luz, hydrophane and cachalong, dendritic opal, and fire opal (both precious and nonprecious and very similar to the Mexican variety). The latter is the most prone to craze and crack of all the types found here, ordinarily developing cracks within mere minutes of exposure to the air. The fire opal ranges from light orange to dark red material, with the dark red tending to be the more stable.

Because all of this is volcanic opal, it is a surprise that so little of the material tends to crack or craze. In those cases where it does occur, if it doesn't happen within minutes, it may wait until the stone is being polished and at other times it takes from days to months for crazing to develop. Putting his cutting skills to the test, Smith often works with pieces that have already crazed, turning out what he terms "crackly" pieces that actually become works or art and emphasize what Smith has always averred—that crazing in opal does not always signify disaster.

By far the greater proportion of Opal Butte material does not craze readily. As Smith puts it, "If crazing or cracking has not occurred by the time it is removed from the thundereggs, it isn't likely to occur later on."[30] This is not an idle or boastful comment. On the whole, stability in these Opal Butte stones is quite high. Kevin Lane Smith kept very close records of this, charting incidents of instability not only immediately after the opal geodes were unearthed and opened, but also during and after the cutting process. Rating them on a percentage scale, with the greatest stability being 100%, the girasol (rainbow), hydrophane, and blue opal ranked highest, at 90%, crystal contra luz at 80%, dendritic at 75%, hyalite and jelly contra luz at 70%, crystal and jelly at 60%, and fire opal (of both varieties) at 20%.

Hyalite ranked as the most abundant opal in the geodes, making up 43% of the total opal recovered. Girasol (rainbow opal) was second, at 25%, blue ranked at 12%, and the remainder were each 6% or less of the total. The girasol/rainbow opal that is recovered not only makes up the largest flawless pieces recovered among all the opal types here—some exceeding 2500 carats—

it is also particularly beautiful, with a POC that makes the transparent stone show the full spectrum in soft tints as light strikes it and the colors changing in awesome loveliness as the angle of the illumination changes.

The hyalite, which also sometimes occurs in large pieces, lends itself especially well to being carved (in conjunction with matrix material) into rather stirring scenes, very much like underwater seascapes of great depth and clarity and inspiring beauty. The best is a pale to vibrant ethereal blue that is well suited for faceting as well as carving and, when faceted, reflects yellow light off the pavilion faces even though the body of the stone is transparent blue. A substantial percentage of the hyalite opal has orange layers or zones. Several flawless pieces of blue hyalite weighing 1500–2500 grams were found in 1987 when the West Coast Gemstones mining began, but only one piece of such size was uncovered subsequently. In those geodes containing contra luz opal, that contra luz almost invariably overlies a girasol layer. The blue opal found here is usually practically opaque and, though normally showing a suggestion of green, is occasionally a pure dark blue. When backlighted, the stone's translucency becomes more apparent.

Smith says that while Dale Huett operates the bulldozer, he follows behind and collects the unearthed thundereggs, separating them into piles roughly by size. When a fair number of geodes have been collected, the bulldozer is shut down and Huett and Smith carefully attack the thundereggs with hammer and chisel. Each geode is first carefully inspected for the presence of natural fracture seams, which, if present, allow the stone to be broken apart with virtually no damage to the opal beyond the natural fracture lines already present. If the specimen shows no such lines externally, however, the thunderegg is apt to be a solid and is taken whole, to be sawed open at a later time.

What they find inside the thundereggs makes the difficult search well worthwhile. The opal within is very often spectacular. Kevin Lane Smith, who is the most skilled gemcutter the author has ever encountered, has faceted many of the Opal Butte opals, cut a great many more into lovely cabochon gemstones and has carved even more than that into exceptionally beautiful pieces—especially the hyalite type, which embody some truly remarkable, often surrealistic scenes.

Sometimes he carves the precious opal as well. He has also developed the knack of deliberately carving—or otherwise cutting—stones that have crazed and, in the process, turns out some amazingly beautiful pieces. As Smith told me, "Most of the time very special care is required to work some of these unstable pieces, but the results can be spectacular (Figure 45). I have found that in the Opal Butte opal, between the stable layers there are often unstable layers where you just know you will get crazings or spontaneous cracking. Often, instead of tying to cut the cracks out of the piece, I'll try to make them an integral part of the finished piece. They add a rather intriguing dimension of sparkle and interest. Every now and then, when I am convinced that a piece is

Figure 45. Deliberately making use of crazed opal is a Kevin Lane Smith trademark. Here he has used a 580-carat slightly crazed piece of light yellow jelly opal with a deeper orange layer to create a freeform carving of considerable interest. Occasionally he will promote further crazing—sometimes before the cutting, sometimes afterward—by gently heating the stone in an oven. (Photo by Kevin Lane Smith)

going to craze or crack when it dries, I will cut it into a simple round shape, keeping it wet during the cutting. After polishing, I leave it out and it cracks spontaneously, within just a few minutes, often very gracefully and into interesting patterns. Most often, such cracking does not make it fall apart. The end result is admittedly a fragile thing, but it's very pretty."

As mentioned, Kevin Lane Smith is highly skilled as a gemcutter. Born in Rolla, Missouri, in 1959, he spent part of his childhood there and in El Paso, Texas, before his family moved to Milton-Freewater, Oregon, on the Walla Walla River. After elementary school he attended high school at Walla Walla Academy, a Seventh Day Adventist institution. From 1978 to 1983 he attended the University of Oregon, majoring in geology, equally studying optics, chemistry, and physics, along with taking minor courses in stonecutting and goldsmithing. He spent his summers studying at the Columbia Art Museum, where, he says, "I came to the conclusion that combining fine art with geology, physics and lapidary skills, would fill a niche not previously filled—sort of a blending of ancient art and high-tech optics."

For Smith, 1983 was a most significant year; after getting his B.Sc. in geology, he moved to Seattle, where he set up a stone and jewelry store in Pioneer Square and attended, off and on, art courses at the University of Seattle. He also started exhibiting his jewelry work at gem and mineral shows and he first started going to Opal Butte with Dale Huett. The place was mostly abandoned then and it was from thunderegg opal recovered there that he began cutting the spectacular pieces he creates. "The very nature of the material," he says, "suited my style quite well and I fell in love with it, working with whatever types of opals we could find."

In 1991, wanting to concentrate more on creating and selling his jewelry—of many different varieties, not just opal—Smith separated himself from the Opal Butte operation and moved to Tucson, where he still lives today. His work has become renowned at such prestigious shows as the Tucson Gem and Mineral Show, the Denver Gem and Mineral Show, and the big International Gem and Mineral Show at Munich, Germany.

I asked him how he decided, when he looked at a piece of rough gemstone material, what he was going to make. He replied, "When I look at a piece of rough, I may see a vague potential or I may envision a very specific form. But I don't act on that immediately; I evaluate it over and again. Sometimes I'll cut a little window on the outside of the stone to see and evaluate what's inside. Sometimes I'll do no initial planning at all, but simply take off all the material that has to go and then the remaining shape will suggest something to sculpt or a treatment or how to enhance what's inside the stone. Sometimes it goes quickly; sometimes it takes years. Sometimes easy; sometimes tough. Sometimes I start a piece that says what it wants, but then, because of unforeseen problems, it has to be changed. Now and then I'll set a piece aside for 8–10 years until a picture comes (Figure 46). You can ruin a stone by trying to force it into being something it doesn't want." When I asked him what he was looking for, what he really wanted, he smiled and replied quietly, "To excel in the craft and to have more demand for my work than can possibly be met."

There seems little doubt he's already achieved the first part of that goal and is rapidly approaching the second. While no longer so closely tied to the operation at Opal Butte as he was some years ago, he remains consulting geologist for West Coast Gemstones and he still enjoys working with the unusual and often uncannily beautiful Opal Butte material. So renowned has his work become that it has been featured on the cover of *Lapidary Journal* magazine as well as inside, and for some of the pieces he is commissioned to complete there is now a waiting period of 2 to 3 years, perhaps more.

Getting back to the matter of Opal Butte material and the way Kevin Lane Smith works with it, he says that in all cases when working with opal he lets the stone itself dictate the form it should take and he tries to work with the natural shapes as much as possible, responding to the problems and limitations of the

Figure 46. The *Dancer* is a fine example of freeform carving with abstract intaglio fashioned around natural formations. The 211-carat piece was created from Opal Butte contra luz opal by Kevin Lane Smith. (Photo by the author)

stone. "I take it one step at a time," he told me, "and hope that it comes together. It usually does."

Finding the thundereggs in the Opal Butte mining operation has not been a guarantee that quality precious opal is being found. Smith states that of the thundereggs recovered, "about 70% contain no opal, some 20% contain common opal only, and only 10% contain gem-quality opal exhibiting prominent play of color." Yet, despite such scarcity, Opal Butte opals, through the efforts of Smith and Huett, are today known and appreciated throughout the world.

Finally, some good news for potential opal miners—Dale Huett inaugurated opal digging on a fee basis in 1996. Further information is obtainable through West Coast Gemstones, P.O. Box 133, College Place, WA 99324, or fax 509-527-1233.

QUEENSLAND

The beauty, variety, and abundance of precious opal from Queensland, Australia, is almost beyond comprehension and deserving of a book devoted to these deposits alone. There are, throughout Queensland, a veritable multitude of very rich fields producing an amazing variety of fine stones—primarily boulder opal, but also seam opal, pipe opal, opal matrix, and Yowah nuts, to say nothing of various volcanic opal deposits in the coastal ranges. The principal opal mining area, however, is the so-called opal belt of western Queensland, which takes in an enormous amount of territory—some say as much as 50,000 square *miles*. Within this area, which runs from the New South Wales border in the vicinity of Hungerford, northwest almost 600 miles [900 km] to Kynuna, in a band that is as much as 155 miles [250 km] wide, high-quality opals have been found in a great variety of places, and it is said that the area is still barely touched where its potential for future development is concerned.

Precious opal was first discovered in Queensland in the 1870s. While the market for Queensland opals has had its ups and downs, the gems are today enjoying an unprecedented popularity, and with good reason: The finest boulder opal can rival in its brilliance and pattern the finest opal from Lightning Ridge or anywhere else. Within each of the numerous principal opal fields there are from a few mines to dozens of them. Among the more prolific opal fields are Bairndale, Black Gate, Brighton Downs, Bull Creek, Bulloo River, Carbine, Chiltern Hills, Depazzie, Duck Creek, Eromanga, Franklin, Hayricks, Hungerford, Jundah, Koroit, Kurran Holding, Kyabra Hills, Kynuna, Listowel Downs, Longreach, Mayneside, Moble, Opalton (discovered in 1888 by George Cragg), Opalville, Quilpie, Springside, Toompine, and Yowah.

The opal deposit in the western Queensland fields is usually discovered through prospecting surface deposits or putting down 9-inch drill bore holes through sandstone and claystone layers to bring up samples of the opal dirt from below and see if it contains any trace of precious opal. If it does, a larger auger drills a 30-inch [76-cm] shaft down to the opal level—usually about 60 feet [18 m] deep and it is checked out carefully by a miner lowered by rope. If it is determined that the prospects are good for an extensive deposit, an open cut is begun using a bulldozer and carefully grading away the overburden. The initial cut is usually 50' wide by 200' long [15 m × 60 m]. Spotters on foot follow behind the bulldozer, carefully studying the material unearthed and at the first sign of precious opal, mechanized work is ceased for the time being and a determination is made as to the extent of the opal and the direction of the deposit, which can then be followed, often altering the shape of the pit. Sometimes these deposits are so extensive that the open cut becomes quite large.

Boulder opal, rough or polished, always includes some of the matrix material, from which the opal alone cannot reasonably be separated without damage to the stone. As boulder opal, it will be one of two classifications: (1) precious opal in associate *with* matrix, normally meaning a layer—often quite thin—of precious opal coating an ironstone backing, but with that backing not visible when the opal is viewed face up; and (2) precious opal *in* matrix, in which some portion of the matrix ironstone is visible when the opal is viewed face up, quite often with half the face of the stone or even more being matrix material.

The matrix in boulder opal is ordinarily dark brown, sometimes so dark it is almost black, and the rich colors of the opal are nicely set off by contrast. Such stones are called boulder blacks, but the background color of boulder opal can also be lighter and of different color—from dark gray to pale gray, from orange to yellowing and sometimes even white. But it is the stones with the dark background that are most desired, since the POC is so saturated and intense in contrast with the darkness (Color Plate 19). Normally the most intense hues displayed are brilliant blue, searing red, and sparkling green. It is the intensity of this color that becomes the principal criterion for judging the boulder opal's value. It is also because boulder opal has matrix material combined with precious opal that rough material or cut stones are usually priced by the piece and not by the carat weight. Pattern will also play an important role in evaluating a particular stone's worth, harlequin being the rarest and most desirable pattern and pinfire, because of being so common, the least valuable. Additionally, even though ideally a boulder opal displays three or more colors, as a general rule the more red exhibited, the more valuable the stone. A piece exhibiting harlequin pattern and three-quarters of the color being red will be the highest-quality boulder opal.

Boulder opal's dramatic increase in popularity in the opal market throughout the world, particularly in the United States, in recent years has been because of the beauty created by a balanced combination of color and background, opal and matrix, pattern and color, and placement of POC. Many jewelry designers and opal fanciers find great aesthetic beauty in these stones, comparable in large measure to the beauty art collectors find in beautiful paintings.

As this is true for boulder opal, so it is also true for its smaller kin, the so-called Yowah nuts, which are mined at Yowah in southwestern Queensland and are named after their usual nutlike exterior appearance. The ironstone involved is most often a very rich red-brown and is so hard that it will polish to just as high a finish as the opal itself.

Since no early records are known to exist, it is not possible to say exactly when the Yowah opal field was discovered, although it was probably some 30 years before the turn of the century. This is a very interesting little field, famed for its brilliant and unusual opals, which appear in the form of small concretions, normally about walnut-sized. These are, of course, the Yowah nuts.

Located about an hour's drive north and west of the town of Eulo, the field is named after Yowah Creek and there is some speculation that the opals may first have been discovered there by stockmen riding across Yowah Paddock. At any rate, the first claim made in the field was a lease registered in 1875 by Herbert Bond as the Southern Cross Mine (Figure 47). The Yowah nuts found here consist of ironstone concretions in which precious opal has formed in hollows or cavities or cracks in brilliant and often very stirring patterns. Quite frequently the "nut" has an outer two-thirds of the red ironstone and an interior kernel of gorgeous opal. Once in a while almost the entire interior will be solid opal inside a thin skin of ironstone, but far more often the opal is intermingled with the ironstone in fascinating patterns, with no two ever being exactly alike. More often than not these concretions are broken or cut in half and then cut and polished with the ironstone into very striking cabochons. Some of these small concretions contain nice specimens of colorfully opalized wood.

When I visited the Yowah field in late 1995, miner Eddie Maguire not only took me into his mine and demonstrated how these unusual stones were recovered, he also showed me as well in his home the remarkable collection of stones he has mined and then polished. They are so beautiful and so fascinating in their variety that one forgets the passage of time and everything else except

Figure 47. There is nothing superficial about Yowah. (Photo by the author)

the intriguing stones one is inspecting. Hours flew by in what seemed the blink of an eye and my chief regret was that so few eyes have seen and appreciated such a treasure. They deserve to be photographed, every one, and preserved in a pictorial book that one could page through at leisure. I will never forget the experience of seeing those beautifully fashioned pieces and the warm hospitality of Tanya and Eddie Maguire during that all too brief visit.[31]

While the opal-bearing from Yowah nuts are still not as well known as some of the boulder opal forms from places such as Quilpie or Opalton, or the fine gem-quality opals of Lighting Ridge, Coober Pedy, Mintabie, and other notable Australian fields, I would not hesitate to predict that Yowah nuts are on the verge of unprecedented popularity. The brilliance of the opal, the variety of the patterns, the marvelous "scenics" that develop in the cutting, the amazing stability of the material, and the joy of working with it are all factors that are bound to increase its popularity throughout the world.

SPENCER, IDAHO

While the state of Idaho can boast more than a dozen sites where precious opal deposits are located, only one of these has developed any real degree of importance on the world opal scene—the Spencer Opal Mine just east of the town of Spencer in Clark Country.[32] The opal deposit that was to become the Spencer Opal Mine was accidentally discovered in 1948 by a pair of deer hunters who became lost in a fog on an Idaho mountainside in the Bitterroot Range some 15 miles south of the Montana border, 60 miles west of Yellowstone National Park, and a few miles east of the town of Spencer. While resting as they waited for the fog to lift, the men discovered pieces of thin-layered, white to pinkish, porcelain like rock that had weathered out of an outcropping ledge of rhyolite. The pieces glittered with brilliant colors such as the hunters had never before seen. They took samples to an expert and learned they were opals. Sample diggings were made on the mountain over the next few years and then, in 1952, the first mining claim was taken out by Franklin W. Argenbright and Jesse Ray Bohney, who called it the Lost Deer Hunters' Mine.

Three years later, in 1955, the claim was relocated as a quartz claim by Bohney and George D. Wright. In 1959, Wright sold his interest in the mine to Charles Casper and not long after that, Bohney sold his interest to Mark Stetler. Eight years of land dispute cases followed, at the end of which time, in 1967, Stetler wound up with sole control of the mine. The following year, Stetler opened the mine to fee digging. It was immediately so popular that in the first year it was visited by rockhounds from every state in the union except Mississippi.

In 1974, a few years after Stetler's daughter, Claudia, married Doyle Haight, the couple took over management of the mine, but Mark Stetler retained ownership. In 1980, though still owning the mine, Stetler turned over its complete operation to Haight and in 1986 gave Haight a full partnership. In 1995, Doyle Haight died. As of this writing the mine was still functioning as a fee-digging operation but rumors were rife that it would soon be closed.

The opals of the Spencer Opal Mine are found as layered material in nodules of hard kaolinite that occur in a strata of much harder rhyolite (Figure 48). These layers of precious opal, sandwiched in a white to beige translucent common opal, are extremely thin. About the thickest ever found are an eighth to a quarter of an inch; normally they're much thinner, all the way down to the thickness of a few sheets of paper and, in some cases, no thicker than a piece of tissue paper. For this reason, most of the Spencer opal is made into triplets, occasionally into doublets, and only rarely are pieces found that are thick enough to cut into solids (Color Plates 1 and 2).

Mark Stetler has always contended that "the play-of-color and flashes of fire in the Idaho opal equal that of opal found anywhere else," and, extravagant though it may seem, there are few who would argue the truth of that statement. The precious opal is very colorful, vying with the best color of the opals of Australia and Nevada. Brilliant reds, greens, golds, oranges, blues, and other

Figure 48. At the Spencer Opal Mine in Idaho, careful blasting has exposed rhyolitic matrix material in which vugs lined with common opal and thin layers of precious opal occur. But even this must be further broken up by hand-wielded sledgehammers into smaller, more manageable chunks. (Photo by Alan A. Vogel)

colors show in an array of POC that is very lovely, not only in color but in pattern as well. Varieties of the latter include pinfire, shortflash, longflash, broadflash, ripple, flagstone, full sheen (highly prized), fanflash, mist, turtleback (unique to Spencer), and many others. In addition, frequently the pieces show interesting pinfire or flash fire over fascinating scenes created by inclusions. It is also said that occasional "star" opals are found that exhibit the same kind of star chatoyancy as seen in sapphires, rubies, and the like.

Doublets and triplets made of Spencer opals have become extremely popular and are often sold at gem shows for very good prices. There is also a substantial international market for the stones. In making the triplet, one side of the stone is carefully ground down to the opal level, exposing it in its full color. To this surface a slice of backing material—usually basinite, black basalt, black obsidian, or other dark or black material—is epoxied. Then the other side of the stone is ground down until again that same opal level is exposed and to that surface is epoxied a quartz dome. The whole stone is then shaped carefully into a pleasing cabochon, which, when set in jewelry, is difficult to differentiate from a solid opal. If the layer of opal is thick enough, a doublet is made instead of a triplet—the same kind of backing, but with the opal itself shaped as the dome, without a quartz cap. Some are made in the reverse—with a dome over the opal, but no backing.

Those who may be interested in collecting their own opals at this fee-digging operation can make reservations or obtain information in regard to admission fees, equipment needed, directions, accommodations, and the like by writing to Mrs. Claudia Haight, The Spencer Opal Mine, Box 113, Spencer, Idaho 83446, or call 208-374-5476.

VIRGIN VALLEY, NEVADA

As with the opals of Lightning Ridge, Andamooka, Quilpie, and other great opal fields, the story of Virgin Valley opals is deserving of a book in its own right because certainly all the wonderful history and anecdotes and informational data cannot possibly be done justice in a short space. Thus, only some high points will be commented upon here. Named after Virgin Creek, which traverses its length, Virgin Valley, roughly 2 miles wide and 12 miles long, is in an uncommonly isolated part of the United States, the high desert country of northwestern Nevada. Five miles south of the central Oregon border and just over 50 miles east of the northern California border, Virgin Valley in Humboldt County is some 32 miles west of the nearest town, which is Denio, whose flexible population averages about 30 individuals.[33] The nearest town of any size is Lakeview, Oregon, some 85 miles west and north, which has a population of around 2500. The nearest city is the Humboldt County seat, Winnemucca, some 130 miles southeast, which itself has a population of only a bit over 6000.

It has been shown in the chapter dealing with the history of opals that black opals were evidently first seen in Virgin Valley during a Chinese expedition to this continent sometime prior to 2250 B.C. But they were not discovered again after that until 1905 when a mining engineer named Marsden Nanson, passing through Virgin Valley, picked up specimen rocks here and there and found one that was beautiful precious opal.[34] His further searching uncovered more and established that the colorful stones were float that was weathering out of a stratum of montmorillonite clay from the side of a towering, basalt-rimmed mesa named Gooch Table (Figure 49).

Nanson wrote about it and before the year was out the first opal mine claim was filed—the Opal Queen Mine. Early the next year the Virgin Opal Mine claim was filed—later to be renamed the Bonanza Mine. With that the floodgates were opened and by the end of 1906, Virgin Valley had become a veritable patchwork of opal claims. The opals, while in volcanic deposits—ash that had become a kaolinitic material that became known as montmorillonite—were primarily wood opal; beautiful black opal and light opal alike that had formed pseudomorphically, filling cavities within wood and very often replacing the wood itself cell by cell in remarkable and incredibly lovely replication. The light opals were as brilliant and colorful as any of the light opals that had ever been mined as so-called Hungarian opals, or those from White Cliffs in New South Wales or Coober Pedy or Mintabie in South Australia. And the black opals . . . Well! They were exquisite and truly black opals—black crystal opal through and through and not relying, as Lightning Ridge black opals typically do, on a thin

Figure 49. Gooch Table looms darkly across Virgin Valley from the main office of the Royal Peacock Opal Mines. The Bonanza Mine, Virgin Mine, and others are located to the left, not far from the area where the light spot shows against the dark slope. (Photo by the author)

layer of crystal opal occurring naturally on a background of dark gray or black potch.

A great deal of incredibly colorful opal was being found in this early mining at Virgin valley and, with it, the discovery that the beautiful opal was all too often inclined to crack or craze, sometimes to such an extent that it actually self-destructed within a matter of minutes or an hour or so. The water content in Virgin Valley opal, while not constant, averages between 6% and 10% and some has been shown to run as high as 13%, as compared to Australian opal with a water content that rarely exceeds 6%. Many miners attribute the stone's instability to this high water content. Even though not all the opal being mined at Virgin Valley was affected with such cracking and crazing, enough was involved that all the opal from there began to be held suspect and was avoided. Miners wishing to sell their opal all too frequently made no attempt to separate the opal that was essentially stable from that which was so prone to crazing. Instead, most of the miners began putting the opals in jars of water, oil, or glycerine as "specimen opal" and this is a process still followed in large measure today. Even though a good bit of Virgin Valley opal is, unfortunately, susceptible to such cracking and crazing, not all of it is and it is unfortunate that practically all of it has been painted with this same brush of ill repute.

It was 6 years after Nanson's original discovery that a second major deposit was found in an area roughly 10 miles southeast from the first. It was found on an elevation called Rainbow Ridge, which was in the nearby Sagebrush Creek drainage.[35] Several prospects were made on the ridge and the first claim was made here and named the McGee Claim after Ed McGee, who registered it. That claim would eventually become one of the most important opal mines in all of North America, the Rainbow Ridge Opal Mine. As with the opal being found on the slope of Gooch Table at the Opal Queen Mine and Virgin Opal Mine, the opal being found here was not only beautifully colored and patterned, it was often being found in remarkably large pieces. The preponderance of what was removed from the ground here was light opal, but a good percentage of beautiful black opal was also coming out.[36] In 1912 a series of claims were made and soon a number of other prospects in which excellent opals were found were registered farther up the Virgin Valley, overlooking Virgin Creek and became collectively known as the Royal Peacock Opal Mines. From these mines would come opals that would vie with those of Rainbow Ridge and Gooch Table as some of the finest opals ever found in America.

One of the most colorful characters of Virgin Valley first made an appearance here in the summer of 1915. This was a 59-year-old woman named Flora Haines Apponyi Loughead Gutierrez—a reporter from the San Francisco *Chronicle*—who was sent to research a feature story on the precious opal being mined here. The daughter of John Penley Haines, a gold rush miner in California in 1849, she was born in 1855 after he returned to White Water, Wisconsin.

A very bright young woman, she graduated from an Illinois college when she was 15 and immediately became a reporter for a Wisconsin newspaper, subsequently getting a better job on a Denver newspaper. It was in Denver that she met and married a Hungarian named Apponyi, who claimed to be an outcast of the ruling Hapsburg Dynasty. They had three children and moved to San Francisco, where she became the first female feature writer for the *Chronicle*. After her divorce from Apponyi, she married a combination artist and hardware merchant named John Loughead—pronounced Lockheed. With him she had two sons, Allan and Malcolm, who became famous in the world of aviation—Allan for founding Lockheed Aircraft, and Malcolm for inventing the hydraulic aircraft braking system. Because of them, she is best known as Flora Loughead, even though after her second husband's death she married one David Gutierrez, who claimed his mother's side were the Castro family, powerful Spanish landowners of early California. She received much acclaim for her personal coverage of the 1906 San Francisco earthquake for the *Chronicle* and so was a good choice to do an in-depth feature about the opal mining that had been going on the past few years in Virgin Valley.

On her arrival, Flora fell in love with the area in general and with the opals in particular. With what money she had, she bought numerous claims, including the Opal Queen Mine—after which she was sometimes referred to herself as the Opal Queen—and the Virgin Opal Mine, as well as Ed McGee's claims at Rainbow Ridge and the Royal Peacock claims well up the valley. She also did a considerable amount of claiming in her own name and, at length, wound up owning as many claims as anyone in Virgin Valley. She also hired J. B. "Ridge" Oliver as her superintendent of mining and he, in turn, hired a considerable number of down-at-the-heels miners to work her mines and claims as salaried employees.

Some truly spectacular opal finds were being made in Virgin Valley at that time. During the summer of 1917, one of Flora's miners uncovered a stone in her claim at Rainbow Ridge that was of great size, beautiful pattern, and spectacular color. Cleaned of all foreign material, the stone was solid opal and weighed a staggering 10,376 carats. Evidently the miner, wanting to set himself up in a mining operation of his own, journeyed to the little stage-stop town of Lovelock, Nevada, halfway between Reno and Winnemucca and there left the magnificent stone as a deposit at the Lovelock Mercantile Company in exchange for a grubstake of mining equipment, food, and other necessaries, details of which can be found under the heading Grubstake Opal in the chapter on famous stones. The following November, Lew Thompson, another of the miners Flora employed at Rainbow Ridge, was working in the main drive of the underground workings when he uncovered a magnificent 3560-carat black opal alive with broad flashes of brilliant scarlet POC—a stone so stupendous that it caused all who saw it to gasp in wonder and admiration. Almost at the same time, a superb stone about half that size with incredibly beautiful harlequin pattern was also found in the Rainbow Ridge mine dump when it was inadvertently struck by a pick and split in half.

Despite these great finds, Flora had spent so much of her money in equipment, salaries, and claim acquisitions that she had virtually wiped out all her own funds and so prevailed upon a rich acquaintance, Mrs. Gardiner Hammond of Santa Barbara, California, to go into partnership with her; Flora would provide the mines and the opal-mining experience—as well as the big black opal and the smaller remarkable harlequin—and Mrs. Hammond, of Hammond Organ fame, would provide the operating capital. They agreed to call their partnership the Rainbow Ridge Mining Company.

The partnership became actuality in April 1918, and shortly thereafter the huge black opal was sold to Ward's Natural History Establishment in Rochester, New York. From them it was purchased by one of the great gemstone collectors of the time, Washington A. Roebling, architect of the Brooklyn Bridge, and was thereafter known as the Roebling Opal. What happened to the two halves of the Harlequin Opal, as some called it, has not been recorded.[37]

After the Great War many of the miners who had gone away to join the army did not return and mining in Virgin Valley entered a period of hiatus that lasted for many years. Surface deposits had all been picked clean long ago and so Flora continued mining as much as she could and as much as the Rainbow Ridge Mining Company could afford, but little by little Mrs. Hammond became less inclined to sink any more of her funds in the venture. Flora, once again relatively destitute, did much of her own mining and was a familiar figure in her high-top white tennis shoes, walking to her claims with a pick held across her shoulder. At length, she hired a miner named Mark Foster to do the work for her that she was physically incapable of doing any longer for herself. Because she had little money with which to pay him, she began giving him some of her claims in exchange for his labors. He soon owned almost all of her upper valley claims in the Royal Peacock group. Although all of these had precious opal deposits, only one was considered at all worthwhile at the time and it was not a mine producing precious opal. The mine was at an elevation well above most of the others and was a consistent producer of large quantities of a pale greenish yellow-tan common opal that fluoresced a brilliant green; a material that was very popular in Europe and was shipped there regularly.

In 1933 another miner in Virgin Valley, Dan Archevaleta, formerly a Basque sheepherder, found a huge opal in his mine, sparking a renewal of interest. This inspired geologist H. C. Dake to visit the area. Before the end of the year, he described the Virgin Valley opal beds in a scientific paper, renewing public interest even more. Four years later the Harry W. Wilson family arrived in Virgin Valley and bought Mark Foster's fluorescent opal mine, as well as many other claims. Foster, as an inducement for the Wilsons to buy, literally "tossed in" the precious opal claims, since they were lying idle and there was no real market for Virgin Valley precious opal anyway. Among those included were the mines that Flora, when she bought them years before, had named The Pebbles, the Northern Lights, Royal Peacock, and others.

Flora's fortunes took another downturn of sorts in 1936 with the appearance of an article by geologist H. C. Drake in the June issue of a magazine called *The Mineralogist*. Because the vast, 539,000-acre Charles Sheldon National Wildlife Range had been formed which encompassed the whole of Virgin Valley and surrounding areas, Dake made comments that Flora interpreted as telling his readers that opal mining was at an end in Virgin Valley and what opal was still there in the mines was available for the taking for whoever wanted to make the journey. Others must have interpreted the article the same way because the result was that a multitude of people converged on the valley and did a great deal of damage to many of the mines, breaking in doors and iron gates, stealing equipment and containers of rough opal, and doing a great deal of vandalizing. Flora wrote vehement letters to the government, demanding protection of the claims and property of other miners and herself in Virgin Valley, but her complaints were largely ignored.

In the late 1930s Flora's family in San Francisco virtually put her under house arrest to keep her from returning to the Virgin Valley mines, where they were sure she would injure herself.[38] As it turned out, however, it was staying home that did her in. In 1938, now 83 years old, she was visiting family members in Los Angeles when she fell from a kitchen stool, broke her hip and never walked again. She was taken back north to the San Francisco area and there, in the Berkeley home of her daughter, Hope Loughead Ledford, she remained, once again a virtual prisoner, until her death at age 87 in January of 1943.

What belonged to the Rainbow Ridge Mining Company, in which the elderly Mrs. Hammond no longer had any interest whatever, was sold off and a man named Harry Foulks of Stockton, California, acquired the six patented claims making up the Rainbow Ridge Mining Company. Mining picked up dramatically in Virgin Valley in 1945, following a quarter-century of near inactivity, but Foulks had bought the claims more as an investment than anything else and he, in turn, subsequently sold them in 1949 to the Hodson family—Glenn and Bea and their son and daughter-in-law, Keith and Agnes. The new owners gave the principal mine—the one where the Grubstake and Roebling and Harlequin opals had been found—the name it still bears today, the Rainbow Ridge Opal Mine. As if it were a signal, opal mining in Virgin Valley suddenly went into a boom and has continued in this way ever since.

Many wonderful finds have been made in the various diggings in Virgin Valley through the years since then—two of the most spectacular made by none other than Keith Hodson himself. One of these was the 14,288-carat Hodson Opal, discovered in the Rainbow Ridge Opal Mine in June of 1952 and valued today at over a million dollars. Two years later the Hodsons bought the old Virgin Opal Mine, renamed Bonanza Mine, from Mark Foster, and 20 years later, in 1974, Keith Hodson discovered by accident at that mine the magnificent 23,586-carat Bonanza Opal.[39]

Glenn Hodson always considered Virgin Valley his "happy place" and when he died in 1959, his ashes were buried in a little private cemetery just above the entrance to the main drive of the Rainbow Ridge Opal Mine. Beside his remains today lie the ashes of his wife, Bea, and their friend, Mark Foster.

In an effort to overcome the lingering reputation Virgin Valley opals have for cracking and crazing, William Kelley, a Cleveland individual who leased mining claims from the Wilson family, developed what he claimed to be a stabilizing process for the stones. He called it the Kelley Process and convinced quite a few people that it worked. Unfortunately, it didn't seem to work all that well and most of the experienced Virgin Valley miners were sure that what opals didn't crack or craze after being subjected to his process were those that wouldn't have cracked or crazed anyway, processed or not.

It was in July of 1970 that another magnificent black opal was discovered in Virgin Valley—this one at the Royal Peacock Number One Mine owned by the Wilsons. A splendid 7370-carat stone, it was cut into a number of very impressive smaller stones, including the 166-carat *Black Peacock* opal and the 20-carat *Little Black Peacock*. Again at the Wilson mines, in 1978, another exceptional black opal was found, this time at the Royal Peacock Number Two Mine. After being cut and polished, it was a scintillating red-on-black oval cabochon weighing 205 carats (Figure 50).

The Wilson family's Royal Peacock Mines and the Bonanza Mine belonging to the Hodsons received their patient in 1980. However, in 1988, after 34 years of owning it, the Hodsons sold the Bonanza Mine and the new owners, in turn, sold shares to individuals and opened the mine for share-digging only. For one of the shareholders, Irene Lovell, it was a good deal. Two years after the new system was inaugurated, she found an enormous opal, now called the *Irene Lovell Opal*, weighing 18,142 carats, which is said to be worth "at least $1 million."

The author himself was fortunate enough to be on hand at Wilson's on 15 June 1992, when a fee digger named Michael Croxwell from Minneapolis, digging in the Northern Lights Mine, encountered an opalized section of log 35 inches long and 16 inches in diameter at its thickest. It took two full days of digging to carefully remove the surrounding dirt and the aid of a front loader to carefully lift it out of the hole. The black opal of which it was in part composed was alive with POC in patterns ranging from pinfire to broadflash and in brilliant red, green, blue, violet, lavender, orange, yellow, and a very unusual fiery pink rarely seen in Virgin Valley opal previously and then only in small pieces (Figure 51).

The 130-pound log, even before being fully cleaned, was estimated to con-

Figure 50. The author works at carefully removing a black opal from the surrounding mont-morillonite clay while his friend, C. William "Bill" Harris, rock shop owner of Sarasota, Florida, looks on. This was at the Northern Lights Mine in Virgin Valley. (Photo by Alan Vogel)

tain at least 30% precious opal—no less than 39 pounds! George Munzing, paleobotanist from Brigham Young University at Provo, Utah, who has been doing a study of fossil woods in Virgin Valley, studied a thin slice of the wood using electron microscopic scanning techniques and determined that the log was a ginkgo, the first of that species ever identified in Virgin Valley. The Royal Peacock opal log was subsequently purchased for an undisclosed sum by long-time Virgin Valley opal miner Slim Houck. Though not confirmed, it is said that when final cleaning of the log was completed, it had an even greater percentage of precious opal than the estimated 30% and the specimen is said to be "a knock-out."

It is the incredibly beautiful black opal that draws would-be opal miners from all over the world. But there are other varieties in Virgin Valley that are also attractive and eagerly sought after. In addition to the black opal, which is a

Figure 51. Walt Wilson, owner of the Royal Peacock Opal Mines of Virgin Valley, with the partially cleaned opalized log recovered from his Northern Lights Mine. When the preliminary cleaning was finished, the log was 35″ [90 cm] long, 16″ [40.6 cm] in diameter, and weighed 130 pounds—294,840 carats! —making it, at this writing, the world's largest officially recognized specimen of fossil opal. (Photo by the author)

true black crystal variety, there is a translucent black opal that glints with color from deep within and there also occurs a transparent brown variety so dark it almost seems black, but which is called root beer opal. Quite often that root beer opal is contra luz, exhibiting its rainbow colors by transmitted light rather than reflected light, but there is also quite a bit of contra luz ranging from translucent white to stones as clear as water. Hydrophane opal is not uncommon, usually white or tan and rich with colors that remain even when the piece is soaked in water and becomes water clear. Cachalong opal is found with relative frequency and there is a good bit of hyalite as well. Bog opal, exhibiting brilliant bits of color intermingled with bits of vegetation in a dark brown translucent base, was discovered by the miner–scientist George Hewitt in his dig close to the Wilson mines. Conk opal—that is, opal that has filled or replaced the pores of wood—is found on occasion. Being very brightly colored and unusually stable, it is a favorite of many, including Keith Hodson.

And, of course, Virgin Valley in general and the Rainbow Ridge Mine in particular are noted for some exceptional transparent, so-called jelly opals, some as clear as water, some colored, which lend themselves well to faceting, either into formal cuts or, more commonly, into freeform pieces in which the POC remains clearly evident and very beautiful (Figure 52). Just as often, these transparent stones, so rich in color and so spectacular in their appearance, are simply cut into nonfaceted freeform pieces.

Fossil woods and plants, often opalized, are very common in Virgin Valley and opalized vertebrate remains are sometimes found. Not uncommonly fossil pine cones are found that are partially—or, rarely, entirely—opalized (Figure 53). They are very beautiful and quite valuable. Agnes Hodson has a collection of these pieces that, by early summer 1996, numbered well over 300. Walter Wilson has in his possession, in addition to the fully opalized carnivore molars mentioned earlier, fossil bones of camels, mastodons, rhinoceroses, and other mammals, some of them partially opalized.

The montmorillonite level in which the opals occur at the Northern Lights Mine is so moist that very often the miner's pick will strike a water-filled cavity that will spew liquid for a considerable while. The opal from this mine is less stable than the opal at the Rainbow Ridge Opal Mine, where the opal level is generally much drier. If carefully and slowly dried over extended periods, how-

Figure 52. In October 1995, at Rainbow Ridge Opal Mine, a blow of a pick broke in half this magnificent jelly opal. In the extraction process, four more grand stones were encountered and removed (one of which, here, is still embedded in the clay). (Photo by Keith Hodson)

Figure 53. This opalized fossil pine cone cabochon was cut by paleobotanist George E. Munzing. (Photo by George E. Munzing, Ph.D.)

ever, the stones become more stable and can often be cut without crazing occurring (Figure 54).

There are at present over 600 opal claims registered in Virgin Valley and some 30 actively working mines. The total number of mines, prospects, and claims is very flexible, however, since old claims regularly expire and just as many or more are filed as new claims. At least two well-producing private operations—one patented, one not—sell practically all their opal to Oriental buyers who ship it to Korea, Taiwan, or Japan for cutting. Rumor has it that the Orientals have developed a process for stabilizing opal from such deposits as Virgin Valley, Querétaro, Honduras, and other sites where cracking and crazing of the material, either as rough or while in the process of being cut, seems to be endemic. While no proof has been found to substantiate these rumors, the very fact that Oriental buyers continue to buy this opal in volume that is reputed to be highly susceptible to cracking and crazing, tends to add a measure of validity to the possibility.

Keith Hodson is only one of many long-time Nevada opal miners who believe there is far more—and better!—precious opal still under the surface at Virgin Valley than has ever seen the light of day. Says Hodson, chuckling, "The only trick is finding it."

There are two principal fee-digging operations at Virgin Valley, for those

Figure 54. Alan A. Vogel, miner/jewelry-maker, of Mequon, Wisconsin, carefully uses an ice pick as an aid in freeing a good-sized black opal that he has encountered in the montmorillonite clay opal level at the Northern Lights Mine in Virgin Valley, during late June 1993. (Photo by the author)

who may be interested in collecting their own opals. One is at the Rainbow Ridge Opal Mine operated by the Hodson family, where collecting is permitted only on the extensive tailings. Another is the open-pit Northern Lights Mine, where digging can be done in the exposed opal level—bank digging, it is called. This is an operation of the Royal Peacock Opal Mines group, owned and operated by the Walter Wilson family, though ownership of this latter group may soon change, since it is presently up for sale. Further information about these fee-digging areas, including rates, reservations, nearby or on-site accommodations, directions, and the like, may be obtained by contacting:

The Hodsons
Rainbow Ridge Opal Mine
P. O. Box 97
Denio, NV 89404, USA
    Ph: 702-941-0270

The Wilsons
Royal Peacock Opal Mines
P. O. Box 55
Denio, NV 89404, USA
    Ph: 702-272-3201

WHITE CLIFFS, NEW SOUTH WALES

Located some 660 miles [1065 km] northwest of Sydney and 183 miles [295 km] northeast of Broken Hill, the White Cliffs opal field, while not the site of the first opals discovered in Australia, was the opal discovery site that most definitely launched Australia as the most important source of opals in the world today. It used to be very difficult to reach this site—sometimes impossible during inclement weather before the roads were sealed. Now only a few miles of unpaved road remains—that portion located between Wilcannia and White Cliffs—and there is usually little problem.

Boulder opal was being mined in Queensland some time before the White Cliffs material was discovered, but the world jewelry market was unprepared for such an unusual form of opal as boulder opal and so a ready market did not exist for it. But White Cliffs opal—ah, that's another matter entirely. Here was a light opal that looked essentially like the best of the so-called Hungarian opal ever produced, only generally much larger and with POC much more brilliant—a scintillating, gorgeous light opal that, initially, seemed in limitless supply. Within only a few brief years the Hungarian opal mines at Dubnik in Slovakia were all but defunct, after having been the principal supplier of the world's gemstone opal for more than 2000 years, supplanted now by the amazing new source "Down Under."

This great change all began in 1889 when precious opals were accidentally found on the ground surface at a place called White Cliffs on Momba Station by a party of kangaroo hunters.[40] The three men—George Hooley, Alf Richardson, and W. H. Clouston—were moving along slowly on the side of a hill, following the trail of a kangaroo they'd wounded and watching the ground carefully for the spots of blood.[41] An extremely brilliant flash of red caught Hooley's attention, but it wasn't blood. He picked up the stone in which the red was glinting, looked curiously at the pebble that had obviously eroded out of the side of the hill, and then showed it to the others, who agreed they'd never seen anything quite like it before.[42] They spread out and found a number of others that had brilliant greens, blues, oranges, and reds glinting from within them, colors that changed as they turned and tilted the stones. None of the three had ever seen opal before, but they'd heard about it and wondered if that was what this was. They had soon collected so many that they were convinced the inside of the hill must be alive with such stones.

At first the three kept their find secret, not quite sure what they should do about it and only too well aware that if the stones were, in fact, opals, there would be a tremendous rush of miners to this place once the word got out. They finally decided to show their find to Charlie Turner, a friend of theirs who was surveying in the area. Turner shook his head, also uncertain what they were, but he knew someone who would know—Tullie Wollaston. He and Wollaston had worked together in the Survey Department somewhat earlier, before the latter had become an opal buyer of material being found in Queensland. Turner boxed up the specimens and sent them to Wollaston in Adelaide, at the same time advising the men that it would be wise to peg out claims in the area where their stones were found at White Cliffs. The men agreed, took Turner with them and all four made claims, the first of these registered at the claims office in 60-mile distant Wilcannia on 21 March 1890.

When Wollaston returned home from his latest buying stint in Queensland, he found the White Cliffs parcel awaiting him and was greatly excited by what he saw inside. He immediately set off on the difficult trip to White Cliffs. The men had collected a considerable amount more by then and a shallow open cut was made from which they were getting more, the opal occurring in abundance in thin horizontal and vertical veins within an orangish sedimentary rock, usu-ally referred to as sandstone or country rock. The opals were occurring in more or less flat bands in those Cretaceous claystone sediments beneath silcrete, shale, and conglomerates, the same material that formed the caps of the numerous mesas of the White Cliffs area. The men had put together a nice parcel and Tullie Wollaston offered them £140 for it, which they readily accepted and, with that, White Cliffs opal field had become a reality. Word of the new field eventually leaked out and there came a trickle of miners that turned into a stream and then a torrent. A village of sorts—primarily tents and shacks called humpies that were made of any kind of junk material—grew and was initially called Kan-garoo Shooters Camp.

Wollaston made out quite well in reselling the opal and soon hired an eager 20-year-old named E. F. "Ted" Murphy as his resident buyer at White Cliffs, and Murphy, in subsequent years, became one of the more renowned figures on the Australian opal fields.[43] German buyers also soon came on the scene and before long the greater portion of what was being mined was being sent for cutting to Kirschweiler, a village in Germany near Idar-Oberstein. All this was the beginning of the end of the Hungarian Opal market, which had been the only game in town for centuries. Wollaston soon initiated steps for establishing a new company here, called the White Cliffs Opal Mining Company, and, as he found eager backers for the venture, the name was changed to the English Company.

Similarly, a group of shrewd businessmen in Wilcannia quickly set them-selves up as the Wilcannia Blocks Syndicate, which proceeded to stake out much of the early White Cliffs field, then established a tribute system of mining, in which they leased 100-foot-square claims to miners in exchange for half of the opal they would find. Ted Murphy, possessed of good business sense, started working as a collector in the tribute system and then became manager for the syndicate. It was not a good or equitable system and trouble soon came. As Murphy himself wrote, "Competition was fast and furious, ever increasingly so.

In their feverish zeal, buyers and sellers alike were none to scrupulous." Robberies and cheating became commonplace and miners began selling their opals outside the tribute system to independent buyers. The abuses of the tribute system eventually inspired reform movements and the system was eventually terminated.

In addition to producing some of the most beautiful light opal the world had ever seen to that point, White Cliffs also began producing some of the most remarkable opalized fossils and opal pseudomorphs ever found anywhere. There were partially or fully opalized shells, foraminifera, wood, plants, brachiopods, tusks, pelecypods and crinoids, bones, teeth, belemnites, and a variety of others, but the most spectacular finds were the fully opalized skeletons of the marine dinosaurs called plesiosaurs, and the remarkable but rather mystifying, spiky formations that bore a resemblance to small, fully opalized pineapples. Though the accepted belief for many years was that these were pseudomorphs after glauberite or gypsum, it was eventually discovered that the original mineral that had been transformed into opal was ikaite.[44]

In 1892 the miners, unable to tolerate the terrible heat, dust, and incredible numbers of files at ground surface at White Cliffs, began digging dugouts to live in or, even more practically, converting old mines into habitations, where the extreme dry heat of the desert air could be escaped. Underground, the temperature remained a very pleasant 72° around the clock. A great many of the old shafts at White Cliffs were converted into the first dug-outs on any Australian opal field.

So productive was this opal field of quality light opal that by 1893 the opal buyers were purchasing £10,000 worth of opal per month from the miners and by the mid-1890s, the name of the mining community was changed from Kangaroo Shooters Camp to the more proper designation of White Cliffs. It soon boasted a population in excess of 5000 individuals and had shops for necessaries, cool underground pubs, and, similarly underground, a large restaurant, a good bakery, and even five hotels for transient buyers. All this while the light crystal opal being produced there was becoming more widely desired and Australia was becoming ever more famous on the world market.

The greatest problem facing the early miners at White Cliffs was lack of water. There was none on the surface and no underground water that could be tapped for drinking. The nearest drinkable water was fully 40 miles away and it had to be carted in by water wagon. Not surprisingly, the White Cliffs community often ran out of water. Diseases—including diphtheria, typhoid, and dysentery—spread rapidly and death claimed many; 500 children alone died there in the first 7 years and over a thousand individuals were buried there by the end of 11 years.

By 1897 the diggings right at White Cliffs covered about a square mile, plus extending over a belt of the country about a mile and a half wide and 9 miles long, from east of Pulpah Head Station to the Yancannia Rush. Some of the early digs were Turley's Hill, Smith's Hill, Lena's Hill, Sullivan's, The Bunker (later renamed Gemville), Walsh's Knob, and, farther out, Gombek.

By 1900, White Cliffs had reached its zenith and had not only swept away Hungarian opal sources as competition, it did the same to Queensland opal. The reasons were basic: It was easier to mine and cut than was boulder opal; there was less risk of loss involved in the cutting; the supply of White Cliffs opal was not only steadier, there was less wide variation than in boulder opal from Queensland, meaning that the opal could be counted on, within certain limitations, for filling preset quotas of size, base color, pattern, quantity, and quality. The result was that Queensland opal production suffered badly and went into a hiatus that lasted about three-quarters of a century. As for White Cliffs, it now had its own post office and a regular newspaper called *The Opal Miner,* in which no less than 14 opal buyers advertised regularly. Social life increased and weekly express coaches ran 120 miles southwest to Broken Hill.

Len Cram told me the story of one of the richest pocket of opals ever found at White Cliffs, which was discovered by an old man named Saul. "He arrived on the field in a covered wagon," Cram said, "along with his wife and son. They made camp just behind Murphy's bark hut, which was a combination home, office, and store and was called Porcupine Villa. Old Saul approached Murphy to negotiate for a tribute lot, but, since reaching the opal level in such a lot usually meant digging down through perhaps 30 feet or more of silcrete, Murphy thought the man was a little too frail and, instead, he took him over to a flat depression on Block No. 7, marked out a claim, and told him he shouldn't have to sink any more than 6 feet before reaching the opal level, figuring he'd quit even before getting down that deep. When the other miners saw old Saul and his wife and son working out on the flat, they gave a little chuckle, believing that Murphy had only put him there to get him off his hands—the usual story of the new chum on all fields. At exactly 6 feet, however, Saul struck an 8' × 10' patch of beautiful opal which took him 3 months to mine. He was the one who laughed last, since he cleared £3290—a small fortune in those days."

Only two years later, in 1902, the demise of White Cliffs began. Opal seams pinched out, pockets of the gemstones were depleted and production dropped over the next year or so by 80% or more. Times grew very difficult and stayed that way. It could have been the demise of Australian opal entirely, except that coincident with the decline of White Cliffs came the rise of Lightning Ridge and its magnificent black opals—an account told elsewhere in this volume.

The miners began drifting away to Lightning Ridge and elsewhere, slowly at first but then in a more pronounced manner when matters at White Cliffs did not improve. The decline became very sharp in 1904. With the increase of poverty and crime, great misery prevailed in the population and the decline in White Cliffs' fortune became sharp. Ted Murphy, who didn't want to give up on the place because he was convinced that its opal resources had not been fully exploited, finally threw in the towel himself in 1905 and went to Lightning Ridge. White Cliffs was, at this point, little more than a ghost town and it has fairly much stayed that way through the intervening years to the present. There have been small flurries of excitement when new pockets of gem-quality opals were found, but they always played out as quickly as they appeared.

A few hardy—or perhaps foolhardy—miners and their families hung on for another decade, but by the end of 1914, no more than a handful of digs were in operation and none of those were producing anything of consequence. Since then hardly any truly serious exploratory work or mining has been done. Occasionally a few hopefuls will show up and dig for a while, but eventually they give up and fade away.

In 1961 the town's population was a mere 20, mostly hopeful miners believing they were the ones who would strike the previously undiscovered glory hole; a tenuous dream at best. There was a return of interest in the area for a short while in 1964, when mechanized mining methods were put into use and bulldozers, excavators, and other heavy equipment began operating, but it didn't last for long and those new operations soon folded just as the old had done. Another flurry of interest flared when some prospectors from Coober Pedy showed up in 1980 and began scratching about and actually found some good opal, but that faded, too, and they drifted away.

Five years later, in 1985, a reintroduction of heavy equipment occurred and interest was maintained into 1986 when good opal was encountered. It was a very nice pocket, but only that; when the pocket played out, so did the interest. Only six mines remained active—and those barely so—in 1989. But something new was occurring: White Cliffs was suddenly not only blooming as a tourist attraction of sorts, it was becoming a retirement village, with retirees moving into the old shafts and turning the drives into quite pleasantly cool underground living quarters where one could, if so inclined, dig into one's own living room wall with a faint hope of encountering some high-quality precious opal. At first such shafts and drives were there for the claiming, and 130 were quickly claimed and refinished as homes. Very soon none remained near town and the government abruptly prohibited the allocation of land for any new ones. During that same year of 1989, a rather posh underground accommodation called the Dug-Out Motel was established by Leon Hornby.

Now the demand for underground housing at White Cliffs is such that in the close vicinity to town, those few that become available for sale are going for some $60,000 to $70,000 apiece, possibly even more. For those visiting White Cliffs, some of the old mines can be toured and there is an interesting "walk-in" mine and several historic buildings to be seen. There are now some underground art galleries as well as subterranean restaurants, pubs, and even a beautifully lighted underground swimming pool.

While there is a remote possibility that at some future time a major new deposit of opals will be found, it is far more likely that this first major developed opal field of Australia will never regain its past glory and that White Cliffs is now essentially dead as a major opal field. But, then, who knows what tomorrow might bring?

EIGHT

Opal Occurrence Worldwide

During the period 1990–1996 a survey was carried out in which the author contacted the chief geologists and leading mineralogists of countries, states, provinces, and territories throughout the world. Many of the initial contacts were accomplished through correspondence and an extensive questionnaire was sent to these individuals; quite often follow-up contacts were made by personal visit, telephone, FAX, or further correspondence. There was, on the whole, remarkable cooperation, for which the author is most appreciative and greatly indebted. Those countries, states, provinces, or territories from whom no response of any kind was received to either the author's initial correspondence or follow-up contacts and of which no information is known concerning the possibility of opal deposits are listed alphabetically at the end of this segment. Information from the countries, states, provinces, territories, and possessions that responded to the queries, are shown alphabetically.

AFGHANISTAN

Letters and questionnaires sent both in 1992 and 1995 to the Department of Geological Survey of the Ministry of Mines and Industries in Kabul were returned with the simple rubber-stamped notation, "Service temporarily suspended".

ALABAMA (United States)

Ernest A. Mancini, state geologist at the Geological Survey of Alabama in Tuscaloosa, reports that while no occurrence of precious opal has been reported in Alabama, both common opal and hyalite occur there, usually in opal-filled veinlets and cavities in granite and gneiss, and as wood replacement in Cretaceous gravels. The opal is found in seams, vugs, and fossil wood, Dr. Mancini says, "occasionally with residual masses of iron oxides encountered in brown ore mines of both the Valley and Ridge and Alabama Coastal Plain provinces. [It is] generally colorless and exhibits mammillary or globular form and somewhat greasy luster." Most of the common opal is found replacing wood in gravels of Tuscaloosa Formation in the northernmost counties of the Alabama Coastal Plain. The hyalite opal found is poor grade "secondary incrustations in granites and gneisses of the Piedmont Province. Some of the Clay County samples from near Millerville are retained in the collection of the Alabama Museum of Natural History at Tuscaloosa, [but] specimens suitable for mineral specimens have not been found in Alabama. The deposits are not mined, either commercially or recreationally, and most finds have been made by rockhounds in search of agate and silicified wood of other types."

ALASKA (United States)

Jill L. Schneider, geologist of the United States Geological Survey at Anchorage, writes:

> I have researched the occurrence of opals in the State of Alaska to the best of my resources and have mighty thin gleanings to show for it. The only reported occurrence of opal in Alaska is found in a private publication by the Chugach Gem & Mineral Society, titled *Alaska: A Guidebook for Rockhounds* (1986, $9.95). It is shown as common opal, but no description of it or of associated matrix is given. Alaska does not have county designations, and the occurrence lies outside any official "borough." The closest description would be to say: South-central Alaska, Mount Hayes Quadrangle, 25–30 miles northwest of Paxson, Alaska, T18/19S, R8/9/10E: in an area approximately 12 miles by 5 miles, bounded by Eureka Creek to the south, the Delta River to the east, small glaciers of the Alaska Range on the north, and Broxson Gulch on the west.

A second letter and questionnaire sent to Tom Smith, state geologist and director of the Division of Geological and Geophysical Surveys in Fairbanks, was answered by Tom Bundtzen, senior economic geologist, who replied, "Unfortunately, very little is known about the existence of opal in Alaska, and, to my knowledge, there are no deposits or occurrences of significance.

ALBERTA (Canada)

Don Scafe, of the Alberta Geological Survey in Edmonton, states that there is no occurrence of opal of any type in the province.

ALGERIA

L. Bitam, chief of the Department of Geological Infrastructure of the Geological Survey of Algeria, stated that while Algeria does have occurrences of an opaque diatomaceous common opal, "We haven't found a precious opal yet in our country." The diatomite *(kieselguhr)* is an important resource produced at the large open-cut Tellait Mine of northwestern Algeria in the Oran region. It is found in association with calcite, iron oxides, and pyrite in a clayey marl deposit of late Miocene sedimentation.

ANTARCTICA

Guy G. Guthridge, manager of the Polar Information Program of the National Science Foundation in Washington, DC, reports that both surface and core samples taken in various locations in Antarctica do show the presence of opal. Submarine geologic analyses of both surface and seafloor specimens collected through deep (600 + meters) seafloor core testing and sediment trap analyses during the continuing 40-year study in Antarctic regions from 1951 to the present show that opal-CT (polymorphs of cristobalite and tridymite) and quartz— including chalcedony—are the two most authigenic silica phases in deep-sea sediments. Such testing shows the presence of biogenic siliceous opal, primarily from diatom skeletal material (diatomaceous opal). The sediments collected in the cores consists of approximately **30%** biogenic opal, while the sediment collected in the surface traps consisted of **60%** to **80%** biogenic opal, the remainder being organic matter, lithogenic and biogenic calcareous particles. Chert, formed by silica from biogenous opal, is found in nodules and in layers or lenses in the Middle Eocene or older sediments, with associated sediments including carbonate, biogenous silica, brown clay, and volcanic ash. Surface and 600 + meters deep seafloor sedimentation testing showed enrichment in organic carbon and biogenic siliceous opal present in Bransfield Strait, Drake Passage, various locations in McMurdo Sound (including Granite Harbor and New Harbor), Powell Basin west of South Orkney Islands, Ross Sea southwestern region, and the Victoria Land Coast fjord basins. At Powell Basin, a large part of the biogenic opal is incorporated into fecal pellets of krill and copepods, these pellets largely consisting of fragmented diatom frustules. Finally, testings at various localities at Prydz Bay showed that mineral occurrence included hornblende, feldspar categories, and calcite mixed with clay minerals in the following percentage ratios: illite (hydrous mica), 55–89%; kaolinite, 2–26% montmorillonite, 2–17%; chlorite, 6–11%.

ANTIGUA and BARBUDA

While no response was received from the Geological Survey of Antigua, there are unconfirmed reports of the occurrence of wood opal in several unspecified locations on Antigua Island.

ARGENTINA

Alejo Brodtkorb, Geological Association of Argentina in Buenos Aires, states that while precious opal does, in fact, occur in Argentina, few studies have been undertaken as to its quality or abundance. Some sample mining has evidently been done but no full-scale commercial opal mining operations yet exist.

ARIZONA (United States)

H. Mason Coggin, director of the Mines and Mineral Resources at the Arizona Mining and Mineral Museum in Phoenix, states that although several deposits of precious opal of volcanic origin have been recorded in Arizona, "In general our opals have not had the exquisite display of colors that we would expect for an area with large outcrops of rhyolite."

Ken A. Phillips, chief engineer of the Arizona Department of Mines and Mineral Resources in Phoenix, replied that in addition to certain deposits of precious opal, Arizona also has common opal that fluoresces bright green and which is found in seams in basalt. The precious opal is found in rhyolite vugs and is mined both commercially and recreationally. It is a translucent light opal with a base coloration ranging from blue to milky white and showing POC that is broadflash green and smudge green. There is presently an unconfirmed report of precious opal having been found at Chalcedony Park, located on the Arizona–Nevada border near Lake Mead, but details remain cloudy.

Locations for known opal occurrences in Arizona include **Cochise Country:** the sole opal claim in this county, the Rex Opal Mine, is presently listed as a past producer and is located on the USGS 7.5-minute Engine Quadrangle topographical map, in the northeast quarter of Section 15, at coordinates T12S R32E, although claims may extend into Section 14, NW; **La Paz County:** there are undocumented reports of fluorescent opal having been found, but without specifics of location, description, etc.; **Maricopa County:** there are similar sketchy, undocumented accounts of fluorescent opal occurrences; **Mojave County:** along with having unconfirmed accounts similar to those of La Paz and Maricopa counties of fluorescent opal occurrences, there is a confirmed precious opal deposit called the Cisco Mine, which is presently listed as not being worked, the opal having originally been discovered during uranium prospecting operations; the mine can be located on the USGS 15-minute Senator Mountain Quadrangle at T30N R20W in the SW Quadrant of Section 23 at coordinates, Lat. N 35°58′23″, Long. W 114°23′52″; **Santa Cruz County:** two adjacent opal mining sites exist in this county, the most prominent of which is the Arizona Blue Fire Opal Mine, located on the USGS Ruby 15-minute quadrangle in Section 25, N2 Quarter at T22S R11E, Lat. N.31°29′30″, Long. W 111°10′10″; the adjacent working mine, at the same coordinates, is called the Jay-R Claim; both are currently producing mines and the opals being obtained are a pale pastel blue with, usually, a distinct but scattered pinfire array of POC, largely of red, green, and yellow; the opals recovered are usually sold by the claim owners to opal cutters and lapidary hobbyists; **Yuma County:** here, too, there are undocumented reports of fluorescent opal occurrence.

ARKANSAS (United States)

J. Michael Howard, geologist–mineralogist with the Arkansas Geological Commission in Little Rock, says

> Arkansas has deposits of precious opal, common opal, and fluorescent opal (hyaline). The precious opal occurs in seams as fracture fillings in pyroxenite alteration; the fluorescent hyaline opal is encountered in vugs as coatings and films on quartz crystals, manganese minerals and on naturalite crystals from gas cavities in syenite, and the common opal replaces wallastonite and/or novaculite adjacent to vanadium deposits. The greater portion of the precious opal is mined recreationally, usually as the result of collecting other minerals. It occurs as both transparent (jelly) opal and translucent milky-white opal, both varieties showing fine play of color in broadflash and pinfire. The fluorescent (hyaline) opal is found over a wide area in Garland, Montgomery, Polk, and Pulaski counties. The common opal occurrence is largely in Garland County. The precious opal was discovered in 1989 in Garland County at the North Wilson Pit during vanadium mining operations. The vanadium deposit was soon depleted and no other opal was encountered.

The North Wilson Pit is located on the Potash Sulphur Springs 7.5-minute quadrangle (USGS) in Section 17, T3S, R18W. Half a quart jar of specimens of this opal was donated to the Arkansas Geological Commission in the Spring of 1990 by Paul Thompson, who, with Dennis Friar, discovered the paper-thin layers in a very moist, extremely rotten matrix rock at a depth of 380 feet. Experience quickly showed the pair that if allowed to dry, the opal irreversibly turned milky and lost almost all its POC. The specimens donated by Thompson were preserved in 70% isopropyl alcohol.

ATLANTIC OCEAN

Brad Butman, geologist with the Branch of Atlantic Marine Geology of the United States Geological Survey (USGS) at Woods Hole, Massachusetts, states that "Precious opal [is] not found in Atlantic Ocean waters."

AUSTRALIA

See listings under state names.

AUSTRALIAN CAPITAL TERRITORY (ACT)

Y. Miezitis, assistant director of Mineral Resources Assessment in the Australian Bureau of Mineral Resources at Canberra, says, "There are no known occurrences of opal of any type in the ACT."

AUSTRIA

Michael Götzinger, Secretary of the Austrian Mineralogical Society and Assistant Professor of the Institute for Mineralogy and Cristallography of the University of Vienna, said that precious opal does occur in Austria. There are, he adds, other varieties.

"In Austria we have three types of opal occurrences: (1) Opals in serpentinite rocks (Bohemian Massif in Lower Austria and in the Pennin-window of Bernstein, Burgenland). These opals occur as white (or white-green or white-yellow) masses in veinlets and clefts and contain dendritic inclusions of Fe- and Mn-oxides ("Dendritenopale"). Mainly they can be found as nodules (between 5 and 20 cm in diameter) in the soil of serpentinite areas. Some collectors produce polished plates and decorative stones. Main occurrences are near Dobersberg–Waldkirchen in Lower Austria and near Bernstein in Burgenland (occasionally mined in a small open pit). X-ray investigations show C-T opals of both types of occurrences. (2) Opals in volcanic rocks occur mainly in the Tertiary volcanic arc in Styria (andesites, latites, rhyolites). Glass-opal (Hyalith) occurs in the volcanics of Hochstraden, red opal masses occur in the alunite-trass (open pit) near Gossendorf, green opal was found near Gleichenberg, and opal as fossil-substance (tertiary mollusks) occurs near Weitendorf. (3) Opals in sedimentary environments: (a) 'Menilithopal' layers occur in the diatomites near Maissau in Lower Austria, they have brownish colour (C-T opal by X-ray investigation). (b) White-coloured opals occur as masses with fossil wood and mollusks near Csaterberg in Burgenland. (c) Near Primmersdorf opal is found with clay-iron-oxides in sediments. (d) In the open pits (graphite mining) near Amstall in Lower Austria white opals are coating veinlets and clefts. These opals may be products of the influence of metamorphism (late stage) in the Bohemian Masif."

Gerhard Niedermayr, Museum of Natural History of Vienna, adds that the five basic types of opal found in Austria are common opal, wax opal, green opal, glass opal (hyalite), and "*menilith*" in diatomite layers, mainly found as seam opal and wood opal. The basic materials are montmorillonite (bentonite) clay, rhyolite and trass (rhyolitic tuff), basalt, serpentinite and lake sediments associated with various gneisses, marble, quartz crystals, clay-iron oxides, andesite, and latite. There is some open-pit mining occurring, but the deposits are largely unmined. The majority of the precious opals are jelly (transparent) with the base coloration predominantly green or yellow, with the most dominant POC being red. There are some precious opal varieties in Austria, however, that are translucent or opaque, with a gray base color, and these occur occasionally in serpentinite rocks. Most of the opals collected in Austria, Dr. Niedermayr adds, "are unmined and collected on a collector's scale only."

Among the Austrian areas where opals occur are the following: **Amstall:** in Niederösterreich (Lower Austria), hyalite quite often occurs in seams on graphitic shist in the open-pit graphite mines; **Asten:** in Oberösterreich (Upper

Austria), hyalite seams occur in siliceous clay; **Bernhards:** in Niederösterreich (Lower Austria), precious opal occurs in vugs in serpentinite; **Bernstein:** at Pennin-window, precious opal occurs in vesicles of basaltic rocks, as crusts on peridotite, and in vugs in serpentinite; **Bodenmossgraben:** in the Salzberg region, hyalite occurs in seams on talc fels; **Buregg:** in the Koralpe area, hyalite opal occurs in crusts in gneisses, pegmatites, and on related rocks; **Burgenland:** in the Casterberg area there occur opalized wood and opalized fossils; **Dietmannsdorf:** in Niederösterreich (Lower Austria), precious opal occurs in vugs in serpentinite; **Dobersberg–Waldkirchen:** in Niederösterreich (Lower Austria), both precious opal dendritic fluorescent opal occur in vugs in serpentinite in the Bohemian Massif; **Dürnberg:** in the Kraubath area, hyalite occurs on serpentinite; **Eibenstein:** hyalite occurs in seams through marble; **Felbertal:** at Salzberg, hyalite occurs in the scheelite mine; **Fiorsthaus Kupper:** at Koralpe, hyalite opal occurs in crusts in gneisses, pegmatites, and on related rocks; **Gleichenberg:** in Steiermark (Styria), precious opal occurs in vesicles of Tertiary basaltic rock; **Gossendorf:** in Steiermark (Styria), precious opal occurs in trass (a sort of rhyolitic tuff); and red opal masses occur in the autenite-trass; **Gleichenberg:** green opal has occurred in excavations made in this area; **Gulsen:** at Kraubath, hyalite occurs on serpentinite; **Hochstraden:** hyalite occurs in volcanic deposits; **Höllgraben:** in Niederösterreich (Lower Austria), precious opal occurs in vugs in serpentinite; **Heüttenberg:** at Kärnten, hyalite and milk opal occur in seams in marble; **Japons:** in Niederösterreich (Lower Austria), precious opal occurs in vugs in serpentinite; **Kalvarienberg:** at bei Seckau, hyalite opal occurs in crusts in gneisses, in pegmatites, and related rocks; **Katzbachgraben:** at Stubalpe, hyalite occurs in crust in gneises, in pegmatites, and on related rocks; **Klause:** in Steiermark (Styria), near Gleichenberg, precious opal occurs in vesicles of basaltic rock; **Kraubath:** hyalite occurs on serpentinite; **Krughof:** at Rabenwald, hyalite occurs on talc; **Laas:** at Fresach, Kärnten, hyalite and milk opal occur in seams on pegmatite rock; **Laufenegg:** at Koralpe, hyalite opal occurs in crusts in gneisses, pegmatites, and on related rocks; **Leckbachrinne:** in the Salzberg area, hyalite occurs in seams on gneiss; **Maissau:** in Niederösterreich (Lower Austria) there are menilithopal layers in diatomites; **North Primmersdorf:** at a.d. Thaya in Niederösterreich (Lower Austria), precious opal occurs in vugs in serpentinite; **Oberdorf a.d. Laming:** hyalite occurs on magnesite; **Oberhaag:** in Steiermark (Styria) near Ebiswald, precious opal occurs in vesicles of basaltic rock; **Oberpullendorf:** in thebiswald, Burgenland region, precious opal occurs in vesicles of basaltic rocks, as crusts in peridotite, and in vugs in serpentinite; **Oberthumeritz:** in Niederösterreich (Lower Austria), precious opal occurs in vugs in serpentinite; **Paselstollen:** in the Salzberg area, hyalite occurs in thin seams in gneiss and on calcite crystals; **Pingendorf:** hyalite occurs on quartz seams; **Primmersdorf:** precious opal occurs in clay-iron oxide sedimentary deposits; **Reinischbruch:** at Pack, hyalite opal occurs in crusts (sometimes surprisingly thick) in gneisses, pegmatites, and on related rocks; **Soboth:** at Koralpe, hyalite opal occurs in crusts on gneisses; **Saint Leonhard:** in Niederösterreich (Lower Austria), precious opal occurs in vugs in serpentinite; **Schabelschmid:** near Koralpe, hyalite occurs in crusts in gneisses, pegmatites, and on related rocks; **Schladming:** in the Salzberg area, hyalite seams occur on talc fels; **Schleibheim:** at Wels in Oberösterreich (Upper Austria), hyalite seams occur in siliceous clay; **Schwagbauer:** at Koralpe, hyalite occurs in crusts in gneisses, pegmatites, and on related rocks; **Steinbach:** in the Burgenland region precious opal occurs in vesicles of basaltic rocks, crusts in peridotite, and vugs in serpentinite; **Steinberg:** in Steiermark (Styria), near Feldbach, precious opal occurs in vesicles of basaltic rock; **Stoffhütte:** at Koralpe, hyalite occurs in crusts in gneisses, pegmatites, and on related rocks; **Tanzenbergtunnel:** hyalite opal occurs in crusts in gneisses, pegmatites, and on related rocks; **Thallein:** at Voitsberg, hyalite occurs in crusts in gneisses, pegmatites, and on related rocks; **Waldenkirchen:** in Niederösterreich (Lower Austria), dendritic fluorescent opal occurs in vugs in serpentinite; **Weitendorf:** in Steiermark (Styria), precious opal occurs in vesicles of basaltic rock; also in this area are found opalized fossils of Tertiary mollusks; **Wilhelmsdor:** in Steiermark (Styria), near Gleichenberg, precious opal occurs in vesicles of basaltic rock; **Zirler klamm:** in the Tirol (Tyrol), precious opal occurs in gibbsite concretions.

BANGLADESH

Mujibur Rahman Khan, director general of the Geological Survey of Bangladesh in Dhaka, reports "no known opal occurrence in the country."

BELGIUM

Ing. R. F. Vochten, at the Laboratory of Chemical and Physical Mineralogy at University Center in Antwerp, reports that no precious opal is known to occur in Belgium. A. Bouckaert, inspector general and head of the Belgium Geological Survey in Brussels, says common opal occurs in the vicinity of Aalter in a rubric quartz matrix and is associated with chalcedony and the cryptocrystalline quartz.

BOTSWANA

Mokwaledi Ntsimanyana, geologist of the Geological Survey Department of Botswana at Lobatse, says, "Yes, precious opal does occur in Botswana." adding regretfully, "but very little prospecting has been done." The opal occurs, he says, in calcareous diatomites that are 14.8% opaline. The matrix material in the diatomaceous earth includes limestone and calicrete (caliche in dry river valleys.) The opal remains unmined. Among the specific locations he cites are **Central District:** at Rakops and on the Boteti River; **Ngwaketse District:** in the Metlojane Pan west of Ramatlabama, and near Sedibeng in the Matletsi dry river valley; **Tuliblock:** on the Kweneng Ranch near the Machaneng Police Camp, on the Dead Mule Ranch, and on the Basinghall Farm.

BRAZIL

Darcy Pedro Svisero of the Institute of Geoscience at the University of Sao Paulo reports that Brazil has occurrences of precious opal as well as common opal, moss opal, and wax opal. The precious opal occurs as amygdules in basalt, associated with arenites, as well as in colorful deposits as wood opal. It is mined commercially with open-pit mining techniques and occurs as opaque specimens with a white (milky) base coloration and POC of red, blue, lavender, green, yellow, and orange. Far less prized are some clear varieties which turn out fair to good faceted gems. The specific locations he lists include **Iraí:** in the Rio Grande do Sul, precious opal occurs in vugs in basalt; **Lageado:** in the Rio Grande do Sul, precious opal occurs in vugs in basalt; **Mata:** in the Rio Grande do Sul, precious opal occurs in sedimentary wood opal deposits; **Piauí:** precious opal occurs as amygdules in basalt at the Pedro II Mine and the Peri-Peri Mine; **Salto do Jacuí:** precious opal occurs in sedimentary wood opal deposits.

BRITISH COLUMBIA (Canada)

Z. D. "Danny" Hora, geologist in the Mineral Resources Division of the British Columbia Geological Survey in Victoria, wrote late in 1991, "Precious opal has been reported and, although the authenticity is not questioned, occurrences in British Columbia are few and very small, amounting to only a few specimens from three or four localities." Actually, a number more than that have been reported. He goes on to say that there have been occurrences of precious opal, wood opal, hyalite, and common opal being found associated with zeolite, agate and calcite, mainly in basalt, adding that "many of the basaltic flows are vesicular or amygdaloidal with opal." The common opal, he writes, has a green base coloration.

None of the opal was being mined at the time Mr. Hora wrote. He was unaware that practically at that same time a significant deposit of precious opal had been discovered in east central British Columbia less than 100 miles southeast of Kamloops, high in the mountains overlooking the Okanagan Valley. Since then a commercial mining operation has begun there. The precious opal is being mined in three different open cuts in close conjunction and the opal, found in basalt in association with gray agate, is of four basic types: (1) a quality precious opal much like Mexican opal with the predominant POC in red and green; (2) a type similar to the boulder opal of Australia but in a softer basalt than the Queensland ironstone; (3) a mixed boulder-and-matrix opal; and (4) a transparent fire opal in clear orange that is said to be ideal for faceting. The operation there has been named the Okanagan Mine and there are indications that this could be a major opal deposit. Greater details of its discovery and the opal being recovered will be found in Chapter 7.

The officially recorded occurrence sites for opal in British Columbia are **Ashcroft area:** Cache Creek area, in Tertiary rocks; also, the 1890–91 Annual Report of the Geological Survey of Canada reported white, pale greenish white, and apple green opal occurring in the Tertiary agglomerate on the Savona Mountains in the Ashcroft Mining Division; **Burns Lake area:** one of the few known precious opal localities in British Columbia; John Shelford of Burns Lake found two pieces of precious opal along Eagle Creek about 4 miles (6.4 km) southwest of Burns Lake village; the locality was staked as a mineral claim, but no further discoveries were made; though common opal is plentiful; **Clinton Mining Division:** good specimens of hyalite are found in dark gray foliated basalt along the Bonaparte River near Hihium Lake and the Canadian National Mineral Collection contains specimens of opal from the head of Loon Lake; **Deadwood:** common opal occurs at the Mother Lode Mine at Deadwood, a sample of which was donated to the National Mineral Collection by P. E. Crane in 1916; **Empire Valley:** opal, agate, jasper, and thundereggs in Tertiary rocks are found on Black Dome Mountain west of Fraser River and south of the Gang Ranch; also similar material is found on the Empire Valley Ranch that is of a quality commensurate with those of Purdy's Ranch in Oregon; **François Lake:** opal, agate, and jasper occur in the Tertiary lavas along the shore of the lake; **Kamloops area:** both precious opal and hyalite are distributed in Tertiary deposits of this region; high-quality precious opal was reported discovered in a nodule found in Watching Creek just north of Kamloops Lake, while hyalite and "a variety of opal" occurs at Stump Lake and Droppingwater Creek in the Kamloops Mining Division; **Kalamalka Lake:** Perry Ranch; partly silicified (opalized) wood of generally poor quality; **Mount Jackson:** silicified (opalized) wood is found 2 miles [3.2 km] southwest of Tulameen on Mount Jackson; **Mount Savona:** about 7 miles [11.3 km] south of Savona, approaching Mount Savona from the southeast, opal occurs along the cliffs below the microwave tower site; **Painted Chasm:** 12 miles [19.3 km] north of Clinton, 2 miles [3.2 km] east of Highway 97, zeolite and opal are abundant in amygdules near the top of the section; **Penicton area:** precious opal has been reliably reported, but the precise locality was not stated, though it is said to be 4 miles [6.4 km] southwest of Princeton and hence may be somewhat north of Yellow Lake, less than 200 feet off the road; **Prince Rupert:** opalized wood occurs along the banks of Barnes Creek 7.5 miles due east of Ashcroft; **Quesnel:** finely laminated massive opal associated with Tertiary argillite and sandstone is found at the Horse Fly Mine, located on the Horse Fly River, about 6.8 miles [11 km] above its entry into Quesnel Lake; **Slocum Mining Division:** Common opal occurs along Fourmile Creek (also known as Silverton Creek); **Silmilkameen Mining District:** a variety of opal listed as semi-opal is found southeast of Princeton on Agate Mountain; **White Lake:** in this area is found partly silicified (opalized) wood of generally poor quality.

BULGARIA

Ryslan I. Kostov, in the Geological Institute of the Bulgarian Academy of Sciences in Sofia, says that small amounts of precious opal with a milky, brown, or yellow base coloration have been found in Bulgaria in the form of cachalong opal, wood opal, and opal pseudomorphs. Hyalite, hydrophane, wax opal, and common opal are also present.

The wood opal deposits, Dr. Kostov says, are "up to 4 to 5 meters [about 13′–16.5′] in length and 40–50 cm [15.76″–19.7″] in diameter, and translucent in thin slices, with inner zone brown or black and outer zone yellowish to white, although on occasion it may be pure gray."

S. Petrusenko, curator of minerals in the Natural History Museum of the Bulgarian Academy of Science in Sofia, says that the hyalite occurs as clear black. The hydrophane opal—in rare instances with pinfire in red, blue, green, and yellow—is transparent when wet and milky white when dry. These opals, presently unmined but sought recreationally by collectors, are found in a matrix of Oligocene volcanic tuff and loose sandstone, as well as rhyolite and limestone. The common opal is pure white.

Specific Bulgarian opal locations are **Bezvodno area:** common opal occurs in the Eastern Rhodope Mountains; **Dsikovo area:** common white opal occurs in the Western Rhodope Mountains; **Golyam Palas area:** common white opal occurs in the Madan Ore Field; **Haskovski area:** opal pseudomorphs, occasionally with POC, occur in the Mineralni Bani; wood opal with some POC occurs at Dragoynovo; **Kardzahlii area:** common white opal occurs in the Eastern Rhodope Mountains; **Komuniga area:** precious opal occurs in the Eastern Rhodope Mountains; **Nakovitsa area:** common opal occurs in the Eastern Rhodope Mountains; **Osikovo area:** precious opal occurs in the Western Rhodope Mountains; **Sofia area:** black hyalite occurs in the Madjaruvo polynetllor deposit on Vitosha Mountain in the Eastern Rhodope Mountains; **Svetoslav area:** common opal occurs in the Eastern Rhodope Mountains; **Zhelezni Vrati**

area: cachalong opal, some with POC, occurs in the Bleogene limestones of the Eastern Rhodope Mountains.

BURUNDI

Audace Ntungicimpaye, director general of Geology and the Mines of Burundi at Bujumbura, le, says, "Yes, we do have opal in Burundi." This includes precious opal, common opal, and wood opal, the latter occasionally with POC. The opal, not presently mined, has a base coloration ranging from yellowish-gray through bluish-gray to bluish-black. The wood opal occurs in the Plaine de la Rusizi in northwestern Burundi near the Rwanda border, while common opal and precious opal occur in basalts of the Mosso area in southeastern Burundi near the border of Tanzania.

CALIFORNIA (United States)

James J. Davis, state geologist, Department of Conservation, Division of Mines and Geology in Sacramento, says that California has nine types of opal—precious, common, hyalite, moss, wood, prase, geyserite, diatomaceous earth, and fluorescent. The precious opal, also locally called [incorrectly] fire opal, is found in seams and vugs in rhyolite and basalt and in some petrified wood; it ranges from transparent to (usually) translucent and often opaque and most frequently exhibits a red pinfire POC and, not uncommonly, broadflash in "fire-like reflections. Common opal," Davis continues, "occurs in white, yellow, brown, bluish, and greenish masses. The hyalite is transparent glassy and found in cavities of volcanic rock. Chrysopal (prase or praseopal) is a greenish opal found associated with chrysoprase." The moss opal is a form of common opal having mosslike inclusions of pyroluscite or chlorite and some of the California specimens have a bright yellow base coloration. The wood opal, Davis adds, "is wood replacement and cavity filling in petrified wood. The geyserite here is a hydrous silica which forms about the vents of geysers and hot springs. Diatomaceous earth (also known as infusorial earth and more properly called diatomite) are deposits of opaline silica formed by diatoms. Fluorescent opal is an opaque light greenish or milky white opal that fluoresces a brilliant green."

While there is some commercial mining of the diatomaceous earth, commercial mining of precious opal is limited to some mines that are open to rockhounds for collecting on a fee basis. The most noteworthy of these is the operation now variously called the Leo Nowak Fire Opal Mine or the Last Chance Opal Mine, in Kern County. It is located in the El Paso Mountains of Mohave Desert, in the upper reaches of Red Rock Canyon at an elevation of 3200 feet [976 m]. It is 125 miles [201.1 km] north of Los Angeles and 25 miles [40.2 km] north of the town of Mohave. The opals, which range in size from pinhead to near 2″ [50.1 mm] in diameter (occasionally even larger), are found embedded in loose basaltic rocks and solid outcrops of basalt.

The base color of the opals is predominantly transparent yellow to transparent orange and they have very bright, attractive POC in red, green, blue, purple, and orange colors and patterns that include pinfire, broadflash, rolling flame, and harlequin. Black opals are found on rare occasions. Leo Nowak, an artist from Los Angeles, became connected with the mine in 1957, when he began to manage it for Janet Cowden, whose family had owned it for over a decade previously. After 8 years of their association, Mrs. Cowdon, unable to participate in mining affairs any longer because of her advanced age, signed the title over to Nowak, who has continued with its operation ever since. The opals from this mine are reputed to be quite stable and able to be cut and polished immediately without any stabilization process. Little digging is done there during the summer because of the intense heat, but fee digging is popular during the winter months. For greater details call 213-899-5744.

Included among the known California opal deposits are **Adams County:** wood opal occurs as float and in sedimentary beds in the Bijou Basin; **Alpine County:** wood opal is widespread in small amounts; **Amador County:** wood opal is widespread in small amounts; **Butte County:** wood opal is widespread in small amounts; **Calaveras County:** wood opal is widespread in small amounts, along with large deposits of a rich, white, nongem common opal, in a subsurface gravel deposit near Mokelumne Hill; first reported in June 1972, by W. Gere and located on the Mokelumne Hill 7.5-minute quadrangle (USGS), Sec. 12, T5N R11E; also in this county, precious opal, common opal, and wood opal occur near Valley Springs on the Hooten Ranch, one mile [1.6 km] from State Route 12 in an occurrence called the Hooten Ranch Deposit, which was first reported in June 1972, by W. Gere and which is located on the Valley Springs Quadrangle, SW-1/4 Sec. 20, T4N R11E; **Elbert County:** wood opal occurs as float and in sedimentary beds in the Bijou Basin; **Fresno County:** there area widespread occurrences of diatomaceous earth (diatomite), and moss opal occurs in the mountains east of Fresno; **Inyo County:** in the Armagosa Desert west of the Greenwater Range, approximately 20 miles [32.2 km] southwest of Death Valley Junction, at the eastern boundary of Death Valley National Monument and on the east slope of the Funeral Mountains, traces of precious opal have been found, though confirmed information is scant and there is some question as to whether this is vug opal from volcanic rock or wood opal from sedimentary deposits; the county also has widespread occurrences of diatomaceous earth; **Kern County:** 18 miles [29 km] west of Johannesburg occurs a deposit of bright yellow moss opal; near Rosamond there is a deposit of milk opal (or resin opal); 25 miles [32.2 km] north of Mohave, precious opal is mined just east of Red Rock Canyon at the Last Chance Opal Mine (Leo Nowak Fire Opal Mine), a fee-digging operation; another deposit, an active mine owned by Shirley and Dick Barnett, is also located in the Red Rock Canyon area some 15 miles [24.1 km] north of California City and is sometimes referred to by the name Opals by Shirley; wood opal deposits are found in the petrified forest at Last Chance Canyon; in the northeastern corner of the county, another precious opal deposit is reported between Ridgecrest and Inyokern, the opal occurring in vugs in the dyke that cuts through the surrounding volcanic material in the El Paso Mountains, a not very extensive site that has no present commercial mining development but which has been significantly attractive to amateur gem and mineral collectors; **Lake County:** diatomaceous earth is widespread and common opal with pale blue base coloration occurs as irregular masses in hydrothermally altered andesite at the Sulphur Bank Mine; **Lassen County:** wood opal deposits are widespread in small amounts, along with diatomaceous earth; **Los Angeles County:** near Lomita, an extensive deposit of diatomaceous earth is being mined; also, there are county-wide deposits of a fluorescent common opal that ranges from milk white through tan to medium brown; **Merced County:** widespread diatomaceous earth deposits throughout county; **Mono County:** diatomaceous earth deposits are widespread in the county, and fluorescent hyalite occurs as thin coatings on joint surfaces at the Morris Claims in the Blind Spring Mining District; **Morgan County:** wood opal occurs as float and in sedimentary beds in the Bijou Basin; **Napa County:** diatomaceous earth is widespread but, also, gem-quality prase opal has been found in a 10-inch vein at the Lone Pine Chromite Mine, 3.5 miles [5.6 km] from Knoxville; **Nevada County:** wood opal deposits are widespread in small amounts, usually intermingled with gravel, with heavier deposits in the area of Little York; **Orange County:** diatomaceous earth deposits are widespread; **Placer County:** diatomaceous earth deposits are widespread; **Plumas County:** wood opal occurs widespread but in small amounts; **Riverside County:** wood opal is widespread in small amounts with gravel, and both common opal and hyalite occur at Crestmore; **San Benito County:** diatomaceous earth is widespread; milky opal is found in the area of San Juan Bautista; **San Bernardino County:** semiprecious pink and amber-colored precious opal occurs in an eastern branch of Black Canyon, on the slope of Opal Mountain, some 25 miles [40.2 km] northwest of Barstow and 15 miles [24.1 km] north of Hinkley; another occurrence of precious opal is reported to have been found 20 miles [32.2 km] northwest of Opal Mountain at Lead Pipe Springs; finally, some 15 miles [24.1 km] northeast of Lead Pipe Springs, close to the western boundary of the China Lake Naval Weapons Center, there is a deposit of nodules and geodes in which occur an almost water-clear opal, some of it containing a fair amount of POC; **San Luis Obispo County:** diatomaceous earth is widespread; **San Mateo County:** diatomaceous earth is widespread; **Santa Barbara County:** near Lompoc, a large, pure deposit of infusorial diatomite is being mined; fossil opalized termite pellets have been found near Santa Maria; **Shasta**

County: widespread deposits of diatomaceous earth; **Sierra County:** wood opal is widespread in small amounts; **Siskiyou County:** near Dunsmuir there is a deposit of precious opal, and a greenish stalactitic and coralloidal opal occurs in "The Catacombs" of Lava Beds National Monument; **Sonoma County:** wood opal is widespread in small amounts, and diatomaceous earth is similarly widespread; precious opal, locally incorrectly termed "fire opal," occurs in kaolinite on the Weise Ranch between Glen Ellen and Kenwood and also in the vicinity of Geyserville; large trees of petrified wood with some opalized matter is found in the petrified forest west of Calistoga; crusts of delicate capillary fibers of geyser opal—geyserite—are found at The Geysers; **Tehama County:** stalactites and stalagmites of opal occur in a lava tunnel on the north side of Inskip Hill; **Tulare County:** wood opal is widespread in small amounts and diatomaceous earth is similarly widespread; fine grade green chrysopal prase occurs in the Chrysoprase Mine near Lindsay; **Tuolumne County:** wood opal is widespread in small amounts, associated with gravels; **Yuba County:** wood opal is found in small amounts county wide.

CANADA (See Also Specific Province Names)

Ann P. Sabina, of Energy, Mines and Resources Canada, Geological Survey of Canada Sector, in her letter of 6 February 1995, stated that: "A number of opal occurrences have been reported in Canada, but only one that we are aware of is of economic significance. This one is currently being worked by Okanagan Opal, Inc., of Vernon, British Columbia."[1]

CANARY ISLANDS

See Spain.

CHILE

Hernan Danús Vásquez, director of the National Service of Geology and Mining at Santiago reports four varieties of opal occur in Chile—common opal, milky precious opal, precious opal in wood, and contra luz opal. The wood opal occurs in sedimentary deposits of silica carbonates, while the two varieties of precious opal and contra luz occur as veinings and amygdules in basalt dikes. The contra luz is transparent, clear to light blue, with the POC usually red, blue, and yellow pinfire; the milky (white) precious opals exhibit the same colors, but usually in broadflash patterns; the POC that often appears in the wood opal is also red, yellow, and blue on a whitish base color, the blue and yellow predominating. No commercial mining of opal occurs but it is prospected for on a recreational basis in the Metropolitan V Area and the Metropolitan XI Area.

COLOMBIA

Eduardo A. Cardoza, geologist of Ingeominas Bogota, states that while there is some occurrence of common opal in Colombia, there are no known deposits of opal in the country that exhibit play of fire. However, Adolfo Alarcón Guzmán, director general of the National Institute of Investigations in Geology and Minerals in the Ministry of Mines and Energy at Bogotá, says precious opal occurs in Colombia in the form of both wood opal and xilopal, the latter being opalized petrified wood and, sometimes, even petrified logs threaded with precious opal. Both the wood opal and xilopal, Dr. Guzmán declares, are found in deposits of montmorillonite, which is mined commercially as well as recreationally. The precious opal is translucent with base coloration that ranges through white, gray, brown, yellow, and green. POC is red, green, blue, indigo, and gold, usually occurring in long streaks. There are, according to Dr. Guzmán, five principal locations in Columbia where this opal is being mined. The first is at Sahagún in the Córdoba Department, the second at Coyaima in the Tolima, and the remaining three—Xampo Alegre, Garzó and LaPlata—are in the Huila Department.

COLORADO (United States)

F. Michael Wahl of the Geological Society of America, Cordilleran Section, Department of Geology at Boulder, wrote that there was "no known opal occurrence in the region." However, a follow-up communication to James A. Cappa, chief of the Minerals and Mineral Fuels Section of the Colorado Geological Survey in Denver resulted in a considerably different response. Dr. Cappa reported that "opals do occur in [the] State—common opal, precious opal (rare), hyalite, moss opal (rare), wood opal, yellow-brown resin precious opal, geyserite, and banded opal. Banded and common opal have been collected in many parts of the State; common (and to a considerably lesser degree, precious) opal is a major to minor constituent of a portion of the petrified wood found in association with beidellite and montmorillonite. Geyserite occurs as a hot-spring deposit that also shows some POC. Quality gem opal, on the other hand, is reported very rarely and probably nowhere abundant or of very fine quality." The precious opal, when found, occurs sometimes as seams in rhyolite and basalt but more usually as amygdule filling in those volcanic rocks. None of the opal is mined commercially and the opal found is usually accidentally by collectors seeking other minerals.

Included in the Colorado sites listed by Dr. Cappa are **Boulder County:** Nederland Tungsten District, common opal is very frequently encountered in the tungsten veins where it is usually associated with beidellite and montmorillonite in vugs; opal crusts indicate they were deposited under gravitational influences; in the Clyde Mine, crusts of opal and beidellite form casts of coarse crystals of ferberite; **Chaffee County:** hyalite is reported as occurring at and near Buffalo Peaks, while milk-white common opal, reports Dr. Cappa, "is abundant as irregular masses several feet in diameter, the central parts opaque flinty chalcedony from which the opal is derived by hydration"; **Cherry County:** wood opal widespread, though not abundant; **Clear Creek County:** in Gilson Gulch near Idaho Springs occurs a deposit of blue-and-yellow opalescent material; **Custer County:** in the Rosita Hills there is a mixture of opaline silica and kaolin, which, according to Dr. Cappa, "results from the alteration of spherulite and pitchstone in the rhyolites, some masses being completely replaced by these minerals, with opal comprising about 65% of the mass"; **Del Norte County:** common opal widespread; **Douglas County:** the Castle Rock Area has petrified wood with opalized pockets and vugs; **Eagle County:** hyalite occurs just below the confluence of the Eagle and Colorado rivers; **Grand County:** at Hot Sulphur Springs there is occurrence of hyalite; **Gunnison County:** hyalite in seams and vugs of basalt along Gunnison River and, says Dr. Cappa, "in the upper part of the Good Hope Mine in the Vulcan District, much opal appears as geyserite, with patches of precious opal, some of which is very rich in gold where, possibly due to terrurium salts, opal is tinted purple"; **Hinsdale County:** a handsome, varicolored opal occurs in jasper boulders along the upper Rio Grande and hyalite occurs in the basalts on Godwins Creek; **Jefferson County:** petrified wood and common opal—but including some precious opal—occur at the Table Mountain and Green Mountain; **Lake County:** Leadville District, common opal and chalcedony occur in large quantities as alteration products of porphyry rocks and ore deposits, but they are significantly rare or absent in the primary ores; in some places there are beautiful opalescent layers as much as a quarter-inch [6.4 mm] thick and 6 to 8 inches [152.4 to 203.2 mm] square on the oxidized ore; in the Ibex Mine and Belgian Mine, common opal, with unverified precious opal on occasion, occurs associated with aurichalite and hemimorphite as fillings in cavities and fractures; **Larimer County:** hyalite occurs at the head of the Cache la Poudre River and one of the few outstanding locations for collecting opal and related forms of silica occurs on Specimen Mountain, a denuded explosive volcano in the northwest corner of Rocky Mountain National Park, where grayish-brown to reddish-brown chalcedony and jasper occur in faults and in pitchstone flows; more important, agate, onyx, opal, and calcite fill or partly fill abundant geodes and, though no precious opal has been found, some is transparent and many beautiful specimens have been collected; here, too, platy calcite is partly or completely replaced by opal and chalcedony in places; **Mesa County:** abundant opalized wood, ranging from milk-white through pea-green and brown to black, occurs four miles [6.4 km] south of Fruita, on Opal Hill and the hills westward into Utah, but there are very few large, unfractured pieces; **Mineral County:** gravel terraces along the Rio Grand contain opal-filled geodes from 3″ [76.2 mm] in diameter upward, and some of the white opal north of Creede locally yields fine precious opal with the POC in beautiful broadflash, short streaks and pinfire; **Park County:** just south of the salt workings occurs a brownish-yellow semi-opal with jasper and chalcedony; **Saguache County:** hyalite is reported to occur in basalt near the head of La Garita Creek; **Teller County:** common opal and sometimes precious opal (unverified) occurs abundantly in the ore deposits of the Cripple Creek District, where it generally represents the last phase of primary vein formation or is in the oxidized ores; the opal is specially abundant in the Zenobia Mine as yellow masses of tangled wires and rods, and here it occurs in vugs to great depths; **Yuma County:** good-quality moss opal that fluoresces a beautiful bright green and which takes a high polish, occurs on the South Forks of the Republican River, 20 miles [32.2 km] north of Burlington.

CONNECTICUT (United States)

Richard C. Hyde, director and state geologist at the Natural Resources Center, Department of Environmental Protection in Hartford, reports "no known opal occurrence in Connecticut."

COSTA RICA

José Francisco Castro Muñoz, director of the Department of Geology and Mines in San José, reports no known occurrence of opals of any variety in Costa Rica. Yet, in view of the opal deposits in the mountainous areas from Mexico southward through Guatemala, Honduras, and El Salvador, chances are good that precious opal is there but not yet discovered in the jungle mountains.

COTE D'IVOIRE

Konan Konakou Gilbert, underdirector of chemical geology and photo geology of the Department of Geology at Abidjan, reports that there is "no known opal occurrence in this country."

CUBA

Luis Gómez Narbona, geologist at the Institute of Geology and Paleontology in Havana, reports that Cuba does have common opal, wax opal, moss opal, chrisopal, and cachalong opal, all these varieties appearing as "weathering cuts of ultrabasites in seams, ledges, and pockets. No transparency occurs in the opals, which range from translucent to opaque." None show any POC. Señor Narbona says all these opals occur in Camagüey Province, where they are mined commercially at Bayatabo, Loma de los Opales, Loma Garcia, La Entrada, Pontezuela, and San Felipe.

CYPRUS (Excluding North Cyprus)

C. Xenophontos, of the Ministry of Agriculture and Natural Resources in the Geological Survey Department, writes: "I am afraid that Cyprus has no deposits of this stone."

CZECH REPUBLIC and SLOVAKIA

The oldest known opal mines in the world are those of what was formerly Czechoslovakia—now the Czech Republic and Slovakia—though over the years the gemstones produced here became generally known as Hungarian opals, due to the Hungarian borders being more extended at that time than now and encompassing portions of that region. The mines of more recent times—about 400 of them—were initiated in 1788, but prospecting for opals, as well as actual rudimentary opal mining, was done at least as far back as the era of the ancient Roman Empire, and possibly even before that, according to what supportive evidence can be gleaned from ancient texts. However, the first actual written notice of opal mines that were located in the present Slovakian region appeared in 1597. Jiri Kourimsky, head of minerals in the Department of Mineralogy and Petrology at Národní Muzeum in Prague, says that tunnel mining occurred from 1750 to 1922 at Dubník and adds that the "first precious opal known of the world from the XI Century may be on the primeval ages/export to Rome." During the period from 1850 through 1897, annual production, almost entirely with relatively primitive hand tools, averaged 20,000 to 30,000 carats of very high-grade precious opal of remarkable stability but generally small size, rarely exceeding two carats in the cut and polished gemstone. The discovery of abundant and very beautiful opals in Australia, however, had a devastating effect on the then Czechoslovakian market. Because of that, as well as from an apparent depletion of the Czechoslovakian opal sources, the annual average of production of gem-grade opal from 1897 to 1900, was only 4500 carats. Over the following 7 years, production dropped to an annual average of 2160 carats. Production continued to wane and in 1922 the total amount of opals mined was 1000 carats and, with that, by the end of the year, commercial opal mining ended, for all intents and purposes. There is still a very small amount of commercial mining done, but it is of little consequence. The only significant opal mining being done in the Czech Republic and Slovakia today is recreational. The single largest precious opal ever found in the mines weighed 600 grams (3000 carats) and that stone today remains a part of the Vienna Museum collection of precious gems.

Rudolf Duda, of the Vychodoslovenské Museum in Kosice, Michal Hamet,

Geological Survey of the Czech Republic in Prague, and Dr. Kourimsky include nine varieties among the opals occurring in that country: precious opal, common opal, bog opal, moss opal, wax opal, hyalite (which is sometimes referred to as pellucid glass opal), chloropal, hydrophane, and ungvarite (green opal colored by nontronite). The precious opals occur in vugs, veinlets, seams, and cavity fillings as amygdaloidal melaphyres as well as concretions, bulbs, tubers, plates, and lenses in matrix composed of basaltic tuff, dolomite, andesite tuff, and dacite and their pyroclastics. The opal deposits are located at considerable depth—100–200 meters [328′–656′ in two layers that are 10–80 meters thick [approximately 33′–263′] and 600–1000 meters long [approximately 1970′–3280′]. The opals are associated with basalt, andesite, serpentinite, iron, nickel, stibnite, and stalactic chalcedony. The common opals are basically opaque. The precious opals range from transparent through translucent and, rarely, to opaque. The translucent and subtranslucent opals occur with base colorations of white or pale blue or green. Base color of the opaque stones is normally milky white, but sometimes tints of red or green. The POC occurs in red, blue, blue-green, green, orange, violet, and lavender, with patterns in pinfire, broadflash, long streaks and smudges, and, occasionally, in the rare harlequin pattern. The transparent stones with POC normally display that color in pinfire, but sometimes in broad smudges. The generally pale, milky "Hungarian opals" mined at Czerwenitza, Dubnik, and other Slovakian mines were so delicate and so susceptible to cracking that they were brought to the surface in stages over extended periods of time, to allow them to acclimate to changes of temperature, humidity, pressure and light.

Among the various opal deposits in the Czech Republic and Slovakia are **Banská Bystrica:** common opal, wax opal and wood opal occur in this central Slovakia area; **Banske:** occurrence here of ungvarite, a green opal colored by nontronite; **Bilina:** opalized fossil logs and limbs and semi-opal in this northern Bohemia location; **Cervenica:** precious opals, often with harlequin pattern, are frequently found in this eastern Slovakia region in the Slansky Vrchy Mountains; these opals are formed of the products of Neogene subsequent volcanism (middle Sarmatian), with the fracture zone in a north–south direction, declination 80°; **Chiahaw:** menilite is found in this Bohemian region; **Dubnik:** at the foot of the highest mountain in the area, Simonka, in this wild, forested location, 30 km [18.6 mi] northeast of Kosice and 15 km [9.3 mi] southeast of Presov, at Libanka, Simonka, and Tancoska in the Slansky Vrchy Mountains of eastern Slovakia, precious opals, frequently with harlequin pattern, are found in seams in andesite tuff as products of Neogene subsequent volcanism (middle Sarmatian); this is the principal Czechoslovakian source of precious opal; hydrophane opal and common opal occur here as well; **Herlany:** common opal, red opal, wax opal, moss opal, and bog opal occur in a matrix of andesite tuff at this location on eastern Slovakia near Kosice; **Kremze:** this location near Ceské

Budejovice, in southern Bohemia produces common opal and moss opal in seams and as pocket material in a serpentinite matrix of serpentinites; the opals are subtranslucent in white, bluish, and greenish base coloration caused by disintegrating serpentinite; accompanied by iron–nickel (FeNi) lateritic mineralization, these opals, in the form of bulbs, tubers, and plates are often cut for use in jewelry as semiprecious stones; **Kuclin:** opalized fossil logs and limbs occur in this northern Bohemian location; **Lubie-Tova:** common opal occurs here on the contact of dolomites and andescites, and is found associated with chalcedony in bluish to pellucid stalactitic forms; **Nagy-Mijaly:** important precious opal deposits occur here on the Laborcza River east of Kashau (Kosice); **Nemcice:** in association with jasper and agates, precious opal occurs in amygdaloidal melaphyres in the Carboniferous and Permian rocks of this eastcentral Bohemian location; **Neudeck:** fine precious opal occurs at Frankfort-on-the-Main in this Bohemian location, largely as pocket and seam material, in andesite tuffs; in the past, this has been one of Czechoslovakia's principal precious opal sources; **Povraznik:** common opal as well as opalized fossil logs in this central Slovakian location; **Romersreuth:** common opal found in this Bohemian area; **Sevba:** opalized fossil logs and common opal are found in this central Slovakian site; **Sitnianska Lehotka:** both precious and common opal occur here, some 25 km [15.5 mi] south of Banska Stiavnica in the Staivnicke Vrchy Mountains; **Tri Vody:** common opal occurs here on the contact of dolomites and andesites, associated with chalcedony in bluish to pellucid stalactitic forms; **Trebíc:** precious opal, common opal, and wax opal occur in the environs of this area in southwestern Moravia; the precious opal occurs as pocket opal in serpentinites; **Valec:** located near Podborany in the Doupovske Mountains of northwestern Bohemia, this is the best locality in Czechoslovakia for crystal-clear hyalite opal (also called pellucid glass opal), which is sometimes tinged transparent reddish; the hyalite occurs in pocket deposits in basaltic tuff (close to 100 articles have been published about this locality since it was first described in an article in 1815); **Walsch:** hyalite is found in this Bohemian area; **Waltsale:** a colorless hyalite is found in this vicinity, in mammillary and botryoidal form and having matrix on the bottom; **Zeleznice:** precious opal, occurring as amygdaloidal melaphyres in the Carboniferous and Permian rocks of this eastcentral Bohemian location; the opal is found in association with jasper and agates; **Zlata Nana:** precious opal with harlequin patterns is found in this location in the Slansky Vrchy Mountains of eastern Slovakia.

DELAWARE (United States)

Thomas E. Pickett, associate director of the Delaware Geological Survey at the University of Delaware in Newark says that "Delaware has no known opal occurrences. However, we do have micro crystalline silica in the weathered gabbro of Iron Hill south of Newark. It does not have the structure of opal, but is somewhat similar chemically. We also have silicified cypress wood in Miocene formations near Smyrna, but no true opal."

DENMARK

Aage Jensen, geological lecturer from the Department of Mineralogy at the University of Copenhagen, says that "Precious opal is not known from Denmark. However common opal occurs . . . on the Faeroe Islands, Iceland, and Greenland." Christian Knudsen, senior research geologist of the Quaternary Geology Division of the Geological Survey of Denmark in Copenhagen reports that while no precious opal occurs in Denmark, in addition to those deposits of common opal known to occur on the Faeroe Islands, Iceland, and Greenland, there are unmined deposits of common opal in association with chert in Denmark proper in the 65-million-year-old Danian Limestone, a bryozoan limestone, that crops out both in Jylland and Sjalland. This is a white, opaque common opal that occurs in veins in black or brown flint (chert) nodules. Dr. Knudsen says the opal is mixed with calcite, which gives the white color and it is called opal flint and the veins are typically from one to ten centimeters in thickness. The material is poor, however, insofar as gemstone quality is concerned.

EGYPT

No response was received from queries sent to the Geological Survey in Cairo, but unofficial reports claim that a type of rose opal, virtually identical to the precious quincyite rose opal of France has been found south of Aswan in southern Egypt.

EL SALVADOR

No response was received from El Salvador officials in respect to precious opal deposits in the Central American nation. Unofficial reports indicate that precious opal deposits do exist in the jungle mountains near the eastern border of the country, not far from where the opal mines of Honduras are located. Although apparently no official note has been taken of these, some confusion exists due to a very definite deposit of precious opal that occurs and is mined at a Mexican locality of some importance, called El Salvador, and located in the state of Jalisco, eastward from Magdalena, north of the town of Tequila and across the Rio Grande de Santiago.

ENGLAND (United Kingdom)

D. E. Highley, of the British Geological Survey in Nottingham, Keyworth, Nottingham, wrote, "The British Geological Survey has little information on the occurrence of opal in the UK. None has been produced commercially, but the mineral has been reported associated with the china clay deposits in south-west England. The china clay deposits have formed from the alteration of the Variscan granites. The Natural History Museum maintains a mineralogical collection and opals are represented." The strong implication in the information received is that any opal occurring in England is simply common opal. Despite this, Jonathan Stewart, of the Mineralogical Society of Great Britain and Ireland, says that there are deposits of opal in England that include precious opal in relatively limited quantities, along with more abundant common opal, cachalong, hydrophane, jasp-opal, ferruginous opal, hyalite, and a form of dull, opaque semi-opal. The precious and common opals that occur, he reports, are "mainly associated with igneous complexes—rhyolite, basalt and chert." This material is mined recreationally but not commercially. The precious opal, according to Mr. Stewart, ranges from transparent to a milky-white base coloration, with some exhibiting a rich POC. The common opal coloration may be white, brown, yellow, greenish-gray or black.

In Cornwall a pleasing common opal occurs with a white to leek-green base color and is found at the Huel Stennach Mine and the Huel Spinster Mine near Saint Day, at the Roskear Mine and the Huel Rosewarne Mine in Camborne, at the Huel Poligine Mine, the Huel Buller Mine, the Huel Damsel Mine and at the Botallack Mine at Saint Just, and also at Gunheath at Saint Austell. Similar material occurs on the Island of Rum. The semi-opal occurs at the Huel Buller Mine and also near Redruth, Saint Ives, Saint Just, and in Devon near Dartmoor at Oakhampton. Precious opal, locally [and incorrectly] called fire-opal, is found at the Huel Spinster mine, at the Huel Rosewarne Copper Mine and at the Huel Gorland Mine and, relatively recently, there was a find of a semi-transparent, light-colored precious opal near Saint Just.

Cachalong opal occurs at Smulgedon in Ulster and in the feldspathic porphyry in Cloger Parish of Tyrone County, as well as in Pomeroy County on Barrack Mountain. The hydrophane opal, which occurs in small amygdaloidal masses, is a brownish-white and is found near Giant's Causeway and at Crossreagh, both in Ballywillin Parish. The occurrence of jasp-opal is at Sandy Braes in Antrim (as well as in some places in western Scotland), and the ferruginous opal occurs near Camborne and at Saint Just, in Cornwall. The hyalite, some of it exhibiting POC, occurs as well-defined specimens from Donald's Hill in County Down; this is an opal material that forms mammillated coatings in concentric layers in cavities of soft claystone amygdaloid and shows the peculiarity of sometimes being studded with small aragonite crystals, and occasionally occurs as a thin mammillated white crust coating granite, the white often quite translucent and pearly. Another deposit of hyalite, also pearly and distinctly iridescent, occurs south of Newcastle, at Quarus.

ESTONIA

Rein Raudsep, research director of the Geological Survey of Estonia in Tallinn, states that there is no known opal occurrence of any type in his country.

ETHIOPIA

An important new source of opals was discovered in Ethiopia in the early 1990s, but was kept secret until the opals began appearing in the Nairobi gem market in 1993. Even then, though the occurrence was confirmed by the government, few details were made public until recently. Located just west of the northern extension of Africa's Great Rift Valley, the site is an expansive volcanic field situated in Ethiopia's Shewa Province, in the district of Menze Gishe and, more specifically, on the northern slope of Yita Ridge about 11 miles [17.7 km] north of the village of Mezezo and 150 miles [241.4 km] northeast of the capital city of Addis Ababa.

The occurrence covers an area roughly 4.5 square miles at a minimum, although those familiar with the area hazard guesses that the field may actually be twice that size or more. Over a dozen separate sites within the known area have produced opal, much of it lower-grade material, but some 15% being gem quality, much of it with pronounced play of color. The gem-quality opals, some of which are contra luz in character, range through milky to transparent and from a base color of brilliant orange through yellow, light tan, root-beer brown, and black. Found largely as nodules in rhyolitic tuff, the rough opals are said to be similar in character and deposit to those found at Opal Butte, Oregon. The Ethiopian opal nodules average about 4 inches [101.6 mm] in diameter and a fair percentage of the gemmy material is prone to cracking or crazing within 24 to 48 hours after exposure. Those that hold up longer than this are being cut into quite handsome gemstones.

Whether this occurrence will develop into a significant factor in the opal market worldwide remains to be seen, but the prospects seem promising.

FAEROE ISLANDS (Denmark)

Common opal occurs regularly in seam deposits in layers, alternating with chalcedony, and in cavities in the basalts; precious opal also occurs as amygdules in gas pockets of the basalt, but in very limited quantities.

FIJI

An unsigned letter from the office of the director of the Mineral Resources Department in Suva states that there is no known occurrence of opal in Fiji.

FINLAND

Kari A. Kinnunen, of the Geological Survey of Finland in Espoo, has studied the opal precipitates of Finland since 1976 when she discovered some very unusual opal precipitates in esker material. She reports:

> Precious opal has not been found in Finland yet. However, there are many localities where common, fluorescent opal, part of it clear hyalite, is known to occur. Opal is quite common as hydromorphic precipitates in eskers in their gravel layers. The precipitates so far found are strongly fluorescent, thin layers occurring on the undersides of boulders and cobbles. Their genesis seems to be quite similar to the precious opal formation in Australia. The eskers are geologically young and therefore the time has been insufficient for the formation of gem-grade opals as in Australia. . . . Opal occurs as silica coatings on vertical rock cliffs in southern Finland. They form coatings on prehistoric rock paintings and have been described in this connection [occurring in] (1) Puumala, Syrjäsalmi, (2) Ristiina, Uittamonsalmi, and (3) Ristiina, Astuvansalmi. . . . Microscopic opal fillings have been found in jasperoid boulders and cobbles from northern Finland: Vuotso, Sodankylä. These opals occur together with chalcedony, quartz and quartzine and have been described in the study of archaeological silica materials used in prehistoric Finland. . . . Recrystallized common white opal has been described from the central nucleus of some agate nodules found from Huittinen in western Finland. . . . Opal is mentioned to have been found in the now exhausted Korsnäs Lead Mine in western Finland. Hyalite has been mentioned to have been found somewhere in the city of Kuopio in central Finland. In southwestern Finland, Parainen, Skarpdal, there is mention of opal.

FLORIDA (United States)

Thomas M. Scott, senior geologist of the Bureau of Geology in the Florida Department of Natural Resources at Tallahassee, says that while no precious opal has been recorded in Florida, common opal and certain trace opal forms are, on rare occasions, exposed by open-pit phosphate mining in Hamilton County and Polk County. In these areas an opal-rich sediment called porcellanite occurs as the result of biogenic Opal-A dissolving and then being reprecipitated as opal-CT, from which felted opal-CT is formed as randomly oriented bundles at or near the sediment-water interface. Some common opal appears as so-called "box-work" geodes in the sediments of Tampa Bay as well as in seams, where it is a replacement of palygorskite clay.

FRANCE

Eric Marcoux, senior geologist of the Department of Geology, National Geographical Survey in Orleans Cedex, stated that "we have several opal occurrences in France: common opal, brown 'resinite' opal, open pit mined diatomites, a particular pink opal called quincyite, etc., but not precious opal variety. . . . We have only 'common opal' *(sensu lato)* in France, located in Massif Central and Bassin de Paris." He evidently erred, however, in unqualifiedly claiming no precious opal for France. There is a high-quality variety of quincyite that occurs on rare occasions in the freshwater limestone at Quincy, France, that is known as rose opal—a magnificent specimen of which was in the famous Green Vaults in Dresden. M. Marcoux goes on to say that the primary opal deposits in France are seam opal, wood opal, ledge opal, and bog opal, and he lists the main varieties as follows:

1. *White common opal:* Veins (up to 0.10 m width) crosscutting Tertiary limestones and volcanic tuffs at Gergovie, 5 km [3.1 mi.] south of Clermont–Ferrand, and impregnations of Tertiary limestones (white, gray, or light brown) in Mezel, located 10 km [6.2 mi] east of Clermont–Ferrand.

2. *Brown "resinite" opal:* Veins crosscutting Tertiary limestones and volcanic tuffs or lava flows in Gergovie, Ceyrat, and Puy Marmant (S. Clermont–Ferrand).

3. *Diatomite opal* (or tripoli—Also called "randanite" because of old mine at Randanne, Massif Central): Marcoux says this material is "Open-pit mined in Auxillac (Murat, Cantal) and La Bade (Riom es Montagne, Cantal) and known in Randanne (Puy de Dome), Menat (Puy de Dome), etc. These diatomites formed either in volcanic craters or in dam lakes created by a lava flow. Their age is 5–6 Ma (Auxillac) and 6–8 Ma (La Bade). They constitute layers of up to several meters thick. These 3 varieties are related to the Tertiary volcanism of French Massif Central.

    "Three other varieties." Marcoux continues "occur in limestones or clay formations and are of sedimentary origin: ménilites, wood opal, quincyite."

4. *Ménilites* (common light grey, grey-blue or cream opal): Usually mixed with calcite; these occur as layered concretions very similar to silex; they are known in Paris (Ménilmontant) and in the Limagne Valley near Clermont–Ferrand, as well as at Pont de Chateau, Romagnat, and Gergovie.

5. *Wood opal:* occurs in alluvial deposits of the Limagne Valley—Aigueperse, Romagnat, Chateaugay, Clermont, Riom, etc.

6. *Quincyite:* A very particular pink opal colored by organic pigments, Marcoux says that "it impregnates the giobertite of oligocene lacustrine siliceous limestones of Quincy and Mehun s/Yevre (10 km NW Bourges). It occurs as

small amounts up to 5–6 cm length. Best specimens are exposed in Paris School of Mines." As mentioned above, rare examples exhibit POC and are called rose opal.

Finally, Marcoux writes that there is a seventh variety—a common gray opal that is "disseminated in Tertiary formations near Orléans but they are of poor interest." Tripolite and hyalite are known to occur in the area of Auvergne.

Jean-Paul Poirot, director of the Public Service for the Control of Diamonds, Pearls and Fine Precious Stones for the Paris Chamber of Commerce and Industry, lists a pink opal he calls *manivi* as a precious stone, though it is devoid of POC. It is a translucent opal that occurs in montmorillonite in a limestone, associated with sepiolite, but it is not mined commercially. This material is evidently the same as that listed by as quincyite by geologist Eric Marcoux, who describes the stone as "very particular pink opal, coloured by organic pigments."

Medard Thiry, director of the Paris School of Mines, says that the common opal of France, "as everywhere in world," occurs in "silcretes paleoweathering" and is associated with silicified limestone and the general "silicification of Tertiary formations." That material, he adds, is mined recreationally in several locations each of the Paris Basin, southeastern France, and the Massif Central.

GEORGIA (United States)

Bruce J. O'Connor, supervisory geologist of the Georgia Geologic Survey in Atlanta, says that while there is no known occurrence of precious opal in Georgia, common opal and hyalite are known to occur as seam opal and wood opal— the latter in fossil wood found in sediments and as fracture fillers in chert and metamorphic rock. Some of the opal is transparent to translucent and is collected recreationally but not otherwise mined. The base coloration ranges from white (milky) to transparent red or green.

Mineralogist Robert B. Cook states that "Opal is known to occur in two distinct modes within Georgia. Common opal infrequently replaces wood of the Tuscaloosa Formation in the northernmost counties of the Coastal Plain. Opal (variety hyalite) occurs as secondary incrustations filling joints and cavities in granite, mafic rocks, and residual masses of iron oxides. Although fire (precious) opal was reported from Washington County in the nineteenth century, no authentic occurrences of precious opal are known today."

Included in the deposits Dr. O'Connor lists for opal occurrence in Georgia are: **Bartow County:** thin seams and mammillary aggregates of colorless hyalite opal fill open spaces in residual iron oxide at many of the iron mines in the Cartersville District; **Brooks County:** waxlike opal has been found on Lot 270, 12th District and, though the occurrence has not been described in the literature, it is assumed that the opal replaces wood; **Burke County:** mammillary incrustations of hyalite coat chert and flint of Eocene Age at Stony Bluff on the Savannah River; **Dekalb County:** (1) thin crusts of hyalite opal coat joint surfaces in granite quarried by the Ethyl Granite Corporation, about 2.5 miles [4 km] southwest of the crest of Stone Mountain, material that fluoresces brilliant green under ultraviolet radiation and is typically associated with uranophane; (2) similar material may be found at the Flat Rock Quarry on the north side of Stone Mountain, the quarry of Stone Mountain Granite Corporation on the south side of the mountain, at the Hayne Quarry, and elsewhere; **Floyd County:** colorless, transparent hyalite opal is relatively abundant in open spaces in residual iron oxide boulders mined at numerous localities in the vicinity of Cave Springs; **Hancock County:** milky opal is found along the shores of Lake Sinclair; **Rabun County:** (1) hyalite occurs as thin incrustations in cracks near the margin of the peridotite body at the Laurel Creek Corundum Mine in the southern part of Lot 72, 3rd District, about 1 mile [1.6 km] southwest of Pine Mountain on Laurel Creek; (2) similar material has been reported from the old Miller Asbestos Mine, Lot 7, 1st District, 3 miles [4.8 km] northwest of Burton on a small branch of Dick's Creek; **Richmond County:** interesting opal replacing wood occurs in Richmond County, several specimens of which are in the museum of the Georgia State Capitol; the material exhibits interesting variations of color, from red through pink to cream-white, and much of it fluoresces ultraviolet light; **Washington County:** (1) the occurrence of "fire opal" (actually, precious opal) is mentioned by Dana (1892 ed., p. 197) from a location near Chalker, where it occurs as small masses in "silicified sandstone" of Eocene Age, which contains calcareous shells, the opal reportedly filled spaces left by the dissolution of the shells; (2) an attempt by R. W. Smith to relocate this occurrence in 1926 resulted in the discovery of opal in identical matrix on the Dick Warthen property, about 2 miles [3.2 km] south of Warthen on the west side of the Sandersville Highway; (3) tan opalized wood is on display in the museum of the Georgia State Capitol from an unspecified location in Washington County; **Webster County:** films and mammillary masses of colorless hyalite opal are occasionally found in cavernous masses of iron oxide in Paleocene and Oligocene sediments and, in an unconfirmed statement, "identical material is reported from Pulaski, Dooly and Stewart Counties" [S. M. Pickering, personal communication]; **White County:** bright green fluorescent, globular hyalite opal is found along seams and fractures in biotite gneiss exposed along a secondary road at the Tesnatee Creek Bridge off Georgia Highway 115, about 3.8 miles [6 km] west of Cleveland.

GERMANY

V. Stein, director of the Geological Survey of Lower Saxony in Hanover, Germany, states that there is no known occurrence of opals of any type in the country. However, a further communication from Hermann Bank, president of the German Gemological Association and German Foundation of Gem Stone Research and German Gemstones Test Institute at Idar-Oberstein, reports that Germany does have opals, including common opal, hyalite, holzopal (wood opal), and, rarely, precious opal. The opal is found, he says, in volcanic matrices, primarily basalt and rhyolite, and usually in association with granulite. It is not mined commercially but is occasional sought by collectors as specimen material. The opal ranges from transparent to translucent and has a base color of brown. The sites Professor Dr. Bank lists include **Kaiserskeuhl:** hyalite occurs at Baden, while precious opal occurs at Eifel, Ihringen, Jechringen, Niedderotweil, Oberrotweil, Obershoffhausen, and Sasbaho; **Kongswinter:** occurrences of semiopal; **Oelberg:** occurrences of semi-opal; **Sachsen und Thüringen:** at Johanngergenstadt, Hubertsburg, Leisnig (precious opal and hyalite), Oberlausitz, Pootelsgrün (precious opal and wood holzopal), and at Tharandt; also occurrences of jasp-opal and semi-opal in the area of Siebengebirg.

GREECE

Kalevi Hokkanen, now with the Geological Survey of Finland at Espoo, has studied the subject of opal occurrence in Greece and reports that silicified fossil wood and opal occurs in Mytilene, stating that "The occurrence of petrified wood of Late Tertiary Age has been previously reported from the Mytilene area (Lesbos, Lesvos) in Greece. The replacement minerals of these fossil trees is mostly Opal-A, as determined by Dr. Kari A. Kinnunen, Geological Survey of Finland. Opal-A is characteristically not older than Tertiary." Some hyalite in insignificant amounts has been reported.

GREENLAND (Denmark)

Peter Appel, geologist of the Geological Survey of Greenland, wrote from Copenhagen, Denmark, that "Opals of good quality are not known from Greenland. All what is known are small samples of a rather poor quality, mostly brownish and intergrown with calcite." He goes on to say common opal is plentiful and there are also deposits wood opal, hyalite, and geyserite—siliceous sinter. One form of the common opal is pure white with a bluish tinge and occurs as separate geodes. A second form, grayish white, appears in limestone deposits, associated with aragonite, calcite, dolomite, and magnesite. A third form occurs as layering in basalt, associated with chalcedony and calcite. This latter common opal, Dr. Appel says, occurs in half-spherical masses, 2 mm–10 mm, on a thin calcite crust in basaltic cavities, its base coloration a semitransparent gray in a fresh state, but soon turning milky white and opaque on decomposed faces. The wood opal occurs only as thin, snow-white fibers resembling asbestos. The hyalite comes in two forms—one that is very clear, colorless, and pure, occasionally exhibiting some small POC, and which is found in black basalt vugs; the other is what Dr. Appel terms "an opaque, white, china-like opal in a brown basalt." Finally, the geyserite is a siliceous sinter that forms a 1- to 2-mm-thick coating on loose pebbles around hot springs, with the surface warty, stalactitic and opaque grayish-white. Dr. Appel says that the opals listed above occur in the East Greenland District at Carlshavn and Brinkley Bjærg, in the Godhavn District at Per Dams Skib, in the Julianehaab District at Unartoq, in the Ritenbenk District at Ujaragsugssuk, and in the Umanak District at Nûgssauaq and Hare Øen.

GUATEMALA

Although no response was received to queries sent to the Geological Survey of Guatemala in regard to the country's opal resources, a small amount of information is known. Some opal, virtually identical to the opal originating in Honduras, has been found in Guatemala, some excellent specimens of which are in the collection of the British Museum collection, but no specific source is shown on the acquisition or collection cards for the specimens in possession of that institution. There is some indication that hundreds of years ago opal deposits were mined, but what limited mining occurs now is apparently haphazard at best and is done more on a prospecting level than anything else. No real modern mining development is known to exist and little is officially recorded about them.

HAWAII (United States)

Glen Bauer, geologist of the Division of Water Resources Management of the Department of Land and Natural Resources in Honolulu, asserts that "common opal does occur in Hawaii, but no precious opal." The common opal, associated with zeolitic materials and appearing as amygdules in basalt, is opaque and usually milky white, though sometimes tinting into a light blue. It is found in the Koolau Caldera of the Kailua area on Oahu Island and in the Iao Valley of Wailuku on Maui.

HONDURAS

Details about the opal deposits of Honduras and the history of the mining for these stones may be found under the Honduras heading in Chapter 7.

HONG KONG (United Kingdom, until 1997)

Raynor Shaw, chairman of the Geological Society of Hong Kong at the University of Hong Kong, reports there is no known occurrence of opal of any variety in Hong Kong.

HUNGARY

Akos Éva Vetó, senior geologist of the Hungarian Geological Institute in Budapest, reports that—in addition to hyalite, a white opaque common opal called milk opal, a brownish semi-opal, a yellow-brown liver opal, a wax opal found near Veresvagas, and scattered occurrences of wood opal—Hungary does have good deposits of precious opal, the best of which occurs in the area 15 miles [24.1 km] to the southeast of Esperias [Presov] at Czerwenitza near Kashau and at Schemnitz and Dubnik. However, the term Hungarian opal more correctly refers to opals historically mined in a broad area taking in (primarily) the Czech and Slovak Republics as well as certain areas southeastward to Turkey. The materials from Hungary proper are found primarily in vugs, seams, and ledges in rhyolite and basalt, associated with andesite, andesite tuffs, and quartz-fluorite; and the quartz-fluorite, while mined recreationally, is not presently mined commercially. This material originates in Borsod-Abauj in Zemplén County, Heves County. Further deposits are noted in the counties of Heves, Nógrád, Vesprém, Fejér, and in the Buda-Hills. See also the section on Czech, Slovakian, and Hungarian Opals.

ICELAND (Denmark)

Aage Jensen stated that in Iceland there are deposits of common opal, some of which exhibits fluorescence under shortwave ultraviolet light. The opal has a varying base coloration of pale green, pale red, faintly yellow, or milky white and ranges from translucent to opaque. It is pocket opal, found in vugs in both rhyolite and basalt. Some has the characteristics of cachalong opal, but none exhibits any POC and it is mined only on a recreational basis. These opals are found in Northern Iceland at Svarfadardalur, in Northeast Iceland at Borgarfjördur Eystri, and in Eastern Iceland at Brattháls.

IDAHO (United States)

Jane E. Jenness, Geologist of the U.S. Geological Survey's Minerals Information Office, said there are a number of important opal deposits in the State of Idaho, a substantial number of which bear precious opal. Much colorful common opal also occurs in Idaho, including blue opal, green prase opal, milk opal, rose opal, yellow "resin" opal, brown and gray "liver" opal, banded "onyx" opal, honey opal, and wood opal. Though found in numerous locations statewide, the primary locations are those in Clark, Lemhi, Latah, and Owyhee Counties. Some of the opal is found within poorly formed "thunderegg" nodules, but most often—particularly in Snake River Valley formations—it occurs in seams or masses embedded in hard compact porphyry, making it uncommonly difficult to extract unfractured pieces.

Probably the most famous Idaho opal deposit is at the fee-digging open-pit operation called the Spencer Mine, located 8 road miles (3 crow-flight miles) east of the Clark County town of Spencer, only 9 miles [14.5 km] south of the Montana border and some 60 miles [96.5 km] directly west of Yellowstone National Park. The Spencer opals are generally thin layers of opal—primarily suitable only for the cutting and construction of doublets and triplets, although some thicker pieces allow solid opal cutting—which occur in a rusty to pale pinkish buff to white common opal that is part of the inclusion in ill-formed very large thunderegg material of rhyolitic composition and originally created by low-grade volcanic activity. The thunderegg material bearing the opals occurs as lumpy geodes and nodular formations of a gritty red rhyolite and (sometimes) black obsidian, with the interior opal-bearing pockets averaging about 2 inches [50.8 mm] in diameter. If opal is inside the pocket, it normally fills only about half the cavity, with from one to several thin parallel layers of precious opal separated by creamy common opal. The POC occurs in red, pink, green, blue, yellow, orange, and lavender, with broadflash red deemed most desirable. Because of its often extremely brilliant displays of color, Spencer opal has been described by some as being as beautiful as Australian opal (Figure 55). Greater details on Spencer opal will be found in Chapter 7.

Among the opal-bearing sites in Idaho are **Canyon County:** unconfirmed reports have both common and precious opal occurring in the vicinity of Nampa; **Clark County:** In addition to the Spencer Mine, there is another fee-digging opal mine nearby—the Jeppeson–Wilson Mine—where much the same type of material is unearthed and collectors are charged $20 per day to dig; **Custer County:** unconfirmed reports claim the occurrence of both common opal and precious opal filling vugs in rhyolite along Squaw Creek; **Idaho County:** quite colorful common opal occurs near Grangeville; **Kootenai County:** a deposit of precious opal has been unofficially reported very close to the Washington border between the Coeur d'Alene Indian Reservation and Nez Perce Indian Reservation, near Whelan; and close by there is an occurrence of very bright lemon-colored transparent opal that is reportedly quite good for faceting, with the stones usually averaging around 25 carats, but with some that reach 100 carats; **Latah County:** a rich pocket of precious opal in basalt was discovered in the Moscow area in 1895 by some men sinking a well, resulting in quite a rush, but the only opal found in that specific area was at the well

Figure 55. The plains of Idaho and Wyoming stretch out eastward from below the Spencer Opal Mine, situated at an elevation of approximately 7000 feet and about 9 miles east and a little south of the town of Spencer. The large rhyolite boulder in the foreground has vugs in it and will be further broken up with a sledgehammer. (Photo by Alan A. Vogel)

discovery shaft; 5 miles [8.1 km] northwest, however, in the Avon District (also called the Mica Mountain District), precious opal was found by T. O'Donnell at a site subsequently called the O'Donnell Opal Occurrence, its present status listed as "developed producer, but inactive" and located on the Pullman 7.5″ topographic quadrangle, Sec. 36, T40N R6W; **Lemhi County:** Cobalt area, in the Salmon River Mountains, 6 miles [9.7 km] northeast in the Blackbird District on the Elk City Quadrangle, Sec. 2, T21N R19E, there is an occurrence, maximum width of 20 feet, [6.1 m], of gem-quality wood opal in fossilized sequoia limbs, roots and logs; the site, called the Cutler Opal Occurrence; another precious opal deposit, called the Panther Creek Opal Occurrence, part of the Yellowjacket Formation, is located 27.5 miles [44.2 km] north of Challis near the mouth of Opal Creek and can be pinpointed on the Challis 7.5″ topographical quadrangle in Section 11, T18N R18E, the opal occurring in veins in a host matrix of Eocene Age quartzite alluvium and also found loose in Challis volcanics and placers at an elevation of 6700 feet; without providing any details, one account enigmatically reports a fee-collecting area of "blue opal of the precious variety" as being located a half-hour's drive from the county seat of Salmon; **Nez Perce County:** a rich pocket of precious opal in basalt country rock was found by well diggers in 1956 not far from Lewiston, but further searching disclosed no other opal occurrences; **Owyhee County:** a fee-digging precious opal operation known as Tallman's Claim at Rock Teepee is located near Marsing; similarly in the same area is located the Tepe Blue Fire Opal Mine; unconfirmed reports mention precious opal occurring along both Squaw Creek and Little Squaw Creek several miles from Marsing; a confirmed report states that "precious opal in many unique opal formations is found at Opal Springs, 23 miles [37 km] south of the Horseshoe Club and just above the Nevada border close to the Owyhee River, and at the Opaline Mining Camp; relatively widespread throughout the county are occurrences of dendritic common opal having a milk white base coloration and bright blue dendrites; **Payette County:** wood opal is widespread but not abundant; **Valley County:** a deposit of lower-grade gem-quality precious opal, called the Gray's Creek Opal Deposit, occurs in the Marble Creek District, 5 miles [8.1 km] north of the Middle Fork Guard Station atop the ridge at the head of Cougar Creek in the Salmon River Mountains, at an elevation of 7600' [2318 m], but it was listed in 1995 as being inactive.

ILLINOIS (United States)

John M. Masters of the Illinois State Geological Survey at Champaign, reports that no varieties of opal occur in Illinois.

INDIA (Including Part of Jammu and Kashmir)

D. Guptasarma, FNA, director of the National Geophysical Research Institute's Council of Scientific and Industrial Research at Hyderabad, states that "we have no systematic information about the occurrence of minerals in the country," but he relayed the query to R. V. Karanth, principal investigator of the faculty of science, Department of Geology at the University of Baroda who, in turn stated both precious and common opal varieties do occur in India, pointing out that "the term opal has derived from the Sanskrit word *'upala'* ", adding that he has been in touch with the gem merchants in various parts of India but "I have not been able to get gem quality opal of Indian origin for my collections and . . . I doubt whether opals are mined in India in recent days." However, he adds that good-quality precious opal was found to some significant extent (along with common opal) as occurrences in pockets and vugs of basalt and chert as a by-product of previous commercially mining for manganese and feldspar, although "the material has not been commercially mined in recent days" and what is found now are "only rare occurrences not available on the market." There is also some occurrence of precious opal in wood opal form. The principal common opal is opaque white, although some occurrence of brown opal has also been noted, as has brownish semi-opal. In ancient times some opal mining is believed to have occurred in areas near Bombay, Hyderabad City, and Madras, although there is no reason to believe that any of this alleged opal production found its way to ancient Rome as the so-called "Oriental opal" gemstones, which actually originated in Slovakian region of southeastern Europe.

Where the opals of India today are concerned, Dr. Karanth lists the following deposits of a white variety of common opal: **Rajasthan:** near Ajmer, Srinagar; **Bihar:** in the Rajmahal Hills, where common opal occurs in nodules up to 2 feet [0.6 m] in diameter in deposits in the Rajmahal Traps and near Sahibganj Railway Station; **Kashmir:** at Ragu in Rupsju; **Andhra Pradesh:** in the manganese mines at Kodur and Kotakarra in the Visakhapatnam District, and in the Deccan Traps in the Pungadi West Godavari District; **Madhya Pradesh:** in the geodes unearthed from the Deccan Traps near Kandri and Kodegaon; **Maharashtra:** in the Deccan Traps of Sitabaldi and Kodegaon in the Nagpur District, and in the Deccan Traps at Gavilgarh in the Amravati District; **Orissa:** at Boirani in the Ganjam District.

Common opal of brown coloration occurs as small seams in the serpentine deposits of Tutland Island in the Andaman Nicobar Islands. Cretaceous wood opal occurrences are reported from Tamil Nadu in the Gondwana Beds near Alundalippur and from near Ariyalur in Malvay.

Dr. Karanth lists the following occurrences of precious opal, which is termed "flame opal" by locals: **Ratanpura:** in a Tertiary Age oligomict conglomerate derived from Deccan Traps; **Karnataka:** in the Deccan traps of the Plains of Bijapur; **Andhra Pradesh:** along the banks of the Sina River between Andargaon and Panda.

INDONESIA

Kingking A. Margawidjaja, director of Mineral Resources for Indonesia in Bandung, says that his country does have good deposits of precious opal, common opal, wax opal, and wood opal. The opal occurs in seams, vugs, pockets, and wood in montmorillonite clay, rhyolite, basalt, and silicious tuff. The base coloration of the precious opal varies considerably, not only in different locations, but even in single deposits, ranging from black, brown, or gray through orange, white (milky), or transparent (jelly) and in optical properties from transparent to translucent to opaque. The POC occurs in broadflash, long streaks, and what Dr. Margawidjaja terms "rainbow," with predominating colors of red, blue, green, blue-green, yellow, lavender, and pink. The black opal, Dr. Margawidjaja states, is particularly attractive. Among the specific locations listed are **Bengkulu:** at Rejanglebong, "where, in association with a very common white potch, precious opal is reported resulting from hydrothermal process in tuffaceous dacite/andesite; the occurrence, on the northwestern coast of Sumatra, is still listed as a probability." he says; **Irianjaya:** on Misool Island, "where precious opal occurs through a water circulation process in sedimentary rocks," according to Dr. Margawidjaja; **Sulawesi:** on the southeastern coast of the province, where there occurs a translucent-to-opaque greenish white potch; **West Java:** at Garut, Sukabumi and Labak, "where precious opal has resulted from the hydrothermal water circulation process," the later deposit being the only one in Indonesia currently (1995) being mined commercially and producing black, white, transparent and brownish (or "tea") opals. Some of the black opals of Java are claimed to be virtually identical to those of Virgin Valley, Nevada, in the United States.

IRAQ

Farazdaq M. Al-Haddad, of the Iraqi Geologist's Union in Baghdad, reports that Iraq has no opal of any variety.

IRELAND (Not Including Northern Ireland)

A. M. Flegg, of the Geological Survey of Ireland in Dublin, says there is "no known opal occurrence in [the] *country*," adding that, "I do not know of any occurrences of opal occurrence in the Republic of Ireland."

However, Jonathan Stewart of the Mineralogical Society of Great Britain and Ireland [see also England], says that there are deposits of opal in Ireland, including precious opal in relatively limited quantities, along with more abundant common opal. This Ireland opal, which is usually white and translucent, but sometimes yellowish and opaque, sometimes shows a vague POC in reds, blues, greens, and yellows, but it can be rated as only marginally gem-quality material. In Antrim, it is found at the Causeway on Rathlin Island, at Crossreagh in Ballywillin Parish and in several locations in the basalt occurring on the northeastern coast of Ireland. At Sandy Braes the opal occurs in variously colored pitchstone porphyry and at times shows distinct opalescence.

ISRAEL

Amit Segev, head of the Minerals and Energy Resources Division of the Geological Survey of Israel in Jerusalem, says that, "Yes, opals do occur in this country, in porcellanite rock." Taliaferro, in 1934, defined porcellanite rock as "impure, usually opaline, rock having the texture and appearance of unglazed porcelain. It is composed mostly of opal and is highly porous (up to 50%) and has a very low permeability (0.08 md.). It sticks to the tongue and is very salty. When immersed in distilled water it takes on approximately a third of its weight, but returns subsequently to its original weight after drying in air for 24 hours." Evidently Taliaferro was here referring to hydrophane opal. Dr. Segev says it is not precious opal but, rather a common opal form that appears in a matrix of porcellanite and chert, associated with brown chert, clay, limonite, chalcedony, calcite, and apatite. He describes the opal as being "white, but becoming grayish with increasing clay content," adding that, while normally opaque, it becomes translucent when heated and transparent when immersed in water, which, of course, identifies it as cachalong opal. Dr. Segev lists two separate occurrences of this opal in southern Israel; the first is in Central Negev, in Arod Pass at the western edge of Makhtesh Ramon, in the porcellainite beds of the Senonian Mishas Formation; the second in Northern Negev, in the Ef'e-Gei Gemalim area, between Arad and Sdom, in the porcellanite beds of the Senonian Mishas Formation.

ITALY

Andrea Todisco, director general of the Italian Ministry of Commercial Mining, reports that the only known opal occurrence in Italy occurs in the Tuscany region, in the South Fiora area, where a translucent milky white xiloide opal (xilopal) occurs in diatomite deposits at Omodeo Lake near Sarolegus.

JAMAICA

Lawrence Henry, director of the Geological Survey Division of the Ministry of Agriculture and Mining in Kingston, states that there is no known opal occurrence in Jamaica.

JAPAN

Michiaki Bunno, director of the Geological Museum, Geological Survey of Japan in Tsukuba, writes that the opal types in Japan include precious opal, common opal and wax opal. This material occurs in rhyolite vugs and is "mined in small scale, but not commercially." The precious opal, he reports, is a transparent (jelly) opal with smudges of POC in red and green and is found at Hosaka in the Fukushima Prefecture.

Ichiro Sunagawa, principal of the Yamanashi Institute of Gemmology and Jewelry Arts at Tohuku University in Tokyo, confirms that precious opals do occur in Japan but that they are mined only on a recreational basis, mainly for mineral specimens, and that no commercial mining has been undertaken. The precious opal is relatively rare and more commonly the opal varieties are hyalite, wood opal (largely without POC), geyserite, and common opal. The precious opal is found in vugs in rhyolite, sometimes in pegmatites, and rarely in fossil wood. The geyserite occurs in precipitates at hot springs. None of the opal is transparent; translucency, sometimes with POC, occurs in white (milky) based specimens. When POC does occur, it is blue pinfire.

Prof. Dr. Sunagawa and Dr. Bunno list, as sites for these opal occurrences **Aomori Prefecture:** at Osore San; **Fukushima Prefecture:** at Abumibata and Nihonmatsu, where translucent nonprecious wood opal is found in sedimentary deposits of ancient volcanic origin; and at Hosaka, where translucent common opal—and occasional translucent precious opal—occurs in rhyolite vugs; *Ishikawa Prefecture:* at Akase, where occasional translucent precious opal occurs in rhyolite vugs; **Nagasaki Prefecture:** at Hazami; **Oita Prefecture (Ni-Mine):** at the Wakayama Mine; **Toyama Prefecture:** at Shin-yu where, in the Tategama Hot Spring, geyserite and nonprecious hyalite occur in precipitates.

KANSAS (United States)

David A. Grisafe, associate scientist of the Industrial Minerals Technological Information Services branch of the Kansas Geological Survey at Lawrence, stated there was no known opal occurrence in State. However, Rex Buchanan of the Kansas Geological Survey, University of Kansas, also at Lawrence, states that moss opal occurs in Kansas and is usually found in the Cretaceous chalks of western Kansas. The material, Dr. Buchanan continued, is unmined and the best known deposits are in Gove County. He adds, "I've never heard Kansas opal described as precious opal" and that true "precious opal is not found in Kansas." Common opal is a relatively common Kansas mineral that is found as a lining or filling in cavities in some rocks, as a deposit formed by hot springs, and as the petrifying material in much fossil wood. It is widespread in the Ogallala Formation in Clark, Ellis, Logan, Ness, and Rawlins Counties. This Ogallala opal is colorless to white or gray and is found with a white, cherty, calcareous rock. Some of it is called moss opal because it contains an impurity, manganese oxide, that forms dark branching deposits (dendrites) like small mosses in the opal. Moss opal (often called moss agate) has been found in Trego, Gove, and Wallace Counties. Opalized fossil bones and shells of diatoms are also found in the Ogallala Formation, as is a green opal that acts as a cement in hard, resistant sandstones.

KENTUCKY (United States)

Warren H. Anderson, geologist of the Kentucky Geological Survey at the University of Kentucky in Lexington, says that while no precious opal occurs in the state, there are some deposits of common opal, although these are "very small, usually microscopic, traces found in vugs of chert or chalcedony." It is nowhere abundant in the state and no deposits of the common opal are mined.

KOREA, SOUTH

Dong Hak Kim, research counsellor for the Korea Institute of Geology, Mining and Materials in Taejon, states unequivocally in regard to opals of any variety, that "they do not occur in my country." However, Lee Dong Jim, principal researcher in the Mineralogical Research Group of KIGAM at Taedok Science Town in Taejon, states that Opal-A and Opal-CT, along with wood opal, occur in the tuffaceous rocks and montmorillonite clays. None of the material is mined. Dr. Lee says that in the Yeongil Area, at Kyungsangbuk, both opal-A and opal-CT are found in the Tertiary tuffaceous rocks, although the opal-A is restricted to the zeolitic zone of the area; opal-CT also occurs as fillings in cavities of smetite rocks. None of the deposits, however, seem to be of any commercial significance.

LIBYA

No response was received from the Geological Survey of Libya in Tripoli, but it is well established that some of the driest opal known to man is found on the Libyan Desert as an extremely desiccated so-called "desert glass," which is opal with virtually no water content whatsoever, due to scores—perhaps hundreds, maybe even thousands—of years of exposure to the dry desert air and scorching sun. It has no commercial importance.

LOUISIANA (United States)

A deposit of precious opal has been discovered in Louisiana that is very similar in composition to the matrix opal found at Andamooka in Australia. Unfortunately, repeated requests for information about this opal, made to the Louisiana Geological Survey, have met with no response. Though events and developments have been shrouded in secrecy, the opal was evidently discovered in the mid-1980s, about 15 miles [24.1 km] west of Leesville in west central Louisiana and the deposit was worked rather intently by a small group of miners from 1989 until about 1994. Lack of demand brought that operation to a close, although there is evidently at least one mine still in operation. The Louisiana opal occurs in a brown to gray-brown to gray-blue quartzite matrix, in which the POC ranges through the spectrum, but with blue and green as the most common colors and red as the rarest. Because the material is not a solid form of precious opal but occurs as an opalescent sandstone and granular quartz, along with traces of pyrite and barium, all cemented together irregularly with bits of precious opal, the stone is easy to cut and polish and does not crack or craze.

The POC is of the pinfire variety and more widely scattered than the pinfire apparent in the Andamooka matrix opal. Much of the material is surface-pitted and almost all has dark inclusions. Base coloration is said to range from blue through brown to black, with the brown tones the most common. Some of the better pieces are reported to have been sold at $50 per carat or more, but the author could discover no proof for the report, and what material is presently available normally sells for between $5 and $20 per gram. Skilled opal cutter Kevin Lane Smith, who has cut some pieces from this material, reported to the author that "it is really pretty, with a terrific play-of-color."

LUXEMBOURG

Jacques Bintz, geologist of the Luxembourg Geological Service at Charlotte, states that "There is no natural occurrence of opals in this country."

MAINE (United States)

Woodrow B. Thompson, physical geologist of the Maine Geological Survey at Augusta, and Vandall T. King, with the Geological Survey in Rochester, state that Maine does have some occurrence of common opal, but no precious opal. The opal occurs as the hyalite variety in granite pegmatites, as coatings on fracture surfaces, and ranges in color from white to colorless, although it has a strong green fluorescence. The Maine opal is unmined and has no value except as mediocre mineral specimens. While no specific locations were given, it is known to occur in Androscoggin, Oxford, and Sagadahoc counties.

Among sites listed for hyalite and/or common opal are **Cumberland County:** close to the south end of Pleasant Lake in a road cut of Route 302 near Casco; also in a road cut of U.S. Route 1 at Freeport; and in the Eagle Gray Quarry at Fryeburg; **Kennebec County:** near Albion, at the Donahue Prospect; **Knox County:** in the Starrett Quarry at Warren; **Oxford County:** in the Bessey Quarry at Buckfield; in the Greenwood area at both the Beryllium Corporation Prospect and in the Emmons Quarry; north of Mount Zircon in a road cut of U.S. Route 2 at Mexico; not far from there, in the Rumford area, at the Black Mountain Quarry; in the Newry area at the Rose Quartz Crystal Locality, and at the Dunton Quarry nearby; and, in the Paris area, at the Hoopon's Ledge Quarry, the Mount Mica Quarry, the Twitchell Quarry and the Whispering Pines Quarry; **Sagadahoc County:** in the Topsham area in an Interstate Route 95 road cut, as well as in the Undivided Quarry, the Willes No. 1 Quarry and the Yedlin Location.

MALAYSIA

Dorani B. Johani, of the Geological Survey of Malaysia in Sarawak, writes that there is no known occurrence of opal in Malaysia.

MANITOBA (Canada)

Richard Gunter, of Manitoba Energy and Mines in Winnipeg, writes that there is no known occurrence of opal in the province.

MARYLAND (United States)

Kenneth N. Weaver, director of the Maryland Geological Survey in Baltimore, said that common opal does occur in Maryland in small seams in serpentine deposits. On the other hand, James P. Reager, chief of the Environmental Geology and Mineral Resources Program of the Maryland Geological Survey, says that the state has occurrences of both common opal of monochromatic base coloration and moss opal. He adds, however, that "the only occurrences of opal in Maryland of which I am aware are essentially chalcedony-filled fractures, small veins and shear zones. All occurrences can be considered rare, and none has revealed any gem-quality materials. Our staff geologists are aware of only three locations where opal has been reported in Maryland." Dr. Reager lists the first two sites, serpentinite quarries, as follows:

1. Hunting Hill Quarry near Rockville, (39°04′45″ N latitude; 77°13′30″ W longitude): opal mixed with magnesite; also as gray to white veins, commonly with manganese oxide dendrites. Veins of white to gray opal, often with mosslike manganese oxide inclusions, have occasionally been found. Brown to green chalcedony veins up to 15 centimeters wide . . . were reported from the northern end of the quarry.

2. Delight Quarry near Reisterstown (39°26′30″ N. latitude; 76°49′45″ W longitude): opal—white, mixed with magnesite and as separate translucent veins, often with dendritic manganese oxides.

Dr. Reager concluded, "A third location was reported during excavation for a business park just west of Baltimore in the 1970s. The location is now under buildings, pavement and lawns. I am not aware of any other information on that site."

Finally, an unconfirmed report without specifics indicates the occurrence of semi-opal in the Bare Hills of Baltimore County.

MASSACHUSETTS (United States)

Joseph A. Sinnot, state geologist in Boston, stated, in regard to opal deposits in the state, that for all intents and purposes, opal does not occur in Massachusetts. He adds, "Sparse or minute quantities would better define the occurrences. I hate NO." However, R. N. Foster, another state geologist, was not so reticent in his comment, remarking that "no opals of any variety occur in the state of Massachusetts."

MAURITANIA

Mohamed Lemine Ould Benahi, director of Mines and Geology in the Ministry of Mines at Geology at Nouakchott, writes, "in Mauritania there do not exist in natural state the mineral Opal."

MEXICO

Jaime Roldán Quintana, of the Geological Institute at Hermosillo in Sonora, reports that there is precious opal, fire opal, common opal, and geyserite in Mexico. Most of this is volcanic opal occurring in vugs as nodules and prune-like concretions in trachytes in very hard pink rhyolitic matrix, although some seam opal is also reported. The opal is, according to Dr. Quintana, "exploited in a small scale" both commercially and recreationally. The precious opal may have a translucent base coloration of blue, red, or milky white and exhibits mainly pinfire, although occasionally broadflash, long streaks and smudges of POC, most frequently red, blue, blue-green, and deep purple.

Despite that claim of opal exploitation on a small scale, for perhaps more than two centuries, Mexico has been one of the world's most important nations in the production of precious opal. Those opals originate mainly from the central volcanic belt in the States of Querétaro, Guanajuato, México, Jalisco, Hidalgo and Nayarit, as well as others. See Chapter 7 for greater details on opal deposits and production.

Among the many locations in Mexico where precious opal occurs and is mined are **Amelaco District:** at the Mina La Purisma; **Aguascaliente:** especially good opal occurs some 150 miles [241.4 km] northwest of Querétaro in the Barranca de Tepezala, Cerro de las Fejas; **Atzcapotzaleo:** in this municipality, quality wood opal is found on the Hacienda de Aspeita; **Cadereyta District:** fine precious fire opal occurs on the Hacienda Foentesuela in the Municipality of Moconi and in the Arroyo de Ramos; **Caja:** both wood opal and volcanic opal in the hills; **Chihuahua, State of:** some 150 miles [241.4 km] west and slightly south of the State's namesake city of Chihuahua, close to the 1000-foot waterfall of the Basaseachic Cascades National Park, in the Sierra

Madre Occidental, precious opal has been found as float along the river just below the falls, but no originating source has yet been located; in the southern region of the state occurs fire opal ranging from transparent brown to brownish red to cherry opal, all with interesting manganese dendritic formations; some 44 mile [70.8 km] southeast of that park, on the ridge dividing the headwaters of the Rio Oteros from that of the Rio Conchos, close to the village of Creel, quality cherry opal is found, ranging in some stones through orange to near yellow; also, a common opal that is pleasantly salmon-colored is widespread in the Sierra Madre Occidental; **Durango, State of:** some 75 miles [120.7 km] due south of the city of Hidalgo del Parral, good milk opal with bright POC is found near the village of Santa Maria del Oro; **Federal District:** some of the finest wood opal in Mexico is found in the municipality of Chiautla on the Hacienda Aspeita; **Guanajuato, State of:** many mines, including some very large operations, produce gem-quality precious opal and cherry opal in this state, including half a dozen just west of the village of Penjamo, one of the best being the Agostinos Mine; **Guerrero, State of:** in a feldspar porphyry in the foothills of the Sierra Madre del Sur, at San Nicolas, occurs fine transparent pale yellow to topaz yellow transparent pale red precious fire opal with strong flashes of red, brilliant yellow and green POC, and 46 miles southeast of Taxco, close to the village of Huitzuco de los Figueroa, is found a fine opal with dark gray to black base color and rich POC, especially in red and green, and very similar to the black opal of Lightning Ridge in Australia; **Hidalgo, State of:** the Cerro de las Fajas produces a top quality volcanic precious opal in reddish rhyolite from the Barranca de Tepezala, and a similar gemmy material from the Barranca Agua Dulce in the Tulancingo District; also, some fire wood opal occurs in several sites in the Cerro de las Silicatas in Tlazacala; **Jalisco, State of:** in the range of high hills running from the southeast to the northwest, east of Magdalena, north of the town of Tequila and north of the Rio Grande de Santiago, just a few miles from the village of El Salvador, is the El Cobano Mine, which produces large quantities of quality precious fire opal and some black opal; the nearby La Unica Mine is also a good producer; most productive mine of the state, however, is the San Simón Mine, about 15 miles [24.1 km] away from Magdalena, where over 100 workers are regularly employed; similarly in the general Magdalena District, there are a number of mines near such villages as San Marcos, Hostotipaquillo, Tequila, and Etzatlan in such mines and prospects as Cerro Viejo, El Conejo, El Muerto, El Toro, Fuentezuelas, La Cuadrillera, La Peineta, and San Augustin; some good opal in small quantities occurs at Guanimero near Guamar; also, some very attractive common opal, both in yellow and in lavender, is fairly widespread; some excellent precious fire opal occurs in the Toliman District, far to the southwest, in the mines on the Hacienda la Jurada; **Michoacan, State of:** a number of mines are scattered throughout the state, mines such as the well known diggings on the Hacienda San

Isidro in the municipality of Contepec, and the Cerro Agustion in the Maravatio District, these mines producing somewhat limited amounts of cherry opal and precious fire opal; **Nayarit, State of:** at least half a dozen mines with fair to good production rates are located south of the state capital of Tepic, close to the village of Compostela; **Oaxaca, State of:** a similar handful of low-producing mines are found in the area of the opal deposits near Tlaxiaco and Magdalena Tequisistlán, but these mines are more often idle than working; **Querétaro, State of:** historically, the location of the most productive precious opal mines in all of Mexico, with the principal mines east of the state capital of Querétaro at elevations up to 11,000 feet [3355 m] in the area of San Juan del Rio, where the centuries-old Aztec mines were rediscovered by a peon working on the Hacienda Esperanza in 1855, although no serious modern mining was inaugurated for 15 years after the discovery; since 1870, when the famed Santa Maria Iris Mine was established here by Don Jose Maria Siurob, it has been the most important mine in this area and one of the most productive in all of Mexico—a large open-cut operation alongside the highway running between Cadereyta and Querétaro, and the precious opal occurring in large blocks of reddish rhyolite; here, too, are the Jurecho Mines of Manuel Villasenor, famed for their production of orange-based transparent opal called girasol—referred to there as *azules*—with POC in brilliant yet delicate red and blue patterns; and the renowned La Carbonera Mine is in this area, also, near the village of La Trinidad[2]; some of these mines in the area of San Juan del Rio are fee-digging mines; included, as well, among the major producing opal operations near San Juan del Rio in Querétaro is the Ontiveros Mine, which has been worked off and on since 1865; **Sonora, State of:** in several locations just south of the Arizona border of the United States, a type of translucent blue-based opal occurs with scattered red, blue and green pinfire, the blue base ranging from pale sky blue to a deeper blue-gray wedgewood blue; **Zacatecas, State of:** in the Sierra Madre Oriental, 60 miles southwest of Saltillo and close to the village of Concepción del Oro, good precious opal is recovered at both the Nocha Buena Mine and the Valenciana Mine.

MICHIGAN (United States)

Robert C. Reed, deputy state geologist of the Michigan Geological Survey in Lansing, states that there is no known opal occurrence in the state and is seconded in his assertion by S. Paul Sundeen, geologist with the Michigan Department of Natural Resources, Geological Survey Division in Lansing.

MINNESOTA (United States)

G. B. Morey, associate director, and Terry Boerboom, geologist, of the Minnesota Geological Survey in Saint Paul, both state that there is no known occurrence of opal of any variety in the state of Minnesota.

MISSISSIPPI (United States)

Michael B. E. Bograd, geologist with the Mississippi Office of Geology in Jackson, states that the only opal occurrence in the state is "a sandstone (quartzite) with opaline silica cement of Miocene origin, which occurs in the Catahoula Formation of central Mississippi. It is not a precious opal and is not mined."

MISSOURI (United States)

Arthur Hebrank, mineralogist and geologist of the Division of Geology and Land Survey in the Department of Natural Resources at Rolla, states that while there is some occurrence of common opal in wood opal variety, "opal is not important or even common in Missouri." What opal does occur, based on reports from mineral collectors, is found as wood opal, along with tripolite, in the clays of sedimentary deposits from a few unspecified locations. None of it is mined.

MONTANA (United States)

Dick Berg, of the Montana Bureau of Mines and Geology in Butte, reports that, while no precious opal has been discovered in Montana, common opal does occur in the state in small amounts, some in ledge deposits at Three Forks in Montana County, where it is found in vugs of rhyolite and some in the form of wood opal in some parts of Yellowstone National Park and in the counties of Gallatin, Jefferson, Park, Ravelli, and Silverbow, where it has been noted in montmorillonite clays and gravels. Not important as a significant deposit anywhere, the opal is unmined.

MOROCCO (Excluding Western Sahara)

M. Addi Azza, chief of the Native Minerals Service of the Department of Geology in Rabat, reports that precious opal occurs in transparent orange in Morocco, and closely resembles some of the precious fire opal of Mexico. There are also occurrences of opaque, beige-colored common opal. Both varieties of opals occur in sedimentary montmorillonite (bentonite) clays as well as in vugs in rhyolite and Triassic basalt, but the opal sites remained unmined. These opals, M. Azza reports, occur at three sites in the country: in the Haut Atlas Occidental region at Tichka, in the Anti-Atlas region at Bouazzer, and at Beni Snaben.

MOZAMBIQUE

João Manuel P. R. Marques, national director of geology at the National Directorate for Geology of Mozambique at Maputo, states that his country does have occurrences of milky white common opal, found in ledges of serpentine rocks in Cabo Delgado Province of Northern Mozambique. There has been, however, no known occurrence of precious opal.

NAMIBIA

Gic Schneider, of the Geological Survey of Namibia in Windhoek, says, "No, opal does not occur in this country."

NEPAL

S. N. Jha, mineralogist and section chief of the Petrology, Mineralogy and Paleontology Section of the Department of Mines and Geology at Kathmandu, notes that there is no known occurrence of opal of any variety in Nepal. K. P. Kaphle, senior divisional geologist of the Department of Mines and Energy in Kathmandu, concurs.

NETHERLANDS

Pieter C. Zwaan, director of the Netherlands Gemological Laboratory of the National Museum of Natural History in Leyden, reports that opal does not occur as a native mineral in the Netherlands.

NEVADA (United States)

Harold F. Bonham, Jr., research geologist at the Nevada Bureau of Mines and Geology at the University of Nevada in Reno, confirms the occurrence of opals of virtually all varieties occurring in the state, including precious, common, moss, fluorescent, prase, wood, hyalite, and geyserite. The opals occur in seams, vugs, wood, and ledges as well as geyser coatings. The major occurrences of the precious variety are found primarily in montmorillonite deposits and in pockets and vugs of both rhyolite and basalt. Mined both recreationally and commercially, in open-pit operations as well as by tunneling, the precious opal is found as transparent, translucent, and opaque, in red, blue, deep purple, green, violet, indigo, lavender, gold, yellow, honey, orange, pink, brown, and gray, with the POC occurring as broadflash, pinfire, smudge, contra luz, etc.

Nevada has by far the richest opal deposits in the United States and most of these are located in the northwestern portion of the state, primarily in the Virgin Valley area of Humboldt County. Yet, before getting into that, it should be noted that a new and perhaps very significant opal deposit has been discovered far distant at the southern tip of the state, in Lincoln County. Well south of Las Vegas, this site, producing reportedly high gem-quality precious opal, was discovered in 1992 by William Webber and his two sons, Layne and Todd, all three of whom established and presently operate the Knobby Hill Mine at that site. Specific details as to its exact location are still not being disclosed, for fear of a rush of miners eager to stake claims adjacent to the Webber claim. It is reported, however, that there is little or no overburden above the opal level and the opal itself is being found in vugs in basinite and rhyolite, associated with quartz crystals, and relatively easily removable in large pieces without undue fracturing. Said to be "quite beautiful and highly stable," the translucent opal's base color ranges from a light blue to a deep wedgewood blue and sometimes to a deep olive coloration. The POC is described as a rolling flash fire of red and green as dominant colors and a gamut of other colors as secondaries. The opal within the vugs is said to be not exactly a true layering but nevertheless in distinct bands that have been likened to the banding that occurs in the black opal nobbies for which Lightning Ridge has become famous in New South Wales, Australia. Some of the Knobby Hill opal fluoresces dark blue and testing by the Gemological Institute of America has shown this opal to have a Mohs hardness rating of 6.5. The stone met with a good reception when introduced to an enthusiastic audience at the American Opal Society Show at Anaheim, California, in November 1994. At the time of this writing, The House of Tibara was acting as exclusive agent for the material and their comment was "We don't want to overstate the importance of this find, but it does appear to be signifi-cant, providing that the mining indications continue to be positive."

Another opal discovery in Nevada, well away from Virgin Valley, is one that may have a climax yet to be written. It began late in the 1940s. At that time a rather remarkable precious opal was found in the vicinity of Sulphur, 40 miles southwest of Winnemucca in Humboldt County. H. C. Dake (in *The Mineralo-gist,* April 1950, p. 172) says that when he was there he encountered an old gold prospector who was carrying around "a silicified claystone nodule filled with a three-inch core of magnificent colored opal." Dake reported that the specimen, which he bought from the prospector for the ridiculously small amount of $2, had been "neatly split in half and was about nine inches in diame-ter." The prospector, who admitted to being glad to get rid of it since it was becoming too heavy to carry around with him, said he had picked up the 9-inch diameter specimen, in his words, "just a mile east and north of Coyote Springs" where he alleged the ground surface was well covered with these cannon balls. Dr. Dake was so absorbed in admiring the specimen that he did not pay close attention to the directions the old man rattled off as to the source. Later, when he spent several days searching for the site in the rolling hills to the east and southeast, even though he did encounter many small spherical nodules, none had cores of solid opal and he was convinced he was not in the proper area. He never did find the cannonball-littered ground the old prospector had described, which Dake concluded must have been in a more northerly direction than he searched. But the mineralogist never got back there and the discovery still waits to be made by some lucky rockhound or miner.

In another Nevada area apart from Virgin Valley, several precious opal occurrences of the volcanic type have been discovered and mining operations established some 80 miles [128.7 km] south in the area of Gerlach in Nevada's Black Rock Desert, greater details of which may be found in the section devoted to Nevada. And, 80 miles [128.7 km] to the east of Virgin Valley, but still in Humboldt county, is the Firestone Mine, an open-pit operation in the Santa Rosa Mountains, where precious opals in rhyolite were mined for a while, but the process is so difficult that the mine was eventually abandoned. And yet another 80 miles [128.7 km] east, in northern Elko County, practically on the Idaho border, opalized wood exhibiting good POC has been reported on the Duck Creek Indian Reservation. A good bit of mining is also done in Nevada for opaline diatomite in bentonite and montmorillonite clays, in such locations as the Reno and Las Vegas areas, Lovelock, Fernley, and Mina. All these opal discoveries and mining operations suggest that Nevada undoubtedly still has significant deposits of opals waiting to be discovered.

Nevertheless, by far the most abundant, extensive and remarkable opal deposits in the state of Nevada—in fact, in all of the United States—and the largest number of opal mines, prospects and claims, are those in the area of Humboldt County's famed Virgin Valley in the northwest section of the state. For greater details about that area, see the section on Virgin Valley in Chapter 7.

Opal mining locations are numerous in Virgin Valley and to simplify locating them in the listing that follows, distances are measured using the old CCC Campground as a point of reference; that well-known campground situated 3 miles [4.8 km] south of State Route 140, on Virgin Valley Road, 1 mile [1.6 km] south of the Sheldon National Wildlife Range field headquarters.

The claims included among the many precious opal mining operations are **Angel Number One Mine:** Located in the Big Spring Butte 7.5″ Quadrangle, Sec. 25, T45N, R26E, 10 miles [16.1 km] southwestwardly from the Campground; highest quality precious opal, wax opal, common opal, conk, contra luz, hyalite, moss opal, and green fluorescent opal; this was one of the earlier developed mines, which was in operation prior to 1920 and was one of 16 original Archevaleta claims filed in the 1920s and 1930s by Rhinehart and Dan Archevaleta; other claims in the group included [see also under specific name listings], Angel Number Two, Blue Ball, Kelly, Little Pebble, Northern Lights, Peacock Number Four, Peacock Number Two, Phantom, Red Ball, Royal Peacock Number One, Royal Peacock Number Two, Skajem, Star Bright, Star Fire, and Yellow Ball; these claims were all relocated in 1937 by Flora Loughead and Mark Foster, from whom Harry Bill Wilson purchased the group in 1942; the elevation ranges from 5000 to 5200' [1525 to 1586 m.]; Lat. 41.79027, Long. 119.09277; first officially reported in March 1981, by D. D. La Pointe, Nevada

Bureau of Minerals and Geology (NBMG); **Angel Number Two Mine:** one of the 16 original Archevaleta claims filed in the 1920s and 1930; adjacent to the Angel Number One [q.v.]; **April Fool Number One Mine:** Big Spring Butte Quadrangle, Sec.24/25/26/34/35; T45N, R25E; local position of the 19 claims in this group is 200 yards [182.8 m] northwest and 300 yards [274.2 m] northeast of the Virgin Valley Ranch house; located in the Virgin Valley District, the 19 claims, all of which were located in 1950, include, in addition to this April Fool Number One, the April Fool Number Two, August, December, February, Fourth of July Number One, Fourth of July Number Two, Friday, January, March, Monday, November, October, Saturday, September, Thursday, Tuesday, Wednesday, Wee Marie; all these claims contain precious opal, uraniferous opal, common opal, and hyalite, associated with carnotite and schringerite; uranium content of the opal on these claims ranges from 0.002% to 0.14%; these 19 claims all together form the group called the Virgin Valley Ranch Deposit [but also called the Crane Claims, after the locators, Jack and Toni Crane, who are also the current owners]; the claims were filed and 20 small pits dug for opal before Crane discovered uranium minerals there in 1950; description of dig: a 315-foot [96.1 m] bulldozer trench and 12 small pits on the east side of the valley, and 3 small pits on the west side of the valley; Miocene Age; uraniferous opal-bearing host horizon matrix is in discontinuous layers parallel to the bedding of the basalt and ash and tuff beds in a dense greenish bentonite (montmorillonite) layer from 1.2″ [30.5 mm] to 4′ [1.22 m] thick and up to 1200 feet [366 m] in length along the strike; carnotite occurs as parting planes and fractures; the uranium occurs as an integral part of the opal here; elevation: 4950′ [1509.8 m]; Lat. 41.78833, Long. 119.10611; opals are scattered specimens, sometimes more abundant in productive "pockets"; deposit size listed as small; deposit first officially reported in February 1981, by D. D. La Pointe, NBMG; **April Fool Number Two:** Big Spring Butte Quadrangle, Sections 24/25/26/34/35.T45N, R25E; part of the 19-claim group owned and operated by Jack and Toni Crane, for details of which, see April Fool Number One; **August Mine:** Big Spring Butte Quadrangle, Sec. 24/25/26/34/35, T45N, R25E; part of the 19-claim group owned and operated by Jack and Toni Crane, for details of which, see April Fool Number One; **Beautiful Opal Mine:** part of the Opal Queen Group of seven mines owned by Ed and Louise Mitchell, for details of which, see Opal Queen; **Becky Mine:** Big Spring Butte Quadrangle, Sec. 17, T45N, R26E; local position is 4 miles [6.4 km] southwest of Dufurrena subheadquarters of Fish and Wildlife Service, in the Virgin Valley District: precious opal, wax opal, common opal, conk, contra luz, hyalite; part of John and Virgie Meyer Group of 5 mines, including Becky, the Black Hope, Moonwalk, Mucket, and White Hills; listed as little developed and inactive (1987); owners, John and Virgie Meyer, but leased to Opals, Inc. (William Kelley, et al.) in 1978; description of dig: consists of 13 bulldozer cuts and one open pit, minable over an area 200' [61m] wide and 6000' [1830m] long, at an elevation of 4400' to 5100' [1342 to 1555.5 m]; Tertiary Age; opal-bearing host horizon matrix is a dense greenish bentonite (montmorillonite) layer up to 10 feet [3.1 m] thick and containing opalized wood fragments and opal nodules; Lat. 41.81444, Long. 119.06027, but the actual workings extend farther east and west than the coordinates given; the Becky (along with the Mucket and White Hills) was first filed in 1954 and leased by the Meyers's to Opals, Inc., from 1969 to 1971; Bentonite deposit (var. Montmorillonite) is volcanic tuff and ash, in association with tuffaceous sandstone and siltstone: opals are scattered specimens, sometimes more abundant in productive "pockets"; deposit size listed as small; first officially reported in January 1981, by D. D. La Pointe, NBMG; **Bell Mine:** Big Spring Butte Quadrangle, Sec. 07/08, T45N, R26E; part of the Opal Queen Group of 7 mines owned by Ed and Louise Mitchell, for details of which, see Opal Queen; **Birdlebough's Mine;** claim patented in 1993; **Black Beauty Mine:** Big Spring Butte Quadrangle, Sec. 07/08, T45N, R26E; part of the Opal Queen Group of 7 mines owned by Ed and Louise Mitchell, for details of which, see Opal Queen; **Black Hope Mine:** Big Spring Butte Quadrangle, Sec. 17, T45N, R26E; local position is 4 miles [6.4 km] southwest of Dufurrena subheadquarters of Fish and Wildlife Service, in the Virgin Valley District; part of the John and Virgie Meyer Group of five mines, for details of which, see Becky; **Black Opal Number One Mine:** Big Spring Butte Quadrangle, Sec. 22/23, T45N, R26E; part of the Rainbow Ridge Opal Company Group of six claims, for details of which, see Rainbow Ridge Opal Mine; **Black Opal Number Two Mine:** Big Spring Butte Quadrangle, Sec. 22/23, T45N, R26E; part of the Rainbow Ridge Opal Company Group of six claims, for details of which, see Rainbow Ridge Opal Mine; **Black Opal Number Three Mine:** Big Spring Butte Quadrangle, Sec. 22/23, T45N, R26E; part of the Rainbow Ridge Opal Company Group of six claims, for details of which, see Rainbow Ridge Opal Mine; **Blue Ball Mine:** Big Spring Butte Quadrangle, Sec. 25, T45N, R26E; one of the 16 original Archevaleta claims filed in the 1920s and 1930; for details, see Angel Number One; **Bonanza Mine:** Big Spring Butte Quadrangle, Sec. 06/07, T45N, R26E; local position is 3.5 miles [5.6 km] south of Dufurrena subheadquarters of Sheldon Antelope Range on Virgin Valley Road, then 1.8 mile [2.9 km] north in the Virgin Valley District: precious opal, wax opal, common opal, conk, contra luz, hyalite; originally called the Virgin Opal and one of the earliest in the Virgin Valley; established in 1908 by Ivan Down, George D. Mathewson, and Alfred Thompson (and others); relocated under the name Virgin Opal 1943 by a Mr. Garaventa; purchased in 1955 by Keith Hodson; description of dig: several sizeable cuts, one adit and a storage building; listed as an open-cut mine employing two persons (1980); current status, quite developed and active (1987); the huge Bonanza Opal, in excess of 6 pounds, but broken in several pieces, discovered by Hodson and valued at over $100,000; mine sold by Hodson in 1987 to group; Tertiary Age; opal-bearing host horizon matrix is a dense greenish bentonite (montmorillonite) up to 6 feet [1.8 m] thick and containing opal pieces up to several inches in diameter, consisting of opalized wood fragments and opal nodules; however, slumping and rotation of blocks made the opal-bearing horizon difficult to trace; elevation: 5200′–5600′ [1586–1708 m]; Lat. 41.83888, Long. 119.0775; discovered and first claim filed in 1908; Bentonite deposit (var. Montmorillonite) is volcanic tuff and ash, in association with tuffaceous sandstone and siltstone: opals are scattered specimens, sometimes more abundant in productive "pockets"; deposit size listed as small; first officially reported in January 1981 by D. D. La Pointe, NBMG; **Charles Eddy Group:** Big Spring Butte Quadrangle, Sec. 05/08, T45N, R26E, for details of which, see Number One; **Claim Number Five Mine:** Big Spring Butte Quadrangle, Sec. 05/08, T45N, R26E, part of the Charles Eddy Group of 21 claims, for details of which, see Claim Number One; **Claim Number One Mine:** Big Spring Butte Quadrangle, Sec. 05/08, T45N, R26E; local position is 5 miles [8.1 km] south of State Route 140 on Virgin Valley Road, then ½-mile [0.8 km] north in the Virgin Valley District: precious opal, wax opal, common opal, conk, contra luz, hyalite; part of Charles Eddy Group of 21 claims and mines, one of which was located in 1948 and the remainder from 1969 to 1974; other claims in group include the Claim Number Five, Claim Number Two, Crazy Indian, Daisy Mae, East Gem Hill Mine, Evening Star, Hidden Valley, Li'l Abner, Lorrie Lee, Lulu, Marvelous, Mayday, Nancy's Nightmare, New Moon, Opal Valley, Richard Patrick, Sparkle Plenty, Sun Valley, West Gem Hill, Windfall; current status, listed as little developed and inactive (1987); owner, Charles Eddy and others (in 1978); description of dig: some 70 pits and bulldozer trenches up to 300' [91.5 m] in length; Tertiary Age; opal-bearing host horizon matrix is a dense greenish bentonite (montmorillonite) up to 6 feet [1.8 m] thick and containing opalized wood fragments and opal nodules; elevation: 5100' [1555.5 m]; Lat. 41.835, Long. 119.05944; discovered in 1940 and first claim filed in 1948, remainder between 1969 and 1974; Bentonite deposit (var. Montmorillonite) is volcanic tuff and ash, in association with tuffaceous sandstone and siltstone: opals are scattered specimens, sometimes more abundant in productive "pockets"; deposit size listed as small; first officially reported in January 1981 by D. D. La Pointe, NBMG; **Claim Number Two Mine:** Big Spring Butte Quadrangle, Sec. 05/08, T45N, R26E; local position is 5 miles [8.1 km] south of State Route 140 on Virgin Valley Road, then ½-mile [0.8 km] north in the Virgin Valley District: part of the Charles Eddy Group of 21 claims, for details of which, see Claim Number One; **Crane Claims:** for details see April Fool Number One; **Crazy Indian Mine:** Big Spring Butte Quadrangle, Sec. 05/08, T45N, R26E; local position is 5 miles [8.1 km] south of State Route 140 on Virgin Valley Road, then ½-mile [0.8 km] north in the Virgin Valley District;

part of the Charles Eddy Group of 21 claims, for details of which, see Claim Number One; **Daisy Mae Mine:** Big Spring Butte Quadrangle, Sec. 05/08, T45N, R26E; part of the Charles Eddy Group of 21 claims, for details of which, see Claim Number One; **Dead Man's Mine:** named after owner Miller, killed [possible suicide] in cave-in; **December Mine:** Big Spring Butte Quadrangle, Sec. 24/25/26/34/35, T45N, R25E; part of the 19-claim group owned and operated by Jack and Toni Crane, for details of which, see April Fool Number One; **East Gem Hill Mine:** Big Spring Butte Quadrangle, Sec. 05/08, T45N, R26E; part of the Charles Eddy Group of 21 claims, for details of which, see Claim Number One; **Evening Star Mine:** Big Spring Butte Quadrangle, Sec. 05/08, T45N, R26E; part of the Charles Eddy Group of 21 claims, for details of which, see Claim Number One; **February Mine:** Big Spring Butte Quadrangle, Sec. 24/25/26/34/35, T45N, R25E; part of the 19-claim group owned and operated by Jack and Toni Crane, for details of which, see April Fool Number One; **Fourth of July Number One Mine:** Big Spring Butte Quadrangle, Sec. 24/25/26/34/35, T45N, R25E; part of the 19-claim group owned and operated by Jack and Toni Crane, for details of which, see April Fool Number One; **Fourth of July Number Two Mine:** Big Spring Butte Quadrangle, Sec. 24/25/26/34/35, T45N, R25E; part of the 19-claim group owned and operated by Jack and Toni Crane, for details of which, see April Fool Number One; **Friday Mine:** Big Spring Butte Quadrangle, Sec. 24/25/26/34/35, T45N, R25E; part of the 19-claim group owned and operated by Jack and Toni Crane, for details of which, see April Fool Number One; **Hidden Valley Mine:** Big Spring Butte Quadrangle, Sec. 05/08, T45N, R26E; part of the Charles Eddy Group of 21 claims, for details of which see Claim Number One; **January Mine:** Big Spring Butte Quadrangle, Sec. 24/25/26/34/35, T45N, R25E; part of the 19-claim group owned and operated by Jack and Toni Crane, for details of which, see April Fool Number One; **Kelley Mine:** Big Spring Butte Quadrangle, Sec. 30, T45N, R26E; local position not stated; precious opal, bog opal, wax opal, common opal, conk, contra luz, hyalite; located in the Virgin Valley District; current status, listed (1985) as an active developed producer employing one person; owner, C. George Hewitt (in 1985); description of dig: listed as an active, open-pit surface mine in 1980; Tertiary Age; opal-bearing horizon matrix is a dense greenish bentonite (montmorillonite) containing pods of ash, rhyolite pebbles, opalized wood fragments, and opal nodules; elevation: not stated; Lat. 41.78138, Long. 119.08166; no data given on discovery or when claim first filed; the Bentonite deposit (var. Montmorillonite) is volcanic tuff and ash, in association with tuffaceous sandstone: opals are scattered specimens, sometimes more abundant in productive "pockets"; deposit size listed as small; first officially reported in March 1981, by D. D. La Pointe, NBMG; **Kelly Mine:** Big Spring Butte Quadrangle, Sec. 25, T45N, R26E; one of the 16 original Archevaleta claims filed in the 1920s and 1930; for details, see Angel

Number One; **Le-Bob Mine:** Big Spring Butte Quadrangle, Sec. 07/08, T45N, R26E; part of the Opal Queen Group of seven mines owned by Ed and Louise Mitchell, for details of which, see Opal Queen; **Li'l Abner Mine:** Big Spring Butte Quadrangle, Sec. 05/08, T45N, R26E; part of the Charles Eddy Group of 21 claims, for details of which, see Claim Number One; **Little Pebble Mine:** Big Spring Butte Quadrangle, Sec. ?, T45N, R25E; part of the 16 original Archevaleta claims filed in the 1920s and 1930; for details, see the Angel Number One; **Lorrie Lee Mine:** Big Spring Butte Quadrangle, Sec. 05/08, T45N, R26E; part of the Charles Eddy Group of 21 claims, for details of which, see Claim Number One; **Lucky Lou Mine:** Big Spring Butte Quadrangle, Sec. 07/08, T45N, R26e; part of the Opal Queen Group of seven mines owned by Ed and Louise Mitchell, for details of which, see Opal Queen; **Lulu Mine:** Big Spring Butte Quadrangle, Sec. 05/08, T45N, R26E; part of the Charles Eddy Group of 21 claims, for details of which, see Claim Number One; **March Mine:** Big Spring Butte Quadrangle, Sec. 24/25/26/34/35, T45N, R25E; part of the 19-claim group owned and operated by Jack and Toni Crane, for detailes of which, see April Fool Number One; **Marvelous Mine:** Big Spring Butte Quadrangle, Sec. 05/08, T45N, R26E; Part of the Charles Eddy Group of 21 claims, for details of which, see Claim Number One; **Mayday Mine:** Big Spring Butte Quadrangle, Sec. 05/08, T45N, R26E; part of the Charles Eddy Group of 21 claims, for details of which, see Claim Number One; **Miserable Mitch Mine:** part of the Opal Queen Group of seven mines owned by Ed and Louise Mitchell, for details of which, see Opal Queen; **Monday Mine:** Big Spring Butte Quadrangle, Sec. 24/25/26/34/35, T45N, R25E; part of the 19-claim group owned and operated by Jack and Toni Crane, for details of which, see April Fool Number One; **Moonwalk Mine:** Big Spring Butte Quadrangle, Sec. 17, T45N, R26E; part of the John and Virgie Meyer Group of five mines, for details of which, see Becky; **Mucket Mine:** Big Spring Butte Quadrangle, Sec. 17, T45N, R26E; part of the John and Virgie Meyer Group of five mines, for details of which, see Becky; **Nancy's Nightmare Mine:** Big Spring Butte Quadrangle, Sec. 05/08, T45N, R26E; part of the Charles Eddy Group of 21 claims, for details of which, see Claim Number One; **New Moon Mine:** Big Spring Butte Quadrangle, Sec. 05/08, T45N, R26E; part of the Charles Eddy Group of 21 claims, for details of which, see Claim Number One; **Northern Lights Mine:** Big Spring Butte Quadrangle, Sec. 25, T45N, R26E; part of the 16 original Archevaleta claims filed in the 1920s and 1930; for details, see the Angel Number One; **November Mine:** Big Spring Butte Quadrangle, Sec. 24/25/26/34/35, T45N, R25E; part of the 19-claim group owned and operated by Jack and Toni Crane, for details of which, see April Fool Number One; **October Mine:** Big Spring Butte Quadrangle, Sec. 24/25/26/34/35, T45N, R25E; part of the 19-claim group owned and operated by Jack and Toni Crane, for details of which, see April Fool Number One; **Opal Claim Number Two Mine:** Big Spring

Butte Quadrangle, Sec. 05/08, T45N, R26E; part of the Charles Eddy Group of 21 claims, for details of which, see Claim Number One; **Opal Queen Mine:** Big Spring Butte Quadrangle, Sec. 07/08, T45N, R26E; local position is 3.5 miles [5.6 km] south of Dufurrena subheadquarters of Sheldon Antelope Range on Virgin Valley Road, then 1/2-mile[0.8 km] north in the Virgin Valley District: precious opal, wax opal, common opal, conk, contra luz, hyalite; part of Opal Queen Group of 7 mines owned by Ed and Louise Mitchell; this Opal Queen was located in 1908 and is probably the earliest claim in Virgin Valley; the remaining six—Beautiful Opal, Bell, Black Beauty, Le-Bob, Lucky Lou, and Miserable Mitch claims—were all located by the Mitchells in 1969 and 1970; current status, quite developed and active (1987); description of dig: some 50 pits and bulldozer trenches, some of which have obscured earlier workings; Tertiary Age; opal-bearing host horizon matrix is a dense greenish bentonite (montmorillonite) up to 6 feet [1.8 m] thick and containing opal pieces up to several inches in diameter, consisting of opalized wood fragments and opal nodules; however, slumping and rotation of blocks made the opal-bearing horizon difficult to trace; elevation; 5100′ [1555.5 m]; Lat. 41.83, Long. 119.07055; discovered and first claim filed in 1908; Bentonite deposit (var. Montmorillonite) is volcanic tuff and ash, in association with tuffaceous sandstone and siltstone; opals are scattered specimens, sometimes more abundant in productive "pockets"; deposit size listed as small; first officially reported in January 1981, by D. D. La Pointe, NBMG; **Opal Valley Mine:** Big Spring Butte Quadrangle, Sec. 05/08, T45N, R26E; part of the Charles Eddy Group of 21 claims, for details of which, see Claim Number One; **Pandora Mine:** Big Spring Butte Quadrangle, Sec. 22/23, T45N, R26E; part of the Rainbow Ridge Opal Company Group of six claims, for details of which, see Rainbow Ridge Opal Mine; **Peacock Number Two Mine:** Big Spring Butte Quadrangle, Sec. 25, T45N, R26E; one of the 16 original Archevaleta claims filed in the 1920s and 1930; for details, see the Angel Number One; **Peacock Number Four Mine:** Big Spring Butte Quadrangle, Sec. 25, T45N, R26E; one of the 16 original Archevaleta claims filed in the 1920s and 1930; for details, see the Angel Number One; **Phantom Mine:** Big Spring Butte Quadrangle, Sec. 25, T45N, R26E; one of the 16 original Archevaleta claims filed in the 1920s and 1930; for details, see the Angel Number One; **Rainbow Ridge Opal Mine:** Big Spring Butte Quadrangle, Sec. 22/23, T45N, R26E; from old CCC Campground, follow signs south another 5 miles [8.1 km] to mine in the Virgin Valley District: highest-quality precious opal, wax opal, common opal, conk, contra luz, hyalite; one of the first developed mines, discovered in 1908 by D. Roop, Ed McGee and G. T. Hill, who found opal chips on east side of small hill; a tunnel was dug 300′ [91.5 m] long and was productive of good opals; in 1917 the Roebling Opal, a fine black opal weighing 2665 carats (553 grams) and valued then at between $50,000 and $250,000 was found here; subsequently donated to

Smithsonian Institution, where it is now; in 1929 six claims were patented by the Rainbow Ridge Opal Company—Black Opal Number 1, Black Opal Number 2, Black Opal Number 3, Pandora, Royal Opal (present Rainbow Ridge Opal Mine), and Rincon Belle; mining activity faded away and not much done from 1920 until 1949 when the claims were purchased by Keith Hodson, who renamed the Royal Opal to Rainbow Ridge Opal Mine and who started several crosscuts and a drift; over 20 acres of minable deposit; in 1952 he discovered the superb black opal called the Hodson Opal, weighing 14,288 carats, then valued at $50,000; for some time after this, little work done by Hodson at the Rainbow Ridge Mine in favor of work at the Bonanza, which was part of the Virgin Opal; later, the Bonanza Mine was sold and Rainbow Ridge opened to rockhounds on a daily fee basis, which still exists; many hundreds of fine gems found here; some 1000 feet [305 m] of underground tunneling, two large cuts and eight smaller pits; Tertiary Age; opal-bearing host horizon matrix is a dense greenish bentonite (montmorillonite) up to 4 feet [1.2 km] thick, with pods of ash and rhyolite pebbles; this is volcanic tuff and ash, in association with tuffaceous sandstone and siltstone, containing opalized wood fragments and opal nodules; opals are scattered specimens, sometimes more abundant in productive "pockets"; the amount of petrified wood increases downward with the opal-bearing horizon; precious opal occurs as conk and in void fillings left where wood has rotted away; "conk" forms when opal fills voids between growth rings in partially petrified wood; the opalescence of the black opals is equal to the best in the word, but high water content increases the possibility of crazing and cracking, though this element has been negatively promoted well beyond justification; elevation: 5050″ to 5100′ [1540.3 to 1555.5 m]; Lat. 41.79527, Long. 119.01416; first officially reported in January 1981, by D. D. La Pointe, NBMG; **Red Ball Mine:** Big Spring Butte Quadrangle, Sec. 25, T45N, R26E; one of the 16 original Archevaleta claims filed in the 1920s and 1930; for details see, the Angel Number One; **Richard Patrick Mine:** Big Spring Butte Quadrangle, Sec. 05/08, T45N, R26E; part of the Charles Eddy Group of 21 claims, for details of which, see Claim Number One; **Rincon Belle Mine:** Big Spring Butte Quadrangle, Sec. 22/23, T45N, R26E; part of the Rainbow Ridge Opal Company Group of six claims, for details of which, see Rainbow Ridge Opal Mine; **Royal Peacock Mine:** [also called **Royal Peacock Number One Mine**]; Big Spring Butte Quadrangle, Sec. 25, T45N, R26E; one of the 16 original Archevaleta claims filed in the 1920s and 1930; for details, see the Angel Number One; **Royal Peacock Number Two Mine:** Big Spring Butte Quadrangle, Sec. 25, T45N, R26E; one of the 16 original Archevaleta claims filed in the 1920s and 1930; for details, see the Angel Number One; **Royal Opal Mine:** part of the Rainbow Ridge Opal Company Group of six claims, for details of which, see Rainbow Ridge Opal Mine; **Saturday Mine:** Big Spring Butte Quadrangle, Sec. 24/25/26/34/35, T45N, R25E; part of the 19-claim group owned and operated by Jack and Toni Crane, for details of which, see April Fool Number One; **September Mine:** Big Spring Butte Quadrangle, Sec. 24/25/26/34/35, T45N, R25E; part of the 19-claim group owned and operated by Jack and Toni Crane, for details of which, see April Fool Number One; **Skajum Mine:** Big Spring Butte Quadrangle, Sec. 25, T45N, R26E; one of the 16 original Archevaleta claims filed in the 1920s and 1930; for details, see the Angel Number One; **Sparkle Plenty Mine:** Big Spring Butte Quadrangle, Sec. 05/08, T45N, R26E; part of the Charles Eddy Group of 21 claims, for details of which, see Claim Number One; **Star Bright Mine:** Big Spring Butte Quadrangle, Sec. 25, T45N, R26E; one of the 16 original Archevaleta claims filed in the 1920s and 1930; for details, see the Angel Number One; **Star Fire Mine:** Big Spring Butte Quadrangle, Sec. 25, T45N, R26E; one of the 16 original Archevaleta claims filed in the 1920s and 1930; for details, see the Angel Number One; **Stone Tree:** add details; **Sun Valley:** Big Spring Butte Quadrangle, Sec. 05/08, T45N, R26E; part of the Charles Eddy Group of 21 claims, for details of which, see Claim Number One; **Thursday Mine;** Big Spring Butte Quadrangle, Sec. 24/25/26/34/35, T45N, R25E; part of the 19-claim group owned and operated by Jack and Toni Crane, for details of which, see April Fool Number One; **Tuesday Mine;** Big Spring Butte Quadrangle, Sec. 24/25/26/34/35, T45N, R25E; part of the 19-claim group owned and operated by Jack and Toni Crane, for details of which, see April Fool Number One; **Vaillant Mine:** Big Spring Butte Quadrangle, Sec. 22/23, T45N, R26E; from old CCC Campground, follow signs south another 5 miles [8.1 km] to mine in the Virgin Valley District, adjacent southward of Rainbow Ridge Mine; **Virgin Mine:** Big Spring Butte Quadrangle, Sec. 24/25/26/34/35, T45N, R25E; **Virgin Opal Mine:** former name of Bonanza Mine, which see for details; **Virgin Valley Ranch Deposit:** see April Fool Number One; **Wednesday Mine:** Big Spring Butte Quadrangle, Sec. 24/25/26/34/35, T45N, R25E; part of the 19-claim group owned and operated by Jack and Toni Crane, for details of which, see April Fool Number One; **Wee Marie Mine:** Big Spring Butte Quadrangle, Sec. 24/25/26/34/35, T45N, R25E; part of the 19-claim group owned and operated by Jack and Toni Crane, for details of which, see April Fool Number One; **West Gem Hill Mine:** Big Spring Butte Quadrangle, Sec. 05/08, T45N, R26E; part of the Charles Eddy Group of 21 claims, for details of which, see Claim Number One; **White Hills Mine:** Big Spring Butte Quadrangle, Sec. 17, T45N, R26E; part of the John and Virgie Meyer Group of five mines, for details of which, see Becky; **Windfall Mine:** Big Spring Butte Quadrangle, Sec. 05/08, T45N, R26E; part of the Charles Eddy Group of 21 claims, for details of which, see Claim Number One; **Yellow Ball Mine:** Big Spring Butte Quadrangle, Sec. 25, T45N, R26E; one of the 16 original Archevaleta claims filed in the 1920s and 1930; for details, see the Angel Number One.

NEW BRUNSWICK (Canada)

W. W. Gardiner, mineral deposits geologist of the Department of Natural Resources and Energy in Fredericton and D. V. Venugopal, nonmetallic minerals geologist of the Mineral and Resources Branch of the Department of Natural Resources and Energy in Fredericton, have both stated late in 1991 that there has been no known opal occurrence in New Brunswick. Nevertheless, opal pseudomorphs (later determined to be pseudomorphs after ikaite) found near New Brunswick's Bay of Fundy and named "fundyite," were described in 1974 as sharp, thin, well-formed crystals upward of a foot in length, similar in composition to the so-called "pineapple" pseudomorphs found at White Cliffs in New South Wales and to the so-called "Hedgehogs" found elsewhere in Canada. For more details on such opal pseudomorphs, see the section devoted to that topic elsewhere in this volume.

NEW HAMPSHIRE (United States)

The office of the State Geologist in Concord states that no opals of any variety are known to occur in New Hampshire, but several unofficial local accounts claim the presence of blue hyalite in an unspecified location in the White Mountain National Forest between the Upper Ammonoosuc River and the town of Berlin in Coos County.

NEW JERSEY (United States)

Richard Volkert, supervising geologist of the New Jersey Geological Survey at Trenton, states that precious opal, common opal, and hyalite do occur in the state. This is seam opal that often occurs as thin crusts coating fractures in ores and trap rocks. The opal, which has a reddish base coloration, is not mined commercially, although some is collected as specimen material. The locations for such occurrences are **Essex County:** Summit area, in New Jersey trap rocks, basalt, and diabase; **Hudson County:** Bergen Hill area, hyalite and precious opal in basalt and diabase; **Passaic County:** Paterson Quarry, in basalt and diabase; **Somerset County:** Great Notch area, in basalt and diabase; **Sussex County:** Franklin area, at Sterling Hill and in the Chimney Rock area, in zinc ore in marble; **Union County:** Upper Montclair area, in basalt and diabase.

NEW MEXICO (United States)

Mark L. Wilson, mineralogist with the New Mexico Bureau of Mines and Mineral Resources at Socorro, states that opal occurrence in the state is relatively widespread and includes precious opal, common opal, moss opal, fluorescent opal, and wood opal. The precious opal, which has a base coloration of white to gray ranges from transparent through translucent to nearly opaque. It occurs as wood opal as well as in seams and vugs in rhyolite, silicified limestone, with cassiterite in rhyolite, as crusted coatings on garnet and quartz, with quartz latite and as a cementing structure in sandstone. It is not of either quantity or quality to justify commercial mining, although some private collecting and mining occurs. Included in the areas of occurrence are **Bernalillo County:** just east of Isleta Pueblo, as a delicately fluorescent milk-white wood opal; **Catron County:** in the Catron Creek District, where it is associated with cassiterite; **Curry County:** in widespread occurrences of diatomaceous earth (diatomite), with 88 species of diatoms identified; **Eddy County:** in the Carlsbad Potash District but only as minute grains identified microscopically in samples of well cuttings; **Grant County:** in both the Santa Rita District and the Central District, where relatively good specimens of precious opals occur; in the same county occur opaline veins in tuffaceous rhyolite in the Black Range and fiorite at Faywood Hot Springs; hyalite occurs in the Burro Mountains District and Central District; white opal outlined by a zone of black chalcedony occurs as "button opal" in the volcanic rocks about a quarter-mile [.4 km] from Fort Bayard Station; fluorescent hyalite occurs at the Merry Widow Mine in the White Signal District; **Hidalgo County:** in the San Simon District, cavities in garnet contain quartz crystals coated with opal and the same material is found in the Hatchet Mountains in the vicinity of Playas Dry Lake; an attractive moss opal occurs in the Peloncillo Mountains, while both uranoan hyalite and common opal occur in the Antelope Wells Prospect; **Lea County:** fluorescent opal is often found at Lovington; **Luna County:** common opal, along with some traces of precious opal, occurs as fillings in cavities in quartz latite near Deming, where some of the opal reportedly occurs at Rockhound State Park; **Rio Arriba County:** in the Petaca District there is occurrence of common opal, again with traces of precious opal and also there is a diatomaceous earth pit along a Jeep trail up Arroyo de la Presa from near Hernandez in the NE quarter of Section 22, T21N, R7E; **Roosevelt County:** another occurrence of diatomaceous earth (diatomite) is widespread in Blackwater Draw and from Sec. 25, T1N, R35E, and Sec. 10, T1S, R35S; **San Juan County:** both common and precious opal occur in the Chuska Mountains in association with banded opal and chalcedony, and is also widespread as a cementing agent in sandstone; **Sandoval County:** precious opal is discovered occasionally among the wood opals that occur in the Cochiti District; the same occurring in a matrix of hydrated quartz over an area 8 miles [12.9 km] long and 2 miles [3.2 km] wide, extending from the north bank of Colla Canyon across a mesa to Peralta Canyon and south from Colla to Bear Canyon; opalized diatoms occur in lake deposits of the Valle Grande; small stalactites of hyalite are known to occur in fissures of the lava near Battleship Rock in the Jemez Sulphur District, along with large wood opal fragments in white, gray, green, and other colors; with similar wood opal fragments occurring as well in the Rio Puerco Valley; **Santa Fe County:** a yellowish-brown opal, occasionally with POC, occurs in the Cerillos District, while common opal occurs in the La Bajada District, and wood opal occurs in the Galisteo Beds; **Sierra County:** common opal (are rarely precious opal) occurs in the Iron Mountain No. 2 District, while a similar deposit occurs as films of bluish white on minerals in vugs; the same material occurs also in the Black Range near Kingston and is abundant in the Jornada del Muerto; in the Hillsboro District and vicinity, most of the lava hills have stones adorned with rosettes and shell-like excrescences of white opaque opal that fluoresces; a similarly fluorescent hyalite occurs in the San Mateo Mountains District at the Uranium Prospect near Monticello; a good-quality gem-grade precious wood opal occurs at the north end of the Fra Cristobal Range and also in the Jornada Valley, along with a moss opal comprised of dendritic pyrolusite in white opal and, in the same area, ribbon opal and opal-filled nodules; good gem-quality wood opal occurs near Hot Springs and is also abundant in lesser quality in the sands and gravels along the east shore of Elephant Butte Reservoir in sand and gravel, this material occurring as opalized stems, limbs, roots, and trunks up to 50 pounds or more and the opal material ranging in color from milky-white and transparent to gray, black, brown, yellow, and mottled; in all these occurrences of both common and precious wood opal, the twigs and branches can be as small as 1/16 inch [2 mm] in thickness to over 1.5 inches [38.1 mm] in diameter, with cell structure well preserved and the base coloration ranging from milk white, cream-white, yellowish, and smoky gray to brownish gray, rusty brown, and black; occasionally the wood opal branches found are hollow; **Socorro County:** common opal occurs in the Iron Mountain No. 2 District as a bluish white film coating other minerals in vugs; the volcanic tuff of the Popotosa Formation is opalized in the Ladron District and brownish in color; veinlets of opal occur in the rhyolite of the Luis Lopez Manganese District immediately north of Black Canyon, and microscopic opal material is found in several rock species of the Magdalena District; fiorite is not uncommon at Socorro Hot Springs; another abundant deposit of good quality wood opal with well-preserved cell structure, occurs just south of the east end of the Bernardo Bridge spanning the Rio Grande (U.S. Highway 60), with colors that ranging from black through brown to gray and often quite large in individual pieces as evidenced in one opalized log section found that was over a foot in diameter and three feet in length—unofficially identified as a genus of ash *(Fraxinus)* and probably Pliocene, though possibly Miocene.

NEW SOUTH WALES (Australia)

F. L. Sutherland, Head of the Mineral Section of The Australian Museum in Sydney, and John Watkins, senior geologist of the Geological Survey of New South Wales in Saint Leonards, heartily affirm that there is an abundance of opal of various types in the state of New South Wales. Precious opal was first discovered in New South Wales in 1875 at Rocky Bridge Creek, 30 km [18.6 mi] south of Blayney, by miners who were following a vein in search of gold. The opal mines there today are located on the west side of the creek above the junction with Abercrombie River. Opal occurs elsewhere in New South Wales as precious opal, common opal, fluorescent opal, moss opal, wax opal, and opal pseudomorphs, the latter as precious opal after ikaite in the formations commonly called pineapples. As to the deposition of precious opal, it is found as seam opal, wood opal, nobby opal, gas opal (also called vug opal or pocket opal), and ledge opal. These precious opal deposits are variously found in rhyolite, basalt, andesite, sedimentary sandstone, mudstone, ironstone, weathered claystone in montmorillonite and bentonite clays, and quartzite. The precious opal is mined commercially and recreationally, both in tunnel mining and open-pit mining. The precious opal may occur as transparent, translucent, or opaque with base colors of black, blue, white (milky), gray, brown, and clear. The POC evidenced includes harlequin, pinfire, broadflash, longstreak, and smudge in red, blue, green, violet, orange, blue-green, deep purple, pink, and yellow. Blue and green predominate in pin points of fire. Red on black is the most valuable combination.

Copeton, Gunnedah, Lightning Ridge, Tintinbar, and White Cliffs are some of the principal opal sites, but it is Lightning Ridge and White Cliffs where the more notable finds have been made throughout the years. The precious opal is primarily seam opal in sandstone; however, locations bearing volcanic opal (also called mountain opal) are so noted. The Grawin opal field, some 35 km [21.7 mi] southwest of the town of Lightning Ridge, produces some very fine gray opals (Figure 56).

Black common opal is reported to occur on the north coast at Point Danger, where fragments of fossil plants are found with the opal. Precious opal was discovered in the Warrambungle Mountains near Tooraweenah in 1899, 8 km [5 mi] off the main road from Gilgandra to Coonabarabran. Both common and precious opal are found at several localities scattered throughout this area. The precious opal occurs as a cavity filling in flat-lying vesicular trachyte flow, which is the basal member of the volcanic sequence in the Warrumbungle Mountains. The cavities in the trachyte are elongate and ellipsoidal in shape, and usually empty or lined with a thin siliceous coating. In some instances the cavities are filled with precious opal showing good play of color. The stones are usually small and difficult to extract from the surrounding hard rock. In the Nandewar

Figure 56. Grawin Opal Field southwest of Lightning Ridge. The vertical mine shafts and tunnels below are protected from stones being dislodged and falling into them by log structures placed around the surface hole. Many miners who cannot afford more modern equipment still use a hand-turned windlass anchored to the logs to bring out the buckets of debris and opal dirt, which is dumped near the hole, then checked carefully for opals before the debris is finally carried away to a dump site. (Photo by Alan A. Vogel)

Mountains area, between Narrabri and Barraba, common opal, sometimes with specks of precious opal, is reported to occur but no specific locations are given. In 1889, the White Cliffs opal field was established and dominated in world opal production for over a decade. In 1900 black opal was discovered at Lightning Ridge and, while at first given short shrift, soon became the most valuable and sought after. In 1904 precious opal, occurring as vesicled filling in basalt, was discovered at Hyandra Creek, 21 km [13 mi] south of Dubbo. In the Nightcap Range area, near Mullumbimby, precious opal and common opal, together with chalcedony and onyx, have been found forming the cores of spherulitic nodules (thundereggs), the centers of which are often filled with transparent, colorless or amber opal; sometimes the opal is opaque milky white or grey with a striking play of color, green being predominant, but red, violet, and yellow are also seen. Greater details of the New South Wales opal occurrences at Lightning Ridge and White Cliffs will be found in Chapter 7.

Numerous opal occurrences, claims, prospects, and workings dot New South Wales, among which are the following:

Bathurst Region

[*Distances from Bathurst unless otherwise noted*]

Bathurst: 160.9 km [100 miles] west-northwest of Sydney; **Bland:** volcanic opal, 193.08 km [120 miles] west-southwest; **Bloomfield:** volcanic opal, 48.27 km [30 miles] west; **Carcoar:** volcanic opal, 48.27 km [30 miles] southwest; **Cowra:** volcanic opal 96.54 km [60 miles] southwest; **Forbes vicinity:** volcanic opal, 144.81 km [90 miles] west; **O'Connell Claim:** volcanic opal, 24.14 km [15 miles] southeast; **Rocky Bridge Creek** (site of first opal discovery in New South Wales, in 1872 near Trunky and 30 km [18.6 miles] south of Blayney): volcanic opal, 56.32 km [35 miles] southwest.

Canberra Region

[*Distances from Canberra unless otherwise noted*]

Bergalia: volcanic opal, 112.63 km [70 miles] southeast; **Braidwood:** volcanic opal, 64.36 km [40 miles] east-southeast; **Gundagai vicinity:** volcanic opal, 96.54 km [60 miles] west-northwest.

Inverell Region

[*Distances from Inverell unless otherwise noted*]

Bingara: volcanic opal, 56.32 km [35 miles] west; **Inverell vicinity:** volcanic opal, 458.57 km [285 miles] northeast of Sydney; **Oban Creek:** volcanic opal, 104.59 km [65 miles] southeast; **Uralla:** volcanic opal, 104.59 km [65 miles] south-southeast; **Vegetable Creek near Deepwater:** volcanic opal, 112.63 km [70 miles] northeast.

Lightning Ridge Region

[*Distances from Lightning Ridge Post Office unless otherwise noted*]

Airport Rush: 2.3 km [1.4 miles] south; **Angledool:** 40.23 km [25 miles] north; **Angledool Mine:** 1.2 km [0.7 miles] northeast; **Bald Hill:** 2 km [3.1 miles] north and slightly east; **Beckett's:** 4 km [2.5 miles] west, just north of Nebea Hill; **Berlin Rush:** 14.48 km [9 miles] northwest; **Bill the Boer Mine:** 2.25 km [1.4 miles] north; **Billy Goat Hill:** 60.25 km [36.15 miles] north; **Bullockies:** 2.6 km [1.6 miles] southeast; **Butterfly:** 1.75 km [1.1 miles] east; **Canada's:** 4.5 km [2.8 miles] south-southwest; **Canfel's Hill:** 1 km [0.6 mile] northeast; **Collarenebri:** 56.32 km [35 miles] east-southeast; **Con's Rush:** 5.75 km [3.6 miles] west; **Darby's:** 2.25 km [1.4 miles] south; **Deep Belars:** 4 km [2.5 miles] southwest; **Deep Four Mile:** 5.25 km [3.3 miles] south-southwest;

Dentist Hill: 10.75 km [6.7 miles] west; **Dry Rush:** 2 km [1.2 miles] southeast; **Eleven Mile:** 9 km [5.6 miles] west and just slightly north; **Eulan:** 2.5 km [1.6 miles] west; **Foley's Six Mile:** 6 km [3.7 miles] west; **Frog Hollow:** 4.15 km [2.6 miles] south; **Frying Pan:** 4.8 km [3 miles] south; **Glengarry:** 54.5 km [32.7 miles] west-southwest **Grawin:** 48.27 km [30 miles] west-southwest; **Gully:** 3.4 km [2.1 miles] south; **Hawk's Nest:** 4.6 km [2.9 miles] southwest; **Hearts and Spices:** 4.2 km [2.6 miles] southwest; **Holden's:** 4.5 km [2.8 miles] southwest; **Hornet's Rush:** 2 km [1.2 miles] north; **Indian's Lookout:** 2 km [1.2 miles] east; **Kingfisher:** 1.2 km [0.7 mile] east-southeast; **Lightning Ridge:** 72.41 km [45 miles] north-northeast of Walgett; **Llandillo:** 48.27 km [30 miles] southwest; **McDonald's Six Mile:** 5.5 km [3.4 miles] west, just north of Cons Rush; **McNamara's:** 4 km [2.5 miles] southwest; **Nebea Hill:** 4 km [2.5 miles] west; **New Chum:** 1.5 km [0.9 mile] north; **New Nobby:** 2.4 km [1.5 miles] southeast; **New Year's Rush:** 0.5 km [0.3 mile] southwest; **Newtown:** 1.15 km [3.1 miles] south-southeast; **Nine Mile:** 15 km [9 miles] west; **Old Chum:** 1.3 km [0.8 mile] north; **Old Nobby:** 2.2 km [1.4 miles] southeast; **Old Town:** 1.5 km [0.9 mile] east; **Phil Herbert's Rush:** 3.5 km [2.2 miles] southwest; **Pony Fence:** 1.5 km [0.9 mile] east-southeast; **Potch Point:** 2.25 km [1.4 miles] north; **Poverty Point:** 2.25 km [1.4 miles] southeast; **Pumpkin Flat:** 1.5 km [0.9 miles] northeast; **Rosso's:** 4 km [2.5 miles] west, just south of Nebea Hill; **Seven Mile:** 11.66 [7 miles] west; **Shallow Belars:** 5 km [3.1 miles] south-southwest; **Shearer's Rush:** 5.75 [3.6 miles] west, just north of Cons Rush; **Sim's Hill:** 1 km [0.6 miles] east; **Snowy Brown's:** 5.75 km [3.6 miles] south-southwest; **Ten Mile:** 8.5 km [5.3 miles] west; **Thorley's Six Mile:** 5 km [3.105 miles] west;**Three Mile:** 3.8 km [2.4 miles] south; **Vertical Bill's:** 3 km [1.9 miles] south; **Walsh's:** 1.5 km [0.9 mile] southeast.

Nundle Region

[Distances from Nundle unless otherwise noted]

Bowling Alley Creek: volcanic opal, 12.87 km [8 miles] north; **Hanging Rock:** volcanic opal, 8.05 km [5 miles] southeast; **Hookanvil:** volcanic opal, 8.05 km [5 miles] southeast; **Nundle:** 185.04 km [115 miles] south of Inverell.

Tweed Heads Region

[Distances from Tweed Heads unless otherwise noted]

Lismore Vicinity: volcanic opal, 72.41 km [45 miles] south-southeast; **Teven:** volcanic opal, 77.23 km [48 miles] south; **Tintinbar:** volcanic opal, 72.41 km [45 miles] south; **Tweed Heads (Tweed River Mouth)** Tweed Heads: 547.06 km [340 miles] northeast of Sydney.

Wellington Area

[*Distances from Wellington unless otherwise noted*]

Cobar Vicinity: volcanic opal, 289.62 km [180 miles] northwest; **Cudgegong:** volcanic opal, 56.32 km [35 miles] east-southeast; **Gulgong:** volcanic opal, 56.32 km [35 miles] east-northeast; **Tooraweenah (Warrambungle Mountains):** volcanic opal, 120.68 km [75 miles] north; **Wellington:** 257.44 km [160 miles] northwest of Sydney.

White Cliffs Region

[*Distances from White Cliffs Post Office unless otherwise noted*]

Barclay's Bunker: 13 km [8.07 miles] southwest; cretaceous sediments are exposed in a scarp caused by erosion along Bunker Creek; shafts have been sunk along the scarp both in Cretaceous sediments and through Tertiary silcrete; **Berlin Rush:** 9 km [5.59 miles] west; just north of Bishops Rush; **Bishop's Rush:** 9 km [5.59 miles] west; **Blocks:** just north and then east of the Wanaaring Road in an area 2.5 km [1.56 mile] long and from 0.3 km to 1.2 km [0.19 mile to 0.75 mile] wide; opal-bearing claystone crops out at the surface over much of this area, which has been worked to depths of 24 m [78.7 feet] this was the center of mining during the most productive years of the field; **Bourke Vicinity:** 289.62 km [180 miles] northeast; **Brewarrina:** 378.12 km [235 miles] northeast; **Bunker Field:** see Gemville; **Clancy's:** in The Blocks area, north of the opal mining area called Yancannia Rush; this area is notable because it was here that precious opal was found in outcrop; the hard silcrete cap has been eroded, allowing much easier sinking; in past mining activity, shafts were apparently restricted to less than 12 m [39.4 feet]; it is of interest that one of the original buildings, Clancy's Hut, is still preserved on this field; **Gemville:** 19 km [11.8 miles] southwest; originally called The Bunker Field, this area has yielded good-quality opal from shafts averaging 6 m [19.7 feet] and seldom exceeding 10 m [32.8 feet]; silcrete capping is not so extensive as at White Cliffs; **Lena's Hill:** 1.2 km [0.75 miles] southwest; prospected by a few shallow shafts and pits along its margin; **Milparinka:** 168.95 km [105 miles] northwest; **Moffat's Hill:** 0.8 km [0.5 mile] northeast of The Blocks and separated by a narrow east-west band of alluvial sediment; in this area mining has been restricted by the thickness of silcrete cover; the main workings are on the northern, western and southern rims of the mesa; large pieces of potch are common; **Purnanga:** 48 km [29.81 miles] north-northeast; discovered in 1896, this area has been prospected by about 50 shafts sunk on the scarp of a Cretaceous plateau; hardened claystone similar to the "shin-cracker" of Lightning Ridge has inhibited exploitation of the area; **Seven Mile:** 7.5 km [4.66 miles] west; **Smith's Hill:** 2.8 km [1.74 miles] south, this hill is capped with silcrete and mining is confined to the margins of the hills; **Sullivan's Hill:** east of and adjacent to The Blocks area; shaft sinking has been restricted because of the thickness of the silcrete cover, with the opal levels recorded to a depth of 11.5 m [37.7 feet]; **Tibooburra:** 193.08 km [120 miles] northwest; **Turley's Hill:** 0.4 km [0.25 mile] east, this hill is capped by Tertiary silcrete; the area has been mined by shafts and by horizontal drives mostly commencing immediately below the conglomerate and silcrete capping; the workings have been concentrated along the margins of the siliceous cap in an endeavor to avoid difficult shaft-sinking conditions; precious opal is recorded (as far back as 1907) to a depth of 12.6 m [41.3 feet]; **Walsh's (aka Welsh):** 11 km [6.83 miles] south; a thick silcrete capping has restricted shaft sinking to the margins of the hills; **White Cliffs:** 201.13 km [125 miles] northeast of Broken Hill; **Yancannia:** 80.45 km [50 miles] northeast; **Yancannia Rush:** a northern extension of The Blocks area and first worked in 1900; the precious opal here has been found to a depth of 11.5 m [37.7 feet].

For considerably expanded details regarding the history, discovery and exploitation of precious opal in this State, see specific headings in Chapter 7.

NEW YORK (United States)

William M. Kelly, associate scientist with the New York State Geological Survey in Albany, confirms that opals do occur in the state of New York, though not precious opal. Varieties noted are a hyalite which fluoresces brilliant green and which occurs as opaque coatings, castings and globular glassy crusts on pegmatite material and in fractures of granite gneiss, usually in association with albite and quartz; and diatomite in the form of a light colored siliceous earth composed principally of opaline fragments of freshwater diatoms (microscopic plants) and secernt siliceous skeletons. None of these opal deposits are mined.

Specific locations are **Essex County:** microscopic botryoidal crusts of hyalite occur on feldspar in a syenitic pegmatite northwest of Crown Point Center; **Herkimer County:** at Beaver Meadow, Big Crooked Lake, Chub Pond, Roilly Pond, and White Lead Lake are reported thick deposits of post Pleistocene diatomaceous earth; **Monroe County:** green prase opal occurs in several localities close to Rochester; **Putnam County:** the Tilly Foster Mine near Brewster hosts a grayish-white hyalite as a coating on hisingerite; **Saratoga County:** an opal deposit has been reported but without indication as to the exact site or the type of opal involved; **Westchester County:** a very highly fluorescent hyalite occurs as crusting on smoky quartz at the Kinkel Quarry in Bedford.

NEW ZEALAND

Geoff Gregory, information program leader for the New Zealand Department of Science and Industrial Research, Geology and Geophysics at Lower Hutt, writes that opals do occur in New Zealand in four varieties—precious opal, common opal, hyalite, and siliceous sinter. Little detail was given in regard to the character of the precious opal found in New Zealand and Gregory remarked that the information on hand about such opals came from "rare reports and not properly authenticated. No specimens at the Department of Science and Industrial Research, Geology and Geophysics." He did remark, however, that the precious opal occurs in sintered pumice and largely in the Coromandel region, adding that "a local farm on the Coromandel Peninsula has a deposit of precious opal, but access is not permitted." Hyalite, he reports, occurs as glassy crusts and "siliceous sinter occurs on a grand scale around hot springs and geysers and accumulates in cauliflower-like encrustations." The common opal is widespread and also found in the Coromandel region in an extinct volcano area and at hot springs associated with rhyolitic volcanism. Opal-CT as a precipitate from silica-saturated water. Opal-CT in chalk at Oxford, Canterbury. The only mining being done is of a recreational nature. The common opal, Gregory says, occurs in: **Canterbury:** near Oxford, Opal-CT occurs in chalk; **Coromandel Peninsula:** common opal occurs in old volcanic zones; precious opal occurs in sintered pumice on a local farm, but access not permitted; **Dunedin Peninsula:** near Waihi, common opal occurs in rhyolite; **Rotura region:** on the North Island, central portion, common opal and siliceous sinter widespread in altered volcanic rocks and hot spring deposits; also, between Rotorua and Atiamura; **Mount Ruapehu:** Opal-CT occurs at Crater Lake as precipitate from silica-saturated water; **Waitaikei Valley:** siliceous sinter occurs commonly in the area of Hot Springs.

NEWFOUNDLAND (Canada)

A questionnaire concerning the occurrence of opal in Newfoundland was sent to Norman Mercer of the Geological Survey Branch of Newfoundland and Labrador, Department of Mines and Energy in Saint John's. It was returned with none of the questions answered but with a comment penned at the top, "Not applicable," which was taken to indicate there is no known occurrence of opal in the Province. A follow-up contact resulted in the comment from Scott Swinden, senior geologist of the Mineral Deposits Section of the Newfoundland Geological Survey at St. John's, that there is no known occurrence of any variety of opal in the province of Newfoundland.[3]

NICARAGUA

No response was received from the Geological Survey of Nicaragua, but there are numerous reports in the records to confirm the existence of precious opal deposits in Nicaragua. There are, in fact, some specimens of Nicaraguan precious opal, almost identical to the Honduras opal, presently in the collection of the British Museum collection. Opal mining in Nicaragua, however, is haphazard at best, and far more often on a prospecting level than anything else, without any real opal mining development having been established. Unfortunately, no specific source is shown for the specimens in possession of the British Museum and accurate source descriptions have not been located by the author elsewhere.

NORTH CAROLINA (United States)

Jeffrey C. Reid, chief geologist of the North Carolina Geological Survey, Department of Environment, Health and Natural Resources in the Division of Land Resources at Raleigh, reports that while there are occurrences of opal in the state, with the exception of one officially recorded specimen, no precious opal has been reported. That single exception was a translucent specimen of a pink base coloration and with faint pinfire POC in red and green discovered near Asheville in Buncombe County. Fluorescent hyalite occurs in limonite geodes at some mines, often in association with peridotite, and incidentally with other mineral mining, primarily feldspar.

Locations involved include **Avery County:** hyalite occurs in the Southers Branch Mine in the Spruce Pine Mining District; **Buncombe County:** a single specimen of precious opal, delicate pink in color, found at a mine (name undisclosed); **Clay County:** hyalite occurs in diggings near Elf; **Macon County:** hyalite occurs at Corundum Hill; **Madison County:** occurrences of hyalite at the Carter Mine; **Mitchell County:** blue hyalite is reported from the Putnam Mine near Little Switzerland; **Stokes County:** hyalite is reported as occurring at Copper Gap; **Vance County:** hyalite occurs near Kittrell; **Yancy County:** in the Spruce Pine Mining District, hyalite occurs at both the McKinney Mine and the Deer Park Mine.

NORTH DAKOTA (United States)

In a telephone conversation in January 1992, Mark R. Luther, geologist with the North Dakota Geological Survey at Bismarck, told the author that "Opal is rare and infrequently found in gravel terraces in the southwest corner of North Dakota. Some bone may also be partially opalized and opal may form thin layers as a weathering product on some flints." He added, however, that there has been "only one known natural opal occurrence of any significance in the state"—

this being a deposit in an undisclosed area of McKenzie County where there was a substantial use of the opal by Indians as knapping material for tools and implements. The opal deposit produces blocky material ranging from transparent to translucent milky white. In early times it was quarried by American Indians for production of flaked-stone tools. The site is considered an archaeological treasure and is now a protected; thus, no mining has occurred there in modern times. Mr. Luther also says there are scattered occurrences of wood opal throughout the Badlands section of North Dakota, but no *specific* locations that are noteworthy. That opal fluoresces only slightly, although it is associated with a rather strongly fluorescent quartz. While some of the opal is found in pockets, most of the occurrences are wood opal in alluvial deposits of a Tertiary kaolinite siltstone-shale.

NORTHERN TERRITORY (Australia)

Andrew Wygralak, geologist of the Northern Territory Geological Survey in Darwin, says that both common opal and precious opal do occur in the Northern Territory. The precious material is seam opal occurring in sandstone, which is mined both commercially and by professional prospectors, and all of it is white (milky) opal with broad flashes of red, blue, and green. Among the specific mining areas he lists are **Beechworth:** precious opal reported but not confirmed; **Buchan area:** good opal in alluvial deposits; **Daylesford:** wood opal in alluvial deposits; **Flemington:** wood opal in alluvial deposits; **Gelantipy:** common opal (yellow-brown); Precious opal reported but not confirmed; **Glenrowan:** precious opal in a granite quarry in northern Victoria; **Helen Springs:** noncommercial diggings just north of due center of territory; **Kulgera region:** noncommercial diggings almost on the border of South Australia; **La Trobe Valley;** common opal; **Sunbury:** common opal in basalt.

NORTHWEST TERRITORIES (Canada)

W. A. Padgham, chief geologist and engineer of mines in the Northwest Territory Geology Division, and Walter A. Gibbins, Arctic Islands District geologist at Yellowknife, both write that there is no known occurrence of opal in the province. Mike Stubley, chief project geologist of Northwest Territories Mineral Initiatives at Yellowknife states that he and his colleagues concur in this assessment.

NORWAY (Including Svalbard and Jan Mayen)

Gunnar Raade, Curator of Minerals at the Minerals-Geology Museum at the University of Oslo, writes: "Opal is a relatively rare mineral in Norway. It is found occasionally as a thin coating along cracks of various rocks or minerals, e.g. in pegmatites, granites, etc. Also covering other minerals in miarolitic cavities of granites and syenites from the Oslo Region. It is usually fluorescent with a yellow to greenish-yellow colour." None of the opal in Norway is mined. There is no precious opal.

NOVA SCOTIA (Canada)

The varieties of opal occurring in Nova Scotia include common opal, cachalong opal, tripolite, silicious sinter, chabazite, analcite, acadialite matrix, and girasol. They are found in the following locations: **Annapolis County:** cachalong opal has been found in an undisclosed location in the North Mountains, a donated specimen of which is presently in the National Mineral Collection; **Cumberland County:** tripolite occurs at Fountain Lake near Amherst, a donated specimen of which is in the National Mineral Collection; also, nodules of common opal the color of beeswax have been found on Partridge Island in this county; **Kings County:** cachalong opal has been found at Cape Blomidon and at Cape Split; **Lunenberg County:** both common opal and girasol occur as veining and in pockets of granite formations situated between New Ross and Lake Ramsay.

OHIO (United States)

Michael C. Hansen, senior geologist of the Ohio Geological Survey in Columbus, states that common opal occurs in Ohio but is of no significance in the state's commercial mining. It occurs in limestone vugs and has a milky-white base coloration. No occurrence of precious opal has ever been recorded. Dr. Hansen adds, "Opal is not a big item in Ohio . . . an occurrence [has been] noted in association with fish bone in the bone beds of the Middle Devonian Columbus and Delaware Limestones. I have collected these bone beds a number of times but do not recall seeing this opal, but I wasn't looking for it either. This occurrence is perhaps not surprising because the bone beds are supposedly high in silica, which some researchers attribute to siliceous volcanic ash. I suspect that the opal is in very small quantities." The opal material Dr. Hansen refers to is a white to gray opal replacing fish fragments, found in the American Aggregates Corporation Marble Cliff Quarry, located in Franklin County west of the Scioto River and about one-half mile [0.8 km] south of Griggs Dam in southeast Norwich Township.

OKLAHOMA (United States)

Kenneth S. Johnson, associate director of the Oklahoma Geological Survey at Norman, relates that there is some occurrence of hyalite in the state of Oklahoma, but no reported instances of precious opal. The hyalite is associated with zeolites and some dolomite and calcite, but is not itself commercially mined. The material occurs in four scattered outcrops in the interior part of the Wichita Mountains of southwestern Oklahoma, in Kiowa County. The northwest of these occurrences is an exposure along the North Fork of Red River, 6 miles [9.7 km] west of Roosevelt. The remaining three, referred to as the southwestern outcrops, occur near Cold Springs. All four of the outcroppings are in the Tepee Creek Formation. The zeolite-opal rock in which the occurrences are noted is normally a dull brick-red color speckled with white and commonly shows small shiny grains of black ilmenite. There are many vuglike openings in the host material which are partly filled with euhedral calcite, analcime, or natrolite. Infrequently, the cavities are coated with crusted opal. Often the opal in these deposits occurs as tiny veins traversing the matrix rock and are a replacement of natrolite, showing that this part of the opal is younger possibly formed through gelatinizing action by ground waters on zeolitic material. This hyalite opal fluoresces a light green and it also forms in transparent botryoidal masses in Government Quarry 6.

ONTARIO (Canada)

John Wood, director of the Ontario Geological Survey in Sudbury, says "Presently, there are no known opal occurrences in the Province of Ontario, Canada. While there is one old (ca. 1890) report of opal in the Bancroft area (Grenville Province), this report has not been substantiated or confirmed. Given the long history of intense gem and mineral collecting in this area, the lack of any substantiated opal occurrences in the Bancroft area likely indicates that the initial report was incorrect or that the opal was local in distribution and was removed with no record."

E. B. Freeman, communication project officer of the Mines and Minerals Division of the Ontario Geological Survey's Ministry of Northern Development and Mines in Toronto, says, "No opals occur in this Province. Our *Catalog of the Ontario Localities Represented by the Mineral Collection of the Royal Ontario Museum,* includes no mention of opal." Mr. Freeman provided a listing of opal occurrences in other Canadian provinces and then went on to say, "These are the only Canadian listings as of 1983. Opal is deposited at low temperatures from silica-bearing waters and can occur in fissures and cavities in any rock type. It is the form of silica secreted by sponges, radiolaria, and diatoms and is an example of a solidified colloidal gel. Opal is essentially amorphous, although X-Ray powder photographs indicate cristobalite-like groupings."

OREGON (United States)

Jerry J. Gray, economic geologist with the Oregon Department of Geology and Mineral Industries at Portland, confirms that precious opal, common opal, moss opal, and fluorescent opal all occur in Oregon. While these occur in seam and vugs in rhyolite, basalt, and zeolite, some occurs in kaolinite and some of the best quality precious opal occurs in geodes of the type generally referred to as thundereggs—some of those geodes as much as 3 to 5 feet in thickness and many hundreds of pounds. The opals are mined both commercially and recreationally. The precious opal ranges from transparent through translucent to opaque and much of it has excellent POC, exhibited in pinfire, broadflash, smudge and harlequin patterns, with a base coloration, if not transparent, generally milky white. Contra luz opal is not uncommon, both in water-clear specimens and in those that are transparent but tinted with color. Since some of the best known material comes from Opal Butte in Morrow County, this material and the Opal Butte site are discussed in considerably greater depth in Chapter 7. The wood opal often shows distinct annular rings and woody cell structure so well defined that the tree species can be identified.

The known opal locations in Oregon include **Baker County:** on the south side of Dooley Mountain at about Section 22 or 23, T12S R40E, several finds of precious opal were reported in newspapers in the early 1900s, but sporadic prospecting over the years turned up no trace of opal until autumn of 1991 when a prospector named Steve Tipton reported finding in that area a few pieces of precious opal with a base coloration of cloudy grayish brown and green, and showing faint red POC; southeast of Auburn, in about Section 25, T10S R39E, there have been persistent reports of precious opal occurring in basalt vesicles, these opals said to be very small; precious opal has been reported from Opal Mine Draw near Rye Valley, Section 10, T13S R43E, on the Huntington 15-minute topo map; there is a deposit of fine white and black banded opalized wood in Pleasant Valley; the Durkee area has long been noted as a locality for precious opal and even though fine specimens were once obtained here with some regularity, very little prospecting has been done in the area in the last decade or so; **Crook County:** Precious opal has been reported from Crook County, but without specific details; **Harney County:** Park, 18 miles [29 km] north of Burns on Highway 395, then 7 miles [11.3 km] west, for good wood opal in alluvium on slopes of Silvies Canyon in Myrtle Park; about 25 miles [40. 2 km] east of Burns, near Buchanan, there is an occurrence at the Desert Dog Mine of Oregon sun opal, which are thundereggs with attractive pale blue-gray common opal interiors, some with "scenic" inclusions; **Jefferson County:** Madras area; fine precious opal occasionally as small seams and veins in thunder-egg "plume beds" of Priday Ranch; precious opal of fine green POC is found on the Warm Springs Indian Reservation in Jefferson and Wasco counties; a single polished slab 2″ [50. 8 mm] in diameter was found by an Indian boy in a ledge outcropping on the surface, the stone said to have "very little red fire but full of large green patches." The area, being on an Indian Reservation, is not open to collecting or mining to other than the Indians themselves. **Lake County:** atop east-sloping basalt-capped Hart Mountain, northeast of Plush, in the steep cliffs on the west facing Plush Valley, are small quantities of precious opal and larger quantities of common opal in gas pockets of the Tertiary Age volcanic rocks; **Malheur County:** in the Homedale area, excellent opalized wood occurs upstream along Sucker Creek to Rockville; **Morrow County:** Opal Butte (originally called Peter's Butte), south of Parker's Mill in the southwestern part of the county was first prospected in 1889 and the first claim filed in 1890, after which some fine common opal was found here, including one mass of precious opal 12″ [304.8 mm] in diameter; great mining difficulty caused mining efforts to be suspended after one season's work and it was not resumed until recently; large nodularlike masses of precious opal occur in thundereggs of varying size (generally spherical and averaging a foot or more in diameter) which are found in a matrix of partly disintegrated basalt.

PAKISTAN (Including Part of Jammu and Kashmir)

Farhat Husain, director general of the Geological Survey of Pakistan in Quetta, reports that there is no known occurrence of opal in Pakistan.

PAPUA NEW GUINEA

Lawrence D. Queen, senior economic geologist of the Geological Survey of Papua New Guinea in Port Moresby, says that there is no opal mining occurring at present in Papua New Guinea and that although "opal is reported to have been mined on New Hanover Island in the 1920s in basaltic serpentine breccia, however, more recent investigations have not confirmed the occurrence of opal." There have also, he said, been unconfirmed reports of opal on Ferguson Island. In addition, officials at the Moresby Copper Mine have reported encountering precious opal in basalt.

PENNSYLVANIA (United States)

R. C. Smith II, of the Pennsylvania Geological Survey in Harrisburg, says that common opal occurs in trace deposits in Pennsylvania, as well as fluorescent hyalite in colorless, transparent yellow or transparent green concretions, but there is no precious opal in the state. The material is found in a York Haven diabase matrix and generally takes the form of small reniform stalactic masses. None of the opal is mined. The common opal is nearly opaque and the color may be green, blue, yellow, red, gray, white or transparent.

Areas of occurrence are **Bucks County:** common opal occurs in Finney's Quarry and the Woodbourne area; **Chester County:** cachalong opal is reported at Barron's, West Goshen; **Delaware County:** common opal in the areas of Avondale, Black Horse, Drexel's Quarry, Gillespie's Quarry, Morton, and

Springfield; **Lancaster County:** cachalong opal occurs in the vicinity of the town of Texas; **Lebanon County:** common opal occurs in the Cornwall area; **Philadelphia County:** common opal and transparent fluorescent hyalite in white, yellow, and green occur in the areas of Branchtown, Cobb's Creek, Fairmount Park, Frankford, Germantown, Overbrook, Rittenhouse Quarry, Wingohocking Creek, and Wissahickon Valley.

PERU

Hugo Rivera Mantilla, executive director of the Institute of Geology, Minerals and Metallurgy in Lima, says that while common opal does occur in Peru, there are no known occurrences of precious opal. The common opal, some red and some milky white, is opaque and found in vugs in rhyolite. The material, he says, is not commercially mined and of so little significance that no record has been kept of those places where the common opal has been found. No mention was made of the Peruvian Blue Opal that has been so popular in the United States in recent years—a common opal that is harder than most other opal, ranging between 6.5 and 7 on the Mohs scale. Mined in the area of San Patricio, the opal has become very popular for jewelry because of its outstanding translucency and the very appealing solid intense color ranging from aquamarine blue through vivid blue-green to sea green. The color is undoubtedly due to microscopic copper inclusions.

PHILIPPINES

Josue L. Perez, supervising geologist of the Lands Geology Division of the Mines and Geosciences Bureau at Quezon City reports that in the Philippine Islands there are occurrences of common opal, including wax opal, moss opal, and nonprecious wood opal. These opals are found in seams and pockets in basalt and chert and though some mining of the material occurs, it is on a very small scale. No occurrence of precious opal is known.

The common opal occurrences are **Ilocos Norte:** occurrences in the Burgos area at Papayas and Siek; **Bulacan:** occurrences at Calawakan and Doña Remedios Trinidad; **Del Gallego Camarines Sur:** occurrences at Tabion; **Romblon:** occurrences at Tablas; **Quinalibugan Island Caramoan:** occurrences at Camarines Sur; **Masbate:** occurrences at Siargao and Claveria; **Davad Orinetal:** occurrences at Makambol and Mati.

POLAND

Wieslaw Heflik, of the Academy of Mining–Metallurgy at the Institute of Geology and Mineral Deposits in Krakow, reports that precious opal, common opal and hyalite do occur in Poland. In fact, says, Professor Dr. Heflik, opal is rather widespread in Poland, but places where it occurs in larger quantities and its utilization as a jeweler's stone would be feasible are scarce. Therefore, first of all, hyalith [hyalite] of Jordanów near Sobótka in Lower Silesia should be mentioned here. Hyalith [hyalite] can also be found in serpentinites of Sobótka and Zabkowice Slaskie in Lower Silesia, cropping out in Wiry, Szklary, Kozmice, Braszowice, and Grochowa as well as in basalts cropping out in Lubien and Slupiec near Jawor. In Wiry, Szklary, Kozmice and Grochowa its amounts are rather larger, but it is nowhere exploited.

Professor Dr. Heflik (who is also the author of *Decorative Stones of Poland,* 1989), adds,

Multicolored, but mostly milk-white opals, showing sometimes opalescence, occur in Jordanów near Sobótka in Lower Silesia and in Naslawice (both localities approximately 1 km apart), within strongly altered serpentinites. Opals build veins or irregular aggregates and could be used as semi-precious decorative stones.
Multicolored opals—milk-white, blue-green, water-white with a pale green tint, white with a blue tint, beige and others—occur also in Szklary near Zabkowice Slaskie, and in Wiry. Their reserves are rather significant there and some of them are of a good jeweler's value.

Professor Dr. Heflik says, concerning these stones, that there is some

small-scale exploitation in the abandoned open-pit mines of Ni-silicate ores and of magnesite respectively.
Szklary near Zabkowice Slaskie, in Lower Silesia is famous, beside the multicolored opal, for its chrysoprase, [which is] green, glassy, locally mat, weakly transparent, having uneven fracture, and forming some varieties. The deposit was formed as a result of intense chemical weathering of serpentinites [where] small exploitation by individuals continues in open pit workings. Several years ago, deposits in Szklary and Marlborough Creek [Australia] had the biggest reserves of chrysoprase in the world.

Professor Dr. Heflik said also that cherts, built of opal in part but more often chalcedony, occur in the Jurassic limestones and marls forming the hills of the Kraków-Wielun Upland, as well as at Góry Swietokrzyskiee in the Holy Cross Mountains. The same type of material occurs in the Cretaceous sediments of the Lublin Upland. They are hard and competent, with variegated colors; gray, black, brownish to red. Some show multicolored streaks and partly are utilized as decorative stones.

Particularly interesting stones called stripped or ribbon cherts, occur within limestones near Ostrowiec Swietokrzski, in the Holy Cross Mts. They were widely exploited by neolithic men who have left in Krzemionki Opatowskie numerous mine workings—trenches, adits and pits. The mine in Krzemionki Opatowskie was one of the biggest mines of the stripped cherts in Europe. The raw material was used by local inhabitants to manufacture hand-axes, bartered around and being found not only throughout the territory of today's Poland, but also in Belorussia, Volhynia, Prussia, and Moravia. Above 70 pits, deep to 11 meters and joined by a network of horizontal galleries, have been preserved. The cherts of Krzemionki Opatowskie take a characteristic multicolored pattern when polished and could be used in manufacturing of decorative items, such as pendants, brooches, ashtrays, paperweights, etc. They take also artificial staining, obtaining an aggregate-like appearance.

The various opal sites in Poland, listed by Professor Dr. Heflik and Teresa Hanahe of the Museum Ziemi PAN in Warsaw, include **Braszowice:** in Lower Silesia, where hyalite crops out in the serpentinites; **Frankenstein:** praseopal occurs in the area of Baumgarten, Lower Silesia; **Góry-Swietokrzyskie:** in the Holy Cross Mountains; occurring in Jurassic limestones and marls forming hills are cherts built of opal in part, but more often of chalcedony; **Grochowa:** in Lower Silesia precious opal occurs in outcrops of the serpentine; there are fairly large amounts, but it is not presently exploited; hyalite is also present; **Jordanów:** near Sobótka, Lower Silesia, 1 km from Naslawice; hyalite occurs here, also milk-white opals within strongly altered serpentine; these latter opals sometimes occur as precious opals with good POC; **Kozmice:** in Lower Silesia, common opal, with some precious opal and hyalite, outcrops in the serpentinites in fairly large amounts, but is not exploited; **Kraków-Wielun Upland:** cherts built of opal in part, but more often of chalcedony, occur in hills formed of Jurassic limestones and marls; **Lubien:** near Jawor in Lower Silesia, common opal with some precious opal crops out in the basalts; **Lublin Upland:** cherts that are partly built of opal but more often chalcedony, occur in Cretaceous sediments; **Naslawice:** in Lower Silesia, near Sobótka and 1 km from Jordanów; milk-white opals, sometimes with POC, occur within strongly altered serpentine; **Slupiec:** in Lower Silesia, near Jawor, precious opal occurs in basalt outcroppings; **Sobótka:** in Lower Silesia; hyalite occurs in outcropping serpentine; **Szklary:** in Lower Silesia, near Zabkowice Slaskie, multicolored opals and hyalite occur in association with chrysoprase, cropping out in fairly large amounts in the serpentine; **Trzebnik:** common opal and moss opal occur in veins in ledges of serpentine; **Wiry:** in Lower Silesia; some precious opal along with hyalite and abundant multicolored common opal, occurs in association with chrysoprase in serpentine outcroppings; **Zabkowice Slaskie:** in Lower Silesia; precious opal and common opal occur in serpentine outcrops.

PORTUGAL

Miguel Montenegro de Andrade of the Museum of Minerals and Geology at the University of Porto, reports that Portugal has deposits of common opal, hyalite, precious opal, and what he calls "cinder ash" opal. In the Beja District of southern Portugal, in the vicinity of Alentejo, the opaque red, yellow, and orange opal occurs in gas pockets of altered peridotite. Here, also, according to Professor Mentenegro de Andrade, "the cinder (ash) opals occur [that] have many red spots." In northern Portugal, at Macedo de Cavaleiros (Trás-or-Montes), the red opal—a precious variety—has POC limited almost entirely to bright red pinfire. It occurs in association with altered peridotite.[4]

PRINCE EDWARD ISLAND (Canada)

Wayne McQuarrie, director of the Prince Edward Island Department of Energy and Minerals in Charlottetown, reports that no opals of any variety occur in his province.

PUERTO RICO (United States)

Ramon M. Alonso, director and state geologist of the Geological Survey Division of the Puerto Rico Department of Natural Resources in Puerta de Tierra, states that there is no known occurrence of opal of any variety in Puerto Rico.

QUEBEC (Canada)

Aïcha Achab of the Geoscientific Center of Quebec at Sainte-Foy and Henri Louis Jacob, geologist with the Geological Service of Quebec, both state that there is "no known opal occurrence in the Province of Quebec." The Ministry of Natural Resources of Quebec at Charlesbourg, concurs.

QUEENSLAND (Australia)

R. W. Day, acting director and chief government geologist of the Geological Survey of Queensland in Brisbane writes:

> A brief summary of opal in Queensland is as follows: Major deposits of opal occur in western Queensland, within a broad zone more than 300 km [186.3 miles] in width and 900 km [558.9 miles] in length over the Great Artesian Basin. This zone, extending from the Queensland/New South Wales state border north to Winton Township, has several hundred deposits sporadically worked by small miners or syndicates over the last 100 years. Queensland is famous for its 'boulder opals' which have been mined mainly in the central portion of the basin in western Queensland. Boulder opals consist basically of a dark or black variety of opal occurring as thin seams within ironstone concretions. Several varieties (sandstone types, ironstone types and nuts) are known. Minor deposits of opal occur in eastern Queensland at Springsure and Maleny. They form fills in vughs [sic] or voids in extrusive volcanic rocks. Non-precious 'potch' opal is widely distributed throughout the state."

The precious opal, in addition to that occurring as boulder opal in ironstone concretions, is primarily seam opal in sandstone; however, locations bearing volcanic opal (also called mountain opal) are so noted. Mining is both commercial and recreational, both as tunnel mining and open-pit mining. The precious opal is of very high quality with base colorations of black, gray, blue, white (milky), and transparent. The POC is chiefly pinfire, broadflash, and harlequin, with blue, green, and yellow predominating. In addition to some mining being done at Baracoo River, Bulla Creek, and Kyabra, there are major mining regions, as listed below. Numerous claims, prospects, and workings dot the area, among which are the following.

Blackall Region

Anzac Hill Workings: 48 km [29.8 miles] southeast of Palparara Homestead; **Arundel Prospect:** 30 km [18.6 miles] northeast of Tonkoro Homestead; **Blad Knob Workings:** 10 km [6.2 miles] southwest of Bareeda Homestead; **Black Boulder Mine:** 11 km [6.8 miles] east of Mayneside Homestead; **Boundary Prospect:** 42 km [26 miles] northeast of Palparara Homestead; **Brilliant Mine:** 1 km [0.6 mile] west of Opalton Homestead Ruins; **Brodie's Hill Workings:** 1 km [0.6 mile] north of Wyola Homestead; **Campover Workings:** 5 km [3.1 miles] north of Eildon Park Homestead; **Carbine Lucky Mine:** 25 km [15.5 miles] northeast of Mayneside Homestead; **Chinaman's Prospect:** 46 km [28.6 miles] north of Palparara Homestead; **Conway's Mine:** 7 km [4.3 miles] southeast of Opalton Homestead; **Coparella Mine:** 3 km [1.9 miles] northeast of Wyola Homestead; **Cragg Boulder Mine:** 9 km [5.6 miles] southeast of Mayneside Homestead; **Dreamtime Workings:** 11 km [6.8 miles] northeast of Dynevor Downs; **Duck Creek Mine:** 2 km [1.2 miles] west of Tirga Homestead; **Elbow Mine:** 7 km [4.3 miles] northeast of Wantha Bluff; **Elusive Prospect:** 5 km [3.1 miles] southeast of Boobara Homestead; **Emu Creek Mine:** 10 km [6.2 miles] south of Tirga Homestead; **Erda Rainbow Workings:** 8 km [5 miles] west-southwest of Yowah. **Fiery Comet Prospect:** 12 km [7.4 miles] southwest of Nooralaba Homestead; **Fiery Cross Mine:** 7 km [4.3 miles] southwest of Parracoonah Homestead; **Flat Prospect:** 5 km [3.1 miles] south-southwest of Coparella; **Gate Mine:** 12 km [7.4 miles] northeast of Dynevor Downs; **Brodie Goodman's Flat Workings:** 6 km [3.7 miles] west-northwest of Tirga Homestead; **Gorringe's 1 Prospect:** 9 km [5.6 miles] south of Berrimpa Homestead; **Great Dragonfly Mine:** 6 km [3.7 miles] southeast of Opalton Homestead; **Harlequin Mine:** 6 km [3.7 miles] north of Highlands Homestead; **Hollaway's Workings:** 13 km [8 miles] southeast of Boobara Homestead; **Hopal Workings:** 27 km [16.8 miles] northeast of Tonkoro Homestead; **Horse Creek Workings:** 24 km [14.9 miles] southeast of

Mayneside Homestead; **Jackson's Mine:** 20 km [12.4 miles] west-west-north-west of Vergemont Homestead; **Jerry's Mine Workings;** 47 km [29.2 miles] southeast of Davenport Downs; **Johnson Mine:** 13 km [8 miles] northeast of Prairie Homestead; **Jundah Mine:** 8 km [5 miles] southeast of Trewallah Homestead (deserted); **Kinder Mine:** 5 km [3.1 miles] southeast of Opalton Homestead; **Koroit Mine:** 10 km [6.2 miles] southeast of Boobara Homestead; **Kyeenee Mine:** 7 km [4.3 miles] northwest of Kyeenee Homestead; **Lightning Gully Mine:** 4 km [2.5 miles] northeast Eildon Park Homestead; **Little Wonder Mine:** 2 km [1.2 miles] west of Opalton Homestead Ruins; **Lushington's Mine:** 2 km [1.2 miles] northeast of Wyola Homestead; **Magic Prospect:** 20 km [12.4 miles] north; Flodden Hills Homestead (deserted); **Mayneside Mine:** 20 km [12.4 miles] south of Mayneside Homestead; **Mud Mine:** 13 km [8 miles] east of Mayneside Homestead; **Never Never Mine:** 9 km [5.6 miles] south of Tinderry Homestead; **Nielsen Mine:** 12 km [7.4 miles] south of Emmett Downs Homestead; **Norah Mine:** 19 km [11.8 miles] east of Mayneside Homestead; **Opalton Homestead Ruins:** in Opalton Mining Field; **Opalville Mine:** 7 km [4.3 miles] north of Hayfields Homestead; **Pride of the Hill Mine:** 8 km [5 miles] southeast of Glen Valley Homestead; **Quartpot Mine:** 11 km [6.8 miles] southeast of Mayneside Homestead; **Red Star Workings:** 11 km [6.8 miles] southeast of Boobara Homestead; **Redhill Workings:** 26 km [16.1 miles] southeast of Mayneside Homestead; **Rocky No. 3 Prospect:** 21 km [13 miles] southeast of Mayneside Homestead; **Sheep Station Creek Mine:** 9 km [5.6 miles] southwest of Tirga Homestead; **Snake Jump Mine:** 5 km [3.1 miles] southeast of Opalton Homestead; **Spur Mine:** 7 km [4.3 miles] north of Highlands Homestead; **Black Tequila Ridge Mine:** 13.5 km [8.4 miles] northeast of Prairie Homestead; **Tyson's Mine:** 24 km [14.9 miles] west-northwest of Vergemont Homestead; **Tyson's Valley Workings:** 20 km [12.4 miles] northwest of Vergemont Homestead; **Wild Horse Mine:** 20 km [12.4 miles] east-southeast of Mayneside Homestead; **Yellow Jimmy Mine:** 18 km [11.1 miles] east of Mayneside Homestead.

Brisbane Region

[Distances from Brisbane]

Buderim Mountain: volcanic opal, 111.02 km [69 miles] north; **Coomrith:** volcanic opal, 362.03 km [225 miles] west; **Glasshouse Mountains:** volcanic opal, 80.45 km [50 miles] north; **Ipswich:** volcanic opal, 32.18 km [20 miles] west-southwest; **Nanango:** volcanic opal, 169.95 km [105 miles] west-northwest; **Nerang Creek:** volcanic opal, 80.48 km [50 miles] south-southeast; **Sandgate:** volcanic opal, 16.09 km [10 miles] northeast; **South Brisbane Station:** volcanic opal, 3.22 km [2 miles] east; **Surat:** volcanic opal, 490.75 km

[305 miles] northwest; **Tamborine Mountain:** volcanic opal, 48.27 km [30 miles] south.

Cairns Region

[Distances from Cairns]

Herberton: volcanic opal, 112.63 km [70 miles] south-southwest; **Mount Garnet:** volcanic opal, 131.93 km [82 miles] southwest; **Palmer River Gold-field:** volcanic opal in the goldfield gravels, 193 km [120 miles] northwest.

Cunnamulla Region

[Distances from Cunnamulla]

Barry's Mine: 41.83 km [26 miles] west-northwest; **Bendena:** 160.9 km [100 miles] east-northeast; **Brandy Gully:** 106.19 km [66 miles] west; **Charlotte Plains:** 18.65 km [30 miles] east; **Dynevor Downs:** 128.72 km [80 miles] west; **Four Mile:** 111.02 km [69 miles] west; **Hungerford:** 168.95 km [105 miles] southwest; **Koroit:** 56.32 km [35 miles] north; **Moble Creek:** 177 km [110 miles] west-northwest; **Rossiter's:** 112.63 km [70 miles] west; **Southern Cross Mine:** 112.63 km [70 miles] west; **Yowah:** 104.59 [65 miles] west.

Eromanga Region

[Distances from Eromanga]

Aladdin: 54.71 km [34 miles] northwest; **Aurora Borealis:** 74.01 km [46 miles] northwest; **Baker and Connell's:** 75.62 km [47 miles] northwest; **Breakfast Creek:** 88.5 km [55 miles] northwest; **Bung Bung:** 57.92 km [36 miles] northwest; **Coleman's Cave Mine:** 88.5 km [55 miles] northwest; **Cunnavalla:** 53.1 km [33 miles] west-northwest; **De Lazra's Mine:** 62.75 [39 miles] northwest; **Fish Ponds Mine:** 72.41 km [45 miles] northwest; **Friday's Mine:** 80.45 km [50 miles] northwest; **Gap Mine:** 56.32 km [35 miles] northwest; **Gem Mine:** 49.88 km [31 miles] northwest; **Gladstone:** 46.66 km [29 miles] northwest; **Gooseberry:** 27.35 km [17 miles] northwest; **Hammond's:** 51.49 km [32 miles] northwest; **Hausington:** 75.62 km [47 miles] northwest; **Hen's Nest Mine:** 53.1 km [33 miles] northwest; **Keroongooloo:** 101.37 km [63 miles] north-northwest; **Kyabra Creek:** 54.71 km [34 miles] north; **Laman's:** 38.62 [24 miles] west-southwest; **Little Wonder Mine:** 53.1 km [33 miles] west; **Malone's Mine:** 51.49 km [32 miles] northwest; **Mascotte:** 49.88 km [31 miles] northwest; **Mat's Hard Mine:** 51.49 km [32 miles] northwest; **Monkey Coolah:** 40.23 km [25 miles] north-northwest; **Mulcahy's Mine:** 28.96 km [18 miles] northwest; **Peppin and Webber's:** 53.1 km [33 miles] northwest; **Pinnacles:** 45.05 km [28 miles] west; **Pitt's Mine:** 86.89 km [54 miles] northwest; **Pott's Mine:** 45.05 km [28 miles] west-southwest; **Quart Pot:** 25.74 km [16 miles] northwest; **Scanlan's Mine:** 75.62 km [47 miles] northwest; **Scotsman:** 56.32 km [35 miles] northwest; **Stanley's:** 77.23 km [48 miles] northwest; **Stoney Creek:** 64.36 km [40 miles] northwest; **Two Jacks:** 51.59 km [32 miles] northwest; **Union Mine:** 67.58 km [42 miles] northwest; **Yellow Nell:** 48.27 km [30 miles] west.

Longreach Region

[Distances are from Longreach]

Bald Knob: 128.72 km [80 miles] west-northwest; **Brilliant Claim:** 120.68 km [75 miles] west-northwest; **Carlyle's Mine:** 152.86 km [95 miles] west; **Conway's Claim:** 128.72 km [80 miles] west-northwest; **Dirri Dirri:** 241.35 km [150 miles] west-southwest; **Fermoy:** 128.72 km [80 miles] northwest; **Horse Creek:** 151.25 km [94 miles] west-southwest; **New Years Creek:** 160.9 km [100 miles] west; **Opalton:** 144.81 km [90 miles] west; **Poison Mine:** 160.9 km [100 miles] west; **Scattery Creek:** 180.21 km [112 miles] west-southwest.

Mackay Region

[Distances from Mackay unless otherwise noted]

Blackwater Creek: volcanic opal, 312.6 km [185 miles] south-southwest; **Britten:** volcanic opal, 120.68 km [75 miles] southwest; **Collinsville:** volcanic opal in near vicinity; **Emerald:** volcanic opal, 289.62 km [180 miles] southwest; **Grosvenor Downs:** volcanic opal, 144.81 km [90 miles] southwest; **Hillsburgh:** volcanic opal, 28.96 km [18 miles] northwest; **Leichardt Range:** volcanic opal in river gravels, 80.45 km [50 miles] west-southwest; **Site Mine:** volcanic opal, 177 km [110 miles] southwest, **Site No. 1 Mine:** volcanic opal, 160.9 km [100 miles] northwest of Collinsville; **Site No. 2 Mine:** volcanic opal, 152.86 km [95 miles] northwest of Collinsville; **Site No. 3 Mine:** volcanic opal, 160.9 km [100 miles] west-northwest of Collinsville; **Site No. 4 Mine:** volcanic opal, 177 km [110 miles] west-northwest of Collinsville.

Maryborough Region

[Distances from Maryborough]

Auburn: volcanic opal, 193.08 km [120 miles] west-southwest; **Burnett River:** volcanic opal, 96.54 km [60 miles] northwest; **Childer's:** volcanic opal, 80.45 km [50 miles] northwest; **Gayndah:** volcanic opal, 128.72 km [80 miles] west; **Gin Gin:** volcanic opal, 120.68 km [75 miles] northwest; **Gympie:** volcanic opal, 120.68 km [75 miles] south; **Miles' Claim:** volcanic opal, 288.01 km [179 miles] west-southwest; **Mondure:** volcanic opal, 80.45 km [50 miles] southwest; **Mount Coffin:** volcanic opal, 257.44 km [160 miles] northwest; **Springsure:** volcanic opal, 490.75 km [305 miles] northwest; **Wondai:** volcanic opal, 54.81 km [90 miles] southwest.

Quilpie Region

[Distances from Quilpie unless otherwise noted]

Adams Mine: 17 km [10.6 miles] southwest of Trinidad Homestead; **Al-E-May Prospect:** 7 km [4.3 miles] west of Yeppara Homestead; **Aladdin Mine:** 7 km [4.3 miles] east of McKinnon's Shed; **Amanda Jane's Workings:** 14 km [8.7 miles] southeast of Pinkilla Homestead; **Black's Prospect:** 20 km [12.4 miles] west of Kyabra Homestead; **Blue Gum Mine:** 48 km [29.8 miles] southwest of Eromanga Homestead; **Booka Workings:** 12 km [7.5 miles] east of Terrachie Homestead; **Boulder Mine:** 56.32 km [35 miles] northwest; **Bowra Creek:** 56.32 km north-northwest; **Bramble Workings:** 15 km [9.3 miles] southeast of Merrigal Homestead; **Breakfast Creek Mine:** 20 km [12.4 miles] west of Yeppara Homestead; **Budgerigar Mine:** 18 km [11.2 miles] east of Budgerigar Homestead; **Buffalo Prospect:** 11 km [6.8 miles] northwest of Bunginderry Homestead; **Bulgroo Mine:** 17 km. [10.6 miles] southwest of Trinidad Homestead; **Bull Creek Mine:** 10 km [6.2 miles] northwest of Bunginderry Homestead; **Bung Bung Workings:** 13 km [8 miles] southwest of Raymore Homestead; **Christiane Prospect:** 5 km [3.1 miles] west, Canaway Downs Homestead; **Coonavalla Mine:** 12 km [7.5 miles] west of Cooma Homestead; **Cunnamulla Prospect:** 11 km [6.8 miles] west of Cooma Homestead; **Depazzie Careno Mine:** 4 km [2.5 miles] northeast; Dillybroo Old Station; **Dingo Flat Mine:** 25 km [15.5 miles] west of Yeppara Homestead; **Donny's Mine Workings:** 15 km [9.3 miles] southwest of Yeppara Homestead; **Double Barrel No. 4 Mine:** 22 km [13.7 miles] southwest; Yeppara Homestead; **Duck Creek:** 101.38 [63 miles] south; **Exhibition Mine:** 13 km [8 miles] southwest of Yeppara Homestead; **Fazarri's Prospect:** 18 km [11.2 miles] southwest of Trinidad Homestead; **Fiery Creek:** 112.63 km [70 miles] south; **Friday Creek Mine:** 6 km [3.7 miles] west of Yeppara Homestead; **Galilee Mine:** 9 km [5.6 miles] northwest of Bunginderry Homestead; **Gem Mine:** 8 km [5 miles] southeast of McKinnon's Shed; **German George Mine:** 19 km [11.8 miles] east-northeast Pieuna Downs Homestead; **Gibgoe Creek Workings:** 16 km [9.9 miles] southwest of Berellem Homestead; **Gidyea Creek Prospect:** 21 km [13 miles] northwest of Berellem Homestead; **Gladstone Mine:** 8 km [5 miles] southeast of McKinnon's Shed; **Golconda Mine:** 112.63

km [70 miles] south; **Goldfinger Mine:** 7 km [4.3 miles] east of McKinnon's Shed; **Goodman's Flat:** 85.28 km [53 miles] south; **Gooseberry Mine:** 11 km [6.8 miles] southwest of Quartpot Homestead (deserted); **Great Mistalop Prospect:** 24 km [14.9 miles] southwest; Berellem Homestead; **Green Show:** 80.45 km [50 miles] north-northwest; **Group Mine:** 23 km [14.3 miles] west of Yeppara Homestead; **Hammond's Mine:** 7 km [4.3 miles] east of Mc-Kinnon's Shed; **Hausington's Mine:** 15 km [9.3 miles] southwest of Yeppara Homestead; **Hayricks Mine:** 6 km [3.7 miles] southwest of Canaway Downs Homestead; **Hewego Prospect:** 26 km [16.1 miles] east of Pieuna Downs Homestead; **Huber Workings:** 40 km [24.8 miles] southwest of Eromanga Homestead; **Joyce Workings:** 15 km [9.3 miles] southeast of Trinidad Homestead; **Johnsons Mine:** 96.54 km [60 miles] south; **Laman's Mine:** 40 km [24.8 miles] southwest of Eromanga Homestead; **Last Card Prospect:** 2 km [1.2 miles] southeast of Pinkilla Homestead; **Listowel Downs:** 225.26 km [140 miles] north-northwest; **Little Gidyea Mine:** 23 km [14.3 miles] northwest of Berellem Homestead; **Little Wonder Mine:** 24 km [14.9 miles] northeast of Berellem Homestead; **Lochray Mine:** 12 km [7.5 miles] east of Terrachie Homestead; **Lushington:** 64.36 km [40 miles] south-southwest; **Marble Arch Mine:** 6 km [3.7 miles] southwest of Dillybroo Old Station; **Marchese Mine:** 24 km [14.9 miles] northeast of Berellem Homestead; **Mascotte Mine:** 8 km [4.7 miles] southeast of McKinnon's Shed; **Maxi Benzine Prospect:** 7 km [4.3 miles] south of Congie Homestead; **May Day prospect:** 5 km [3.1 miles] southeast of Pinkilla Homestead; **McGeorge's (Boa) Mine:** 8 km [4.7 miles] southeast of McKinnon's Shed; **Mercedes' Mine:** 16 km [9.9 miles] west of Yeppara Homestead; **Monkey Coolah Mine:** 13 km [8.1 miles] west-northwest of Quartpot Homestead (deserted); **Monte Carlo Prospect:** 20 km [12.42 miles] west of Kyabra Homestead; **Mulcahy's Mine:** 17 km [10.6 miles] west of Cottesmore Homestead (deserted); **Nickaville:** 32.18 km [20 miles] north; **Old Country Workings:** 15 km [9.3 miles] west of Yeppara Homestead; **One Mile Workings:** 102.98 km [64 miles] south; **Opal Cheek Mine:** 13 km [8.1 miles] southwest of Trinidad Homestead; **Opex Prospect:** 14 km [8.7 miles] east of Pieuna Downs Homestead; **Peppin and Webber's Mine:** 8 km [5 miles] southeast of McKinnon's Shed; **Pinkilla Mine:** 6 km [3.7 miles] southeast of Pinkilla Homestead; **Pinnacles Prospect:** 17 km [10.6 miles] northwest of Berellem Homestead; **Pott's Mine:** 48 km [29.8 miles] southwest of Eromanga Homestead; **Poulston's Prospect:** 9 km [5.6 miles] southwest of Raymore Homestead; **Pride of the Hills:** 72.41 km [45 miles] south; **Quail's Workings:** 12 km [7.5 miles] southwest of Quartpot Homestead (deserted); **Quartpot Mine:** 7 km [4.3 miles] west of Quartpot Homestead (deserted); **Rainbow Mine:** 21 km [13 miles] east of Pieuna Downs Homestead; **Red Show Workings:** 7 km [4.3 miles] southeast of Canaway Downs Homestead;

Redflag Prospect: 5 km [3.1 miles] southeast of Pinkilla Homestead; **Russell's Mine:** 46 km [28.6 miles] southwest of Eromanga Homestead; **Sandstone Mine:** 57.92 km [36 miles] northwest; **Saratov Mine:** 25 km [15.5 miles] west of Kyabra Homestead; **Scotchman Mine:** 7 km [4.3 miles] east of McKinnon's Shed; **Second Choice Workings:** 17 km [10.6 miles] southeast; Trinidad Homestead; **Seven Wonders Mine:** 24 km [14.9 miles] northeast of Berellem Homestead; **Shaff Gully Mine:** 8 km [5 miles] southeast of McKinnon's Shed; **Sheep Station Creek:** 93.32 km [58 miles] south; **Stony Creek Workings:** 25 km [15.5 miles] west of Kyabra Homestead; **Suzanne Prospect:** 45 km [27.9 miles] southwest of Eromanga Homestead; **Top Mine:** 7 km [4.3 miles] east of McKinnon's Shed; **Top of the World Mine;** 11 km [6.8 miles] northeast of Pieuna Downs Homestead; **Toompine:** 64.36 km [40 miles] south; **Trinidad's Prospect:** 11 km [6.8 miles] north of Trinidad Homestead; **Valdare Mine;** 12 km [7.5 miles] east of Terrachie Homestead; **Why Not?:** 32.18 km [20 miles] southwest; **Yellow Nell Workings:** 24 km [14.9 miles] northwest of Berellem Homestead.

Winton Region

[Distances from Winton unless otherwise noted]

Allen Range: 24.14 km [15 miles] south-southwest; **Blue Speck Mine:** 28km [17.4 miles] east-northeast Denbigh Downs Homestead; **Carters:** 128.72 km [80 miles] west; **Coathworth Mine Workings:** 20 km [12.4 miles] west of Franklin Homestead: **Hudson's Claim:** 119.07 km [74 miles] northwest; **Kynuna:** 128.72 km [80 miles] northwest; **Kynuna Mine:** 27 km [16.8 miles] west of Dagworth Homestead: **L.B.J. Historic Mine:** 10 km [6.2 miles] east-northeast of Carisbrooke; **Longreach:** 209.17 km [130 miles] southeast; **Macpherson's Claim:** 112.63 [70 miles] northwest; **Mount View:** 16.09 km [10 miles] east-southeast; **Muttaburra:** 152.86 km [95 miles] east-southeast; **Opal Den Mine:** 28 km [17.4 miles] east-northeast of Denbigh Downs Homestead: **Opalton Mining Field:** Opalton area; many old workings; **Pinnacle Hill:** 112.63 km [70 miles] northwest; **Red Flash Mine:** 28 km [17.4 miles] east-northeast of Denbigh Downs Homestead; **Stuart's Claim:** 115.85 km [72 miles] northwest.

Yaraka Region

[Distances from Yaraka]

Black Mine: 128.72 km [80 miles] west; **Corrikie:** 193.08 km [120 miles] west-northwest; **Johnsons Claim:** 128.72 km [80 miles] west; **Jundah Old**

Field: 131.94 km [82 miles] west; **Magic Mine:** 168.95 km [105 miles] west; **Mick's Mine:** 148.03 km [92 miles] west; **Mount Edinburgh:** 128.72 km [80 miles] east-southeast; **Mount Square Top:** 233.31 km [145 miles] west-north-west; **Opalville:** 128.72 km [80 miles] west; **Tomkin's Mine:** 141.59 km [88 miles] west; **Tommy Dod:** 152.86 km [95 miles] west; **Top Flat:** 130.33 km [81 miles] west.

REUNION (France)

Patrick Bachèlery, volcanologist of the science faculty at the University of Reunion in St. Denis, says that no opal of any variety is known to occur on the island of Reunion.

RHODE ISLAND (United States)

J. Allan Cain, state geologist and professor in the Department of Geology at the University of Rhode Island in Kingston, reports that there are occurrences of both common opal and hyalite in the state, but no precious opal. Both forms of opal are found associated with graphite and usually in lime rock matrix as a by-product of quarrying operations. The hyalite occurs as a white coating that fluoresces green in the Johnston area and brown at Copper Hill Mine location.

Areas where this material occurs include **Pawtuxet County:** hyalite and common opal in the Lincoln area at the Dexter Lime Quarry; common opal only in lime rock at Conklin's Lime Quarry (also called Harris Quarry); **Providence County:** in the Cumberland area, common opal occurs at Beacon Pole Hill in an inactive quarry; at Catamint Hill (also called Calumet Hill) at the Diamond Hill Granite Co. Quarry; in an inactive quarry at the Iron Mine Hill in an inactive quarry; and in the road cuts at Greenville Avenue and Route 6; brown hyalite occurs in an inactive quarry at the Copper Mine Hill; in the Johnston area, brown hyalite occurs in the Route 295 roadcut at coordinates R250/U413; **Washington County:** in the Cranston area, white fluorescent hyalite occurred in the graphite mine at, but that mine is now filled; and common opal occurs in beach outcrops at Bonnet Shores in the Narragansett area.

ROMANIA

Dan P. Radulescu of the Department of Mineralogy, Bucharest University, states that Romania has no deposits of precious opal and, in fact, the only opal occurring in the country is common opal found in rhyolite, chert, sandstones, organic silica rocks, and pyroclastics, but the material is unmined. The common opal has a base coloration ranging from white (milky) to bluish. According to Dr. Radulescu, this opal occurs as

1. A product of the hydrothermal activity related to the Mesozoic ophiolytes in the Apuseni Mountains (e.g., at Techerau, District Hunedoara) or in the Neogene volcanics in the East Carpathian Mountains (e.g., in the area Seini-Ilba, District Maramures) and in the Apunsi Mountains (e.g., at Craciunesti, District Hunedoara, and at the Almasul Mare, District Alba) and as gangue in ore veins, geodes and diaclases.

2. In various sedimentary rocks of different ages as (a) cement of sandstones, (b) together with jasper as epigenetic product in diatomites, radiolarites (e.g., Racosul de Sus, District Brasov, and Pojorata, District Suceava), and (c) substituting the wood substance of fossil trees (e.g., in the volcano-sedimentary formation of the East Carpathian Mountains.

RUSSIA

No response was received to the several queries sent to the Russian Geological Survey in Moscow during the period 1990–1995. Frank Leechman, in *The Opal Book* reports that there are deposits of precious opal in Siberia, but does not elaborate as to where or of what type.

RWANDA

Reliable information about the possible occurrence of opal in Rwanda was unavailable in 1992 and 1995 due to what was termed a temporary suspension of the geological service of the Ministry of Commerce.

SASKATCHEWAN (Canada)

P. Guliov of Saskatchewan Energy and Mines in Regina states that Saskatchewan has "no known opal occurrence." R. Macdonald, chief geologist of the Saskatchewan Geological Survey in Regina, concurs.

SCOTLAND (United Kingdom)

David H. Land, of the Edinburgh Geological Society, states that while there is "no native opal occurrence in Scotland, we do have an opalescent quartz," which may be a reference to iris quartz. However, Kamal S. Siddiqui, of the Mineralogy and Petrology Group of the British Geological Survey at Keyworth, Nottingham, states that opal deposits exist in several Scottish locations, including Galston at Ayershire; at Peeble Knowe and Ballindean, Perthshire; at Campbelltown and Kilkerton Point, Argylshire; at Kincaedinshire Blue Hole, Usan; and at Cliff Foot south of Stack, Talisker on the Island of Skye.

SIERRA LEONE

A. C. Wurie, director of the Sierra Leone Geographical Survey Division at Freetown, reports no known occurrence of opal of any type in his country.

SLOVAKIA

See Czech Republic and Slovakia.

SOLOMON ISLANDS

Nicholas Bilpki, director of Geology at Honiara, states that the Solomon Islands have no occurrences of opal of any type.

SOUTH AFRICA

C. Frick, director of the Geological Survey of South Africa at Pretoria, states that his country has occurrences of precious opal, hyalite, common opal, and wood opal. Herbert S. Pienaar, of the Department of Geology of De Beers Laboratory at Stellénbosch University, however, says, "No precious opal or gem opal has yet been found in South Africa. Some wood opalization has been noted in Kwa-Zulu." The majority of the opal, associated with albite, occurs as inclusions in the gossans, which develop as weathered crusts on basic and ultra-basic rocks which may contain metallic sulphides, or which are the leading products of sulphide-rich pipes such as those found north of Rustenburg. Although none of this material is commercially mined, small amounts are regularly dug by gem collectors. Chris C. Callaghan, of the Geological Survey of South Africa, and author of the article *Opal in South Africa,* concurs with Dr. Pienaar, stating that "True precious opal is not known in South Africa." See Zimbabwe in this section concerning reports of precious opal occurring on the border of South Africa and Zimbabwe at Beit Bridge.

The chief occurrences of opal in South Africa are **Geigas area:** about 2.5 km [1.6 miles] south, in the northwest Cape, so-called "opaline quartz" of a brown to black color cements the brecciated Kaigas dolomite Member (Gariep Suite); Callaghan writes, "This opaline material was very popular in the stone age for making implements"; **Gordonia district:** hyalite and semitransparent opals with marked iridescence are reported occurring in a pegmatite on the farm Zoovoorby 458; **Henkries vicinity:** black opal (color imparted by manganiferous ferric oxide) and hyalite occur coating platy albite crystals deposited during the late hydrothermal stage of mineralization in a beryl pegmatite; **Ingwavuma vicinity:** near Swaziland, occurrences of light blue common opal; **Jakkalswater:** 3 km [1.9 miles] west, north of Steonkopf, in a beryl pegmatite, hyalite occurs as a coating on albite, this material deposited during the late hydrothermal stage of mineralization; **Karoo Basin:** silicified wood (probably not opal) is abundant in the northern part of this area in the Upper Beaufort Group; **Mapula Lodge:** 30 km [18.6 miles] west of Warmbaths, brown common opal occurs in association with a hydrothermal vein deposit; **Marico district:** near Pella in the northwest Cape Province, ferruginous opal forms the groundmass in a gossan on the farm Goudini 30 JP, and the same type of deposit occurs near Postmasburg in the northeast Cape on the farm Alewyns Poort 29 JP; and, on the farm Riekersdam 109 JP, are found semitransparent pinkish-brown opals with marked iridescence is found; **Rustenberg district:** near Ingwavuma, on the farm Otterfontein 438 JP is found semitransparent opals with marked iridescence, in a light blue variety, associated with agates; also, 60 km [37.2 miles] south, common opal occurs in gossan over sulphide-rich basic and ultrabasic rocks such as gabbro and peridotite 60 km north of Rustenberg; also in this area, a milk-white common opal occurs on the farm Otterfontein 438 JP; **Swartwater area:** in northwestern Transvaal, small deposits of common opal are widespread; **Vivo vicinity:** common opal deposits are located in the western part of the Soutpansberg in the Pilansberg Mountains.

SOUTH AUSTRALIA (Australia)

Jack Townsend of the Department of Mines and Energy of South Australia at Eastwood states that the opals of South Australia include precious opal, common opal, fluorescent opal and wax opal, all of which are translucent. These opals are basically seam opal and pocket opal found in deposits of claystone and kaolinitic sandstone. The base coloration may be black, transparent, milky white, gray, or yellow, with POC that is pinfire, broadflash, longstreak, and harlequin, in all colors, but especially red, blue, green, blue-green, yellow, violet, and orange. The opals are mined both commercially and recreationally.

South Australia precious opal was first discovered in 1849 at Angaston, 63 km [39.1 miles] northeast of Adelaide. Since then there have been discoveries of some of the most famed precious opal deposits known in the world today, including the phenomenally important and productive precious opal fields called Andamooka, Mintabie, and Coober Pedy. For much greater details, see the sections in this book devoted to these specific opal fields in Chapter 7. The precious opal is primarily seam opal in sandstone. Numerous opal occurrences, claims, prospects and workings dot South Australia, among which are Andamooka, Charlie Swamp [also called Charley's Swamp], Coober Pedy, Coward Cliff, Eeavinna Hill, England Hill, Granite Downs, Lambina, Mintabie, Mount Brady, Myall Creek, Ouldburra Hill, Sarda Bluff, Stuart Creek, Teal Waterhole, Vesuvius, Wallatinna, Welbourn Hill, William Creek, and Yarra Wurta Cliff.

SOUTH CAROLINA (United States)

Arthur H. Maybin III, chief of the Mineral Resources Department of the South Carolina Geological Survey in Columbia, reports no known occurrence of opal in the state.

SOUTH DAKOTA (United States)

Eric Fritzsch, of the Museum of Geology at the South Dakota School of Mines and Technology in Rapid City, reports that there are occurrences of common opal, both fluorescent and nonfluorescent, in South Dakota. This opal occurs in seams and pockets in pegmatites as late stage hydrothermal fracture fillings, as well as in prairie hydrothermal associated with chalcedony. Some is reported in iron formations, perhaps as a collapsed sinter deposit. There is also the occurrence of opal as a cement that supports clasts up to cobble size, and wood opal pseudomorphs are relatively common. None of the opal, however, shows any POC. There is some collecting of opal specimens occurring, but only on a very limited basis, and no active mining of the material anywhere.

Sarah Chadima, geologist with the South Dakota Department of Environment and Natural Resources in the Science Center at the University of South Dakota at Vermillion, however, reports that in addition to common opal and wood opal, there are also occurrences of hyalite which fluoresces a brilliant green and precious opal. These opal varieties occur as botryoidal, reniform, globular or ropey-surfaced crusts and films along fracture and joint surfaces in pegmatites, granites, siltstones and other rocks, and as botryoidal incrustations on chalcedony. Some of the opal occurs shaped into small stalactitic to coralloidal formations as well as in irregular concretionary masses. Most commonly as a cavity filling and as veinlets. The opal is normally found in association with autunite, minutely crystalline purple fluorite, limonite, feldspar, quartz, black tourmaline, urananite, and chalcedony. It is to some extent found by collectors who are searching for other materials, such as agate, but more often is seen as a byproduct of mining operations for other minerals and metals. The opal ranges from transparent through translucent to nearly opaque, with base colorations of gray to brown in the common opal and precious opal and pastel blue, green, or yellow in the hyalite. The precious opal, says Sarah Chadima, exhibits rich internal POC, usually red, green, and blue, but also white and yellow from secondary uranium minerals.

Among the locations Geologist Chadima lists are **Custer County:** there are scattered occurrences of common opal and wood opal (some with rich POC) throughout the Badlands; a colorless hyalite that fluoresces brilliant green is found in the November Mine, which is located on the west side of Highway 87 a mile and a half [2.4 km] southeast of the Needles Eye Tunnel; **Lawrence County:** in the Bald Mountain District, thin, colorless crusts of hyalite are found in great abundance on siltstones at the Davier Mine located on Annie Creek, 5 miles [8.1 km] west of Lead; **Pennington County:** occurrences of common opal, precious opal and wood opal (some with intense POC) throughout the Badlands, but more specifically at the Ferguson Lode Claim, located a half-mile [0.8 km] northwest of the Wood Tin Lode, 3 miles [4.8 km] southeast of Keystone; similar material occurs in the Etta Mine at Keystone; also several small deposits of like material 2.5 miles [4 km] south of Scenic in the northwest quarter of Section 34, T3S, R13E; finally, there are quite exceptional specimens of highly fluorescent hyalite occurring as thick botryoidal incrustations on chalcedony over a large area in the vicinity of Scenic, especially 5 [8.1 km] miles south, in the southwest quarter of Section 9, T4S, R13E; **Shannon County:** the Badlands area has numerous occurrences of common opal and wood opal, some of the latter exhibiting distinct POC.

SPAIN (Including Canary Islands)

Angel Paradas Herrero, of the GeoMineral Technological Institute of Spain at Madrid, reports, "There is no known precious opal occurrence in Spain, although opaline silcretes and semi-opal deposits are known." He does not elaborate beyond that remark. However, Luis Alcala, director of Paleontology of Vertebrates in the Division of Prehistory and Geology at the National Museum of Natural Sciences in Madrid, writes that his country has deposits of xilopal, cachalong, hyalite, and common opal, including wood opal, which occurs in basalt and chert. Not commercially mined, this material is opaque. Dr. Alcala included a listing of 111 opal deposits for Spain that has heretofore never been published and was previously found only in the files of the National Museum in Madrid.

Said listing includes **Alava Province:** (1) a tan-colored, massive, cachalong opal deposit occurs at La Guardia, Peña Revilla; **Albacete Province:** (2) reddish xilopal occurs in massive form at La Cañada; (3) tan-colored lenses of the same material occur at Elche de la Sierra, as does (4) massive white tripoli (diatomite); (5) at Hellin occurs deposits of white tripoli as crusting material and (6) in massive form, along with (7) massive reddish tripoli; also at Hellin occurs (8) laminates of tan common banded opal and (9) tan-colored lenses of xilopal, along with (10) gray banded common opal and (11) a concretional menilitic tan common opal; **Almerica Province:** (12) an ivory-colored massive common opal is widespread; (13) at Cuevas de Vera there is an occurrence of both yellowish-beige and (14) yellowish-brown common opal; (15) at Rodalquilar-Nijar occurs some massive white common opal; **Bandajoz Province:** (16) a fine bluish common opal occurs at Chaparral; **Baleares Province:** (17) a pure white common opal occurs widespread; **Cordoba Province:** (18) a clear, transparent green massive common opal occurs in the Sierra de Cordoba Campo Bajo Cuarzo; **Cuenca Province:** (19) yellowish-brown massive common opal is widespread; **Gerona Province:** (20) at Caldas de Malavella, a dull gray menilitic opal occurs in massive form, as well as (21) deposits of massive common opal in solid black and also (22) in maroon; while (23) concretions in the same region carry common opal of tan coloration as well as (24) a similar menilitic opal that is cloudy black, gray, and brown, often with bits of brighter yellow or red; **Gran Canaria Province:** (25) a globular, transparent to milky white, glassy hyalite occurs in vugs of volcanic rock; (26) an arriñonado white opal occurs in the White Cliffs of Sardina; (27) at Galiva occurs a globular opal that is white and tan; (28) widespread on the Canary Islands is massive white common opal, and (29) a tan-colored massive common opal deposit is found at Llanos de Barrera; **Granada Province:** (30) a yellowish maroon common opal is widespread and (31) a tan massive common opal occurs at Baza; **Guipuzcoa Province:** (32) at Montrico there are concretions containing menilitic opal that is gray with black markings; **Huelva Province:** (33) a very fine-grade, porcelanitic, pale greenish, massive common opal occurs in the pyrite deposits at Almonaster la Real; **Islas Canarias Province:** (34) a massive clear golden-colored common opal occurs in the vicinity of Tenerife; **La Coruña Province:** (35) at Santiago in La Mañoca Cuarzo occurs a massive, caramel-colored common opal; **Madrid Province:** (36) a massive, deep red semi-opal occurs in the Casa de Campo pyrolusite deposits; (37) in the Black Hills (Cerro Negro) of the province occur deposits of banded (sometimes referred to as striped) grayish massive common opal; (38) in the Vallecas foothills are deposits of a very pale tan, globular, massive common opal; (39) in the grasslands of Parla are deposits of interlaced, hollow strands of beige common opal as well as (40) beige massive common opal; (41) a similarly beige, massive semi-opal is found in deposits of the Getafe area; (42) a massive opal deposit with striped tan coloration occurs at Segovia Point; there is (43) widespread clean, massive common dendritic opal with a reddish gray base coloration occurring throughout the province; (44) milky white massive common opal occurs at Vallecas; (45) nodules of dull gray menilitic opal occurs in the area of Puente de la Princes; (46) black massive common opal occurs at El Pardo; (47) gray-speckled common opal in massive form occurs in the sloped hills of Ribas de Jarama; (48) in the Silex at Valdemoro occurs a massive brown cachalong opal; (49) a white resinous opal with dendrites occurs in massive form at Ribas de Jarama, while (50) a similar dendritic tan-colored massive common opal is found in deposits at Cerro de Ribas; (51) massive common pure white (milky) opal and (52) massive common beige opal are found in deposits in the foothills at Vallecas, as does (53) a beautiful banded blue-and-gray massive common opal; (54) geodes lined with an opal drusy called "white teeth" occur in the area of Vallecas; (55) shiny, massive common opal in deep red also occurs near Vallencas; (56) massive maroon menilitic opal is found in the Casa de Campo area; (57) deep red opal pseudomorphs after calcite are found in the chalcedony of Vallecas; (58) in the Cedro de la Trapa at Getafe occurs a very interesting botryoidal, transparent hyalite; (59) a globular gray-and-blue opal occurs at the Silex near Parla; (60) a virtual pavement of tan-colored menilitic opal occurs at Arganda; (61) in the Vallecas foothills are deposits of a fine-grade translucent white massive semi-opal; (62) a pale maroon twinned opal pseudomorph formation occurs at Getafe; (63) at Parla a massive common opal occurs in beige-maroon and white chalcedony; (64) at Las Alcantueñas there occurs a fine gray-blue massive common opal; (65) a tan-colored massive common opal formation occurs at Parla in Las Cantueñas calcite; (66) massive maroon common opal in Las Alcantueñas chalcedony occurs at Parla; (67) massive oscuro (black) opaque common opal occurs at Vallecas; (68) massive beige common opal occurs in the foothills of Ribas de Jarma; (69) a massive gray-blue common opal occurs in sandstone at Vallecas; (70) a fine banded beige common opal occurs at an undisclosed location in the province; (71) pure white common opal in massive form is found at Alcala de Henares; (72) an occurrence of massive bone semi-opal occurs at Montarco; (73) dendritic beige massive opal occurs in the hills near Ribas del Jarama, as does (74) a pure white common opal in massive form; (75) translucent gray common opal occurs in massive form in association with chalcedony at Vallecas; (76) a very nice, clean massive dark red common opal occurs at Vallecas; (77) a good pure black massive common opal similar to that found at El Pardo occurs at Vallecas; (78) a solid tan massive common opal occurs in the foothills at Ribas de Jarama; (79) an opalized breccia of sepiolite occurs at Vallecas; (80) a formation of massive maroon opal pseudomorphs after fluorite occurs at Getafe; (81) a massive maroon common opal occurs associated with quartz chalcedony at Vallecas;, as does (82) a beautiful white and blue common opal in massive form; (83) solid beige massive common opal occurs at Parla; (84) a massive magnesium opal formation of tan coloration is widespread in the province; (85) a lovely massive gray with red common opal occurs on the Camino de Paracuellos in the Silex at Torrejon de Ardoz; (86) a massive light tan common opal occurs in the Vallecas area, as does (87) a fine maroon resin opal and (88) a grayish white massive common opal; (89) a sapphire blue massive common opal occurs in association with the chalcedony of the Casa de Campo region; **Melilla Province:** (90) at Afra-Beni-Ifur there is a deposit of olive green massive common opal; (91) a massive common opal of tan coloration occurs in the Nador area on the Camino de Hardu a Nador; **Murcia Province:** (92) there is a deposit of light brown massive common opal at Cartagena; **Tenerife Province:** (93) a common white oqueroso opal deposit is found in the teide and (94) massive dark red common opal occurs widespread in volcanic rocks; (95) at

Arico-Güimar there is a deposit of massive common opal called honey-beige; (96) a massive grayish common opal occurs throughout the province in volcanic rocks; **Teruel Province:** (97) massive tan common opal is widespread in the province; **Toledo Province:** (98) massive tan common opal is also found in the Magan hills; (99) at Villaluenga there is a deposit of white common opal and (100) a similar bluish-white common opal; (101) a tan massive common opal occurs at Rielves; (102) at Villaluenga there is a deposit of attractive gray-blue massive opal and (103) at Esquivias there is a deposit of clean, massive common dendritic opal with a reddish-gray base coloration occurring in association with fossil remains; also (104) at Esquivias, in association with the Silex chalcedony, there is a very interesting deposit of globular common opal that is mottled white, blue and gray, as well as (105) a tan massive common opal; a deposit of (106) black massive common opal occurs in the Villaluenga hills; (107) a very bright red massive common opal occurs at Cabañas, as does (108) a massive common opal that is an attractive yellow-red; (109) dark red common opal in massive form occurs at Esquivias, and (110) a very similar material occurs at Magan; (111) a tan-colored menilitic opal in concretions occurs widely throughout the province.

SWAZILAND

Leslie K. C. Strachan, senior geologist of the Geological Survey and Mines Department at Mbabane, reports no known opal occurrence in Swaziland.

SWEDEN

Anders Dauegberg, senior state biologist of the Geological Survey of Sweden at Uppsala, writes that opals do occur in Sweden, but not precious opals. They occur in diatomaceous clays and are dull, yellow-brown, common opal varieties, usually opaque but sometimes translucent. Carl-Magnus Backman, of the Geological Survey of Sweden adds that "these opals are associated with bog ore (ferrous) recovered through tunnel mining. I have been in contact with Professor Bengt Lindquist at the Museum of Natural Sciences in Stockholm, who has said that he has specimens in the museum, however, he would be reluctant to describe them as opal." Among the locations listed where this type of common opal is found are the iron ore mines in the Bergslagen Mining District of south-central Sweden, including those at Koppaiberg, Nordmark, and Taberg.

SWITZERLAND

Beda A. Hofmann, curator of the Earth Science Department of the Natural History Museum at Berne, writes that "Unfortunately, there are only a few opals in Switzerland, and no precious ones." The museum, he says, has a number of these opals in their collection—including hyalite and common opal. Of the reported common opal in chert matrix, occurring at Le Locle in the Juro Mountains, Dr. Hofman says, "It has never been investigated in detail and might be a fine-grained chert. The hyalite, colorless, is usually only detectible under ultraviolet light, where it fluoresces green, and it occurs in pegmatites in the Tessin Region at Claro, Iragua and Sementine." According to Dr. Hofman, "all the above opals are ugly."

TAIWAN

Chen-Hong Chen of the Institute of Geology, National Taiwan University in Taipei, says that opals do occur in his country, in the Tatun Volcano Group of northern Taiwan, but that they are common opals found in seams and vugs in andesitic agglomerate and "not worth being mined." Chao-Hsia Chen, chief of Mineralogy and Petroleum Division of the Central Geological Survey, also in Taipei, adds that some opal of the same character is found in the Coastal Range in eastern Taiwan and that all of the opal material is "gray and not of commercial value."

TANZANIA

Precious opal with brilliant green POC was reported discovered in 1962 but no further details have been forthcoming. Two separate queries sent to the Tanzanian Director of the Ministry of Water, Energy and Minerals in Dodoma requesting further information about the report have gone unanswered.

TASMANIA (Australia)

L. Matthews of the Division of Resources and Energy at Rosny Park, Tasmania, says, "Yes, opals do occur in Tasmania, but these are common opal. No precious opal has been recorded in Tasmania. The common variety is seam opal in basalt and sedimentary wood opal." The known common opal deposits in Tasmania are mined recreationally, but probably more often than not the prospector is hoping to find heretofore unrecorded precious opal.

TENNESSEE (United States)

Edward T. Luther, state geologist with the Department of Environment and Conservation of the Division of Geology in Nashville, reports that there is no known occurrence of opal of any variety in Tennessee.

TEXAS (United States)

Allan Standen, geologist with the Texas Geological Survey, and L. E. Garner, Bureau of Economic Geology, both in Austin, state that opal occurs in several varieties in the state, including precious opal, common opal, hyalite, wood opal (some with POC), and llanite, the latter not truly an opal but an opal-appearing blue quartz in granite. The wood opal and some precious opal occur in deposits of Bentonite clay (montmorillonite). Common opal and other precious opal occurs in vugs in rhyolite and basalt. None of the opal material is commercially mined, although the Woodward Ranch in Brewster County (see below) has an active mine where collectors may do fee-digging for precious opal. The precious opal occurrences in Texas are translucent to opaque, the base coloration a milky white to pale bluish-white and exhibit rather small blue, blue-green, green, fiery red and orange pinfire and broadflash POC.

Among the listed locations are **Brewster County:** probably the best known location for precious opal in Texas is the Frank Woodward Ranch, a fee-digging area located in the Cathedral Mountain Quadrangle, on Texas Route 118, 12 miles [19 km] south of intersection U.S. 90 at Alpine; both common and precious opal occur here as fillings of vesicles and amygdules in Tertiary basalt and rhyolite and Quaternary gravels derived from basalts; the deposits are located in the Sheep Canyon and Cottonwood Springs basalts; most of the precious opal from this location is small, though colorful, and is most often found as small seams and gas-pocket fillings rarely more than a quarter-inch diameter in a very hard pinkish-brown rhyolite from which it is very difficult to extract the opal; because of that, most often cabochons cut from this material incorporate matrix with the gemstone for stability and a larger finished stone; more widespread in the county is a translucent (approaching opaque) common opal that occurs in such colors as red, blue, green, white, gray, and yellow, usually found in the areas of wet-weather lakes (playas); **El Paso County:** a number of deposits of diatomaceous earth (diatomite) occur in this county; this soft opaline material is comprised chiefly of the skeletons of diatoms, which are minute one-celled plants that live in fresh or salt water and have the capability of absorbing silica from the water to make opal skeletons for themselves; these diatom skeletons collect on the beds of lakes or seas in vast abundance and form a crumbly, earthy material that is usually gray, white, or cream-colored and which is, in essence, an impure form of opal called diatomite, which has commercial value in the manufacture of filters, insulation, and polishing agents; there are numerous localities in this county and other west Texas counties where opal is found that has some degree of POC, but the pieces are so small and the fire so limited that collecting it as gem material is not usually considered worthwhile; **Duval County:** near Freer is a deposit of very attractive common opal which occurs in soft tints of yellow, blue, and pink, sometimes cemented together by clear chalcedony and often more than one color in the same piece; the material is favored by many lapidaries for making particularly handsome cabochons, and the area of occurrence, while never commercially developed, is frequently hunted by collectors and gemcutters; **Fayette County:** Tertiary age wood opal, usually in bentonite clay deposits or in association with chalcedony, is not uncommon in this county and other counties of the Texas Gulf Coastal Plain; **Gonzales County:** there are a number of occurrences in this county of wood opal such as that in Fayette County; **Hale County:** diatomaceous earth deposits similar to those mentioned for El Paso County are relatively widespread; **Hudspeth County:** common opal similar to that mentioned in Brewster County occurs around some of the wet-weather (playa) lakes, this opal formed from underground waters containing silicon gel that deposits itself on rocks and in cracks and cavities as the solution moves through them; **Jeff Davis County:** deposits of common opal similar to that occurring in Brewster County and wood opal akin to that found in Fayette County, plus several deposits countywide of diatomaceous earth; **Karnes County:** relatively abundant bentonite deposits yield wood opal, some of which has slight POC, though normally not enough to make the material valuable as a commercial operation; **Lavaca County:** wood opal occurs in bentonite clay (montmorillonite) deposits and sometimes elsewhere associated with chalcedony; **Llano County:** clear hyalite, commonly botryoidal and icelike in appearance, occurs in masses filling cavities and cracks in the Catahoula sandstones and similar sandstone deposits elsewhere, as well as in sedimentary rock crevices and pockets; wood opal is also relatively common; there is also a midnight black common opal that occurs mixed in a jelly white opal that forms in a matrix of white wollestonite; **Mason County:** similar to a deposit found in Llano County, there is an occurrence of black common opal mixed in a jelly white opal that forms in a matrix of white wollestonite; **Presidio County:** hyalite occurs in a number of locations throughout the county, similar to the hyalite that occurs in Llano County; also deposits of common opal of the same nature as that occurring in Brewster County; **Starr County:** common opal associated with chalcedony is relatively common in Tertiary formations.

THAILAND

Prayong Angsuwathana, deputy director general of the Department of Mineral Resources in Bangkok, states that there is colorful common opal in Thailand, as well as a very small amount of precious opal. The common opal, which is translucent, occurs both as wood opal and as fillings in vugs and pockets in rhyolite and chert, its color ranging from black, brown, or yellow through a milky white, green, or pink. "There is no play of color," says Mr. Angsuwathana, "except at the Ban Pang Fluorite Mine in Lum Phun, where the opal exhibits [a] very small amount of play of color, but not enough for commercial purpose." The precious opal that does occur has POC that is largely blue or green. None of the opal in Thailand is commercially mined. Among the sites where opal occurs, Mr. Angsuwathana listed **Lopburi Province:** in the Chai Badan District; **Lum Phun Province:** in the Li District at the Ban Pang Fluorite Mine; **Nan Province:** in the Mae Charim District; **Nakhon Ratchasima Province:** in the Muang District.

TRINIDAD AND TOBAGO

Curtis Archie, secretary of the Geological Society of Trinidad and Tobago in La Romain, reports no known occurrence of opal on the islands of Trinidad or Tobago.

TURKEY

Turkish opal was one of the principal opal resources known before the turn of the century, but the opal production of the Turkish mines was long overshadowed by that from the Czech-Slovak deposits under the general heading of Hungarian opal. Nonetheless, some of those early Turkish deposits are still being mined today. Murat Erandil, head of Ores Department in the Mineral Research and Exploration Institute in Ankara, reports that both precious opal and common opal still occur in Turkey. The common opal has a red to milky white base coloration and is opaque. The precious opal varies from transparent to translucent with vibrant POC, usually in broadflash red, violet, and lavender. The common opal occurs in a matrix of dacite, while the precious opal, volcanic in origin, is found in rhyolite. The precious variety is commercially mined in the central portion of northwest Anatolia, at Polatli in Ankara Province, near Karaman in Karaman Province, at Simav in Kütahya Province, and at Bayramic in Qanakkale Province.

UGANDA

John Odida, senior documents officer at the Geoscience Data Centre of the Geological Survey and Mines Department at Entebbe, reports that opal of any variety in Uganda remains "so far not yet discovered."

URUGUAY

Henri C. Masquelin, geologist of the Uruguay Department of Geology in Montevideo, reports no known occurrence of precious opal in his country, but there are indicators that such may well exist along with the nonprecious wood opal and opaque milk opal that does occur in deposits of montmorillonite clay at kilometer marker 15 on the Posta del Chuy Road near the city of Melo in the Cerro Largo Department. None of the common opal is mined and some research and exploration is presently underway to determine whether precious opals may be present.

UTAH (United States)

M. Lee Allison, state geologist with the Utah Geological Survey in Salt Lake City, confirms that opal varieties, including precious opal, common opal, wood opal, and girasol, do occur in the state. The precious variety occurs primarily in wood opal specimens, but also occasionally as fillings in vugs and seams of igneous rocks, where it occurs in botryoidal, stalactitic, and massive form. Specimens are usually transparent to translucent with base coloration ranging from colorless or white through pale yellow, brown, gray, green, or blue and with the POC, as Mr. Allison puts it, "a wide range in fine display."

He lists the following locations: **Beaver County:** Beaver area, in the Lincoln District at the Creole Mine; in the San Francisco District, near Milford, at the Horn Silver Mine; also in that same area, at the Opal Mine, located in the Adamsville Quadrangle, 6 miles [9.7 km] northeast of Milford, in the southwest quarter of the northwest quarter of the northeast quarter of Section 16, T27S R9W, at an elevation of 5770 feet [1760 m] in the Mineral Mountains above the Escalante Desert; Lat. 38.46666, Long. 112.86833; the opal occurring as a small hot spring hydrothermal vein deposit struck at N 40° W, with a 40° southeast dip; previous production at the site has been limited, the diggings established in several bulldozer cuts 10′ to 15′ wide [3.1 to 4.6 m] by 500′ [152.5 m] long; the deposit is a north-trending normal fault traceable for some 3 miles [4.8 km]; the matrix material being a granite dated by K-AR as 9.2 million years old; current (1995) status of the mine is shown as inactive; the occurrence was first officially reported in May 1979 by Mike L. Everts, geologist of the BLM, following an on-site investigation with Utah Geological and Mineral Survey; **Daggett County:** opalized wood occurrence at Red Creek, in the Yellow Canary Uranium Deposit; **Grand County:** an extensive opalized wood field along the Colorado River stretching from western Colorado into eastern Utah near Cisco; **Iron County:** at the Cima Mine; **Juab County:** deposit on the Orme Property in the San Pitch Mountains: equally on Topaz Mountain in the Thomas Range at the Autenite Number Eight Claim, at the Buena Number One Claim and at the Nonella Prospect; also, opalized palmwood near Nephi; **Piute County:** at the J & L Alunite Mine in the Silica Hills of the Marysvale District: **Salt Lake County:** at the Old Jordan Mine and the Galena Mine in the Bingham District; **Sevier County:** girasol and wood opal at Fish Lake, and unofficial reports of black precious opal near Salina; **Tooele County:** in the Gold Hill District at the Alvarado Mine, the Gold Hill Mine (aka U.S. Mine), the Monoco Mine and the Unadine Mine; **Wasatch County:** wood opal occurs in the vicinity of Heber City.

VANATU

Stanley Temakon, deputy director of the Department of Geology, Mines and Rural Water Supply at Port Vila, states that "there is no known occurrence of opal in this country."

VENEZUELA

Queries sent to the Geological Survey of Venezuela in Caracas have gone unanswered and in the abundance of other sources checked by the author, there is only one authenticated account of opal being found in this South American country. This was the mention of one solitary specimen of precious opal having been found in the mountains by emerald prospectors. Virtually no details of the find are available apart from the fact that it is volcanic opal that was retrieved from a vug in pink rhyolite.

VERMONT (United States)

Diane Conrad, geologist in the Office of the State Geologist at Waterbury, reports no opal of any variety is known to occur in Vermont.

VICTORIA (Australia)

William D. Birch of the Department of Mineralogy and Petrology at the Museum of Victoria reports that opals definitely do occur in Victoria, in "too many locations to list them all." The state, he says, has common opal that occurs mainly in Tertiary basalts, wood opal found primarily in Tertiary alluvial deposits, and precious opal (including hyalite) in granite and basalt. None of this is as yet being commercially mined, although a certain amount of recreational prospecting does occur, as in the area of Lillicur. The precious opal is largely jelly opal (transparent) with broad flashes of blue, green, and violet. The precious opal is primarily seam opal in sandstone. Numerous opal occurrences, claims, prospects, and workings dot Victoria, among which are the following:

Albury Region

[Distances are from the Albury Post Office]

Beechworth: 40.23 km [25 miles] south-southwest; **Chiltern:** 16.09 km [10 miles] south; **Mitta Mitta:** 67.59 km [42 miles] southeast; **Woolshed:** 40.23

km [25 miles] southwest; **Yackandandah:** 32.18 km [20 miles] south-southwest.

Melbourne Region

[*Distances are from the central Melbourne Post Office*]

Bairnsdale: 241.35 km [150 miles] east; **Gisborne:** 48.27 km [30 miles] northwest; **Moe:** 125.50 km [78 miles] east-southeast; **Morwell:** 144.81 km [90 miles] east-southeast; **Mount Blackwood:** 64.36 km [40 miles] northwest; **Riddell's Creek:** 48.27 km [30 miles] northwest; **Sunbury:** 33.79 km [21 miles] northwest; **Woodend:** 53.1 km [33 miles] northwest.

VIRGINIA (United States)

A query addressed to Julia A. Jackson, director of publications at the American Geological Institute (Eastern Region) at Alexandria, brought the response that there is "No known opal occurrence in Region. . . . Nothing showed up in GeoRef database about opals occurring in this area." However, a follow-up query to D. Allen Penick, state geologist with the Virginia Division of Mineral Resources at Charlottesville, resulted in a considerably different response. According to Dr. Penick,

> Opals are present in Virginia, including not only frequently occurring common opal, fluorescent opal and hyalite, but also unconfirmed reports of precious opal that can be transparent, translucent or opaque with base color in white, black, pale brown, or dark gray, and the POC in scintillating red, orange, yellow, green, and blue, in broadflash, smudges and pinfire. These opal varieties occur in seams, wood pseudomorphs, surface incrustations in fractures, colloform masses, small glassy spheres, arborescent masses, surface glazes, stalactitic masses, and botryoidal coatings. The matrix materials for these occurrences are generally granite, diabase, sandstone, pegmatite, dolomite, mica, quartz, and feldspar, with associated minerals including goethite, limonite, diatomaceous earth, quartz, barite, blue beryl, and albite. Some of the opals are said to contain cristobalite.

Dr. Penick says that the opals, per se, are "unmined, although collectors may work individual sites to a small degree."

He lists the following sites of opal occurrence in Virginia: **Albemarle County:** small glassy spheres of hyalite opal occur as incrustations on quartz at the Stony Point Iron-Copper Mine on State Route 640, 1.5 miles [2.4 km] northeast of Stony Point; **Amelia County:** opal occurs rarely in the pegmatites and country rocks near Amelia Courthouse; **Botetourt County:** fine fluorescent opaline silica occurs as small botryoidal masses atop clusters of barite crystals at the James River Hydrate and Supply Company Quarry, a mile [1.6 km] east of

Buchanan; **Clarke County:** hyalite opal occurs in the Berryville Mine located 1.3 miles north-northeast of Castleman's Ferry; **Culpeper County:** hyalite opal has occurred in an abandoned quarry on the Rapidan River near Rapidan; **Fairfax County:** hyalite occurs between Camp Washington and Centreville; **Hanover County:** wood opal deposits occur near Ashland; **Henrico County:** fluorescent hyalite opal occurs sporadically on granite in Forest Hill Park in Richmond; **Henry County:** glassy, botryoidal masses of nearly colorless opal that fluoresces a brilliant green occur as sporadic coatings on fractures in a coarse-grained mica-quartz-feldspar rock exposed in roadcuts at Axon; **King George County:** opaline material occurs in the diatomaceous earth at Greenlaw's Wharf; **Loudoun County:** common opal occurs as sporadic coatings on fractures at the Bull Run Quarry, the Old Goose Creek Quarry, and the Virginia Traprock Quarry; **Lunenburg County:** hyalite opal occurs at a small unidentified granite quarry near Kenbridge; **Powhatan County:** a sort of botryoidal hyalite opal has been found in bubbly-type frosted coatings on blue beryl and albite at the Herbb No. 2 Pegmatite Mine; this opal fluoresces a vivid white-blue under short-wave ultra-violet light; yellow, brown, reds and (rarely) green masses are abundant in the creek on the Coleman Jones Farm near Macon; **Prince William County:** common (and possibly precious) opal, from white to yellow, occurs in botryoidal coatings on fracture surfaces at the Manassas Quarry, with one piece recorded that exhibiting a district blue POC; **Richmond:** opaline material occurs in the diatomaceous earth at Carter Wharf; **Roanoke County:** a nearly colorless hyalite occurs as botryoidal crusts on some limonite matrix material of the breccia that serves as bedrock along U.S. 220, about a mile [1.6 km] south of the Blue Ridge Parkway overpass; **Wise County:** both gray and brown common opal (and, in unconfirmed reports, precious opal), some of which comprises banded mixtures of the two colors, occur in arborescent masses, botryoidal coatings, surface glazes, and stalactitic masses, sporadically on joints and other exposed surfaces within the Lee Formation sandstone in two separate areas—one southwest of Norton, the other southwest of Coeburn.

WASHINGTON (United States)

Raymond Lasmanis, state geologist with the Department of Natural Resources of the Geology and Earth Resources Division at Olympia, states that opals do occur in the state of Washington in three varieties—wood opal, common opal, and precious opal. The wood opal (some of it exhibiting POC) occurs in Tertiary deposits of montmorillonite, while the common opal and precious opal occurs as fillings in seams and in nodules of basalt and rhyolite. The translucent opals are mined both commercially and recreationally; the base coloration ranging from colorless to milky white, with the POC reported as primarily pinfire in blue, green, yellow, red, and orange. Some of the wood opal has such well-defined bark, annular rings, and cell structure that paleobotanist are able to determine the tree species involved. A number of accounts have made a point of mentioning that the opal from Washington state is singularly unstable, but those specimens observed by the author seemed to be as stable as the volcanic opal from other locations.

Specific locations cited by Dr. Lasmanis include **Benton County:** widespread in the Horse Heaven Hills; **Douglas County:** semi-opal reported as common throughout the country; **Garfield County:** at and north of Lower Granite Lake in vicinity of Chief Timothy State Park, at Moses; and 7 miles [11.3 km] northeast of Pullman almost on the Idaho border, where precious opal was originally mined in 1891 **Grant County:** in the diatom pits of both the Vantage area and the White Bluffs area; **King County:** in the Burma Road area; **Kittitas County:** south of Ellensburg and west of the Yakima River, in the Umtanum Ridge; **Klickitat County:** in both the Roosevelt area and the Goodnoe area; **Lincoln County:** near Reardan; **Skamania County:** in the Rock Creek area.

WEST VIRGINIA (United States)

Hobart M. King, head of the Economic Minerals and Geologic Hazards Section of the West Virginia Geological and Economic Survey in Morgantown, reports that both precious opal and common opal occur in the state, in Monongalia County. Here the opal occurs as small stalactitic deposits up to about an inch [25.4 mm] long, clinging to the underside of large sandstone overhangs, both at Coopers Rock, 2 miles [3.2 km] south of U.S. 48, and beneath the large cliffs of Pottsville sandstone. This material is not mined, although some private collecting is done for mineral specimens.

WESTERN AUSTRALIA (Australia)

P. E. Playford, Director of the Department of Mines, Geological Survey of Western Australia in East Perth confirms that opals do occur in Western Australia—both precious opal and common opal, including moss opal. This opal occurs, Dr. Playford says, primarily in veins

in thin-bedded metamorphosed granite shalls and tuff beds within amphibolite, in association with auriferous quartz, quartz porphyry, kaolin, graphite–chlorite schist, and limestone calcareous gravels. Potch [common opal] veins are to a thickness of 75 mm [3″] and maximum thickness of precious opal veinlets is 12 mm [0.48″]. Host rocks appear to extend for several kilometers north of the prospect area and possibly to the south. Transition from quartz to common opal to precious opal with 25 to 50 mm [0.99″ to 1.98″] in the same vein has been noted. Also, fire opal [precious opal] occurs in nodules.

Dr. Playford reports that, while the precious opal occurs in transparent and translucent varieties, the most common base colorations are white and black. "The white precious opal," he says, "is of higher quality than the average white Coober Pedy opal. Black is high quality. Fire opal [no POC] is rich red-brown." He adds that the common opal varieties include a very beautiful translucent green moss opal, an opaque yellow variety called "*gold lace*", milk white, opaque pale coffee color, deep brown, and a "bright emerald green." There is also, he said, "yellow to mauve variegated opal." The most frequently occurring POC in the precious opals is green, blue, yellow, bright red, and blood red. All of this opal is mined recreationally.

A fair number of opal occurrences, claims, prospects, and workings are found in Western Australia, among which are **Antrim Plateau:** 289.62 km [180 miles] south of Wyndham; **Bamboo Springs:** quartzite and basaltic rocks contain veins of inferior opal; 450.52 km [280 miles] east of Carnarvon; **Belele:** occurrences have been reported of green chromiferous opal; **Bullfinch:** massive milk-white opaque opal, known locally as "enamel," has been found at Manxman, 8 km. north [4.97 miles]; **Bulong:** moss opal, sometimes called lace opal, associated with magnesite on hills of serpentinite, occurs between Bulong and Lake Yindarlgooda; a similar occurrence is located 6 km [3.73 miles] northeast in the Taurus group of mines; Bulong is 32.18 km [20 miles] east of Kalgoorlie; **Carnarvon Basin:** opalized wood of specimen quality rather than polishing quality, some containing abundant bivalve borings and similar to the "peanut wood" found at Gascoyne Junction, occurs near Kalbarri, north of the Murchison River on Murchison House Station; **Coolgardie:** thin slivers of black opal that are cut and mounted as doublets or triplets occur 4.8 km [2.98 miles] northeast of Coolgardie, which itself is 38.62 km [24 miles] southwest of Kalgoorlie; **Copperfield:** 128.72 km [80 miles] northwest of Kalgoorlie; **Cossack:** site of the first discovery of precious opal in Western Australia, 1860; 611.42 km [380 miles] northeast of Carnarvon; **Cowarna Station Homestead:** 13 miles east, at Mineral Claim 28/392; **Cranbrook:** opalized wood occurs at the base of the Stirling Range; **Cue:** striking red- and black-banded common opal; **Gabanintha:** bright green common opal occurs 30 km [18.6 miles] east of Nannine and 514.88 km [320 miles] east-southeast of Carnarvon; **Gascoyne Junction:** opalized black wood with marine bivalve borings infilled with white opaline silica is found here and on Mooka Station and is known locally as "peanut wood"; 178.6 km [111 miles] east of Carnarvon; **Gnowangerup:** opalized wood occurs 12 km [7.45 miles] north of Albany, at the base of the Stirling Range; **Grants Patch:** variously colored breccia opal occurs 10 km [6.2 miles] southeast of Ora Banda; **Iniagi Well:** small amounts of gem-quality opaline silica occur 1 km (0.62 mile) northwest and north of Meegea Hill; **Jutson's Rocks:** precious opal of a rich red-brown color and high translucency occurs 37 km [23 miles] northeast of Laverton, toward Jutson's Rocks; a 4-ct. piece was brilliant and flawless when cut about 1926, but after three years' storage it developed many cracks; **Kanowna:** 32.18 km [20 miles] north of Kalgoorlie; **Kennedy Range:** opalized black wood with marine bivalve (Teredo) at the southwestern end of the range; **Kookynie:** 152.86 km [95 miles] north of Kalgoorlie; **Marillana:** opaline silica is found in limestone and calcareous gravels in the center of a large outcrop of Oakover Formation, in a prospecting area 32 km [19.9 miles] east-northeast Marillana Homestead, in the valley of the Fortescue River; **Mooka:** Mooka Mine Area, 16 km [9.9 miles] east-northeast of Mooka Homestead; **Mundiwindi:** precious opal of rich red-brown color and high translucency on nodules up to 2 cm [0.79″] or more in diameter; 643.6 km [400 miles] east of Carnarvon; **Nannine:** occurrence of milk-white moss opal 40 km [24.8 miles] south of Meekatharra in the Nannine District; **Norseman:** white common opal and moss opal in colors ranging from opaque yellow (called "gold lace"), translucent green, opaque pale coffee-color, and opaque white; **Ongerup:** opalized wood occurs at the base of the Sterling Range; **Ora Banda:** scattered about on the surface on the west side of Black Flag Road are small angular pieces of common opal, ranging in color from white, brown and yellow to emerald green, 2 km [1.24 miles] west-southwest of town; **Paris:** at the Paris group of mines, massive yellow to mauve variegated opal; **Poole Range:** opalized wood occurs in the Kimberly Division; **Poona:** bright green chromiferous opal occurs in a glassy quartz vein on former ML 59/94; also common opal that is milk-white, grayish-white, dull green, and brown; 3 km [1.86 miles] east of Government Well, 434.43 km [270 miles] southeast of Carnarvon; **Quinn's:** 555.11 km [345 miles] southeast of Carnarvon; **Rothsay:** large masses of deep-green common opal, pigmented by chromium, occur 1 km [0.62 mile] north of the shaft of the main lode; **Smithfield:** precious opal of good rich color occurs in irregular masses and veinlets in an auriferous quartz, 10 km [6.2 miles] and 40.23 km [25 miles] northwest of Kalgoorlie; **Spargoville:** almost opaque golden to yellow moss opal; **Wadara Hills:** 458.57 km [285 miles] east-northeast of Carnarvon; **Westonia:** chromigerous green opal occurs a little north of the railway line between Merredin and Southern Cross, 241.35 km [150 miles] east-northeast of Perth; **Widgiemooltha:** bright red to black streaky common opal found here, and, a little distance eastward, large masses of silicified wood; **Yarra Yarra Creek:** 321.8 km [200 miles] southeast of Carnarvon; **Yundamindera:** extra fine fire opal in the form of nodules an inch or more in diameter, ranging from colorless to rich amber, with the best being identical to Mexican fire opal is found in deeply weathered granite breakaways, 10 km [6.2 miles] west-northwest of Yundamindera Homestead and 4 km [2.48 miles] northeast of Bulla Rocks Well; also, on this same station, 3 km [1.86 miles] north of Pyke Well, lace opal and honey opal are found in open-cut operations; Yundamindera is 185.04 km [115 miles] north-northeast of Kalgoorlie.

WISCONSIN (United States)

Thomas J. Evans, of the Mineral Resources and Mining Information Branch of the Wisconsin Geological and Natural History Survey at Madison, states that there is no known occurrence of opal in Wisconsin.

WYOMING (United States)

W. Dan Hausel, deputy director of the Wyoming Geological Survey at Laramie, lists five varieties of opal as occurring in the state of Wyoming—precious opal, common opal, geyserite (silicious sinter), moss opal, and a true fire opal that is lovely translucent bright red to yellow without POC. The Wyoming opal varieties, Dr. Hausel says, "occur in seams, as wood replacement, as deposits on and in hot spring cones and terraces near geysers, these deposits precipitated from silica-rich waters as fissure and void fillings in the Yellowstone and Absaroka volcanics; tuffaceous silty sedimentary Tertiary deposits in which the opal occurrence ranges from botryoidal to stalactitic to veins and seams." The geyserite occurs in a matrix of white tuffaceous sandstone. Dr. Hausel adds that these various varieties of opal "are associated with uranium, quartz, chalcedony, barite, red quartz, and monzonite. There is," he adds, "no mining of opal on a commercial scale, but a considerable amount of the opal is prospected for and mined recreationally." The precious opal may be transparent, translucent, or opaque, had a base coloration of transparent to milky white, yellow, brown, black, pink, green, cream, orange, or red, and the POC is predominantly intense blues, reds, yellows, in broad flashes and/or pinfire.

The specific locations Dr. Hausel lists are **Carbon County:** white precious opal was at one time found in limited quantity near the Pathfinder Reservoir; **Fremont County:** geyserite occurs in the tuffaceous Tertiary deposits of the Oligocene White River Formation along the Beaver Divide and in the northern part of the Hartville uplift, along the Sweetwater River in the Granite Mountains; precious opal with traces of uranium were reported in 1956 in Section 26, T33N, R90W, from the Vitro Uranium Company Pit in the middle to upper Eocene Wind River Formation in the Gas Hills area; **Natrona County:** white precious opal was at one time found in quantity near the Pathfinder Reservoir and in the Granite Mountains area along the Sweetwater River; **Park County:** precious opal has been found in the volcanics of Yellowstone National Park and in the Absaroka Range; **Sweetwater County:** precious opal is found with some degree of regularity in the vicinity of Cyclone Ridge; **Teton County:**

precious opal found in the volcanics of Yellowstone National Park and the Absaroka Range, as well as along Sage Hen Creek, Agate Lake and Jackson Lake; **Yellowstone County:** common opal, moss opal, and precious opal are found in the volcanics of Yellowstone National Park and the Absaroka Range; the common opal is particularly abundant in several locations, including Specimen Ridge and Amethyst Mountain; precious opal occurs in seams in the volcanics on the north flank of Mount Washburn; opalized wood (some with POC) is abundant in several areas of the park's petrified forest; it should be noted here that *no* rock and mineral collecting of any kind is permitted in Yellowstone National Park. **Other locations:** in Section 16, T42N, R60W, opal was found in 1956 in association with uranium mineralization in the Lower Cretaceous Fall River Formation, possibly on or near the Wicker-Baldwin property; opal associated with quartz and chalcedony in the tuffaceous silty sediments of the Oligocene White River Formation in conjunction with a series of northeast-southwest tending fault zones was discovered in 1955 and 1956 in Section 28, T32N, R69W, where these zones are silicified and form discontinuous sharp ridges up to 30 feet wide and are found throughout the south half of the township; precious opal was reported in 1966 in the northwest Section 2, T21N, R85W, along the northern edge of a shear zone in contact with red quartz monzonite, along with an associated pod of barite; an opal "sulfogel" closely associated with uranium mineralization was found on the Lucky Mac Property in Section 23, T33N, R90W; a particularly attractive clear moss opal and white common opal was found in 1989 in Section 32, T27N, R84W, from center of this Section on west side of Pathfinder Reservoir, the deposit appearing to occur in white tuffaceous sandstone of Miocene Split Rock Formation, with common white opal also reported from the same sedimentary unit east of Pathfinder Reservoir; in Section 32, T22N, R112, and 113W, an opal bench extends east–west across the bottom edge of these townships, with Quaternary sand on top of the Bridger Formation making up the bench: In northeast Section 21, T21N, R114W, Opal Springs is underlain by the Laney Shale Member of the Green River Formation and, though the name "Opal" is also found in Section 26 of this township, the source of these place names is not known.

YUGOSLAVIA

Predrag Srbljanovic, of the Geoinstitute in Belgrade, wrote to the author that, "First of all, I would like to point out that exploration of opal has not been carried out on a larger scale and that it wasn't mined commercially in Serbia. . . . Most interesting are the localities of Ramaca (near Ktagujevac), and Golesh (in Kosovo)." Dr. Srbljanovic went on to say there are three varieties of opal found in Yugoslavia, most important of which is the precious opal, which, in Serbia, is called blazing opal, and which has play of colors embracing the whole spectrum. There is also a semi-opal of hydrothermal origin, which fills cracks and pores in the andesitic volcanites of Kratovo-Zletovo region (Macedonia) and, finally, a chrysoprase of opal-chalcedonic composition, found in the weathering crusts of serpentized ultramafites in different spots in Serbia, as at Ljig, Vrnjacka banja, Pristina. These opal variations embrace such offshoots as brown-ocher opal, dendritic opal, and an abundance of common opal. They may be transparent, translucent, or opaque and usually, especially in the case of precious opal, have a base coloration of blue, gray, green, or yellow. The hydrothermal semi-opal, in addition to a cavity-filling material in andesitic volcanites, also regularly occurs in rounded kidneylike to grapelike nodules and in thin sheets. There are also relatively frequent precious opal occurrences as fillings in the internal cavities of irregularly shaped geodes, the base coloration of these opals colors ranging from red, gray, and dim blue to black. Matrix for the opal varieties includes chrysolite as hydrothermal amethyst in fissures of porphyric phenocrystals, as well as matrix of chrysoprase, crysopal and limonite. The opals are associated with amethyst, rock quartz, smoky quartz and chrysoprase.

None of the opal occurrences, according to Dr. Srbljanovic, are presently being mined. Throughout the country there are occurrences of common opals of typical conchoidal or uneven fracture; they are brittle and mulleable, have a glassy to greasy lustre, and fit the criteria of wax opals or resin opals. The colors of these common opals are diverse: light to dark green, brown, and rarely red, often multicolored or mottled varieties. The common opal is often intersected by veinlets of chalcedony, or contains irregularly scattered chalcedony geodes.

Among the Yugoslavian opal locations listed by Dr. Srbljanovic are **Bolija:** precious opal and semi-opal; **Boraca:** precious opals occur within the volcanogenic-intrusive complex but they are of insignificant nature except for the occurrence at Gornja Trepea; **Goles region:** an abundance of common opal occurs in association with crysopal and chrysoprase; **Golesh region:** milky-white dendritic opal and brown-ocher opal occur in the area of Mirena; **Klobucar:** brown common opal occurs abundantly in masses within the volcanic-intrusive complex of Novo Brdo; **Kosovska Kamenica:** opal–chalcedonic breccia occurs in the Crni Kamen locality; **Kratovo-Zletovo region:** both common and precious opal occur in the Macedonian deposits; **Krezenac;** precious opal and semi-opal are frequently found filling cracks and pores of volcanic andesites; **Lece region:** in the Bucomet area and at Kameno rebro, Vrtaca and Cvorovici, are found large amounts of Tertiary volcanic precious opal-chalcedonic masses, with base color ranging in a wide spectrum from white, light yellow, yellow, brown, and black, and POC in "iridescent" reds and greens as well as different combinations of colors and patterns and these are generally called "blazing opal" by miners; **Popina:** in this region are scattered occurrences of precious opal with morion (smoky quartz); **Ramaca region:** precious opal occurs at Dobraca (where there are large reserves of very heterogenous raw materials), Gaj, Lazine

[Gaj-Lazina], Ugljarevac, and Vuckovica; with all specimens found representing completely silicified (opalized) serpentinites; **Semedraz region;** high-quality precious opal has been noted from this area; **Serbia:** the precious opal here reportedly occurs "in various colors ranging from blue, gray, green, and yellow, up to brilliant red, often in different combinations, forming in this manner the so-called multicolored opal, particularly at Ramachka Glavica, a Ramacha village near Kragujevac"; **Shumadia district;** in 1981–1984, precious opal was discovered in the serpentinite zone during an exploration for semiprecious stones carried out by Geozavod, the Institute for Mineral Resources Investigations; **Strezovci region:** scattered occurrences of extraordinary precious opal-chalcedonia breccia that is ordinarily black, but occasionally green and blue colored; **Vuckovica:** common opal material that is light green in color, the veins themselves consisting of spherically shaped grains, although these veins occasionally swell to kidneylike masses that are occasionally intensively impregnated with limonite and around which occur radially shaped aggregates of elongated clear dolomite crystals of green shaded color.

YUKON TERRITORY (Canada)

The only reported occurrence of opal in Yukon Province is a common opal, specimens of which were collected in 1972 at an elevation of 1575' [480 m] on Porcupine Hill at the open-cut Clinton Creek Mine. Trevor J. Bremner, of the Exploration and Geological Services Division at Whitehorse states (31 January, 1995) that considerable common opal is known to exist in the Yukon but is unmined. Representative material occurs at the Clinton Creek Mine associated with serpentinite intruding schist, quartzite, gneiss and crystalline limestone—the common opal generally found near the surface of the pit and varying in color from pea-green to olive-green and from reddish-brown to darker brown, each background color mottled with tones of other colors. The deposit was discovered in 1957. It is located some 139.7 miles [225 km] south of the Arctic Circle at an elevation of 1580' [481.9 m] on Porcupine Hill, which overlooks Clinton Creek.

ZIMBABWE

It was reported in 1968 that precious opal had been discovered in southern Zimbabwe almost on the border of South Africa in the vicinity of Beit Bridge. However, in response to queries made in 1991, J. L. Orpen, director of the Department of Geological Survey, and A. E. Roberts, senior economic geologist at the Institute of Mining Research, both at Harare, refuted that report and replied that while common opal does occur in Zimbabwe, precious opal does not. The common opal occurs in dyke material and as wood opal in alluvial beds, both types varying from opaque to translucent and in color is milky-white, blue-green, and brown, frequently with these colors mixed in individual specimens. The dyke common opal is found in sandstone matrix in association with serpentinite, in the area of, and adjacent to, the Great Dyke. The wood opal occurs in numerous locations in the Petrified Forest of Zimbabwe Valley.

CONCLUDING NOTE

There were a fair number of countries, states, provinces, possessions, and other political entities that made no response whatever, either to the first query sent out to them or to subsequent queries sent over a five-year period. Opal may, of course, be present in some of these places, but the author has been unable to determine this. Among those countries not responding were the following: Albania, American Samoa, Andorra, Angola, Anguilla, Anhwei (China), Armenia, Aruba, Azerbaijan, Bahamas, Bahrain, Barbados, Belarus, Belize, Benin, Bermuda (United Kingdom), Bhutan, Bolivia, Bosnia, British Virgin Islands, Brunei, Burkina Faso, Caicos Islands (United Kingdom), Cambodia, Cameroon, Cape Verde, Cayman Islands (United Kingdom), Central African Republic, Chad, Chekiang (China), China (including Taiwan), Christmas Island (Australia), Cocos (Keeling) Islands (Australia), Comoros (excluding Mayotte), Congo, Cook Islands (New Zealand), Croatia, District of Columbia (United States), Djibouti, Dominica, Dominican Republic, Ecuador, Equatorial Guinea, Eritrea, Falkland Islands (United Kingdom), French Guiana, French Polynesia, Fukien (China), Futuna, Gabon, Gambia, Gaza Strip, Georgia (former USSR), Ghana, Gibralter (United Kingdom), Golan Heights, Grenada, Grenadines, Guadaloupe [including dependencies] (France), Guam (United States), Guernsey [including dependencies] (United Kingdom), Guinea, Guinea-Bissau, Guyana, Hainan (China), Haiti, Heilungkiang (China), Herzegovina, Honan (China), Hopeh (China), Hunan (China), Hupeh (China), Inner Mongolia (China), Iowa (United States), Iran, Isle of Man (United Kingdom), Jersey (United Kingdom), Jordan, Kansu (China), Kazakhstan, Kenya, Kiangsi (China), Kiangsu (China), Kiribati, Kirin (China), Korea (North), Kwangsi Chuang (China), Kwangtung (China), Kweichow (China), Kyrgyzstan, Laos, Latvia, Lebanon, Lesotho, Liaoning (China), Liberia, Liechtenstein, Lithuania, Macau (Portugal), Macedonia, Madagascar, Malawi, Maldives [including dependencies], Mayotte (France), Micronesia (Federated States of), Midway Islands (United States), Miquelon (France), Moldova, Monaco, Mongolia, Montserrat (United Kingdom), Myanmar, Nauru, Nebraska (United States), Netherlands Antilles, Nevis, New Caledonia (France), Niger, Nigeria, Ningsia Hui (China), Niue, Norfolk Island (Australia), North Cyprus, Northern Ireland (United Kingdom), Northern Mariana Islands, Oman, Palau, Panama, Paraguay, Peking (China), Pitcairn [including dependencies] (United

Kingdom), Principe, Qatar, Saint Helena [including dependencies] (United Kingdom), Saint Kitts, Saint Lucia, Saint Pierre (France), Saint Vincent, San Marino, Sao Tome, Saudi Arabia, Senegal, Seychelles, Shanghai (China), Shansi (China), Shantung (China), Shensi (China), Singapore, Sinkiang Uighur (China), Slovenia, Somalia, South Georgia (United Kingdom), South Sandwich Islands (United Kingdom), Spanish North Africa, Sri Lanka, Suriname, Syria, Szechwan (China), Tajikistan, Tibet (China), Tientsin (China), Tobago, Togo, Tokelau (New Zealand), Tonga, Tsinghai (China), Tunisia, Turkmenistan, Turks (United Kingdom), Tuvalu, Ukraine, United Arab Emirates, Uzibekistan, Vatican City, Vietnam, Virgin Islands (United States), Wake Island (United States), Wales (United Kingdom), Wallis, West Bank (including Jericho), Western Sahara, Western Samoa, Yemen, Yunnan (China), Zaire, and Zambia.

A Glossary of Opal-Related Terms

alluvial opal Any opal that has eroded out of the deposit in which it was originally formed and that may be found loose on the surface, in which circumstance it is called a "floater," or mixed in with the general detritus of the area.

amphibolite A dark-colored, coarse-grained rock consisting mainly of amphibole and plagioclase; a product of metamorphism of dolerite and basalt.

amorphous A mineral that has formed from a solidified gelatinous base and lacks true crystal structure, as in opal, obsidian (volcanic glass), and man-made glass.

auger A drilling system used primarily in Australia to prospect for opals. [See also Calweld drill.]

Back of Beyond, The A term formerly used to mean the vast desert country of interior Australia; synonymous with The Outback, The Bush, and The Never-Never.

ballroom An area of a tunnel (or drive) that has been widened into a extensive open room area as the result of a broadening search for opals in particularly productive area.

band, the, or bandstone See steel band.

basalt A hard, dark-colored, fine-grained, volcanic (igneous) rock, sometimes having vugs (gas pockets) in which precious opal has formed.

base color The pervasive general background color of an opal irrespective of the amount or pattern of POC it exhibits; also called basic color or body color.

basic color Synonymous with base color.

belemnite A fossilized squidlike creature that had tentacles similar to the modern-day squid, but the body of which was encased in a long, conical tube that in some cases filled with precious opal in the fossilization process, or in some cases metamorphosed into opal, and that are occasionally found at Coober Pedy in Southern Australia, where they are often incorrectly called pipe opal.

bentonite A crystalline kaolinite mineral that is a highly plastic, colloidal, swelling clay formed from altered volcanic ash (first described as occurring in the Fort Benton Formation in Wyoming), and that, in a more refined state that is richer in aluminum, is called montmorillonite—the species of volcanic tuff or clay in which precious opal forms.

blob A pancake-shaped piece of rough opal common to Andamooka that is similar to the Lightning Ridge nobby except for being flatter and rounder.

body color Synonymous with base color.

boulder doublet A two-part cut stone usually fashioned from thin precious opal or precious opalized shells that are epoxied to an ironstone backing.

boulder splits The matching halves of a boulder opal that has split in half along an opal vein line; if the exposed surfaces are made up mostly of precious opal with good POC, the matching halves can be quite valuable.

breccia A sedimentary rock in which the coarse-grained fraction is of broken angular fragments.

brightness The intensity of the fiery flashes of POC exhibited by a precious opal. [See also intensity of fire.]

broad flashfire pattern Alternative name for broadflash opal pattern.

Bush, The A term used to mean the vast desert country of interior Australia; synonymous with The Outback, The Bush, The Back of Beyond, and The Never-Never.

cabochon An unfaceted cut gemstone of domed, flat, or convex form.

Calweld Drill A mechanized, extendable, broad-diameter auger to drill holes as shafts by which to reach subterranean opal dirt levels; capable of drilling to depths exceeding 100 feet [30 m]; drills holes usually 30″ or 36″ in diameter.

cantera Spanish term meaning ore.

cantera limpia The Spanish term meaning "clean ore" and applied to a material that is partly volcanic rock matrix and partly precious opal, which is cut, carved, and polished into the shapes of living creatures or simple cabochons and provide attractive, inexpensive precious opal gemstones. Also called *cantera pulida,* meaning "polished ore."

capped doublet A form of doublet constructed with a cap but without backing material. [See doublet.]

carat A measure of gemstone weight: 5 carats equal one gram; 141.75 carats equal one ounce.

chatoyancy Commonly known as the cat's-eye effect; silky sheen which is concentrated in a band of light that changes its position as the mineral is turned; occurs in such stones as cat's-eye and tiger's-eye.

cheaps Inexpensive opal rough; the least valuable opals in a find or a parcel.

Chinese hat A nobby (nodule) of rough opal that has an outer form resembling a Chinese coolie hat.

chips Small pieces of bright precious opal, too small to reasonably be cut into gemstones but often purchased by cutters in Hong Kong and elsewhere in the Orient for decorative or secondary use in other jewelry.

claiming The American term for staking out a claim for mining; synonymous with the Australian term, pegging.

clarity The quality and degree of transparency in an opal.

classer On the Australian opal fields, this is an expert in rough opal value who prices a miner's opal and who may help separate it into priced parcels for sale.

clay See kaolinite.

clearing the field Australian term for buying at any given time all the available rough opal on a field.

cobwebs Threadlike impurities in opal, giving the appearance of cobwebs or open-weave knitting.

color band See color bar.

color bar Also called color band or line of color. A layer of color in precious opal that differs from the color layers that adjoin it above or below, or that separates the precious opal from common opal. [See also color separation line.]

color separation line A fine line of color variation in precious opal where different colors adjoin; often mistaken for a crack by the inexperienced. The line of adjoinment usually not as straight or level as with a color bar. See also structure line.

copi Alternative spelling for kopi; alternative term for kaolinite.

concrete Common terminology for a clay that has been cemented together naturally with opal, either common or precious; also a very soft and porous matrix opal mined at the Andamooka opal field in South Australia. It is often dyed dark to simulate black opal.

consistency A general sameness in all the important characteristics of an opal, including color, pattern, intensity of fire, density of background, and color of background.

Coober Pedy One of the foremost precious opal fields of Australia, this one located in the state of South Australia and famous for the large quantities of high-quality light opal mined here. The name stems from the dialectic aboriginal term *kupa piti,* meaning "boy's waterhole," referring to the discovery made by Willie Hutchison here at the same time he discovered the opals in 1915—the discovery of the water being of far more importance to the aboriginals than the discovery of the opals. Some sources claim the name means "white man in the ground" and alludes to white miners who not only work underground but also, in an effort to escape the heat, live in underground dugouts.

costean A shallow pit or trench that has been excavated to expose opals (or any other specific rocks of interest.)

cotton A threadlike impurity in precious opal.

cottoning Term for a phenomenon in which a piece of boulder opal that is opened has intensely fiery transparent opal veins inside, but within a few days that opal turns opaque white and loses its POC.

coyotes A derisive term applied by locals to intermediate buyers who appear at intervals during the week at the Mexican opal mines before the major buyers fly in to make their large purchases on the weekends; the "coyotes" buy up the stones of lesser value, including those collected by the pepinadores and usually leave by Friday.

crack A fracture in opal that greatly reduces the value of the gemstone.

crazing Also called checking. The process of a series or network of fine cracks appearing spontaneously in opal, especially in precious opal, both in rough opal or cut stones; a process that can, if the crazing continues, cause the stone to disintegrate. Such crazing is usually attributed to accelerated drying, resulting in the loss of internal moisture, which, many believe, causes a weakening in the alignment of the molecules of which the opal is constructed. Such crazing also results from intense light and equally from excessive heat occurring within the stone during the cutting process. Crazing often affects only the surface or near-surface of the stone and can sometimes be peeled away, as opposed to cracking, which runs more deeply through the stone.

crystal A homogenous mineral body which has plane and often lustrous faces and which shows a regularity in its arrangement; a particular crystal shape is characteristic of that mineral.

cut The quality and specific shape into which an opal has been cut and polished; the act of cutting or shaping an opal.

cutting Actually a misnomer, since there is little actual cutting of opal, as with a saw, in fashioning it into a finished stone; cutting refers to the process of rough-shaping an opal through coarse grinding, then sanding it to the finished smooth shape, and, finally, polishing it to a high luster.

decrepitation The action of breaking up, or otherwise fracturing, when a mineral such as opal is heated.

diatomaceous earth   Also known as diatomite; a light, friable siliceous material resembling chalk that is derived chiefly from the remains of diatoms—one-celled algae; used as a fine polishing abrasive, a filtering substance, an absorbent, and as a filler in various paints and plastics.

diffraction   The breaking up of a beam of white light into its individual spectral colors.

directionality of fire   The degree to which an opal's fire retains its POC and overall brilliance when viewed from different angles.

dolerite   A dark-colored, medium-grained igneous rock which commonly cuts across other rocks in tabular-shaped intrusive masses.

dome   The curved face arching across the surface of an opal cabochon; may be classed as high dome, medium dome, and low (or flat) dome.

dominant color   The color most apparent in the POC of any particular opal.

doublet   A thin layer of precious opal (normally light opal or transparent opal) that is cemented to a thicker backing that will help prevent its breaking, the opal itself forming a carefully polished veneer over the protective backing, which may be potch (common opal), basinite, obsidian, black onyx, black (or dark) glass, plastic, or other material more sturdy than the precious opal itself. A doublet is constructed not only to safeguard a piece of opal too thin to be used as a solid opal on its own, but also to simulate black opal by cementing transparent or thin light translucent opal to a dark backing material. In times past, when the backing was a natural material, such as potch or basinite, the finished stone was called a "true doublet"; when constructed with man-made backing material such as glass or plastic, the stone was called a "false doublet." Such terms are rarely used in present times. On rare occasions, a doublet may be constructed where the thin opal slice is cemented to the underside of a domed quartz cap with no other backing, and this is called a capped doublet. [See also triplet.]

drive   A mining tunnel that is usually a horizontal (or slightly angled) underground excavation, normally extending outward in an opal level from a vertical shaft, but sometimes following an emergent opal level horizontally (or nearly so) into a slope, hillside, or mountainside; in essence, a tunnel driven along the trend of the reef.

duffer   An unproductive opal hole, shaft, tunnel, claim, or mine.

fault   A distinct break in the ground usually associated with earth movement and usually showing a displacement of a certain stratum to a greater or lesser degree; considered an indicator for the presence of opal; also called a slide or slip.

field   See opal field.

fire   Common term for the diffracted play of color (POC) in a precious opal, providing a single color, two or three colors, or a whole spectrum of color combinations. Sometimes referred to as fire color.

fire pattern   See pattern.

flaw   Any mark, crack, inclusion, mist, or impurity within a precious opal that diminishes the value of the stone.

floaters   See alluvial opal.

fluorescent opal   Opal, either precious or common, that, when exposed to ultraviolet light, glows brightly with a different color than is seem under daylight or ordinary artificial light.

fossicking   Australian term meaning the searching for minerals (usually opals) and/or fossils (often opalized) as a recreation on the surface of debris removed from mines and dumped in piles of tailings called mullock heaps. The term may also embrace general surface fossil hunting or prospecting. In New South Wales, a permit is required for fossicking. Usually fossicking may be done only without the use of tools, whereas tool use is permitted in noodling.

fuller's earth This material has been described as "any clay which has an adequate decolorizing and purifying capacity to be used commercially in oil refining without chemical treatment"; fuller's earth is composed of attapulgite, kaolinite, or minerals of the montmorillonite group; the U.S. Bureau of Mines reports production and use of fuller's earth separately from bentonite in the *Minerals Yearbook,* although it is sometimes difficult to make a distinction between the two types of clay.

gambusinos Spanish term for miners, especially those miners employed in the Mexican mines, who removed the opal-bearing rhyolitic host material from the blast zones with a rock hammer.

ghost opal A term used primarily in Virgin Valley, Nevada, in reference to what is called elsewhere, phantom opal—opal that creates a ghostly image of itself within or outside of itself. [See phantom opal.]

gibbers Term used by Australian opal miners to designate weather-worn siliceous stones that are reddish-gray in color, rounded, and usually about the size of an average man's fist.

ginger whiskers A term usually meaning thin, rust-colored imperfections in precious opal; such imperfections are often associated with cracks.

glory hole Any place in an opal level where a number of good opals are found more or less clustered together, the term more commonly used in United States mining than Australian.

gneiss (pronounced "nice") An igneous rock that is characterized by being light-colored, coarse-grained, and primarily composed of quartz, feldspar, and mica; usually formed in large masses.

gouger An Australian term formerly applied to the opal miner as he used hand tools to "gouge" opals out of the clay and sandstone in his mine, but this is a term rarely used at present; modern miners are normally called "diggers," not "gougers."

Grawin An opal field near Lightning Ridge which has produced some very nice precious opals, often with gray base coloration.

gypsum A mineral often found as an impurity in precious opal (especially in Australia) and which, in a needlelike crystal, may penetrate entirely through the stone and, as such may be referred to as kopi.

hectorite A clay mineral similar to montmorillonite, but instead of being rich in aluminum, it is a magnesia- and lithia-rich species.

humpy Australian slang for a hutlike makeshift living quarters used by a miner in the field. Sometimes spelled humpie.

Icelandic agate See Icelandic opal.

Icelandic opal An alternative term for the siliceous sinter that coats rocks in and near thermal springs or vents in Iceland.

ikaite A mineral that forms and crystallizes into bladed clusters in frigid submarine conditions and that disintegrates within moments of being exposed to air or warmer water; the mineral that is the basis for the pseudomorphic opal pineapples found at White Cliffs opal field in New South Wales.

imperfection Any inclusion, mist, crack, crazing, or anything else that diminishes the value of a precious opal.

impurity Any foreign material, such as a sand spot or gypsum needle, that appears in precious opal and diminishes its value.

inclusion A nonopal material or common opal within a precious opal.

intarsia An artistic piece of worked opal or jewelry in which precious opal and other gem materials are fitted together with great exactitude in an intricate and very pleasing geometrical design.

intensity of fire The brightness of the POC in any given piece of precious opal. [See also brightness.]

ironstone Australian term for the very hard, dark brown, ferruginous sandstone that occurs particularly in Queensland, on and in which precious opal is found in the form of boulder opal.

kaolinite The clay in which sedimentary Australian opal forms, though not limited to Australia. Also sometimes incorrectly called kopi.

kieselguhr See diatomaceous earth.

knobby Synonymous with nobby.

kopi Sometimes spelled copi. Generally, gypsum in one or more of several forms: (1) at Lightning Ridge the term refers to certain significantly flattened selenite crystals; (2) at Andamooka it refers to a light-colored (often pure white) earthy clay of which a principal constituent is gypsum; (3) most frequently elsewhere in Australia and around the world it refers to a white impurity in opal that appears as needlelike fibrous crystals with a silky lustre formed of the variety of gypsum known as satin spar; (4) sometimes used incorrectly to mean kaolinite.

level A horizontal or near-horizontal stratum or layer associated with opal formation.

Lightning Ridge One of the premiere opal fields in all of Australia; located in the state of New South Wales near the Queensland border. Producer of the majority of the world's finest black opals. Lightning Ridge opals characteristically exhibit a base coloration ranging from dark gray to black.

line of color Precious opal flashes formed in nature in an individual piece of opal or within an opal seam as one or more relatively straight lines where one color is separated from another or from common opal. [See also color bar.]

lineaments In Australia, these are ground surface indicators of fault lines, which, in turn, may be indicators of the presence of precious opal deposits.

lousing Searching for accidentally discarded opals in the mullock heaps in Australia; synonymous with "noodling."

mafic Descriptive of an igneous rock consisting mainly of dark-colored minerals, the word derived from a combination of magnesium and ferric.

matrix of opal The mother rock in which opal is found and which encloses the opal forming in it; in volcanic deposits, this matrix is usually rhyolite or basalt; in sedimentary opal it is usually montmorillonite clays or sandstones. Not the same as matrix opal.

mineral jelly A naturally occurring form of silica gel.

Miner's Right A Provision of the Australian Mining Act which makes it legal for any person, on payment of a very minimal yearly fee, to peg out a claim, after which, any mineral or gemstone recovered on this claim while the Miner's Right is in effect becomes the personal property of the miner.

Mintabie One of the most important opal fields in South Australia.

monkey A shaft in the floor of a mine, dug to connect two different opal levels or to search downward for a new opal layer, but which does not go through the roof of a drive to the surface.

montmorillonite A fine-grained aluminum magnesium silicate clay mineral in which opal is prone to form, particularly precious opal. A form of kaolinite, montmorillonite was first described from Montmorillon, France, in 1847 by Damout and Salvetat, although a similar clay material had been known since 1788 as smectite or smectis. Most deposits of montmorillonite are derived from volcanic ash and rocks, usually pyroclastic materials of Tertiary or Quaternary Age, and an igneous nature is normally retained by the clay, which hampers the growth of vegetation and which effectively resists erosion, as can be seen by the many well-rounded knolls of montmorillonite that occur in the American West, especially in Nevada and Utah, but only in the foothill regions of the mountains rather than at higher elevations. In addition to being the source mineral for much of the world's precious opal, montmorillonite clay is a valuable mineral resource with a multitude of industrial uses, notably in foundry molding sands, rotary-drilling muds, iron-ore concentrate pelletizing, and oil refining, as well as uses as a binder of animal feeds in pellet form, in insulation, as a plasticizing agent in cement and grout, and similarly in brick, sewer-pipe, ceramic, and refractory mixes, as a thickener in fire-retardant slurries dropped from aircraft and as both thickener and stabilizer of latex and rubber adhesives, to say nothing of more refined uses as a thickening, suspending, and absorptive ingredient in medicines, pharmaceuticals, and cosmetics, as a gelling agent in greases and lubricants, as a suspending and thixotropic agent in water- and oil-base paints, porcelain enamels, and glazes, as an emulsifying agent and detergent in soaps, as a strong absorbent of oil or grease on floors, and equally as an absorbent in animal bedding and for animal sanitation, as a food supplement for poultry and domestic stock, as a clarifying and purifying material for wines, other beverages, and domestic water, and as a filler in paper to absorb wood pitch and improve printability . . . and other uses that are rapidly being developed.

mosaic opal doublet A form of doublet where small pieces of opal are fitted together to form a geometric pattern or a picture on a piece of backing material, usually black, covering the face of the stone.

mosaic opal triplet A picture created by pieces of opal glued onto a backing (usually black) and covered over with a clear quartz dome or, sometimes, a specially painted glass.

mullock Waste rock and debris, usually from mining activities, that is normally dumped in piles or heaps outside the mine.

Never-Never A term formerly used to mean the vast desert country of interior Australia; synonymous with The Outback, The Bush, and The Back of Beyond.

nobby A small nodule of rough opal, ranging in size from pea to (more commonly) walnut, usually round or only slightly elongated on one side, and usually with a dull crust or skin, within which may be potch that is gray or black, and possibly some gem-quality precious opal. Ideally, the nobby interior should be largely black potch through which is a line of precious opal and, when the stone is ground down to that line on one side, the potch forming the underside provides the background for a fine black opal; even better, occasionally the line of precious opal can be thick enough to be split and then a fine black opal can be cut from each half. Derivation of nobby (plural is nobbies) is unclear, though the most accepted belief is that it stemmed from nodule. Some insist it derived from the Cockney word nobby, which implies stylish, smart, or showy. Nobbies are thought by some to show evidence of being fossil remains of aquatic seed pods, but others claim this is absolutely untrue. Nobbies rarely exceed a diameter of 2 inches [50.8 mm], whereas nodules are generally larger, more oblong in shape, and with a surface more uneven than a nobby, and nodules are apparently merely lumps of potch or potch-and-color that are apparently not fossil related. Nobby has also erroneously been written as knobby. While the nobby is essentially thought of by many as being exclusive only to Lightning Ridge in New South Wales, a similar type of nodule, usually called a "pebble," is found in some of the workings at the Royal Peacock claims in Virgin Valley, Nevada.

nodule Rounded lump of opal of an irregular shape.

nontronite a clay mineral similar to montmorillonite, but instead of being rich in aluminum, it is an iron-rich species.

noodling The act of searching with hand tools, screens, and the like through heaps of rejected mining material for precious opal that may have been inadvertently discarded. The term is said to derive from nodules, the lumps of material often composed of precious opal, a word that was supposedly corrupted to "noodles" and, thus, looking for opals became "noodling." Originally, when noodling was done primarily by women and children, the term was used rather contemptuously, but that no longer applies. Synonymous with "lousing," noodling is not the same as fossicking, in which the use of tools is not permitted.

opal brightness kit A kit designed for opal buyers (and sometimes used by jewelers) that contains a set of opals of various brightness for use as a standard against which the brightness of any particular opal may be measured and its carat value more accurately established.

opal dirt The material comprising the layer (or stratum) in which opal occurs naturally; in Australia this is usually a relatively soft sandstone and in Virgin Valley it is a dense greenish-gray montmorillonite clay when moist and light gray to tan when dry.

opal field A contiguous area of varying size and/or extent where opal occurs naturally and is mined; a major opal field, such as Lightning Ridge, may take in a number of minor or smaller opal fields (or workings), such as Three Mile, Six Mile, New Chum, Bald Hill, Hawk's Nest, Grawin, and Glengarry.

opal layer A stratum of opal dirt which is usually horizontal in Australia and located directly beneath a hard layer variously called the steel band, the bandstone, or merely the band; also a stratum of opal dirt which, more often than not, angles downward from the horizontal in Virgin Valley.

opalescent A term commonly used (and much abused) in describing any gem material in which vague bluish to pinkish light plays back and forth as the specimen is turned. The term was derived from opal, but widely and erroneously used to describe the fluctuating and/or iridescent bands or stars of colors or white light reflected from the moonstone feldspars (better described as adularescence), the coloration of mother-of-pearl iridescence (better described as nacreous), and the chatoyancy in chrysoberyl, tiger-eye, cat's-eye, etc.

opalized fossils Fossil wood, shells, teeth, bones, invertebrate, and vertebrate creatures that have been changed into opal by the chemical action of ground waters percolating through siliceous deposits, causing the organic remains to become opalized rather than merely petrified. A large proportion of these consist of common opal, but precious opal does occur as well and such pieces can be very valuable, both from a paleontological standpoint and as precious gemstones.

open cut An opal mining method in which a large open pit is dug by a bulldozer to reach and then follow the opal level.

orange peel A term to describe a certain poorly finished opal surface, in which the finished opal shows on its surface a series of indentations resembling those found on the skin of an orange.

Outback, The A term used to mean the vast desert country of interior Australia; synonymous with Back of the Beyond, The Bush, and The Never-Never.

parcel A packet of opals within a specific type range and price range, made up by sellers on the field and useful to miners and buyers alike in assuring the sale of inferior quality opals along with those of greater quality, to stabilize the market and keep prices within reason.

pastelite Unofficial name applied to both common opal and chalcedony of similar colors and which similarly fluoresce a bright chartreuse color under shortwave ultraviolet light.

pattern The distribution of the POC in a precious opal, as to the mixture, size, and positioning; many patterns occur frequently enough that they are known by specific names, such as harlequin, pinfire, and broadflash. Such patterns are a very important factor in the ultimate value of precious opal. [See also rare pattern.]

pegging The Australian term for staking out a claim for mining; synonymous with the American term, claiming.

pegging party In Australia, the rush to stake claims adjacent to an area where a good opal discovery has been made. Synonymous with rush.

pepinadores Spanish term meaning "breakers" and referring to the large number of Mexican mine workers who use hand tools to break up large blocks of dynamited rhyolite and expose the opal embedded in vugs and pockets, for which service their only wage is the right to take the smaller waste pieces of matrix from the mine and further break them up in the hope of finding previously undiscovered vugs or small pockets filled with precious opal.

petrified wood Wood that, through fossilization, has turned to stone, not necessarily opal.

phantom opal A term used in reference to opal that displays a ghostly image of itself within or outside of itself. Called ghost opal in Virgin Valley.

pillar In a drive, this is an upright section of the opal dirt that is left standing in place from floor to ceiling in a sort of pillar formation, to act as a support for the roof of the tunnel.

pintas (1) A term used in Latin American countries to describe the small bright "indicators" of color in the rocks on the surface that signify opal presence in certain localities; (2) Mexican name for a pattern of bright specks of color, that pattern about the same as pinfire opal, except that in Mexico the term is sometimes applied to stones where the points of light are larger than pinpoints.

plant A cache of opals hidden (usually buried in a tin or sturdy pouch of canvas or leather) by an Australian miner for safekeeping. [See also springing a plant.]

play of color The characteristic that makes precious opal differ from common opal; it is that phenomenon in precious opal of exhibiting scintillating iridescent colors in one or more of a variety of patterns, appearing, disappearing, shifting, and moving as bands, patches, streaks, geometric figures, lines, smudges, blotches, fogs, flashes, and pinpoints. For the sake of convenience and brevity, often throughout this work the author has taken the liberty of using the term POC as an acronym to signify combined play of color and play of pattern.

POC See play of color.

polishing See cutting.

porcelainite A fused white clay that is not a form of opal but rather a porcelain–jasper, or gypsite.

puffball A ball of pumicelike material ranging from fist-size to several feet in diameter, occurring in the opal level and thought by many to be an indicator for the presence of opals to the sides or directly beneath the ball (Figure 57). Common in the mines of Virgin Valley.

rare pattern A rare or unusual pattern of POC, which does not readily fit under a specified pattern type. [See also pattern.]

refraction The deflection of a ray of light when passing obliquely out of a substance.

rotten stone A powdery polishing compound formed naturally by the weathering of siliceous limestones.

rough opal Opal of any kind in its natural, unpolished state; uncut opal.

rubbing The process of gently grinding down the exterior of a rough opal to get an idea of its interior opal content and position in order to plan the subsequent cutting.

rush The action that occurs when a new find of opal becomes known (even though most miners will try to keep it secret as long as possible) and a large number of the miners in the area leave the claims upon which they are working and rush to peg out new claims adjacent (or at least close) to where the new opal discovery has been made.

saponite A clay mineral similar to montmorillonite, but instead of being rich in aluminum, it is a magnesia-rich species.

self-tipper A large mining bucket which, when filled with mining waste at the bottom of the shaft, automatically rises to the surface where it also automatically dumps the mine waste and then descends to the shaft bottom to once again be filled.

sheen Alternative term for especially wide broadflash in opal, where the flash of color may be broad enough to cover the whole surface of the stone or may nearly do so but be surrounded by one or more of other POC; a type of color display often found in the opals from the Spencer Opal Mine in Idaho.

shell doublet An opal doublet in which the precious opal originates from opalized clamshell. [See also solid shell.]

silica gel The chemical name for opaline silica manufactured by man.

slide See slip.

slip A fault line that is vertical or near-vertical and that displaces the level; very often considered an indicator for the presence of opal. Often called (especially in Australian mines) a slippery-back.

slippery-back See slip.

snide A term used in Queensland, Australia to designate worthless common opal; synonymous with the term "potch" used elsewhere in Australia.

soak A place, natural or artificial, where an opal miner could find water to sustain himself while he mined, even though he might have to carry it long distances.

solid shell A fossil shell, often a bivalve, that has become filled with precious opal. If this piece is fashioned into a doublet, it is then called a shell doublet.

specking Looking for previously undiscovered specks of "color" on mullock heaps, dumps, or tailings in the opal fields, particularly when those specks are newly exposed after a rain has washed the opal clean of dust; or noodling for opal through mine debris that has just newly been brought to the surface and dumped.

spider A piece of wire (often fencing wire) that has been bent into a candle-holder on one end and a sharpened point on the other, which can be stuck into the wall of a mine and a candle thus held stationary as a sort of sconce that becomes an underground light source to illuminate a work area.

Figure 57. The author while digging in the montmorillonite clay opal level at the Northern Lights Mine in Virgin Valley, June 1995, (1) encountered a so-called puffball (the oblong light spot of pumicelike material), which is believed by some to be an indicator of the presence of opal. Having dug away the puffball and continued digging, (2) the author encountered a section of log containing pockets of precious opal. When a section of the log was freed, (3) it was pulpy wood on the large end but opalized on the pointed end, and contained (4) both black opal and light opal. The remainder of the log broke apart as excavation continued, but there were (5) several good pockets of black opal in the surrounding clay. (Photos by Alan A. Vogel)

Figure 57 *(Continued)*

Figure 57 *(Continued)*

split-face boulder A boulder opal that has been split at the seam to expose opal on both sides of the split seam.

spotters People who follow behind a bulldozer engaged in open-cut mining and search for precious opal exposed by the equipment.

springing a plant The act of a miner moving out to retrieve a cache of opals from where he has hidden it.

spud-bag A cloth sack used to put opals into that have been found; such cloths are usually folded and used by miners to kneel upon while digging until opal is found, then the floor area cleared of debris and the cloth spread open to safely catch whatever opals may be dislodged from the wall and drop before they can be caught.

steel band, the A hard band of stratum seldom exceeding a foot in thickness, this band occurring directly over the opal level in most sedimentary opal deposits; also known as the bandstone or simply the band. Because the soft layer of "opal dirt" almost always underlies the steel band, the Australian opal miner usually finds the steel band is the roof of his drive. At Lightning Ridge the steel band is a very hard sandstone and often dark gray, but elsewhere it may vary from light beige to nearly white. Some patches of it have precious opal in small cracks or veins, or even simply between the grains of sand, so that a delicate suffused glow or flush of opal colors may be seen over the whole surface. Where suitable cracks occur, it closely corresponds to the modern meaning of angel stone, which is precious opal in baked, cracked clay, while the original meaning, the steel band of today, applies to cracked hard sandstone. Thus, when similar cracking occurs, the two materials resemble each other, which may account for the same name being used for two different kinds of bands, one in smooth white clay and the other in coarse and gritty sandstone.

structure lines Lines in an opal where the internal structure of an opal, its size, and/or alignment of the silica spheres has changed; often erroneously mistaken for a crack. Where such a structure line affects mainly the color, as a change from one band of color to another, it is called a line of separation.

tailings The waste from mines that is deposited outside the mine in piles or spread out by heavy equipment; also, mainly in Australia, called mullock.

tops (1) The highest-quality portion of the opal found in a specific location; (2) the highest-quality parcels in multiple opal parcels.

traces Tiny isolated bits, often hardly more than pinpoints, of opal in the opal level, which may be indicators of concentrations of precious opal nearby; similar traces include very thin lines of precious opal in the opal level.

tribute system An early opal mining system in Australia under which a land syndicate would lease opal mining rights on a particular claim to a miner in exchange for that miner paying to the syndicate a "tribute" of 50% of whatever opals he dug.

tributors Former term for miners in the early days of Australian opal mining who worked their claim on the tribute system.

triplet A thin slice of light opal attached to a black background with a protective crystal (usually a clear quartz dome) glued to the top as a protective cap, forming a sort of three-layer sandwich. The layer of precious opal may in some cases be thinner than a piece of tissue paper (Color Plate 20). Triplets have in some instances been called triplex.

triplex Synonymous with triplet.

tripolite An infusorial earth, often called diatomite, which occurs in vast beds of the minute siliceous skeletal remains of simple freshwater and saltwater plants called diatoms; also called diatomaceous earth.

tuff A rock formed of compacted fine ash and other debris initially deposited by explosive volcanic action.

value The market price for any given opal or parcel of opals as established and agreed upon by a buyer and seller. In gem-quality opal, the value is usually established as its worth per carat; in boulder opal, the value is generally established by the finished piece.

vermiculite A clay mineral related to montmorillonite, of which opal is formed by the alteration of certain silicate minerals.

vesicle A small round cavity in a volcanic rock; the cavity is actually a pocket formed by the entrapment of a gas bubble during solidification of the lava.

weight (1) The weight of a cut opal, usually measured in carats; (2) the weight of a parcel of opal rough, usually measured in grams or ounces.

White Cliffs One of the very first major opal fields discovered in Australia. Located in the state of New South Wales near the famous Broken Hill Mines, White Cliffs was noted for its production of quality light opals and the abundance of fossils found there, many of which (including the famous "pineapples") were partially or wholly opalized. This opal field enjoyed its greatest boom from about 1890 to 1905. Though sporadic finds of opal have occurred through the years since then, the field is considered played out insofar as commercial production is concerned and has been designated a hobby field.

windlass A hand winch comprising a supported axle spanning the mouth of a shaft, with a rope or cable wound about that axle, and a bucket for debris, tools, etc., attached to the outer end of the line and capable of being lowered to the bottom of the shaft, or lifted to the top.

Notes

FOREWORD

1. There are those who would today add to the list of stones considered precious (as opposed to semiprecious) the gemstones alexandrite, tanzanite, and pearl.
2. Pliny's *Natural History* is the most important source of information about gemstones and minerals in ancient times. At least 222 editions of the work have appeared and, of course, a number of variations of the translation of this passage occur in the literature. The one quoted here is the first English translation, by the scholar Philomen Holland in 1601.

CHAPTER 1

1. *Nano*-signifies a one-billionth part; ergo, a nanometer is the one-billionth part of a meter.
2. Technically speaking, when the silica spheres are less than 200 nm and are correctly stacked, they will still diffract light, but not in the white wave lengths that human eyes detect; in many cases, under ultraviolet light that "invisible" color may become visible.
3. A phenomenon called opalescence frequently occurs in transparent common opal, which, when exposed to light on one side, will display a milky to bluish coloration on that side and a yellowish to reddish color on the other side, but this particular phenomenon has no connection with the POC of gem-quality opal.
4. Oddly enough, for reasons not yet fully understood, precious opal in some areas will fluoresce, while that from others will not. In the case of Australian opal, for example, the precious opal from Andamooka will normally fluoresce; a fair portion of the precious opal from Coober Pedy will fluoresce, a meager amount of Queensland precious opal will fluoresce, and virtually none of the precious opal from Lightning Ridge will fluoresce.
5. In regard to cleavage planes in precious opal or potch, opal expert Len Cram told me that "Common potch doesn't have a cleavage plane because of the shape and arrangement of the spheres, but precious opal does. The perfect stacking of the spheres in precious opal not only creates color, it also creates planes of cleavage. The proof is simple. Without it you would never be able to split beautiful seams of thin boulder into such lovely faces of such clean opal and, as you know, most of these pieces are split with a tomahawk. The blow follows the line of least resistance, straight down the center of the opal, which has to be a cleavage plane. If there was no cleavage plane, it would just shatter into pieces."

6. Opal pseudomorphs of fossil animal material—shells, belemnites, plesiosaurs, etc.—are not uncommon at such fields in Australia as White Cliffs, Lightning Ridge, and Coober Pedy. In the western United States—in Washington, Oregon, Idaho, and Nevada—fossil forests exist where opalized tree trunks and limbs of considerable size occur. In Virgin Valley, Nevada, whole limb sections are found that have been entirely morphized to precious opal.

7. Two closely related types of opal, hydrophane and cachalong, are so porous that they are a light opaque or light translucent color when dry but become entirely transparent in mere minutes upon being immersed in water (see Color Plate 6)

CHAPTER 2

1. In at least one case at Lightning Ridge, a piece of wood was found of which one end was soft and woody, while the other end, that had extended into an opal dirt level, had become well opalized. There have been several cases where fenceposts erected across an opal field have had their buried portions turned into opal within a period as short as 20 years. Similar occurrences of fossil branches, limbs and even logs are found not uncommonly at Virgin Valley, where one end is soft and pulpy, the middle portion petrified and the other end has pseudomorphosed into precious opal.

2. Keith Hodson, owner of the Rainbow Ridge Opal Mine of Virgin Valley, Nevada, showed the author a jar in which he stored some of his opals in water for a long time and the interior of that jar is now evenly coated with a fine film of very colorful precious opal, obviously the product of a spontaneous electrolytic action and resultant ion exchange.

3. Sanders and Darragh had even earlier, in 1965, published a very important scientific paper based on extensive investigations into the microstructure and origin of precious opal, investigations assigned to them by their superior, E. Ralph Segnit of Deakin University near Melbourne. In their paper, entitled "The Origin of Color in Opal Based Upon Electron Microscopy," they showed, through electron microscopy of some Andamooka Opal, for the first time and conclusively, how color in precious opal is caused by light passing through and around a neat lattice-like arrangement of submicroscopic spheres, finally putting to rest the multitude of then-existing theories erroneously describing how the color phenomenon in precious opal occurred.

4. John V. Sanders, the only person to whom Len Cram revealed the secret of his process and the type of electrolyte used, died only a short time after his visit with Cram and, so far as Cram knows, never revealed the secret to anyone.

CHAPTER 3

1. It is likely that prior to World War I, Mr. Ralston saw the Pandora displayed in London and for sale at £2000, but it was not until the war had ended that he flew to Australia, bought the Pandora, and returned with it to Canada.

CHAPTER 4

1. Czernowitz is also referred to in various texts as Cervenica, Czervenetz, Cernowitz, and Vörösvagas.

2. Marbodus is also referred to in the literature as Marbod, Marbode, Marboddel, and Merbode.

3. It should be taken into consideration by readers that no comment blaming opal for the deaths appeared at the time of the Plague and, in fact, not for some 500 years, when abruptly certain writers of the nineteenth and twentieth centuries were stating it as fact.

4. At least once source claims the company was not formed until 1898.

5. The most prevalent story is that Murray's children, wandering about and playing on the ridge, found the opals on the ground and began collecting them, and were playing with them as if they were marbles when their father saw what they were doing and realized what they had found. An amusing story, but not true; Jack Murray's oldest child at this time was a toddler barely able to walk.

6. When the author visited Tintinbar in October 1995, he found considerable work being done at the site with heavy equipment and a full-scale mining operation underway. However, the miners on hand were very secretive about what was being found and made it quite clear that strangers were unwelcome.

7. The digs originally called Nobby Hill are now better known as the Shallow Nobby, which, in later 1995, was being worked as an open cut.

8. Nettleton, in many works, has been given credit as being the discoverer of the Lightning Ridge opal field because he was first to bring stones to Murphy. That, of course, as is shown here, is untrue.

9. Only 5 years later, a parcel of black opal of this size and quality would have netted them £750.

10. Again, these were stones that, in the 1996 market, could have brought upwards of $1000 per *carat,* roughly.

11. A number of different stories exist in respect to how opals were first discovered in Virgin Valley this year. Three of the most repeated tales are that (1) a cowboy riding along sees a stone glinting in the sunlight, gets off his horse to investigate, and finds it is opal; (2) a Basque sheepherder, tending his flock, found the opal on the ground next to where he was sitting when he paused briefly to rest; (3) a Pony Express rider, thundering through, saw the stones glinting and stopped to pick one up. There is no known authentication for either of the first two versions and the third is, of course, ridiculous, since the Pony Express existed for only about 18 months during 1860–61. As nearly as can be officially documented, the discovery was made by Marsden Manson as noted.

12. For a full account of how, in 1963, the mystery was solved regarding what the opal "pineapples" actually are, see the section in this book entitled Opalized Fossils and Pseudomorphs.

13. Over the years numerous efforts have been made to find new deposits at White Cliffs and rekindle the opal boom there. This seemed to be occurring when, in 1986, good opals were encountered by a miner, but the find unfortunately turned out to be only an isolated pocket. There were only about 20 full-time miners working this field when the author visited it in late 1995.

14. Details of the three-year struggle between the miners and the organized station mangers could very nearly fill a book by themselves. It involved the horses and mules of the miners being shot, the waterholes fenced off or deliberately poisoned, and other

vicious activities. Len Cram says he may, in the opal book he is preparing, go into considerable detail about the conflict and its ultimate resolution.

15. Conflicting accounts that cannot be resolved indicate that the date of this find may not be exact and it may not even have been Nettleton who discovered Three Mile.

16. What Pappa Francis, in turn, received for the stones is not known, but in today's market just a one-ounce black opal like the big one of that lot, which would produce at least 50 carats of top gem quality opal, would be worth half a million dollars. If that whole parcel of 320 stones was found, cut, polished, and sold today, it would certainly be worth in excess of $1 million.

17. In some of the accounts the miner's name is spelled Dunston.

18. Considerable confusion exists in practically all the documents in regard to these three opals identically named *Aurora Australis*. There is much juxtaposing of data in the records regarding original uncut weight, cut weight, shape, value, and disposition of these stones. The author has endeavored to sort this all out, but the record is so confused, some error may still exits and, if so, the author apologizes.

19. In years to come, much of this material will be sawn into slabs and polished. The source, now all but depleted, still occasionally gives up some foat material, including some precious opal.

20. The first and most productive opal field discovered in South Australia, it is at first named the Stuart Range Opal Mines. A few years later, as will be shown, it was agreed that something more suitable might be appropriate and the place was re-named to what is renowned as today, an aboriginal term—Coober Pedy. The find of precious opals on the surface was made by Willie Hutchison in the area that is presently the upper reaches of Crowder's Gully (now a road with underground houses lining it), directly behind a present tourist attraction called the Big Winch.

21. It is the written account of Wollaston that has led many following writers to parrot his error about how and when the Stuart's Range Opal Field (later Coober Pedy) was discovered and by whom. As has been shown it was by the party led by James R. Hutchison. The O'Neils remained and worked the field for five years.

22. One source says the newspaper involved was the San Francisco *Examiner* and another says it was the San Francisco *Call*.

23. Greater details of the occasion of these stones being discovered will be found in the section under Famous Opals.

24. Some writers have identified the place as Lone Tree Hill, but One Tree Hill is correct.

25. See also 1909 and 1989 for the two other stones given the same name.

26. John Altmann and Rudi Cherny began business in 1948 as gem cutters and whole-salers, buying opal rough directly from Coober Pedy, Andamooka, White Cliffs, and Lightning Ridge.

27. Valued at $1 million in 1995, the *Aurora Australis* is owned by Altmann & Cherney and presently on exhibit at their branch store, Regent Jewellers, in the Regent Hotel, Melbourne.

28. The date for this event is an estimate and it may have occurred somewhat earlier.

29. The date of 1973 is approximate for the introduction of Opalite; some sources say 1976.

30. This remarkable opal was purchased in the field by a representative of the Sydney firm of E. Gregory Sherman, Pty., Ltd. It was seen in October 1976, by Louis Moyd, then curator of the Canadian Museum of Nature, who was in Sydney attending an International Museums Association Conference. Expressing a keen interest in buying the stone, he conferred with Mr. Sherman, who agreed to send it to Canada on approval, and the purchase was finalized a short time later.

31. Getting claims patented has never been easy and despite such approbation for their opals, the Birdleboughs continued to seek their patent for more than another decade before it was finally granted.

32. Doyle Haight has recently died.

33. The author was on hand at the time of this find and his article about it, entitled *Opal-logue,* appeared in the June 1993 issue of *Lapidary Journal.*

CHAPTER 5

1. All weights are given in avoirdupois weight, not troy weight.

2. There was enough of the original stone left when the principal cutting was finished that John Altmann cut another fine quality stone—a 45-carat oval cab subsequently sold to a private collector from Chicago, Illinois.

3. At least two different accounts state that this stone was subsequently cut into a rectangular stone of 27 carats and sold for $300,000, with present whereabouts not divulged.

4. The former Marie Josephine Rose Tascher de la Pagerie, 1763–1814.

5. Keith Hodson's father was Glenn Hodson.

6. Almost a half-century later, about 1960, two quite good stones—one valued at perhaps £40—were picked up on the surface of the same claim by noodlers picking through the white dumps.

7. That mine eventually became the Rainbow Ridge Opal Mine presently owned by Agnes and Keith Hodson.

CHAPTER 6

1. In another section of this book, there is a glossary of opal-related terms that does not concern itself with types of opal.

CHAPTER 7

1. It is believed that Andamooka Station was named after what the aboriginals called the area originally, variously written as *Jantamuka* or *Jandarimoko.*

2. Some of the accounts give the name of this hill as Lone Tree Hill. That hill is today sometimes called Treloar's Hill and is in the center of the town of Andamooka.

3. In some sources, Yahloo is spelled Yarloo, the phonetic spelling of the Aussie pronunciation.

4. Woomera is an aboriginal word meaning "throwing stick," but that does not necessarily mean a boomerang.

5. The permanent population of Andamooka in 1996 was recorded as 700 individuals, but without notation of how many of these were actual miners.

6. Some texts have credited the discovery of the Coober Pedy opal field to the brothers Jim and Dick O'Neil. Indeed, they were early on the field, but did not arrive until several months after the discovery of the opals.

7. In New South Wales a fossicking permit is required, which limits the fossicker to searching in specified, limited areas or on private mullock heaps with permission of the owners.

8. These same formations continue occurring westward into El Salvador, but the opal resources in that country have been little exploited.

9. Erandique is pronounced eh-RAHN-dee-kay.

10. Official records show that, in accordance with existing mining laws at the time, 16 actively producing opal mines in the Erandique area alone were registered in 1850 with the Honduran government.

11. This may well have been the case with the superb stone, alleged to be a Hungarian opal mined at Czernowitz, presented to the Empress Josephine by Napoleon Bonaparte at the beginning of the nineteenth century—the stone that was named the *Burning of Troy* opal. For further details, see the entry under that stone's name in the chapter on famous opals.

12. It was in honor of Dr. Kunz that the gemstone kunzite was named.

13. There are no less than a dozen confirmed reports of unusually high-quality Lightning Ridge black opals from the New Coocoran field selling for $12,500 per carat. One source lists the finest blacks as selling for as much as $18,000 to $20,000 per carat, but the author has been unable to locate any documentation substantiating opal sales at prices over $12,500 per carat.

14. Some accounts give the number of sheep as 200 and some say 300. The figure of 600 has been given by several sources, including Len Cram, whom the author considers to be a careful researcher, and so that figure has been accepted.

15. Lightning Ridge is 770 km [478.17 miles] from Sydney along the Mitchell Highway to Gilgandra and then north on the Castlereagh Highway through Walgett and then an addition 75 km [46.58 miles] to Lightning Ridge. Although Brisbane is closer than Sydney, the road is merely graded dirt in some areas and prone to closings during inclement weather. The road from Sydney is entirely paved (bitumen sealed, the Aussie's call it) into the town of Lightning Ridge.

16. In all fairness, it should be noted that the black opal of Lightning Ridge was not the first Australian black opal to appear on the market. A true black opal was discovered almost 20 years earlier and mined to a considerable extent in a dig called the Black Mine in the Jundah field of Queensland, more than 200 miles north of Lightning Ridge. Though in an area where boulder opal prevails, this was pipe opal—a magnificent true crystal black with superb depth, color, and pattern.

17. By LRMA guidelines, Virgin Valley black opal and Honduras pure black opal are definitely acceptable; Honduras matrix opal on black basalt is not.

18. The exception to this rule is the seam—or sheet—opal mined at the southwestern Lightning Ridge fields, Grawin, Glengarry, and Sheepyards. Even though that material is largely black opal, it is of a different caliber, easier to find and far more abundant than the nobby black opal and is frequently sold as rough.

19. Marla, situated on the Stuart Highway, is 22.4 miles [36 km] east of Mintabie. It is approximately 600 miles [1000 km] from Adelaide to Lambina, 64 miles [103 km] due north from Lambina to the Northern Territory border, and 224 miles [360 km] from the new diggings to Alice Springs.

20. The figure is only an estimate, since accurate governmental figures are not kept and what record-keeping is done is normally accomplished in a haphazard manner at best. The best estimates the author could find were some unofficial production figures for the year 1994 in which it was reported that the market was very favorable for Mexican opal and that the total amount produced for that years was just under $5 million. It would appear that since about 1988, annual production of Mexican opal has probably exceeded $4 million annually.

21. Even the more famous stones of Mexican origin are generally stones weighing less than 50 carats. An example is the renowned *Phoebus* opal in the Hope Collection—a superb carving of the head of Phoebus, the Sun, the finished stone measuring 1.75″ × 1″ [44.45 mm × 25.4 mm], weighing 35 carats, and having POC in vibrant blue, green, and red. Another is the famous 32-carat *Aquila Azteca—Aztec Eagle Opal.*

22. There is account, possibly apocryphal, that about the year 1958 a very large uncut black opal was found lying on the dirt floor in the corner of a peon mine worker's hut in Huitzuco. Recognized for what it was, the finder gave the peon a dollar or two for it, then had it cut and polished. Later he is said to have taken it to New York, where it was allegedly appraised for nearly a quarter-million dollars, and named it the *Peon Black.*

23. The author personally knows a number of well-experienced opal miners and dealers in America who have never had the pleasure of seeing a top gem-quality Mexican opal.

24. The Stuart Trail eventually became today's Stuart Highway, which runs from Port Augusta to Alice Springs.

25. Mintabie is situated 22 miles [35 km] west of the Stuart Highway at the turnoff 2½ miles [4 km] northwest of the present town of Marla, 93 miles [150 km] south of the Northern Territory border, and 600 miles [1000 km] northwest of Adelaide.

26. Similar geodes, though more often chalcedony-filled, are common throughout much of Oregon and the Northwest and are most familiar under the name "thundereggs"—a term first used by the Indian tribes of that region to designate the egg-shaped rocks that were often exposed through erosion following thunderstorms, although the Indians believed such stones fell from the heavens when lightning split the skies and thunder rolled heavily over the hills.

27. The name Opal Butte was officially recognized in the United States Geological Survey Report for 1893.

28. Smith told the author that he and Huett soon discovered that there were eight separate layers of material involved finding the Opal Butte opal: (1) topsoil, followed by (2) a gravellike layer of rhyolitic pieces; then (3) a layer of larger chunks of the same material, followed by (4) a zone of thunderegg-bearing perlite in which 95% of the geodes have no opal in their interiors but occasional rare translucent blue opal geodes turn up; followed by (5) the principal zone, in which, again, the thundereggs, though compacted through the layer, are roughly 95% devoid of opal. The (6) next layer, the principal perlite zone, is where most of the opal is found,

followed by (7) a layer of darker green perlite that is essentially devoid of opal and, (8) the eighth layer, which is simply a large ledge of rhyolite. The partners did not explore beyond this level.

29. A number of sites exist where opal occurs in Oregon apart from Opal Butte, some of very good quality but, so far as can be determined, lacking in commercial quantity. A deposit of rather fine precious opal with excellent green POC occurs in Jefferson and Wasco counties on the Warm Springs Indian Reservation. It was discovered by an Indian boy, who found a large chunk in a ledge outcrop; that chunk was cut and polished into a single square slab two inches to the side and almost an inch thick and was said to be "uncommonly beautiful." The area, being on an Indian Reservation, is not open to collecting or mining except by the Indians themselves. Another occurrence of quality precious opal was discovered about 1914 on the edge of the western escarpment of Hart Mountain in Lake County, some six miles east of the town of Plush. While no commercial exploitation has been undertaken of this opal deposit, it is said that "hundreds of fine stones have been picked up by casual wanderers over this area." That, of course, was in the first years after the discovery. What opal is recovered now is dug out by hand. Greater details of the Hart Mountain occurrence can be found in an article by H. C. Dake in *The Mineralogist,* February 1954.

30. Kevin Lane Smith states that he knows of three private collections in the United States today that include numerous precious opals collected from Opal Butte almost a quarter-century ago; all remain stable, entirely unblemished by cracks or crazing.

31. The Maguires also operate a tourist stop in Yowah called the Opal Bus Stop—a large blue bus converted into a combination tea and gift shop—where visitors can relax and have a spot of tea, learn about Yowah, and perhaps buy a few opals.

32. Details about other opal deposits in Idaho will be found in the chapter of this book entitled Opals . . . Worldwide.

33. Denio is pronounced to rhyme with Ohio.

34. At least one account states that the precious opal in Virgin Valley was discovered in 1905 by a cowhand named James Flinders. So far as the author has been able to determine, this is not true.

35. Nearly all references to Rainbow Ridge and the Rainbow Ridge Opal Mine place them in Virgin Valley. Technically, as Keith Hodson frequently points out, this is not true. They are in the Sagebrush Creek drainage, although Sagebrush Creek does, in fact, eventually empty into Virgin Creek.

36. The McGee Claim, later to become the Rainbow Ridge Opal Mine, subsequently became the first patented opal mine in the world—meaning that having proven itself as a commercially productive mine, it was patented as a true taxable property now belonging to McGee and no longer a claim on state-owned land, which was required to have a certain amount of "improvement" work done each year for the claim to be maintained, lest it revert to the state, and meaning as well, among other things, that permanent structures could now be built upon it.

37. Additional details about the Roebling Opal will be found in the chapter dealing with famous and noteworthy stones. As for the Harlequin Opal, as some called the split stone, Allan Ledford, grandson of Flora Loughead Gutierrez, stated that he saw it when he was a little boy, saying: "Never have I seen a more beautiful stone. The halves were each about four or five inches long and a couple inches deep of

solid multihued pinfire. I have never heard of its disposition, but I understood from grown-ups' conversation that Mrs. Hammond's advisors recommended that she sell everything possible to recover her substantial investment, as she was paying all the bills."

38. One very prevalent story, believed by many but nevertheless thought to be apocryphal, states that Flora threw notes out of the bathroom window at passersby, telling them she was being held prisoner and that at one point she managed to "escape" from the house, hired a taxicab, and had the driver take her all the way to Virgin Valley—some 380 miles distant. That there may be some element of truth to the story derives from the fact that a notation in the family papers shows that a "motorcar belonging to the family was sent to fetch her back home."

39. Detailed accounts of the finding of both the Hodson Opal and the Bonanza Opal will be found in the chapter dealing with famous stones.

40. The date of 1889 for the discovery of opals at White Cliffs is the most generally accepted date, although several accounts give different dates, some occurring as early as 1884.

41. In some accounts, Hooley's name is spelled Holley.

42. At least one account states the stone they found was kicked up by the hoof of one of their horses.

43. Full details of the discovery of the White Cliffs opal field have been told in both Wollaston's 1924 book entitled *Opal: The Gem of the Never Never* and in E. F. "Ted" Murphy's 1948 book, *They Struck Opal!* Murphy was soon to become Wollaston's resident opal buyer at White Cliffs.

44. For greater details about opalized fossils and opals pseudomorphs after ikaite, see Chapter 3.

CHAPTER 8

1. See expanded information about the discovery and development of the Okanagan Mine under the British Columbia heading in Chapter 7.

2. La Carbonera, one of the more productive of the smaller mines, was quite a profitable venture but was unfortunately first badly neglected and then wholly deserted from 1940 to 1946 as a direct result of a lawsuit over ownership.

3. Frank Leechman in *The Opal Book* says there are opal deposits in Newfoundland, but gives no idea of where or of what kind.

4. Oddly, a returned questionnaire from the office of the director general of Geology and Mines, Ministry of Industry and Energy in Lisbon, flatly states that opals are not known to occur in Portugal. And Margarida C. Simoes, geologist and gemmologist of the Institute of Geology and Mines of the Ministry of Industry and Energy of Portugal in Mamede de Infesta, concurs that opal does not occur in Portugal in any varieties.

Bibliography

PRINCIPAL AND SECONDARY SOURCES

Alexander, G. B., with W. M. Heston and H. K. Iler. "The Solubility of Amorphous Silica in Water." *Journal of Physical Chemistry* 58 (1954): 453–455.

Altmann, J. D. "Australia Calls." *Lapidary Journal* (December 1955): 432, (February 1956): 544, (June 1956): 168, (October 1956): 372, (February 1957): 545, (April 1957): 98, (August 1957): 358.

———. "The Big New Opal Strike." *Lapidary Journal* (December 1956): 420.

———. "On Our Cover . . . Australian Opal." *Lapidary Journal* (October 1975): 1228.

———. "Spotlight on Australian Opals, Part 1." *Lapidary Journal* (August 1954): 266.

———. "Spotlight on Australian Opals, Part 2." *Lapidary Journal* (October 1954): 304.

———. "Today's Opal Market." *Lapidary Journal* (December 1961): 524.

———. "The Truth About Large Australian Opals." *Lapidary Journal* (June 1959): 290.

———. "World-Wide Popularity for Australian Opal." *Lapidary Journal* (October 1960): 338.

American Gemcutter. "Opal." no. 94 (December 1994): 16.

———. "Tips on Making Opal Doublets." no. 63 (May 1992): 13.

Anderson, C., with H. S. Jevrons. "Opal Pseudomorphs from White Cliffs, New South Wales." *Records of the Australian Museum* 6, Part 1 (16 June 1905): 31–36.

Anderson, W. "Occurrence of Opal in New South Wales." *Records of the Geological Survey of New South Wales, 1892.* Department of Mines, New South Wales, Australia.

Andrews, E. C. "Geology of the Lightning Ridge (Wallangulla) Opal Field." *Annual Report, 1924, Department of Mines,* New South Wales, Australia.

Anonymous. "Discovery of Coober Pedy." *South Australian Mining Review,* no. 22 (1915).

Audubon Society. *The Audubon Society Field Guide to North American Rocks and Minerals.* Audubon Society, New York, 1978.

Baggeto. Reno, Nevada. "Humboldt's Opal Fields to be Worked Again." Reno, NV (17 May 1941).

Baier, E. "Optics of Opal." *Zeitschrift für Kristallographie* 81 (1932).

Bailey, J. W. "On Silicified Wood Found Near Fredericksburg, Virginia." *Academy of Natural Sciences of Philadelphia Proceedings* 1 (1888): 75.

Baker, L., Jr. "Opal Doublets and How to Make Them." *Lapidary Journal* (June 1957): 232.

Ball, S. H. *A Roman Book on Precious Stones.* Gemological Institute of America, Santa Monica, CA, 1950.

Bancroft, P. *Gem and Crystal Treasures.* Fallbrook, CA, 1984.

Barbour, T. R. "A Description of Honduras Opal, with Some Cutting Tips." *Lapidary Journal* (April 1965): 66.

———, with J. Barbour. "Country of Opals—Honduras, Part 1: Finally We Enter the Country." *Lapidary Journal* (November 1964): 948; Part 2, "We Leave the Pan-American Highway Far Behind." *Lapidary Journal* (December 1964): 1066; Part 3, "We Continue on Toward Siguatepeque." *Lapidary Journal* (January 1965): 1158; Part 4, "The Opal Search Is On, We See the Back Country." *Lapidary Journal* (February 1965): 1236; Part 5, "We Go to La Esperanza." *Lapidary Journal* (March 1965): 1320; Part 6, "Erandique at Last!" *Lapidary Journal* (April 1965): 46.

———. "Querétaro . . . Gem Cutting Center of Mexico." *Lapidary Journal* (January 1964): 992.

Barnes, L. C., with I. J. Townsend. *Opal: South Australia's Gemstone.* Handbook no. 5, South Australia Department of Mines and Energy, 1972.

Bartley, N. *Opals and Agates.* Gordon & Gotch, Brisbane, 1892.

Bartoli, F., et al. "Role of Aluminium in the Structure of Brazilian Opals." *European Journal of Mineralogy* 2, no. 5 (1990): 611–619.

Bauer, M. (revised by Prof. Dr. K. Schlossmacher). *Edelsteinkunde.* Bernhard Tauchnitz, Leipzig, 1932.

Beckwith, J. A. *Gem Minerals of Idaho.* Caxton Printers, Caldwell, ID, 1961.

Behrens, H. "Structure of Opal." *Sitzungsperichte der Kaiserliche Akadamie der Wissenschafter,* no. 64 (1871).

Benham, R. H. "Presto! You, Too, Can Make Black Opal Doublets." *Lapidary Journal* (May 1969): 396.

Bernstein, L. R. *Minerals of the Washington, D.C. Area.* no. 5 in the Maryland Geological Survey Educational Series, Baltimore, 1980.

Berrington, M. D. *Stones of Fire.* Private, Melbourne, 1958.

Berta, Z., with D. Berta. "Opals Can Affect You That Way." *Lapidary Journal* (February 1980): 2356–2362.

Bingham, L. P. "Opals from Australian Deserts." *Canadian Mining Journal* 74 (1953).

Birdsall, M. "Coober Pedy." *Lapidary Journal* (November 1978): 1800–1809.

———. "Lightning Ridge: Black Opal Capital of Australia." *Lapidary Journal* (June 1986): 26.

Blazek, M. "Unusual Property Noted in Precious Opal." *Lapidary Journal* (December 1973): 1466.

Bøggild, O. B. *The Mineralogy of Greenland.* Medd. om Grønland, vol. 149, no. 3, Kovnhagen, 1953.

Boodt, A. *Gemmarium et Lapidarium historia.* Antwerp, 1609.

Boot, A. B. *Le Parfaict Joaillier.* Chez Jean-Antoine Hygyetan, Lyon, France, 1644.

Borner, R. *Minerals, Rocks and Gemstones.* Macmillan & Co., Ltd., London, 1938.

Bostock, J., with H. T. Riley. *The Natural History of Pliny.* Henry G. Bohn, London, 1857.

Bower, C. E. "Digging for Black Opals at the Royal Peacock Opal Mines, Virgin Valley, Nevada." *Lapidary Journal* (July 1977): 526.

Boyd, R. T. "Big New Find of Andamooka Opal." *Lapidary Journal* (August 1958): 374.

Brard, C. P. *Minéralogie Appliquée aux Arts.* 3 vols. Chez F. G. Levrault, Paris, 1821.

Brewster, D. "On the Study of Opal." Appendix to *Report of the British Association for the Advancement of Science,* 1844.

Briggs, H. E. *An Encyclopedia of Gems.* Sawyer Press, Los Angeles, 1944.

Brooks, J. H. "A Prospector's Guide to Opal in the Yowah-Eromanga Area." *Queensland Government Mining Journal* 68, Brisbane, 1967.

Broughton, P. "A Recent Discovery of Blue Opal in Western Idaho. *Lapidary Journal* (October 1974): 1102.

Brown, G. "Treated Andamooka Matrix Opal." *Gems & Gemology* 27, no. 2, 1991.

———, with G. Lambert. "A Brief Report on Indonesian Opal." *Australian Gemmologist* 18, no. 11 (1994): 359–361.

Brown, R. W. "Paleobotany: A Miocene Grapevine From the Valley of Virgin Creek in Northwestern Nevada." *Journal of the Washington Academy of Sciences,* Menasha, WI 32 (1942): 287–291.

Bruce, G. *Lightning Ridge: Home of the Black Opal.* Lightning Ridge, Australia, 1983.

Bruderer, R. "Modern Methods Now Used in Australian Opal Mining." *Lapidary Journal* (October 1959): 488.

Buchanan, M. S. *Prospecting for Opal.* Bowles, Sydney, 1931.

Butkovic, S. *Historia slovenskeho drahého opálu z Dubníka.* Alfa, Bratislava, 1970.

———. *Z historie lokality Dubník [The Mining History of Opals in Dubník];* Acta Musei Nationalis Pragae 29 B, 1973, pp. 131–136.

Butler, G. A. "Opal in Virgin Valley." *Rock & Gem* (September 1987): 36–38.

———. "Staking Your Claim!" *Rock & Gem* (March 1992): 22–27.

Butschli, O. "Cellular Structure of Amorphous Silica." *Verhandlungen des Naturhistorich-medizinischen Vereins zu Heidelberg* 6, (1901).

Campbell, D. A. "Fiery Opals in Southern California." *Gems and Minerals* (March 1983): 37–62.

Camsell, C. *Canada Mining Institute Journal* 14 (1911): 606.

Carlisle, T. R. "Opal: Second Thoughts." *Lapidary Journal* (June 1981): 660–663.

———. "Opalholic." *Lapidary Journal* (December 1980): 1958.

Carlson, E. H. *Minerals of Ohio.* "Catalog of Mineral Localities." Bulletin no. 69 of the Ohio Department of Natural Resources, Division of Geological Survey, Columbus, 1991, p. 120.

Carter, C. F., et al. "Mineral Resources of the Idaho Primitive Area and Vicinity, Idaho." *USGS Bulletin 1304,* 1973, p. 431.

Cathrall, J. B., et al. "Mineral Resources of the Charles Sheldon Wilderness Study Area," in *USGS Opal File Report 78-1002,* 1978.

Chalmers, R. O. "A New Occurrence of Precious Opal of Volcanic Origin near Mullumbimby, New South Wales, Australia." *Lapidary Journal* (February 1970): 1541.

————. *Australian Rocks, Minerals and Gemstones.* Ure Smith, Sydney, 1967.

————. "New Occurrences of Gem Materials in Australia." *Lapidary Journal* (April 1972): 14.

Church, A. H. *Handbook to the Victoria and Albert Museum Collection.* V & A Museum Soc., London, 1913.

————. *Precious Stones.* 4th ed. V & A Museum Soc., London, 1913.

Cody, A. *Australian Precious Opal.* Mount Press, Melbourne, 1991.

————. "Valuation of Australian Precious Opal." *Gemological Association of Australia,* 1988.

Coetzee, C. B., ed. *Mineral Resources of South Africa,* 5th ed. Handbook 7 of the Geological Survey of South Africa, 1976.

Colen, M. "The Fire of Opal." *Rock & Gem* 21, no. 10 (October 1991): 24–30, 86–88.

————. "Little Green Opals." *Rock & Gem* (October 1991) 44–46.

Collin, H. E. "Opal Matrix, the Poor Man's Opal." *Rock & Gem* (November 1971): 1164.

Connah, T. H. *A Prospector's Guide to Opal in Western Queensland.* Queensland Government Mining Journal 72, Brisbane, 1966.

Cook, R. *Minerals of Georgia: Their Properties and Occurrences,* by R. B. Cook, *Georgia Geological Survey Bulletin Number 92,* Atlanta, 1978, pp. 158–159 B.

————, with W. E. Smith. *Mineralogy of Alabama.* Alabama Geological Bulletin 120, n.d., 206–209.

Cooksey, T. "The Cause of Colour in Opal Pseudomorphs from White Cliffs." *Records of the Australian Museum,* vol. 2, part 2, 1896.

Copisarow, A. C., with M. Copisarow. "The Opalescence of Silicic Acid Gels." *Journal of the American Chemical Society* 67 (1945).

————. "Formation of Hyalite and Opal." *Science* (new series), no. 104, (1946).

————. "The Structure of Hyalite and Opal." *Science* (new series), no. 157, (1946).

Correspondence and manuscript matter:

Congrave, Alan, owner, House of Opals, Honolulu, Hawaii; manuscript letter to Donna Birdlebough regarding being distributor for opals from Virgin Valley mine belonging to the Birdleboughs; 30 December 1980.

Koivula, John I., Research gemologist, Gemological Institute of America, Santa Monica, CA.: Manuscript letter to Donna Birdlebough, Seattle, Washington, regarding analysis of Virgin Valley black opals; 21 February 1981.

————. Manuscript letter to Harold Birdlebough, Seattle, Washington, regarding analysis of black opals from Virgin Valley; 3 December 1980.

Ledford, Allan, of Honolulu, Hawaii, grandson of Flora Haines Lockheed. Manuscript letter and biographical sketch entitled "The Opal Queen" to a Ms. Warrington, 10 November 1987.

Lockheed, Flora Haines Gutierrez; Manuscript letter to E. R. Sans, Superintendent, Charles Sheldon Antelope Preserve, regarding public depredations to opal mines in Virgin Valley, 26 April 1938.

————. Manuscript letter to Hon. Hiram Johnson, U.S. Senator from California, regarding depredations to opal mines in Nevada; 17 January 1938.

———. Manuscript letter to Hon. W. M. Rush, regarding depredations occurring by misinformed public; 18 September 1938.

———. Manuscript letter to Hon. W. M. Rush, regarding donation of her opal mines to U.S.; 4 June 1939.

———. Manuscript Statement entitled "Nevada Opal Fields Statement"; 4 pages, typescript; undated, but evidently 1937 or 1938.

Murray, T. B., acting regional director, USDA Bureau of Biological Survey. Manuscript letter to E. R. Sans, superintendent, Charles Sheldon Antelope Range, describing offer of Flora Lockheed as "ravings of the Opal Queen"; 14 June 1939.

———. Manuscript letter to Hon. W. M. Rush, Regional Director, U.S. Geological Survey, regarding her potential donation of opal mines to U.S.; 4 June 1939.

———. Manuscript letter to Hon. W. M. Rush, Regional Director, U.S. Geological Survey, regarding her potential donation of opal mines to U.S.; 4 June 1939.

Rush, W. M., of Bureau of Biological Survey, USDA; Manuscript letter to E. R. Sans, supt., Sheldon National Antelope Range, regarding letter received from Flora Haines Loughead; 23 September 1938.

———. Manuscript letter to Flora Haines Loughead, responding to letter from her dated September 18, 1938; 23 September 1938.

———. Manuscript letter to Hon. James G. Scrugham, regarding opal claim of Mrs. Tillie McLeod of Dayton, Nevada, 14 July 1936.

Sans, E. R., Superintendent of Charles Sheldon Antelope Range, Cedarville, California, to Flora Haines Loughead Gutierrez, refusing offer of opal mines, 21 June 1939.

———. To T. B. Murray, acting regional director, Bureau of Biological Survey, regarding Flora Loughead's offer of opal claims to U.S.; 21 June 1939.

Court, A., with I. Campbell. *Minerals*. Van Nostrand Reinhold, New York, 1974, p. 17.

Crabtree, D. R. "Picea Wolfei, A New Species of Petrified Cone from the Miocene of Northwestern Nevada." *American Journal of Botany* 70, no. 9 (1983): 1356–1364.

Cram, L. *Beautiful Australian Opals*. Robert Brown & Assoc., Carina, Queensland, 1990.

———. *Beautiful Australian Opals: A Field Guide*. Robert Brown & Assoc., Coorparoo, Queensland, 1994.

———. *Beautiful Lightning Ridge*. Robert Brown & Assoc., Buranda, Queensland, 1991.; same, revn., 1993; same, revn., 1996.

———. *Beautiful Queensland Opals*. Robert Brown & Assoc., Buranda, Queensland, 1991.

———. *Beautiful Opals: Australia's National Gem*. Robert Brown & Assoc., Buranda, Queensland, 1994.

———. *Beautiful Opals of the Desert*. Brisbane, Queensland, 1992.

———. *Beautiful Yowah, Black Gate & Koroit*. Len Cram Publ., Lightning Ridge, New South Wales, Australia, 1995.

———. *Journey with Colour*. Lightning Flash, Lightning Ridge, New South Wales, Australia, 1988.

Cribb, H. G. S. "Opal Deposits and the Hayricks Opal Mine, Quilpie." *Queensland Government Mining Journal* 49 (1948): 48–51.

Croll, I. C. H. "Report on the Opal Industry in Australia." *Bulletin of the Bureau of Mineral Resources,* no. 17, Canbarra, Australia, 1950.

Crooks, E. R. "A Visit to the Lost Deer Hunt Opal Mine." *Lapidary Journal* (November 1977).

Curran, J. M. "On the Occurrence of Precious Stones in New South Wales." *Proceedings of the Royal Society of New South Wales* 30, Sydney, 1897, p. 46.

Cuthbert, D. L. "Precious Opal, Queen of Gems, in Idaho." *Lapidary Journal* (October 1969): 928.

Dabdoub, T. "A Cut Above." *Lapidary Journal* 47, no. 6 (September 1993): 83–88.

———. *Opal Report From Honduras: The Fire Still Burns.* Tropical Gem Explorations, Los Angeles, 1985.

Dake, H. C. "The Gem Minerals of Oregon." *Oregon State Department of Geological and Mineral Industries,* Bulletin no. 7, 1938, Portland, Oregon.

———. "Opal at Sulphur." *The Mineralogist* (April 1950): 172.

———. "Opal in Oregon." *The Mineralogist* 22, no. 2 (February 1954): 68–70.

———. "Opal near Lewiston, Idaho." *The Mineralogist* (January 1958): 13.

———. "Opal near Moscow, Idaho." *The Mineralogist* (January 1958): 18.

Dana, E. S. "A Crystallographic Study of the Thinolite of Lake Lahontan." *Bulletin of the United States Geological Survey,* no. 12. Government Printing Office, Washington, DC, 1884.

Darragh, P. J., with A. J. Gaskin and J. V. Sanders "Opals." *Scientific American* (April 1976): 8495.

———. "The Origin of Color in Opal Based Upon Electron Microscopy." *Scientific American* (December 1965): 1052.

———. "Origin of Precious Opal." *Nature* 209 (1966): 13.

———. "The Nature and Origin of Opal." *Australian Gemmologist* 66 (1966): 5–9.

———. "Precious Opal: Developments Towards Synthesis." *Australian Gemmologist,* 73 (1973): 17–21.

David, T. W. E., with T. G. Taylor. "Occurrence of the Pseudomorph Glendonite in New South Wales." *Records of the Geological Survey of New South Wales* 8, part 2 (1905): 161–179.

———, with W. R. Browne. *The Geology of Australia.* A. Burton, London, 1950.

Davies, J. E. "The Opals of Mexico." *Lapidary Journal* (February 1963): 1063.

Dawson, G. M. *Geological Survey of Canada Annual Report* 3 (1887–88): p. 11OR.

Delius, C. T. *Nachricht von ungarischen Opalen und Weltaugen.* Abhandlungen de Private-gesellschaft 3, 1777, 227–252.

Denton, V., ed. *Pages from the Diaries of Shelley Wright Denton,* V. Denton, Wellesley, MA, 1949.

Desautels, P. E. *Treasures in the Smithsonian: The Gem Collection.* Smithsonian, Washington, DC, 1979.

Dietz, R. W. "Play of Colors in Precious Opal." *Gems and Minerals* (June 1965): 16–18.

Downing, P. B. "America's Outback Opal." *Lapidary Journal* 48, no. 3 (June 1994): 53–57.

———. "An Australian Love Affair." *Lapidary Journal* (June 1989): 32–40.

———. "Australian Opal Discoveries." *Rock & Gem* 20, no. 9 (September 1990): 48–51, 88–89.

———. "Evaluating Cut Opal." *Rock & Gem* (December 1987): 16–21.

———. "New Fire in British Columbia." *Rock & Gem* 24, no. 10 (October 1994): 41–45, 82.

———. "Okanagan Opal." *Lapidary Journal* 46, no. 11 (February 1993): 63–66.

———. *Opal Adventures.* Majestic Press, Tallahassee, FL, 1990.

———. *Opal Cutting Made Easy* 6th ed. Majestic Press, Tallahassee, FL, 1990.

———. *Opal Identification and Value.* Majestic Press, Tallahassee, FL, 1992.

———. "Valuing Cut Opal." *Cornerstone* (July 1990).

———. "World Opal Supply and Prices." *Rock & Gem* (September 1986): 26–32.

Drucker, R. B. *Gemworld Pricing Guide,* vol. 9. Gemworld International, Chicago, IL., 1991.

Duncan, M. "Crazing of Stones." *Gemline, Australian Gem Industry Association,* October 1988.

Dunstan, B. "Queensland Mineral Index and Guide." *Geological Survey of Queensland,* Publication no. 241, 1913.

Duron, J. F. "Opals and Opal Hunters, as a Native Honduran Sees the Scene." *Lapidary Journal* (December 1965): 1060.

Dwyer, F. P., with D. P. Mellor. "A Note on the Occurrence of Beta-Crystobalite in Australian Opals." *Journal and Proceedings of the Royal Society of New South Wales* 66 (1932).

———. "An X-Ray Study of Opals." *Journal and Proceedings of the Royal Society of New South Wales* 68 (1934).

———. "X-Ray Diffraction Studies of the Crystallization of Amorphous Silica." *Journal and Proceedings of the Royal Society of New South Wales* 67 (1933).

Eckert, A. W. "Opal-Logue." *Lapidary Journal* 47, no. 3 (June 1993): 36–40.

Ein, D. A. "Over the Rainbow." *Lapidary Journal* 46, no. 3 (June 1992): 79–81.

Etheridge, R. "Opalised Remains from Lightning Ridge." *Proceedings of the Royal Society of Victoria* 29 (1917).

Evans, J. *History of Jewellery, 1100–1870.* Faber & Faber, London, 1953.

Eyles, W. C. *The Book of Opals.* Charles E. Tuttle, Rutland, VT, 1971.

———. "Opal Boom Continues." *Lapidary Journal* (October 1963): 755.

———. "They Still Dig for Opal at Lightning Ridge." *Lapidary Journal* (October 1963): 736.

———. "A Trip to the Australian Opal Fields." *Gems & Minerals* (August 1953): 22.

Falz, E. *Die Idar-Oberstein Schmuckstein-Industrie.* Carl Schmidt, Idar-Oberstein, 1926.

Farmington, O. C. *Gems and Gem Minerals.* A. W. Muford, Chicago, 1903.

Feather, R. C., II. "Amphibole in Opal." In Inclusion of the Month column, *Lapidary Journal* 48, no. 3 (June 1994): 16.

Federman, D. "Fire Opal: Pride of Mexico." *Modern Jeweler,* brochure, n.d.

Fenton, C. L., and M. A. Fenton. *The Rock Book* Fenton, New York, 1940.

Ferguson, W. H. "Occurrence of Opal in East Gippsland." *Records of the Geographical Survey of Victoria,* 1902.

Fleischer, M. "New Mineral Names: Ikaite." *American Mineralogist* 49 (March–April 1964): 439.

Fletcher, M. "Faceting Opal Triplets." *Gems & Minerals* (December 1979): 68.

Florer, D. "The Elusive Opal." *Lapidary Journal* (October 1952): 266.

Ford, W. E. *Dana's Textbook of Mineralogy.* Frederick A. Stokes, New York, 1947.

Foshag, W. F. *Gems and Gemmology* (Spring 1953): 282.

Frank, A. L. "Dig Your Own Opal at the Pato de Gallo Mine." *Lapidary Journal* (December 1973): 1469.

———. "Querétaro, the Opal Capital of Mexico." *Lapidary Journal* (October 1974): 1146.

Franks, M. "The Deadly Lure: A Story from the Lightning Ridge Opal Fields." *Lapidary Journal* (March 1981): 2662–2670.

Frazier, S., and A. Frazier. "Cleavage in Quartz." part I, *Lapidary Journal* 44, no. 7 (October 1990); part II, 44, no. 8 (November 1990).

———. "Idar's Opal Village." *Lapidary Journal* 46, no. 3 (June 1992): 34–39.

———. "Lore, Lies, & Misinformation." *Lapidary Journal* 47, no. 3 (June 1994): 48–52, 78–82.

———. "Museum Idar-Oberstein." *Lapidary Journal* (December 1988: 41–57.

———. "Opal or Iris?" part I; *Lapidary Journal* 48, no. 3 (June 1994): 58–66; part II; *Lapidary Journal* 48, no. 5 (August 1994): 48–57.

———. "Pineapples." *Lapidary Journal* 48, no. 3 (June 1994) 32–43.

Gemological Instiitute of America. *Gem Reference Guide.* Santa Monica, CA, 1988.

———. *Gems Made by Man.* Santa Monica, CA, 1980.

Gems & Gemology. "Faceted Synthetic Opal." In Gem News column, 30 (Summer 1994): 131.

———. "Black Opal From Brazil." (spring 1991): 49.

———. "Brief Report on Indonesian Opal." (spring 1995): 79.

———. "Black Cat's-Eye Opal From Jalisco, Mexico." (winter 1990): 304.

———. "Plastic-Coated, Sugar-Treated Opal." (fall 1990): 236.

———. "Opal," in Gem News column, 19 (winter 1993): 294.

———. "Opal From Ethiopia." in Gem News column 30 (spring 1993): 52.

———. "Opals With an Unusual Inclusion." (fall 1990): 222.

Gentile, C. "How to Polish Opal." *Lapidary Journal* (November 1977).

Gipps, H. F. de V. "Some Notes on the White Cliffs Opal Fields." *Transactions of the Australasian Institution of Mining Engineers* 2 (1894).

———. "White Cliffs." *Engineering and Mining Journal* 59 (1895).

Girard, R. M. *Texas Rocks and Minerals: An Amateur's Guide.* Texas Bureau of Economic Geology, Guidebook 6, Austin, February 1964.

Glackin, J. J. "Opal Idiosyncrasies." *Lapidary Journal* (December 1972): 1368.

Glenn, C. E. "More Light on the Honduras Opal Story." *Lapidary Journal.* (September 1971): 873.

Goronov, A., with T. Todořova. "Opal Siliceous Rocks from the Eastern Rhodopes." *Bulletin of the Academy of Bulgarian Science* 38, no. 3 (1985): 353–355.

Gray, M. "Faceted Opals." *Lapidary Journal* 46, no. 6 (June 1992): 93–95.

Greg, W. L., with R. Lettson. *Mineralogy of Great Britain and Ireland*. n.d., J. Wheeler, London.

Greig, J. W. "Crystallites in Opal." *Journal of the American Chemical Society* 54 (1932).

Gourlay, A. J., with D. H. McColl, and B. R. Senior. "Review of the Opal and Sapphire Industries." *Australian Mineral Industry Quarterly Review* 28 (1976): 1–12.

Griesmeyer, G. "Our Search for Opal." *Lapidary Journal* (June 1977) 724–730.

———. "Rock Hunting in the City Down Under." *Lapidary Journal* (October 1978): 1624–1626.

Griffith, J. "Arizona Blue Fire Opal Goes to Europe." *Lapidary Journal* (November 1980): 1750–1754.

Gübelin, E. J. "New Fakes to Simulate Black Opal." *Gemmologist* 28 (1959): 141.

———. "Opal from Mexico." *Australian Gemmologist* 16, no. 2 (1986): 45–51.

———. "Opale aus Mexiko." *Lapis* 10, no. 1 (1985): 23–30.

Gurich, G. "Opal Pseudomorphs from White Cliffs." *Neues Fahrbuch für Mineralogie, Geologie, und Paläontologie* 4 (1901).

Hadley, W. D. "A Carved Opal Pendant." *Rock & Gem* (September 1985): 33–35.

———. "Carving Opal." *Rock & Gem* 20, no. 9 (September 1990): 52–54, 86–87.

———. "Gemstone Carvings." *Rock & Gem* (January 1988): 53–55.

———. "Opal Folklore and Facts." *Rock & Gem* (September 1987): 32–35.

———. "Working with Opal." *Rock & Gem* 21, no. 10 (October 1991): 40–43.

Halenar, L. "Opal Prospecting in Australia and How to Prepare an Opal Doublet." *Lapidary Journal* (October 1947): 128.

Hanchildt, J. "The Spencer, Idaho, Opal Episode." *Lapidary Journal* (May 1978): 540–543.

Harshbarger, K. "A Preliminary Study of Calcite after Ikaite." Unpublished monograph, 1993.

Haüy, L'Abbé. *Traité de Mineralogie*. Paris, 1801.

Haverland, S. "A Passion for Opal." *Rock & Gem* 24, no. 10 (October 1994): 36–38.

Hawley, D. "World's Largest Black Opal." *Lapidary Journal* (August 1970): 684.

Hawley, H. Fabergé and His Contemporaries: *The India Early Minshall Collection of the Cleveland Museum of Art*. Cleveland Museum of Art, Cleveland, 1967.

Heath, D. E. "Coober Pedy Opal." *Lapidary Journal* (November 1968): 1001.

———. "Coober Pedy Today." *Lapidary Journal* (October 1965): 818.

———. "Opal Cutting Tips from Coober Pedy." *Lapidary Journal* (February 1966): 1264.

Heddle, M. F. *The Mineralogy of Scotland*. Publisher unknown, Edinburgh, 1901.

Heflik, W. *Decorative Stones of Poland*. Ladislas Czerny, Krakow, 1989.

———, with W. Parachoniak. "Hyalite From Jordanów near Sobótka (Lower Silesia)." *Mineralogia Polonica* 3 (1972).

Hewitt, C. G. "Adventures with Virgin Valley Opals." *Lapidary Journal* (December 1977): 1995–1998.

Heylmun, E. B. "Four Opal Localities in Mexico." *Lapidary Journal* (September 1983): 880.

———. "The Magdalena Opal District." *Gems and Minerals* (June 1984): 54–57.

———. "Map of the Querétaro Opal Mines, Mexico." *Lapidary Journal* (May 1983): 344.

———. "Varieties of Mexican Opal." *Lapidary Journal* (August 1984): 746–752.

———. "Virgin Valley. *Lapidary Journal* (June 1987): 33–44.

Hiern, M. N. *Opal Deposits in Australia,* Geological Survey of South Australia, Quarterly Geological Notes, vol. 16, 1966.

Hill, J. *A General Natural History; or New and Accurate Descriptions of the Animals, Vegetables and Minerals of the Different Parts of the World,* 3 vols. Thomas Osborne, London, 1748.

Hiss, D. A. "Opal: The Down Under Wonder." *Lizzadro Museum* (summer-fall 1990).

Hodson, K. "Mining Rainbows." *Lapidary Journal* (June 1989): 41–43.

———. "Opal Mining at Virgin Valley." *Lapidary Journal* (December 1961): 530.

Hoffeld, H. " 'Opalitis': An Article Concerning its Pathogenesis and Treatment." *Lapidary Journal* (July 1977).

Holmes, I. "Fireworks at Midnight on the Isle of Java." *Opal Express* (July 1986): 3–6.

Hoover, D. B. "An Historical Note on the Colour Phenomenon in Precious Opal." *Australian Gemmologist* 18, no. 5 (1993): 145–148.

Hudson, S. "Cutting Opal." *Rock & Gem* (September 1987): 40–46.

———. "Opal in Dixie." *Rock & Gem* (September 1987): 20–22.

Huett, D. E. "A Centennial Celebration: Gem Quality Opal in Oregon." *Lapidary Journal* 44, no. 8 (November 1990): 22–29.

———. "A Real Beaut!" *Lapidary Journal* 47, no. 3 (June 1993): 75–80.

Humboldt Star, Winnemucca, Nevada. "Bureau Proposes Changes in Mine Reclamation Bond Requirements." July 1991.

———. "The Opal Beds of Humboldt County." 13 November 1914.

Hunek, E. "Regenerated Precious Opal." *Gemmologist* 30 (1961): 101.

Hurlbut, C. S. *Dana's Manual of Mineralogy.* 16th ed. John Wiley & Sons, New York, 1952.

Hurlbut, C. S., Jr., with G. S. Switzer. *Gemology.* Macmillan, New York, 1979.

Hutchison, J. R. "Discovery of Coober Pedy." Adelaide *Chronicle,* 7 April 1938.

Idriess, I. L. *Lightning Ridge.* T. Windsor, Sydney, 1940.

Ingebritson. D. "A Gem Cutter on the Opal Fields of South Australia." *Lapidary Journal* (November 1973): 1309.

Ingram, J. A. "Drilling for Opal In Queensland." *Queensland Government Mining Journal* 70 (1969): 451–454.

Jack, R. L. "Report on the Geology of the Region to the North and North-West of Tarcoola." *Bulletin of the Geological Survey Australia* no. 15 (1931).

Jackson, C. F. V. "The Opal Mining Industry and the Distribution of Opal Deposits in Queensland." *Report of the Geological Survey of Queensland,* Queensland Publication no. 177, 1902, 112–114.

Jacquet, J. B. *Report on the White Cliffs Opal Field.* Department of Mines, New South Wales, 1892.

Jauncey, W. M. *Queensland. (Map) 1:250,000 scale, Geological Series, with Explanatory Notes Sheet SF/54–16.* Department of National Development, Bureau of Mineral Resources, Geology and Geophysics, Canberra, Australia, 1967.

Johnson, P. W. *A Field Guide to the Gems and Minerals of Mexico.* Mentone Press, Mentone, CA, 1965.

Jones, B. "A Bust of Black Basaltic Opal." *Rock & Gem* 24, no. 4 (April 1994): 68–70.

———. "Colorful Minerals of the Great Southwest." *Rock & Gem:* (September 1987) 24–30.

———. "The Fire of Opal." *Rock & Gem* (February 1978): 32–36, 77–78, 87.

———. "G'day Opal." *Rock & Gem* (September 1988): 32–36, 80.

———. "Idaho Blue Fire Opal." *Rock & Gem* (February 1989) :56–59.

———. "Opal News." *Rock & Gem* (Februrary 1995): 40–48.

Jones, J. B., et al. "Stucture of Opal." *Nature* 204 (1964): 990.

Kalokerinos, A. *Australian Precious Opal.* Thomas Nelson, Melbourne, 1971.

Kammerling, R. C., with J. I. Koivula. "Novel Assembled Opals from Mexico." *Australian Gemmologist* 18, no. 1 (1992): 19–21.

Kaplan, S. E. "My Favorite Gem, the Opal." *Lapidary Journal* (May 1970): 390.

Keller, P. C. *Gemstones and Their Origins.* Van Nostrand Reinhold, New York, 1990.

Kennedy, G. S. "Opal Carving (Gem Carving Instruction no. 13). *Lapidary Journal.* December, 1955; 392.

Kennedy, E. J. "Gem Opal [White Cliffs]." *Bulletin of the Geological Survey of New South Wales,* Mineral Resources Bulletin no. 36, 1934.

King, C. W. *Antique Gems: Their Origin, Uses, and Value.* John Murray, London, 1860.

———. *The Natural History of Precious Stones and Gems.* John Murray, London, 1865.

King, E. A. Jr. *Texas Gemstones.* Texas Bureau of Economic Geology Report of Investigations, no. 42, Austin, TX (February 1961).

Koch, S. *Magyarország Ásványa.* Akadémiai Kiardó, Budapest, Hungary, 1985.

Kodera, K. "Topograficka mineralogias." *Slovenska I–III.* Bratislava, Veda, 1382 s., 1990.

Koivula, J. I., et al. "Microscopic Features of Imitation Phenomenal Gems." *Colored Stone* (January/February 1990): 194–196.

———. Fryer, C., with P. C. Keller. "Opal from Querétaro, Mexico: Occurrence and Inclusions," *Gems & Gemology* 19, no. 2 (summer 1983): 87–96.

Kosminsky, I. *The Magic and Science of Jewels and Stones.* T. Y. Crowell, New York, 1922.

Kostov, R. I., with I. M. Pogarevski. "Electron Paramagnetic Resonance of Opal and Silicified Wood from the Haskovo District in South Bulgaria." *Bulletin of the Academy of Bulgarian Science,* 41, no. 7 (1988): 63–66.

Kourimsky, J. *Die Edelsteine der Tschechoslowakei.* Universitätsverlag, Mainz, 1981.

———. *Die Edlen Steine der CSSR.* Staatliches Museum für Mineralogie u. Geologie, Dresden, 1982.

———. *Edle Steine u. Schmuck aus der CSSR.* Natur-historisches Museum, Wien, 1983.

———. *Katalog sbírky drahych kamenu Národního muzea v Praze [Catalog of the Collection of Precidious Stones of the National Museum in Prague].* Národního muzeum, Praha, 1968.

———. *Minerals & Rocks.* Octopus, London, 1977.

Kovac, P. "White Cliffs and the Lure of Opal." *Lapidary Journal* (March 1982): 2354.

Kratochvil, M. "Topograficka mineralogie." *Czech I–VIII.* Praha, NCSAV, 1956.

Kraus, E. H., with C. B. Slawson. *Gems and Gem Materials,* 5th ed. McGraw-Hill, New York, 1947.

Kraus, P. D. "Opal and Tourmaline: Birthstones for October." *Lapidary Journal* (October 1964): 788; (October 1976): 1608.

Krosch, N. J. "A Summary of Opal Mining Activity, Western Queensland, 1970–1983." *Queensland Government Mining Journal.* Government Press, Brisbane, Australia, 1983, p. 273.

Kruta, T. "Topograficka mineralogie Moravy." *Brno. Moravske Muzeum,* 380 s., 1966.

Kunz, G. F. *The Curious Lore of Precious Stones.* J. B. Lippincott, Philadelphia, 1913.

————. *Gems and Precious Stones of North America.* 2d ed. Peter Smith, New York, 1890.

————. *Gems, Jewelers' Material, and Ornamental Stones of California.* California Division of Mines Bulletin, no. 37, 1905.

————. "Precious Stones" (D. T. Day, ed.) *Mineral Resources of the United States, Calendar Year 1892.* Government Printing Office, Washington, DC, 1893.

Kurtzeman, J. "Conk Opal." *Rock & Gem* (October 1989): 76–77.

Ladd, N. B. "A New Nevada Opal Discovery." *Lapidary Journal* (June 1957): 208.

Lapidary Journal. "Advice on Buying Opal Rough." (August 1955): 280.

————. "Anyone Can Work Precious Opal by Hand." (August 1968): 716.

————. "Black Opals at Lightning Ridge." (October 1960): 320.

————. "The Black Opals of Lightning Ridge." (June 1987): 49.

————. " 'El Tortolito'—An Account of Present Day Opal Mining Conditions in Mexico." (July 1968): 512.

————. "Elusive in Louisiana." (June 1986): 54.

————. "Eye of the World—Occulus Mundi." (December 1961): 562.

————. "Fiery Favorites." Editorial. 47, no. 3, (June 1993): 4.

————. "Fireworks at Midnight." (June 1986): 20.

————. "The Gem Minerals of Mexico." (April 1958): 4.

————. "Glossary of Opal Terms."(December, 1961): 558.

————. "Jade—Sapphires—Fire Opal, Part 2." (August 1973): 756.

————. "Japanese Manmades." (January 1982): 2004.

————. "Lapidary Treatment of Opalized Woods." (July 1947): 57.

————. "Lightning Ridge Black Opal Knobby." (March 1974): 1796.

————. "Living Under Ground." (February 1953): 434.

————. "Louisiana Opal." From Facets column. 46, no. 3 (June, 1992): 10.

————. "Mexican Opals." (June 1974): 496.

————. "More Plesiosaur." (January 1972): 1368.

————. "New Variety of Opal Found Near Sonoma, California." (June 1978).

————. "Not So Basic Black." Facets column. 47, no. 3 (June 1993): 10.

————. "Opal as an Investment." Opal Spectrum. (October 1977): 1492.

————. "Opal from Magdalena." June, 1986; 49.

————. "Opal Hunting in Mexico." (December 1958): 602.

————. "Opal Localities in West Central Mexico." (July 1983): 598.

————. "Opal Terminology." (June 1987): 51.

———. "Opals in Brazil." (July 1968): 597.

———. "Rare Faceting Minerals—Silicates, Part 14." (January 1966): 1142.

———. "So You Want to Cut Opal." (August 1952): 214.

———. "Some Record Setting Gems of the World." (February 1984): 1574.

———. "Star Opal from Idaho." (February 1976): 1986.

———. "Tips on Rock Importations from Mexico." (June 1953): 116.

———. "Treated Opal Gets Mixed Reaction." (February 1986): 8.

———. "Ultraviolet Recovery." (June 1986): 36.

———. "Varieties of Mexican Opal." (August 1984): 746.

———. "Virgin Valley?" December (1973): 1467.

———. "What Makes Fire in Opal?" (November 1971): 1139.

———. "Zimapan Opal: Are the Mines Lost?" (September 1984): 794.

Leaming, S. *Paper 72–53. Geological Survey of Canada, 1973,* 25–29.

Ledford, A. Unpublished manuscript, biographical sketch of Flora Haines Loughead Gutierrez (his grandmother), entitled "The Opal Queen." November 1987.

Leechman, F. *The Opal Book.* Ure Smith, Sydney, 1961.

———. "The Origin of the Roman Opal." *The Gemmologist,* 26, no. 315, (1957): 175–177.

Leechman, G. F. "Bibliography on Opal." *Journal of Gemmology* 5, no. 1 (1955).

———. "The Formation of Opal." *Commonwealth Jeweller and Watchmaker* (March 1951).

———. "Further Notes on the Cause of the Colour in Opal." *Journal of Gemmology* 4, no. 7 (1954).

———. "Introductory Bibliography on Opal." *Commonwealth Jeweller and Watchmaker* (September 1954).

———. "Lattice Structure in Precious Opals." *Gems & Gemmology* 8, no. 5 (1955).

———. "Observations on Opal Fields." *Journal of Gemmology* 5, no. 7 (1956).

———. "The Occurrence of Opal." *Commonwealth Jeweller and Watchmaker* (April 1956).

———. "The Origin of the Colour in Precious Opal." *Journal of Gemmology* 4, no. 5 (1954).

———. "Thoughts on the Cause of Colour in Opal." *Gemmology* 7 (1953).

Leiper, H. "Is There Precious Opal in Honduras?" *Lapidary Journal* (October 1959): 568.

———. "Some Notes on the Early History of Honduras Opal." *Lapidary Journal* (April 1965): 62.

Leitmeier, H. "Opale aus Kleinasein, Kupfererze aus Bulgarien und Kacholong aus Steiermark." *Centralblatt für Mineralogie, Geologie und Paläontologie,* 1910.

Leonardus, C. *The Mirror of Stones.* J. Freeman, London, 1750.

Liddicoat, R. T., Jr. *Handbook of Gem Identification,* 11th ed. Gemological Institute of America, Santa Monica, CA, 1981.

———. "Notes on Recent Synthetics and the Blackening of Natural Opals." *Journal of the Gemmologist* 12 (1971): 309.

———. "Unusual Opals." *Gems & Gemmology* 13 (1970): 148.

Lindhe, H. E. "There Is Opal in Honduras." *Lapidary Journal* (December 1961): 500.

Linot, F. *Les Lapidaires Indiens: Bibliothéque de L'école des Hautes Études*. Libraire Émile Bouillon, ed., Paris, 1896.

Livstrand, U. "The Black Opals of Lightning Ridge." *Lapidary Journal* (June 1987): 49–56.

Loneck, A. *Opals: Rivers of Illusions*. Gemcraft, East Malvern, Victoria, Australia, 1986.

Lyons, D. D. H. "Black Opal Prices Stabilized." *Colored Stone* (September/October 1989): 8–14.

Mallory, L. D. "Opal Mining in Western Mexico, Part 1." *Lapidary Journal* (June 1969): 420.

———. "Opal Mining in Western Mexico, Part 2." *Lapidary Journal* (July 1969): 570.

Mayers, D. E. "Gems of Mexico." *Journal of Gemmology*, London (July 1947).

———. "Mexican Black Opal." *Gems & Gemology* 5 (1947): 475.

McCleod, E. "Fluorescent Opal in Virgin Valley." *The Desert Magazine* (July 1941): 30–32.

McDonald, R. M. *Opals and Gold*. J. B. Lippincott, Philadelphia, 1928.

McIver, J. R. *Gems, Minerals and Rocks in Southern Africa*. Purnell & Sons, Cape Town, 1966.

McNevin, A. A., with G. Holmes; "Mineral Industry of New South Wales no. 18." *Gemstones*, 2d ed. New South Wales Geological Survey, Sydney, 1980.

Melon, T., with P. Bourguignon and A. M. Fransolet. *Les Minéraux de Belgique*, LeLotte, Dison, Belgium, 1976.

Merriam, J. C. "Tertiary Mammal Beds in Virgin Valley and Thousand Creek in Northwestern Nevada," Part 1, Geologic History, California University Department Geology Bulletin V-6, no. 2, pp. 21–53, 1910.

Merrill, G. P. *Handbook* [to collection in U.S. National Museum/Smithsonian]. Washington, 1922.

Merritt, C. A. *Igneous Geology of the Lake Altus Area, Oklahoma*. Bulletin 76 of the Oklahoma Geological Survey, January 1958, Norman.

———, with W. E. Hamm. "Pre-Cambrian Zeolite-Opal Sediments in Wichita Mountains, Oklahoma," in *Bulletin of the American Association of Petroleum Geologists* 25, no. 2 (February 1941): pp. 287–299.

Metzger, R. L. "Australian Opal." *Lapidary Journal* (November 1982): 1452.

Miers, H. A. *Mineralogy: An Introduction to the Scientific Study of Minerals*, 2d rev. ed. by H. L. Browman. Macmillan, London, 1929.

Miller, H. F., with R. L. Olson. "Adventuring 'Off the Beaten Track' in Mexico, Part 1: Opals, Opals, Everywhere." *Lapidary Journal* (May 1966): 284.

Mineral Digest. "Opal." *Mineral Digest*, no. 1 (spring 1972): 88–89.

———. "Passion for Opals." no. 1 (pring 1972): 79–85.

Mitchell, J. R. "Agate, Chalcedony, and Precious Opal Near Tecopa, California." *Lapidary Journal* (January 1984): 1422.

———. "Agate, Jasper, and Opalite Near Eureka, Nevada." *Lapidary Journal* (March 1984): 1734.

———. "Agate, Jasper, and Opalized Wood between Homedale, Idaho, and the Oregon Border." *Lapidary Journal* (March 1982): 2538.

————. "Southeast Oregon." *Rock & Gem* (August 1990): 60–65.

————. "Southwest of Virgin Valley." *Rock & Gem* (October 1991): 52–54, 84–85.

————. "Virgin Valley Opal." *Rock & Gem* 20, no. 9 (September 1990): 56–59, 78–80.

Mitchell, R. K. "Oiled Opals." *Journal of the Gemmologist* 18 (1982): 339.

Moore, T. "Frail Princess of Gems." *Lapidary Journal* 46, no. 3, (June 1992): 22–26.

Morse, J. "A Quest for Oregon Opal." *Lapidary Journal* 13 (August 1959): 418.

Morrison, M. "Report on the Tintinbar Opal Discovery." *Annual Report of the New South Wales Department of Mines,* 1919.

Mulkey, J. E. Jr. "Opal Hill Fire Agate Mine." *Rock & Gem* (April 1992): 53–56.

Munzing, G. E., with W. D. Tidwell. *Sequoiadendron Hodsonii Sp. November, from the Middle Miocene Virgin Valley Flora of Northwestern Nevada.* Unpublished abstract, University of Utah.

Murdoch, J., with R. W. Webb. *Minerals of California.* California Division of Mines and Geology, Bulletin 189, San Francisco, 1966.

Murphy, E. F. *They Struck Opal!* Associated General Productions, Sydney, 1948.

Murray, W. "Andamooka Mining." Parts 1 and 2. *American Gemcutter* no. 81 (November 1993): 11–14; no. 82 (December 1993): 25–27.

Museo Nacional de Ciencias Naturales. Unpublished list of opal occurrences in Spain. Madrid, 1995.

Myatt, B. *Australia and New Zealand Gemstones.* Summit Books, Sydney, 1970.

————. *Where to Find Gemstones in Australia and New Zealand.* Summit Books, Sydney, 1972.

Nevada Bureau of Mines and Geology. "Directories of Nevada Mine Operations Active, 1981–1985," Reno, 1986 (also MRDS Report of January 1992).

————. "Major Mines of Nevada, 1990." Special publication no. 11, Mackay School of Mines, University of Nevada, Reno, 1991.

Nevada Department of Minerals. Press release about Virgin Valley Black Fire Opal being named State Precious Gemstone; n.d.

Nichols, R. A. "Opal Mines of Nevada." *Lapidary Journal* (October 1979): 1638–1644.

Nicols, T. *A Lapidary; or the History of Precious Stones.* Thomas Buck, Cambridge, UK, 1652.

Noel, A. G. "Treating Opal Matrix." *Lapidary Journal* (October 1970): 914; (October 1976): 1787.

Noorbergen, R. *Secrets of the Lost Races.* Barnes & Noble, New York, 1978.

Northrup, S. A. *Minerals of New Mexico.* Albuquerque, 1966.

Nowak, G. "Fire Opals in the Mojave Desert." *Lapidary Journal* (April 1974): 52.

Oakley, P. "An Opal Prospecting Tour through Australia." *Lapidary Journal* (August 1974): 778.

O'Leary, B. *A Field Guide to Australian Opals.* Rigby, Adelaide, South Australia, 1977.

————. "Fire Forever." *Lapidary Journal* (October 1977): 1498.

————. "Opals of Indonesia." *Lapidary Journal* (February 1977): 2484.

Opals, Inc., bill of lading; holograph by Bob Simmons; shipment of 21 pounds gem opal and 85 pounds of gem opal rough from Peacock no. 1 Mine, 14 and 23 August 1969.

Osterstock, A. *Andamooka Opal.* Roling Press, Adelaide, South Australia, 1976.

Panczner, B. "Mexican Opal: The Hummingbird Stone." *Rock & Gem* 24, no. 10 (October 1994): 58–62.

Parker, R. E. "Hunting Fire Agates and Opals in Mexico." *Lapidary Journal* (October 1963): 740.

Parkin, L. W. "The Opal Industry in South Australia." *Mining Review of the South Australia Department of Mines,* no. 84 (1901).

Parser, D. "1963 Conditions at the Opal Mines in Australia." *Lapidary Journal* (June 1963): 366.

Payne, J. M. "Rockhounding in British Columbia." *Rock & Gem* (November 1978): 30–34.

Pearson, G. "Opal Pineapples from White Cliffs." *Australian Mineralogist* 2, no. 2 (1986): 143–151.

———. "Opal Pineapples from White Cliffs, New South Wales." *Australian Gemmologist* 16, no. 4 (1987): 7–12.

Perry, N., with R. Perry. *Australian Gemstones in Colour.* A. H. and A. W. Reed, Sydney, 1979.

———. *Australian Opals in Colour.* A. H. and A. W. Reed, Sydney, 1980.

———. *Gemstones in Australia.* A. H. and A. W. Reed, Sydney, 1978.

———. *Prospectors Guide to Gemstones in Australia.* A. H. and A. W. Reed, Sydney, 1982.

Petrusenko, S., with R. I. Kostov. *Gem and Decorative Minerals of Bulgaria.* Publisher unknown, Sofia, 1988.

Phillips, W. R., with D. T. Griffen. *Optical Mineralogy: The Nonopaque Minerals.* McGraw-Hill, New York, 1981.

Piers, H. Paper in *Transactions of the Nova Scotia Institute of Science* 12 (1908–1910): 446.

Pittman, E. J. "Opal" in *The Mineral Resources of New South Wales* as the *Annual Report of the New South Wales Department of Mines, 1901.*

Pough, F. H. *A Field Guide to Rocks and Minerals.* Houghton Mifflin, Boston, 1955.

———. "Gem Treatment: Opal." *Lapidary Journal* (October 1986): 16–18.

———. "The Genesis of Opal." *Jewelers' Circular-Keystone* (October 1959).

———. "Spectral Gemstones, Frozen Rainbows." *Lapidary Journal* 39 (September 1985): 19–21.

Praed, R. C. *Opal Fire* [Novel]. Macmillan, London, 1910.

Prichard, K. S. *Black Opal* [Novel]. Periwinkle Books, Sydney, 1946.

———. *Potch and Colour* [Novel]. Periwinkle Books, Sydney, 1944.

Profile of the Gemstone Industry in Queensland. Department of Industry and Regional Development, Brisbane, Australia, 1992.

Queensland Opal. Queensland Department of Mines, Mapping Series, Brisbane, Australia, 1988.

Queensland Yearbook, 1992. Queensland Department of Resource Industries, Brisbane, Australia, 1992.

Ralph, R. E. "The White Cliffs Opal Field, New South Wales." New South Wales Department of Mines, Technical Report 7, for 1959; 1961, pp. 7–18.

Raman, C. V., with A. Jayaraman. "Iridescent Quartz Crystals." *Proceedings of the Indian Academy of Sciences.* 32 (1950).

————. "The Origin of the Colours in Precious Opal." *Current Science* 22 (1953).

————. "Structure of Iridescent Opal." *Proceedings of the Indian Academy of Sciences* 38 (1953).

Ransom, J. E. *Gems and Minerals of America.* Harper & Row, New York, 1975.

Reed, E. "An Opal Tip." *American Opal Society Newsletter* (6 December 1972).

Reidenbach, K.-T. *Achatschleiferers und Wasserschleifen am Idarbach Idar-Oberstein.* Raiffeisenbank, Idar-Oberstein, 1986.

Reisen, F. E. "Opals." *Gems & Minerals* (June 1982): 8, 46–47.

Renton, J. L. "Opal or Agate Filled 'Thunder Eggs'." *The Mineralogist* 4 (1936): 12, 46–52.

Report of the Royal Commission to Inquire into the Opal Industry at White Cliffs, New South Wales. Sydney, 1901.

Roberts; W. L., with G. Rapp, Jr. *Mineralogy of the Black Hills.* Rapid City, 1968.

Robertson, D. "The Duffields' Little Jo Opal Mine—A New Place to Dig!" *Lapidary Journal* (October 1972): 1096.

Rocks & Minerals. "Metallic Oxides in Precious Opal." 17 (1942).

Rogers. P. A., and R. Beard. *Five Thousand Years of Gems and Gemology.* J. B. Lippincott, Philadelphia, 1947.

Rose, W. A. "Treating Matrix Opal." *Gems & Gemology* 14 (1974): 306.

Ross, C. P. "The Metal and Coal Mining Districts of Idaho, with Notes on the Nonmetallic Mineral Resources of the State," *Idaho Bureau of Mines and Geology Pamphlet 57* (1941): 263.

————. "Ore Deposits in the Tertiary Lava in the Salmon River Mountains, Idaho," *Idaho Bureau of Mines and Geology Pamphlet 25* (1927): 20.

Roth, B. "Glendonites." *Pacific Discovery* (October 1979): 29–31.

Rothstein, J. "Hydrophane." *Lapidary Journal* (December 1982): 1490.

Rowe, G. *Saltbush Rainbow—The Early Days at White Cliffs.* Gwen Rowe, 1983.

Ruppenthal, P. *Edelsteine-Handel und Industrie im Raum Idar-Oberstein von 1923 bis 1985.* A. Ruppenthal, Idar-Oberstein, 1985.

Sanders, M. B. "New Mexico's Opal Trail." *Lapidary Journal* (December 1961): 544.

Sanders, J. V., et al. "Colour of Precious Opal." *Nature* 204 (1964): 1151.

Schowalter, M. "Slocum Stone—A New Man-Made Material." *Lapidary Journal.* (September 1976): 1320.

Schumann, W. *Gemstones of the World.* Sterling, New York, 1977.

Scott, Sir Walter. *Anne of Geierstein; or, The Maiden of the Mist,* 3 vols., Cadell, Edinburgh, 1829.

Segnit, R. W. "Andamooka Opal Field." *Mining Review* 62 (1935), South Australia Department of Mines.

————. "The Pre-Cambrian-Cambrian Succession in South Australia." *Bulletin of the Geological Survey of South Australia* no. 18 (1939).

Seiple, E. "Buffalo Canyon Opal." *Lapidary Journal* (September 1988): 22–26.

Seke, L., with M. Pejcic and M. Milenkovic. "Physical-mineralogical Properties of Semiprecious Stones from the Serpentinite Zone of Shumadia District." *Gemstones of Serbia.* Publisher not identified, Belgrade, 1985, pp. 62–63.

———, with M. Pejcic and N. Malesevic. "Semiprecious and Ornament Stone Deposits and Occurrences at Serbia." *Gemstones of Serbia.* Publisher not identified, Belgrade, 1985.

Selbert, P. "Opal Oasis." *Lapidary Journal* 47, no. 3 (June 1993): 65–74.

Senior, B. R., et al. "The Geology and Magnetic Characteristics of Precious Opal Deposits, Southwest Queensland." *BMR Journal of Australian Geology and Geophysics* 2 (1977): 241–251.

Shaub, B. M. "The Origin of Fire Opals." *Rock & Gem* (August 1987): 35–39.

Shiach, W. S. *An Illustrated History of Morrow County.* W. H. Lever, Eugene, OR, 1902.

Shigley, J. E., et al. "Gem Localities of the 1980s." *An Illustrated History of Morrow County* 26, no. 1 (spring 1990): 4–31.

Shipley, R. M. *Dictionary of Gems and Gemology.* Gemological Institute of America, Los Angeles, 1945.

Shockey, P. N. "Reconnaissance Geology of the Leesburg Quadrangle, Lemhi County, Idaho." *Idaho Bureau of Mines and Geology Pamphlet 113* (1957): 42.

Simpson, E. S. *Minerals of Western Australia,* vols. 1,2,3. Perth Govt. Printer, 1948, 1951, 1952.

Sinkankas, J. *Gemology: An Annotated Bibliography.* 2 vols. Scarecrow Press, Metuchen, NJ, 1993.

———. *Gemstones of North America.* Van Rostrand Reinhold, New York, 1959.

———. "Opal Cutting Tips." *Lapidary Journal* (December 1961): 550.

———. *Prospecting for Gemstones and Minerals.* Van Nostrand Reinhold, New York, 1961.

———. *Sinkankas' Catalog of Gem Values.* Geoscience Press, Prescott, AZ, 1968.

———. *Standard Catalog of Gems.* Van Nostrand Reinhold, New York, 1968.

Skalicky, J. "Interesting Opals from Czechoslovakia." *Lapidary Journal* (July 1983): 578–584.

Skertchly, S. B. J. *The Story of the Noble Opal.* Gordon & Gotch, Brisbane, 1908.

Smith, G. "Report on Lightning Ridge Opal Field." *Annual Report of the New South Wales Department of Mines,* 1923.

Smith, G. F. H. *Gemstones.* Shoe String Press, London, 1912, revised 1958.

Smith, C. P. "Unusual Natural Opal." *Gems & Gemology* (spring 1990): 96–97.

Smith, K. L. "Opals from Opal Butte, Oregon." *Gems & Gemology* 24, no. 4 (winter 1988): 229–238.

Sosman, R. B. "Crystobalite and Opal." *Journal of the American Chemical Society* 54 (1932).

———. *The Properties of Silica.* Academy Press, New York, 1927.

South Australian Department of Mines and Energy. *Opal in South Australia.* Mineral Information Series, Parkside, September 1938.

Spence, G. W. "Opalized Wood in Colombia, South America." *Lapidary Journal* (March 1967): 1454.

Spencer, L. J. *Key to Precious Stones,* 2d ed. Macmillan, London, 1946.

———. *The World's Minerals.* Macmillan, New York, 1911.

Spencer, R. J., with A. A. Levinson and J. I. Koivula. "Opal from Querétaro, Mexico: Fluid Inclusion Study." *Gems & Gemology* 28, no. 1 (spring 1992): 28–34.

Staatz, M. H., with H. L. Bauer, Jr. *Virgin Valley Opal District, Humboldt County, Nevada.* U. S. Geological Survey Circular 142, Washington, DC, 1952.

Staples, L. W. "Origin and History of the Thunder Egg." *The Ore Bin* 27 (1965): 189–204.

Steinoff, J. M. "Famous Opals of the World." *Lapidary Journal* (December 1976): 2208–2209.

Sterrett, D. B. "Gems and Precious Stones." *Mineral Resources of the United States,* Washington, DC, 1911.

———. "Gems and Precious Stones." *Mineral Resources of the United States,* Washington, DC, 1910.

———. "Precious Stones." *Mineral Resources of the United States,* Washington, DC, 1908.

———. "Precious Stones." *Mineral Resources of the United States,* Washington, DC, 1909.

Stetler, M. "Free Basis Collecting Sites." *Lapidary Journal* (December 1976): 2034–2040, 2074.

Stivens, D. "Opal—Queen of Gems." *Lapidary Journal* (November 1964): 882.

Stone, D. M., with R. A. Butt. *Australian Precious Opal.* Periwinkle Books, Sydney, 1976.

Streeter, E. W. *Precious Stones and Gems.* 5th ed. Gordon Press, London, 1892.

Stutzer, O., with W. Fr. Eppler. *Die Lagerstätten der Edelsteine und Schmucksteine.* Verlag von Gerbréder Borntraeger, Wien, 1935.

Talliafero, L. N. "Some Properties of Opal." *American Journal of Science* 30 (1935).

Taylor, J. S. "The Story of White Cliffs Opal Field." *Gems & Gemology* (fall 1971): 334–343.

Themelis, T. "Flashes in Black Opal." *Lapidary Journal* (March 1988): 12.

Thomson, I. D. "Australia's Lightning Ridge, Home of the Black Opal." *Lapidary Journal* (December 1969): 1308.

Thorndike, L. *A History of Magic and Experimental Science* 8: *The Seventeenth Century.* Columbia University Press, New York, 1958.

Towner, J. M. "Crinoids and Opal in the Heart of Texas." *Lapidary Journal* (August 1974): 832.

Townsend, I. J. "The Mintabie Opalfield." *Australian Gemmologist* 18, no. 1 (1992): 7–12.

Traill, R. R. Paper 80-18 in *Catalogue of Canadian Minerals,* revised 1980.

Turley, D. "A Summer of Fire." *Rock & Gem* (July 1987): 48–50.

United States Geological Survey. *Opal File Report 78–1002,* Washington, DC, 1978.

United States Government Printing Office. *Minerals Yearbook, 1939.* Washington, DC, 1939, p. 1934.

Utah Geological Association. "Geology of the Milford Area." *Utah Geological Association Publication no. 3.* Salt Lake City, UT, 1973.

Vakanjac, B. "Potentiality of Yugoslavia Regarding Precious, Semi-precious and Ornamental Stones." *Gemstones of Serbia.* Publisher not identified, Belgrade, 1985.

Van Bebber, J. S. "The Opal—Lucky Gemstone of Hope." *Lapidary Journal* (October 1975): 1338.

van Calker, F. J. P. "Beitrage zur Kenntniss des Pseudogaylussit und übedr dessen Vorkommen in Holland." *Zeitschrift für Kristallographie* 28, band 6 (1897): 556–572.

Van Leuvan, E. P. "Opal Gemlore." *Gems & Minerals* no. 253 (October 1958): 34–35.

Van Nostrand, D., Co., Inc. "Opal." *D. Van Nostrand's Scientific Encyclopedia,* 4th ed. Van Nostrand, Princeton, NJ, 1968, p. 1239.

Verrill, A. H. *Minerals, Metals and Gems.* Houghton Mifflin, Boston, 1939.

Wain, H. C. *The Story of Fluorescence.* Stafford Springs, CT, 1965.

Waite, G. G. "The Unusual Opals of Mexico." *Lapidary Journal* (December 1969): 1220.

Wake, P. V. *Opal Men.* A. H. & A. W. Reed, Sydney, 1969.

Walker, B. G. *The Book of Sacred Stones.* Harper & Row, New York, 1989.

Walker, C. "The Onyx and Opal Cutting Industry." *Lapidary Journal* (April 1970): 281.

Walker, D., with C. Walker. "Crosscountry Mining." *Lapidary Journal* (April 1990): 81–83.

———. "Hunting for Opals." *Lapidary Journal* (August 1990): 97.

———. "Idaho's Blue Heaven." *Lapidary Journal* 45, no. 7 (October 1991): 75–76.

Walker, G. W. *Geological Map of Oregon East of the 121st Meridian.* United States Geological Survey, Department of the Interior, Renton, VA, 1977.

Walker, W. H. "A New Type of Simulated Heat-treated Black Opal." *Lapidary Journal* 17 (1963): 655.

———. "Black Opal Matrix." *Gems and Minerals* (September 1963): 35–37.

Walton, Sir James. *Physical Gemology.* Oxford University Press, New York, 1952.

Ward, L. K. "The Stuart Range Opal Field." *Mining Review* 25 (1916) South Australia Department of Mines.

Watkins, J. J. "Future Prospects for Opal Mining in the Lightning Ridge Region." *New South Wales Geological Survey, Report GS1985/119* (unpubl.); 1985.

Watkins, J. "Opaltalk." *Lapidary Journal* 47, no. 3 (June 1993): 27–29.

Webster, R. *Gems in Jewelry.* Shoe String Press, London, 1975.

———. *Gems: Their Sources, Descriptions and Identification.* 3rd ed. Archon, London, 1975.

———. *Practical Gemology.* Wehman Brothers, London, 1952.

———, with V. Hinton. *Introductory Gemology,* vol. 5 of *Jeweler's Library.* Gramercy Press, Los Angeles, 1945.

Weinstein, M. *Precious and Semi-Precious Stones,* 3d ed. Gordon Press, New York, 1939.

Whiting, J. W., with R. E. Ralph. "The Occurrence of Opal at Lightning Ridge and Grawin, with Geological Notes on Country Finch." *New South Wales Department of Mines, Technical Report 6, for 1985,* pp. 7–21.

Whitlock, H. P. *The Story of Gems,* 2d ed. Harvey House, New York, 1940.

Wild, K. E. *Die Idar-Obersteiner Edel-Und Schmuck-Steinverabeitende Industrie 1834–1960, Heimatchroniken der Stäste und Kreise des Bundesgebietes, Idar-Oberstein im Landkreis Birkenteld.* Band 24 der Reihe, 1961.

———. "Australische Opale und ihre Bearbeitung in Kirschweiler, in Kirschweiler Beiträge zur Wirtschaft, Struktur und Geschichte." *Metteilungen des Vereins für Heimatkunde im Landkreis Birkenfeld.* Sonderheft 29, 1977, pp. 75–86.

Willden, R. *Nevada Bureau of Mines and Geology Bulletin 59,* 1964.

Wilson Mines. Bulletin, undated, for treating matrix opal to make it a "treated black opal."

Wise, R. W. "Australia, Thy Name Is Opal." *Colored Stone* 4, no. 2 (1991): 9.

———. "Queensland Boulder Opal." *Gems & Gemology* 29, no. 1 (spring 1993): 4–15.

Wollaston, T. C. *Opal: The Gem of the Never Never*. Thomas Murby, London, 1924.

Wood, J. "The World's Largest Opal." *Rock & Gem* 20, no. 12 (December 1990): 52–54.

Woolnough, W. G. "The Duricrust of Australia." *Journal and Proceedings of the Royal Society of New South Wales* 61 (1924).

Wright, D. "The Craze for Opal." *Lapidary Journal* (February 1974): 1726.

Zegarac, S. "Gems Processing from the Occurrences at Serbia Region." *Gemstones of Serbia*. Publisher not identified, Belgrade, 1985, p. 79.

Zeitner, J. C. "Doublets and Triplets." *Lapidary Journal* (June 1987): 45–48.

———. "Opal, Anyone?" *Lapidary Journal* (June 1989): 52–56.

———. "The Opal of Querétaro." *Lapidary Journal* (July 1979): 868.

———. "Opals That Made History." *Lapidary Journal* (June 1989): 23–30.

———. "Precious and Blue." *Lapidary Journal* (June 1990): 76–80.

———. "Precious Opal from Nevada." *Lapidary Journal* (March 1971): 1534.

———. "Precious Opal in the United States." *Lapidary Journal* (June 1986): 42.

———. "Querétaro Opals." *Lapidary Journal* (June 1987): 20–24.

———. "Tally, Opal!" *Lapidary Journal* 46, no. 3 (June, 1992): 83–90.

Zielinski, R. A. "Uraniferous Opal, Virgin Valley, Nevada: Conditions of Formation and Implications for Uranium Exploration." *Journal of Geochemical Exploration,* 16 (1982): 197–216; The Netherlands.

Index

Aalter, Belgium, 270
Abercrombie River, NSW, 70, 322
Abidjan, Cote D'Ivoire, 280
Aboriginal Council, 229
Aboriginals, 89, 91–94, 98, 146, 187, 191, 199, 200, 229, 231, 375
Absaroka Range, WY, 366
Abumibata, Jpn., 300
Achab, Aïcha, 338
Adams County, CA, 275
Adavale, Qld., 70
Addis Ababa, Eth., 286
Adelaide, S. Austral., 42, 68, 74, 83, 84, 89, 90, 100, 120, 121, 141, 187, 189, 191, 193, 196, 200, 224, 229, 257, 349
Adelaide Advertiser, 141
Afghanistan, 263
Afra-Beni-Ifur, Sp., 353
Agate Lake, WY, 367
Agate Mountain, B.C., 273
Aguascaliente, Mex., 304
Aigueperse, Fr., 288
Ajmer, In., 297
Akase, Jpn., 300
Akos, Éva Vetó, 293
Alabama, 263, 264
Al-Haddad, Farazdaq M., 298
Alaska, 55, 264
Alava Province, Sp., 351
Albacete Province, Sp., 351
Albania, 370
Albany, NY, 327
Albany, W. Austral., 364
Albemarle County, VA, 361
Alberta Province, Can., 264
Albion, ME, 302
Albury Region, Vic., 360
Alcala, Luis, 351
Alcala de Henares, Sp., 353
Alentejo, Port., 337
Alexandria, VA, 361
Alfonso X, King, 62
Alfonso XII, King, 72
Algeria, 264
Alice Springs, N.T., 89, 117, 224, 229, 231

Allen Range, Qld., 345
Allison, M. Lee, 359
Almasul Mare, Rum., 347
Almerica Province, Sp. 351
Almodad (ancient explorer), 54
Almonaster la Real, Sp., 352
Alonso, Ramon M., 338
Alpine, TX, 356
Alpine County, CA, 275
Altmann, John, 96, 101, 120, 121, 147, 189, 201
Altmann & Cherney, Ltd., 101
Alturas, CA, 132
Aluminum oxide, 25, 34
Alundalippur, In., 297
Amador County, CA, 275
Amelaco District, Mex., 304
Amelia County, VA, 361
Amelia Courthouse, VA, 361
America, xi, xii, 16, 36, 54, 55, 64, 70, 72, 73, 81, 84, 86, 87, 89, 91, 94, 101, 102, 104, 107, 110, 112, 120, 122, 132, 136, 137, 154, 169, 183, 202, 204, 207, 213, 228, 246, 278, 284, 309, 330, 331, 360, 361, 370, 374, 379, 381
American Samoa, 370
Americus Australis opal, 101, 120, 156
Amethyst Mountain, WY, 367
Amherst, N.S., 331
Amorphous, 1, 41, 173, 182, 332, 373
Amravati District, In., 297
Amstall, Aus., 268
Amygdaloidal nodules, 21
Amygdules, 21, 23, 205, 206, 271, 272, 277, 278, 286, 292, 356
Anaheim, CA, 309
Anatolia, Turk., 358
Anchorage, AK, 264
Andaman Nicobar Islands, In., 297
Andamooka Opal, 26, 29, 98, 100, 120, 121, 146, 154, 158, 188, 189, 375
Andamooka opal, 29, 121, 146, 188, 189, 375

Andamooka, S. Austral., 8, 22, 26, 29, 31, 94–96, 98, 100, 101, 104, 109, 116, 120, 121, 146, 149, 154, 156, 158, 175, 178, 187–193, 195, 198, 200, 244, 301, 302, 349, 373, 375, 378
discovery of precious opal, 94
Andamooka Station, 187, 188
Andamooka Township, S. Austral., 193
Andargaon, In., 297
Anderson, C., 85
Anderson, Warren H., 300
Andes, MT, 54
Andes Mountains, 204
Andhra Pradesh, In., 297
Andorra, 370
Andrew Cody, Pty., Ltd., 42
Androscoggin County, ME, 302
Angaston, S. Austral., 68, 349
Angledool, Lightning Ridge, 44, 86, 94, 109, 114, 121, 156, 209, 211, 324
Angola, 370
Angsuwathana, Prayong, 357
Anguilla, 370
Anhwei (China), 370
Animas Peak, NM, 54
Ankara Province, Turk., 358
Ankartra, Mal. Rep., 96
Anna Creek, S. Austral., 78, 89
Annapolis County, N.S., 331
Anne of Geierstein, 67
Annie Creek, SD, 351
Antarctica, 50, 111, 265
Anti-Atlas Region, Mor., 307
Antigua, W.I., 265
Antolovich, Mario, xiv
Antony, Marc (Marcus Antonius), 58
Antrim, G.B., 285
Antrim, Ire., 298
Antrim Plateau, W. Austral., 364
Antwerp, Belg., 270
Aomori Prefecture, Jpn., 300
Appel, Peter, 291
Apponyi, 246, 247
Apuseni Mountains, Rom., 347
Aquascaliente, Mex., 97, 102

Aquila Azteca (Aztec Eagle) opal, 60, 226
Arabana aboriginals, 92
Arabia(n), xii, 2, 56, 60, 151, 371
Arad, Isr., 299
Archangel, Russ., 51, 95
Archevaleta, Dan, 248, 310
Archevaleta, Rhinehart, 310
Archevaleta Opal, 96, 156
Archie, Curtis, 358
Arganda, Sp., 353
Argenbright, Franklin W., 99, 242
Argentina, 265
Argylshire, Scot., 347
Arico-Güimar, Sp., 354
Ariyalur, In., 297
Arizona, xiv, 115, 128, 140, 145, 162, 180, 266, 306
Arkansas, 267
Armagosa Desert, CA, 275
Armenia, 370
Arod Pass, Isr., 299
Arrowhead, 132, 133
Arroyo de la Presa, NM, 320
Arroyo de Ramos, Mex., 304
Aruba, 370
Ashcroft, B.C., 272, 273
Asheville, NC, 152, 329
Ashland, VA, 362
Assembled opal, 162. *See also* Doublets; Triplets
Asten, Aus., 268
Astoria, OR, 51, 69, 73
Astrakhan, Russ., 173
Astuvansalmi, Fin., 287
Aswan, Eg., 284
Athens, Greece, 55
Atlanta, GA, 289
Atlantic City, NJ, 137
Atlantic Ocean, 267
Atom migration, 23, 25, 26, 37. *See also* Ion exchange
Atzcapotzaleo, Mex., 304
Auburn, OR, 333
Auburn, Qld., 342
Augusta, ME, 302
Aurora Australis opal, 87, 96, 114, 121, 131, 149, 156, 158, 201, 222
Aurora Borealis, Qld., 341
Austin, TX, 356
Australia(n), x, xiii, 3, 4, 10, 12, 13, 17, 22, 23, 29, 35, 36, 40, 42, 45, 46, 49, 50, 53, 68–70, 72–78, 80, 82–95, 97–101, 104, 106, 109, 110, 112–114, 116, 117, 120–122, 128–132, 134, 136, 140–142, 145, 146, 148, 149, 151–160, 162, 164, 165, 167–170, 174– 176, 178, 179, 182, 184, 185, 187, 189, 191, 193– 199, 200, 203, 205, 206, 213, 214, 222, 224, 227, 229, 239, 242, 243, 245, 246, 256–259, 261, 267, 272, 281, 287, 294, 301,

305, 309, 322, 330, 336, 338, 349, 355, 360, 363, 364, 370, 373–382, 385, 386
first discovery of opal, 68; first discovery of precious opal, 70; first opal mining leases, 70; seam opal discovered, 74; second discovery of opals, 68; underground living begins, 80
Australian Capital Territory, 267
Australian Gem Trading Company, 189
Australian Mining Act, 100
Australian Mining Journal 140
Austria(n) 85, 91, 93, 126, 268– 270
Auvergne, Fr., 289
Auxillac, Fr., 288
Avery County, NC, 329
Avon District, ID, 295
Avondale, PA, 334
Axon, VA, 362
Ayershire, Scot., 347
Azacualpa, Hon., 208
Azerbaijan, 370
Aztec, 60, 64, 69, 129, 158, 171, 180, 184, 205, 226–228, 306
Aztec Sun God opal, 60, 158
Azza, M. Addi, 307

Bachèlery, Patrick, 346
Bachelor Mountain, OR, 55
Backman, Carl-Magnus, 354
Backus Opal, 121, 156
Backus, Standish (Mrs.), 121
Baden, Ger., 291
Badlands, SD, 350
Bad luck reputation of opals, 61, 62, 67–69, 149, 173
Baghdad, Ir., 298
Bahamas, 370
Bahrain, 370
Bailey, George, 86
Bairndale, Qld., 239
Bairnsdale, Vic., 361
Baker County, OR, 333
Bald Mountain District, SD, 351
Baldy Peak, NM, 54
Baldy Peak, TX, 54
Baleares Province, Sp., 352
Ballindean, Scot., 347
Ballroom in mines, 192, 373
Ballywillin Parish, G.B., 285
Ballywillin Parish, Ire., 298
Baltimore County, MD, 303
Bamboo Springs, W. Austral., 364
Bancroft, Ont., 332
Bancroft, Peter, 124
Bandajoz Province, Sp., 351
Bandung, Indon., 297
Bangkok, Thai., 357
Bangladesh, 270
Bank, Hermann, 291
Banská Bystrica, Slov., 282
Banska Stiavnica, Slov., 283

Banske, Slov., 282
Baracoo River, Qld., 339
Barbados, 370
Barbuda, W.I., 265
Bare Hills, MD, 303
Barnes Creek, B.C., 273
Barnett, Dick/Shirley, 276
Barraba, NSW, 323
Barrack Mountain, G.B., 285
Barranca Agua Dulce, Mex., 305
Barranca de Tepezala, Mex., 97, 102, 304, 305
Barron's, West Goshen, PA, 334
Barstow, CA, 276
Bartow County, GA, 289
Basque, 85, 96, 132, 248
Bassin de Paris, Fr., 288
Batho, F., 72
Bathurst, NSW, 70, 324
Battleship Rock, NM, 321
Bauer, Glen, 292
Baumgarten, Lower Silesia, Pol., 337
Bayatabo, Cu., 281
Bay of Fundy, N.B., 108, 319
Bayramic, Turk., 358
Baza, Sp., 352
Beacon Pole Hill, R.I., 346
Bear Canyon, NM, 320
Beautiful Yowah, Black Gate & Koroit, 118
Beaver, UT, 359
Beaver County, UT, 359
Beaver Divide, WY, 366
Beaver Meadow, NY, 327
Beckett, Joe, 82, 211, 324
Bedford, NY, 327
Bedouins, 56, 166, 56
Beechworth, N.T., 330
Beechworth, Vic., 360
Behrens, H., 3
Bei Seckau, Aus., 269
Beit Bridge, Zim., 106, 369
Beja District, Port., 337
Belarus, 370
Belele, W. Austral., 364
Belgium, 270
Belgrade, Yug., 367
Belize, 370
Belorussia, 337
Benahi, Mohamed Lemine Ould, 304
Bengkulu, Indon., 297
Beni Snaben, Mor., 307
Benin, 370
Benton County, WA, 363
Berchtold, 117
Berg, Dick, 307
Bergalia, NSW, 324
Berkeley, CA, 98, 249
Berlin, NH, 319
Bermuda, 370
Bernalillo County, NM, 320
Berne, Switz., 354
Bernhards, Aus., 269
Bernhardt, Sarah, 78
Bernstein, Aus., 268, 269
Bezvodno, Bulg., 273

Bhutan, 370
Biesiada, Gieny, 42
Big Ben opal, 98, 121, 156
Big Crooked Lake, NY, 327
Bihar, In., 297
Bijou Basin, CA, 275, 276
Bilina, Cz. Rep., 282
Bilpki, Nicholas, 348
Bingara, NSW, 324
Bingham District, UT, 359
Bintz, Jacques, 302
Birch, William D., 360
Bismarck, ND, 329
Bitam, L., 264
Bitterroot Range, ID, 242
Black Canyon, CA, 276
Black Canyon, NM, 321
Black Dome Mountain, BC, 272
Black Hills, Sp., 352
Black Horse, PA, 334
Black opal, xii, 10, 18, 29–31, 35,
    44–47, 54, 55, 59, 67, 69,
    73, 74, 81, 83–87, 90, 91,
    93, 96, 98–101, 107, 108,
    110, 111, 114–117, 121,
    126–131, 135, 136, 146–
    148, 150, 153, 155, 161,
    163, 164, 168, 171, 174,
    175, 180, 182, 183, 190,
    191, 200, 206–208, 210–
    214, 221, 222, 225, 227,
    229–231, 245–248, 250–
    252, 259, 275, 297, 298,
    305, 309, 312, 316, 317,
    323, 348, 364, 370, 375,
    376, 379. *See also* Types of
    opal: Black crystal opal;
    Black jelly opal
  collected by ancient Chinese, 55;
    description of, 213; discov-
    ered at Lightning Ridge, 81
Black Peacock opal, 107, 158, 250
Black Prince opal, 91, 122, 132,
    134, 137, 151, 158, 222
Black Range, NM, 320, 321
Black Rock Desert, NV, 106, 110,
    117, 132, 310
Blackall Region, Qld., 339
Blackbird District, ID, 295
Black Sea, 57
Blackwater Creek, Qld., 342
Blackwater Draw, NM, 320
Blanca Peak, CO, 54
Bland, NSW, 324
Blayney, NSW, 322
Blind Spring Mining District, CA,
    276
Bliss, ID, 87
Bloomfield Hills, MI, 121
Bloomfield, NSW, 324
Blue Web opal, 107, 122, 158
Bodell, Fred, 149
Bodenmossgraben, Aus., 269
Boerboom, Terry, 306
Bogota, Col., 278
Bograd, Michael B. E., 307
Bohemia, 282, 283
    Cz. Rep., 283; Cz. Slov., 282

Bohemian Massif, Aus., 268, 269
Bohney, Jesse Ray, 99–101, 242
Boirani, In., 297
Boise, ID, 78
Bolija, Yug., 368
Bolivia, 370
Bombay, In., 297
Bonanza Opal, 109, 116, 123–125,
    156, 250, 312
Bonanza Opal Mine Corporation,
    116
Bonaparte, Napoleon, 66, 67, 126,
    146, 205
Bonaparte River, B.C., 272
Bond, Herbert, 70, 241
Bonham, Harold F., 308
Bonnet Shores, RI, 346
Boraca, Yug., 368
Borgarfjördur Eystri, Ice., 293
Borgia, Cesare, 63
Borsod-Abauj, Hung., 293
Bosnia, 370
Bosporus, 57
Boston, MA, 304
Boteti River, Bot., 271
Botetourt County, VA, 361
Botryoidal formations, 12, 171,
    182, 283, 327, 332, 350,
    351, 353, 357, 359, 361,
    362, 366
Botswana, 270
Bouazzer, Mor., 307
Bouckaert, A., 270
Boulder County, CO, 278
Boulder opal, 12, 18, 22, 29, 30,
    70, 74, 76, 78, 80, 99, 101,
    107–109, 113, 115–117,
    131, 135, 144, 145, 152,
    161, 164, 170, 175, 178,
    185, 190, 195, 206, 212,
    239, 240, 242, 256, 259,
    272, 338, 339, 374, 375,
    378, 385, 386. *See also*
    Queensland opal
  boulder black opal, 164; boulder
    brown opal, 164; boulder
    matrix opal, 164; boulder
    white opal, 164; first discov-
    ered, 70; Yowah nut opal,
    118, 164, 174, 175, 185,
    239–242
Bourges, Fr., 288
Bowling Alley Creek, NSW, 325
Bradley, Walter, 132–134, 149
Braidwood, NSW, 324
Branchtown, PA, 335
Bransfield Strait, Ant., 50, 111, 265
Brard, C. P., 67
Braszowice, Lower Silesia, Pol.,
    336, 337
Brattháls, Ice., 293
Brazil, 111, 164, 193, 271
Brazilian opal, 164, 193, 194, 207
Breakfast Creek, Qld., 341
Breccia, 185, 225, 334, 353, 362,
    364, 368, 369, 374
Bremner, Trevor J., 369
Brewster County, TX, 356, 357

Brewster, David (Sir), 3
Brewster, NY, 327
Brian Hodson Opal, 125, 158
Bridger Formation, WY, 367
Brighton Downs, Qld., 239
Brindle, Joe, 70, 74
Brinkley Bjærg, Green., 292
Brisbane, Qld., 72, 135, 209, 223,
    338, 340
British Columbia, Can., 55, 116,
    169, 177, 194, 196, 271,
    272, 277
British Virgin Islands, 370
Brodtkorb, Alejo, 265
Broken Hill, NSW, 118, 256, 259,
    327, 386
Brooklyn Bridge, 152, 248
Brooks County, GA, 289
Brooks, Sam, 94–96, 187–191
Brown, George, 131
Brown, Snowy, 151
Broxson Gulch, AL, 264
Bruce, Gan, 111
Bruce, Son, 86, 289
Brunei, 370
Brussels, Belg., 270
Buchan, N.T., 330
Buchanan, OR, 333
Buchanan, Rex, 300
Buchanan, VA, 362
Bucharest, Rum., 346
Bucharia, Russ., 165
Buckfield, ME, 302
Buckley, Bob, 82
Bucks County, PA, 334
Bucomet, Yug., 368
Buda-Hills, Hung., 293
Budapest, Hung., 293
Buderim Mountain, Qld., 340
Buenos Aires, Arg., 265
Buffalo Peaks, CA, 279
Bujumbura, le, Burundi, 274
Bulacan, Phil., 335
Bulgaria, 273
Bulong, W. Austral., 364
Bulla Rocks Well, W. Austral., 365
Bullarenda, Qld., 71
Bullfinch, W. Austral., 364
Buncombe County, NC, 329
Bundtzen, Tom, 264
Bunno, Michiaki, 299
Buregg, Aus., 269
Burgenland, Aus., 268–270
Burgos, Phil., 335
Burke County, GA, 290
Burkina Faso, 370
Burlington, CO, 280
Burma. *See* Myanmar
Burma Road, WA, 363
Burnett River, Qld., 342
Burning of Troy opal, 67, 85, 92,
    93, 126, 156, 205
Burns, OR, 333
Burro Mountains District, Mex.,
    320
Burroughs Opal, 12
Burroughs, Wilbur Greely, 126
Burton, Des, 115

Burton, GA, 290
Burundi, 274
Butman, Brad, 267
Butte County, CA, 275
Butte, MO, 307
Butterfly Opal (Red Admiral), 127
Byro Station, W. Austral., 80
Byzantium, 57, 58

Cabañas, Sp., 354
Cabo Delgado Province, Moz., 308
Cachalong opal (kalmuk agate/kal-
    mut opal/kaschts-chilon
    opal), 13, 16, 164–166,
    168, 172–174, 178, 179,
    234, 252, 273, 274, 280,
    285, 293, 299, 331, 334,
    335, 351, 352
Cache Creek, B.C., 272
Cache la Poudre River, CO, 279
Cach River, Russ., 165
Cadereyta District, Mex., 304, 306
Caicos Islands, 370
Cain, J. Allen, 346
Cairns, Qld., 70, 341
Cairo, Eg., 284
Caja Hills, Mex., 70, 304
Calabah Flame opal, 107, 128, 156
Calaveras County, CA, 275
Calawakan, Phil., 335
Caldas de Malavella, Sp., 352
California, 35, 51, 55, 73, 90, 98,
    101, 103, 120, 132, 169,
    176, 177, 187, 244, 246–
    249, 274, 275, 276, 309
California City, CA, 276
Calistoga, CA, 277
Callaghan, Chris C., 348
Calumet Hill, RI, 346
Camagüey Province, Cu., 280
Camarines Sur, Phil., 335
Cambodia, 370
Camborne, G.B., 285
Camel, 45, 74, 95, 253
Cameroon, 370
Camino de Hardu a Nador, Sp.,
    353
Camino de Paracuellos, Sp., 353
Campbelltown, Scot., 347
Camp Washington, VA, 362
Canada, 42, 54, 108, 111, 116,
    127, 150, 177, 194, 203,
    211, 264, 271, 272, 277,
    303, 319, 324, 328, 330–
    332, 338, 347, 369
Canada Bill, 127
Canal Zone, 204
Canary Islands, 277, 352, 351, 352
Canberra, ACT, 267
Candle-box trade, 80
Canfell brothers, Jim/Mick/Tom,
    82, 153, 211
Cantal, Fr., 288
Canterbury, NZ, 328
Canyon County, ID, 294
Cape Blomidon, N.S., 331
Cape Province, S. Afr., 349
Cape Split, N.S., 331

Cape Verde, 370
Capitol Peak, NV, 55
Cappa, James A., 278
Caracas, Venez., 360
Carbon County, WY, 366
Carcoar, NSW, 324
Cardoza, Eduardo A., 278
Carisbrooke, Qld., 345
Carlsbad Potash District, NM, 320
Carlshavn, Green., 292
Carnarvon Basin, W. Austral., 364
Carnarvon, W. Austral., 364, 365
Carpathian Mountains, 35, 56–58,
    63, 66, 84, 347
Carroll, Lisa/Peter, xiii
Cartagena, Sp., 353
Carter Wharf, VA, 362
Cartersville, GA, 289
Casa de Campo, Sp., 352, 353
Casco, Maine, 302
Casper, Charles W., 101, 242
Caspian Sea, 165, 173
Casterberg, Aus., 269
Castile, Sp., 62
Castle Creek, ID, 77
Castle Rock, CO, 279
Castleman's Ferry, VA, 362
Castro family, 247
Catahoula Formation, MS, 307
Catamint Hill, RI, 346
Catron County, NM, 320
Catron Creek, NM, 320
Cattrell, Eric, 104
Cave Springs, GA, 290
Cayman Islands, 370
CCC Campground, Virgin Valley,
    310
Cedro de la Trapa, Sp., 353
Ceduna, S. Austral., 203
Central African Republic, 370
Central America(n), 64, 72, 101,
    102, 204, 284
Central District, NM, 320
Central Negev, Isr., 299
Centreville, VA, 362
Cerillos District, NM, 321
Cerro Agustion, Mex., 306
Cerro de Ribas, Sp., 352
Cerro Largo Department, Urug.,
    359
Cerro Negro, Sp., 352
Cervenica, Slov.., 282
Ceské Budejovice, Cz. Rep., 282
Ceyrat, Fr., 288
Chad, 370
Chadima, Sarah, 350
Chaffee County, CO, 279
Chai Badan District, Thai, 358
Chain of Opal Mountains, Hon.,
    205
Chalker, GA, 290
Challis, ID, 81, 295
Champaign, IL, 296
Chaparral, Sp., 352
Charlesbourg, Que., 338
Charlie Swamp, S. Austral., 349
Charlotte, Lux., 302
Charlottesville, VA, 361

Charlottetown, P.E.I., 338
Chateaugay, Fr., 288
Chatoyancy, xi, 244, 374, 380
Chekiang (China), 370
Chen, Chao-Hsia, 355
Chen, Chen-Hong, 355
Cherry County, CO, 279
Chester County, PA, 334
Chiahaw, Cz. Rep., 282
Chiapas, Mex., 225
Chiautla, Mex., 305
Chicago, IL, 60, 121, 129, 153
Chicoma Peak, NM, 54
Chihuahua, Mex., 225, 304
Chile, 277
Chiltern Hills, Qld., 239
Chiltern, Vic., 360
Chimney Rock, NJ, 319
China, 16, 54, 179, 203, 276, 285,
    292, 370, 371, 370
China Lake Naval Weapons Center,
    CA, 276
Chinati Peak, TX, 54
Chinese, 54, 55, 70, 166, 178, 245,
    374
Christie's, Ltd., 142
Christina, Queen, 73
Christmas Beetle opal, 128, 158
Christmas Island, 370
Chub Pond, NY, 327
Chuska Mountains, NM, 320
Cisco, UT, 359
Clark County, ID, 99, 242, 294
Clark County, KS, 300
Clarke County, VA, 362
Claro, Switz., 355
Classic of Eastern Mountains, 54, 55
Classic of Mountains and Seas, 54
Claveria, Phil., 335
Clay County, NC, 329
Clear Creek County, CO, 279
Cleopatra, Queen of Egypt, 58
Clermont-Ferrand, Fr., 288
Cleveland, GA, 290
Cleveland, OH, 250
Cliff Foot, Scot., 347
Cliffs, ID, 78
Clinton Mining Division, B.C., 272
Cloger Parish, G.B., 285
Clouston, Wil H., 74, 256
Clover Creek, ID, 87
Coacoyula, Mex., 97, 102
Coastal Range, Tai., 355
Cobalt, ID, 295
Cobar, NSW, 326
Cobb's Creek, PA, 335
Cochise County, AZ, 266
Cochiti District, NM, 320
Cocos (Keeling) Islands, 370
Cody, Andrew, 42
Coeburn, Virginia, 362
Coeur D'Alene Indian Reservation,
    ID, 294
Coggin, H. Mason, 266
Cold Springs, OK, 332
Colla Canyon, NM, 320
Collinsville, Qld., 342
Colombia, 204, 278

Colon, Mex., 102
Colorado, 54, 89, 162, 278, 279, 359
Colorado River, 162, 279, 359
  Colorado, 279; Utah, 359
Columbia River, 231
Columbia, SC, 350
Columbus, OH, 331
Common opal (snide), 1, 3, 7, 8, 10–13, 21, 22, 24, 29, 31, 33, 41, 42, 44, 48, 53, 55, 56, 64, 67, 73, 81, 84, 87, 93, 97, 99, 101–104, 106, 112, 115, 116, 126, 134, 145, 155, 161–164, 166–168, 169–171, 173–180, 182–185, 195, 201, 207, 208, 210, 211, 221, 225–228, 231, 234, 238, 243, 246, 248, 263, 264, 266–280, 282–294, 296–305, 307, 308, 310–314, 316, 319–323, 325, 326, 328, 330–335, 337, 338, 346, 348–370, 363–366, 374, 376, 378–382
  agate opal, 162; agaty potch, 162; amber opal, 162, 323; amber potch, 162; blackmorite, 163; black potch, 31, 81, 87, 163, 210, 246, 379; blue opal, 29, 112, 115, 163, 234, 235, 293, 295, 335, 353; brown-and-gray opal 164; chloropal, 166, 167, 282; chrysopal, 166, 274, 277; corencite opal, 167; dendritic opal, *see* Types of opal: dendritic opal; enhydro potch, 168; fire opal, 8, 11, 13, 53, 56, 64, 67, 69, 73, 93, 97, 101, 102, 104, 106, 112, 116, 145, 161, 162, 164, 166, 169–171, 174, 175, 177, 179, 183, 184, 195, 196, 207, 225–228, 234, 266, 272, 274, 275, 277, 290, 296, 304–307, 363–366, *see also* Types of opal: precious fire opal; gold opal, 170; green opal, 116, 170, 268, 269, 272, 282, 300, 365; green-and-yellow opal, 171; half-opal, 171, 182, *see also* Semi-opal, below; isopyre, 173; magpie potch, 174; moss opal, 168, 175, 183, 271, 274, 275, 278, 280, 282, 283, 300, 303, 310, 320–322, 335, 337, 363, 364–367; onyx opal, 162, 176; orange opal, 177; potch, 11, 24, 29, 31, 33, 44, 48, 81, 87, 134, 162, 163, 166, 168, 174, 176, 179, 201, 210, 211, 221, 246, 297, 298, 325, 326, 338, 363, 376, 379,

382; potch-and-color, 48, 134, 179, 379; red opal, 166, 180, 268, 269, 282, 338, 353; resin opal, 11, 166, 180, 182, 275, 353; semi-opal, 171, 182, 184, 273, 280, 282, 285, 291, 293, 297, 303, 351–353, 363, 368, *see also* half-opal, above; vermilite opal, 184; wax opal, 11, 166, 179, 180, 182, 184, 268, 271, 273, 280, 282, 283, 293, 297, 299, 310–314, 316, 322, 335, 349; yellow opal, 171, 185
Comoros, 370
Compillary fuel converter, 20
Compostela, Mex., 306
Comtesse de Castiglione, 72
Concepción del Oro, Mex., 306
Concord, NH, 319
Congo, 370
Connecticut, 154, 280
Conrad, Diane, 360
Constantinople, 57, 59, 69
Contepec, Mex., 306
Coober Pedy, 8, 12, 13, 22, 29, 34, 41, 47, 89, 90, 93–96, 98, 100, 101, 109, 110, 112–115, 120, 130, 136, 141, 142, 147, 154, 156, 158, 167, 187, 189–193, 196–200, 202, 203, 208, 213, 227–231, 242, 245, 260, 349, 364, 373, 375
  discovery of precious opal, 89; flooded, 114; Flying Doctor of S. Austral., 203; named, 93; underground living, 92, 197; water reservoir, 90
Coober Pedy opal, 110, 154, 167, 189, 196, 197, 202, 364
Coocoran Flame opal, 118
Coocoran Lake, 114, 115
Cook Islands, 370
Cook, Robert B., 289
Cooks Peak, NM, 54
Coolgardie, W. Austral., 78, 84, 116, 156, 364
Coomrith, Qld., 340
Coonabarabran, NSW, 78, 322
Coopers Rock, WV, 363
Coos County, NH, 319
Copán, Hon., 205
Copenhagen, Den., 284, 291
Copeton, NSW, 322
Copper Gap, NC, 329
Copperfield, W. Austral., 364
Cordillera Opala, Hon., 205
Cordoba Province, Sp., 352
Córdoba, Col., 278
Cornucopia opal, 128, 158
Cornwall, G.B., 285
Cornwall, PA, 335
Coromandel Peninsula, NZ, 328
Corrikie, Qld., 345
Cortes, Hernando, 64

Cossack, 69
Cossack, W. Austral., 364
Costa Rica, 280
Cote D'Ivoire, 280
Cottonwood Springs, TX, 356
Cougar Creek, ID, 296
County Down, G.B., 285
County Durham, G.B., 68, 94
Coward Cliff, S. Austral., 349
Cowdon, Janet, 98, 275
Cowra, NSW, 324
Coyaima, Col., 278
Coyote Springs, NV, 309
Craciunesti, Rum., 347
Cracking. *See* Opal: crazing/cracking of opal
Cragg, Fred, 106
Cragg, George, 74, 239
Cram, Len, xiii, 11, 15, 17–37, 40, 43, 46, 47, 79, 85, 108, 118, 179, 209, 213, 259, 259
Cranbrook, W. Austral., 364
Crane, Toni/Jack, 311, 313–315, 318
Crane Mountain, OR, 55
Crane Opal, 129
Crane, P. E., 272
Crane, R. T., Jr., 129
Cranston, RI, 346
Crater Lake, NZ, 328
Crazing. *See* Opal: crazing/cracking of opal
Creede, CO, 280
Creel, Mex., 305
Crestmore, CA, 276
Cretaceous Period, 21, 53, 191, 196, 225, 257, 263, 297, 300, 326, 336, 337, 367
Crevoshay, Paula, xii
Cripple Creek, CO, 280
Crni Kamen, Yug., 368
Croatia, 370
Crook County, OR, 333
Crossreagh, G.B., 285
Crossreagh, Irc., 298
Crown Point Center, NY, 327
Crowning Glory opal, 111, 129, 156
Croxwell, Michael, 250
Crystals, 1, 3, 40, 41, 48, 50, 51, 67, 77, 95, 114, 178, 191, 207, 212, 221, 225, 229, 230, 232, 234, 245, 252, 267–269, 279, 283, 285, 302, 309, 319, 320, 348, 361, 369, 373, 375, 377, 378, 386
  crystalline, ix, x, 1, 50, 173, 284, 350, 369, 373; crystalline structure, x, 50
Csaterberg, Aus., 268
Cuauhtemoc, 129, 130
Cuauhtemoc Opal, 129
Cuba, 280
Cudgegong, NSW, 326
Cue, W. Austral., 364
Cuenca Province, Sp., 352
Cuevas de Vera, Sp., 351

Cukliacan, Mex., 55
Culpeper County, VA, 362
Cumberland County, ME, 302
Cumberland County, N.S., 331
Cumberland, RI, 346
Cunnamulla, Qld., 341, 343
Cunnavalla, Qld., 341
Cupid's gem. *See* Types of opal: Cupid's gem
Curry County, NM, 320
Custer County, CO, 279
Custer County, ID, 294
Custer County, SD, 350
Cutting of opal: baroque opal, 163, 169; calibrated opal, 165, 169; cameos, 144, 165, 175, 178; critical angle, 14; doublets, *see* Doublets, Triplets under main headings; freeform opal, 165, 169; freeshape opal, 163, 169; freesize opal, 169; intarsia, 378
Cvorovici, Yug., 368
Cyclone Ridge, WY, 366
Cyprus, 281, 370
Czechoslovakia(n), 57, 58, 281, 283
Czech Republic, 171, 281, 282, 348
Czernowitz, Slov., 57, 67, 205

Daggett County, UT, 359
Dake, H. C, 96, 234, 248, 249, 309
Dampier Archipelago, W. Austral., 69
Dana, Edward S., 51, 69, 73
Dana, James Dwight, 51, 68
Danube River, 57
Dark Jubilee opal, 85, 130, 158
Darragh, Peter J., 3, 26, 31
Dartmoor, G.B., 285
Darwin, N.T., 330
Daueberg, Anders, 354
Davad Orinetal, Phil., 335
Davenport Downs, Qld., 340
David, T. W. E., 85
Davis, James J., 274
Day, R. W., 338
Daylesford, N.T., 330
Deadwood, B.C., 272
De Andrade, Miguel Montenegro, 337
Death Valley Junction, CA, 275
De Boot, Anselm, 65
De Gemmis et Lapidus, 65
De Monpensier, Duc and Duchesse, 73
Decrepitation. *See* Opal
Deepwater, NSW, 324
Dekalb County, GA, 290
Del Gallego Camarines Sur, Phil., 335
Del Norte, CO, 279
del Pila, Infanta Maria, 73
Delaware, 283, 331, 334
Delaware County, PA, 334

Delpard Station, 70
Delpard, Laura, 71
Delpard, Lucy, 71, 72
Delta River, AK, 264
Deming, NM, 320
Dendrites, 176, 183, 234, 268–270, 296, 303, 305, 321, 352–354, 368. *See also* Types of opal: dendritic opal
Denio, NV, xiv, 244, 255
Denmark, 111, 284, 286, 291, 293
Denver, CO, 237, 247, 278
Depazzie, Qld., 239
Des Burton, 115
Desert Beauty Opal, 130, 158
Detroit, MI, 182
Devon, G.B., 285
Dhaka, Bang., 270
Diana, Princess, 107, 122
Diatomaceous, 168, 173, 180, 183, 264, 265, 271, 274–277, 320, 327, 354, 356, 357, 361, 362, 376, 378, 386. *See also* Types of opal: diatomaceous opal *and* Minerals/rocks: diatomite; Fuller's earth
Diatoms, 16, 168, 274, 300, 320, 327, 332, 356, 376, 386. *See also* Minerals/rocks: diatomite
Dick's Creek, GA, 290
Dietmannsdorf, Aus., 269
Disease, 62, 63, 73, 82, 258
    Bubonic plague (Black Death), 62, 63; Cholera, 73; Diphtheria, 82, 258; Dysentery, 82, 258; Typhus, 82, 258
District Alba, Rum., 347
District Brasov, Rum., 347
District Hunedoara, Rum., 347
District Maramures, Rum., 347
District of Columbia, 370
District Suceava, Rum., 347
Djibouti, 370
Dobersberg-Waldkirchen, Aus., 268, 269
Dobraca, Yug., 368
Dodoma, Tanz., 355
Dominican Republic, 370
Donald's Hill, G.B., 285
Doña Remedios Trinidad, Phil., 335
Dooley Mountain, OR, 333
Dooly County, GA, 290
Double G Opal, 95, 130, 156
Double Wedding, The (movie), 136
Doublets, 100, 112, 162, 163, 176, 179, 195, 206, 208, 212, 243, 244, 294, 364, 373, 374, 376, 379, 382, *see also* Triplets; boulder, 373; capped, 374, 376; shell, 382
Douglas County, CO, 279
Douglas County, WA, 363
Doupovske Mountains, Cz. Rep., 283
Dover, NJ, 173

Down Under, 69, 76, 130, 158, 222, 256. *See also* Australia
Down Under Opal, 130
Dragoynovo, Bulg., 273
Drake Passage, Ant., 265
Drake, Francis (Sir), 64
Dream Cloud opal, 131, 156
Dreamtime, 199, 200, 339
    aboriginal beliefs, 200
Dresden, Ger., 181, 288
Droppingwater Creek, B.C., 272
Dsikovo, Bulg., 273
Dubbo, NSW, 84, 323
Dublin, Ire., 298
Dubois, ID, 108
Duck Creek, 239, 310, 339, 343
Duck Creek Indian Reservation, NV, 310
Duda, Rudolf, 281
Duffield Opal, 106, 156
Duffield, Ray, 106, 156
Duke of Devonshire opal, 99, 131, 158, 222
Dunedin Peninsula, NZ, 328
Dunsmuir, CA, 277
Dunstan, 87, 121, 131, 133, 149, 158, 222
Dunstan's Stone opal, 87, 121, 131, 149, 158
Durango, Mex., 305
Durkee, OR, 333
Dürnberg, Aus., 269
Dutch, 65
Duval County, TX, 356
Dynevor Downs, Qld., 339, 341

E. Gregory Sherman, Pty., Ltd., 146
Eagle County, CO, 279
Eagle Creek, B.C., 272
Eagle River, CO, 279
East Africa, 53
East Carpathian Mountains, Rum., 347
East Greenland District, Green., 292
East Perth, W. Austral., 363
Eastern Rhodope Mountains, Bulg., 273
Eastwood, S. Austral., 349
Ecuador, 370
Eddy County, NM, 320
Edinburgh, Scot., 347
Edmonton, Alta., 264
Ef'e-Gei Gemalim, Isr., 299
Egypt, 56, 58, 180, 284
Eibenstein, Aus., 269
Eifel, Ger., 291
Eighty-Quid Opal, 87, 156, 87
El Pardo, Sp., 352, 353
El Paso County, TX, 356
El Paso Mountains, CA, 274, 276
El Salvador, 280, 284
El Salvador, Mex., 104, 305
Elche de la Sierra, Sp., 351
Electrolyte, 23–26, 28, 30, 32, 33, 35, 36, 213; electrolytic, 25, 26, 40, 46, 50

Electron microscopy, 3, 26, 31, 103, 31
Elephant Butte Reservoir, NM, 321
Elf, NC, 329
Elizabeth I, Queen, 64
Elizabeth II, Queen, 100, 120, 189
Elko County, NV, 310
Ellensburg, WA, 363
Ellis County, KS, 300
Empire Valley, B.C., 272
Empress opal, 66, 67, 85, 91, 122, 126, 128, 131, 132, 134, 142, 151, 153, 156, 205, 222
England, 3, 51, 64, 68, 94, 103, 121, 150, 285, 349
English Company, 79, 257
Entebbe, Ugan., 358
Enterprise, ID, 77
Equatorial Guinea, 370
Equipment. *See* Mining equipment/machinery
Erandil, Murat, 358
Eritrea, 370
Eromanga, Qld., 239
Escalante Desert, UT, 359
Esperias, Hung., 293
Espoo, Fin., 287, 291
Esquivias, Sp., 354
Essex County, NJ, 319
Essex County, NY, 327
Estonia, 286
Ethiopia, 54, 96, 118, 286
    Menze Gishe District, 286; Shewa Province, 286
Ethridge, Bill, 127
Etzatlan, Mex., 305
Eulan, Lightning Ridge, 325
Eulo, Qld., 185
Eureka Creek, AK, 264
Evans, Paddy, 94, 188
Evans, Thomas J., 366
Everts, Mike L., 359
Eye-Of-The-World opal, 168

Faeroe Islands, 284, 286
Fairbanks, AK, 264
Fairfax County, VA, 362
Fairmount Park, PA, 335
Fairview, MT, 54
Falkland Islands, 370
Fall River Formation, WY, 367
Father's Day Opal. See Hodson Opal
Fault, 115, 150, 359, 367, 376, 378, 382
Favell Arrowhead Opal, 132
Favell, Gene, xiv, 126
Fayette County, TX, 357
Faywood Hot Springs, NM, 320
Feather, Russell C., II, 122, 155
Federal District, Mex., 305
Fee-digging for opals, 48, 104, 106–108, 110, 112, 116, 117, 121, 147, 196, 234, 239, 242–244, 250, 254, 255, 274, 275, 294–296, 306, 317, 356
    Jeppeson-Wilson Mine, Spencer,

ID, 294; Last Chance Opal Mine (Leo Nowak Fire Opal Mine), CA, 104, 274, 275; Lemhi County opal mine, ID, 295; Northern Lights Mine, Virgin Valley, 48, 107, 116, 250; Okanagan Opal Mine, B.C., 116, 196; Rainbow Ridge Opal Mine, Virgin Valley, 112, 121, 147, 254, 255, 317; Royal Peacock Mine Number 2, Virgin Valley, 110; Royal Peacock Opal Mines, Virgin Valley, 107, 254, 255; Royal Rainbow Mine, Black Rock Desert, NV, 117; San Juan del Rio mines, Mex., 306; Spencer Opal Mine, ID, 106, 108, 112, 242, 243, 294; Tallman's Claim at Rock Teepee, near Marsing, ID, 296; West Coast Gemstones Mine, Opal Butte, OR, 234, 239; Woodward Ranch, Brewstewr County, TX, 356
Fejér County, Hung., 293
Felbertal, Aus., 269
Feldbach, Aus., 270
Ferguson, Peter, 82
Fernley, NV, 310
Fiji, 287
Finland, 287, 291
Fiorsthaus Kupper, Aus., 269
Fish Lake, UT, 359
Flame Queen opal, 91, 133, 134, 149, 158, 222
Flamingo Opal, 91, 122, 132, 134, 143, 151, 156, 222
Flegg, A. M., 298
Flemington, N.T., 330
Flinders Range, S. Austral., 68, 94, 187
Florida, xiii, 287
Floyd County, GA, 290
Fluorescence, 8, 10, 293, 302, 381. *See also* Types of opal: fluorescent opal
Folshag, W. F., 140
Forbes, NSW, 324
Forms of opal:
    alluvial opal (wasch opal), 162, 184, 373, 376; amygdaloidal opal, *see* volcanic opal, below; animal opal, 16, 72; basaltic opal, 129; blob, 22, 95, 189, 192, 373; boulder opal, *see* Boulder opal in main headings; conk opal (speck opal), 166, 183, 184, 252, 310–314, 316, 317; contra luz opal, *see* Types of opal: contra luz opal; crystal opal, *see* Types of opal: crystal opal; mountain opal, *see* volcbaic opal, below; pipe opal, 22, 31, 41, 74, 161,

179, 181, 184, 212, 239, 373; seam opal, 30, 74, 90, 161, 166, 181, 182, 184, 207, 239, 268, 288, 289, 304, 319, 322, 330, 339, 349, 355, 360; vegetable opal, 16, 161, 166, 178, 183; vein opal, 183, 206; vertical opal, *see* pipe opal, above; vertical seam opal, 182, 184; volcanic opal (amygdaloidal opal), 13, 14, 22, 35, 40, 69, 70, 81, 84, 91, 98, 100, 103, 110, 116, 161, 162, 174, 176, 184, 234, 239, 304, 322, 324–326, 339–343, 360, 363; wasch opal, *see* alluvial opal, above; white speck opal, 166, 183, 184, *see* conk opal, above
Forest Hill Park, VA, 362
Fort Bayard Station, NM, 320
Fortescue River, W. Austral., 365
Fossicking, 193, 203, 223, 376, 377, 380
Fossils, opalized/petrified, vii, 4, 12, 17, 22–25, 30, 35, 37, 39–48, 50, 54, 56, 71, 76, 77, 85, 87, 91, 94, 96, 103, 111, 114, 119, 120, 126, 142, 147, 150, 151, 154, 156, 168, 169, 178, 179, 182–184, 190, 191, 199, 201, 213, 226, 251, 253, 258, 263, 268–270, 276, 278, 282, 283, 289–291, 295, 300, 311, 312, 321, 322, 327, 329, 331, 341, 347, 353, 354, 356, 359, 364, 365, 373, 376, 379, 380, 382, 386. *See also* Fossicking, in main headings
    ammonite, 39, 41; bat, flying fox, 45; belemnite, 12, 39, 41, 119, 169, 179, 258, 373; bivalve, 39, 364, 365, 382; bone, 25, 37, 39, 41, 42, 44, 76, 114, 142, 150, 169, 253, 258, 300, 329, 331, 353, 380; brachiopod, 39, 258; brachiosaur, 39, 41, 114; camel jawbone, 45; cat skeleton, 22, 40; cave bear, 94; cephalopod, 39, 41; clam, 39, 119; cockleshell, 39; coral 39, 46; crinoid, 39, 41, 76, 258; crocodile, 39, 45; *Crocodilus selas-lopheosis,* 45; dinosaur, 39, 41, 44, 114, 120, 154, 169, 258; dogfish, 39; fish, 39, 45, 46, 89, 311, 312, 331, 341, 359; foraminifera, 39, 258; ginkgo wood, 48; hardwood, 48; human, 43, 44; limb, 12, 22, 91, 111, 126, 147, 151, 156, 282, 283,

Fossils *(Continued)*
295, 321; log, 17, 22, 48,
87, 233, 278, 282, 283,
295; mammal part, 39, 253;
marine creature, 39; mussel
shell, 47; palm, 48; pelecy-
pod, 39, 258; petrified
wood, *see* Minerals/rocks:
petrified wood; pine, 48;
plant, 39, 47, 54, 71, 168,
253, 258, 322, 327, 356,
386; plesiosaur, 12, 22, 39,
41, 42, 120, 150, 169, 190,
191, 258; protozoa, 39; reptile, 22, 39, 41, 120; roots,
56, 179, 295, 321; shark,
39, 45, 77; shell, 4, 12, 25,
39, 41, 47, 76, 169, 178,
182, 183, 199, 258, 290,
300, 321, 373, 380, 382;
snake, 39, 201; snake skeleton, 46; teeth, 39, 45, 46,
258, 353, 380; tortoise, 39,
42, 169; trigonia, 39; turtle,
39, 43, 183; tusk, 39, 46,
76, 258; vertebrae, 41, 76;
wood, xiv, 1, 10, 17, 22, 24,
25, 35, 37, 39–41, 47, 48,
87, 88, 124, 146, 147, 151,
166, 169, 174, 177, 178,
184, 185, 206, 226, 241,
245, 251, 252, 258, 263–
265, 268, 269, 271, 272–
279, 282, 284, 288–291,
293–297, 299–301, 304,
305, 307, 308, 310, 312–
314, 316, 317, 320–322,
330, 332–335, 347–351,
355–362, 364–367, 369,
370, 379–381, *see also* Types
of opal: wood opal; wood
borer, 39; wooden fence-
posts, 22
Foster, Mark, 96, 100, 248, 250,
310, 327
Foster, R. N., 304
Foulis, Mr., 94, 188
Foulks, Harry, 98, 99, 249
Fountain Lake, N.S., 331
Fra Cristobal Range, NM, 321
Fracture, *See* Opal: fracture
France, 36, 55, 67, 68, 94, 135,
170, 174, 178, 180, 203,
284, 288, 289, 346, 370,
371, 379
Francis, Pappa, 87
François Lake, B.C., 272
Frankenstein, Pol., 337
Frankford, PA, 335
Frankfort-on-the-Main, Cz. Rep.,
283
Franklin County, OH, 331
Franklin, NJ, 319
Franklin, Qld., 239
Fraser River, B.C., 272
Frazer, Harold, 150
Frazer, Polly, 150
Fredericton, N.B., 319

Freeman, E. B., 332
Freeport, ME, 302
Freer, TX, 356
Freetown, S.L., 348
Freiesleben, Johan Katrk, 67
Fremont County, WY, 366
French, 66, 67, 126, 135, 288
French Guiana, 370
French Polynesia, 370
French Rose opal, 135
Fresach, Aus., 269
Fresno County, CA, 275
Fresno, CA, 275
Frick, C., 348
Fritzsch, Eric, 350
Fruita, CO, 279
Fryeburg, ME, 302
Fukien (China), 370
Fukushima Prefecture, Jpn., 299,
300
Fuller's earth. *See* Minerals/rocks: di-
atomite: Fuller's earth
Funeral Mountains, CA, 275
Futuna, 370

Gabanintha, W. Austral., 364
Gabon, 370
Gaj, Yug., 368
Galaxy opal, 115, 135, 156, 205
Gallatin County, MT, 163, 307
Galloping Sixty opal, 135
Galman brothers, 136
Galston, Scot., 347
Gambia, 370
Gang Ranch, B.C., 272
Ganjam District, In., 297
Gardiner, W. W., 319
Garfield County, WA, 363
Garland County, AR, 267
Garner, L. E., 356
Garut, Indon., 298
Garzó, Col., 278
Gas Hills, WY, 366
Gascoyne Junction, W. Austral.,
364
Gavilgarh, In., 297
Gay Paree opal, 76, 135, 156
Gaza Strip, 370
Gearhart Mountain, OR, 55
Geigas, S. Afr., 348
Gelantipy, N.T., 330
Gem City, ID, 76–78, 84
Gem of the West opal, 136
Gem quality opal, xi, 42, 46, 73,
87, 147, 170, 181, 191,
206, 225, 242, 278, 286,
296, 348, 364
Gem Starstone Co., NY, 122
Gemmarium et Lapidarium Historia,
65
*Gems and Precious Stones of North
America,* 73, 207
Gemstones (excluding opal):
alexandrite, ix, 2; patite, 50, 226,
299; citrine, 207; color-
change stones, 2; crystals, *see*
Crystals in main headings; di-
amond, ix, x, 1, 2, 64, 65,

86, 121, 137, 141, 144,
145, 152, 171, 208, 289,
346; emerald, ix, x, 1, 2, 7,
58, 65, 360; garnet, 11, 58,
320, 341; kunzite, 2, 73,
207; moonstone, 165, 166,
177, 380; ruby, ix, x, 1, 58,
64, 65, 266; sapphire, ix, 1,
25, 58, 65, 141, 353; star
stones, xi; topaz, 11, 97,
101, 151, 174, 305, 359;
turquoise, 12, 205; zircon,
171, 302
Genesis of Natural Opal, The, 26, 28
Geneva, Switz., 142
Georgia, xiv, 289, 290, 371
Georgia (former USSR), 370
Gere, W., 275
Gergovie, Fr., 288
Gerlach, 106, 110, 310
Gerlach, NV, 106, 117, 156, 158,
310
German/Germany, 3, 50, 51, 61,
67, 68, 77, 80, 85, 91, 93,
96, 103, 111, 128, 135,
144, 165, 168, 172, 178,
184, 191, 199, 203, 237,
257, 290, 291, 343
Germantown, PA, 335
Gerona Province, Sp., 352
Getafe, Sp., 352, 353
Geyserville, CA, 277
Ghana, 370
Giant's Causeway, G.B., 285
Gibber, 187
Gibbins, Walter A., 330
Gibraltar, 370
Gilgandra, NSW, 78, 209, 322
Gilson Gulch, CO, 279
Gilson, Pierre, 108, 170
Gisborne, Vic., 361
Gladstone, Qld., 341
Glasshouse Mountains, Qld., 340
Gleichenberg, Aus., 268, 269
Glen Ellen, CA, 277
Glenburndale Creek, 71
Glendon, NSW, 51, 68–70, 85
Glenrowan, N.T., 330
Glomer Challenger (ship), 51, 111
Gnowangerup, W. Austral., 364
Goascoranand, Hon., 205
Goddard, Dr., 146, 147
Godhavn, Green., 292
Godwins Creek, CO, 279
Golan Heights, 370
Golden Jubilee Opal, 136, 158
Gold Hill District, UT, 359
Goldsworthy, R , 120
Goles, Yug., 368
Golesh, Yug., 367, 368
Golyam Palas, Bulg., 273
Gomez, Alejandro, 129
Gonevy, 130
Gonzales County, TX, 357
Gooch Table, Virgin Valley, 245,
246
Gooding County, ID, 87
Goodnoe, WA, 363

Gooseberry, Qld., 341
Gordonia, S.A., 348
Gornja Trepea, Yug., 368
Góry Swietokrzyskiee, Pol., 336
Gossendorf, Aus., 268, 269
Götzinger, Michael, 268
Gove County, KS, 300
Government Well, W. Austral., 365
Gracios à Dios, Hon., 205
Gran Canaria Province, Sp., 352
Granada Province, Sp., 352
Grand Canyon, 55
Grand County, CO, 279
Grand County, UT, 359
Grangeville, ID, 294
Granite Downs, S. Austral., 349
Granite Harbor, Ant., 265
Granite Mountains, WY, 366
Grant County, 320, 363
    New Mexico, 320; Washington,
    363
Grants Patch, W. Austral., 364
Gravel Range District, ID, 81
Gray, Jerry J., 332
Gray, R., 136
Grays Peak, WY, 54
Great Artesian Basin, Qld., 338
Great Depression, 94
Great Dividing Ridge, 70
Great Dyke, Zim., 370
Great Lakes, 55
Great Notch, NJ, 319
Great Rift Valley, 286
Great War, 91, 92, 248
Greece/Greek, xii, 40, 41, 55, 56,
    61, 172, 177, 199, 203, 291
Green Goddess opal, 96, 136, 158,
    136
Greenland, 50, 103, 284, 291, 292
Greenlaw's Wharf, VA, 362
Green Mountain, CO, 279
Green River Formation, WY, 367
Green Vaults, Dresden, Ger., 181,
    288
Greenwater Range, CA, 275
Greenwood, ME, 302
Gregory, Geoff, 328
Grenada, 370
Grenadines, 370
Grenville Province, Ont., 332
Grguranic, Josip, 135
Griggs Dam, OH, 331
Grisafe, David A., 300
Grochowa, Pol., 336, 337
Groningen, Hol., 94
Grubstake Opal, 91, 94, 136, 137,
    156, 247, 249
Grywacheski, Tony, 116, 195
Guadalajara, Mex., 225
Guadaloupe, 370
Guadalupe Peak, TX, 54
Guam, 370
Guamar, Mex., 305
Guatemala(n), 169, 205, 225, 280,
    292
Gübelin, Edward J., 35
Guernsey, 370
Guinea, 370

Guinea-Bissau, 370
Guinness Book of World Records, 100,
    114, 141, 142, 147, 201
Guipuzcoa Province, Sp., 352
Gulf Coastal Plain, TX, 357
Gulf of Fonseca, Hon., 205
Gulgong, NSW, 326
Guliov, P., 347
Gulsen, Aus., 269
Gundagai, NSW, 324
Gunheath, G.B., 285
Gunnedah, NSW, 322
Gunnison County, CO, 279
Gunnison River, CO, 279
Gunter, Richard, 303
Guptasarma, D., 296
Guthridge, Guy G., 265
Guyana, 370
Guzmán, Adolfo A., 278
Gyges, King, 55, 56

Haggarty, Irish, 133
Haight, Doyle, 108, 110–112,
    242–244
Hainan (China), 370
Haines, John Penley, 90, 246
Haiti, 370
Hale County, TX, 357
Hamet, Michal, 281
Hamilton County, FL, 287
Hamlin, A. C., 73
Hammond, Gardiner (Mrs.), 90,
    91, 152, 248, 249, 341, 344
Hanahe, Teresa, 337
Hancock County, GA, 290
Hands, Bobby, 43
Hanging Rock, NSW, 325
Hanover County, VA, 362
Hanover, Ger., 290
Hansen, Michael C., xiv, 331
Hapsburg Dynasty, 247
Harare, Zim., 369
Hare Øen, Green., 292
Harlequin Opal, The, 248
Harlequin Prince opal, 122, 137
Harney County, OR, 333
Harris, Bill, xiii
Harrisburg, PA, 334
Hart Mountain, Man., 54
Hartford, CT, 280
Hartville, WY, 366
Harwood, Spencer, 99. *See also*
    Spencer Opal Mine under
    main headings
Haskovski, Bulg., 273
Hatchet Mountains, NM, 320
Hatton Garden, London, G.B.,
    137
Hausel, W. Dan, 366
Haut Atlas Occidental Region,
    Mor., 307
Häuy, Abbé René Just, 41
Havana, Cu., 280
Hawaii, 110, 292
Hazami, Jpn., 300
Head of Queen Victoria Opal, 137
Heber City, UT, 360
Hebrank, Arthur, 307

Heflik, Wieslaw, 335
Heilungkiang (China), 370
Helen Springs, N.T., 330
Helena Rubenstein Opal necklace,
    137, 371
Hellin, Sp., 351
Henkries, S.A., 348
Hennissey, Walter, 82
Henrico County, VA, 362
Henry, Lawrence, 299
Henry County, VA, 362
Heppner, OR, 232
Herberton, Qld., 341
Herkimer County, NY, 327
Herlany, Slov., 282
Hermanecz, Hung., 94
Hermione, 67
Hermosillo, Mex., 304
Hernandez, NM, 320
Herrero, Angel Paradas, 351
Herzegovina, 370
Heüttenberg, Aus., 269
Heves County, Hung., 293
Hewitt, George, xiv, 47, 252, 314
Hidalgo County, NM, 70, 304,
    305, 320
Hidalgo del Parral, Mex., 305
Hidalgo, Mex., 304, 305
Higginbotham, H. N., 153
Highley, D. E., 285
Hihium Lake. B.C., 272
Hill, G. T., 316
Hill, John, 66
Hillsboro, NM, 321
Hillsburgh, Qld., 342
Hinkley, CA, 276
Hinsdale County, CO, 279
Hispalensis, Isidorus, 60
*Historia General de las Cosas de
    Neuve España,* 60
Historia Naturalis, ix
Hobden, Keith, 128, 147
Hochstraden, Aus., 268, 269
Hodson, xii, 26, 45, 99–101, 110–
    113, 116, 123–126, 129,
    138–140, 142, 147, 152,
    156, 158, 246, 249, 250,
    252–255, 312, 313, 317
Hodson, Agnes, v, xiii, 45, 99, 101,
    111, 112, 125, 129, 147,
    249, 253
Hodson, Bea, 99, 249, 250
Hodson, Glenn, 99, 101, 139, 249,
    250
    dies, 101
Hodson, Keith, xii, xiii, 26, 99–
    101, 110, 113, 116, 123–
    125, 138, 139, 152, 249,
    250, 252, 254, 312, 317
    family buys Bonanza Mine, 100;
    family buys/names Rainbow
    Ridge claims, 99; sells Bo-
    nanza Mine, 113
Hodson Opal, 100, 125, 138, 140,
    142, 156, 158, 249, 250,
    317, 100, 138, 249; descrip-
    tion of, 140
Hofmann, Beda A., 354

Hogarth and Warren's Station,
   S. Austral., 78
Hokkanen, Kalevi, 291
Holland, 94
Höllgraben, Aus., 269
Holy Cross Mountains, Pol., 336,
   337
Homedale, OR, 334
Honan (China), 370
Honduras/Honduran, 64, 67, 73,
   126, 156, 166, 169, 171,
   175, 203–208, 213, 254,
   280, 284, 292, 329, 204
Honduras opal, 73, 171, 207, 329
Hong Kong, 42, 176, 191, 293,
   374
Honiara, Solomon Islands, 348
Honolulu, HI, 292
Hookanvil, NSW, 325
Hooley, George, 74, 256
Hooten Ranch, CA, 275
Hopeh (China), 370
Hora, Z. D. "Danny," 271
Hornby, Leon, 115, 260
Horse Heaven Hills, WA, 363
Horseshoe Club, ID, 296
Hosaka, Jpn., 299
Hot Springs, NM, 321
Hot Springs, NZ, 328
Hot Sulphur Springs, CO, 279
House of Opal, HI, 110
House of Tibara, 309
Howard, J. Michael, 267
Huasteca Indians, 60
Hubertsburg, Ger., 291
Hudson County, NJ, 319
Hudspeth County, TX, 357
Huelva Province, Sp., 352
Huett, Dale E., 233–235, 237, 238
Huila, Col., 278
Huittinen, Fin., 287
Huitzuco de los Figueroa, Mex.,
   227, 305
Huitzuco, Guerrero, Mex., 227
Humboldt County, NV, 86, 88,
   100, 109, 132, 244, 308–
   310
Humpies, 85, 117, 192, 257, 377
Hunan (China), 370
Hungarian opal, 35, 56–58, 62, 63,
   65–67, 69, 72, 74, 76, 84,
   93, 144, 154, 156, 160,
   161, 171, 177, 184, 196,
   197, 205, 245, 247, 256,
   257, 259, 281, 282, 293,
   358
   description of, 57; first noted historically, 56; opal mining
   ceases, 95; original source,
   57
Hungary, 57, 94, 156, 171, 203,
   293
Hungerford, 78, 239, 341
Hupeh (China), 370
Husain, Farhat, 334
Hutchison, James R., 78, 90
Hutchison, Willie, 89, 92, 196,
   200, 375

Hutchison Street, Coober Pedy, 90
Hyandra Creek, NSW, 84, 323
Hyde, Richard C., 280
Hyderabad, In., 296, 297

Iao Valley, HI, 292
Iceland, 284, 293, 377, 284
ID, 12, 35, 76–78, 81, 84, 87, 99,
   101, 104, 107, 108, 115,
   140, 141, 158, 162, 166,
   174, 180, 182, 183, 187,
   242–244, 279, 293, 294,
   310, 363, 382
Idaho County, ID, 294
Idaho Shirley opal, 104, 140, 158
Idaho Springs, CO, 279
Idar-Oberstein, 77, 85, 165, 257,
   291
Ihringen, Ger., 291
Illinois, 121, 247, 296
Ilocos Norte, Phil., 335
Imitation opal, 104, 107, 108, 118,
   173, 174, 176, 182, 104. *See
   also* Opalite; Simulated opal:
   myrickite opal, 176
Imperial Reservoir, CO, 162
Imperial Treasury, Vienna, Aus.,
   154
Inamori Division, 110
India, 16, 57, 59, 60, 183, 296,
   297
Indian, 69, 132, 137, 208, 211,
   232, 234, 294, 296, 310,
   313, 325, 333
Indian's Lookout, Lightning Ridge,
   211, 325
Indians:
   Huasteca, 60; Otomi, 60
Indonesia, 297, 298
Ingwavuma, S.Afr., 348, 349
Inner Mongolia (China), 370
Inskip Hill, CA, 277
Interference colors, 3, 8
Intibucá, Hon., 205
Intibucat, Hon., 205
Inverell, NSW, 324
Inyo County, CA, 275
Inyokern, CA, 276
Ion exchange, 23, 25, 26, 28–30,
   35, 40, 46, 50, 213. *See also*
   Atom migration
Iowa, 370
Ipswich, Qld., 340
Iragua, Switz., 355
Iraí, Braz., 271
Iran, 370
Iraq, 298
Ireland, 285, 298, 370
Irene Lovell Opal, 109, 250
Irianjaya, Indon., 298
Iridot, 173
Iron County, UT, 359
Iron Hill, DE, 284
Iron Mountain No. 2 District, NM,
   321
Irwin, 131, 151
Irwin, Tom, 131, 151
Ishikawa Prefecture, Jpn., 300

Island of Rum, G.B., 285
Island of Skye, Scot., 347
Islas Canarias Province, Sp., 352
Isle of Man, 370
Isleta Pueblo, NM, 320
Israel, 298, 299
Italy/Italian, 65, 70, 203, 299
Ivigtut, Green., 50

Jackson, Julia A., 361
Jackson, MS, 307
Jackson, Stuart, 141
Jackson Lake, WY, 367
Jacob, Henri Louis, 338
Jakkalswater, S.Afr., 348
Jamaica, 299
Jandarimoko, 94, 187
Jantamuka, 94, 187
Japan(ese), 18, 51, 110, 111, 118,
   170, 203, 226–228, 254,
   299
Japanese market, 18
Japons, Aus., 269
Jarrow, G.B., 51, 68
Jawor, Pol., 336, 337
Jechringen, Ger., 291
Jeff Davis County, TX, 357
Jefferson County, 279, 307, 333
   Colorado, 279; Montana, 307;
   Oregon, 333
Jemez Sulphur District, NM, 321
Jenness, Jane E., 293
Jensen, Aage, 284, 293
Jersey, 370
Jerusalem, Isr., 298
Jevons, H. Stanley, 85
Jewelry Box, 199
Jha, S. N., 308
Jim, Lee Dong, 301
Johani, Dorani B., 303
Johannesburg, CA, 275
Johanngergenstadt, Ger., 291
Johnson, Kenneth S., 331
Johnston, RI, 346
Jordan, 370
Jordanów, Pol., 336, 337
Jornada del Muerto, NM, 321
Jornada Valley, NM, 321
Josephine, Empress, 67, 85
Juab County, UT, 359
Julianehaab, Green., 292
Jupiter-Five opal, 101, 109, 114,
   141, 142, 147, 150, 156
Juro Mountains, Switz., 355
Jutson's Rocks, W. Austral., 364
Jylland, Den., 284

Kabul, Afghan., 263
Kailua, HI, 292
Kaiserskeuhl, Ger., 291
Kaiserstuhl, Ger., 91
Kalamalka Lake, B.C., 272
Kalbarri, W. Austral., 364
Kaleidoscope Queen opal, 131, 142
Kalgoorlie, W. Austral., 364–366
Kalvarienberg, Aus., 269
Kameno Rebro, Yug., 368
Kamloops, B.C., 271, 272

Kandri, In., 297
Kangaroo Shooters Camp, 257, 258, 257
Kanowna, W. Austral., 365
Kansas, 130, 175, 183, 300
Kansu (China), 370
Kaphle, K. P., 308
Karaman (Karamandjik) Province, Turk., 69, 358
Karanth, R. V., 296
Kardzahlii, Bulg., 273
Karelian Coast, Russ., 51, 95
Karnataka, In., 297
Karnes County, TX, 357
Kärnten, Aus., 269
Karoo Basin, S.Afr., 349
Kaschan, 57
Kashau, Slov., 283
Kashmir, ID, 297
Kathmandu, Nep., 308
Katzbachgraben, Aus., 269
Kazakhstan, 370
Kelley, William, 103, 250
Kelly, William M., 327
Kenbridge, VA, 362
Kennebec County, ME, 302
Kentucky, 126, 300
Kenwood, CA, 277
Kenya, 53, 97, 370
Keraunios, 56, 173
Kern County, CA, 274, 275
Keroongooloo, Qld., 341
Keystone, SD, 351
Keyworth, G.B., 285
Keyworth, Scot., 347
Khan, Mujibur Rahman, 270
Kiangsi (China), 370
Kiangsu (China), 370
Kilkerton Point, Scot., 347
Kim, Dong Hak, 301
Kimberly Division, W. Austral., 365
Kincaedinshire Blue Hole, Scot., 347
King County, WA, 363
King George County, VA, 362
King, Hobart M., 363
King, Vandall T., 302
Kingfisher (goddess), 200
Kings County, N.S., 331
Kingston, Jam., 299
Kingston, NM, 321
Kingston, RI, 346
Kinnunen, Kari A., 287, 291
Kinzua Pine Mills Corporation, 112, 233, 234
Kiowa County, OK, 332
Kiribati, 370
Kirin (China), 370
Kirschweiler, Ger., 257
Kittitas County, WA, 363
Kittrell, NC, 329
Klamath Falls, OR, xiv, 126, 132, 137
Klause, Aus., 269
Klein, William, 143
Klickitat County, WA, 363
Klobucar, Yug., 368

Knehr, Joe, 144
Knox County, ME, 302
Knoxville, CA, 276
Knudsen, Christian, 284
Kodegaon, In., 297
Kodur, In., 297
Komuniga, Bulg., 273
Kongswinter, Ger., 291
Kontis, Jim, 104
Kookynie, W. Austral., 365
Koolau Caldera, HI, 292
Kootenai County, ID, 294
Kopi, 191, 375, 377, 378
Koppaiberg, Swed., 354
Koralpe, Aus., 269, 270
Korea, 203, 254, 301, 370
Kosice, Slov., 57, 281–283
Kosovo, Yug., 367
Kosovska Kamenica, Yug., 368
Kostov, Ryslan I., 273
Kotakarra, In., 297
Kourimsky, Jiri, 281, 282
Kozmice, Pol., 336, 337
Kragujevac, Yug., 369
Krakow, Pol., 335
Kraków-Wielun Upland, Pol., 336, 337
Kratovo-Zletovo Region, Yug., 368
Kraubath, Aus., 269
Kremze, Cz. Rep., 282
Krezenac, Yug., 368
Krughof, Aus., 269
Krzemionki Opatowskie, Pol., 336, 337
Ktagujevac, Yug., 367
Kuclin, Cz. Rep., 283
Kulgera, N.T., 330
Kunz, George Frederick, 73, 207
Kuopio, Fin., 287
Kupa piti, 92, 200, 375
Kurran Holding, Qld., 239
Kütahya Province, Turk., 358
Kwa-Zulu, S.A., 348
Kwangsi Chuang (China), 370
Kwangtung (China), 370
Kweichow (China), 370
Kyocera Corporation, 110
Kyrgystan, 370
Kyungsangbuk, S.Kor., 301

La Bade, Fr., 288
La Bajada District, NM, 321
La Cañada, Sp., 351
La Coruña Province, Sp., 352
La Entrada, Cu., 281
La Esperanza, Hon., 205
La Garita Creek, CO, 280
La Guardia, Sp., 351
La Mañoca Cuarzo, Sp., 352
La Paz County, AZ, 266
La Pointe, D. D., 310
La Romain, Trin., 358
La Trinidad, Mex., 306
La Trobe Valley, N.T., 330
Laas, Aus., 269
Labak, Indon., 298
Laborcza River, Slov., 283
Ladron District, NM, 321

Lageado, Braz., 271, 276, 279, 333
Lake County, 276, 279, 333
 California, 276; Colorado, 279; Oregon, 333
Lake Mead, AZ, 266
Lake Ramsay, N.S., 331
Lake Sinclair, GA, 290
Lake Torrens, S. Austral., 94
Lake Winnipeg, Man., 54
Lake Yindarlgooda, W. Austral., 364
Lakeview, OR, 244
Lamb, Mabel, 154
Lambina, S. Austral., 117, 189, 198, 208, 224, 225, 349
Lambina Station, 224
Lancaster County, PA, 335
Land, David H., 347
Lansing, MI, 306
Laos, 370
Lapidario del rey, 62
Lapidarium, 61
Lapidary Journal, xii, 117, 237
LaPlata, Col., 278
Laramie, WY, 366
Larimer County, CO, 279
Las Alcantueñas, Sp., 353
Las Cantueñas, Sp., 353
Las Colinas, Hon., 206, 208
Las Piedras, Hon., 205
Las Vegas, NV, 308, 310
Lasmanis, Raymond, 362
Lassen County, CA, 276
Last Chance Canyon, CA, 276
Latah County, ID, 76, 294
Latvia, 370
Laufenegg, Aus., 269
Lavaca County, TX, 357
Laverton, W. Austral., 365
Lawrence County, SD, 350
Lawrence, KS, 300
Lazine, Yug., 368
Le Locle, Switz., 355
Le Pasale, Hon., 205
Lea County, NM, 320
Lead Pipe Springs, CA, 276
Lead, SD, 351
Leadville, CO, 279
Leakey, Louis S. B., 53, 97
Lebanon, 370
Lebanon County, PA, 335
Lece, Yug., 368
Leckbachrinne, Aus., 269
Ledford, Allan, 91, 98, 248, 249
Ledford, Hope Loughead, 98, 249
Leechman, Frank, x, xi, 134, 142, 156, 328, 347
Leechman's Loss opal, 142, 156
Leichardt, Qld., 342
Leisnig, Ger., 291
Lemhi County, ID, 81, 84, 294
Leòn, 62
Leonard Opal, 94, 143, 158
Leonard, R. W., 143
Leonardus, Camillus, 63
Lesbos, Gr., 291
Lesotho, 370
Levy, Sam, 79

Lewiston, ID, 296
Leyden, Neth., 308
Liaoning (China), 370
Libanka Mountain, Slov., 84, 282
Liberia, 370
Libya, 301
Libyan Desert, Lib., 301
Li District, Thai., 358
Liechtenstein, 370
Light of the World opal, 101, 143, 156, 222
Lightning Ridge, NSW, xiii, xiv, 8, 12, 13, 15, 17, 18, 22, 26, 29–31, 34, 41–46, 53, 79, 81–87, 90, 91, 93, 94, 96, 98, 99, 101, 104, 106–111, 114, 115, 117, 118, 121, 122, 127, 128, 130, 131–133, 135, 136, 142, 143, 145–151, 153, 156, 158, 161–164, 174, 175, 178, 179, 181, 183, 189, 192, 198, 200, 206, 208–214, 222, 223, 227, 230, 231, 239, 244, 245, 259, 260, 305, 309, 322–326, 373, 377–380, 385
  discovery of black opals, 81; hotel, 132; Miners Association, 163, 212; Mining Syndicate, 82, 83, 85; opal, 83, 94, 114, 128, 133, 161, 174; Waterholes poisoned, 211
Lightning Ridge, Home of the Black Opal, 111
Lillicur, Vic., 360
Lima, Peru, 335
Limagne Valley, Fr., 288
Lincoln County, NV, 308
Lincoln County, WA, 363
Lincoln District, UT, 359
Lincoln, RI, 346
Lindhe, Henry E., 206
Lindquist, Bengt, 354
Lindsay, CA, 277
Lismore, NSW, 325
Lithika of Orpheus, 59
Lithuania, 370
Little Black Peacock opal, 107, 158, 250
Little Rock, AR, 267
Little Squaw Creek, ID, 77, 296
Little Switzerland, NC, 329
Little York, CA, 276
Living Fire (Red Show) opal, 93, 144, 158
Lizard Opal, 144
Ljig, Yug., 368
Llandillo, Lightning Ridge, 325
Llano County, TX, 357
Llanos de Barrera, Sp., 352
Lobatse, Bot., 270
Lockheed Aircraft, 247
Logan County, KS, 300
Loma de los Ópales, Cu., 281
Loma Garcia, Cu., 281
Lomita, CA, 276
Lompoc, CA, 276

London, 42, 70, 72–75, 77, 85, 86, 137, 142
Longs Peak, CO, 54
Longs Peak, WY, 54
Loon Lake, B.C., 272
Lopburi Province, Thai., 358
Los Angeles, CA, 101, 104, 249, 274–276
Los Gatos, CA, 55
Loudoun County, VA, 362
Loughead, Allan, 247
Loughead, Flora (Flora Haines Loughead Gutierrez), 90, 91, 96, 98, 152, 246–249, 310
  dies, 98
Loughead, John, 247
Loughead, Malcolm, 247
Louis XIII, King, 144
Louis XIII Opal, 144
Lovell, Irene, 109, 116, 250. *See also Irene Lovell Opal*
Lovelock Mercantile Company, NV, 136, 247, 310
Lovington, NM, 320
Lower Granite Lake, WA, 363
Lower Hutt, NZ, 328
Lower Saxony, Ger., 290
Lower Silesia, Pol., 336, 337
Loy, Myrna, 136
Lubie-Tova, Cz. Rep., 283
Lubien, Pol., 336, 337
Lublin Upland, Pol., 336, 337
Lucerne, Switz., 35
Luis Lopez Manganese District, NM, 321
Lum Phun Province, Thai., 358
Luna County, NM, 320
Lunenberg County, N.S., 331
Lunenburg County, VA, 362
Luther, Edward T., 355
Luther, Mark R., 329
Luxembourg, 302
Lydia, 55, 56, 55

Macau, 370
Macdonald, R., 347
Macedo de Cavaleiros, Port., 338
Macedonia, 370
Macedonia, Yug., 368
McGee, Ed, 88, 246
Machaneng Police Camp, Bot., 271
Machinery. *See* Mining equipment/machinery
Mackay, Qld., 71, 342, 71
MacKenzie brothers, 144
McKenzie County, ND, 330
McKenzie, Mel, 89
MacKenzie's Opal, 82, 144, 156, 82, 144
McMurdo Sound, Ant., 265
MacNeill, J. B. (Mrs.), 131
McNichol, Jock, 42, 149, 150
McQuarrie, Wayne, 338
Macon County, NC, 329
Macon, VA, 362
Macquarie Lake, NSW, 18
Madagascar, 370

Madero, Mex., 55
Madhya Pradesh, In., 297
Madison County, NC, 329
Madison, WI., 366
Madjaruvo, Bulg., 273
Madras, In., 297
Madras, OR, 333
Madrid, Sp., 73, 351, 352
Mae Charim District, Thai., 358
Mafic, 289, 378
Magan, Sp., 354
Magdalena District, NM, 321
Magdalena Tequisistlán, Mex., 306
Maguire, Eddie/Tanya, xiv, 241, 242
Magyar language, 58, 177
Maharashtra, In., 297
Mahogany Peak, OR, 55
Maine, 302
Maine, Jack, 86
Maissau, Aus., 268, 269
Makambol, Phil., 335
Makhtesh Ramon, Isr., 299
Malawi, 370
Malaysia, 303
Maldives, 370
Maleny, Qld., 338
Malheur County, OR, 334
Malvay, In., 297
Man-made opal. *See* Synthetic opal
Mancini, Ernest A., 263
Manganese oxide, 168, 300, 303
Manitoba, 54, 303
Mantilla, Hugo Rivera, 335
Manxman, W. Austral., 364
Manzano Peak, NM, 54
Mapula Lodge, S.A., 349
Maputo, Moz., 307
Maravatio District, Mex., 306
Marble Creek District, ID, 296
Marbodus, Bishop of Rennes, 61
Marcoux, Eric, 288, 289
Margawidjaja, Kingking A., 297
Margrethe, Queen of Denmark, 111
Marico, S.A., 349
Maricopa County, AZ, 266
Marillana, W. Austral., 365
Marla Station, S. Austral., 93, 224, 229
Marques, Joao Manuel P. R., 307
Marsing, ID, 107, 296
Maryborough, Qld., 342
Maryland, 303
Marysvale District, UT, 359
Masbate, Phil., 335
Mason County, TX, 357
Masquelin, Henri C., 358
Massachusetts, 267, 304
Massif Central, Fr., 288, 289
Masters, John M., 296
Mata, Braz., 271
Mati, Phil., 335
Matletsi River, Bot., 271
Matrix, 12, 60, 69, 74, 83, 95, 98, 100, 102, 109, 115, 116, 129, 131, 135, 136, 144–146, 148, 152, 154, 160,

161, 164, 174–176, 180–
185, 188, 190–195, 205–
208, 213, 226, 228, 235,
239, 240, 264, 267, 270–
273, 282, 283, 290, 295,
299, 301, 302, 304, 311,
312–314, 316, 317, 320,
331, 332, 334, 346, 355–
359, 361, 362, 366, 368,
370, 374, 375, 378, 381. *See
also* Types of opal: matrix
opal
Matthews, L., 355
Matthey, 81, 116, 117
Matthey, Theodore, 81, 116
Maui, HI, 292
Mauritania, 304
Maxmiliano, Emperor, 60
Maya culture, 205
Maybin, Arthur H., 350
Mayneside, Qld., 239
Mayotte, 370
Mazatlan, Mex., 55
Mbabane, Swaz., 354
Medicine Bow Peak, WY, 54
Meegea Hill, W. Austral., 364
Meekatharra, W. Austral., 365
Mehun, Fr., 288
Melbourne, Vic., 26, 42, 72, 89,
96, 100, 101, 120, 121,
135, 147, 152, 201, 361
Melilla Province, Sp., 353
Melo, Urug., 359
Menat, Fr., 288
Menge, Johannes, 68, 69
Menil-Montant, Fr., 174
Merced County, CA, 276
Mercedes, Princess, 72
Mercedes, Queen, 73
Mercer, Norman, 328
Merredin, W. Austral., 365
Mesa County, CO, 279
Meteor (ship), 50, 111, 50
Metropolitan V Area, Chile, 277
Metropolitan XI Area, Chile, 277
Mexico/Mexican, 10, 11, 13, 15,
53–56, 60, 64, 67, 69, 70,
72, 89, 97, 99, 101–104,
106, 115, 116, 145, 151,
158, 161, 162, 164, 166,
169–171, 174, 175, 177,
183, 184, 187, 195, 196,
204, 205, 207, 225–229,
234, 272, 280, 284, 302,
304–307, 319, 365, 375,
377, 381
Mexican Dragon opal, 145
Mexican opal, 64, 67, 69
fire opal, 11, 145, 162, 164, 166,
170, 171, 175, 183, 184,
195, 365; first noted historically, 60; precious fire opal,
11, 13, 53, 56, 64, 67, 69,
73, 97, 101, 102, 106, 161,
169, 170, 179, 207, 225,
226–228, 304–307
Mexican Sunrise opal, 145, 158
Mexico City, 69, 70, 97, 101, 225

México State, Mex., 304
Mexico, ME, 302
Mezel, Fr., 288
Mezezo, Eth., 286
Mica Mountain District, ID, 295
Michigan, 104, 121, 146, 182, 306
Michoacan, Mex., 305
Micronesia, 370
Middle Fork Guard Station, ID,
296
Midway Islands, 370
Miezitis, Y., 267
Milford, UT, 359
Miller, 89
Millerville, AL, 264
Milnic, Peter, 116, 156
Milton-Freewater, OR, 236
Mina La Purisma, Mex., 304
Mina, NV, 310
Mineral County, CO, 279
Mineral Mountains, UT, 359
Mineralni Bani, Bulg., 273
Mineralogists, 3, 67–69, 73, 124,
206, 234, 249, 267, 289,
307–310, 319
Mineralogist, The, 249
Minerals/rocks:
agate, 1, 59, 162, 165, 167, 173,
175, 177, 232, 264, 271–
273, 279, 283, 287, 300,
349, 350, 367, 377
black moss agate (mocha
stone), 175; kalmuk agate,
see Cachalong opal, in main
headings; moss agate, 175,
300
amethyst, ix, 1, 58, 367, 368; andesite, 57, 205, 268, 276,
282, 283, 293, 297, 322;
angel stone, 46, 162, 385;
see also dog stone, below;
apophyllite, 50, 226; aragonite, 50, 226, 285, 291;
bandstone, 373, 380, 385;
basalt, 12, 21, 23, 70, 76–
78, 100, 116, 129, 174,
175, 184, 194, 195, 205–
207, 213, 226, 231, 244,
245, 266, 268–271, 272,
274, 275, 277–280, 282,
283, 285, 286, 291–298,
307, 308, 311, 319, 322,
323, 330, 333–337, 351,
355, 356, 360, 362, 364,
373, 378; basinite, 244,
309, 376; calcite, 12, 50, 51,
226, 265, 269, 271, 279,
284, 288, 291, 299, 332,
353; carnelian, 1, 58; cat's–
eye, xi; celestial opal. *See*
Minerals
moonstone, 165, 166, 177
ceylonese opal. *See* Minerals
moonstone, 165, 166, 177
chalcedony 1, 56, 77, 166, 170,
171, 173, 176, 178, 232,
265, 266, 270, 279, 280,
282, 283, 286, 287, 291,

299, 301, 303, 320, 323,
336, 337, 350, 351, 353,
354, 356, 357, 366, 367,
368, 381; chert, 176, 265,
284, 285, 289, 290, 296,
299, 301, 335, 346, 351,
355, 357; cristobalite, 3,
265, 332, 361; cryptocrystalline silica, 1; crystalline silica,
1, 284; crystals, *see* Crystals
in main headings; diatomite,
168, 264, 268, 274–276,
288, 299, 310, 320, 327,
351, 356, 376, 386
Fuller's earth, 16, 168, 377
dog stone, 46, *see also* Angel
stone, above; dolerite, 373,
376; feldspar, 23, 97, 265,
296, 305, 327, 329, 350,
361, 362, 377; flint, 1, 284,
290; glauberite, 50, 77, 85,
103, 258; glendonite, 51,
68, 85, 103, 68; gneiss, 263,
269, 290, 327, 369, 377;
gold, ix, xi, 55, 59, 70, 72,
78, 89, 90, 100, 143, 144,
151–153, 155, 167, 169,
170, 191, 246, 278, 279,
308, 309, 322, 359, 364,
365; granular quartz silica,
1; gypsum, 50, 103, 226,
258, 377, 378; hectorite,
377; ikaite, 50, 51, 77, 103,
108, 111, 112, 118, 155,
178, 226, 258, 319, 322,
377; iris quartz, 59, 167,
347; ironstone, 12, 108,
116, 131, 135, 145, 164,
170, 175, 180, 182, 185,
195, 240, 241, 272, 322,
338, 339, 373, 378; jarrowite, 51, 68, 94, 103, 68;
jasp-opal (jasper/opal), 168,
173, 176, 285, 291; jasper,
1, 173, 176, 225, 272, 279,
280, 283, 347, 381; jas-
peroid, 287; jasperoidal silica, 80; kaolinite, 21, 25,
243, 265, 277, 330, 333,
373–375, 377–379, *see also*
montmorillonite, below;
limestone, 180, 271, 273,
284, 288, 289, 291, 320,
331, 363, 365, 369; mocha
stone, *see* black moss agate,
above; montmorillonite, 25,
107, 174, 181, 184, 229,
245, 253, 265, 268, 278,
289, 297, 301, 307, 308,
310, 311–314, 316, 317,
322, 356–358, 362, 373,
377–380, 382, 386. *See also*
kaolinite, above
description of, 379; geology
of, 379
mother-of-opal, 175, 180; obsidian (volcanic glass), 1, 11,
173, 176, 205, 244, 294,

Minerals/rocks *(Continued)*
373, 376; black, 244, 294; layered, 173; perlite, 112, 162, 178, 208, 231–234; petrified wood, 1, 10, 41, 185, 274, 277–279, 291, 317, 381; pink chalcedony, 5, 178; plagioclase, 373; porphyry, 84, 97, 162, 171, 205, 207, 231, 279, 285, 294, 298, 305, 363; pseudogaylussite, 51, 94; quartz, 1, 3, 12, 56, 59, 78, 89, 100, 167, 173, 178, 179, 185, 193, 232, 242, 244, 265, 267–270, 287, 293, 301, 302, 309, 320, 327, 330, 347, 348, 350, 353, 356, 361, 362, 363, 365–368, 376, 377, 379, 386
   rose, 1, 56, 178, 302; smoky, 1, 368
   quartzite, 1, 81, 146, 178, 180, 189, 190, 295, 301, 307, 322, 364, 369; rhyolite/rhyolitic, 12, 23, 35, 64, 69, 77, 99, 102, 112, 115, 146, 174–176, 181, 184, 205–207, 225, 226, 228, 231–234, 242, 243, 266, 268, 269, 273, 274, 278, 285, 286, 291, 293, 294, 297, 299, 300, 304–310, 314, 317, 320, 321, 322, 328, 333, 335, 346, 356–358, 360, 362, 377, 378, 381; sandstone, ix, 70, 95, 141, 142, 144, 145, 148, 149, 161, 162, 164, 170, 175, 178–183, 185, 194, 196, 201, 229, 239, 257, 273, 290, 301, 307, 312–314, 316, 317, 320, 322, 330, 338, 339, 345, 349, 353, 357, 360–363, 366, 367, 370, 377, 378, 380, 385; silica dioxide, 1; silica gel, 17, 21–26, 30, 40, 45, 168, 175, 184, 213, 378, 382; silica, soluble, 21; silver, 11, 129, 359; thinolite, 51, 73, 103; discovery of, 73; thundereggs, 75, 112, 183, 208, 231–235, 237, 238, 272, 294, 323, 333, 334, *see also* Types of opal: thunderegg opal; *and* Types of opal: thunderstone opal; trachyte, 205, 206, 322; tridymite, 3, 265; tuff, 205, 268, 269, 273, 282, 283, 286, 297, 311–314, 316, 317, 321, 363, 373, 386; volcanic glass, *see* obsidian, above; zirconium oxide, 36
Miner's Right, 79, 85, 100, 378
Mines/mining operations, ix, xi, xiii, 1, 12, 18, 20, 26, 45, 46,

48, 69, 70, 74–76, 78, 80–82, 84–86, 88–91, 93, 94, 96, 98–104, 106–118, 120–122, 124–130, 135, 136, 138, 141, 146–147, 149, 151–153, 156, 158, 177, 178, 188, 191, 192, 194–196, 199, 202, 203, 206, 211, 222, 225, 230, 232, 234, 239, 242, 245–247, 249, 250, 253, 255–257, 259, 266, 267, 271–277, 279, 284, 285, 287, 290, 294–296, 302, 303, 305, 306, 309–318, 320, 321, 324–327, 329, 331–335, 339–346, 348–351, 357–359, 361–364, 366, 369, 374–375, 377, 380–382
Adams Mine, Qld., 343; Agostinos Mine, Mex., 305; Aladdin Mine, Qld., 70, 341, 343; Alewyns Poort 29 JP Farm, S.Afr., 349; Alvarado Mine, UT, 359; Amanda Jane's Workings, Qld., 343; Angel Number 1 Mine, Virgin Valley, 310–312, 315–318; Angel Number 2 Mine, Virgin Valley, 311; Antelope Wells Prospect, NM, 320; Anzac Hill Workings, Qld., 339; April Fool Number 1 Mine, Virgin Valley, 311, 313–315, 318; April Fool Number 2 Mine, Virgin Valley, 311; Arundel Prospect, Qld., 339; August Mine, Virgin Valley, 311; Autenite Number 8 Claim, UT, 359; Baker and Connell's Dig, Qld., 341; Bald Knob Workings, Qld., 339, 342; Ban Pang Fluorite Mine, Thai., 357, 358; Barclay's Bunker, White Cliffs, 326; Bareeda Homestead, Qld., 339; Barry's Mine, Qld., 341; Basinghall Farm, Bot., 271; Beautiful Opal Mine, Virgin Valley, 311; Becketts Tank, Lightning Ridge, 82, 324; Becky Mine, Lightning Ridge, 311, 312, 315, 318; Belgian Mine, CO, 279; Bell Mine, Virgin Valley, 312, 316; Bendena, Qld., 341; Berellem Homestead, Qld., 343, 345; Berrimpa Homestead, Qld., 339; Berryville Mine, VA, 362; Beryllium Corporation Prospect, ME, 302; Bessey Quarry, ME, 302; Bill the Boer Mine, Lightning Ridge, 211, 324; Birdlebough's Mine, Virgin Valley, 110, 312; Black Beauty Mine, Virgin Valley,

94, 312, 316; Black Boulder Mine, Qld., 339; Black Hope Mine, Virgin Valley, 311, 312; Black Knobby Dig, Lightning Ridge, 211; Black Mine, Qld., 345; Black Mountain Quarry, ME, 302; Black Opal Number 1 Mine, Virgin Valley, 312; Black Opal Number 2 Mine, Virgin Valley, 312; Black Opal Number 3 Mine, Virgin Valley, 312; Black Tequila Ridge Mine, Qld., 345; Black's Prospect, Qld., 343; Blocks Diggings, White Cliffs, 326; Blue Ball Mine, Virgin Valley, 312; Blue Fire Opal Mine, AZ, 266; Blue Gum Mine, Qld., 343; Blue Speck Mine, Qld., 345; Bluebird Pit, B.C., 116, 195, 196; Bonanza Mine, Virgin Valley, 86, 88, 90, 100, 109–111, 113, 116, 124–126, 128, 129, 156, 245, 250, 312, 317, 318
   first established as Virgin Mine, 86; patented, 110; sold by Hodson, 113
Boobara Homestead, Qld., 339, 340; Booka Workings, Qld., 343; Botallack Mine, G.B., 285; Boulder Mine, Qld., 343; Boundary Prospect, Qld., 339; Bourke Diggings, White Cliffs, 326; Brace Brothers Ranch, ID, 78; Bramble Workings, Qld., 343; Breakfast Creek Mine, Qld., 70, 74, 341, 343; Brewarrina Diggings, White Cliffs, 326; Brilliant Mine, Qld., 339, 342; Britten Digs, Qld., 342; Brodie Goodman's Flat Workings, Qld., 339; Brodie's Hill Workings, Qld., 339; Budgerigar Mine, Qld., 343; Buena Number One Claim, UT, 359; Buffalo Prospect, Qld., 343; Bulgroo Mine, Qld., 343; Bull Creek Mine, Qld., 239, 343; Bull Run Quarry, VA, 362; Bulla Creek Mine, Qld., 339; Bullock's Head Diggings, Lightning Ridge, 211; Bullockies Diggings, Lightning Ridge, 211, 324; Bung Bung Workings, Qld., 341, 343; Bunginderry Homestead, Qld., 343; Butterfly Claim Diggings, Lightning Ridge, ix, 20, 46, 86, 127, 128, 151, 158, 211, 222, 324; Butterfly Number 2 Diggings, Lightning Ridge, 128; Buza

Workings, Andamooka, 191; Campover Workings, Qld., 339; Canada's Workings, Lightning Ridge, 211, 324; Canaway Downs Homestead, Qld., 343, 344; Canfell's Hill Diggings, Lightning Ridge, 82, 153, 211, 324; Caramel Pit, B.C., 116, 195; Carbine Lucky Mine, Qld., 339; Carlyle's Mine, Qld., 342; Carter Mine, NC, 329; Carter's Workings, Qld., 345; Cerro Viejo Mine, Mex., 102, 305; Charles Eddy Group Mines, Virgin Valley, 313–318; Childer's Diggings, Qld., 342; Chinaman's Prospect, Qld., 339; Christiane Prospect, Qld., 343; Chrysoprase Mine, CA, 277; Cima Mine, UT, 359; Cisco Mine, AZ, 266; Claim Number 1 Mine, Virgin Valley, 313; Claim Number 2 Mine, Virgin Valley, 313, 315; Claim Number 5 Mine, Virgin Valley, 313; Clancy's Prosect, White Cliffs, 326; Clinton Creek Mine, YT., 369; Clyde Mine, CO, 279; Coathworth Mine Workings, Qld., 345; Coleman Jones Farm, VA, 362; Coleman's Cave Mine, Qld., 341; Congie Homestead, Qld., 344; Conklin's Lime Quarry, RI, 346; Conway's Claim, Qld., 342; Conway's Mine, Qld., 339; Cooma Homestead, Qld., 343; Coonavalla Mine, Qld., 343; Coparella Mine, Qld., 339; Copper Hill Mine, RI, 346; Coster's Hill Diggings, Andamooka, 96, 121; Cottesmore Homestead, Qld., 344; Cowarna Station Homestead, Western Austral., 108, 364; Cragg Boulder Mine, Qld., 339; Cragg Mine, Qld., 74, 78, 106; Crane Claims, Virgin Valley, 311, 313; Crazy Indian Mine, Virgin Valley, 313; Creole Mine, UT, 359; Crystal Valley Dig, Mintabie, 230; Cunnamulla Prospect, Qld., 343; Daisy Mae Mine, Virgin Valley, 313, 314; Dagworth Homestead, Qld., 345; Darby's Diggings, Lightning Ridge, 211, 324; Davier Mine, SD, 351; De Lazra's Mine, Qld., 341; Dead Man's Claim, Virgin Valley, 96, 314; Dead Man's Gully, Coober Pedy, 199;

Deadman's Dugout, Coober Pedy, 199; Dead Mule Ranch, Bot., 271; Denbigh Downs Homestead, Qld., 345; December Mine, Virgin Valley, 311, 314; Deep Belars, Lightning Ridge, 211, 324; Deep Four Mile, Lightning Ridge, 136, 324; Deer Park Mine, NC, 329; Delight Quarry, MD, 303; Depazzie Careno Mine, Qld., 343; Desert Bog Mine, OR, 333; Dexter Lime Quarry, RI, 346; Diamond Hill Granite Co. Quarry, RI, 346; Dingo Flat Mine, Qld., 343; Dirri Dirri Diggings, Qld., 342; Discovery Pit Mine, B.C., 116, 195; Donahue Prospect, ME, 302; Donny's Mine Workings, Qld., 343; Double Barrel No. 4 Mine, Qld., 343; Dreamtime Workings, Qld., 339; Drexel's Quarry, PA, 334; Duck Creek Mine, Qld., 239, 339; Dunton Quarry, ME, 302; Eagle Gray Quarry, ME, 302; East Gem Hill Mine, Virgin Valley, 313, 314; El Cobano Mine, Mex., 305; El Conejo Mine, Mex., 102, 305; El Muerto Mine, Mex., 102, 305; El Toro Mine, Mex., 102, 305; Elbert County, CA, 275; Elbow Mine, Qld., 339; Elusive Prospect, Qld., 339; Emerald Diggings, Qld., 342; Emmons Quarry, ME, 302; Empire Valley Ranch Mine, B.C., 272; Emu Creek Mine, Qld., 199, 339; Erda Rainbow Workings, Qld., 339; Ethyl Granite Corporation Quarry, GA, 290; Etta Mine, SD, 351; Etzatlan Mine, Mex., 103, 305; Evening Star Mine, 313, 314; Exhibition Mine, Qld., 343; Fazarri's Prospect, Qld., 343; February Mine, Virgin Valley, 89, 196, 222, 234, 277, 311, 314; Ferguson Lode Claim, SD, 351; Fiery Comet Prospect, Qld., 339; Fiery Cross Mine, Qld., 339; Finney's Quarry, PA, 334; Firestone Mine, NV, 100, 109, 310; abandoned, 109 Firestone Opal Mine (No. B), NV, 100; Fish Ponds Mine, Qld., 341; Flat Prospect, Qld., 339; Flat Rock Quarry, GA, 290; Four Mile Diggings, Qld., 341; Four

Nations Diggings, Andamooka, 191; Fourmile Creek, B.C., 273; Fourteen Mile Mine, Coober Pedy, 199; Fourth of July Number 1 Mine, Virgin Valley, 311, 314; Fourth of July Number 2 Mine, Virgin Valley, 311, 314; Friday Creek Mine, Qld., 343; Friday Mine, Virgin Valley, 149, 311, 314, 341, 343, 375; Friday's Mine, Qld., 341; Frying Pan Diggings, Lightning Ridge, 211, 325; Fuentezuelas Mine, Mex., 102, 305; Fuentezuelas Prospect, Mex., 305; Galena Mine, UT, 359; Galilee Mine, Qld., 343; Gap Mine, Qld., 341; Gate Mine, Qld., 339; Gem Mine, Qld., 341, 343; German George Mine, Qld., 343; Gibgoe Creek Workings, Qld., 343; Gidyea Creek Prospect, Qld., 343; Gillespie's Quarry, PA, 334; Gin Gin Diggings, Qld., 343; Gladstone Mine, Qld., 130, 341, 343; Gloria Dia Mine, AZ, 115; Golconda Mine, Qld., 343; Gold Hill Mine, UT, 359; Goldfinger Mine, Qld., 344; Good Hope Mine, CO, 279; Gooseberry Mine, Qld., 344; Government Quarry 6, OK, 332; Gorringe's One Prospect, Qld., 339; Goudini 30 JP Farm, S.Afr., 349; Grasshopper Dig, Mintabie, 230; Great Dragonfly Mine, Qld., 339; Great Mistalop Prospect, Qld., 344; Green Show Diggings, Qld., 344; Group Mine, Qld., 344; Hallion Diggings, Andamooka, 191; Hammond's Mine, Qld., 341, 344; Harlequin Mine, Qld., 339; Harris Quarry, RI, 346; Hausington's Mine, Qld., 341, 344; Hayne Quarry, GA, 290; Hayricks Mine, Qld., 18, 80, 239, 344; Hearts and Spices Mine, Lightning Ridge, 211, 325; Hen's Nest Mine, Qld., 341; Herbb Number Two Pegmatite Mine, VA, 362; Hewego Prospect, Qld., 344; Hidden Valley Mine, Virgin Valley, 313, 314; Holden's Diggings, Lightning Ridge, 325; Hollaway's Workings, Qld., 339; Hoopon's Ledge Quarry, ME, 302; Hopal Workings, Qld., 339; Horn Silver

Mines/mining operations *(Cont'd)* Mine, UT, 359; Horse Creek Workings, Qld., 339; Horse Fly Mine, B.C., 273; Hostotipaquillo Mine, Mex., 103, 305; Huber Workings, Qld., 344; Hudson's Claim, Qld., 345; Huel Buller Mine, G.B., 285; Huel Damsel Mine, G.B., 285; Huel Poligine Mine, G.B., 285; Huel Rosewarne Mine, G.B., 285; Huel Spinster Mine, G.B., 285; Huel Stennach Mine, G.B., 285; Hunting Hill Quarry, MD, 303; Ibex Mine, CO, 279; J & L Alunite Mine, UT, 359; Jackson's Mine, Qld., 340; James River Hydrate and Supply Company Quarry, VA, 361; January Mine, Virgin Valley, 74, 98, 122, 249, 311–314, 316, 317, 329, 369; Jay-R Opal Mine, AZ, 266; Jepperson-Wilson Mine, ID, 294; Jerry's Mine Workings, Qld., 340; Johnson Mine, Qld., 340; Johnson's Claim, Qld., 345; Joyce Workings, Qld., 344; Jundah Mine, Qld., 340; Jurecho Mines, Mex., 70, 306; Kelley Mine, Virgin Valley, 311, 314; Kelly Mine, Virgin Valley, 314; Kinder Mine, Qld., 340; Kinkel Quarry, NY, 327; Knobby Hill Mine, NV, 309; Koroit Mine, Qld., 78, 118, 239, 340, 341; Korsnäs Lead Mine, Fin., 287; Kyeenee Mine, Qld., 340; Kynuna Mine, Qld., 78, 239, 345; L.B.J. Historic Mine, Qld., 345; La Cuadrillera Prospect, Mex., 102, 305; La Carbonera Mine, Mex., 70, 306; La Jurado Mine, Mex., 102; La Peineta Mine, Mex., 102, 305; La Unica Mine, Mex., 305; Laman's Mine, Qld., 341, 344; Larkin's Folly Diggings, Coober Pedy, 199; Last Card Prospect, Qld., 344; Last Chance Opal Mine, CA, 274; Laurel Creek Corundum Mine, GA, 290; Le-Bob Mine, 315, 316; Leo Nowak Fire Opal Mine, CA, 104, 274, 275; Li'l Abner Mine, Virgin Valley, 313, 315; Little Gidyea Mine, Qld., 344; Little Jo Mine, NV, 106; Little Pebble Mine, Virgin Valley, 89, 310, 315; Little Wonder Mine, Qld., 70, 74, 340, 341, 344; Lochray Mine,

Qld., 344; Lone Pine Chromite Mine, CA, 276; Lorrie Lee Mine, Virgin Valley, 313, 315; Lost Deer Hunters Mine, 99, 101, 104, 242, 99. *See also* Spencer Opal Mine
becomes Spencer Opal Mine, 104
Lucky Lou Mine, Virgin Valley, 315, 316; Lulu Mine, Virgin Valley, 313, 315; Lucky Mac Property, WY, 367; Lunatic Mine, Andamooka, 96; Lushington's Mine, Qld., 340, 344; Luz Nueva Mine, Mex., 130; MacPherson's Claim, Qld., 345; Magdalena Opal Mine, Mex., 103, 145, 225; Magic Prospect, Qld., 340; Magic Mine, Qld., 346; Malone's Mine, Qld., 341; Manassas Quarry, VA, 362; Marble Arch Mine, Qld., 344; Marble Cliff Quarry, OH, 331; Marchese Mine, Qld., 344; March Mine, Virgin Valley, 75, 81, 90, 121, 257, 310, 311, 314, 315; Marvelous Mine, Virgin Valley, 315; Mascotte Mine, Qld., 344; Mat's Hard Mine, Qld., 341; Maxi Benzine Prospect, Qld., 344; May Day Prospect, Qld., 344; Mayday Mine, Virgin Valley, 313, 315; Mayneside Mine, Qld., 340; McGee Claim, Virgin Valley, 88, 90, 246, 247, 316; McGeorge's (Boa) Mine, Qld., 344; McKinney Mine, NC, 329; McKinnon's Shed, Qld., 343, 345; McNamara's Mine, Lightning Ridge, 325; Mercedes' Mine, Qld., 344; Merry Widow Mine, N. Mex., 320; Mick's Mine, Qld., 346; Miles' Claim, Qld., 343; Miller Asbestos Mine, GA, 290; Mineral Claim 28/392, W. Austral., 364; Mintabie, *see* Mintabie in main headings; Miserable Mitch Mine, Virgin Valley, 315, 316; Monday Mine, 311, 315; Monkey Coolah Mine, Qld., 341, 344; Monoco Mine, UT, 360; Monte Carlo Prospect, Qld., 344; Mooka Mine, W. Austral., 365; Moonwalk Mine, Virgin Valley, 315; Moresby Copper Mine, Pap. N.G., 334; Morris Claims, CA, 276; Mother Lode Mine, B.C., 272; Mount Mica Quarry, ME,

302; Mucket Mine, Virgin Valley, 311, 312, 315; Mud Mine, Qld., 340; Mulcahy's Mine, Qld., 341, 344; Nancy's Nightmare Mine, Virgin Valley, 313, 315; Never Never Mine, Qld., 340; New Moon Mine, Virgin Valley, 313, 315; New Nobby Mine, Lightning Ridge, 325; New Rush Diggings, Lightning Ridge, 127; Nielsen Mine, Qld., 340; Nocha Buena Mine, Mex., 306; Nonella Prospect, UT, 359; Norah Mine, Qld., 340; North Wilson Pit, AR, 267; Northern Lights Mine, Virgin Valley, 48, 89, 90, 116, 249, 250, 253, 255, 310, 315; November Mine, SD, 350; November Mine, Virgin Valley, 315, 350; Okanagan Opal Mine, B.C., 116, 177, 194– 196, 271, 272, 277; Old Country Workings, Qld., 344; Old German Diggings, Quilpie, 93; Old Goose Creek Quarry, VA, 362; Old Jordan Mine, UT, 359; One Mile Workings, Qld., 344; Ontiveros Mine, Mex., 69, 306; Opal Claim Number Two Mine, Virgin Valley, 315; Opal Creek Mine, Qld., 344; Opal Den Mine, Qld., 345; Opal Queen Mine, Virgin Valley, 85, 88, 245–247, 311, 312, 315, 316
established, 85
Opal Valley Mine, Virgin Valley, 316; Opaline Mining Camp, ID, 296; Opalville Mine, Jundah, 115, 135, 239, 340, 346; Opex Prospect, Qld., 344; Orion Mine, Virgin Valley, 89; Otterfontein 438 JP Farm, S. Afr., 349; Pandora Mine, Virgin Valley, 316; Paterson Quarry, NJ, 319; Peacock Number 1 Mine, Virgin Valley, 89, 250, 310, 317; Peacock Number 2 Mine, Virgin Valley, 89, 250, 310, 316, 317; Peacock Number 3 Mine, Virgin Valley, 89; Peacock Number 4 Mine, Virgin Valley, 89, 310, 316; Pebble Mine, Virgin Valley, 89, 178, 256, 310, 315, 380; Pedro II Mine, Braz., 271; Peppin and Webber's Mine, Qld., 341, 344; Peri-Peri Mine, Braz., 271; Phantom Mine, Virgin Valley, 89, 310, 316, 377, 381; Pinkilla

Mine, Qld., 344; Pitt's Mine, Qld., 342; Poison Mine, Qld., 342; Pott's Mine, Qld., 342, 344; Poulston's Prospect, Qld., 344; Pride of the Hill Mine, Qld., 340, 344; Putnam Mine, NC, 329; Quail's Workings, Qld., 344; Quartpot Mine, Qld., 340, 344; Rainbow Mine, Qld., 344; Rainbow Ridge Opal Mine, Virgin Valley, xiii, 26, 45, 48, 88, 99–101, 112, 121, 125, 138, 146, 147, 152, 246, 249, 250, 253, 255, 312, 316, 317, 399; Red Ball Mine, Virgin Valley, 310, 317; Red Flash Mine, Qld., 345; Red Rock Opal Mine, 98, 101, 104; Red Show Workings, Qld., 344; Red Star Workings, Qld., 340; Redflag Prospect, Qld., 345; Redhill Workings, Qld., 340; Rex Opal Mine, AZ, 266; Richard Patrick Mine, 317; Riekersdam 109 JP Farm, S. Afr., 349; Rincon Belle Mine, Virgin Valley, 317; Rittenhouse Quarry, PA, 335; Rocky No. 3 Prospect, Qld., 340; Roskear Mine, G.B., 285; Rossiter's, Qld., 341; Rosso's Diggings, Lightning Ridge, 211, 325; Royal Opal Mine, Virgin Valley, 317; Royal Peacock Number 1 Mine, Virgin Valley, 89, 250, 310, 317; Royal Peacock Number 2 Mine, Virgin Valley, 89, 250, 317; Royal Peacock Opal Mines, 8, 45, 48, 89, 90, 96, 107, 110, 116, 156, 246, 255, 380 patented, 110

Royal Rainbow Mine, NV, 117; Russell's Mine, Qld., 345; San Augustin Mine, Mex., 102, 305; San Augustin Prospect, Mex., 305; San Marcos Mine, Mex., 103; San Simón Mine, Mex., 305; Sand Pebbles Number 1 Mine, Virgin Valley, 89; Sand Pebbles Number 2 Mine, Virgin Valley, 89; Sand Pebbles Number 3 Mine, Virgin Valley, 89; Sandstone Mine, Qld., 345; Santa Maria Iris Mine, 70, 101, 102, 225, 306; Saratov Mine, Qld., 345; Saturday Mine, Virgin Valley, 311, 317; Scanlan's Mine, Qld., 342; Scotchman Mine, Qld., 345; Second Choice Work-

ings, Qld., 345; September Mine, Virgin Valley, 311, 318; Seven Wonders Mine, Qld., 345; Shaff Gully Mine, Qld., 345; Shallow Nobby Mine, Lightning Ridge, 82, 85, 96, 121, 127, *see also* Old Nobby; Sheep Station Creek Mine, Qld., 340, 345; Shirley Mine, ID, 104, 141; Site Mine Nunber 1, Qld., 342; Site Mine Nunber 2, Qld., 342; Site Mine Nunber 3, Qld., 342; Site Mine Nunber 4, Qld., 342; Skajum Mine, Virgin Valley, 318; Snake Jump Mine, Qld., 340; Snowy Brown's Diggings, Lightning Ridge, 325; Southern Cross Mine, Qld., 241, 341; Southers Branch Mine, NC, 329; Sparkle Plenty Mine, Virgin Valley, 318; Spencer Opal Mine, *see* Spencer Opal Mine under main headings; Spur Mine, Qld., 340; Stan's Hill Diggings, Andamooka, 191; Stanley's Workings, Qld., 342; Star Bright Mine, Virgin Valley, 310, 318; Star Fire Mine, Virgin Valley, 310, 318; Starrett Quarry, ME, 302; Stevens Creek Diggings, Andamooka, 96, 98, 100, 120, 191, 192; Stony Creek Workings, Qld., 342, 345; Stony Point Iron-Copper Mine, VA, 361; Stuart's Claim, Qld., 345; Sulphur Bank Mine, CA, 276; Suzanne Prospect, Qld., 345; Tablon Mine, Hon., 206; Tallman's Claim, ID, 296; Tellait Mine, Alg., 264; Tepe Blue Fire Opal Mine, ID, 107, 296; Tequila Mine, Mex., 103, 104, 284, 305, 340; Thursday Mine, Virgin Valley, 311, 318; Tilly Foster Mine, NY, 327; Tomkin's Mine, Qld., 346; Top Mine, Qld., 345; Top of the World Mine, Qld., 345; Trinidad's Prospect, Qld., 345; Tuesday Mine, Virgin Valley, 318; Undivided Quarry, ME, 302; Union Mine, Qld., 342; Vaillant Mine, 318; Valdare Mine, Qld., 345; Valenciana Mine, Mex., 306; Vertical Bill's Mine, Lightning Ridge, 325; Virgin Mine, Virgin Valley, 85, 88, 90, 100, 318; Virgin Opal Mine, Virgin Valley, 245–247, 250, 312, 317, 318, 245; Virginia Traprock

Quarry, VA, 362; Vitro Uranium Company Pit, WY, 366; Walsh's Diggings, Lightning Ridge, 211, 325, 327; Wednesday Mine, Virgin Valley, 311, 318; Wee Marie Mine, Virgin Valley, 311, 318; West Gem Hill Mine, Virgin Valley, 318; Whispering Pines Quarry, ME, 302; White Hills Mine, Virgin Valley, 318; Why Not? Diggings, Qld., 345; Wicker-Baldwin property, WY, 367; Wild Horse Mine, Qld., 340; Willes No. 1 Quarry, ME, 302; Windfall Mine, Virgin Valley, 313, 318; Woodward Ranch opal mine, TX, 356; Yellow Ball Mine, Virgin Valley, 318; Yellow Canary Uranium Deposit, UT, 359; Yellow Jimmy Mine, Qld., 340; Yellow Nell Workings, Qld., 342, 345; Zenobia Mine, CO, 280; Zoovoorby 458 Farm, S. Afr., 348

Mining equipment/machinery, 104, 115, 214, 222, 341, 344, 373, 374, 378
automatic self-tip bucket hoist, 104; Calweld drill, 115, 214, 222, 373, 374 nine-inch bore, 214; thirty-six-inch bore, 222
monkey, 341, 344, 378; puddler, 101; self-tipping bucket hoist, 104; tunneling machine, pneumatic, 114, 141, 214; windlass, 104, 214, 386

Minneapolis, MN, 250
Minnesota, 306
Mintabie opal, 109, 129, 175, 176, 202, 229, 230
Mintabie, S. Austral., 13, 93, 108–112, 114, 117, 129, 156, 160, 175, 176, 189, 193, 198, 200, 202, 208, 224, 225, 229–231, 242, 245, 349, 378
flooded, 114; heavy mining equipment initiated, 108
Miquelon, 370
Mirena, Yug., 368
Misool Island, Indon., 298
Mississippi, 55, 106, 242, 307
Mississippi Valley, 55
Missouri, 236, 307
Mitchell County, NC, 329
Mitta Mitta, Vic., 360
Moble, Qld., 239
Moconi, Mex., 304
Moe, Vic., 361
Mohave, CA, 274, 275
Mohave Desert, CA, 274

Mohs scale, 12, 176, 193, 335
Mojave County, AZ, 266
Mokelumne Hill, CA, 275
Moldova, 370
Momba Station, NSW, 74, 256
Monaco, 370
Mondure, Qld., 343
Monet, Claude, xii
Mongolia, 370
Mono County, CA, 276
Monongalia County, WV, 363
Monroe County, NY, 327
Montana, 54, 99, 163, 242, 294, 307
Montana County, MT, 307
Montarco, Sp., 353
Montevideo, Urug., 358
Montgomery County, AR, 267
Monticello, NM, 321
Montrico, Sp., 352
Montserrat, 370
Mooka Station, W. Austral., 364, 365
Moonbeam Opal, 145
Moose Mountain, Sask., 54
Moravia, Cz. Rep., 283, 337
Morey, G. B., 306
Morgan, J. P., 131, 137
Morgan, John Junius, 131
Morgan County, CA, 276
Morgantown, WV, 363
Morocco, 53, 307
Morris County, NJ, 173
Morrow County, OR, 75, 112, 208, 231, 333, 334
Morton, PA, 334
Morwell, Vic., 361
Moscow, ID, 76, 84, 294, 347
Moses, WA, 363
Mosso, Burundi, 274
Mount Blackmore, MT, 163
Mount Blackwood, Vic., 361
Mount Brady, S. Austral., 349
Mount Burkett, AL, 55
Mount Coffin, Qld., 343
Mount Edinburgh, Qld., 346
Mount Fairweather, AL, 55
Mount Garnet, Qld., 341
Mount Harvard, CO, 54
Mount Hayes, AL, 264
Mount Hood, OR, 55
Mount Jackson, B.C., 272
Mount Olympus, WA, 55
Mount Princeton, WY, 54
Mount Ranier, WA, 55
Mount Ruapehu, NZ, 328
Mount Savona, B.C., 272
Mount Shasta, CA, 55
Mount Square Top, Qld., 346
Mount Vesuvius, It., ix
Mount View, Qld., 345
Mount Waddington, B.C., 55
Mount Washburn, WY, 367
Mount Zircon, ME, 302
Mountain Home, ID, 77
Moyd Opal, 108, 145, 156, 108, 145
Moyd, Louis, 146

Mozambique, 307, 308
Muang District, Thai., 358
Mullock, 26, 203, 214, 223, 376, 378, 379, 382, 386
Mullumbimby, NSW, 323
Mundiwindi, W. Austral., 365
Munich, Ger., 237
Muñoz, José Francisco, 280
Munro, D., 81
Munzing, George, xiv, 48, 178, 251
Murat, Fr., 288
Murchison House Station, W. Austral., 364
Murchison River, W. Austral., 364
Murcia Province, Sp., 353
Murphy, Edward F. "Ted,", 42, 45, 46, 48, 49, 75, 76, 79, 83–85, 99, 127, 153, 210, 212, 257, 259
Murray, Jack, 81–83, 96, 210
Murray, James "Jimmy," 127
Murray, Willis "Murray the Miner," 192
Murray River, 68
Murray the Miner, 192
Museums, 21, 42, 54, 60, 73, 88, 91, 107, 114, 121, 122, 126, 129, 130–132, 137, 140, 141, 143, 145–147, 151–155, 160, 205, 226, 236, 264, 266, 268, 272, 273, 281, 292, 317, 329, 332, 337, 360,
  Alabama Museum of Natural History, 264; American Museum of Natural History, 91, 94, 122, 136, 137, 154; Arizona Mining and Mineral Museum, 266; Australian Museum at Sydney, 42, 88; British Museum, 292, 329; Bulgarian Academy of Sciences, 273; Canadian Museum of Nature, 146; Canadian National Mineral Collection, 272; Colburn Gem and Mineral Museum, 152; Columbia Art Museum, 236; Cranbrook Institute of Science, 121, 146, 147; Favell Museum of Western Art and Indian Artifacts, 132, 137; Field Museum of Natural History, 60, 129, 153; *Grainger Hall of Gems,* 129, 153, 154; Hamlin Collection, Harvard University, 205; Harvard University Mineralogical Museum, 54, 73, 205; Hof (Natural History Museum), Aus., 160; Hope Collection, 151, 226; J. P. Morgan Hall of Gems, 137; Museum of Natural History, Aus., 268; Museum of Victoria, Austral., 360; Museum Ziemi

PAN, Warsaw, Pol., 337; Národní Muzeum, Cz. Rep., 281; National Museum of Mexico, 60; Royal Ontario Museum, Can., 131, 143, 160, 332; Smithsonian Institution, 91, 107, 114, 121, 122, 130, 140, 141, 145, 152, 155, 317; Vychodoslovenské Museum, Kosice, 281; Washington A. Roebling Gem Collection, 152, 155; Wilbur Greely Burroughs Geologic Museum, 126
Myall Creek, S. Austral., 349
Myanmar, 16, 370
Myrtle Park, OR, 333
Myths and superstitions. *See* Chapter 4
Mytilene, Gr., 291

Nador, Sp., 353
Nagasaki Prefecture, Jpn., 300
Nagpur District, In., 297
Nagy-Mijaly, Slov., 283
Nairobi, E. Afr., 286
Nakhon Ratchasima Province, Thai., 358
Nakovitsa, Bulg., 273
Nakuru, E. Afr., 53, 97
Namibia, 308
Nampa, ID, 77, 294
Nan Province, Thai., 358
Nanango, Qld., 340
Nandewar Mountains, NSW, 322
Nankai Trough off Japan, 51, 111
Nannine, W. Austral., 364, 365
Nanson, Marsden, 84, 245, 246
Napa, CA, 101, 120
Napa County, CA, 276
Napoleon, *see* Bonaparte, Napoleon
Napoleon Opal, 146
Narbona, Luis Gómez, 280
Narbri, NSW, 323
Narragansett, RI, 346
Nashville, TN, 355
Naslawice, Pol., 337
National parks/reserves, 99, 242, 249, 266, 275, 279, 294, 304, 307, 310, 312, 316, 319, 320, 363, 366
  Basaseachic Cascades National Park, Mex., 304; Chalcedony Park, AZ, 266; Charles Sheldon National Wildlife Range, 249, 310, 312, 316; Chief Timothy State Park, WA, 363; Death Valley National Monument, 275; Lava Beds National Monument, CA, 277; Petrified Forest of Zimbabwe Valley, Zim., 370; Rockhound State Park, NM, 320; Rocky Mountain National Park, CO, 279; White Mountain National Forest, 319; Yel-

lowstone National Park, WY, 99, 242, 294, 307, 366
Natrona County, WY, 366
Nauru, 370
Nayarit, Mex., 304, 306
Nebraska, 370
Nederland Tungsten District, CO, 278
Needles Eye Tunnel, SD, 350
Nemcice, Cz. Rep., 283
Nepal, 308
Nephi, UT, 359
Ness County, KS, 300
Netherlands, 308, 370
Netherlands Antilles, 370
Nettleton, Charlie, 82, 83, 85, 86, 210–212
Neudeck, Cz. Rep., 283
Neusohl, Hung., 94
Nevada, xii, xiii, xiv, 8, 12, 13, 26, 35, 51, 53–55, 73, 84, 85, 88, 92, 94, 98–101, 103, 106, 109, 110, 111, 121, 123, 125, 126, 128, 129, 132, 136, 146, 147, 151, 155, 156, 158, 166, 169, 177, 178, 187, 243, 244, 247, 254, 266, 276, 296, 298, 308–310, 377, 379, 380
Nevada County, CA, 276
Nevis, 370
New Brunswick, 319
New Caledonia, 370
New Canaan, CT, 154
New Hampshire, 319
New Hanover Island, Pap. N.G., 334
New Harbor, Ant., 265
New Jersey, 137, 173, 319
New Mexico, 54, 319
New Ross, N.S., 331
New South Wales, xiii, xiv, 17, 18, 22, 41, 48, 51, 53, 68–70, 73, 74, 78, 80, 81, 84, 85, 89, 91, 94, 96, 98, 99, 101, 103, 108, 110, 122, 130, 143, 146, 148, 154–156, 158, 178, 187, 203, 208, 209, 211, 239, 245, 256, 309, 319, 322–324, 338, 377–379, 386
Department of Mines, 84; Minister of Mines, 85
New York, 86, 91, 94, 122, 137, 142, 152, 154, 227, 248, 327
New Zealand, 171, 179, 182, 328, 370, 371
Newark, DE, 283
Newcastle, G.B., 68, 286
Newcastle, NSW, 17, 18
Newcastle County, G.B., 51
Newfoundland, 328
Newry, ME, 302
Nez Perce County, ID, 295
Nez Perce Indian Reservation, ID, 294

Ngwaketse District, Bot., 271
Nicaragua, 64, 329
Nickaville, Qld., 344
Nickel, 170, 179, 282, 283
Niedderotweil, Ger., 291
Niedermayr, Gerhard, 268
Niederösterreich, Aus., 268–270
Niger, 370
Nigeria, 370
Nightcap Range, NSW, 323
Nihonmatsu, Jpn., 300
Ningsia Hui (China), 370
Niue, 370
Noah, 54
Nobby/nobbies, 22, 30, 33, 46, 47, 81–83, 85–87, 96, 101, 114, 121, 127, 132, 134, 135, 142, 150, 161, 163, 170, 181, 210, 211, 213, 214, 221, 222, 309, 322, 325, 373, 374, 378, 379
Nógrád County, Hung., 293
Nonius, Roman senator, 58, 63, 146, 158
Nonius Opal, 146
Noodling, 377, 378, 380, 382
Noolinga Nera opal, 98, 146, 154, 156
Nordmark, Swed., 354
Norfolk Island, 370
Norman, OK, 331
Norseman, W. Austral., 365
North America, 54, 55, 73, 207, 246
North Carolina, 152, 329
North Creek, S. Austral., 89
North Cyprus, 370
North Dakota, 329, 330
North Fork Red River, OK, 332
North Mountains, N.S., 331
North Primmersdorf, Aus., 269
North Truchas Peak, N.M., 54
Northern Ireland, 370
Northern Mariana Islands, 370
Northern Negev, Isr., 299
Northern Territory, 224, 229, 231, 330
Northwest Territories, 330
Norton, VA, 362
Norway, 330, 331
Norwich Township, Franklin County, OH, 331
Nottingham, G.B., 285
Nottingham, Scot., 347
Nouakchott, Mauri., 304
Nova Scotia, 108, 111, 131, 331
Novo Brdo, Yug., 368
Nowak, Leo, 101, 104, 275, 275
Ntsimanyana, Mokwaledi, 270
Ntungicimpaye, Audace, 274
Nuclearite, 26
Nûgssuaq, Green., 292
Nundle Region, NSW, 325

O'Brien, Paddy, 70, 72
O'Connor, Bruce J., 289
O'Donnell, T., 295
O'Neil, Colin, 128

O'Neil, Dick, 90, 196
O'Neil, Jim, 90
Oahu Island, HI, 292
Oakhampton, G.B., 285
Oakover Formation, W. Austral., 365
Oaxaca, Mex., 97, 225, 306
Oban Creek, NSW, 324
Oberdorf, Aus., 269
Oberhaag, Aus., 269
Oberlausitz, Ger., 291
Oberösterreich, Aus., 268, 270
Oberpullendorf, Aus., 269
Oberrotweil, Ger., 291
Obersdorf, Thuringia, Ger., 51
Obershoffhausen, Ger., 291
Oberthumeritz, Aus., 269
Obtalus/Obtalmius, 63
Odida, John, 358
Oelberg, Ger., 291
Ogallala Formation, KS, 300
Ohio, xiv, 244, 331
Oita Prefecture, Jpn., 300
Okanagan Opal, Inc., 277
Okanagan Valley, B.C., 271
Oklahoma, 331, 332
Oliver, J. B. "Ridge," 91, 247
Olson, Edward, 129, 153
Olympia, WA, 362
Olympic Australis opal, 109, 140, 142, 147, 156, 199–202, 223
Oman, 370
Omodeo Lake, It., 299
Ongerup, W. Austral., 365
Onomacritus, 55, 56, 178, 55, 56
Ontario, 131, 143, 160, 332
Ontiveros, 69, 306
Oodnadatta, 78
Oodnadatta, S. Austral., 78
Opal:
    alleged medical attributes, 59, 64; bad luck reputation begins, 61, 68, 69, 73; blazing, 368; called indivisible quartz, 173; cheaps, 374; chemical composition of, 1; cleavage, 11, 173; color bar, 163, 168, 221, 374, 375, 378; collected by ancient Chinese, 55; crazing/cracking of opal, x, 3, 11–16, 21–23, 30, 34, 37, 66, 71, 81, 95, 103, 109, 110, 113, 124, 125, 126, 147, 152, 155, 162, 169, 175, 176, 181, 184, 189, 190, 191, 194, 195, 206, 208, 226, 227, 229, 234–236, 241, 246, 250, 254, 282, 286, 290, 302, 317, 330, 357, 365, 368, 375, 377, 385, *see also* decrepitation, fracturing, and self-destruction, below; critical angle, *see* Cutting of opal: critical angle; decrepitation, 375; derivation of name, 56–58; diffraction, 3,

Opal *(Continued)*
4, 6, 7, 31, 103, 179, 194, 376; dyed opal, 168, 190; first named stone, 67; floater, 74, 373; fluorescence; *see* Fluorescence, in main headings, and Types of opal: fluorescent opal; formation of, 17; fracture, 11, 13, 14, 178, 181, 185, 235, 267, 279, 282, 289, 290, 302, 303, 311, 319, 327, 336, 350, 361, 362, 368, 375; habit, 11; hardness, 12, 31, 34, 185, 193, 309; heat sensitivity, 12; impurities in, 3, 10, 31, 168, 175, 180, 300, 374, 375–378; inclusions in, 10, 136, 147, 168, 175, 176, 178, 180, 181, 208, 244, 268, 274, 302, 303, 333, 335, 348; instability of, 13, 181, 226, 227, 234, 246; lamellae, 3; luster, 11, 165, 178, 180, 185, 264, 375; metamorphism, 25, 45, 268, 373; mineraloid, 1; nomenclature, 161; opacity/opaque, 11, 13, 14, 16, 50, 56, 60, 61, 155, 161, 163, 164, 168, 170, 172, 173, 175, 177, 179, 183, 184, 185, 190, 195, 235, 264, 268, 271, 274, 279, 280, 282, 284, 285, 291–293, 296– 299, 307, 308, 320–323, 327, 333–335, 337, 350, 351, 353, 354, 356, 358, 361, 364–366, 368, 370, 375; opal matrix, 115, 144, 176, 190, 195, 239; protector (patron stone) of thieves (patronus furum), 61, 178; refraction, 6, 10, 13, 103, 347, 381; rough opal, 77, 171, 181, 249, 373–375, 379, 381, 382; rub/rubbing/ rubbed opal, 96, 121, 132, 181, 221, 382; scintillation, 182; sedimentary, 14, 161, 174, 182, 378, 385; self-destruction, 14, 15, 184, 227, 246; sheen, 164, 190, 244, 374, 382; smoked opal process, 99; sobriquet: "eye of the world," 61; solid, 24, 40, 41, 98, 100, 108, 111, 114, 116, 124, 136, 141, 142, 146, 163, 177, 182, 189, 200, 201, 241, 244, 247, 294, 309, 376; specific gravity, 12; specimen opal, 13, 15, 103, 111, 206, 246; stability, 13, 15, 16, 66, 109, 112, 125, 167, 169, 193, 199, 208, 234, 242, 281, 356, 380

Kelley Process for opal stabilization, 103, 250
structure of, 3; storage of, 13, 15, 21, 312, 365
glycerin, 13; mineral oil, 13; silicone, 13
sugar-acid treatment, 191; translucent opal, 10, 11, 13, 14, 16, 130, 143, 145, 155, 161–164, 166–172, 174, 177–179, 182–185, 193, 206, 207, 213, 225, 227, 234, 243, 252, 266–268, 273, 274, 278, 280, 282, 286, 289, 291, 293, 297– 300, 303, 304, 306, 308, 309, 320, 322, 329, 330, 333, 349, 350, 353, 354, 356–359, 361, 362, 364– 366, 368, 370, 376, *see also* Translucency, in main headings; transparent opal, 6, 7, 11, 13, 14, 31, 32, 50, 51, 61, 64, 121, 122, 126, 135, 145, 151, 155, 160–164, 166–175, 177–179, 182, 183, 185, 193, 195–197, 206–208, 226, 227, 234, 235, 252, 253, 267, 268, 272–275, 277, 279, 282, 283, 285, 286, 289–291, 294, 297–300, 305–308, 320–323, 330, 332–336, 339, 349, 350, 352, 353, 358–361, 364, 366, 368, 375, 376, *see also* Translucency, in main headings; treated opal, 183, *see also* stability: Kelley Process, above, and sugar-acid treatment, above; tri-color, 140; water content, 3, 7, 10, 12, 13, 34, 193, 195, 246, 301, 317
Opal Book, The, x, 85, 134, 328, 347
Opal Butte, OR, 53, 75, 77, 78, 112, 181, 208, 231–235, 237, 238, 286, 333, 334
fee-digging, 239
Opal dirt, 15, 22–26, 28–33, 35, 37, 40, 46, 96, 134, 150, 163, 182, 185, 213, 239, 374, 380, 381, 385. *See also* Opal level
Opal Essence. *See* Synthetic opal
Opal fields:
airport Rush, Lightning Ridge, 211, 324; Al-E-May Prospect, Qld., 343; Andamooka, *see* Andamooka in main headings; Bald Hill, Lightning Ridge, 87, 91, 131, 133, 149, 211, 324, 380; Benito's Folly, Coober Pedy, 199; Bergen Hill, NJ, 319; Bergslagen Mining District, Swed., 354; Berlin

Rush, Lightning Ridge, 211, 324; Berlin Rush, White Cliffs, 326; Big Flat, Coober Pedy 90, 198, 199; Billy Goat Hill, Lighting Ridge, 109, 209, 211, 324; Bishop's Rush, White Cliffs, 326; Black Flag, Coober Pedy, 199, 365; Black Gate, Qld., 118, 239; Blackboy, Andamooka, 96, 191; Boundary Riders, Andamooka, 96, 181; Bowra Creek, Qld., 343; Brandy Gully, Qld., 341; Brooks', Andamooka, 96; Bulloo River, Qld., 70, 239; Bunker, White Cliffs, 80, 259, 326; Burns Lake, B.C., 272; Canaway opal deposits, Qld., 53; Carter's Rush, Lightning Ridge, 211; Cerro de las Fejas, Mex., 97, 102, 304; Cerro de las Silicatas, Mex., 305; Charlotte Plains, Qld., 341; Chum, Lightning Ridge, 86; Con's Rush, Lightning Ridge, 211, 324; Collarenebri, Lightning Ridge, 324; Coober Pedy, *see* Coober Pedy in main headings; Coocoran, Lightning Ridge, xiv, 98, 114, 115, 118, 208, 209, 211, 222; Corundum Hill, NC, 329; Crater, Coober Pedy, 199; Crowder's Gully, Coober Pedy, 89, 90, 199; Cutler Opal Occurrence, ID, 295; Deccan Traps, In., 297; Dentist Hill, Lightning Ridge, 325; Dillybroo Old Station, Qld., 343, 344; Dingo, Coober Pedy, 199, 343; Dora Gully, Coober Pedy, 199; Dubnik, Slov., 56, 57, 62, 72, 84, 93, 95, 256, 281, 282, 293; Dry Rush, Lightning Ridge, 325; East Pacific, Coober Pedy, 115, 199; Eeavinna Hill, S. Austral., 349; Eight Mile, Coober Pedy, 90, 98, 100, 147, 198–202; Eildon Park Homestead, Qld., 339, 340; Eleven Mile, Lightning Ridge, 325; Emmett Downs Homestead, Qld., 340; England Hill. S. Austral., 349; Erandique, Hon., 171, 205– 208; Eromanga Homestead, Qld., 239, 341, 343–345; Ferguson Island, Papua New Guinea, 334; Fermoy, Qld., 342; Fiery Creek, Qld., 343; Flats, Coober Pedy, 199; Flodden Hills Homestead,

Qld., 340; Foley's Six Mile, Lightning Ridge, 211, 325; Four Mile Claim Area, Lightning Ridge, 86, 199, 211, 324; Four Mile Flat, Lightning Ridge, 211; Four Mile, Coober Pedy, 90; Franklin Homestead, Qld., 345; Frog Hollow, Lightning Ridge, 211, 325; Galisteo Beds, NM, 321; Gayndah, Qld., 342; Gemville, NSW, 80; Gemville, White Cliffs, 259, 326; Geraghty Hill, Eight Mile, Coober Pedy, 98, 198, 199; German Gully, Andamooka, 96, 191, 199; Glen Valley Homestead, Qld., 340; Glengarry, 98, 106, 107, 128, 147, 156, 158, 209, 211, 214, 325, 380; Gombek, White Cliffs, 259; Gondwana Beds, In., 297; Goodman's Flat, Qld., 344; Grawin, Lightning Ridge, 44, 98, 101, 106, 143, 156, 209, 211, 214, 231, 322, 325, 377, 380; Gray's Creek Opal Deposit, ID, 296; Greek Gully, Coober Pedy, 199; Grosser's, Andamooka, 96, 191; Grosvenor Downs, Qld., 342; Guanajuato, Mex., 106, 304, 305; Guanimero, Mex., 305; Guerrero, Mex., 97, 101, 187, 227, 305; Gully Diggings, Lightning Ridge, 325, 345; Gunn's Gully, Andamooka, 96, 191; Gympie, Qld., 71, 343; Haan's Peak, Coober Pedy, 113–115; Hacienda de Aspeita, Mex., 304; Hacienda Esmeralda, 70; Hacienda Esperanza, 69, 225, 306; Hacienda Foentesuela, Mex., 304; Hacienda la Jurada, Mex., 305; Hacienda San Isidro, Mex., 306; Hard Hill Diggings, Andamooka, 191; Hart Mountain, OR, 54, 100, 234, 333; Hawk's Nest, Lightning Ridge, 86, 211, 325, 380; Hayfields Homestead, Qld., 340; Highlands Homestead, Qld., 339, 340; Hopeful Hills, Coober Pedy, 199; Hornet's Rush, Lightning Ridge, 211, 325; Horse Creek, Qld., 342; Horse Paddock, Andamooka, 96, 191; Iniagi Well Hill, W. Austral., 80, 364; Iron Bark Claim Area, Lightning Ridge, 86, 211; Iron Mine Hill, RI, 346; Jalisco, Mex., 99, 103, 104, 145, 158, 187, 225, 228,

284, 304, 305; Jubilee, Andamooka, 85, 96, 130, 136, 158, 191; Jundah, Qld., 74, 80, 115, 135, 144, 156, 212, 239; Jundah Old Field, Qld., 345; Jungle, Coober Pedy, 90, 199, 204, 225, 280, 284; Kangaroo, 74, 223, 256–258; Kingfisher Workings, Lightning Ridge, 211, 325; Koska's, Andamooka, 96, 191; Kweneng Ranch, Bot., 271; Kyabra, Qld., 78, 339; Kyabra Creek, Qld., 70, 74, 78, 239, 339, 341, 343–345; Kyabra Hills, Qld., 70, 74, 239; Kyabra Homestead, Qld., 343–345; Kyeenee Homestead, Qld., 340; Lambina, *see* Lambina in main headings; Lena's Hill, White Cliffs, 259, 326; Lennon, Coober Pedy, 199; Lightning Ridge, *see* Lightning Ridge in main headings; Listowel Downs, Qld., 70, 77, 239, 344; Lone Tree Hill, Andamooka, 96; Longreach, Qld., 239, 342, 345; Lunatic Hill (Grosser's) Diggings, Andamooka, 96, 154, 191; Madan Ore Field, Bulg., 273; Magdalena District, Mex., 103, 145, 158, 225, 228, 284, 305, 306, 321; Marillana Homestead, W. Austral., 365; Mayneside Homestead, Qld., 236, 339, 340; McDonald's Six Mile, Lightning Ridge, 82, 211, 325; Mehi, Lightning Ridge, 86, 94, 98, 109, 114, 121, 133, 149, 209; Merrigal Homestead, Qld., 343; Metlojane Pan, Botswana, 271; Millionaire's Gulch, Glengarry, 106, 107, 128, 147; Millionaire's Gully, Glengarry, 211; Milparinka, White Cliffs, 73, 326; Mintabie, S. Austral., *see* Mintabie, in main headings; Moble Creek, Qld., 341; Moffat's Hill, White Cliffs, 326; Mohave Valley mines, CA, 35; Mooka Homestead, W. Austral., 365; Muttaburra, Qld., 345; Nebea Hill, Lightning Ridge, 211, 324, 325; Nerang Creek, Qld., 340; New Chum Claim Area, Lightning Ridge, 86, 200, 211, 259, 325, 380; New Coocoran, xiv, 98, 114, 115, 118, 208, 209, 211, 222 discovered, 114; flooded, 115 New Field, Coober Pedy, 30, 86,

90, 100, 113, 202, 224, 257; New Nobby Claim Area, Lightning Ridge, 86, 101, 150, 211, 325; New Rush, Lightning Ridge, 127; New Year's Creek, Qld., 342; New Year's Rush, Lightning Ridge, 211, 325; Newtown, Lightning Ridge, 325; Nine Mile, Lightning Ridge, 211, 325; Nobby Hill, Lightning Ridge, 81–83, 85–87, 142; Nooralaba Homestead, Qld., 339; O'Connell Claim, NSW, 324; O'Donnell Opal Occurrence, ID, 295; Old Chum, Lightning Ridge, 211, 325; Old Four Mile, Coober Pedy, 199; Old Nobby, Lightning Ridge, 85, 96, 121, 127, 211, 325; Old Town Area, Lightning Ridge, 85, 86, 211, 325; Olympic, Coober Pedy, 98, 100, 101, 115, 120; One Tree Hill, Andamooka, 94–96, 187, 188, 191; Opal Butte, *see* Opal Butte in main headings; Opal Creek, Andamooka, 94, 187, 191, 192; Opal Creek, ID, 81, 295; Opal Mine Draw, OR, 333; Opal Mountain, CA, 276; Opal Springs, ID, 296; Opal Springs, WY, 367; Opalton, Qld., 78, 106, 239, 242, 342; Opalton Homestead Ruins, Qld., 339, 340; Opalton Mining Field, Qld., 345; Ouldburra Hill, S. Austral., 349; Palmer River Goldfield, Qld., 70, 341; Palparara Homestead, Qld., 339; Panther Creek Opal Occurrence, ID, 81, 84, 295; Parracoonah Homestead, Qld., 339; Perfecto, Coober Pedy, 199; Peter's Butte, 75, 334, *see also* Opal Butte; Phil Herbert's Rush, Lightning Ridge, 211, 325; Phone Line Diggings, Lightning Ridge, 122, 127, 128, 131, 151, 211; Pieuna Downs Homestead, Qld., 343, 344; Pinkilla Homestead, Qld., 343, 344; Pinnacle Hill, Qld., 345; Pinnacles Prospect, Qld., 342, 344; Pluto, Coober Pedy, 199; Pony Fence Claim Area, Lightning Ridge, 86, 211, 325; Post Office Hill, Coober Pedy, 90, 199; Potch Point, Lightning Ridge, 211, 325; Pott's Point claim area, Lightning Ridge, 86, 211; Poulston's

Opal fields *(Continued)*
Prospect, Qld., 344; Prairie Homestead, Qld., 340; Pumpkin Flat, Lightning Ridge, 211, 325; Pungadi West Godavari District, In., 297; Purnanga, White Cliffs, 326; Querétaro, Mex., *see* Querétaro in main headings; Quilpie, Qld., 80, 93, 99, 108, 144, 145, 152, 156, 158, 239, 242, 244, 343; Quinn's, W. Austral., 365; Raymore Homestead, Qld., 343, 344; Red Rock Canyon, CA, 98, 274–276, 275; Rose Quartz Crystal Locality, Maine, 302; Roxby Downs, S. Austral., 193; Russo's Folly, Coober Pedy, 199; Saddle, Andamooka, 96, 191; Saddle, Coober Pedy, 199; San Juan del Rio, Mex., 69, 70, 102, 225, 306; San Nichola del Oro, Mex., 97; Sandgate, Qld., 340; Santa Maria del Oro, Mex., 305; Seven Mile, Lightning Ridge, 202, 211, 325, 327; Seven Mile, White Cliffs, 327; Seventeen Mile, Coober Pedy, 199; Shallow Belars, Lightning Ridge, 211, 325; Shearer's Rush, Lightning Ridge, 211, 325; Sheepyard, Lightning Ridge, 174, 209, 211; Shell Patch, Coober Pedy, 199; Sierra de Celaque, Hon., 205; Sierra de Cordoba Campo Bajo Cuarzo, Spain, 352; Sierra de Tarahaumare, Mex., 97; Sierra Madre del Sur, Mex., 129, 305, 305; Sierra Madre Occidental, Mex., 129, 305; Sierra Madre Oriental, Mex., 306; Sierra Opalaca, Hon., 205; Sim's Hill, Lightning Ridge, 85, 86, 211, 325; Smith's Hill, White Cliffs, 259, 327; Stevens Creek, Andamooka, 96; Stuart Range Opal Mines, 89–92, *see also* Coober Pedy under main headings; Sullivan's Hill, White Cliffs, 259, 327; Taurus Group Mines, W. Austral., 364; Teatree Flat, Andamooka, 191; Telephone Line claim area, Lightning Ridge, 86, 91; Ten Mile, Lightning Ridge, 211, 325; Terrachie Homestead, Qld., 343, 344; Thirty-two Mile, Coober Pedy, 199; Thorley's Six Mile, Lightning Ridge, 211, 325; Three Mile Flat, Lightning Ridge, 43, 128, 380; Three Mile, Lightning Ridge, 86, 128; Tibooburra Diggings, White Cliffs, 327; Tinderry Homestead, Qld., 340; Tintinbar, NSW, 81, 91, 322, 325; Tirga Homestead, Qld., 339, 340; Tommy Dod, Qld., 346; Tonkoro Homestead, Qld., 339; Top Flat, Qld., 346; Treloar Hill, Andamooka, 95; Treloar's, Andamooka, 96; Trewallah Homestead, Qld., 340; Triangle, Andamooka, 96, 191; Trinidad Homestead, Qld., 343–345; Treloar's Workings, Andamooka, 96, 187, 188, 191; Turley's Hill, White Cliffs, 259, 327; Twelve Mile, Coober Pedy, 90, 199; Twenty Mile, Coober Pedy, 93, 198, 199; Two Jacks, Qld., 342; Twitchell Quarry, ME, 302; Tyson's Mine, Qld., 340; Tyson's Valley Workings, Qld., 340; Unadine Mine, UT, 360; U.S. Mine, UT, 359; Vegetable Creek, NSW, 324; Vergemont Homestead, Qld., 340; Virgin Valley, *see* Virgin Valley in main headings; Wadara Hills, W. Austral., 365; Walsh's Knob, White Cliffs, 259, 327; Wantha Bluff, Qld., 339; Warden Hill, Andamooka, 191; White Cliffs, *see* White Cliffs in main headings; White Dam, Andamooka, 191; Willis' Ridge, Andamooka, 96; Wondai, Qld., 343; Wyola Homestead, Qld., 339, 340; Yahloo, Andamooka, 96; Yahloo Extension, Andamooka, 191; Yahloo South, Andamooka, 191; Yahloo West, Andamooka, 191; Yancannia Rush, White Cliffs, 259, 326, 327; Yaraka, Qld., 345; Yedlin Location, ME, 302; Yarra Wurta Cliff, S. Austral., 349; Yeppara Homestead, Qld., 343; Yellow Lake, B.C., 273; Yowah, Qld., xiv, 78, 118, 164, 174, 175, 185, 239–242, 339, 341; Yundamindera Homestead, W. Austral., 365; Zorba, Coober Pedy, 199

Opal Hill, CO, 279

Opal level/layer, xi, 44, 82, 86, 87, 127, 149, 162, 184, 190–192, 196, 198, 201, 213, 214, 225, 229, 239, 244, 253, 255, 259, 309, 376–378, 380, 381, 385, 386. *See also* Opal dirt

Opal Miner, The, 81, 130, 144, 259

Opal: The Gem of the Never Never, 74, 93

Opalbanya, 56–58, 158, 177

Opalescent, 162, 184, 279, 301, 347, 380

Opalholic, xi

Opaline, ID, 104

Opalite. *See* Simulated opal: opalite

Opalized fossils. *See* Fossils, opalized

Opals by Shirley, 276

Ora Banda, W. Austral., 364, 365

Ops (Roman goddess), 56

Oran Region, Alg., 264

Orange County, CA, 276

Oreana, ID, 77

Oregon, xiv, 12, 51, 53, 55, 69, 73, 75, 77, 78, 100, 103, 112, 126, 132, 137, 169, 181, 183, 187, 193, 208, 231, 232, 234, 236, 244, 272, 286, 332, 333

Organizations. *See* Societies/organizations

Orient(al), xi, 14, .6, 55, 57, 59, 65, 97, 103, 110, 165, 166, 194, 226, 228, 254, 306, 374

Orient Queen opal, 107, 128, 147, 158

Originum seu Etymologiarum, Libri XX, 60

Orissa, In., 297

Orleans Cedex, Fr., 288

Orme Property, UT, 359

Orpen, J. L., 369

Osikovo, Bulg., 273

Oslo, Norw., 330

Osore San, Jpn., 300

Ostrowiec Swietokrzski, Pol., 336

Other Half opal, 112, 147, 150, 156

Ottawa, Can., 146

Otto's Stone opal, 93, 148, 156, 148

Overbrook, PA, 335

Owyhee County, ID, 77, 294, 296

Owyhee River, ID, 296

Oxford County, ME, 302

Oxford, NZ, 328

Padgham, W. A., 330

Painted Chasm, B.C., 272

Painted Lady opal, 104, 148

Pakistan, 334

Palau, 370

Palestine, 211

Pall Mall, London, 70

Pamachic, Mex., 55

Panama, 102, 204, 370, 102, 370

Panda, In., 297

Pandora Opal, 26, 42, 94, 149, 150, 156, 222, 316, 317

Panther Creek, 81, 84, 295

Papayas, Phil., 335

Papua New Guinea, 334

Paradise Valley, NV, 100, 109
Paraguay, 370
Parainen, Fin., 287
Paris, Fr., 61, 65, 94, 136, 170, 174, 288, 289, 302, 365
Paris, ME, 302
Paris, W. Austral., 365
Paris Basin, Fr., 289
Paris School of Mines, 289
Park County, 280, 307, 366
    Colorado, 280; Montana, 307; Wyoming, 366
Park, OR, 333
Parker's Mill, OR, 334
Parla, Sp., 352, 353
Partridge Island, N.S., 331
Patrick, Richard, 313, 317
Paselstollen, Aus., 269
Passaic County, NJ, 319
Pat's Stone opal, 81, 101, 150, 156, 150
Pathfinder Reservoir, WY, 366, 367
Patterson, Virgil, xiv
Paua shell (sea opal), 182
Pauly, Hans, 50, 103
Pawtuxet County, RI, 346
Paxson, Alaska, 264
Payette County, ID, 296
Pearson, Grant, 49, 112
Peeble Knowe, Scot., 347
Peineto, Mex., 70
Peking (China), 370
Pelayo, Francisco de Asís Fernando Pío Juan María Gregorio, 72
Pella, S. Afr., 349
Peloncillo Mountains, N. Mex., 320
Pendleton, OR, 232
Penick, D. Allen, 361
Penicton, B.C., 272
Penjamo, Mex., 106, 305
Pennington County, SD, 351
Pennsylvania, 334
Peña Revilla, Sp., 351
Per Dams Skib, Green., 292
Peralta Canyon, N. Mex., 320
Perez, Josue L., 335
Perry Ranch, B.C., 272
Persephone opal, 114, 141, 142, 150, 156
Persian, 151
Perth, W. Austral., 365
Perthshire, Scot., 347
Peru, 335
Petaca District, N. Mex., 320
Peter Ferguson, 82
Peter of Arles, 63
Petrusenko, S., 273
Philadelphia County, PA, 335
Philippines, 335
Phillips, Jack, 133
Phillips, Ken A., 266
Phoebus Opal, 151, 158, 226
Phoenix, AZ, 266
Piauí, Brazil, 111, 194, 271
Pickering, S. M., 290
Pickett, Thomas E., 283
Pienaar, Herbert S., 348
Pilansberg Mountains, So. Afr., 349

Pine Mountain, GA, 290
Pingendorf, Aus., 269
Pioneer Square, Seattle, WA, 237
Pitcairn, 370
Pitjantjatjara Land Rights Act, 229
Pitjantjatjara, Anangu, 231
Piute County, UT, 359
Placer County, CA, 276
Plaine de la Rusizi, Bur., 274
Plains of Bijapur, In., 297
Plato, 55, 56
Play of color (POC), xi, 2–4, 6, 7, 11, 13, 14, 29, 31, 47, 49, 56, 57, 61, 67, 97, 102, 103, 107, 108, 112, 114, 115, 118, 121, 122, 124, 126–132, 134–137, 143–147, 149–155, 160–164, 166–180, 182–185, 189–191, 193–197, 199, 203, 206–208, 210, 213, 214, 221, 225–227, 230, 234, 235, 240, 244, 247–250, 252, 253, 256, 266–268, 271–278, 280, 282, 283, 285, 286, 289, 292–295, 297, 298, 299–302, 304–306, 308–314, 316, 321, 322, 329, 333, 335, 337–339, 349–351, 353, 355, 356, 357–359, 361, 362, 364, 366–368, 373–376, 378, 381, 382;
bandfire opal, 162; bar opal, 163; block opal, 163; blue opal, 29, 112, 115, 163, 234, 235, 293, 295, 335, 353; broadflash xi, 2, 47, 67, 108, 122, 126, 129, 130, 132, 134, 136, 137, 143–147, 149, 151, 152, 154, 155, 160, 161, 164, 167–169, 174, 193, 206, 207, 226, 244, 250, 266, 267, 274, 275, 277, 280, 282, 294, 297, 304, 308, 322, 333, 339, 349, 356, 358, 361, 374, 381, 382; chaff opal, 166; Chinese hat, 374; Chinese writing opal, 166, 178; columnar fire opal, 166; confetti opal, 166; contra luz opal (iris opal), 112, 140, 145, 166, 167, 173, 197, 207, 227, 234, 235, 252, 277, 286, 308, 310–314, 316, 333; exploding flash opal, 168; fan harlequin opal, 168; fan opal, 168; fancy pattern opal, 168; fan-flash opal, 244; flagstone opal, 169; flame opal, 107, 118, 169; fire opal, 169; flash opal, 168, 169, 180; flashfire opal, 2, 57, 164, 169, 180, 374; full sheen opal, 244; harlequin opal, 2, 67, 102, 114, 122, 124, 127, 128, 137,

155, 161, 167–169, 171, 175, 208, 240, 248, 249, 275, 282, 283, 322, 333, 339, 349, 381; iridot, 173; mackerel sky opal, 174; mosaic opal, 171, 175, 379; multicolor opal, 176; multifire opal, 176; palette opal, 178; pinfire, 2, 47, 100, 108, 126, 130, 136, 145, 149, 155, 161, 163, 164, 166, 167, 169, 174, 178, 179, 183, 193, 201, 207, 226, 229, 240, 244, 248, 250, 266, 267, 273–275, 277, 280, 282, 300, 302, 304, 306, 308, 322, 329, 333, 338, 339, 349, 356, 361, 362, 366, 381; pinpoint pattern, 179; red flash opal, 180; red-on-black opal, 180; ribbon opal, 174, 180, 321; rolling blue dot opal, 180; rolling flash opal, 180; rolling flashfire opal, 180; straw opal, 183; sun stone, 183; sunflash opal, 163, 183, 213; turtleback opal, 244; turtleflash opal, 183; twinkle opal, 183
Playas Dry Lake, N.M, 320
Playford, P. E., 363
Plaza Obregon, Querétaro, Mex., 228
Pleasant Lake, ME, 302
Pleasant Valley, OR, 333
Pliny the Elder (Gaius Plinius Secundus), ix, 59, 190
Plush Valley, OR, 333, 334
Poached Egg Opal, 134
POC. *See* Play of color
Podborany, Cz. Rep., 283
Point Danger, NSW, 322
Poirot, Jean-Paul, 289
Pojorata, Rum., 347
Poland, 57, 179, 335–337
Polatli, Turk., 358
Polk County, 267, 287
    Arkansas, 267; Florida, 287
Pollon, Joff, 122
Pollon, Jonathan S., 122
Pomeroy County, G.B., 285
Pont de Chateau, Fr., 288
Pontezuela, Cu., 281
Poole Range, Austral., 365
Poona, W. Austral., 365
Pootelsgrün, Ger., 291
Popina, Yug., 368
Popotosa Formation, NM, 321
Porcupine Hill, YT, 369
Porcupine Villa, 259
Port Augustus, S. Austral., 89, 187, 193
Port Curtis, 71
Port Moresby, Pap. N.G., 334
Porta, Giovanni, 64
Port Vila, Vanatu, 360
Portland, OR, 332

Porto, Port., 337
Portugal, 337, 338, 370
Postmasburg, S. Afr., 349
Pough, Frederick, 122, 140
Povraznik, Slov., 283
Powell Basin, Ant., 265
Powell, William, 136
Powhatan County, VA, 362
Precious Stone Prospecting Permit, 203
Precious Stones and Gems, 136
Preschau, Hung., 57
Presidio County, TX, 357
Presov, 57, 282, 293
   Hungary, 57, 293; Slovakia, 282
Pretoria, S. Afr., 348
Priday Ranch, OR, 333
Pride of Australia opal, 91, 122, 128, 132, 134, 151, 158, 222
Primmersdorf, Aus., 268, 269
Prince Edward Island, 338
Prince Rupert, B.C., 55, 273
Prince William County, VA, 362
Princess Diana. *See* Diana, Princess
Princeton, B.C., 273
Principe, 371
Pristina, Yug., 368
Prospecting, 104, 108. *See also* Noodling
   geophysical aerial prospecting, 104, 108
Providence County, RI, 346
Provo, UT, 251
Prussia, 337
Prydz Bay, Ant., 265
Puente de la Princes, Sp., 352
Puerta de Tierra, PR, 338
Puerto Rico, 338
Pulaski County, 257, 290
   Arkansas, 267; Georgia, 290
Pullman, WA, 363
Pulpah Head Station, NSW, 259
Purdy's Ranch, OR, 272
Purnanga, NSW, 78, 80, 326
Putnam County, NY, 327
Puumala, Fin., 287
Puy de Dome, Fr., 288
Puy Marmant, Fr., 288
Pyke Well, W. Austral., 365

Qanakkale Province, Turk., 358
Qatar, 371
Quarus, G.B., 286
Quebec, Can., 338
Queen Elizabeth I, 64
Queen Elizabeth II, 100, 120, 189
Queen Margrethe, 111
Queen Victoria, 68, 69, 137
Queen, Lawrence D., 334
Queensland, Australia, xiii, xiv, 8, 12, 18, 29, 53, 58, 70, 71, 74, 76–80, 93, 99, 104, 106–110, 113–118, 131, 135, 144, 145, 152, 156, 158, 164, 174, 175, 179, 180, 182, 185, 187, 195, 206, 209, 212, 214, 239, 240, 256, 257, 259, 272, 338, 378, 382
Department of Mines, 76
Queensland opal, 76, 78, 80, 108, 180, 259. *See also* Boulder opal
Querétaro, Mex., 60, 69, 70, 97, 102, 151, 158, 187, 225, 228, 254, 304, 306
   opal mines, history of, 306
Quesnel Lake, B.C., 273
Quesnel, B.C., 273
Quetta, Pak., 334
Quetza-litzle-pyollitli, 60
Quezon City, Phil., 335
Quilpie Artesian Basin, Qld., 152
Quinalibugan Island Caramoan, Phil., 335
Quincy, Fr., 135, 180, 288
Quintana, Jaime Roldán, 304

Raade, Gunnar, 330
Rabat, Mor., 307
Rabenwald, Aus., 269
Rabun County, GA, 290
Racosul de Sus, Rum., 347
Radulescu, Dan P., 346
Rainbow Ridge, xiii, 26, 45, 48, 88, 90, 91, 94, 96, 98–101, 112, 121, 125, 136, 138, 146, 147, 152, 246–250, 253, 255, 312, 316–318
Rainbow Ridge Mining Company, 91, 98, 99, 248, 249
Rajasthan, In., 297
Rajmahal Hills, In., 297
Rajmahal Traps, In., 297
Rakops, Bot., 271
Raleigh, NC, 329
Ralston, John Prosper, 42, 150
Ramaca, Yug., 367, 368
Ramachka Glavica, Yug., 369
Ramatlabama, Bot., 271
Rapid City, SD, 350
Rapidan River, VA, 362
Rapidan, VA, 362
Ratanpura, In., 297
Rathlin Island, Ire., 298
Raudsep, Rein, 286
Ravelli County, 307
Rawlins County, KS, 300
Reager, James P., 303
Reardan, WA, 363
Red Admiral Opal, 127, 151, 158. *See also* Butterfly Opal
Red Creek, UT, 359
Red Show Opal, 93, 344
Redruth, G.B., 285
Reed, Robert C, 306
Reeve, Paul, xiv
Regina, Sask., 347
Reid, Jeffrey C., 329
Reinischbruch, Aus., 269
Reisterstown, MD, 303
Rejanglebong, Indon., 297
Reno, Nevada, xiv, 247, 308, 310

Reserves. *See* National parks/reserves
Reunion, 346
Rhode Island, 346
Rhodesia, 106
Ribas de Jarama, Sp., 352
Ribas de Jarama, Sp., 353
Ribas del Jarama, Sp., 353
Richardson, Alf, 74, 256
Richmond County, GA, 290
Richmond, VA, 362
Riddell's Creek, Vic., 361
Ridgecrest, CA, 276
Rielves, Sp., 354
Rio Arriba County, NM, 320
Rio Conchos, Mex., 305
Rio Grande de Santiago, Mex., 305
Rio Grande do Sul, Braz., 271
Rio Grande, CO, 279
Rio Grande, NM, 321
Rio Oteros, Mex., 305
Rio Puerco Valley, NM, 321
Rio San Jose Lepasite, Hon., 208
Riom es Montagne, Fr., 288
Riom, Fr., 288
Ristiina, Fin., 287
Ritenbenk District, Green., 292
Riverside County, CA, 276
Roanoke County, VA, 362
Roberts, A. E., 369
Rochester, ME, 302
Rochester, MI, 104, 182
Rochester, NY, 152, 327, 248
Rock & Gem Magazine, xii
Rock Creek, WA, 363
Rock Teepee, ID, 296
Rocks. *See* Minerals/rocks
Rockville, MD, 303
Rockville, OR, 334
Rocky Bridge Creek, NSW, 70, 322, 324
Rocky Mountains, 102, 204, 102
Rodalquilar-Nijar, Sp., 351
Roebling, John A., 152, 155
Roebling, Washington A., 152, 155, 248
Roebling Opal, 91, 125, 151, 155, 156, 158, 248, 316, 91, 151, 248, 249, 316
Roeburn, W. Austral., 69
Roilly Pond, NY, 327
Rolla, MO, 236, 307
Romagnat, Fr., 288
Roman, ix, x, 68, 177
Roman Empire, 58, 59, 65, 171, 281
Roman Lovers opal carving, 152, 158
Romblon, Phil., 335
Rome, 58, 146, 281, 297
Romersreuth, Cz. Rep., 283
Ronasco, Dan, 138
Roosevelt County, NM, 320
Roosevelt, OK, 332
Roosevelt, WA, 363
Rosamond, CA, 275
Rosenove, 80
Rosita Hills, CO, 279

Rosny Park, Tas., 355
Ross Sea, Ant., 265
Rothsay, W. Austral., 365
Rotura, NZ, 328
Rough Times Company, 118
Royal Peacock opal, 251
Rumania(ns), 58, 181
Rumford, ME, 302
Rupsju, In., 297
Ruskin, John, xi
Russia(ns), 51, 103, 203, 347
Rustenberg, S. Afr., 348, 349
Rwanda, 274, 347, 274
Rye Valley, OR, 333

Sabina, Ann P., 277
Sachsen und Thüringen, Ger., 291
Sacramento, CA, 274
Sagadahoc County, ME, 302
Sage Hen Creek, WY, 367
Saguache County, CO, 280
Sahagún, Col., 60, 278
Sahara Desert, 56, 166, 307, 371
Sahibganj, In., 297
St. Austell, G.B., 285
St. Day, G.B., 285
St. Helena, 371
St. Ives, G.B., 285
St. John's, Nfld., 328
St. Just, G.B., 285
St. Kitts, 371
St. Leonards, NSW, 322
St. Leonhard, Aus., 270
St. Lucia, 371
St. Paul, MN, 306
St. Pierre, 371
St. Vincent, 371
Sainte-Foy, Que., 338
Salina, UT, 359
Salmon, ID, 295
Salmon River, ID, 81, 295
Salmon River Mountains, ID, 295, 296
Salt Lake County, UT, 359
Saltillo, Mex., 306
Salto do Jacuí, Braz., 271
Salzberg, Aus., 269
San Antonio Mountains, Hon., 171, 206, 207
San Benito, CA, 276
San Bernardino County, CA, 276
San Diego, CA, 118
San Felipe, Cu., 281
San Francisco Bay, CA, 55
San Francisco Chronicle, 90, 246, 247
San Francisco District, UT, 359
San José, CR, 280
San Juan Bautista, CA, 276
San Juan County, NM, 320
San Luis Obispo County, CA, 276
San Marcos, Mex., 305
San Marino, 371
San Mateo County, CA, 276
San Mateo District, NM, 321
San Nicolas, Mex., 305
San Patricio, Peru, 335
San Pitch Mountains, UT, 359

San Simon District:
  Arizona, 115; New Mexico, 320
Sanders, John V., 3, 26–28, 31, 36
Sandoval County, NM, 320
Sandy Braes:
  England, 285; Ireland, 298
Sangerhausen, Ger., 67, 68
Sanskrit language, 56, 58, 177, 296
Santa Barbara County, CA, 55, 90, 248, 276
Santa Cruz County, AZ, 180, 266
Santa Fe County, NM, 321
Santa Maria, CA, 276
Santa Rita District, NM, 320
Santa Rosa Mountains, NV, 310
Santa Rosa, Hon., 205
Santiago, Chile, 277
Santiago, Sp., 352
Sao Tome, 371
Saratoga County, NY, 327
Sarawak, Malaysia, 303
Sarda Bluff, S. Austral., 349
Sarolegus, It., 299
Saskatchewan, 54, 347
Saturn (Roman god), 56
Saturnalia, 56
Saudi Arabia, 371
Saul, 79
Savannah River, GA, 290
Savona Mountains, B.C., 272
Scafe, Don, 264
Scattery Creek, Qld., 342
Scenic, SD, 351
Schabelschmid, Aus., 270
Schladming, Aus., 270
Schleibheim, Aus., 270
Schneider, Gic, 308
Schneider, Jill L., 264
Schwagbauer, Aus., 270
Schwalm, 91
Schwencke Opal, 99, 152, 156, 99
Scioto River, OH, 331
Scotland, 285, 347
Scotsman, Qld., 342
Scott, Thomas M., 287
Scott, Walter (Sir), 67
Scottsdale, AZ, 140
Sdom, Isr., 299
Sedibeng, Bot., 271
Segev, Amit, 298
Segovia Point, Sp., 352
Seini-Ilba, Rum., 347
Semedraz, Yug., 369
Sementine, Switz., 355
Senegal, 371
Senonian Mishas Formation, Isr., 299
Serbia, 367, 369
Sevba, Slov., 283
Sevier County, UT, 359
Seville, 60
Seychelles, 371
Shan Hai King, 54, 55,
Shaner, Levi, 232
Shanghai (China), 371
Shannon County, SD, 351
Shansi (China), 371

Shantung (China), 371
Sharp, Gene, xiv
Shasta County, CA, 276
Shaw, Raynor, 293
Sheep Canyon, TX, 356
Shelford, John, 272
Shensi (China), 371
Shepherd, Roy, 94, 187–189
Sherman, Ernest G., 98, 108, 122, 132, 134, 146, 147, 151, 200, 201, 212
Sherman, Greg, 146, 147, 201
Shin-yu, Jpn., 300
Shumadia District, Yug., 369
Siargao, Phil., 335
Siddiqui, Kamal S., 347
Siebengebirg, Ger., 291
Siek, Phil., 335
Sierra Blanca, NM, 54
Sierra County, 277, 321
  California, 277; New Mexico, 321
Sierra Leone, 348
Silesia, Pol., 179
Silex, Sp., 352, 353
Silica Hills, UT, 359
Silmilkameen Mining District, B.C., 273
Silverbow County, MT, 307
Silverton Creek, B.C., 273
Silvies Canyon, OR, 333
Simav, Turk., 358
Simonka Massif, Slov., 57, 282
Simulated opal (imitation opal), 104, 107, 108, 118, 173, 174, 176, 182, 183. *See also* Synthetic opal; Paua shell myrickite, 176; Opal Essence, 107; opalite, 108, 118, 176; paua shell (sea opal), 182; Slocum Stone, 36, 108, 182
Sina River, In., 297
Singapore, 371
Sinkankas, John, 145, 227
Sinkiang Uighur (China), 371
Sinnot, Joseph A., 304
Sioux Pass, MT, 54
Siskiyou County, CA, 277
Sisoquichic, Mex., 97
Sitabaldi, In., 297
Sitnianska Lehotka, Slov., 283
Siurob, Jose Maria, 70
Sjalland, Den., 284
Skamania County, WA, 363
Skarpdal, Fin., 287
Skertchly, S. B. J., 58
Slánsky highland, Slov., 57
Slansky Vrchy Mountains, Slov., 282, 283
Slocum, John, 104, 107, 182
Slocum Mining Division, B.C., 273
Slovakia(n), 56–58, 63, 69, 72, 84, 93, 95, 126, 156, 158, 171, 177, 256, 281–283, 293, 297, 348
Slovenia, 371
Slupiec, Pol., 336, 337

Smith, Kevin Lane, xiv, 12, 128,
    145, 233–238, 259, 290,
    302, 327, 334
Smith, R. C., II, 334
Smith, R. W., 290
Smith, Tom, 264
Smithfield, W. Austral., 365
Smulgedon, G.B., 285
Smyrna, DE, 284
Smythe, Hodge, 88, 155
Snake River, 77, 294
Snake River, ID, 294
Soboth, Aus., 270
Sobótka, Pol., 336, 337
Societies/organizations, 3, 26, 31,
    36, 89, 92, 257, 265, 268,
    291
    American Opal Society, 309; Aus-
    tralian Mineralogical Society,
    268; Commonwealth Scien-
    tific Industrial Research Or-
    ganization (CSIRO), 3, 26,
    31, 36; German Gemmologi-
    cal Association, 291; Na-
    tional Science Foundation,
    265; New Colorado Pros-
    pecting Syndicate, South
    Australia, 89; Progress Com-
    mittee of Coober Pedy, 92;
    Wilcannia Blocks Syndicate,
    257
Socorro County, NM, 321
Socorro Hot Springs, NM, 321
Socorro, NM, 319
Sodankylä, Fin., 287
Sofia, Bulg., 273
Solomon Islands, 348
Somalia, 371
Somerset County, NJ, 319
Sommer Camp, ID, 77
Sonoma County, CA, 277
Sonora, Mex., 225, 304, 306
Sotheby's, 160
South Africa, 53, 106, 348, 369
South America(n), 16, 183, 360
South Australia, 22, 68, 69, 78,
    89–91, 94, 97, 98, 101,
    110, 120, 121, 129, 130,
    136, 146, 149, 153, 154,
    156, 158, 160, 167, 175,
    187, 189, 195, 196, 203,
    214, 224, 229, 245, 330,
    349, 375, 378
    Department of Mines, 91; Flying
    Doctor of South Australia,
    203
South Brisbane Station, Qld., 340
South Carolina, 350
South Dakota, 350
South Fiora, It., 299
South Fork Republican River, CO,
    280
South Georgia (United Kingdom),
    371
South Orkney Islands, Ant., 265
South Pacific, 199
South Sandwich Islands, 371

Southern Cross, W. Austral., 365
Soutpansberg, S. Afr., 349
Spain, 64, 72, 73, 277, 351
Spanish, 60, 62, 153, 158, 161,
    162, 166, 167, 171, 173–
    175, 177, 247, 371, 374,
    377, 381
Spanish North Africa, 371
Spargoville, W. Austral., 365
Specimen Ridge, WY, 367
*Speculum Lapidum Clarissima Ar-
    tium,* 63
Spencer Harwood, 99
Spencer Opal Mine, 35, 99, 100,
    104, 108, 110–112, 166,
    182, 183, 242–244, 382
    address, phone, etc., 244; discov-
    ery of, 99; fee-digging, 242
Spencer, ID, 99, 242, 294
Split Rock Formation, WY, 367
Springfield, PA, 335
Springside, Qld., 239
Springsure, Qld., 70, 72, 77, 338,
    343
Spruce Pine Mining District, NC,
    329
Squaw Creek, ID, 77, 294, 296
Srbljanovic, Predrag, 367
Sri Lanka, 371
Srinagar, In., 297
Stack, Scot., 347
Staivnicke Vrchy Mountains, Slov.,
    283
Standen, Allan, 356
Star of Bethlehem Opal, 153
Starr County, TX, 357
Steel band, 127, 162, 181, 214,
    373, 380, 385
Steiermark (Styria), Aus., 269, 270
Stein, V., 290
Steinberg, Aus., 270
Steonkopf, S. Afr., 348
Sterling Hill, NJ, 319
Sterling Range, W. Austral., 365
Stetler, Claudia, 108, 242
Stetler, Mark, 101, 104, 108, 110,
    112, 242, 243
    owns/names Spencer Opal Mine,
    104. *See also* Spencer Opal
    Mine
Stevens, Kurt, 143
Stewart, GA, 290
Stewart, Jonathan, 285, 298
Stirling Range, W. Austral., 364
Stockholm, Swed., 354
Stockton, CA, 98, 249
Stoffhütte, Aus., 270
Stokes County, NC, 329
Stone Mountain Granite Corpora-
    tion, 290
Stone Mountain, GA, 290
Stone, Garry, 153
Stony Bluff, GA, 290
Strachan, Leslie K. C., 354
Streeter, E. W., 136
Strezovci Region, Yug., 369
Stuart, H. H., 132

Stuart Creek, S. Austral., 349
Stuart Range, 89–92, 196, 197
Stuart Range, S. Austral., 89
Stuart Trail, 229
Stubalpe, Aus., 269
Stubley, Mike, 330
Stump Lake, B.C., 272
Sucker Creek, OR, 334
Sudbury, Ont., 332
Sulawesi, Indon., 298
Sulphur, NV, 309
Sumatra, 297
Summit Peak, CO, 54
Summit, NJ, 319
Sunagawa, Ichiro, 299
Sunbury, N.T., 330
Sunbury, Vic., 361
Sundeen, S. Paul, 306
Sun-downers, 70
Sun God Opal, 153
Superstitions and myths. *See* Chap-
    ter 4
Surat, Qld., 340
Suriname, 371
Sussex County, NJ, 319
Sutherland, F. L., 322
Suva, Fiji, 287
Svarfadardalur, Ice., 293
Svetoslav, Bulg., 273
Svisero, Darcy Pedro, 271
Swartwater, S. Afr., 349
Swaziland, S. Afr., 348, 354
Sweden, 203, 354
Sweetwater County, WY, 366
Sweetwater River, WY, 54, 366
Swinden, Scott, 328
Switzerland, 35, 142, 170, 329,
    354, 355
Sydney, NSW, 41, 42, 72, 82, 83,
    88, 108, 120, 122, 130,
    134, 146, 148, 154, 155,
    209, 210, 212, 256, 322,
    324–326
    Botanical Gardens, 41
Synthetic opal, 36, 104, 107, 110,
    108, 170, 173, 174, 183. *See
    also* Imitation opal; Simu-
    lated opal
    Gilson Opal, 36, 108, 170
Syria, 371
Syrjäsalmi, Fin., 287
Szechwan (China), 371
Szklary, Pol., 336, 337

Taberg, Swed., 354
Tabion, Phil., 335
Tablas, Phil., 335
Table Mountain, CO, 279
Taejon, S. Kor., 301
Taipei, Tai., 355
Tairua, NZ, 179
Taiwan, 254, 355, 370
Tajikistan, 371
Taliaferro, 298
Talisker, Scot., 347
Tallahassee, FL, 287
Tallinn, Est., 286

Tamborine Mountain, Qld., 341
Tamil Nadu, In., 297
Tampa Bay, FL, 287
Tancoska, Slov., 282
Tanzania(n), 53, 102, 111, 274, 355, 102, 274, 355
Tanzenbergtunnel, Aus., 270
Tapia, 130
Tapia, Rafael, 130
Tarrawilla, 68
Tartan Queen opal, 131, 153
Tartar, 165, 173
Tasmania, 130, 355
Tategama Hot Spring, Jpn., 300
Taxco, Mex., 130, 305
Taylor, Les, 18
Teal Waterhole, S. Austral., 349
Techerau, Rum., 347
Tegucigalpa, 207
Tegucigalpa, Hon., 207
Tehama County, CA, 277
Teller County, CO, 280
Temakon, Stanley, 360
Tenerife Province, Sp., 353
Tenerife, Can. Is., 352
Tennessee, 355
Tepee Creek Formation, OK, 332
Tepezala, Mex., 97, 102, 304, 305
Tepic, Mex., 306
Tequesquipan, Mex., 70
Terry, Oxford, 153
Tertiary, 21, 53, 225, 231, 268–270, 272, 273, 288, 289, 291, 297, 301, 312–314, 316, 317, 326, 327, 330, 334, 356, 357, 360, 362, 366, 368, 379
Teruel Province, Sp., 354
Tesnatee Creek, GA, 290
Tessin Region, Switz., 355
Teton County, WY, 366
Teven, NSW, 325
Texas, 54, 70, 236, 335, 356, 357
Texas, PA, 335
Thailand, 357, 358
Thallein, Aus., 270
Tharandt, Ger., 291
Thargomindah, Qld., 70
Theodore Matthey, 81, 116, 117
They Struck Opal!, 99, 153, 257
Thiry, Medard, 289
Thomas Range, UT, 359
Thompson, Alfred, 312
Thompson, Lew, 91, 152, 247
Thompson, Paul, 267
Thompson, Woodrow B., 302
Three Forks, MT, 307
Thuringia, 51, 67, 68, 95
Thuringia, Ger., 51
Tibet (China), 371
Tichka, Mor., 307
Tientsin (China), 371
Tiffany's, 86
Tipton, Steve, 333
Titheradge, Frank, 100, 147, 200, 201
Tlaxiaco, 97, 306

Tlaxiaco, Mex., 97, 306
Tlazacala, Mex., 305
Tobago, 358, 371
Todisco, Andrea, 299
Togo, 371
Tokelau, 371
Tokyo, Jpn., 299
Toledo Province, Sp., 354
Tolima, Col., 278
Toliman District, Mex., 305
Tonga, 371
Tooele County, UT, 359
Toompine, Qld., 239, 345
Tooraweenah, NSW, 78, 322, 326
Toowoomba, Qld., 70
Topaz Mountain, UT, 359
Topsham, ME, 302
Toronto, Ont., 131, 143, 160, 332
Torrejon de Ardoz, Sp., 353
Townsend, Jack, 349
Toyama Prefecture, Jpn., 300
Translucency, 11, 171, 180, 182, 183, 227, 235, 300, 335, 364, 365. *See also* Opal: translucent opal
Transparency, 11, 31, 163, 164, 169, 170, 172–174, 181, 182, 227, 280, 374. *See also* Opal: transparent opal
Transvaal, S. Afr., 349
Trás-or-Montes, Port., 338
Trebíc, Cz. Rep., 283
Trego County, KS, 175, 183, 300
Treibs, Emil, 79
Treibs, Ltd., 77
Treloar, Alan, 94, 96, 188
Trenton, NJ, 319
Tri Vody, Cz. Rep., 283
Triangulo, Mex., 55
Trident Peak, NV, 55
Trinidad, 306, 335, 343–345, 358
Triplets, 100, 112, 162, 163, 179, 195, 206, 208, 212, 243, 244, 294, 364, 376, 379, 386. *See also* Doublets
Tripoli, Libya, 301
Tripp Opal, 153, 158, 153
Tripp, Chester D., 154
Trzebnik, Pol., 337
Tsinghai (China), 371
Tsukuba, Jpn., 299
Tucson, AZ, xiv, 128, 145, 237
Tufra Mountains, 94
Tulameen, B.C., 272
Tulancingo District, Mex., 305
Tulare County, CA, 277
Tuliblock, Bot., 271
Tunisia, 371
Tuolumne County, CA, 277
Turkey, 58, 69, 199, 203, 293, 358, 371
Turkmenistan, 371
Turley, Dick, xi, 259, 327
Turner, Charlie, 74, 256, 257
Tuscaloosa, AL, 263
Tuscany, It., 299
Tutland Island, In., 297

Tuvalu, 371
Tweed Heads Region, NSW, 325
Tyne River, 51, 68
Types of opal. *See also types listed under* Common opal, in main headings:
abanderado, *see* abanderos opal, below; abanderos opal (abanderado/flag opal), 161, 162, 169; common opal, *see* Common opal in main headings; arananjado opal, 162; azule opal, 162, 170, 227, 306; banded opal, 162, 173, 278, 320, 351; barleycorn opals (gerstenkörner), 51, 67, 68, 95, 103; black jelly opal, 163; Brazilian opal, *see* Brazilian opal in main headings; cachalong opal, *see* Cachalong opal in main headings; cat's-eye opal, 1; ceraunium opal, 56, 166, 173, 183; chamälconstein opal, *see* Hydrophane opal; cherry opal, 166, 169, 225, 227, 305, 306; chromite, 170, 276; chrysoberyl, 2, 380; chrysoprase, 1, 170, 274, 277, 336, 337, 368; claro opal, 166; claro-o-translucente, 166; cloudy opal, 166; conk opal, *see* Forms of opal: conk opal; crystal opal, 29, 31, 32, 42, 87, 112, 118, 145, 151, 163, 164, 167, 168, 173, 174, 182, 189, 193, 195, 196, 203, 213, 230, 231, 234, 245, 246, 258, *see also* jelly opal, below
  black, 87, 151, 163, 167, 245; brown, 164, 167; clear, 167; light, 163, 173, 174, 234, 258; orange, 167; red, 42; yellow-orange, 195
Cupid's gem, 55, 178, *see also* rose opal, below; dark opal, 163, 168, 174, *see also* light opal, below; dendritic opal, 112, 168, 175, 234, 352, 354, 368, *see also* Dendrites, in main headings; diatomaceous earth, *see* tripoli; diatomaceous opal (infusorial opal/kieselguhr opal), 168, 173, 180, 183, 264, 265, 378, *see also* Diatomaceous, in main headings, diatomite, below; *and* Fossils: opalized/petrified; diatomite, *see* tripolite, below; egg opal, *see* huevos opal, below; eisen opal, 168; eye of the world, *see* hydrophane opal, below; eye-stone, 59, 177; fiorite opal, *see* geyserite, below;

Types of opal *(Continued)*
flag opal, *see* abanderos opal, above; fluorescent opal, 248, 266, 267, 269, 270, 274, 287, 310, 320, 322, 333, 349, 361, 376, *see also* Fluorescence, in main headings; fun-stone opal, 170; fundyite, 108, 111, 319, 108; gelite opal, 170; gerstenkörner, *see* barleycorn opals, above; geyserite (fiorite/geyser opal), 12, 169, 170, 173, 181, 182, 274, 277–279, 291, 292, 299, 300, 304, 308, 366, *see also* siliceous sinter; girasol opal (hyacinth opal/rainbow opal/lluviznados opal), 162, 170, 171, 174, 175, 177, 179, 180, 185, 234, 235, 306, 331, 359.; glass opal, *see* hyalite, below; gray opal, 161, 164, 170, 182, 289, 303, 331; gummisteen opal, *see* hyalite, below; heliotrope opal, 171, 180, *see also* pyrophane, below; honey opal, 171, 183, 227, 294, 365; hornlet, 51, 95, 103; huevos opal (egg opal), 134, 171; hummingbird stone, *see* vitzitziltecpatl, below; hyacinth opal, *see* girasol, above; hyalite opal (glass opal/gummisteen/Müller's glass opal), 11, 48, 53, 112, 155, 166, 170–172, 176, 227, 234, 235, 252, 263, 264, 268–274, 270, 276, 278, 279, 280, 282, 283, 285–287, 289–293, 299, 300, 302, 308, 310–314, 316, 319, 320, 321, 327–329, 331, 332, 334, 335, 337, 346, 348, 350–353, 355–357, 360–362; hydrophane opal (chamälconstein/eye of the world/oculus mundi/weltaug), 13, 16, 61, 99, 112, 164–166, 168, 172–174, 176, 178, 180, 184, 195, 227, 234, 252, 273, 282, 285, 299; Icelandic opal, 173, 377, *see also* siliceous sinter, below; infusorial opal, *see* diatomaceous opal, above; iris opal, *see* Play of color: contra luz opal; jelly opal (water opal), 124, 140, 163, 168, 173, 183, 184, 196, 207, 209, 213, 228, 234, 360, *see also* crystal opal, above
black, 87, 151, 163, 167, 245; brown, 164, 167; clear, 167; light, 163, 173, 234, 258;

orange, 167; red, 42; yellow-orange, 195
kalmuk opal, *see* Cachalong opal, in main headings; kaschtschilon opal, *see* Cachalong opal, in main headings; kieselguhr opal, *see* diatomaceous opal, above; layered opal, *see* Icelandic opal, above; lechosos opal, 173, *see also* milk opal, below; lemon opal, 174; levin opal, 174; light opal, 29, 31, 59, 70, 73, 74, 81, 86, 88, 90, 98, 110, 143, 150, 155, 161, 163, 167, 168, 174, 182, 184, 189, 210, 213, 226, 229, 234, 245, 246, 256, 258, 266, 375, 376, 386, *see also* dark opal, above; lithoxyl opal, 174; liver opal (menilite opal), 164, 174–176, 282, 293; lluviznados opal, *see* girasol opal, above; Louisiana opal, 115, 175, 301; magic stone, 165, 172, 174, *see* cachalong opal, in main headings, *and* hydrophane opal, above; manivi, *see* pink opal, below; matrix opal, 60, 95, 98, 129, 161, 164, 174–176, 180, 205, 213, 272, 301, 302, 375, 378; menilite opal, *see* liver opal, above; Mexican flag opal, 161; Mexican opal, *see* Mexican opal, in main headings; milk opal, 8, 77, 91, 97, 102, 173–175, 184, 196, 269, 275, 276, 290, 293, 305, 358, *see also* lechosos opal, above; mother-of-pearl opal, 175; Müller's glass opal, *see* hyalite opal, above; neslite opal, 174, 176; night stone opal, 163, 176; noble opal, 73, 176; nodular opal, 181; oculus mundi, *see* hydrophane, above; opal-A, 287, 291, 301; opal-CT, 265, 268, 287, 301, 328; opalia, 56; opaline, 141, 176, 271, 298, 307, 310, 320, 327, 348, 351, 356, 362, *see also* matrix opal, above; opaline silica, 1, 80, 274, 279, 307, 361, 364, 365, 382
byro opal, 80
opallion/opallios, 56, 177; opalus, 56–59, 177; ophthalmis lapis, 59; Oriental opal, 60, 177, 297; orphanus opal, *see* pyrophane, below; paederos, 55, 56, 178; painted lady opal, 95, 101, 104, 148, 156, 178, 190; peacock's tail

opal, 178; pearl opal, *see* Tabasheer; pebble opal, 178; perlmutter opal, 165, 178, *see also* cachalong opal, in main headings, *and* hydrophane opal, above; picture opal, 178, *see also* Scenic opal; pineapple opal, 48–51, 77, 81, 85, 94, 95, 103, 111, 112, 116, 117, 155, 178, 258, 319, 322, 377, 386. *See also* Pseudomorphs
discovery of, 77
pink opal (manivi), 116, 179, 288, 289; pipe opal, *see* Forms of opal: pipe opal; pitch opal, 11, 179, 180; prase opal, 166, 179, 274, 276, 277, 293, 308, 327; precious fire opal, *see* Mexican opal, in main headings; prime d'opal, 175, 180; pseudomorphic, 12, 16, 45, 50, 103, 112, 178, 190, 226, 377; pseudomorphs, vii, 12, 39–41, 45–48, 50, 51, 67–70, 73, 77, 81, 85, 94, 95, 103, 108, 111, 112, 116, 155, 178, 184, 191, 258, 273, 319, 322, 350, 353, 361; pyrophane opal (orphanus opal/waise opal/zeazite opal), 171, 173, 177, 180, 184, 185, *see also* heliotrope opal, above; quartzite opal, 180; quinzite opal, 178, 180; radiolite opal (smoky opal), 171, 180; rainbow opal, 112, 170, 180, 234, *see also* girasol, above; randannite, 180, *see also* diatomaceous opal, above; rose opal, 55, 56, 60, 178–180, 284, 288, 289, 293; rumanite, 181; sandstone opal, 161, 181; santillite opal, 181; scenic opal, 178, 181, *see also* Picture opal; sea opal, *see* Paua shell, in main readings; siliceous sinter (fiorite/geyserite/geyser opal), 12, 162, 169, 170, 173, 178, 182, 291, 292, 328, 377, *see also* Icelandic opal; smoky opal, *see* Radiolite opal, above; snakeskin opal, 182; snakestone, *see* tabasheer, below; speck opal, *see* Forms of opal: speck opal; specimen opal, *see* Opal: specimen opal, in main headings; sun opal, 183, 333; tabasheer opal (pearl opal/snakestone), 16, 166, 175, 182, 183; thunдеregg opal, 75, 112, 183, 208, 231–235, 237,

238, 272, 294, 323, 333, 334; thunderstone opal, 56, 60, 166, 183; trego opal, 175, 183; tripoli (diatomaceous earth), 16, 168, 180, 183, 288, 351; tripolite (diatomite), 183, 289, 307, 331, 386.; vitzitziltecpatl (hummingbird stone), 60, 171, 184, 227; waise opal, *see* pyrophane, above; water opal, *see* jelly opal, above; weltauge, *see* hydrophane opal, above; white opal, 46, 73, 81, 93, 140, 164, 174, 175, 184, 207, 227, 267, 269, 273, 274, 280, 287, 320, 321, 336, 337, 352, 357, 367, *see also* Milk opal; White Sea hornlet opals, *see* hornlet, above; wood opal, 48, 124, 146, 147, 151, 166, 174, 177, 178, 184, 185, 206, 245, 265, 268, 271, 273, 274, 275–279, 282, 288, 289, 291, 293–297, 299–301, 304, 305, 307, 320–322, 330, 333, 335, 348, 350, 351, 355–360, 362, 369, 370, *see also* Fossils, opalized/petrified: wood; zeazite opal. *See* pyrophane

Tyrell, Clement, 71, 72, 156
Tyrone County, G.B., 285

Uganda, 358
Ugljarevac, Yug., 369
Uittamonsalmi, Fin., 287
U.S. Geological Survey, 232, 293
Ujaragsugssuk, Green., 292
Ukraine, 57, 371
Ulster, G.B., 285
Umanak District, Green., 292
Umtanum Ridge, WA, 363
Unartoq District, Green., 292
Underground living, 80
Union County, NJ, 319
United Arab Emirates, 371
United States, 10, 12, 53, 54, 75, 76, 78, 84, 85, 87, 89–91, 96, 101, 103, 106, 115, 118, 120, 141, 151, 152, 156, 158, 166, 168, 176, 187, 197, 203, 209, 225, 228, 232, 234, 240, 244, 263, 264, 266, 267, 274, 278, 280, 283, 287, 289, 292, 293, 296, 298, 300, 301–304, 306–308, 310, 319, 327, 329, 331, 332, 334, 335, 338, 346, 350, 355, 356, 359–363, 366, 370, 371, 377
Universities, xiv, 126, 130, 141, 236, 237, 251, 268, 271, 283, 284, 293, 296, 299–

301, 308, 330, 346, 348, 350, 355
Berea, Kentucky, 126; Brigham Young, Provo, UT, xiv, 251; Bucharest University, 346; Kansas Newman College, Wichita, 130; National Taiwan University, Taipei, 355; Stellénbosch University, S. Afr., 348; Taedok Science Town, Taejon, 301; Technical & Further Education College, 141; Tohuku University, Tokyo, 299; University of Baroda, In., 296; University of Copenhagen, Den., 284; University of Delaware, Newark, 283; University of Hong Kong, 293; University of Kansas, Lawrence, 300; University of Kentucky, Lexington, 300; University of Nevada, Reno, 308; University of Oregon, 236; University of Oslo, Norway, 330; University of Reunion, St. Denis, 346; University of Rhode Island, Kingston, 346; University of Sao Paulo, Braz., 271; University of Seattle, 237; University of South Dakota, Vermillion, 350; University of Vienna, Aus., 268; Yamanashi Institute of Gemmology, 299
Unnamed Andamooka Opal, 154
Unnamed Hungarian Opal, 154
Unnamed Lady opal, 141
Unnamed Opalized Clamshell opal, 154
Unnamed Opalized Dinosaur Jawbone opal, 154
Unnamed Pineapple opal pseudomorph, 155
Unnamed Virgin Valley Opal, 155
Unnamed White Cliffs Opal No. 1, 155
Unnamed White Cliffs Opal No. 2, 155
Úpala, 56
Upper Ammonoosuc River, NH, 319
Upper Montclair, NJ, 319
Uppsala, Swed., 354
Uralla, NSW, 324
Uruguay, 358
Usan, Scot., 347
Utah, xiv, 251, 279, 359, 379
Uzibekistan, 371

Vaillant, Paul/Serjean, xiv, 318
Valdemoro, Sp., 352
Valec, Cz. Rep., 283
Vallecas, Sp., 352, 353
Valley County, ID, 296
Valley Springs, CA, 275
Vanatu, 360

Vance, Bill, 118
Vance County, NC, 329
Vantage, WA, 363
Vásquez, Hernan D., 277
Vatican City, 371
Venezuela, 360
Venugopal, D. V., 319
Venus, 199
Vermont, 360
Vernon, B.C., 277
Vesprém County, Hung., 293
Vesuvius, S. Austral., 349
Victoria, Austral., 22, 265, 271, 330, 360
Victoria, B.C., 271
Victoria, N.T., 330
Victoria Land Coast, Ant., 265
Victoria, Queen, 68, 69, 137
Vienna, Aus., 85, 91, 93, 126, 154, 156, 160, 268, 281
Vienna Imperial Opal, 160
Vietnam, 371
Vila Seca, 70
Villaluenga, Sp., 354
Villasenor, Manuel, 306
Vino, 199
Virgin Creek, NV, 244, 246
Virgin Islands, 371
Virgin of Alumdena, 73
Virgin Valley, xiii, xiv, 8, 10, 12, 13, 15, 22, 26, 35, 45, 47, 48, 53–55, 84, 85, 88–92, 94, 96, 98, 99, 100, 101, 103, 106, 109–112, 116, 117, 121, 123, 125, 126, 128, 129, 136, 137, 146, 147, 151, 155, 156, 158, 161, 163, 166, 175, 177, 178, 184, 206, 208, 213, 244–251, 253, 254, 298, 308–314, 316, 318, 377, 380, 381
discovery of precious opal, 85; fee-digging, 254; fire opal, 184; opal, 90, 91, 96, 98, 146, 155, 161, 184, 246, 248, 250, 251; ranch opal deposit, 311, 318
Virginia, 361–363
Visakhapatnam District, In., 297
Vitosha Mountain, Bulg., 273
Vivo, S. Afr., 349
Vochten, Ing R. F., 270
Vogel, Alan A., xiii
Voitsberg, Aus., 270
Volhynia, 337
Volkert, Richard, 319
Von Brandt, Fred, 101, 120
Vrnjacka banja, Yug., 368
Vrtaca, Yug., 368
Vuckovica, Yug., 369
Vuotso, Fin., 287

Wahl, F. Michael, 278
Waihi, NZ, 328
Wailuku, HI, 292
Waitaikei Valley, NZ, 328

Waite Opal, 160
Waite, G. Grant, 156, 160
Wakayama, Jpn., 300
Wake Island, 371
Waldenkirchen, Aus., 270
Wales, 371
Walgett Spectator, 136
Walgett, NSW, 135, 136, 151, 209, 325
Walla Walla River, WA, 236
Wallace County, KS, 300
Wallangulla Station, Lightning Ridge, 81, 84, 209
Wallatinna, S. Austral., 349
Wallis, 371
Walsch, Cz. Rep., 283
Walsh, Michael, 135
Waltsale, Cz. Rep., 283
Ward's Natural History Establishment, 126, 152, 248, 126, 152
Warmbaths, S. Afr., 349
Warm Springs Indians Reservation, OR, 333
Warrambungle Mountains, NSW, 322, 326
Warrangulla Station, NSW, 81
Warren, ME, 302
Warrnambool Downs, Qld., 78
Warsaw, Pol., 337
Warthen, GA, 290
Wasatch County, UT, 360
Wasco County, OR, 333
Washington A. Roebling, 152, 155, 248
Washington County, 289, 290, 346
Georgia, 289, 290; Rhode Island, 346
Washington, D.C., 12, 55, 76, 91, 114, 122, 140, 265, 294, 362, 363
Watching Creek, B.C., 272
Waterbury, VT, 360
Watkins, John, 322
Waverly Novels, The, 67
Weaver, Kenneth N., 303
Webber, Layne, 309
Webber, Todd, 309
Webber, William, 309
Webster County, GA, 290
Weise Ranch, CA, 277
Weitendorf, Aus., 268, 270
Welbourn Hill, S. Austral., 349
Wellington, NSW, 326
Wendt's Jewelers, Adelaide, 121
West Bank, 371
West Coast Gemstones, 112, 233–235, 237, 239
West Java, Indon., 298
West Virginia, 363
West, Herb, xiv
Westchester County, NY, 327
Western Australia, 69, 80, 84, 116, 156, 363, 364
Western Rhodope Mountains, Bulg., 273
Western Sahara, 371

Western Samoa, 371
Westonia, W. Austral., 365
Weymouth, N.S., 131
Whelan, ID, 76, 294
White Bluffs, WA, 363
White Cliffs, NSW, 12, 22, 41–51, 53, 70, 73–86, 88, 89, 92, 94–96, 100, 103, 109–112, 114, 116, 118, 130, 144, 145, 154–156, 162, 178, 179, 184, 197, 210, 213, 245, 256–261, 319, 322, 323, 326, 327, 352, 377, 386
Dug-Out Motel, 115, 260; first opal claims established, 75; heat exhaustion, 82; officially designated as "hobby field," 118; post office established, 81; tribute system, 79, 257–259, 386; underground living, 114, 118, 260
White Cliffs Number Two Opal, 88, 109
White Cliffs opal, 73, 75, 76, 79–81, 89, 118, 130, 144, 155, 178, 184, 256, 257, 259, 323, 377
White Cliffs Opal Miner newspaper, 81, 130, 144
White Cliffs Opal Mining Company, 79, 257
White Cliffs of Sardina, Sp., 352
White County, GA, 290
White Lake, B.C., 273
White Lead Lake, NY, 327
White River Formation, WY, 366
White Signal District, NM, 320
White Water, WI, 246
Whitehorse, YT, 369
Wichita, KS, 130, 332
Wichita Mountains, OK, 332
Widgiemooltha, W. Austral., 365
Wilcannia, NSW, 74, 256, 257
Wilhelmsdor, Aus., 270
William Creek, S. Austral., 78, 95, 349
Wilson, Harry W. "H.," 96, 110, 248
Wilson, Mark L., 319
Wilson, Mary Ann, xiv, 116
Wilson, Walter, xiv, 8, 45, 116, 253, 255
Winch, P. J., 89
Wind River Formation, WY, 366
Windhoek, Nam., 308
Wingohocking Creek, PA, 335
Winnemucca, NV, 244, 247, 309
Winnipeg, Man., 303
Winton, Qld., 103, 116, 345
Winton District, Qld., 74
Winton Township, Qld., 338
Wiry, Pol., 336, 337
Wisconsin, xiii, 246, 247, 366
Wise County, VA, 362
Wissahickon Valley, PA, 335
Wolf Mountain, WY, 54

Wollaston Tullie Cornthwaite, 46, 73–76, 83–85, 90, 93, 120, 153, 212, 256, 257
Wood, John, 332
Woodbourne, PA, 334
Woodend, Vic., 361
Woods Hole, MA, 267
Woolshed, Vic., 360
Woomera Rocket Base, S. Austral., 191, 193
World War, 42, 93, 94, 98, 126, 127, 133, 181, 189, 200, 230;
World War I, 42, 126, 127, 133, 200
World War II, 93, 94, 98, 126, 181, 230, 189
Wright, George D., 100, 242
Wurie, A. C., 348
Wygralak, Andrew, 330
Wyndham, W. Austral., 364
Wyndomen, Qld., 70, 72
Wyoming, 54, 366, 373

Xampo Alegre, Col., 278
Xenophontos, C., 281

Yackandandah, Vic., 361
Yahloo, S. Austral., 96, 191
Yakima River, WA, 363
Yancy County, NC, 329
Yarra Yarra Creek, W. Austral., 365
Year of the Opal, 118
Yellowjacket Formation, ID, 295
Yellowknife, NWT, 330
Yellowstone County, WY, 367
Yemen, 371
Yeongil, S.K., 301
Yita Ridge, 286
York Haven, PA, 334
Yuba County, CA, 277
Yugoslavia, 367
Yukasapa, 205
Yukasapa, Hon., 205
Yukon Territory, 369
Yuma County:
Arizona, 162, 266; Colorado, 280
Yunnan (China), 371

Zabkowice, Pol., 336
Zabkowice Slaskie, Pol., 336, 337
Zacatecas, Mex., 306
Zagar, Steven, 141, 142
Zaire, 371
Zale Corporation, 130
Zambia, 371
Zeleznice, Cz. Rep., 283
Zemplén County, Hung., 293
Zhelezni Vrati, Bulg., 273
Ziggy, 141, 142
Zimbabwe, 53, 106, 348, 369, 370, 106
Zirler klamm, Aus., 270
Zlata Nana, Slov., 283
Zwaan, Pietere, C., 308